INTRODUCTION

TO

REAL ESTATE LAW

By

The Institute for Paralegal Training

Russell C. Bellavance, Volume Editor

Caroline S. Laden, Institute Series Editor

PARALEGAL SERIES

William P. Statsky, Editor

David Matz, Editor

ST. PAUL, MINN.

WEST PUBLISHING CO.

1978

Library of Congress Cataloging in Publication Data

Institute for Paralegal Training.
    Introduction to real estate law.
    (Paralegal series)
    Includes index.
    1. Real property—United States. 2. Vendors and purchasers—United States.
3. Mortgages—United States. I. Bellavance, Russell C. II. Title.
KF570.I55   346'.73'0437   78–7930

ISBN 0–8299–2006–4

Inst.Par.Train.Real Estate Law
3rd Reprint—1984

Jeannie, Joy and Ned
"Carpent tua poma nepotes"
Virgil

*

III

INTRODUCTION

If form follows function, then the first task of an author or an editor must be to determine the purpose of both this volume and of the series of which this volume is a part. My own resolution of the issue has been determined in large measure by what I have perceived to be the law firm approach to the training and utilization of new paralegals and associate attorneys.

Although new associate attorneys have received more legal training than a new legal assistant, the legal assistant will usually have received considerably more training in the practicalities of the practice of law. The attorney may have had two or three semesters of real property law, but may never have even seen a deed or a lease, much less prepared one. However, the law firm will expect that a new legal assistant will be familiar with the preparation of deeds, mortgages and leases. The first purpose of this book, then, is to assist the instructor in preparing the student to satisfy the expectation of the law firm employer that the legal assistant will have the technical knowledge to prepare basic documents.

Technical knowledge can only be a starting place. A legal assistant must also have comprehension of background and context, in order to develop professionally. The second purpose of this book, co-equal with the first, is to assist in developing the comprehension of background and context.

There are several areas in which this development should take place. Since a legal assistant will be working with lawyers, he must be familiar with the way that lawyers think and talk. The discussions in the book concerning the negotiation process, and of the concerns of the negotiating attorneys, should provide some insight into the thought processes of commercial lawyers. Examples of legal and real estate jargon have been included, with definitions, so that the language barrier will not be insurmountable.

The legal profession and the real estate industry are by no means completely congruent. The real estate industry also includes accountants, architects, developers, construction lenders, permanent mortgage lenders, major tenants, brokers, syndicators and government agencies of every kind and function. We have used a transactional approach in the book in order to help develop "the big picture". The first subject chapter is Chapter II, Agreements of Sale. An agreement to purchase is often the first active step in a complex

INTRODUCTION

series of real estate transactions. Between the agreement of sale and actual settlement (Chapter XI) some or all of the following steps might be taken by the proposed purchaser: ordering a title insurance report (Chapter IV), obtaining commitments for permanent and/or construction financing (Chapter VIII) and negotiating leases for the property (Chapter IX). Although each of these activities may seem discrete and distinct, they are in fact all interrelated. No attorney can function effectively with respect to any one of the activities if he is ignorant of any of the others.

This volume assumes a high degree of involvement and competence from the instructors. The instructors must choose their own emphasis and must select from among the suggested problems and discussions those that best serve their purposes. The instructors must have sufficient technical expertise to correct the problems, and must be able to breathe life into the attempts at developing comprehension. It is a difficult task, and I wish them well.

No author or editor works in a vacuum, and many persons have contributed to this volume, in one way or another. My employer, Cohen, Shapiro, Polisher, Shiekman and Cohen, forebore the diversion of many hours of my time. Cal Laden and Flora Wolf provided truly constructive criticism. The classes I taught at The Institute for Paralegal Training served as a laboratory for my pedagogical experiments. Finally, there was the strong family support from Jean, who carried and bore our son Ned during the time I worked on the volume, and from Joy, who accepted having both parents undergoing separate, simultaneous gestation processes.

RUSSELL C. BELLAVANCE

Philadelphia, Pennsylvania
June, 1978

PREFACE

This book is intended as an introduction to real estate law for legal assistants and other real estate specialists. Instructors utilizing this text will want to supplement this book with local practice customs and forms. Students will want to review local forms and procedures and compare them with the examples in the text.

The text itself can be used in a survey course or in a more sophisticated real estate law course by careful selection of reading topics and the utilization of assignments which are appropriate to the level of the course.

This book and its companion volumes are the result of the activities of a unique institution, The Institute for Paralegal Training in Philadelphia, Pennsylvania. Since its founding in 1970 more than 2500 persons have graduated from The Institute, many trained in Real Estate Law. The text has benefited from the experience of those students and their concerned instructors.

This text is the product of many minds and pens working over the last six years to create course materials especially for the instruction of paralegal students. The Institute owes a debt of gratitude to all who have been involved in the effort. The original materials for the General Practice Real Estate Course and the Real Estate Specialty Course at The Institute for Paralegal Training were authored by Philadelphia attorneys Stuart Ebby, Paul Baron, Daniel Litwin, Ronald Glazer, James Rosenstein, Julian Rackow, and Paul E. Shapiro, and edited by Paul E. Shapiro, a founder and former Director of The Institute.

The present text owes its life to the editorial efforts of Russell C. Bellavance, Esq. who has worked diligently to create a text which will be enormously useful to students from a variety of backgrounds studying real estate from the logical viewpoint.

Charles Zall, Esq., an instructor in Real Estate and staff members Flora B. Wolf, Irwin A. Schein and Ruth Scott of The Institute were most helpful in the process of making this book a reality.

CAROLINE S. LADEN
THE INSTITUTE FOR PARALEGAL TRAINING

Philadelphia, Pennsylvania
June, 1978

*

SUMMARY OF CONTENTS

SUMMARY OF CONTENTS

SUMMARY OF CONTENTS

CHAPTER SEVEN. PARTNERSHIP AGREEMENTS

CHAPTER EIGHT. REAL ESTATE MORTGAGES

PART ONE. RESIDENTIAL MORTGAGES

PART TWO. COMMERCIAL–INDUSTRIAL MORTGAGES

PART THREE. CONSTRUCTION MORTGAGES

PART FOUR. FEDERAL HOUSING ADMINISTRATION (FHA) MORTGAGES

SUMMARY OF CONTENTS

PART FIVE. INDUSTRIAL DEVELOPMENT AUTHORITY LOANS

PART SIX. FORM AND SUBSTANCE OF THE NOTE AND MORTGAGE

PART SEVEN. ASSIGNMENT, SATISFACTION AND RELEASE OF MORTGAGES

PART EIGHT. MORTGAGE FORECLOSURE

CHAPTER NINE. LEASING

PART ONE. BASIC ELEMENTS OF A LEASE

PART TWO. SPECIAL TYPES OF LEASES

SUMMARY OF CONTENTS

PART THREE. OFFICE BUILDING LEASES

CHAPTER TEN. DEEDS OF CONVEYANCE

CHAPTER ELEVEN. SETTLEMENTS AND CLOSINGS

*

TABLE OF CONTENTS

TABLE OF CONTENTS

TABLE OF CONTENTS

TABLE OF CONTENTS

TABLE OF CONTENTS

TABLE OF CONTENTS

TABLE OF CONTENTS

TABLE OF CONTENTS

TABLE OF CONTENTS

TABLE OF CONTENTS

TABLE OF CONTENTS

CHAPTER EIGHT. REAL ESTATE MORTGAGES

PART ONE. RESIDENTIAL MORTGAGES

PART TWO. COMMERCIAL–INDUSTRIAL MORTGAGES

TABLE OF CONTENTS

TABLE OF CONTENTS

TABLE OF CONTENTS

TABLE OF CONTENTS

TABLE OF CONTENTS

TABLE OF CONTENTS

I. COMMERCIAL AND SHOPPING CENTER LEASES—Continued

XXXI

TABLE OF CONTENTS

CHAPTER TEN. DEEDS OF CONVEYANCE

TABLE OF CONTENTS

TABLE OF CONTENTS

TABLE OF CONTENTS

TABLE OF CONTENTS

TABLE OF CONTENTS

INTRODUCTION

TO

REAL ESTATE LAW

Chapter One

INTRODUCTION TO REAL PROPERTY

This book has two major purposes. The first is to develop in the prospective legal assistant an understanding of the basic information, concepts and jargon necessary to perform in any phase of a real estate transaction in the United States. The second is to develop certain skills and techniques, some of which, such as drafting skills, are of general application to a legal assistant's career and others of which, such as preparing a deed, are of particular application for a real estate paralegal.

The scope of this book is limited to *basic* real estate transactions for which a legal assistant may expect to be given some measure of responsibility. Such basic transactions include the purchase and sale of real estate, mortgage loans and leasing. A legal assistant must be familiar with the individual basic transactions, with the integration of the component transactions and with the jargon employed by lawyers and clients in the real estate field.

It is intended that the text treat the major component transactions of a comprehensive real estate development in logical sequence. In actual practice, not all real estate transactions will involve every aspect of the materials provided in this book. However, an understanding of at least the basics of all facets of real estate is necessary to comprehend the forces that shape even the most elemental of transactions, such as the purchase of a house for cash.

The first important concept which must be understood fully by a legal assistant is the definition of the term "real estate".

I. INTRODUCTION

"Real estate", or as it is referred to in technical terms, "real property," is defined as land and all structures permanently affixed to land. All other property, such as automobiles, jewelry, stocks and

1

cash, is called "personal property" or "personalty". From a legal standpoint, therefore, all property is classified either as real property or personal property. The distinction is important because in many situations the law governing or affecting real property is different from the law governing personal property, and a different result will be obtained depending on whether the property in question is real property or personal property.

Sometimes it is quite difficult to determine whether a given item of property is real or personal. For example, a window air conditioner which has been built to the window frame could be viewed as permanently affixed to a building, and therefore be considered real property, or as not permanently affixed, and therefore be considered personal property.

Historians and sociologists, may debate the reasons, but no one will deny that the desire of human beings to possess and control land has been a dominant force and theme in the course and development of human civilization. Among various cultures, the need to use land for survival has resulted in strikingly different social and legal patterns. Our own concepts of ownership and property rights are by no means the necessary or logical result of such desire and need. Many societies, including many American Indian tribes, have had no concept of "ownership" of land at all, but only of rights of use, often common to an entire tribe. Other societies have stressed the stewardship concept, that the present user of the land has an obligation to society and to future users to maintain the property and not permit it to go to waste.

Our own system of property law, as well as most of our other laws, is derived most directly from English principles of law such as existed during the colonial period of our history. The derivation is not pure, and in various parts of our country Spanish and French law have had considerable influence. More remotely, many of our legal principles go back to Roman civil law, and some concepts extend even further back.

Most of the English law that existed during the colonial period was judge made law as contrasted with legislatively enacted law. There were few statutes, and those that existed were subject to significant judicial interpretation. Courts and judges make laws by deciding actual cases and by announcing in an opinion the legal principles upon which they have based their decision. In order that the law be consistent, prior decisions and principles are generally followed by later judges, such prior cases being called precedents. The resultant body of law, consisting of precedents and stated principles, is called the common law. English common law continues to be a source for American judges. Each American state has also developed it own state common law. Since the Industrial Revolution, and especially since the Depression, the common law in America has been increasingly supplemented, and sometimes supplanted, by statutory law.

II. BASIC CONCEPTS OF REAL PROPERTY RIGHTS

We generally think of land and real estate only in the physical sense. Certainly land does have measurable physical characteristics, and these must be ascertained with considerable precision in order to avoid disputes. However, lawyers also think of real estate as consisting of a bundle of rights, both actual and potential. Very broadly, there are four aspects of real property which are included in the bundle of rights, elements of which might be separated from the bundle and granted to different persons. These four are: **ownership,** which is the core element of the bundle; **possession,** which may be granted to another, such as by a lease, and which involves the *general* right to use the property during the period of possession; **use,** which may be separate from possession in the case of an easement or other *limited* right of use; and **control,** which may be granted to another by means of private agreement, or to society by law. We shall briefly review some of these elements, all of which will be discussed in greater detail in the various chapters.

A. PHYSICAL

The first object of real estate law is to define a parcel of land so that it can be precisely identified and distinguished from other parcels of land. In order to distinguish various parcels of land, each is said to have certain boundaries which define where one parcel ends and another begins. Boundaries are generally defined in relation to some established landmark. The landmark in an urban area may be a street. In the country it may be a stone fence, an unusual tree or a boulder. Using surveyor's instruments and starting at a particular landmark as a point of reference, a parcel of land can then be defined.

B. A BUNDLE OF RIGHTS

There are various interests which one may own in a piece of land.[1] The rights in and to real estate that a person owns are sometimes referred to as that person's "interest in the real estate". Some, but not all, examples of these components are listed below:

1. Fee

The ultimate core of ownership is called the "fee". If one person has the entire ownership interest and if such interest cannot be taken from him or his heirs and assigns without his consent (subject to the right of the state of eminent domain), then he is said to have title in "fee simple absolute".

---

[1] A further semantic confusion is that one who possesses an interest in real estate is sometimes said "to own that interest," even though the interest itself is not an ownership interest; that is, it does not involve ownership of the land. Thus, one who possesses a possessory interest in land, such as a tenant under a lease, may be said to "own that interest."

It is possible for more than one person to own a share of a fee interest in land. Persons having an undivided [2] fee interest are said to be co-owners and to own the property as <u>tenants in common</u>.

2. Lease

A person [3] may not own the fee but still have the right to use the land, a portion of the land, or a portion of a building located on the land for a specific period of years. Such a person may be called a tenant or lessee. A tenant's right to possession may be derived from the fee owner or from an existing tenant. A person giving such rights is referred to as the landlord or lessor.

3. Mineral Interest or Air Rights

A person may have merely the right to mine or drill for and remove minerals from a parcel of land. Such right is usually derived from the fee owner who, according to legal principles, owns the subsurface of his land to the center of the earth and the airspace above his land (subject to the public's right to use the airways for transportation). When the owner of the entire fee grants a right to remove minerals or timber from real property, such a right is called a profit, from the Norman term *profit à prendre*. This should be distinguished from the practice common to many mining areas in the United States of horizontal division of a property into different strata, with different persons having fee ownership of different strata. In certain coal mining regions, for example, entire towns are sometimes built entirely on surface ownership of the ground, with one or more coal companies holding fee title to the ground beneath the surface. The coal companies may mine the subsurface property which they own with no restrictions except an obligation to provide physical support to the owner of the surface rights, and sometimes they do not even have any obligation to provide physical support.

A landowner can also grant air rights from any level above the surface of the ground. One purpose of acquiring air rights is preventive. For example, a person owning land may want to acquire air rights above a level of 50 feet on adjoining property so that high buildings that would block light and air to his own land will never be built on the adjoining property. A second purpose would be for the right to build. For example, in New York City, the Pan Am Building is built in the air over Grand Central Station. In such an instance, the person acquiring the air rights would also need an easement of support.

2. Undivided means that each has an interest in the whole, not just in a part.

3. The word "person" can refer to human individuals, whether male or female, or to people in a non-individual capacity, such as trustees or executors, or to entities, such as a corporation, association, or partnership. The term "individual" refers only to people acting in their own capacity.

4. Easements, Rights of Way

One may merely own the right to travel over a piece of property or to string and maintain a wire over the property, or to use a portion of the land in some other limited way. Such a right may be referred to as an easement or right of way.

At common law there were only seven kinds of easements which could be created and there were very special conditions to their creation. With the development of modern recording statutes many other kinds of easements have been developed. For example, the owner of a large residential tract may develop it in separate stages of midrise apartments, each of which stages may ultimately be owned by a separate entity. There may be common security systems, woods and recreational facilities. In order to tie the project into a single unit for purposes of using the roads, sidewalks, parking and other facilities and in order to allocate the costs of maintaining these facilities, the developer may record a declaration of easements covering the entire project and granting cross-easements throughout.

The holder of an easement and the owner of the subject land have certain mutual obligations with respect to the use and maintenance of the property and of the easement area. Unlike a lease situation, the grantor of an easement does not usually grant possession or exclusive use, but merely a right of use.

5. Life Estate

A life estate in realty is the right of a person (called the "life tenant") to use real property until death. This right cannot be passed on to an heir, but terminates at the death of the user. A variation of a life estate is a life estate *pur autre vie*, which means that the life by which the term of the estate is measured is the life of someone other than the user. There is a substantial amount of common law dealing with the specific rights which pertain to a life estate, such as whether the holder of the life estate can cut and remove timber, and with the rights and duties of the remaindermen to whom the property will come upon the expiration of the life estate. There is also considerable law dealing with the valuation of the respective interests of a life tenant and a remainderman in the event of a forced sale, such as a condemnation.

6. Future Interests

Future interests are present rights in real property that give the right to future possession or use. There are many kinds of future interests. For example, the remainderman who has a right to use or possession of real property upon the expiration of a life estate possesses a future interest. Remaindermen have certain present rights in the property, such as the right to certain protections against the commission of waste by the life tenant.

C. METHODS OF ACQUIRING TITLE TO REAL ESTATE

1. Purchase

Our system of law permits and protects the right to transfer interests in real estate, including the right to sell such interests. There are relatively few restrictions upon these rights. One restriction is that if only a portion of a parcel is to be sold, the owner may be required to obtain approval of the local government prior to such a sale. The approval required is called "subdivision" approval since the owner is proposing to divide his land. The type of subdivision that requires approval and the body whose approval must be obtained are matters of state law. Generally, such powers of approval are constitutionally limited to a determination that the subdivision will not violate local requirements with regard to parking, lot size, setback limitations and the like. The local authority would not have the power to disapprove arbitrarily or for a prohibited reason, such as dislike of the proposed grantee.

2. Inheritance and Gift

Interests in real estate may be transferred from one person to another as a gift. In addition, a person may transfer interests in real property at death by a will. If no will exists the interests will be transferred to certain heirs of the deceased owner as directed by state intestacy [4] law. Again, free rights of transfer by gift or by will are protected rights, subject, of course, to tax laws such as federal gift taxes and federal and state estate and inheritance taxes.

3. Adverse Possession

The doctrine of adverse possession was derived from the English common law, although many states have enacted statutes governing the subject. The doctrine provides that one may obtain ownership of real estate interests by taking possession for a certain period of time and holding it in a manner adverse to the legal owner. The term "adverse" includes a requirement that the party claiming title by adverse possession shall not have been in possession by permission of the legal owner.

D. LEGAL INTERESTS OF A SPOUSE

1. Dower

At common law, upon the death of her husband a widow was entitled to receive a one-third interest in all real property owned by her husband in fee at the time of and after their marriage, whether or not the property was owned by her husband at the time of his death. In

---

4. The term "intestacy" relates to the local law governing distribution of the property of a person who dies "in-testate", that is, without having left a valid will.

changed June 17, 1978

most states this right, known as the "right of dower", has either been abolished or changed in some manner by statute. In Pennsylvania, for example, a widow receives a one-half or a one-third fee interest in all real estate owned by her husband, in his name alone, during their marriage. Any transfer during his lifetime of his interest in the real estate without her joinder in the deed would be made subject to her dower rights. Therefore, if the wife survives the husband, such a purchaser from the husband would not own the real estate in its entirety.

2. Curtesy

The common law also provided that a widower received, upon the death of his wife, a life estate in all real property owned by his wife in fee at any time during their marriage. This right was called the right of curtesy. The general principles governing dower applied also to curtesy. Most states have revised the common law right of curtesy and, in lieu thereof, give a surviving husband rights similar to those given to a surviving wife.

The rights of dower and curtesy, and their statutory equivalents, apply to property owned by a spouse in his or her own name and to which the other spouse has no present rights of use. A person taking an interest in real estate from a married person without the joinder of the other spouse in the document transferring the interest, is gambling that the spouse transferring the interest will be the survivor of the two.

III. PUBLIC CONTROL OVER LAND USE

The right of an owner of real estate to use the land is not absolute. Society, acting through various government agencies, often has a voice in the manner to which land may be used. The use which an owner makes of his land can have a definite effect upon his neighbors, sometimes to their serious detriment. In order to control such situations, the common law of nuisance, and its statutory counterpart, zoning, have been developed.

A.   NUISANCE

In general terms, the law of nuisance regulates the use of land so as to prevent uses which unduly interfere with a neighbor's use and enjoyment of the neighbor's own land. For example, a manufacturing plant might not be permitted to foul the air that residents of adjoining properties are forced to breathe. Usually common law nuisance cases involve a balancing process by the courts, which try to balance the harm caused against the economic benefit and property rights of the alleged offender.

B. ZONING

Many communities have enacted zoning laws which dictate the manner in which land within the community can be used and developed. As a general proposition, such laws, while clearly infringing on rights of private ownership, have been held to be constitutional. However, many specific zoning laws, patterns, practices and even motivations have been declared to be constitutionally invalid. Exclusionary zoning designed to exclude particular economic or social groups or certain kinds of housing is not legally permissible. The permissible rationale underlying zoning is that certain uses of land are not compatible with other uses.

C. PRIVATE RESTRICTIONS

In addition to the common law of nuisance and zoning laws, it is possible to restrict the use of land by agreement among the individual owners. An owner or group of owners of land may voluntarily agree in writing to restrict the use of their land. Such restrictions may affect and bind future owners.[5] Examples of private restrictions would be those which prohibit building within a certain distance from roads, prohibit non-residential use, or prohibit certain uses such as raising livestock. Some, but not all of these private restrictions, will be enforced by courts of law. For example, restrictions on sale to, or ownership by, persons of a particular religion or race, are unenforceable.

D. LIENS

Under certain circumstances one who is owed money can protect his position as a creditor by acquiring an interest in his debtor's real estate or personal property. Such an interest is called a lien. An example of a type of lien is a "mortgage", which is a lien voluntarily given on an interest in real estate to secure performance of an obligation, usually the payment of money. Sometimes a creditor can unilaterally obtain a lien on the debtor's property in order to secure repayment, or a lien may be created by statute. For example, a contractor who performs services or supplies materials for construction or repair of a building may be entitled by statute to a lien on security for payments for services rendered or materials supplied. Having a lien usually gives the holder the right, after following certain procedures, to force a sale of the property subject to the lien to yield proceeds to pay ("satisfy") the debt.

---

5. When a promise to do something (a "covenant") or to refrain from doing something (a "restriction") is imposed upon the ownership of land and binds future owners, then the covenant or restriction is said to "run with the land".

IV. DETERMINATION OF OWNERSHIP

A. TITLE SEARCHING

It is possible to determine the various interests which people hold in a particular parcel of land by examining public records kept for such purpose. All states have systems for recording interests in land. By reviewing ("searching") such records, it is possible to trace back the various interests in a piece of land hundreds of years. In some states, it is possible to trace interests in land back to the time of its colonization. By searching title a prospective purchaser is able to determine whether an interest in a parcel of real estate to be acquired is subject to the rights of others. For example, Greene might offer to sell to White a parcel of real estate on which Greene lives. A search of the real estate records might reveal that the land is really owned by Rodman who has merely rented it to Greene. Thus, the search of the records has revealed to White that Greene cannot transfer fee title to the land.

B. DOCUMENTS

Transfers of interests in real estate are normally evidenced by means of a formal written document. The format of such documents is often highly stylized due to their historical origins and the formalities imposed by statutes governing public recording. As shall be seen, the usual document for a transfer of a fee interest in real property is a deed.

V. SUMMARY

The concepts we have introduced in this first chapter are the building blocks necessary to function in the real estate field. Out of context, these concepts may seem difficult to understand, easy to forget and even unimportant. Subsequent chapters will provide that context by discussing various kinds of real estate transactions. As you study these subsequent chapters, you may find it helpful to reread this chapter.

Chapter Two

BUYING AND SELLING REAL ESTATE

I. INTRODUCTION

A contract for the sale and purchase of real estate is customarily called an agreement of sale. For reasons which will be discussed below, an agreement of sale for an interest in real estate is almost always embodied in a written document signed by both the seller and the purchaser. Execution of the agreement of sale by both parties fixes the relative rights and obligations of the seller and purchaser. For this reason the agreement of sale is a critical document in a transaction involving a sale and purchase of real estate. It is the basic charter, the constitution, governing the transaction.[1]

Although the legal assistant will rarely represent a client in negotiating the terms of an agreement of sale, the paralegal may be given responsibility for preparing an agreement of sale for a supervising attorney either (a) as an initial proposal prior to negotiation, or (b) as an initial draft subsequent to the negotiation of the major business and legal terms. Even if the paralegal is never given the responsibility for preparing a draft of an agreement of sale, he must be able to comprehend the legal terms of an agreement of sale in order to be able to prepare for settlement. For this reason, the chapter is written as if you as a paralegal would be first negotiating and then drafting an agreement of sale. You may receive the impression that every provision of every agreement of sale is both negotiable and actually negotiated in every transaction. In many transactions, however, and especially in residential transactions, few or none of the provisions are actually negotiated, and common form agreements are used virtually unchanged. Indeed, in many cases the client does not even seek legal counsel until after he has executed an agreement of sale and thus already fixed his rights and obligations. If the client seeks legal counsel before executing the agreement of sale, the decision as to which provisions to negotiate is properly the decision of the attorney, utilizing professional judgment.

It is the purpose of the chapter to familiarize you with some of the negotiating and drafting considerations which may arise in connection with agreements of sale for various types of real estate. One technique that this chapter will employ is to indicate what the rights and responsibilities of the parties would be if the agreement of sale

---

1. "Execution" refers to the performance by a party of all of the formal requirements necessary to bind that party to a contract or other legal document, including signing and physical delivery of the document. The term "seller" is interchangeable with the term "vendor" and the term purchaser is interchangeable with the terms "buyer" and "vendee".

did not deal with an issue or if typical form agreements of sale were used, and then to contrast that result with the rights and responsibilities of each party that would result if a provision were used favoring the seller or a provision were used favoring the purchaser. This will help illustrate the first rule of negotiating and drafting: consider every issue with regard to the position and requirements of your present client, either purchaser or seller. A provision which you may insist upon when your client is the seller of real estate may lose its charm when your client is the purchaser.

A.   THE NEED FOR AN AGREEMENT OF SALE

As previously indicated, an agreement of sale for real estate is a contractual undertaking by the owner of real estate to sell his interest in a real estate to another party, and an undertaking on the part of the purchaser to acquire the real estate, usually for the payment of a stated purchase price.[2]

Parties usually enter into an agreement of sale to be consummated at a future date instead of exchanging title and the purchase money immediately upon reaching an agreement. The principal reason for the delay in time is that there are many matters which both the purchaser and seller must attend to between the time that they agree upon the terms of the sale and the time when the actual exchange of title for purchase money can be made. Such matters include establishing the "marketability of title" (discussed in section E of this chapter) and arranging for a loan to pay for the purchase price (purchase money financing). The agreement allocates responsibility among the parties to insure that these and other matters to be resolved prior to, or as a condition of, consummation of the sale (referred to as the "settlement" or "closing") are accomplished in a satisfactory manner.

Since both parties normally invest considerable time and expense in making arrangements for settlement, both purchaser and seller want to be assured that they have an agreement that they can legally enforce against the other party. Furthermore, without a legal commitment the seller would not want to agree to refrain from seeking another purchaser for his real estate and the purchaser would not want to cease looking at other properties.

B.   THE NEED FOR A WRITTEN AGREEMENT OF SALE

One of the oldest statutes in Anglo-American jurisprudence is the "Statute of Frauds" which deals with the problem of the enforceability of various agreements and instruments by establishing minimum requirements which must be met before the courts will enforce the agreement or instrument. The lawsuit for enforcement of an

---

2. In this chapter we shall assume that the purchaser is paying money and/or assuming a mortgage in exchange for the real estate. There are many other items of value, the promise of which will be legally sufficient to act as consideration for the promise to convey real estate.

agreement of sale for real estate is called an action for specific performance. The remedy of specific performance means that a court will compel the recalcitrant party to perform that party's obligations under the contract. Normally, if one party breaches a contract, the remedy of the other party would be to receive money damages to compensate for any loss occasioned by the breach. However, each parcel of land is unique and money cannot really satisfy a disappointed purchaser, because the purchaser cannot replace exactly something which is unique. Specific performance can mean that a seller can force an unwilling purchaser who has signed an agreement of sale to buy the seller's property, provided that the Statute of Frauds has been implied with. The terms of many agreements of sale specifically deny this remedy to one or both of the parties.

The Statute of Frauds is still a vital part of the real estate law of the United States. Every state has enacted some version of the Statute of Frauds. Generally, modern versions of the Statute of Frauds contain the requirement that in order for a party to compel specific enforcement of an agreement to convey real estate, or to recover loss of bargain remedies, the essential terms of the agreement must be contained in a writing signed at least by the party against whom specific performance is sought (and in some jurisdictions by the party seeking specific performance as well).

PROBLEM

1. Find the Statute of Frauds of your jurisdiction relating to the sale of real estate.

2. What are the essential terms that the Statute of Frauds for your jurisdiction requires to be contained in a writing in order to enforce an agreement of sale for an interest in real estate?

Without a writing which satisfies the Statute of Frauds, a purchaser is not able to recover money damages from the seller for loss of the bargain. Loss of bargain is the difference between the purchase price and the market value of the property.[3]

There are a number of common exceptions to the Statute of Frauds. The Statute of Frauds is intended to protect the owners of real estate from fraudulent claims. In many states, therefore, if the seller can prove the existence of a written agreement signed only by the purchaser but orally accepted by the seller, the courts will force the purchaser to complete the transaction or to pay the seller's damages, notwithstanding the fact that seller's agreement is oral. The

---

3. Some relief from the harshness of the non-enforceability consequences of the Statute of Frauds is provided if the purchaser can prove that there was an oral agreement of sale for the real estate. Most jurisdictions permit the buyer to recover from the seller reimbursement for expenses which the purchaser incurred on the strength of the oral agreement and also any payments made to the seller.

seller's damages equal the amount purchaser agreed to pay less the sum of money paid by a new purchaser. In addition, seller is entitled to recover the expenses incurred in obtaining a new purchaser. In such jurisdictions, the purchaser can help to protect himself against enforcement of an oral contract by providing in any agreement of sale which he executes that the offer to purchase contained in the agreement may only be accepted in writing by executing and delivering a copy of the agreement of sale to purchaser within a specified period of time.

Another exception is that an informal writing signed by the party against whom enforcement is sought, which sets out sufficient details of the agreement so that the court can ascertain the important terms of the transaction, is deemed to be a sufficient writing to satisfy the requirements of the Statute. The party seeking enforcement will be entitled to specific performance even though no formal agreement of sale was ever signed.

Where property is owned by more than one person, or more than one person has a legal interest in the property (such as the spouse of a married owner), all of those persons must sign a writing before a court will compel a conveyance. If one of the co-owners of the property does not sign the alleged "agreement", the courts of most states will not compel a conveyance of any interest in the property, not even the interests of those persons who have signed the agreement.

C. LEGAL CONSEQUENCES OF EXECUTING AN AGREEMENT OF SALE FOR REAL ESTATE

An extensive body of law has developed over the years concerning the legal consequences of executing an agreement of sale. Many jurisdictions have held that the execution of an agreement of sale causes the immediate transfer of beneficial (or "equitable") ownership of the real estate to the purchaser, leaving the seller with mere title which he holds as trustee for the purchaser and as security for the balance of the purchase price due from the purchaser. The important legal consequences which flow from this event can best be illustrated by the use of several examples:

(a) As soon as an agreement of sale has been executed the law views the purchaser as having an interest in the real estate. If the purchaser should die before the transaction is consummated, his rights (and obligations) under the agreement of sale would pass to his heirs in the same manner as his other real estate interests, and not in the manner provided for other contract rights he might have.[4] As with other real estate interests, the purchaser's in-

---

4. At common law, the property of a person who died intestate (without a will) would be distributed in certain shares to the closest relatives of the deceased. The relatives to whom the property would go and the shares of the property they would get differed depending on whether the property in

terest in the property described in the agreement of sale may be mortgaged, may become subject to a lien for unpaid debts of the purchaser, and, absent agreement between the purchaser and the seller to the contrary, may be transferred to other parties in the same manner as real estate is normally transferred.

(b) In the absence of an agreement to the contrary, upon execution of the agreement of sale, the risk of loss of the real estate passes from the seller to the purchaser, giving the purchaser an insurable interest in the property. This means that if, for example, the property which the purchaser has just agreed to buy should be damaged or destroyed by fire between the time the agreement is executed and settlement, the seller can still compel the purchaser to purchase the property at the full price stated in the agreement of sale, notwithstanding the damage to or destruction of the property.

(c) Absent an agreement to the contrary, if the seller remains in possession of the property between the date of execution of the agreement and settlement (which is the usual case), the law imposes on him an obligation to use reasonable efforts to maintain and protect the property on behalf of the purchaser until settlement.

It should be noted, however, that the execution of an agreement of sale does not normally affect rights in the real estate of persons who are not parties to the agreement of sale. Consequently, a seller cannot object to the entry of a lien filed by one of his creditors against the real estate between the date of execution of the agreement and settlement by claiming that he is no longer the equitable owner of the real estate. Similarly, if the title which purchaser would receive at settlement would be subject to the rights granted to an innocent third party (such as a tenant) by the seller in the period between execution of the agreement and settlement. The concept of an innocent third party without notice will be discussed at greater length in Chapter 3.

II. TERMS COMMON TO AGREEMENTS OF SALE FOR ALL TYPES OF REAL ESTATE

This section of the chapter will focus on terms of agreements of sale which are essential terms to the transaction, and are therefore common to all purchase-sale transactions. Unless specified to the contrary, it will be assumed in this chapter that the parties will be following the order of events customary to most transactions involving the sale of real property. Typically, a prospective purchaser makes an offer by signing an agreement of sale prepared either by a real estate broker or by his own attorney. This signed agreement as presented to the seller constitutes an offer to purchase the property upon

question was real property or personal property. Most jurisdictions have specific intestacy distribution statutes, and in many of them the distinction between real and personal property has been eliminated.

the terms contained therein. The seller may accept the offer, usually be executing and delivering to the purchaser a copy of the agreement, although the seller may also accept orally, unless the offer requires written acceptance. After his own review or review by his attorney, the seller may object to certain terms and provisions of the offer, instead of accepting the offer. Negotiation may follow. Once the parties have agreed upon all of the terms and conditions to be included in the written agreement, then either the existing offer is changed accordingly and executed by the seller, with both parties initialling the changes, or a new agreement is submitted by one party or the other embodying the agreed terms and conditions. Although the new agreement of sale contains all the terms and conditions which both parties have orally agreed to, the new agreement is technically only an offer being submitted by a party. The other party is not legally bound to accept the offer and is not bound by the agreement until he does accept the offer.[5]

A. DATE

Frequently the date is the first item appearing on the agreement of sale. We have noted that the purchaser becomes the equitable owner of the property on the date of the agreement. If there is damage to the premises by fire, or a taking by eminent domain, the precise date on which purchaser became the equitable owner may be of great importance. When an agreement is to be signed by all parties, the best practice is to date the agreement on the date of execution by the last party to execute.

The question sometimes arises of when the last party to execute has in fact executed. Some forms of printed agreements of sale contain a signature line where the broker signs the agreement as agent for the owner. Where the agent has legal authority to bind the owner to the agreement, the agreement would be effective upon the date on which it is signed by the agent and the purchaser. Where, however, the agent lacks such authority, the effective date of the agreement would be the date on which the owner approved the agreement of sale. The rules which govern the appointment of an agent for purposes of entering into an agreement of sale on behalf of either the purchaser or the seller are discussed in more detail in subsection B below.

B. PARTIES

It is extremely important that the nature and status of all parties to an agreement of sale be fully and accurately described in the agree-

5. Remember, the Statute of Frauds can be satisfied by something less than a full, formal written agreement of sale. Thus an initialled memorandum of proposed agreement of sale can sometimes bind a party. Such memo-randa and similar "agreements to agree" can be very dangerous to those who believe that they are protected by the Statute of Frauds until they sign a formal document labelled "Agreement of Sale".

ment. For example, the seller or the purchaser may be co-tenants, a partnership, limited partnership, corporation, trust or estate. The parties should be carefully identified and the status in which they are to execute should be delineated. In the case of a party which is not a natural person, e. g. a corporation, the capacity of the person executing the agreement on behalf of the entity should be stated. The student will recall from the discussion of the Statute of Frauds that where the property is owned by more than one person, each co-owner should be named as a seller and should execute the agreement.

Care must be taken when dealing with any party other than an individual to obtain all the signatures necessary to bind the party. Thus, for a corporation one commonly requires the signature of one officer plus the attesting signature of another officer, with a clear indication that they are signing on behalf of the corporation in their capacity as officers. You should be careful to understand that the signature of a person to an agreement in one capacity does not bind that person in any other capacity, and another signature by that same person may be required. For example, if Joan Smith Buggy Whip, Inc., a corporation, is selling property to Herman and Joan Smith, husband and wife, the agreement should contain the following signature lines:

SELLER

Joan Smith Buggy Whip, Inc.

By: _____
Joan Smith, President

Attest: _____
Fred Brown, Secretary

PURCHASER

_____
Herman Smith

_____
Joan Smith

PROBLEM

Greenacre is co-owned by (1) Wanda Wylie and Sanford Tunney, Executors of the Estate of Robert Wylie, Deceased and (2) Sanford Tunney and Ida Tunney, his wife. The owners have agreed to sell Greenacre to Greenacre Associates, a general partnership consisting of Wanda Wylie, Ida Tunney and Jack Parris. Please prepare the signature lines necessary and appropriate to bind all of the parties to the agreement.

1. Seller

For the protection of the purchaser, it is advisable that the seller or sellers be named in the agreement of sale in precisely the same way that the grantee is described in the deed by which title is held. The draftsman can obtain this information from the seller's deed, a copy of which should be inspected, if possible, prior to preparing the agreement. Information concerning the grantor is also reflected in title report ordered by buyer (if title insurance is used), but typically a title report is not available until after the agreement of sale has been signed.

(a) Agent as Seller

Some printed form agreements of sale name the seller's real estate agent as the seller. This is not a desirable practice from the purchaser's point of view because even though the agent may produce written evidence of his authority, the purchaser has no way of knowing whether that authority has been revoked by a later act. Therefore, purchaser should require that the actual owner of the property be named as the seller and that the seller also execute the agreement.

(b) Joinder of Spouse

The laws of many states give one spouse an automatic contingent property interest in any real estate owned or acquired by the other spouse, as an individual, during the period of the marriage, notwithstanding the fact that only one spouse is named in the deed as grantee of the property. In order for the purchaser to receive good title to the real estate in such a jurisdiction, it is necessary for the spouse of the seller to join in the deed, thereby conveying his or her contingent interest to the purchaser. In those jurisdictions granting the spouse an interest in real estate, it is imperative that the purchaser ascertain prior to executing the agreement of sale whether any of the sellers is or has ever been married. Based on this information, the purchaser's attorney can decide whether it is necessary for the spouse or former spouse of seller to join in the execution of the deed. If it is determined that the joinder of a spouse is needed, then it is important to the purchaser that the spouse agree in writing to join in the deed. Otherwise, the purchaser will have no right to compel the seller's spouse to join in the deed. One way of requiring the spouse to join in the deed is to make him or her a party to the agreement of sale, and this procedure is often followed. However, naming the spouse as a party would make the spouse responsible for all of the seller's obligations under the agreement of sale, which may not be the intended result. The purchaser will be adequately protected if the spouse simply obligates himself or herself to join the deed if settlement is consummated. This can be done by having the spouse sign a short statement below the signatures on the agreement of sale, substantially as follows:

"For good and valuable consideration, and intending to be, undersigned, legally bound, the wife (husband) of the seller in the above agreement, without becoming a party thereto, hereby joins in the sale for the purpose of approving the sale and to indicate her (his) agreement to join her (his) husband (wife) in executing and acknowledging the deed."

2. Purchaser

The purchaser or purchasers of the property should be named and described in the agreement in the same way that they will take title to the property. This insures that the seller will deliver to the purchaser a deed which correctly describes the purchaser, and the nature of the tenancy by which they are to hold title. It also avoids questions as to whether the agreement has been assigned in violation of its terms, where the agreement bars assignments. For example, assume the agreement of sale was signed by John Smith intending to acquire the property for his business, John Smith, Inc. If John Smith requested seller to name John Smith, Inc. as grantee in the deed, the seller could legitimately refuse to deliver the deed to and in the name of anyone other than the purchaser named in the agreement of sale or his assignee if assignment [6] was permitted by the agreement of sale. Indeed, absent proof of proper assignment of the agreement of sale by the named purchaser, the seller would act at legal peril in conveying the property to anyone else, even an apparently related party.

C. DESCRIPTION OF PROPERTY BEING SOLD

In order to comply with the Statute of Frauds, the property intended to be conveyed must be identified, not necessarily in an elaborate manner, but with sufficient detail to preclude confusion as to which property is involved in the transaction.

1. Methods of Description

There are several ways customarily used to describe the real property which is subject to an agreement of sale.

---

6. A party having legal rights set forth in an agreement or contract generally has the right to convey those benefits to another party. The conveyance is called an "Assignment", the conveyor an "assignor" and the recipient an "assignee". Usually an assignment also conveys to the assignee the assignor's responsibilities and obligations in the agreement or contract. Not all contracts or agreements are assignable. Some are not assignable because the agreement itself so specifies, and this is often the case with agreements of sale for the sale of real estate.

(a) Description by Reference to a Plan

One way of describing property is by reference to a plan of the property, which plan is then attached as an exhibit to the agreement of sale. An example of a provision setting forth this type of description follows:

> "All that certain parcel of ground with any buildings or improvements thereon and the appurtenances thereto, situate in Bellfield Township, Lakes County, Illinois as outlined in red on the plan attached hereto as Exhibit 'A' and hereby made a part hereof."

(b) Legal Description

The agreement of sale may contain a full legal description of the property as taken from a recent survey or the seller's deed, either written out in its entirety or incorporated into the agreement of sale by reference to an attached exhibit. If the survey plan from which the legal description was taken was not prepared in connection with this particular conveyance or if the legal description is taken from a prior deed, or title report, the parties must carefully verify that the property intended to be conveyed by the agreement of sale is indeed identical to that described in the legal description.

(c) Recorded Plan, Street Number

If neither a plan nor a legal description of the property is available for inclusion in the agreement of sale, it may be adequate to identify the real estate merely by reference to a recorded plan, a lot number, a prior conveyance, a street name and number or even by the name by which the property has been popularly known for an extended period of time. Chapter 5 will deal at greater length with forms of legal description and their use in an agreement of sale.

2. Items to be Included in Description

(a) Reference to Buildings

Regardless of the method chosen to identify the property, it is a good practice to include with the description of the land certain additional references to improvements on the property such as, "together with the buildings and improvements thereon and the appurtenances thereto". To the extent that improvements, air rights or subsurface rights are not being conveyed, it is imperative that the agreement of sale specifically exclude the property or rights which the parties do not intend to convey. Where the principal improvement being purchased is a commercial or industrial building, it is desirable to identify the building by its commonly used name, or by a reference to the number of floors and present use of the building:

> "All that certain piece or parcel of land situate in the County of Philadelphia, Pennsylvania, bounded and described as follows: Beginning at a point in the intersection of the North side of Walnut Street (50 feet wide) and the West side of Fourth Street (50 feet

wide); thence in a Westerly direction along the North side of Fourth Street One Hundred (100') Feet to a point; then in a Northerly direction parallel to Fourth Street Two Hundred (200') Feet to a point; thence in an Easterly direction, parallel to Walnut Street, One Hundred (100') Feet to a point on the Westerly side of Fourth Street; thence along said Westerly side of Fourth Street a distance of Two Hundred (200') Feet to the point and place of beginning. Being No. 401 Walnut Street. Together with the 15 story office building erected thereon known as the 'Stern Electronics' building."

(b) Acreage

When representing the purchaser, it is usually a good practice, where the information is available, to include at the end of the description a statement as to the approximate number of acres contained in the tract to be conveyed. If there is a misunderstanding between the parties as to the property being sold, this device often brings the disagreement into the open at an early stage.

(c) Reference to Public Streets

Where one or more of the boundaries of the real estate lie along a public thoroughfare, a prudent draftsperson will include in the agreement of sale and in the deed a clause stating that the conveyance includes all rights of the seller in and to the beds of streets, highways and alleys abutting the property. This is done to make it clear that the conveyance includes all the property rights of the seller, a fact which would be relevant if some time in the future the course of the street is changed or the street is closed to traffic or stricken as a street.

(d) Condemnation Awards

For reasons discussed in subsection II(K) of this chapter, if there is any possibility that the property or any part of the property has been condemned prior to the conveyance to purchaser, the purchaser's attorney should add to the description of the property a clause substantially as follows:

> "and all awards in condemnation, or damages of any kind, to which the Seller may have become entitled or may hereafter be entitled, by reason of any exercise of the power of eminent domain with respect to, or for the taking of, the premises sold hereunder, or any part thereof."

If such a provision is not included the purchaser could end up with a condemned property and the seller would have the right to the proceeds of the condemnation.

(e) Other Property Included in Sale

Just as it is important to describe adequately the real estate which is the subject of the agreement of sale, it is equally important to describe any property intended to be included in the sale which is not, or might not be considered to be, part of the real estate and, conversely, to describe property not intended to be covered by the sale, such as "fixtures". As we discussed in Chapter 1, "fixtures" is a legal term which includes such items as plumbing, electrical wiring, heating and sprinkler systems, television antennas, curtain rods and lighting fixtures. Unless specifically excepted in the agreement of sale, fixtures are automatically included in the conveyance of the real estate to which they are attached. Often, however, it is unclear whether a particular item is a fixture. Especially where it is important to one party or the other that a particular item be included or excluded from the sale, an express provision should state whether the item is or is not intended to be included in the sale. The problem of fixtures is discussed in more detail in section VI of this chapter, dealing with agreements of sale for commercial improved real estate.

PROBLEM

Prepare a short provision for an agreement of sale for a residence indicating that the Lalique chandelier in the dining room is not included in the sale, and that the washer and dryer are.

D. PURCHASE PRICE AND PAYMENT TERMS

1. Standard Provision

The agreement of sale should set forth the amount of the purchase price and the method of payment. Often part of the purchase price is paid at the time the agreement of sale is executed and the balance is paid at settlement. The following is a typical provision setting out the purchase price and payment terms in a cash transaction: [7]

> "The total consideration or purchase price for the premises shall be $_____, and shall be paid as follows:
> (a) $_____ on the signing of this agreement in cash or by plain
>
> check, drawn to the order of _____ to be held in escrow by Agent, and (b) $_____ at settlement in cash or by certified check."

In order to satisfy the Statute of Frauds, the purchase price for the property must be ascertainable from a writing signed by the seller. The writing may simply state the purchase price or may give a formula from which the purchase price may be derived, as where the purchase price is stated in terms of a specified number of dollars to be paid per acre of land.

---

7. In this chapter, a cash transaction is one in which the seller receives the purchase price entirely in cash. This is in contrast to transactions in which the seller receives the purchase price partly in cash and partly in a purchase money note and mortgage at settlement. The purchaser in a cash transaction may well have obtained the cash needed to complete settlement from a mortgage loan made by a third party.

In the absence of language to the contrary, it is presumed that the purchase price is payable in cash. It is rare, however, that the seller insists on payment in cash. The initial deposit at the signing of the agreement of sale is frequently paid by purchaser's plain check (as distinguished from a certified check). For his own protection, the seller should indicate that he accepts the check subject to collection. The seller will not normally, however, accept the balance of the purchase price in the form of purchaser's plain check because of the possibility that the check might be dishonored, leaving the seller with nothing more than a large money claim against the purchaser, who has received and probably recorded the deed. In some parts of the country where settlements are customarily held at the offices of a title insurance company, the title company acts as the collection and disbursing agent. In such areas, one form of acceptable payment of balance of the purchase price is for the title insurance company to issue its check to the seller. The title insurance company will normally be willing to issue its check if it first receives a certified check from the purchaser. If the title insurance company and the bank upon which the title insurance company's check is drawn are financially solvent, there is little danger that the title insurance company's check will be dishonored. Where there is some doubt as to the financial stability of either the title insurance company or its bank, the seller should insist that payment be made by the bank or treasurer's check of a reliable bank. Once such a check has been issued and delivered to the seller, the purchaser has no right to stop payment on the check.

The use of purchase money mortgages and installment sales agreements is more common in commercial real estate transactions, and the discussion of their use and the drafting and negotiating considerations attendant to their use are reserved for later sections of this chapter.

2.   Escrow Account

An extremely desirable practice followed in many parts of the country is to provide in the agreement that deposit monies paid by the purchaser will be placed in an escrow account, the control over which will be in the hands of a neutral party, frequently an attorney, a real estate broker or a title insurance company, who has been designated by the parties to act as the "escrowee." Payment to an escrowee negates the obvious advantage in the seller's position if he has received a substantial downpayment and a dispute arises before settlement. The duties of the escrowee and the conditions upon which he will pay the monies over to one party or the other should be set forth in the agreement or in a separate letter.

The drafting of the escrow provision is a good example of the process by which a careful draftsperson, by consideration of the possibilities and claims, creates a provision that a lay reader would judge to be overly complex for a fairly simple idea. <u>The idea of an escrow is truly simple</u>: <u>to have a trusted neutral party hold the money</u>. Many agreements of sale would say very little more than that, and would leave the definition of the duties of the escrow holder (known as an "escrowee") to be determined by other provisions of the agreement of sale and by the law of the state dealing with escrows. In the great bulk of real estate transactions, that is, those transactions which are successfully concluded, the role of the escrowee would not require any greater definition. However, since the very idea of requiring an escrow suggests that something may go wrong, that some dispute may arise, the drafter of an escrow provision should consider dealing with some of the following issues:

The first and most basic question is to whom the escrowee should pay the deposit monies if nothing goes wrong and the transaction is consummated. The following provision might be used:

"At settlement under this Agreement of Sale, the escrowee shall pay all deposit monies to the Seller, who shall apply them towards the purchase price to be paid the Seller by the Purchaser hereunder."

The next concern for the escrowee is the question of what to do with the deposit monies if either party shall clearly default:

"If Seller, fails, refuses or is unable to make settlement, and Purchaser elects not to sue for specific performance or Purchaser is precluded from suing for specific performance by the terms of this agreement, in addition to Purchaser's remedies other than specific performance, Purchaser shall, upon giving written notice thereof to escrowee and Seller, become entitled to the return of all deposit monies held by escrowee pursuant to this agreement. If Purchaser fails, is unable or refuses to make settlement, upon giving written notice thereof to escrowee and Purchaser, Seller shall forthwith, in addition to Seller's other remedies, become entitled to receive all monies held by escrowee pursuant to this agreement."

An escrowee will not want to take it upon himself to decide whether one party or the other is in default, especially if both claim the money. He might, therefore, add to the foregoing provision, language substantially as follows:

"The escrowee shall pay the monies held in escrow to the party making a demand for payment of the escrow as above provided, unless within five (5) days after receiving notice of the demand for payment of the monies escrowee shall have received notice in writing from the other party that such other party denies the right of the demanding party to receive such monies. The objecting party shall set forth in his notice, under oath, the reason(s) why he denies the right of the demanding party to receive these monies. In the event the escrowee receives conflicting demands for the monies held in escrow or in the event the parties do not agree in writing as to whom the monies belong, escrowee shall have the right to hold the monies until he has received a written agreement between the parties as to its disposition. If the escrowee is sued, he shall have the right to interplead the parties and deposit the money in court."

It is advisable to state what compensation, if any, the escrowee will receive and from whom. In addition, the escrowee may insist upon the inclusion of a provision indemnifying the escrowee against liability, costs and expenses, incurred as escrowee. The following sample provision may be added to deal with the above problems:

"In any action taken relative to this Agreement, the escrowee shall not be liable for any mistake of fact or error of judgment, or for any acts or omissions of any kind unless caused by its own willful mistake, gross negligence or bad faith.

The escrowee may act in reliance upon the advice of counsel satisfactory to it in reference to any matter connected with the escrow and shall not incur any liability for any action taken in accordance with such advice.

The parties agree to pay the escrowee its fees for acting as such, the amount of which fee shall be $_____, and to indemnify the escrowee and hold it harmless from all damages, costs and expenses, including counsel fees, incurred by the escrowee, except such as result from its own breach of this Agreement, and the escrowee shall have a security interest in the subject matter of this escrow for the payment of all fees, charges, costs and expenses."

If the sum being held by the escrowee is large, it may be advantageous to deposit it into an interest bearing account. However, because savings accounts are not entirely risk free, the escrowee might want specific authorization to deposit the money in a savings account. If this is done, the agreement must clearly indicate who is entitled to this interest both in the situation where the transaction is completed and when there is a default.

PROBLEM

Draft a clause of the escrow provision authorizing the escrowee to deposit the deposit monies in an interest bearing account at any local commercial bank or savings and loan association, and providing that interest will be paid to the party entitled to receive the deposit monies (but note that if the Seller receives the interest, the amount of the interest is not credited towards the purchase price).

E.   CONDITION OR QUALITY OF TITLE TO BE CONVEYED

The escrow provision was the first truly lawyerly term which we have so far discussed. Any intelligent layman would probably include in an agreement a brief description of the parties, the purchase price and the property being sold. Few laymen would think to include an escrow provision. As few or fewer would think to include a provision dealing with the quality of title. Yet this is an important term. The description of the premises indicates the physical boundaries of what is being conveyed. The quality of title indicates the legal boundaries of the real estate interest being conveyed. As you will recall from Chapter 1, many kinds of interests or estates in real property can be conveyed, and real property can be subject to a virtually limitless number of interests, estates, rights, powers, restrictions, easements, liens and encumbrances. Each state has decided according to its own state laws what quality of title the seller must convey and the purchaser must accept if the agreement of sale is silent as to quality of title. The state law in this respect could vary all the way from requiring the seller to provide title in fee simple absolute, subject to no easements, restrictions, agreements, liens or encumbrances whatsoever; to requiring the purchaser to accept only a quitclaim deed conveying whatever interest (if any) seller has, subject to easements, liens and encumbrances.

The drafter of the quality of title provision must be aware of this range of possibilities. If poorly drawn from the standpoint of the seller, the provision can be so restrictive in terms of what the seller must provide that the purchaser, in effect, has an option to buy or reject the property at settlement. On the other hand, if the provision is poorly drafted from the standpoint of the purchaser he can be forced to complete the transaction and pay the full purchase price for a piece of real estate which a title search reveals to be worth to the purchaser but a fraction of what the purchaser has agreed to pay for the property. Printed below are four provisions, each of which deals with the problem in a different way.

EXAMPLE 1:

"The premises are to be conveyed free and clear of all liens, encumbrances, and easements, Excepting however, the following: Mortgage encumbrances as above mentioned, existing building restrictions, ordinances, easements of roads, privileges or rights of public service companies, and any other restrictions or conditions of record, if any; otherwise the title to the herein described lot or piece of ground shall be good and marketable or such as will be insured by a reputable Title Insurance Company in the City of Philadelphia, or the adjacent counties, at the regular rates."

EXAMPLE 2:

"Title to the Premises shall be good and marketable and free and clear of all liens, restrictions, easements, encumbrances, leases, tenancies and other title objections, and shall be insurable as such at ordinary rates by any reputable title insurance company selected by Buyer."

EXAMPLE 3:

"Title to the Premises shall be good and marketable and free and clear of all liens, restrictions, easements and other encumbrances and title objections excepting, however, those title objections set out in Exhibit 'A' attached hereto and hereby made a part hereof; and shall be insurable as such at regular rates by any responsible title insurance company selected by Buyer."

EXAMPLE 4:

"Title to the Premises shall be good and marketable and free and clear of all liens, encumbrances and easements; Excepting however the following: existing building restrictions, ordinances, easements of roads, privileges or rights of public service companies, and any other restrictions of record, if any; provided, however, that the present use of and improvements to the Premises are not in violation of any of the above and none of the above shall restrict or prevent the use of the Premises as a single family dwelling or impose any monetary or maintenance obligations (except in the case of ordinances) upon the owner of the Premises, otherwise, the title to the Premises shall be good and marketable and insurable as such by First National Land Title Insurance Company at its regular rates."

Example 1 of the condition of title clause is so broad as to impose hardly any obligation at all upon the seller, other than to pass title. **Example 2,** on the other hand, is so narrow that very few owners of real estate in urban or suburban areas could comply with it. **Examples 3 and 4** are fairly typical of quality of title provisions that have been negotiated by the attorneys for the purchaser and the seller.

Let us now examine the language of these provisions more closely to determine exactly how the language of each is advantageous to one party or the other. Ideally, a purchaser wants title to his property to be entirely free and clear of all liens, encumbrances, and easements. If he has no alternative but to take title to certain relatively minor title objections, as is normally the case in a populated area, he would like to know, prior to committing to purchase the property, precisely what those title objections will be. In that manner the purchaser can make an informed judgment as to the price he is willing to pay for the property or whether he wants the property at all; i. e., whether the title objections prevent the buyer from putting the real estate to the intended use. For this reason the language in the first version of the condition of title clause dealing with liens, encumbrances, and easements may not be acceptable to a purchaser. Most sellers, when confronted by a knowledgeable purchaser, are willing to obligate themselves to deliver a title which is free and clear except for a certain number of limited objections to the title which are impossible or impractical to remove and which either are specifically enumerated in the agreement of sale (or an exhibit to it) and agreed upon by the parties, as in Example 3, or which are not of the sort to restrict the purchaser in his intended use of the property, as in Example 4.

If a title search on the property has been completed shortly before the agreement of sale is executed, both parties can decide prior to executing the agreement which of the title objections appearing on such a report will be acceptable. Frequently, however, a title search is not available prior to execution of the agreement of sale. If the seller obtained title insurance when he bought the property, the parties can refer to that title insurance policy for the purpose of enumerating the acceptable title objections. Of course, that title insurance policy will not show any liens, encumbrances or easements which may have arisen while the seller was the owner of the property. It is very important, therefore, when representing a seller, to question the seller very closely to determine whether anything has happened during the seller's ownership of the property to encumber the title and, if something has occurred, to add that to the list of objections obtained from the seller's title insurance policy.

In some circumstances the seller will not know what title objections, if any, exist. In such instances, the approach demonstrated in Example 4 is often used as a substitute for the more exact, and therefore preferable, approach shown in Example 3.

1. Good and Marketable Title

Each of the sample provisions quoted above refers to a good and marketable title. What does this term mean? In exploring the meaning of good and marketable title in Chapter 4, you likely will find the definition hard to grasp. It is a term which legal writers have also found difficult to define in a non-circular manner. One authority defined marketable title as follows:

> "[The term marketable title] was coined by the equity courts to designate a title which, although it may be clouded by some uncertainties or defects, is sufficiently free from all fair or reasonable doubt, so that they would compel a purchaser to accept it in a suit for specific performance. Conversely, an unmarketable title, although not necessarily bad, is one that has apparent defects or encumbrances which will cause such a doubt in the mind of a reasonable, prudent, and intelligent person that he will refuse to take the property, or to take it at its full value. In fact, it has frequently been held that a doubt sufficient to impair a title's quality of marketableness must be such as to affect the selling value of the property or to interfere with the making of a sale. The good title which a purchaser may require need not be free from all clouds or suspicions; it need only be such a title as prudent men, well ad-

vised as to the facts and their legal bearings, would be willing to accept . . . [It is generally conceded that for title to be good and marketable the following elements must be established:]

1. Rightful ownership of the entire property, or of the entire interest or estate contracted for, free from all fair or reasonable doubts . . . [which in some states, as a matter of law, and under most agreements of sale, is satisfied by production of appropriate record evidence of ownership].

2. Freedom of the estate or interest involved from liens, charges or other encumbrances.

3. Rightful possession of the property." [8]

2. Insurable Title

A second test stated in the sample provisions for determining the condition of title to the premises is the requirement that the title will be insurable. In order to forestall any arguments as to whether the requirement is satisfied if at least one title company will issue or whether every title company must be willing to issue, the parties can specify a particular title company. The seller may agree to let a single designated title insurance company be the arbiter if that company also issued the seller's policy. If this approach is used and the Real Estate Settlement Procedures Act of 1974 applies (this Act, also known as RESPA, is discussed in detail in Chapter 11) the agreement of sale should make it clear that the purchaser chose the particular title company or that the company is being referred to only as the judge of quality of title, with no requirement that Purchaser obtain title insurance from them.[9] Failure to make this clear may subject the seller to substantial penalties under RESPA. Since the title insurance company which insured the seller when he bought the property is already obligated to pay for unexcepted defects in the title occurring prior to the seller's ownership, it will often insure the purchaser's title in circumstances where other title insurers would not. The reason for this is that by so doing the title insurance company may avoid having to pay damages to the seller under the seller's policy, although it might have liability to the purchaser at a later time.

The purchaser will not be adequately protected if the agreement of sale merely states that the title will be insurable. It is necessary to add the words "at regular rates." If paid a sufficient premium, some title insurance companies can be induced to assume an unusually high risk. If this short phase were omitted, the purchaser could be required to purchase a property with a serious defect and, if he

8. American Law of Property § 18.7 (A. J. Casner ed. 1952).

9. The provision is included in response to the restriction in RESPA forbidding a seller or financer from requiring a purchaser to employ a certain title company. It is essentially an anti-kickback provision.

desired title insurance, be subject to payment of an extremely high premium.

If you read again the four provisions quoted above, you will note three of them provide that title is to be good and marketable, *and* such as will be insurable at regular rates while Example 1 provides that title is to be good and marketable *or* such as will be insurable at regular rates. There is a meaningful difference between the two phrases. In the one case, the title must be both good and marketable *and* also meet with the approval of the title company. In the second, the title could actually be unmarketable, but be insurable by some title insurance company, or else it could be good and marketable but not insurable by any title insurance company. If the purchaser is to be adequately protected, he should insist that the quality of the title meet both tests.

F. TIME AND PLACE OF SETTLEMENT

Chapter 11 contains a detailed description of what transpires at a "settlement" or "closing." For purposes of this chapter, you need only understand that it is at settlement that the seller delivers an executed deed to the purchaser in exchange for the purchase price (which may include a purchase money note and mortgage), and the other obligations contained in the agreement of sale are also generally satisfied.

The courts will interpret an agreement of sale which does not specify the time and place of settlement as meaning that the parties intended settlement to be held within a reasonable time following execution of the agreement, at a place reasonably convenient to the parties. However, the time and place of closing should be specified in the agreement of sale in order to avoid the delay and risk of litigation.

Many printed forms of agreement of sale attempt to cover time of settlement by merely providing that "settlement shall be made on or before _____ day of _____, _____", without specifying the time of day or place where the settlement is to be held. If the parties cannot agree as to the time and place of settlement, one party might have a very difficult time establishing that the other party breached the agreement by failing to complete settlement. Of course, the fact that a time and place of settlement is expressly stated in the agreement does not preclude the parties from changing the time and place of settlement. For this reason, a good agreement of sale will normally contain a provision similar to the following:

"Settlement will be made at the offices of _____, [*insert address*] _____, at _____ o'clock on _____, 19___, or at such other definite place and time and prior date as Seller and Purchaser (or their respective attorneys) may agree upon in writing."

By specifying a time and place for settlement either party can properly "make tender" in the event the other party breaches the agreement of sale. "Tender" is a legal term which means that one party produces and offers the requisite money or property to the other party as required by the agreement of sale. Tender is usually followed by a demand that the other party meet its corresponding obligations. In most jurisdictions, unless the agreement of sale provides for a waiver of formal tender of the deed, the seller must appear at the time and place designated for settlement with a signed, sealed and acknowledged deed before he has the right to declare the buyer in default under the agreement of sale. The above rule would apply even if the purchaser declared bankruptcy or fled the country the week before settlement. Similarly, in the absence of the agreement of sale providing a waiver of formal tender of the purchase money, the purchaser must appear at the time and place designated for settlement with the balance of the purchase price in hand, (in the form specified in the agreement of sale) if he is to have the right to declare the seller in default. Many standard agreements of sale now provide that formal tender of both the deed and the purchase money are waived.

Many agreements of sale provide that the times set for the performance of various obligations (such as the obligation to pay the purchase price or to deliver the deed) are "of the essence" of the agreement. This phrase is used to designate those obligations which are sufficiently important to the parties so that if they have not been satisfied by the designated time, the resulting default will be deemed to be a material breach of the entire agreement. Such a breach entitles the non-defaulting party to obtain rescission of the agreement, which is a judicial cancellation of the agreement accompanied by a return to the *status quo ante*. In the absence of an express stipulation that time is of the essence, the general rule is that courts will grant a defaulting party a reasonable time in which to cure his default and will not grant a non-defaulting party rescission of the agreement if the breach is cured in a reasonable time. If the defaulting party does cure his breach, then a court will limit the non-defaulting remedies to compensation for damages caused by the delay.

Where the parties wish to provide that the failure on the part of either to perform punctually all of the obligations under the agreement shall be deemed to be a material breach of the contract, a provision such as the following should be used:

"The time set for settlement hereunder and all other times referred to for performance of any of the obligations of this agreement shall be of the essence."

G. POSSESSION

The final act in consummating a real estate transaction is for the seller to surrender possession of the property to the purchaser.

Because the seller cannot deliver possession of a piece of real estate by handing it to the purchaser, a symbolic form of delivery of possession takes place at settlement. A fairly typical provision relating to symbolic delivery states:

> "Possession of the Premises shall be given to Purchaser at the time of settlement (the Premises being then unoccupied and free of any leases, claims to or rights of possession) by delivery of the keys to the Premises and Seller's special warranty deed (with release of dower, curtesy and homestead rights, if any) in proper recordable form, duly executed and acknowledged by Seller."

The foregoing provision requires delivery of the premises "unoccupied and free of any leases, claims to or rights of possession." If the property or part of the property is under lease at the time of sale and the buyer desires to purchase the property subject to the lease(s), the language would have to be amended to so provide. In addition, the agreement should then obligate the seller to assign all of the leases to the purchaser at the settlement and produce a signed notice to each tenant, directing the tenant to make future rental payments to purchaser. Furthermore, since the purchaser will be responsible for return of security deposits to the tenants, a provision is normally included allowing the amount of those deposits as a credit to the purchaser. The seller should insist that the purchaser agree to assume all of the obligations of landlord under the leases being assigned.[10]

There is a particular problem when real estate is sold to the tenant of the property. Pennsylvania courts have held that execution of an agreement of sale by a tenant, or exercise of an option to purchase, terminates the landlord-tenant relationship. This is seldom the intended result as far as a seller is concerned, and it is therefore necessary to state specifically that the lease survives until settlement.

Sometimes the purchaser wishes to take possession of the real estate prior to the date scheduled for settlement, or conversely, the seller wishes to remain in possession of the property after settlement has been completed. Both of these conditions are normally undesirable from the standpoint of the party out of possession. The problem is that the party out of possession may experience difficulty in getting the party in possession to vacate the premises at the appointed time. When it is necessary to permit the non-owner of the property to have possession, the rights of the parties should be defined by a written lease which contains appropriate legal remedies if the non-owner fails to vacate on time. If the seller desires to remain in possession until a specified date, the purchaser will normally be well advised to insist upon postponing settlement for the period the seller needs to re-

---

10. The other side of an assignment of an agreement or contract is the agreement of the assignee to perform all of the assignor's obligations under the agreement being assigned. When an assignee agrees to become personally and primarily responsible for assignor's obligations, then the assignee is said to have "assumed" the agreement.

main in possession rather than to complete settlement and have the seller as a tenant. Problems such as deterioration of the property between the date of settlement and the date of possession become more difficult to remedy if settlement has occurred.

If the purchaser is to take possession of the property prior to settlement, both the agreement of sale and the lease for the property for the interim period prior to settlement should provide that the purchaser's possession is governed exclusively by the terms of the lease and that he is not a purchaser in possession under an agreement of sale. Furthermore, the lease should provide that its term expires upon the date set for settlement, so that if the purchaser fails to complete settlement, the seller will have the right to evict the purchaser. Frequently the lease incorporates liquidated damages provisions which make it extremely onerous for a defaulting purchaser to remain in possession after his default.

H. APPORTIONMENTS

At the settlement for almost all real estate sales there are certain expenses relating to the property which must be apportioned between the parties. The apportionments arise because of charges which must be paid by the owner of the property at a specified time, but which relate to the use of the premises during a period of time which spans ownership by seller and purchaser. It would not be equitable to expect one party or the other to bear the entire amount of these expenses, depending upon the mere chance of which party is in possession at the time the charge is payable. It is customary, therefore, for the purchaser and seller to allocate the charges between themselves on the basis of the percentage of the period for which the charge is imposed that each one of them is in possession of the property.

A typical printed form of agreement of sale deals with this apportionment problem in the following manner:

> "Taxes, Rents, Water Rents, Interest on Mortgage Encumbrances, and Sewer Rental, if any, shall be apportioned pro rata as of the date of settlement, which apportionments shall be based upon the actual fiscal period for which the charges are assessed or levied."

The proper way to handle the apportionment problems and the safeguards which are necessary to protect the purchaser and seller will depend greatly on the law and practices of the jurisdiction governing the transaction. In any case the first steps are to determine the period for which the charge is imposed and whether the charge is imposed in arrears, in advance or partly each. Taxes often are assessed for a twelve month period, but the twelve month period does not always coincide with the calendar year. If, for example, the taxes are for a July 1—June 30 fiscal year and settlement is held on August 1, for purposes of apportioning this particular charge, the seller has been in possession of the property for only $\frac{1}{12}$th of the year, not $\frac{7}{12}$ths. By this example, the seller would be responsible for $\frac{1}{12}$th of that annual tax and the purchaser would be responsible for $\frac{11}{12}$ths. If the tax is payable in advance and has actually been paid by the seller, then the seller is entitled to receive compensation from the purchaser for $\frac{11}{12}$ths of the tax. If the tax is not yet due or is due but has not yet been paid by the seller,[11] then the purchaser is entitled to credit for $\frac{1}{12}$th of the tax.

In some areas, one set of taxes is imposed for one twelve month period while a second set is imposed for a different twelve month period. For example, a tax imposed by a school district may be based on a fiscal year starting July 1, while a tax to support general municipal services is based on a calendar year. Sometimes both taxes are assessed in one bill, in which case various portions of the bill will be treated differently in regard to apportionments. Some charges are imposed for periods of less than twelve months, such as quarterly or semi-annually.

Another variation is that in some areas taxes are paid by one or more estimated installments during the taxable period. The estimated tax is usually based upon the final tax for the previous tax period. A final reckoning is made at the end of the tax period based upon the actual budgetary expenses of the taxing authority. Taxpayers are entitled to a credit if the final tax is less than the estimated tax they have paid. However, the usual experience in the recent inflationary times is for taxing authority expenses to increase, and the taxpayer in such areas usually must anticipate an increase every year. For purposes of apportionments, the paralegal in such areas must realize that the actual tax to be paid for the entire tax period is attributable to the entire period. Thus, at settlement in areas using estimated tax payments, the ultimate tax liability of the seller for the period prior to settlement may not be known until several months after settlement. Local practice will usually make some accommodation for this fact, by way of escrows or estimated increases.

PROBLEMS

How many local taxes are imposed upon real estate in your area? What taxing periods do the taxing authorities use? Are taxes paid in advance or in arrears? Are taxes paid in installments, and, if so, are they estimated installments?

It is advisable to determine whether the charge creates a personal liability against the owner of the property or whether it merely results in a lien against the property. In some states, for example, real estate taxes are assessed and become liens as of the time the rate is determined or as of the beginning of the tax fiscal year. In those

---

11. A properly drafted clause should impose upon the seller the full burden of any penalties due for taxes which are overdue.

states, the owner of real estate becomes personally liable for payment of taxes as of the day of assessment, regardless of the fact that he sells the property the next day and has no interest in the property for the balance of the year. Because of this personal liability, the seller must assure himself not only that real estate taxes assessed against the property during his ownership are apportioned, but also that both his share and the purchaser's share of the taxes are paid in full to the taxing authority at settlement even though they are not yet due. If any particular charge does not result in personal liability to the seller, his only real concern is that it is properly apportioned.

Apportionment of rents payable under leases on the property is discussed in section VI of this chapter. Apportionment of interest on mortgages which are remaining on the property after the property is conveyed will be discussed in Chapter 11 and will be discussed further in subsection III(A) of this chapter.

I. REAL ESTATE TRANSFER TAXES

Many states and municipalities tax the transfer of real estate or the recording of a deed. These taxes are similar in some respects to sales taxes imposed upon the sale of personal property.[12] The name by which the tax on the transfer of real estate is known and the amount of the tax varies with the jurisdiction.

The statute enacting a transfer or recording tax may specify that the purchaser, the seller, or both are responsible for payment of the tax. Local custom may also dictate who is responsible for its payment. In Pennsylvania, for example, it is customary for the burden of the realty tax to be split evenly between the purchaser and the seller. In New Jersey, on the other hand, it is customary for the seller to pay the full amount of the transfer fee. Notwithstanding the prevailing law or custom, it is preferable for the agreement of sale to fix responsibility for payment of a transfer or recording tax.

J. MUNICIPAL IMPROVEMENTS AND VIOLATIONS OF LAWS, ORDINANCES OR REGULATIONS

Normally, assessments which have been made for municipal improvements, such as street paving and curbing and installation of water and sewer lines, are encumbrances upon the property and must be removed as title objections before the seller can convey title which is free and clear of all liens and encumbrances.

The problem is that occasionally assessments have not been made by the time of settlement for improvements which have been com-

---

12. One difference between transfer taxes and sales taxes relates to the federal income tax consequences of the tax. Unlike most state sales taxes, transfer taxes may not be included on Schedule A of an itemized income tax return in the category of "taxes paid". Transfer taxes are a cost of selling or purchasing real estate and are included within the tax basis of the property for purposes of determining gain or loss upon sale.

pleted, or which are close to completion. If the purchaser has not adequately provided for this eventuality in the agreement of sale, he may be in the unpleasant position of receiving an unexpected assessment after he takes possession of the property. Consequently, the purchaser should question the seller as to whether the local authorities have contemplated making, are in the process of making, or have recently made any improvements which might result in an assessment against the property. In addition, the subject should be covered in the agreement of sale. If the seller is willing to pay for improvements begun before the agreement is executed and the purchaser, as the equitable owner, is willing to bear the burden thereafter, the following provision might be included in the agreement of sale:

"Seller warrants and represents that as of the date hereof no assessments for public improvements have been made against the premises which remain unpaid. Seller shall be responsible for the payment of any assessment or charge hereafter made for any public improvement begun before the date hereof. Purchaser shall be responsible for the payment of any assessment or charge hereafter made for any public improvement begun after the date hereof."

If the seller refuses the above, the purchaser may be willing to settle for the following type of provision, although in that case the purchaser should make a particularly close inspection of the property to determine whether any recent municipal improvements have been made:

"Seller warrants and represents that the premises will not be assessed for any street improvements, or installation of or connection to sewer or water lines heretofore made. Purchaser will be responsible for any public improvements, no matter when begun, which have not yet been completed."

The purchaser must also be careful that he will not be burdened with the costs of bringing the property into compliance with the health, building, safety, zoning and related laws of the jurisdiction in which the property is located. He might request that an inspection of the property be made by the appropriate officials or require the seller to produce at settlement certificates from the local authorities stating that the property is in compliance with all applicable laws. The seller will often refuse to agree to provisions of this type, either because he knows that there are violations, or for fear that an inspection will reveal one or more technical violations of the law. If the seller is unwilling to have the property inspected or to produce certificates of compliance at settlement, a clause substantially similar to the one which follows is often used:

"Seller covenants and represents that, prior to the execution of this agreement, no notice from any governmental authority has been served upon the premises, or upon Seller, or Seller's agent, requiring, or calling attention to the need for any work, repairs, construction, alterations or installations on or in connection with the premises, which have not been complied with. If Purchaser takes title to the premises, Purchaser will be responsible for the cost of all such work, repairs, construction, or installations which may be required or called attention to, by any notice served by any of the said authorities at or after the execution of this agreement."

The problem with the provision set forth above is that since the purchaser is not being presented with a certificate from the local authorities, he may not learn of a violation of covenant until sometime after settlement. At such time his only remedy will be a lawsuit against seller (who may be unavailable or without assets) to recover the cost of correcting the violations. Indeed, unless the warranty "survives" the settlement, it is possible that the warranty will not be operative after settlement, in which case the purchaser will have no remedy. (See Section P(2) of this Chapter).

K.   CONDEMNATION

Under certain circumstances, federal and state governments political subdivisions thereof, and some public utilities, have the power (referred to as the power of condemnation or eminent domain), to acquire interests in real estate without the consent of the owner or the possessor of the property affected. The taking may be accomplished with little or no notice to the owner of the property or the party in possession. The Fifth Amendment to the U. S. Constitution requires that the condemning authority compensate the owner for the interest taken. In most jurisdictions, the identity of the owner is determined as of the date of the condemnation, which is sometimes prior to the actual taking of possession by the condemning authority. A possible result is that if property subject to an agreement of sale is condemned prior to settlement, the purchaser will ultimately suffer the loss, but the condemning authority will pay the condemnation award to the seller, as the owner of record, even if the award is not actually paid until after settlement is made.

If the agreement of sale is silent as to the respective rights of the parties in the event of a condemnation, the purchaser in most jurisdictions would have the right to rescind the transaction or, if the taking was of only a party of the property, to obtain a reduction of the purchase price if he discovered the condemnation prior to settlement. However, if the purchaser does not discover the condemnation prior to the time of settlement and he pays the full purchase price and accepts the deed, in most jurisdictions he will have no right to recover anything from the seller, unless the seller delivered a deed of general warranty rather than special warranty or "quitclaim".

For the purchaser to be fully protected in this situation, the draftsman must include in the agreement of sale an assignment of any condemnation award received or receivable by the seller. The agreement should also provide that any award actually received by the seller will be credited to the purchase price if settlement is concluded. From the purchaser's standpoint it is advisable, notwithstanding the assignment of any award, also to reserve the right, at the purchaser's option, to terminate the agreement in the event of a condemnation of all or part of the property.

Many printed forms of agreement of sale do not contain any provision dealing with the condemnation problem. It is necessary, therefore, when using such a printed form, to add a condemnation clause. One suggested provision is as follows:

> "In the event of the taking of all or any part of the premises by eminent domain proceedings or the commencement of any such proceedings prior to settlement, Purchaser shall have the right, at his option, to terminate this agreement by giving written notice thereof to Seller on or before the date fixed for settlement hereunder. If Purchaser does not so terminate this agreement, the purchase price for the premises shall be reduced by the total of any awards or other proceeds received by Seller at or prior to settlement with respect to any taking, and at settlement Seller shall assign to Purchaser all rights of Seller in and to any awards or other proceeds payable by reason of any taking. Seller agrees to notify Purchaser of eminent domain proceedings within five days after Seller learns thereof. Notwithstanding the fact that neither Purchaser nor Seller knows of the taking of all or any part of the premises by eminent domain proceedings at the time of settlement, Seller shall execute, acknowledge and deliver at settlement, an assignment of all the rights of Seller in and to any awards or other proceeds payable by reason of any such taking, whether known or unknown. At Purchaser's option, such assignment may be included in the deed from Seller to Purchaser or may be in the form of a separate assignment."

L. DEFAULTS AND REMEDIES

1. The Law Absent Agreement by the Parties

The statutory and common law of each state provides for certain rights and remedies to a party to an agreement of sale upon the default of the other party, whether or not the agreement itself specifies any such rights or remedies. The following are typical categories of remedies available in some form in most states.

(a) Default by the Purchaser

In most jurisdictions, if the purchaser fails to complete settlement, the following remedies are available to the seller:[13]

(i) Suit for Damages

The seller may sue the purchaser for damages suffered by the seller, of which one measure would be the difference between the pur-

---

13. Remember that the seller may have to tender a deed as discussed earlier in this chapter.

chase price stated in the agreement of sale and the amount (less costs of the sale) received by the seller at a subsequent fair sale of the property, sometimes with interest on such damages.

(ii) Specific Performance

In lieu of a suit for damages, the seller may maintain an action for specific performance of the agreement of sale in order to obtain from the purchaser the balance of the purchase price.

(b) Default by Seller

In most jurisdictions, if the seller fails to complete settlement, the following remedies are available to the purchaser:

(i) Suit for Damages

The purchaser can bring a suit for damages suffered by the purchaser in an amount equal to any unreturned deposit made by the purchaser plus his actual expenses (such as cost of a title search and preparing a survey), plus interest.

(ii) Specific Performance

The purchaser may maintain an action for specific performance of the agreement of sale, and purchase the property in accordance with the agreement of sale.   The purchaser may be given a reduction in the purchase price to compensate for the damages suffered by the purchaser by reason of the delay (one measure of such damages being the amount by which the net income produced by the property during the period of the delay exceeds the interest on the balance of the purchase price during that period).

(iii) Loss of Bargain

If the seller wilfully breaches the agreement or is guilty of bad faith in an attempt to escape his obligations under the agreement, such as by conveying or agreeing to convey the property to a second purchaser, the purchaser may be able to recover not only the deposit money paid, plus interest and expenses, but also damages for the loss of the bargain.[14]

2.   Agreement of the Parties

Often, the parties wish to alter the respective rights and liabilities of the parties that the state law would provide upon default of a party. This may be done by specifying in the agreement what their respective rights will be in the event of breach.   Within certain broad limitations, the parties to an agreement of sale can agree to expand upon or limit the remedies that would otherwise be available to them.

---

14.   See section P of this chapter regarding loss of bargain damages.

(a) Purchaser's Default

The following is an example of a typical provision dealing with default by a purchaser:

> "Should the Purchaser violate or fail to fulfill and perform any of the terms or conditions of this agreement, then and in that case all sums paid by the Purchaser on account of the purchase price or consideration herein may be retained by the Seller, either on account of the purchase price, or as liquidated damages for such breach, as the Seller shall elect, and in the latter event the Seller shall be released from all liability or obligation and this agreement shall become null and void."

The above provision is largely declaratory of the law in the absence of a default clause in the agreement. An attorney representing the purchaser will want to amend the provision to eliminate the right of the seller to bring suit for the purchase price. That will leave the seller with damages equal to the down payment made by the purchaser. The change may be accomplished by the following language:

> "Should the Purchaser violate or fail to fulfill and perform any of the terms or conditions of this agreement then and in that case all sums paid by the Purchaser on account of the purchase price or consideration herein shall be retained by the Seller as liquidated damages. In such event both parties shall be released from all liability or obligation to the other under this agreement and this agreement shall become null and void. The retention of such damages shall be Seller's sole remedy in the event of default by the Purchaser; and the Seller hereby waives any right to recover the balance of the purchase price or any part thereof not already paid by the Purchaser."

(b) Seller's Default

The following provision (also favorable to the seller) limits the usual state law remedies to which the purchaser would be entitled in the event of the seller's default:

> "In the event the Seller is unable to give a good and marketable title or such as will be insured by any reputable title insurance company, as above set forth, Buyer shall have the option of taking such title as the Seller can give without abatement of price, or of being repaid all monies paid on account by Purchaser to Seller and the Purchaser shall also be reimbursed for any Title Company charges incurred; and in the latter event there shall be no further liability or obligation by either of the parties hereunder and this agreement shall become null and void."

The attorney for the purchaser might want to restore most or all of the purchaser's usual state law remedies as previously set forth.

M. ZONING

Zoning is the generic name for municipal ordinances which regulate the use of real property within a municipality by restricting a landowner in a particular zone to certain specified classes of use. The issue of zoning raises some problems to which the parties might wish to address themselves in an agreement of sale. The purchaser may attempt to include in the agreement of sale a provision by which the seller warrants to the purchaser that the present use is permitted under the existing zoning classification, and which conditions settlement upon continued legality of use. A provision to that effect follows:

> "Seller hereby represents and warrants that the zoning classification of the premises is _____, that the present use of the premises as _____ is in compliance with the zoning laws and all ordinances pertaining thereto, and that Purchaser's intended use of the premises as _____ is also in compliance therewith. If, prior to settlement, an amendment to the zoning ordinances or any other law, ordinance or regulation comes into effect, which prohibits the operation of _____ upon the premises, Purchaser shall have the right, upon giving written notice thereof to Seller, at or before settlement, to cancel this agreement and to recover all monies paid to Seller on account of the purchase price."

Normally, if the agreement of sale contains no representation or warranty as to zoning or legality of use, then the purchaser is wholly subject to the zoning laws and any changes in the zoning laws, and may not refuse to make settlement because he discovers that his intended use is not permitted. However, to safeguard himself, the seller should negate any warranty or representation, as follows:

> "Buyer hereby acknowledges that he has ascertained the zoning classification of the premises and the legality of the present use thereof. Buyer further acknowledges that Seller has made no representation or warranty relating to zoning or use notwithstanding any statute, or customs to the contrary."

If the purchaser knows that he cannot put the property to his intended use without first obtaining a variance or special exception under the zoning code, he should condition his obligation to complete the sale upon his ability to obtain whatever approval of local authorities are needed. Due to the possibility of appeals and other delays, it may take a long period of time to obtain and finalize such approval. Therefore, the purchaser wants to provide himself ample time to obtain the approvals. The seller, on the other hand, does not want the property removed from the market for a long period of time. Accordingly, it is advisable in this type of situation for the parties to establish an outside date at which time the agreement will become null and void and the purchaser's purchase money will be returned if the necessary approvals have not been received and the possibility of appeal foreclosed. The agreement should make clear which of the seller and the buyer will be responsible for obtaining the necessary zoning approval. If the seller is to obtain the approval, the purchaser should make provision for the right to take over and carry on the procedure if the seller fails to pursue the matter diligently, which might occur if the seller receives a better offer for the property. A provision dealing with the problem of zoning approval from the viewpoint of the purchaser follows:

"Purchaser's obligation to complete settlement under this agreement is conditioned, in accordance with the provisions hereinafter stated, upon the issuance to Purchaser by the duly constituted public authorities of such permits, certificates, variances, exceptions, licenses, authorizations, approvals and changes (including by way of illustration and not limitation, zoning variances, zoning exceptions, subdivision approval and building permits), (each being referred to in this agreement as a "Permit") as may be required or desired by Purchaser to permit the use of the premises as a _____. Seller agrees to cooperate with Purchaser in obtaining the Permits and prosecuting any appeals in connection therewith and to execute any documents submitted by Purchaser with respect thereto. If at the time of settlement hereunder all of the Permits are not validly issued and received by Purchaser or the time within which an appeal may be taken from the issuance of any Permit has not elapsed or an appeal has been taken from the issuance of a Permit and for any reason has not been finally determined in favor of the applicant for the Permit, then, in any such event, Purchaser shall have the right, at its option, to terminate this agreement by giving written notice thereof to Seller."

The attorney for the seller would want to make sure that the Purchaser makes a good faith effort to obtain the necessary Permits.

PROBLEM

Add the necessary language to the above provision requiring the Purchaser to try to obtain the Permit, including a waiver of the condition if he does not try to do so.

N. PURCHASER'S RIGHT OF INSPECTION

Shortly before the time scheduled for the settlement, the purchaser should inspect the premises in order to verify that they are in the condition required by the agreement, that all fixtures which the seller has agreed to leave on the property have indeed been left and that they are in good operating condition.[15] It may be desirable for the purchaser to have the property inspected prior to settlement by experienced inspectors. However, unless the purchaser has reserved the right to come onto the property for the purpose of conducting such inspections, the seller can legally bar the purchaser's entry until after settlement. A provision granting the purchaser a right of inspection follows:

"Purchaser, or Purchaser's employees or agents, shall have the right to inspect the premises prior to settlement at reasonable times

---

15. Please remember that there is no legal requirement that the fixtures or any personalty included in the sale be in good operating condition unless the agreement of sale specifically imposes such a requirement.

on reasonable advance notice from time to time for the purposes of obtaining estimates for any work to be done to the premises after settlement and verifying that the provisions of this agreement have been complied with."

O. BROKERS

It is not common practice for the agreement between the broker and the party who engaged him to be made part of the agreement of sale. However, occasionally serious disputes arise over the questions of whether a particular broker is entitled to a commission and who is to pay the commission. Therefore, it is often advisable for the parties to raise the issue as to whether any broker has become involved in the transaction and to allocate the responsibility for compensating the broker. In addition to containing representations from each party as to whether that party engaged any broker, such a provision might contain an indemnification by each party of the other party against any claim for broker's commissions.

PROBLEMS

1. Draft a broker's commission provision for an agreement of sale regarding which the seller has agreed to pay XYZ Realty a 6% commission.

2. Draft a broker's commission provision for an agreement of sale regarding which no broker has been involved.

P. MISCELLANEOUS PROVISIONS [16]

1. Merger (Survival of Settlement)

The "merger doctrine" provides that, unless the parties indicate a contrary intent, the delivery of the deed at settlement in exchange for the purchase money terminates all covenants in the agreement of sale which are inconsistent with the parties' actions in completing settlement. This doctrine may be grounded on the theory that, by their acts at settlement, the parties demonstrate their intention to modify the agreement of sale by waiving all covenants, representations and warranties not also contained in the deed. For all practical purposes, therefore, absent express agreement to the contrary, agreements of sale die once the settlement is concluded and all provisions in such an agreement are considered to have merged into the deed, and the covenants and warranties contained in the deed.

Therefore, the benefits to a seller or purchaser of real estate of a well negotiated, well drafted agreement of sale can be lost after settlement by virtue of the "merger doctrine" unless proper precautions are taken. As to most matters, it is the attorney's responsibility

---

16. In lawyer's jargon, fairly standard provisions of agreements and other le-gal documents are often referred to as "boiler plate".

to protect his client adequately by insisting at settlement that all provisions of the agreement be strictly complied with as a prerequisite to his client concluding settlement. However, some agreement of sale contain warranties and representations which are of a nature either such that a breach of the warranty is not likely to be discovered until after settlement or such that the party benefitting from the warranty desires the effect of the warranty to continue after settlement. In some cases a covenant contained in the agreement can be preserved by inserting a similar covenant in the deed itself, but this is not appropriate in all cases. If it is important to the client that a particular covenant survive settlement and it is an inappropriate covenant to include in the deed, then the draftsman should rebut the presumption of merger by specifically providing in the agreement of sale that a particular covenant is intended by the parties to survive settlement. Alternatively, the draftsman may wish to include a general survival provision affecting all the covenants, representations and warranties contained in the agreement. The survival provision may limit the survival to a specified period of time following settlement.

2.   Recording the Agreement of Sale

The agreement of sale does not have to be recorded to be effective as between the parties. However, as discussed in Chapter 3, in most jurisdictions, an unrecorded agreement of sale is ineffective as against third parties who acquire an interest in the real estate by purchase, by operation of law, or otherwise, without having received notice of the existence of the outstanding agreement of sale. It is to the advantage of the Purchaser, therefore, to record the agreement of sale, especially when a long period of time will elapse between the execution of the agreement of sale and the scheduled date for settlement. The seller, however, has a very strong interest in not recording. The seller's principal objection to recording the agreement of sale is that it creates a cloud on his title which might be difficult and expensive to remove if the purchaser defaults and does not complete settlement. For this reason, many form agreements of sale expressly prohibit the purchaser from recording the agreement.

3.   Notices

Agreements of sale frequently require the delivery of certain papers and provide for various notices to be given by one party to the other. For example, the date fixed for settlement may be changed by notice from either party to the other. It is a good practice to specify the acceptable method by which delivery of notice and other papers is to be made. The following is an example of one such notice provision:

"All notices to be given by either party to the other, shall be in writing and shall be mailed by Registered or Certified United States mail, postage prepaid, return receipt requested, addressed to Seller at _____ with a copy to _____ and to Pur-

(Seller's attorney)

chaser at _____ with a copy to _____ ; or to such

(Purchaser's attorney)

other address as either party may designate by written notice to the other given pursuant to this section. Notice will be considered to have been given upon the postmark date of mailing. The title report, form of deed or other papers which either party desires or is required to deliver may be mailed in the same manner."

The requirement that the notices be sent by registered mail, return receipt requested, is desirable because the return receipt provides a simple and effective method of ascertaining that the addressee has indeed received a communication sent to him. Some notice provisions go further and provide that a return receipt is the only acceptable evidence that a notice has been sent.

4. Parties Bound

Most agreements of sale include a provision, largely declaratory of the law, stating that neither the death of a party nor his assignment of the agreement shall affect the obligations under the agreement.

(a) Assignment Permitted

If the agreement of sale does not by its terms prohibit assignment, the draftsman can use a clause similar to the following:

"This agreement shall be binding upon the parties hereto and their respective heirs, administrators, executors, successors and assigns."

(b) Assignment Not Permitted

If, on the other hand, there is a restriction on the right of the purchaser to assign the agreement, the following clause would be more appropriate:

"Subject to the said provision regarding assignment by Purchaser this agreement shall extend to and bind the heirs, executors, administrators, successors and assigns of the respective parties hereto."

5. Captions

If an agreement contains captions or headings at the beginning of the various provisions, the draftsman might consider indicating in the agreement that the captions themselves are not part of the agreement. This will preclude someone from later trying to support a particular interpretation of the agreement based on language found in a caption. For this purpose, a clause similar to that which follows is appropriate:

"The captions contained herein are not a part of this agreement. They are intended solely for the convenience of the parties and they are not relevant in the construction of this agreement, nor do they in any way modify, amplify, or give full notice of any of the terms, covenants or conditions of this agreement."

6. Integration (Entire Agreement)

Although it is also largely declaratory of the law, the prudent draftsman should include a provision which attempts to preclude one party or the other from claiming that various oral covenants had been made regarding the sale in addition to or modifying those contained in the written agreement. Such a clause is commonly called an "integration clause." The following is typical of the type of integration clause used in agreements of sale:

> "This is the entire agreement between the parties, covering everything agreed upon or understood in the transaction. There are no oral promises, conditions, representations, undertakings, interpretations or terms of any kind as conditions or inducements to the execution hereof or in effect between the parties. No change or addition is to be made to this agreement, except by written agreement executed by the parties."

7. Negation of Representations by the Seller

In seller's forms of agreement of sale it is not uncommon to find, in addition to an integration clause, a provision expressly negating any representation or warranty by the seller that is not expressly stated in the agreement of sale. A typical provision of this kind reads as follows:

> "It is understood and agreed that Purchaser has inspected the premises and that Purchaser has agreed to purchase same as a result of such inspection and not because of or in reliance upon any representation by Seller or any agent of Seller. It is also understood and agreed that Seller shall not be responsible nor liable for any agreement, condition or stipulation not expressly set forth herein relating to or affecting the physical condition of the premises, or otherwise."

Of course, if the purchaser is indeed relying upon a representation made to him by the seller or a real estate agent, it is incumbent upon the purchaser's attorney to include that representation in the agreement of sale and expressly to negate the above provision. In recent years some jurisdictions have developed doctrines which imply by law certain warranties as to the condition of the property, especially regarding the sale of newly constructed residences. These warranties exist even though no express statement of condition has been made by seller. Many seller's forms of agreements of sale attempt to negate the implied warranties, with more or less success.

8. Preparation of Documents

In the absence of express agreement to the contrary, the custom of the particular community usually dictates whether the seller's or buyer's attorney will draw the deed, and the various debt instruments if the seller is taking back a purchase money mortgage. If it is intended that the prevailing custom in the community will not be followed in this regard, express language in the agreement of sale will be needed in order to negate the custom. Even where the custom is to be followed, however, it is good practice to include a short statement assigning the responsibility for the preparation of the various instruments needed at the closing.

Q. SIGNATURES

1. In General

The signature lines of the agreement should provide a place for signatures of all of the parties to the agreement of sale. As mentioned previously in subsection II(B), the signatures should be obtained both of all persons who have any interest in the real estate and of all persons who will be taking title. In addition, there should be signature lines provided for the witnesses to the signing of the agreement by the parties.

2. Co-Owners

The student will recall that if property is owned by more than one person as co-owners, an agreement of sale which lists all of the co-owners but does not include the signatures of all of the co-owners will not, in most jurisdictions, bind any of the co-owners.[17] Consequently, it is important for the purchaser to verify that all co-owners of the property have signed the agreement of sale as sellers.

3. Partners

Although partnership law in most jurisdictions permits any general partner to execute an agreement and thereby bind the entire partnership, it is wise to require that all of the general partners execute the agreement. Otherwise, the attorney representing the other party might be compelled to examine the partnership agreement in order to determine whether the partnership agreement itself places restrictions upon the ability of a single partner to sign an agreement of sale on behalf of the partnership.

4. Corporation

The signature of a corporation is made by the signature of its president or one of its vice presidents, with an attestation (by its secretary, treasurer, assistant secretary or assistant treasurer) to the effect that the president or vice president is authorized to sign the agreement on behalf of the corporation. In addition, the corporate seal is generally affixed next to the signature of the officers.

17. The signature of one or more, but less than all, of the co-owners might give rise to a lawsuit for damages against the executing co-owners under some circumstances.

Although the use of a corporate seal is no longer mandatory in some states, it is typically used in executing documents relating to real estate.

5. Agent

As discussed previously, the practice of permitting a person to be a party to an agreement solely in the capacity of an agent for another is to be avoided. Where it is necessary, however, for an agent to execute the agreement on behalf of his principal, it is important that a provision be added requiring the principal to ratify the act of his agent in writing, preferably by signing the agreement itself, within a specified time from the date of the agreement. This provision should also state that failure to ratify within the time limit specified will cause the agreement to be null and void in which event all deposit monies will be returned to the purchaser.

III. TYPICAL ADDITIONAL PROVISIONS OF AGREEMENTS OF SALE FOR SINGLE FAMILY RESIDENCES (EXISTING BUILDING)

Because of the vast number of sales of single family residences and the relatively small amount of money usually involved in these transactions, it is uncommon for a "custom-made" agreement of sale to be used. In most instances the real estate broker representing the seller will present the prospective purchaser with a printed form of agreement of sale on which the blanks have been filled in and perhaps several other minor changes have been made to reflect any special terms of the transaction. The typical printed form of agreement of sale for residential real estate is prepared for use by the seller's broker. Therefore, the form can be expected to provide fairly adequate protection for the seller while seldom providing the purchaser with the protection which he requires. It is usually up to the purchaser's attorney, if the purchaser consults an attorney prior to executing the agreement, to modify, supplement, and in some cases delete, the printed provisions of the agreement of sale so that the agreement includes more adequate protection for the purchaser.

Most of the provisions of a typical agreement of sale for a single family residence, which will require the particular attention of the purchaser's attorney, have already been discussed in detail in section II of this chapter. This Section will be devoted to a study of additional provisions which are needed to protect sellers and purchasers of single family "used" dwellings and which are peculiar to this type of transaction.

A. MORTGAGES

Most real estate purchases are financed, partially or entirely, by some form of time payments. Generally, the financing takes the form of a note or bond secured by a mortgage or a deed of trust, all of which will be discussed at greater length in Chapter 8. The discussion which follows will deal with a mortgage as the form of security instrument. The deed of trust form of security instrument has virtually the same effect as a mortgage and, consequently, the provisions discussed in this section would apply with little change if a deed of trust were used in lieu of a mortgage.

There are basically three types of provisions dealing with the subject of mortgages which may be found in agreements of sale. If the property being purchased is already encumbered by a mortgage, and if the mortgage so permits, the seller and purchaser may agree to transfer the property subject to the lien of the mortgage. The effect of this is that the amount of cash which the purchaser is required to pay at the settlement will be reduced by the principal balance of the mortgage, and the purchaser will be obligated to pay off that balance over the life of the mortgage. A second alternative method of financing is for the seller to agree to accept as part of the purchase price a purchase money mortgage. A purchase money note and mortgage constitute an extension of credit by the seller to the purchaser for a portion of the purchase price. The third form of financing is for the purchaser to obtain a mortgage loan from an outside source such as a bank, a savings and loan association or other lending institution. These three alternatives will be discussed below:

1. Purchase with Mortgage Remaining (Subject to Mortgage)

As will be discussed in Chapter, the purchaser's liability for payment of the principal and interest owing on a mortgage which will remain on the property can be any one of three different types and it is important to state in the agreement of sale what liability, if any, the purchaser will bear with respect to the existing mortgage.

(a) No Personal Liability

If the seller of the property himself has no personal liability [18] under the mortgage, the seller will be assuming no risk if he agrees that the purchaser will not be personally liable, either to the seller or to the mortgagee, for the payment of the mortgage debt. A sample provision for this situation is set forth below. The sample provision assumes a total purchase price of $100,000.

> "The total consideration to be paid by Buyer shall be One Hundred Thousand ($100,000) payable as follows:
> (a) Ten thousand dollars ($10,000) shall be paid to the Escrowee at the signing of this agreement by Purchaser's check, subject to collection; receipt of which check is hereby acknowledged;

18. This means that, if the mortgage is not paid, then the mortgagee's (lender's) remedies and rights of repayment are limited to the mortgagor's (borrower's) interest in the mortgaged property. If the value of the mortgaged property is less than the amount due the mortgagee, the mortgagee may not sue the mortgagor for the deficiency.

(b) Ninety thousand dollars shall be paid to Seller by Purchaser at settlement as follows:

(i) $40,000 shall be paid in cash, certified check or check of the Title Insurance Company,

(ii) The balance, being $50,000, shall be paid by Purchaser accepting the premises encumbered by the lien of a certain mortgage on the premises which, as of the date of settlement, shall have a principal balance due of $50,000. Said mortgage was made by Seller to XYZ Bank on April 5, 1958, and is recorded in Mortgage Book 3, page 102. Purchaser will not indemnify Seller against the mortgage obligation nor will Purchaser assume the aforementioned mortgage."

(b) Purchaser Personally Liable to Seller

If the terms of the existing mortgage are such that the seller is personally liable under the mortgage in the event of a default, the seller normally will be unwilling to sell the property with the existing mortgage on it unless he extracts from the purchaser an agreement to indemnify the seller in the event of purchaser's default under the mortgage. In many states all that need be done to accomplish this result is to provide in the deed that purchaser shall take the premises "under and subject" to the mortgage. The following provision can be employed:

"The total consideration to be paid by Buyer shall be One Hundred Thousand ($100,000) Dollars, payable as follows:

(a) Ten thousand dollars ($10,000) shall be paid to the Escrowee at the signing of this agreement by Purchaser's check, subject to collection; receipt of which check is hereby acknowledged;

(b) Ninety thousand dollars shall be paid to Seller by Purchaser at settlement as follows:

(i) $40,000 shall be paid in cash, certified check or check of ABC Title Insurance Company,

(ii) The balance, being $50,000 shall be paid by Purchaser accepting the premises under and subject to a certain mortgage on the premises which as of the date of settlement shall have a principal balance due of $50,000. Said Mortgage was made by Seller to XYZ Bank on April 5, 1958, and is recorded in Mortgage Book 3, page 102."

Use of the phrase "under and subject" to the existing mortgage does not make the purchaser personally liable to the mortgagee for such payments. The courts have construed that phrase to obligate the purchaser to indemnify the seller against any loss actually suffered by the seller. Of course, unless and until the seller suffers such a loss, he has no cause of action against the purchaser.

(c) Purchaser Personally Liable to Seller and Mortgagee

A seller who is personally liable for the payment of an existing mortgage debt may want more protection than a mere indemnity from the purchaser against actual loss. In some jurisdictions, he can get this added protection by using the phrase "assumes and agrees to pay" wherever the existing mortgage is referred to. In such a case, section (b)(ii) would read as follows:

> (ii) The balance, being $50,000 shall be paid by Purchaser accepting the premises under and subject to a certain mortgage on the premises which Purchaser hereby assumes and agrees to pay. As of the date of settlement said mortgage shall have a principal balance due of $50,000. Said mortgage was made by Seller to XYZ Bank on April 5, 1958, and is recorded in Mortgage Book 3, page 102."

The purchaser's agreement to "assume and pay" the mortgage debt has the effect of making the purchaser personally liable for payment of the debt, regardless of whether the seller suffers any actual loss and regardless of whether the purchaser is still the owner of the property at the time the mortgage is in default. The agreement to "assume and agree to pay" has the additional effect, at least in some jurisdictions, of permitting the mortgagee to sue the purchaser directly on the note. The mortgagee does not have this right if the purchaser has only agreed to accept the premises under and subject to the mortgage.

An extremely cautious seller may not be willing to convey the property with the mortgage on it, even though the purchaser has agreed to assume and pay the mortgage, unless the seller has obtained from the mortgagee a release of the seller's personal liability under the mortgage. Agreements of sale for residences are seldom conditioned upon the ability of the seller to obtain a release of personal liability under the mortgage, for the reason that few mortgagees are willing to grant such a release. In the absence of such a release, the seller must rely on the value of the real estate and the financial ability of the purchaser to pay off the mortgage debt as security for the mortgagee.

Where an existing mortgage is to remain a lien on the property after conveyance, it is common to add to the section of the agreement of sale dealing with apportionments that interest payable on the mortgage will be apportioned between the seller and the purchaser as of the date of settlement. No such apportionment is made with respect to payments on account of principal since the parties have presumably already considered what the amount of the unpaid balance of the mortgage would be at the time of settlement when they fixed the purchase price. If, however, settlement is not held as scheduled and the seller is thereby relieved from making a mortgage payment or is required to make an additional mortgage payment, provision should be made in the agreement of sale to either decrease or increase the amount of cash the purchaser must pay in order to complete settlement.

2.   Purchase Money Mortgage from Purchaser to Seller

Where a purchase money mortgage is used, the purchaser gives the seller a note, secured by a mortgage on the property, in lieu of cash for all or a portion of the purchase price. It is often advisable to agree upon the terms of the note and mortgage at the time the agreement of sale is negotiated. The form of note and mortgage can then be attached to the agreement as an exhibit. If this degree of completeness is not practicable, then the essential terms of the note or bond and mortgage should be spelled out in the agreement.

3.   Mortgage Contingency

If the purchaser intends to finance part of the purchase price by obtaining a mortgage loan from someone other than the seller, the purchaser will want to be able to regain his deposit in the event that he is unable to obtain a mortgage on terms and conditions satisfactory to him. Therefore, it is important from the purchaser's standpoint that the agreement of sale contain a provision (often called a mortgage contingency clause) making the purchaser's obligations contingent upon obtaining a commitment for a satisfactory mortgage. On the other hand, before the seller will agree to take his property off the market, he will want some assurance that the purchaser will make a good faith effort to obtain a mortgage.

The mortgage contingency provision should state which of the two parties is obligated to attempt to obtain the mortgage. Furthermore, the provision should set forth at least the most important terms which such a mortgage is to contain, such as the principal sum, interest rate, maturity date, the amount and frequency of installments, the number of points [19] to be paid, the absence of personal liability on the part of the mortgagor, if applicable, and the source of the mortgage funds such as "any reputable bank, trust company, insurance company or pension fund". Although the source of the funds may seem to be an immaterial fact to the purchaser, he has a definite interest in knowing that the lender, with whom he is likely to have a long association, is reputable and reasonable to deal with.

Often the parties provide that the purchaser will be given a fixed period of time to try to obtain mortgage financing and, if he is unable to obtain financing, the seller will have the opportunity for a fixed period of time to obtain it for him. If such a scheme is used, the agreement should spell out specific time periods during which the respective parties may act and provide for giving notice to one another not later than the end of their respective time periods as to whether they have been successful in obtaining financing.

---

19. A "point" is 1% of something. Thus, if a lender is charging a commitment fee of 3½ points, then the commitment fee on a $200,000 loan would be $7,000 ($200,000 × 0.035).

PROBLEM

Incorporate the above comments into mortgage contingency clause which provides that the agreement is contingent upon the purchaser obtaining within 45 days an institutional self-amortizing [20] mortgage of $40,000 at 8% interest payable monthly over a term of 25 years and having a service or commitment fee of not more than 1%. Do not forget to provide for proper notices and for the results if the mortgage is not obtained in time.

B. FIRE OR OTHER CASUALTY AND RISK OF LOSS

As discussed in section I of this chapter, in some jurisdictions, absent an express agreement by purchaser and seller to the contrary, the purchaser has the risk of loss of the property commencing with the date of execution of the agreement of sale. As a consequence, the purchaser is deemed to have an insurable interest in the property from that date. Having an "insurable interest" means that the purchaser may obtain an insurance policy on the property prior to settlement, even though he has not taken possession and is not yet the record owner of the property. Furthermore, if the real estate is damaged between execution of the agreement of sale and settlement and the seller, as record owner of the property, receives proceeds as compensation for the damage, the seller must hold the proceeds in trust for the purchaser and as security for the purchaser's performance of the agreement. As a consequence, the purchaser is entitled to have the proceeds paid over to him at settlement.

To avoid duplication of costs, the seller and purchaser often agree among themselves that the seller will maintain his insurance in force until settlement. If such an arrangement is made, the agreement should require that the seller add the purchaser to the existing policy as an insured, "as his interest may appear," to ensure that the seller fulfills his obligation to pay any insurance proceeds to the purchaser. A clause similar to the following can be used:

"Insurance against fire and extended coverage risks is now carried by Seller in the amount of One Hundred Thousand Dollars ($100,-000). Said insurance shall be maintained by Seller, and forthwith upon the execution of this agreement all such policies shall be endorsed or amended to make the proceeds payable to Seller and Purchaser, as their interests may appear in regard to any damage occurring between the date hereof and conveyance of the premises to Purchaser. A certificate to that effect, issued by the insurance company will be delivered to the Purchaser within ten (10) days after the date hereof. This agreement will not be cancelled or affected by reason of damage or destruction due to fire or other casualty.

20. Self-amortizing means that the combinded installment payments of principal and interest are such that the loan will be fully repaid during the term of the loan.

The net proceeds of any insurance collected prior to settlement will be paid or credited to Purchaser on account of the purchase price at settlement. All unpaid claims and rights in connection with losses under any policies will be assigned to Purchaser at settlement but will not be credited to Purchaser. If this agreement is cancelled or becomes void, for any reason Purchaser hereby authorizes Seller, to sign any letter or instrument or do any other thing necessary to cancel the amendment or endorsement under which Purchaser was named as a party in interest in the said insurance."

If there is fire or other insured damage to the property after the purchaser has been added as a named insured, the proceeds of the insurance will be payable to both seller and purchaser. If, for some reason, settlement is not held, the seller may have a very difficult time getting the purchaser to endorse the proceeds of the insurance check over to the seller. The purchaser, on the other hand, is obligated to complete settlement regardless of whether the premises have been destroyed by fire or other casualty, and some kinds of casualties, such as floods, are not covered by even an "extended coverage" insurance policy. If the purchaser is concerned about the property being damaged or destroyed by such casualties, he should obtain insurance coverage for these risks himself.

The amount of insurance carried by the seller may be substantially less than the present value of the property. This is particularly likely to be true if the seller has owned the property for a long period of time. If this is the case, the seller will rarely agree to increase his insurance. Thus, the purchaser in this situation should obtain his own policy for an appropriate amount.

C. TERMITE INSPECTION AND CERTIFICATE

The purchaser of residential real estate is, of course, concerned that the house he is buying is in as good condition as it appears from his visual inspection. One condition which is not always readily apparent is infestation and damage caused by termites and other wood-boring insects. The following type of provision is intended to provide the purchaser with protection in this regard:

"At settlement Seller shall, at Seller's expense, provide Purchaser with a certificate from a reputable exterminator (a) certifying that the building on the premises is free and clear of infestation and any resulting wood damage caused by termites and other wood-boring insects, and (b) guaranteeing the same for at least one (1) year after the date of settlement. Should such infestation or damage be found, Seller, at Seller's expense, shall promptly have any infestation cured and/or repair and restore any damage caused to the premises by termites or other wood-boring insects."

There can, of course, be many variations on this provision, including the requirement that the purchaser obtain the certificate at his own expense, but with the obligation of the seller to repair if damage is discovered. Another alternative would be to require the seller to repair all damage up to a certain dollar amount of damage. If the repairs would cost more than the dollar limit, the seller might retain the option of terminating the agreement rather than expending the funds to make the repairs.

D. CONDITION OF THE PREMISES

There are other conditions about which purchasers may have particular concerns, including the condition of the roof and the plumbing system, the condition of mechanical and electrical equipment such as the heating and air-conditioning systems, and, in those houses that have basements, possible water leakage or excessive moisture in the basement. If the purchaser's bargaining position is strong enough, he may be able to get the seller to agree to a provision similar to the following:

> "Seller covenants, represents and warrants that the plumbing, heating, air-conditioning, and electrical systems serving the building on the Premises are in good working order and condition and shall be in good working order and condition at the time of settlement. In the event that Seller is unable to make the foregoing warranty as of the time of settlement, Purchaser shall be entitled to an abatement of the purchase price in the amount which the parties agree is reasonably required to restore the defective equipment to good working order and condition, and in the absence of such agreement the provisions of the foregoing sentence shall survive and continue after settlement and shall not merge therein so that Purchaser shall be entitled to pursue all legal and equitable remedies available to Purchaser. Seller covenants that the Premises will, at the time of settlement, be in substantially as good condition as on the date hereof, and Seller agrees, at Seller's expense, to make any and all repairs required to maintain such condition between the date hereof and the time of settlement."

A seller is likely to resist such a provision. Indeed, a seller will sometimes insist that a provision be included in the Agreement that negates any warranties and provides that the premises are being purchased "as is".

PROBLEM

Prepare an "as is" clause for an Agreement of Sale.

E. FIXTURES AND ARTICLES OF PERSONAL PROPERTY INCLUDED IN THE SALES

One of the most frequent disputes occurring at settlement between the parties to a residential real estate transaction arises as a result of verbal understandings as to what items of personal property are included in the sale. In order to eliminate or minimize these disputes, it is highly desirable that the parties reduce these understandings to writing in as much detail as is possible. The following is an example of one such provision:

> "All plumbing, heating and lighting fixtures and systems appurtenant thereto and forming a part thereof, as well as all ranges, laundry tubs, dishwashers, TV antennas and rotors, storm sash and/or doors, shades, awnings, venetian blinds, couplings for automatic washers and dryers, window air-conditioners, radiator covers, cornices, kitchen cabinets, wall to wall carpeting in living room and front bedroom, draperies and drapery hardware, curtain rod hardware including traverse rod hardware and fixtures, if any, and all trees, shrubbery and plantings now in or on the property are included in the sale and purchase price. If Purchaser so requests, Seller shall execute a bill of sale in form satisfactory to counsel for Purchaser, enumerating all or any part of said personal property, fixtures and equipment to be included in the conveyance."

Items that the seller wants to remove, and that are even arguably includible among the above, should be listed with an indication that they are not included in the sale and that the seller has the right to remove them. Depending on the items and the difficulty of removal, the purchaser may want to insist upon replacement of certain items (e. g., lighting fixtures) to be removed.

An example of an agreement of sale for residential property follows:

EXAMPLE: Agreement of Sale for Residential Property

Copy No.
of   Copies

Agreement for the Sale of Real Estate

THIS AGREEMENT made this   day of October   A.D.1977 BETWEEN John Smith and Cecily Smith, husband and wife, hereinafter called Seller, and Robert Brown and Joan Brown, husband and wife, hereinafter called Buyer,

WITNESSETH:

PROPERTY AND TERMS

1. Seller hereby agrees to sell and convey to Buyer, who hereby agrees to purchase ALL THAT CERTAIN lot or piece of ground, together with improvements and buildings thereon erected situate in the township of Easttown, County of Chester, State of Pennsylvania, being known and numbered 123 Laureleaf Lane, Brynwood, Pennsylvania. Being all of the real property owned by Seller at this address and to be more fully described in Deed from Seller to Buyer at the time of settlement and containing approximately one (1) acre of ground.

for the sum of SIXTY THOUSAND	dollars ($60,000.00)

which shall be paid to the Seller by the Buyer as follows:

Cash at the signing of this Agreement	$ 1,000.00
Cash to be paid on or before two weeks from signing of this agreement	$ 5,000.00
or Title Insurance Company check	$
Cash at Settlement	$54,000.00
TOTAL	$60,000.00

SETTLEMENT

2. Settlement shall be made on or before January 28, 1978
The said time for settlement and all other times referred to for the performance of any of the obligations of this Agreement are hereby agreed to be of the essence of this Agreement.

TITLE

3. The premises are to be conveyed free and clear of all liens, encumbrances, and easements, EXCEPTING HOWEVER, the following: existing building restrictions, ordinances, easements of roads, privileges or rights of public service companies, if any; or easements or restrictions visible upon the ground, provided, however, that none of the foregoing shall prohibit the use of the premises for all single family residential purposes and shall not impose any financial burden upon the Buyer. Further such privileges or rights of public service companies shall be limited to providing service to the building on the premises, otherwise the title to the above described real estate shall be good and marketable and such as will be insured by any reputable Title Insurance Company at the regular rates.

In the event the Seller is unable to give a good and marketable title and such as will be insured by any reputable Title Company, subject as aforesaid, Buyer shall have the option of taking such title as the Seller can give without abatement of price or of being repaid all monies paid by Buyer and held in escrow on account of the purchase price together with such Title Company charges as Buyer may have incurred; and in the latter event there shall be no further liability or obligation on either of the parties hereto and this Agreement shall become null and void.

If any surveys are necessary or desired, they shall be secured and paid for by the Buyer.

Seller covenants and represents as of the approval date of this Agreement of Sale, that no assessments for public improvements have been made against the premises which remain unpaid and that no notice by any governmental or other public authority has been served upon Seller or anyone on the Seller's behalf, including notices relating to violations of housing, building, safety or fire ordinances which remain uncorrected unless otherwise specified herein. Buyer will be responsible for any notices served upon the Seller after the approval date of this Agreement and for the payment of any assessments and charges hereafter made for any public improvements, if work in connection therewith is hereafter begun in or about said premises and adjacent thereto. Seller will be responsible for any such improvements, assessments or notices received prior to the date of this Agreement, unless the improvements consist of sewer or water lines not in use on or prior to the date of approval hereof.

POSSESSION

4. Possession is to be delivered by special warranty deed, keys and physical possession at day and time of settlement, or by special warranty deed and assignment of existing lease at time of settlement if premises is tenant occupied at the signing of this Agreement, unless otherwise specified herein. Buyer will acknowledge existing lease by initialing said lease at time of signing of this Agreement of Sale if tenant occupied.

TAXES AND ADJUSTMENTS

5. All apportionable debits and credits, including taxes, rents, interest on encumbrance (if any), sewer rent (if any) for the current term shall be calculated as levied and pro-rated as of date of settlement. (School taxes are levied on a fiscal year basis, Township and County taxes are levied on a calendar year basis.) All Real Estate Transfer Taxes imposed by any governmental authority shall be divided equally between Buyer and Seller.

TENDER PAYMENT OF DEPOSIT

6. Formal tender of an executed deed and purchase money is hereby waived.

7. Deposit or hand monies shall be paid to Boris B. Broker who shall retain the same in escrow until consummation or termination of this Agreement as required in accordance with the Act of Assembly of Pennsylvania of July 9, 1957, Public Law 608, Section 4. Said deposit monies shall be placed in an interest bearing account, and the interest earned thereon shall be paid to Buyer at settlement. If settlement does not take place for any reason, then the interest shall be paid to whichever party is entitled to the deposit monies.

FIXTURES, TREES, SHRUBBERY, ETC.

8. All plumbing, heating and lighting fixtures and systems appurtenant thereto, and forming a part thereof, as well as all ranges, laundry tubs, dishwasher, refrigerators, disposals, TV antennas, mail box, door knockers, and other permanent fixtures, together with screens, storm sash and/or doors, shades, awnings, venetian blinds, valances, curtain rods, drapery rods, or traverse rods, radiator covers, and all trees, shrubbery and plantings now in or on the property, unless specifically excepted in this Agreement, are to become the property of the Buyer and are included in the purchase price. None of the above mentioned items shall be removed by Seller from the premises after the date of this Agreement. Seller hereby warrants that Seller has good legal title free and clear of any claim and encumbrance to all the articles described in this paragraph. It is further agreed that all fuel oil remaining in the tank at final settlement shall become the property of the Buyer and is included in the purchase price.

Seller agrees to remove all rubbish and debris from the premises and garage and leave broom-clean prior to settlement, or accept the liability for its removal.

INSURANCE

9. Any loss or damage to the property caused by fire, or loss commonly covered by the extended coverage endorsement of reputable insurance companies between the date of this Agreement and the time of settlement shall not in any way void or impair any of the conditions and obligations hereof. It is the Buyer's responsibility, at Buyer's own cost and expense, to carry such insurance on said premises as he may deem desirable.

DEFAULT

10. Should the Buyer fail to make any additional payments as specified in paragraph no. 1, or violate or fail to fulfill and perform any of the terms or conditions of this Agreement, then and in that case all deposits and other sums paid by the Buyer on account of the purchase price, whether required by this Agreement shall, may be retained by the Seller either on account of the purchase price or as liquidated damages for such breach, as the Seller may elect, and, in the latter event, the Seller and Buyer shall be released from all further liability or obligation and this Agreement shall become null and void.

REPRESENTA-TIONS

11. It is understood that Buyer has inspected the property and that Buyer has agreed to purchase it as a result of such inspection and not because of or in reliance upon any representation made by Seller or by any agent of Seller and that Buyer has agreed to purchase it in its present condition unless otherwise specified herein. It is further understood that the Seller agrees to maintain the grounds and the improvements and buildings thereon in the same condition as prevails at the time of the signing of this Agreement. This Agreement contains the whole Agreement between the Seller and the Buyer and there are no other terms, obligations, covenants, representations, statements or conditions, oral or otherwise of any kind whatsoever concerning this sale. Any changes or additions to this Agreement must be made in writing and executed by the parties hereto. The Seller shall maintain the premises, including the roof, heating, electrical and plumbing systems therein, in good order and working condition to the date of settlement, provided that to the extent this provision is inconsistent with paragraph 9 above, paragraph 9 shall control.

The Buyer shall have the right to inspect the premises at all reasonable times between the date hereof and the date of settlement.

RECORDING

12. This Agreement shall not be recorded in the Office for the Recording of Deeds or in any other office or place of public record and if Buyer shall record this Agreement or cause or permit the same to be recorded, Seller may, at Seller's option, elect to treat such Act as a breach of this Agreement.

ASSIGNMENT

13. This Agreement shall be binding upon the respective heirs, executors, administrators, successors and, to the extent assignable on the assigns of the parties hereto, it being expressly understood, however, that the Buyer shall not transfer or assign this Agreement without the written consent of the Seller being first had and obtained. This Agreement is to be construed and interpreted in accordance with the laws of the Commonwealth of Pennsylvania.

AGENT

14. It is expressly understood and agreed between the parties hereto that Boris B. Broker is acting as agent only and will in no case whatsoever be held liable to either party for the performance of any terms or covenants of this Agreement or for damages for the non-performance thereof. It is understood and agreed that said agent(s) is (are) the sole moving cause of this sale, and Seller agrees to pay to said agent(s) a real estate commission in the amount of six per cent of sales price to be divided equally between them for services rendered.

In the event Buyer defaults hereunder, any monies paid on account shall be equally divided between Seller and Agent(s) but in no event will the sum paid to Agent(s) be in excess of the above specified commission.

DESCRIPTIVE HEADING

15. The descriptive headings used herein are for convenience only and they are not intended to indicate the matter in the sections which follow them. Accordingly, they shall have no effect whatsoever in determining the rights or obligations of the parties.

16. Mortgage Contingency attached hereto.

17. At settlement Seller shall deliver to Buyer the original of the Terminex International, Inc. Certification and Service Warranty, a photocopy of which has already been delivered to Buyer, and Seller hereby warrants that Seller will have paid at or prior to settlement the $10.00 fee to Terminex set forth on said Certification and Service Warranty at Seller's own cost.

18. This Agreement shall be null and void if the Buyer does not receive a fully executed copy of this Agreement on or before 11:59 p. m. Monday, November 3, 1977.

WITNESS WHEREOF, the individual parties hereto have hereunto set their hands and seals, and the corporate parties hereto have caused these presents to be executed and their corporate seal to be attached by their proper officers thereunto duly authorized, the day and year first above written.

WITNESS: DATE:

_____   _____   _____ [Seal]
                                                John Smith
_____   _____   _____ [Seal]
                                                Cecily Smith
_____   _____   _____ [Seal]
                                                Robert Brown
_____   _____   _____ [Seal]
                                                Joan Brown
_____   _____   _____ [Seal]

MORTGAGE CONTINGENCY

1. It is mutually understood and agreed that within five days from the date hereof, Buyer will prepare and file an application with a reputable lending institution for a direct reduction first mortgage loan to be secured upon the property in the amount of $40,000.00 for a term of not less than 25 years at an interest rate not to exceed prevailing rate to enable Buyer to finance the purchase of this property.

2. Should Buyer be unable to obtain a written commitment for a mortgage loan on the terms set forth above, Buyer shall advise Seller in writing by certified mail on or before 45 days after the date hereof of such condition and Seller shall thereupon have 14 days from date of receipt of such notice within which to obtain such a mortgage commitment for and on behalf of the Buyer. Buyer agrees to execute any application at Seller's request and Buyer agrees to pay a service charge not in excess of one per cent plus appraisal fees.

3. If Buyer fails to make application for such mortgage loan or notify Seller of his inability to obtain a written commitment as herein set forth or fails to execute any application for such mortgage loan at Seller's request, the condition and contingency provided for shall no longer prevail and this Agreement shall be and remain in full force and effect according to its terms in the same manner as if the condition and contingency were not a part hereof.

4. Should neither Buyer or Seller be able to obtain such a mortgage commitment on the terms set forth above within the period above referred to, Buyer, at Buyer's election may (a) proceed with consummation of this contract without regard to the failure of the condition or (b) may cancel this Agreement, in which event all monies paid hereunder by Buyer on account of the purchase price will be returned to Buyer upon receipt by Seller of (1) Buyer's written notice of intention to cancel, (2) return to Seller of all copies of the agreement of sale. Thereafter all rights and liabilities of these parties shall cease and determine, anything herein contained to the contrary notwithstanding. Buyer shall notify Seller in writing of Buyer's election under (a) or (b) within ten days after date Seller notifies Buyer that Seller is unable to obtain mortgage in accordance with Section II above by certified mail after being notified by Seller that a mortgage commitment loan was not obtained. In the event that Buyer fails to notify Seller of his election to cancel the contract under (b) above within the prescribed time limit, Buyer shall be obligated to proceed with consummation of the Agreement.

WITNESS

_____   _____ [*Seal*]
                              John Smith

_____   _____ [*Seal*]
                              Cecily Smith

_____   _____ [*Seal*]
                              Robert Brown

_____   _____ [*Seal*]
                              Joan Brown

IV. TYPICAL ADDITIONAL PROVISIONS OF AGREEMENTS OF SALE FOR NEW CONSTRUCTION SINGLE FAMILY RESIDENCES

An agreement of sale for residential real estate entered into at a time when the house is not yet completed is substantially the same as that for completed homes. However, certain additional provisions must be added, especially provisions describing the obligations of the seller as the builder. This section will deal with some additional agreement of sale provisions relating to the construction of new homes.

Very often in the purchase of newly constructed or under construction housing, especially where the house being purchased is part of a larger development, the purchaser is handed a printed agreement of sale prepared by the seller. The agreement is likely to be extremely favorable to the seller. Depending upon the relative bargaining power of the two parties, changes can sometimes be made to these agreements which make them more equitable.

A. ADDITIONAL PROTECTION WHICH THE BUYER REQUIRES WHEN PURCHASING A NEWLY COMPLETED RESIDENCE

1. Description of Property

It is important for the purchaser of a new construction residence that the agreement of sale require the seller to produce at or prior to settlement an "as built" survey plan of the premises prepared after all construction has been completed. Such a survey will show (a) any encroachments of the buildings and other improvements upon a neighbor's land or encroachments by a neighbor's buildings upon the land being sold, (b) possible easements and other physical conditions which the surveyor has observed, (c) the exact location and dimension of the buildings, (d) the location of buildings and improvements with respect to setback and side yard and rear yard restrictions, (e) party walls and openings therein, (f) the boundaries including adjoining properties and streets, (g) the courses and distances of the boundaries, and (h) the locations of markers on the boundaries, if any.

2. Warranties From Seller Relating to the Premises Themselves

(a) Subdivision Approval

The seller might be requested to warrant that the house was erected in compliance with the zoning requirements and that all necessary subdivision approvals, building permits and certificates of occupancy have been obtained. If new streets have been opened, the seller should be required to warrant that the streets have all been completed or that a bond to insure completion of such streets has been posted with the local government. Seller should also covenant to dedicate the streets and maintain them until such dedication has been accepted by the local municipality.

(b) Water and Sewer Hooked-Up

The seller should identify the source of the fresh water supply to the premises and warrant that such water service has been installed, connected and fully paid for by the seller. Similarly, if applicable, the seller should warrant that the premises are served by a sanitary sewer system that has been installed and connected and that all charges in connection with the system have been paid by the seller.

(c) Mechanic's Liens

Most state legislatures have created statutory remedies for unpaid contractors or material suppliers in connection with any kind of real estate development and construction. The remedies vary from state to state but are commonly referred to as mechanic's liens. Mechanic's liens permit a lien to be filed upon the property and in many states such mechanic's liens are granted a priority which dates back to the visible commencement of any work on the property. The effect of this priority is that a grantee taking title prior to the filing of a mechanic's lien could find at a later time that the property is subject to mechanic's liens filed by contractors who had performed work for the grantor. A purchaser should require the seller to include in the agreement of sale a warranty that at the settlement the seller will have paid all monies due the general contractor and all subcontractors and materialmen. The condition of title clause should make it clear that the title delivered by the seller must be free and clear of all mechanic's and materialmen's liens.

A mechanic's lien might become superior to a mortgage, by the same sort of relating-back of priority. Many mortgage lenders will insist upon having a mortgagee's title policy issued without an objection relating to mechanic's liens. Title insurers will often remove the objection for mechanic's liens upon payment of an additional premium. The purchaser usually pays for all title insurance which he obtains, including that for the mortgagee. If the seller is to pay any additional premium for mechanic's lien insurance, this obligation should be specifically set forth. In addition, the title company may require some form of assurance from the builder that all contractors and materialmen have been paid or have waived their right to file a lien.

3. Warranties From Seller With Respect to Construction and Equipment

The purchaser would like to obtain from the seller as many warranties as possible, which may include a one year guarantee by the seller against defects in workmanship and material and an assignment of all manufacturer's warranties on equipment. Some builders include in their agreements of sale warranties of the kind described above, and some provide their standard warranty booklet at settlement. The entire area of new home warranties is undergoing change. The change has come in part from the courts, which have sometimes held builders to have made implicit warranties. Additionally, passage of the Magnuson-Moss Act regarding consumer warranties and the development of group warranty plans, such as the current Home Owners Warranty plan developed by the National Association of Home Builders, have created impetus for change. Care should be taken in reviewing warranties proposed by a seller, since they often attempt to limit the obligations of the seller that would otherwise be imposed under state law.

4. Uncompleted Items

If, at the time the agreement of sale is executed, the house has not been fully completed, it is desirable from the purchaser's standpoint to attach to the agreement of sale a list of all uncompleted work which is to be done by the seller prior to settlement. The agreement should specify that it will be a condition precedent [21] to purchaser's obligation to complete settlement that the specified work has been completed. The purchaser should not sign any instruments certifying that the work has been completed until an inspection of the property has been made which verifies the completion, and the agreement should provide for a pre-settlement inspection by the purchaser accompanied by an agent of the seller authorized to sign a "punch list" of items that remain to be completed and corrected after settlement. The punch list should contain appropriate time limits and remedies.

An example of an agreement of sale for a newly completed residence follows.

EXAMPLE: Agreement of Sale for a Newly Completed Residence

Copy No.
of   Copies

Agreement for the Sale of Real Estate

THIS AGREEMENT made this   day of July A.D. 1977 BETWEEN Smith Development Co., Inc. hereinafter called Seller, and William White and Brenda White, husband and wife hereinafter called Buyer,

WITNESSETH:

PROPERTY AND TERMS

1. Seller hereby agrees to sell and convey to Buyer, who hereby agrees to purchase ALL THAT CERTAIN lot or piece of ground, together with improvements and buildings thereon erected situate, known and numbered as 781 Smith Terrace, Upper Marion Township, Montgomery County, Pa., according to a plan made for Smith Development Co., by Jones Engineering Co., Dated May 15, 1971, together with a building to be completed thereon in a good and workmanlike manner. Being all the real property owned by Seller at such location. The whole to be more fully described in legal description which is to be contained in Deed which will be executed and delivered from Seller to Buyer at time of Final Settlement. Said lot to contain 0.509 acres.

for the sum of Seventy Four Thousand Five Hundred Forty Five dollars	($74,545.00)
which shall be paid to the Seller by the Buyer as follows:	
Cash at the signing of this Agreement	$ 1,000.00
Cash to be paid on or before July 30, 1977	$ 6,454.50
	$
Cash at Settlement	$67,090.50
TOTAL	$74,545.00

SETTLEMENT

2. Settlement shall be made on September 30, 1977

The said time for settlement and all other times referred to for the performance of any of the obligations of this Agreement are hereby agreed to be of the essence of this Agreement.

TITLE

3. The premises are to be conveyed free and clear of all liens, encumbrances, and easements, EXCEPTING HOWEVER, the following: existing building restrictions, ordinances, easements of roads, privileges or rights of public service companies, if any; or easements or restrictions visible upon the ground, otherwise the title to the above described real estate shall be good and marketable and such as will be insured by any reputable Title Insurance Company at the regular rates. See Rider A.

In the event the Seller is unable to give a good and marketable title and such as will be insured by any reputable Title Company, subject as aforesaid, Buyer shall have the option of taking such title as the Seller can give without abatement of price or of being

21. When an agreement is contingent upon the satisfaction of a particular item, then that item is a condition precedent to the obligations of the parties under the agreement; that is, the satisfaction of the condition must occur before (precede) the settlement under the agreement. This is to be distinguished from conditions subsequent, which indicate that the status of the parties, having been settled by a closing, may be altered if something occurs at a later time (subsequently).

repaid all monies paid by Buyer and held in escrow on account of the purchase price together with such Title Company charges as Buyer may have incurred; and in the latter event there shall be no further liability or obligation on either of the parties hereto and this Agreement shall become null and void.

See Rider M.

If any surveys are necessary or desired, they shall be secured and paid for by the Buyer. Seller shall provide stakes at all corners of the property.

Seller covenants and represents as of the approval date of this Agreement of Sale, that no assessments for public improvements have been made against the premises which remain unpaid and that no notice by any governmental or other public authority has been served upon Seller or anyone on the Seller's behalf, including notices relating to violations of housing, building, safety or fire ordinances which remain uncorrected unless otherwise specified herein. Buyer will be responsible for any notices served upon the Seller after the approval date of this Agreement and for the payment of any assessments and charges hereafter made for any public improvements, if work in connection therewith is hereafter begun in or about said premises and adjacent thereto. Seller will be responsible for any such improvements, assessments or notices received prior to the date of this Agreement, unless the improvements consist of sewer or water lines not in use on or prior to the date of approval hereof, provided settlement shall be completed hereunder.

POSSESSION

4. Possession is to be delivered by special warranty deed, keys and physical possession at day and time of settlement, premises to be vacant, unoccupied and in broom-clean condition.

TAXES AND ADJUSTMENTS

5. All apportionable debits and credits, including taxes, rents, interest on encumbrance (if any), sewer rent (if any) for the current term shall be calculated as levied and pro-rated as of date of settlement. (School taxes are levied on a fiscal year basis, Township and County taxes are levied on a calendar year basis.) All Real Estate Transfer Taxes imposed by any governmental authority shall be divided equally between Buyer and Seller.

TENDER

6. Formal tender of an executed deed and purchase money is hereby waived.

PAYMENT OF DEPOSIT

7. Deposit or hand monies shall be paid to Seller who shall retain the same in escrow until consummation or termination of this Agreement as required in accordance with the Act of Assembly of Pennsylvania of July 9, 1957, Public Law 608, Section 4.

FIXTURES, TREES, SHRUBBERY, ETC.

8. All plumbing, heating and lighting fixtures and systems appurtenant thereto, and forming a part thereof, as well as all ranges, laundry tubs, dishwasher, disposals, TV antennas, mail box, door knockers, and other permanent fixtures, together with screens, storm sash and/or doors, shades, awnings, venetian blinds, valances, curtain rods, drapery rods, or traverse rods, radiator covers, and all trees, shrubbery and plantings now in or on the property, unless specifically excepted in this Agreement, are to become the property of the Buyer and are included in the purchase price. None of the above mentioned items shall be removed by Seller from the premises after the date of this Agreement. Seller hereby warrants that Seller has good legal title free and clear of any claim and encumbrance to all the articles described in this paragraph. It is further agreed that all fuel oil remaining in the tank at final settlement shall become the property of the Buyer and is included in the purchase price.

Seller agrees to remove all rubbish and debris from the premises and garage and leave broom-clean prior to settlement, or accept the liability for its removal.

. . .

DEFAULT

10. Should the Buyer fail to make any additional payments as specified in paragraph no. 1, or violate or fail to fulfill and perform any of the terms or conditions of this Agreement, then and in that case all deposits and other sums paid by the Buyer on account of the purchase price, whether required by this Agreement or not, may be retained by the Seller, as liquidated damages for such breach, and the Seller and Buyer shall be released from all liability or obligation and this Agreement shall become null and void.

The foregoing shall be Seller's sole remedy.

REPRESENTA-TIONS

11. It is understood that Buyer has inspected the property and that Buyer has agreed to purchase it as a result of such inspection and not because of or in reliance upon any representation made by Seller or by any agent of Seller and that Buyer has agreed to purchase it in its present condition unless otherwise specified herein. It is further understood that the Seller agrees to maintain the grounds and the improvements and buildings thereon in the same condition as prevails at the time of the signing of this Agreement. This Agreement contains the whole Agreement between the Seller and the Buyer and there are no other terms, obligations, covenants, representations, statements or conditions, oral or otherwise of any kind whatsoever concerning this sale. Any changes or additions to this Agreement must be made in writing and executed by the parties hereto.

RECORDING

12. This Agreement shall not be recorded in the Office for the Recording of Deeds or in any other office or place of public record and if Buyer shall record this Agreement or cause or permit the same to be recorded, Seller may, at Seller's option, elect to treat such Act as a breach of this Agreement.

ASSIGNMENT

13. This Agreement shall be binding upon the respective heirs, executors, administrators, successors and, to the extent assignable on the assigns of the parties hereto, it being expressly understood, however, that the Buyer shall not transfer or assign this Agreement without the written consent of the Seller being first had and obtained. This Agreement is to be construed and interpreted in accordance with the laws of the Commonwealth of Pennsylvania.

. . .

DESCRIPTIVE HEADING

15. The descriptive headings used herein are for convenience only and they are not intended to indicate the matter in the sections which follow them. Accordingly, they shall have no effect whatsoever in determining the rights or obligations of the parties.

16. See mortgage contingency addendum attached and made a part hereof.

17. See Description of materials and specifications addendum attached and made part hereof.

18. See Rider attached hereto and made a part hereof containing provisions A through M.

IN WITNESS WHEREOF, the individual parties hereto have hereunto set their hands and seals, and the corporate parties hereto have caused these presents to be executed and their corporate seal to be attached by their proper officers thereunto duly authorized, the day and year first above written.

WITNESS:　　　　　　　　　　DATE:

_____　　_____　　_____ [*Seal*]
　　　　　　　　　　　　　　　　　　　　　　　　　　　Smith Development Co., Inc.
_____　　_____　　By: _____ [*Seal*]

_____　　_____　　Attest: _____ [*Seal*]

_____　　_____　　_____ [*Seal*]
　　　　　　　　　　　　　　　　　　　　　　　　　　　Brenda White
_____　　_____　　_____ [*Seal*]
　　　　　　　　　　　　　　　　　　　　　　　　　　　William White

MORTGAGE CONTINGENCY

1. It is mutually understood and agreed that within 5 days from the date hereof, Buyer will prepare and file an application with any reputable lending institution for a direct reduction first mortgage loan to be secured upon the property in the amount of $35,000.00 for a term of not less than 30 years at an interest rate not to exceed prevailing rate to enable Buyer to finance the purchase of this property.

2. Should Buyer be unable to obtain a written commitment for a mortgage loan on the terms set forth above, Buyer shall advise Seller in writing, by certified mail on or before August 23, 1976 of such condition and Seller shall thereupon have twenty (20) days from date of receipt of such notice within which to obtain such a mortgage commitment for and on behalf of the Buyer. Buyer agrees to execute any reasonable and customary application at Seller's request and Buyer agrees to pay a service charge not in excess of 1% of loan amount plus $75.00 to the lender.

3. If Buyer fails to make application for such mortgage loan or notify Seller of his inability to obtain a written commitment as herein set forth or fails to execute any application for such mortgage loan at Seller's request, the condition and contingency provided for shall no longer prevail and this Agreement shall be and remain in full force and effect according to its terms in the same manner as if the condition and contingency were not a part hereof.

4. Should neither Buyer or Seller be able to obtain such a mortgage commitment on the terms set forth above within the period above referred to, Buyer, at Buyer's election may (a) proceed with consummation of this contract without regard to the failure of the condition or (b) may cancel this Agreement, in which event all monies paid hereunder by Buyer on account of the purchase price will be returned to Buyer upon receipt by Seller

of (1) Buyer's written notice of intention to cancel, (2) return to Seller of all copies of the agreement of sale. Thereafter all rights and liabilities of these parties shall cease and determine, anything herein contained to the contary notwithstanding. Buyer shall notify Seller in writing of Buyer's election under (a) or (b) within 3 days by certified mail after being notified by Seller that a mortgage commitment loan was not obtained. In the event that Buyer fails to notify Seller of his election to cancel the contract under (b) above within the prescribed time limit, Buyer shall be obligated to proceed with consummation of the Agreement.

WITNESS   Smith Development Co., Inc.

_____   By: _____ [*Seal*]

_____   Attest: _____ [*Seal*]

_____   _____ [*Seal*]
                                          William White
_____   _____ [*Seal*]
                                          Brenda White

UPPER MERION TWP., MONTGOMERY CO., PA

1. CHIMNEYS—Material—Brick; Flue lining—terra cotta; Heater flue size 8½ x 8½.

2. SIDING—⅝″ Texture III, stained at factory, Olympic stain Color #718.

3. FIREPLACES—Fireplace flue, size 9 x 12; Brick, full wall, raised hearth with 2″ x 8″ wood mantel.

4. FLOORS—Basement floor: concrete slab, mix 1—2—4 3″ thick; Garage: concrete slab, mix 1—2—4 4″ thick; Finished floor: center hall, living room, dining room, family room, all bedrooms and center hall upstairs and closets will be ⁵⁄₁₆ hardwood floors, #2 oak 2″ width resin top nailed paper, filled and sanded, finished natural throughout with 2 coats of shellac.

5. GUTTERS & DOWNSPOUTS—Aluminum 4″ (white) Gutter—Aluminum 3″ (white) Downspout—1′ x 2′ splash block.

6. INTERIOR WALLS—½″ drywall, joint treatment taped; 2 coats white latex (prime & finish); 2 coats white latex enamel (prime & finish) on interior trim and windows.

7. DOORS—type: Hollow core mahogany 1¾″, finished natural throughout, Main entrance door—1—¾″ x 36″ Wood (Frame wood); other entrance doors, wood 2′ 8″ wide. Attic louvered, aluminum 14″ x 18″.

8. WINDOWS—Anderson casement style. Storm panels & screens available at extra cost.

9. CABINETS & INTERIOR DETAIL—Kitchen cabinets & wall units by Triangle Pacific. Liberty style. Approximately 13 cabinets. Counter top—Spanish Oak #344, Wilson Art Series.

10. STAIRS—Basement & main—wood 1″ thick, strings 2 x 10, handrail 2 x 3.

11. SPECIAL FLOORS—2nd floor bathrooms—hall bath—ceramic in wet bed (floor only); Master bedroom bath—ceramic in wet bed (floor only). Ceramic tile to be chosen at John Trevisan—390 E. Pembroke Ave., E. Lansdowne, Pa. MA6—6793. Kitchen

and laundry rooms ⅟₁₆″ vinyl asbestos to be chosen at Fred Callaghan's—555 Abbott Dr., Broomall, Pa. K14–2644.

12. PLUMBING—Hall bathroom: Fixtures will be Kohler Wellworth —water closet #K3510, color cerulion blue, tub #K715 Villager, color cerulion blue. Master bedroom bath: Fixtures will be Kohler, water closet #K3510, color Mexican Sand. Powder room: Fixture will be Kohler: water closet #K3510, color Fresh Green. Total extra cost for Kohler fixtures will be $310.00. 80 gallon electric hot water heater, Bradford glass-lined or equal. House drain: inside, copper; outside—cast iron.

13. HEATING—Bryant 85,000 furnace, model #390A048125 air conditioner—3 ton Bryant or equal, same quality as heat model.

14. ELECTRIC—Service: overhead circuit breaker, 200 amp service. Wiring: non metallic cable. Special outlet: range, dryer and heating system. Door bell—push bell, location—front door.

15. LIGHTING FIXTURES—$75.00 allowance at builder's supplier —David Tori, 60 Old State Road, Media, Pa. LO6—1972.

16. INSULATION—Ceiling, 6″ blown fibreglass; Walls, 3″ batts, exterior walls only.

17. APPLIANCES—GE J767 Americana Double Oven Range vented or equal $525.00 extra. Color—Avocado. Dishwasher—GE #SD281, 2 cycle sound insulated or equal, color—Avocado. Disposal—GE–FC110 or equal.

18. GARAGE DOOR—7 x 16 wood composition, installed by Buranich.

19. VANITIES—2—30 x 22 Bellwood vanities to be selected from Knock on Wood—3721 West Chester Pike, Newtown Square, Pa. 353–3333.

20. FINISH GRADE & SEED—all disturbed ground and planting of 6 shrubs.

21. DRIVEWAY—Asphalt—9′ entrance, 2 car width in front of garage. Concrete walk from drive to entrance.

22. Deck in rear of house to be extended to 10′ width at extra charge of $610.00. See Rider H.

23. Wood hand rail installed on hall stairs in lieu of wrought iron.

24. Seller shall transfer, assign and deliver to Buyer at settlement all warranties and guarantees that Seller has received or may then have received and/or which may thereafter be received.

25. Seller shall furnish at his sole cost and expense the labor, materials, and equipment required to make repairs and to correct any and all poor workmanship or defective materials installed in or on the property, for a period of one year following settlement. Seller shall not be responsible for normal wear and tear or repairs made necessary by the negligence on part of the Buyer.
See Rider D.

26. Seller is not responsible for shrinkage of lumber, trim, millwork, and hardwood floors or the results thereof including drywall,

cracks which are normal in new house construction. Buyer understands and is aware that shrinkage and results thereof may not be an indication of poor workmanship or defective materials, and Buyer understands that the repairs thereof may be maintenance and therefore the responsibility of the Buyer. However, Seller agrees to repair at his own expense in the year warranty period, all nail pops, cracked seams and repair swelling or shrunk doors.

27. Buyer to have the right of continuing inspection after reasonable notice.

28. Seller is given the option, in Seller's discretion, to make substitutions of material whenever Seller shall find it necessary or expedient to do so. It is understood that no changes in construction or in completion ordered by Buyer will be made unless authorized in writing by the Buyer at a cost agreed upon and approved by the Seller in writing. The cost of any such changes requested by Buyer and so approved by Seller shall be added to the total cost named herein and will be paid in cash by Buyer prior to the commencement of such changes, Seller may, at Seller's option, require additional deposit money to be paid under this Agreement in the event that the Seller agrees to any such changes in construction requested by Buyer.

29. Seller extends new home guarantee by Home Owners Warranty Corp. to Buyer at time of final settlement.

_____

_____

_____

_____

RIDER TO AGREEMENT OF SALE BY AND BETWEEN SMITH DEVELOPMENT CO., INC. ("SELLER") AND WILLIAM WHITE AND BRENDA WHITE, HIS WIFE ("BUYER") PREMISES: 781 SMITH TERRACE GULPH MILLS, UPPER MERION TOWNSHIP

A. Seller represents and warrants that title to the premises at settlement shall be free and clear of all liens, encumbrances, easements, restrictions, agreements and other matters of record, except for easements to public utility companies for the purpose of providing service to the premises.

B. Seller represents and warrants that all construction will be performed in compliance with, and that the completed premises will, at settlement, be in compliance with all applicable zoning ordinances, building codes and other governmental requirements. Seller will obtain and deliver to Buyer at settlement all necessary governmental permits or certificates of occupancy.

C. Seller shall, prior to the date of settlement, complete the premises in all respects in accordance with the Description of Materials and Specifications attached hereto and made a part hereof. In the event that any substitutions of material shall be deemed necessary or expedient by Seller, as provided in Section 28 of the Description of Materials and Specifications, said substitutions shall be of equal or better quality to those materials set forth on said Description of Materials and Specifications. Seller shall give Buyer at least three (3) days' prior notice of any substitutions which are contemplated.

In the event that the premises shall not be completed prior to the date scheduled for settlement hereunder, Buyer shall have the right to extend said date for an additional thirty day period.

D. Seller shall and does hereby unconditionally guarantee the work and materials and equipment furnished hereunder against defects in materials and workmanship for a period of one year from the date of settlement. Seller shall, within a reasonable time after receipt of notice thereof, make good any defects in materials, equipment and workmanship which may develop within such period for which said materials, equipment and workmanship are guaranteed and also make good, at seller's expense, any damage to other work caused by the repairing of such defects.

E. In addition to all of the guaranties referred to herein, seller shall deliver to owner at settlement, all guaranties extended by manufacturers or suppliers, including, without limitation, heating and air-conditioning equipment, appliances, roofing shingles and hot water heater.

F. Seller represents and warrants, on the date hereof and on the date of settlement, that all utilities and street improvements (including streets, curbs, sidewalks, water and sewer lines) and all other installations at or abutting the premises have been completed and paid for by the Seller.

G. In the event that the premises are substantially damaged or destroyed prior to settlement, Buyer shall have the option, exercisable by notice in writing to the Seller, of terminating this Agreement. In the event of such termination, all deposit money paid by Buyers pursuant to this Agreement of Sale shall be returned to Buyers and neither party shall have any further liability hereunder.

Seller shall maintain full fire and extended coverage insurance for the premises up to the date of settlement and shall make the proceeds of any such insurance available to Buyers in the event of loss or damage to the premises, provided that Buyers shall not have elected to terminate this Agreement as provided in the first paragraph of this Section G.

H.   The deck to be constructed in the rear of the house as specified in Section 22 of the Description of Materials and Specifications shall be _____ feet in length.

I.   Seller shall, prior to settlement hereunder, install a fence across the entire rear of the premises at such location as shall be designated by Buyer.   Said fence shall be of the following material:

J.   At settlement, Seller shall provide Buyer with a certification from a reputable exterminating company certifying that there is no infestation by wood-destroying insects (including termites) and that there is no uncorrected damage from prior infestation, if any.

K.   In the event of any conflict or inconsistency between this Rider and the printed portion of this Agreement of Sale, the provisions of this Rider shall be controlling.

L.   All provisions, agreements, representations and warranties hereof, shall survive settlement hereunder.

M.   Seller shall provide Buyer and Buyer's mortgagee with mechanics' liens insurance from Gulph Title Insurance Company, insuring against mechanics' liens and the possibility thereof.

Smith Development Co., Inc.
By: _____ [*Seal*]
Attest: _____ [*Seal*]

_____

William White

_____

Brenda White

B.   ADDITIONAL PROVISIONS TO PROTECT THE PURCHASER OF RESIDENCES TO BE CONSTRUCTED OR IN THE PROCESS OF CONSTRUCTION AT THE TIME THE AGREEMENT OF SALE IS EXECUTED

In addition to the provisions discussed in the preceding section with respect to the purchase of recently completed residential real estate, there are several types of provisions which should be added to an agreement of sale in order to protect a purchaser of a residence which is to be constructed or is in the process of construction.

1. Description

In the portion of the agreement dealing with the description of the property the land should be identified by legal description, by lot identification on a filed subdivision plan or on a survey plan or by reference to the lot's location with respect to streets and other lots, plus its area and front footage (length of the side of the property abutting a street).   The buildings and improvements should be described not merely by reference to a particular sample house, but, rather, to a specific set of plans and specifications showing all the details of construction.

2. Deposit

To protect against the loss of the deposit money in the eventuality that the builder becomes bankrupt or insolvent during the course of construction of the building, it is important to the purchaser that the deposit be placed in escrow with a reputable real estate broker, attorney or title company, rather than paid directly to the seller.

3. Settlement Date

Because of the vagaries of the construction business, sellers of homes to be constructed or under construction are frequently loath to include a firm settlement date in the agreement of sale. In order to help protect the purchaser, the agreement of sale should recite the dates by which construction must commence and be completed and give the purchaser the option to terminate the agreement and receive back all monies paid on account of the purchase price in the event that either of these deadlines is not met. A sample provision follows:

"Construction of the dwelling to be built on the premises shall commence on or about August 15, 1977 and shall be completed on or before March 15, 1978. The parties agree that such time shall be of the essence; provided, however, that Seller shall not be responsible for, and is hereby relieved and discharged from all liability by reason of any delay in completion of the premises or of settlement if such delay is caused by conditions beyond the control of Seller. In any event, if the premises are not completed by April 15, 1978 or, due to no fault of Purchaser, settlement is not held by April 15, 1978, Purchaser may cancel this agreement by giving notice to Seller no later than April 16, 1978. In the event Purchaser cancels this agreement, pursuant to this paragraph, all hand money paid by Purchaser shall be forthwith returned to Purchaser and this agreement shall be null and void."

V. TYPICAL ADDITIONAL PROVISIONS OF AGREEMENTS OF SALE FOR RAW LAND TO BE DEVELOPED

If a purchaser is interested in purchasing raw land for development purposes, certain terms should be added to the agreement of sale. These relate to conditions of the land which are peculiar to undeveloped real estate and which, if not adequately provided for in the agreement, could make the buyer's proposed development of the real estate impossible or burdensome. The ability to develop the land and to use it as the Purchaser desires may hinge upon such factors as zoning approval, subdivision approval, building permits and mortgage commitments.

A. SUBDIVISION APPROVALS

Many jurisdictions have legislation which provides that no one may divide a parcel of land, or erect a building on land in a subdivision, unless a subdivision plan has been approved by a designated authority, usually a county or local governmental authority. If the purchaser's proposed use of the tract in question will eventually necessitate obtaining subdivision approval, he should make the obligation to complete settlement conditional upon obtaining such approval. As in the case of zoning approval, it is important to specify (a) which party has the obligation to prepare and submit to the appropriate authorities the subdivision plan upon which subdivision approval may be based, and (b) which party is to pay the cost therefor. Each party requires the same sorts of conditions as those discussed in section II(M) of this chapter. If the purchaser is purchasing a tract of land which is part of a subdivision, the agreement of sale should provide that an approved subdivision plan will be filed of record not later than the date of settlement. This requirement is important because many subdivision ordinances prohibit the sale of land in a subdivision before such a plan has been approved. In any event, the parties should agree who will be responsible for making any improvements to, or for the benefit of, the premises (such as the installation of streets and specified utility lines) which are required by the local officials as conditions of obtaining final subdivision approval.

B. MUNICIPAL APPROVAL; STREETS, WATER SERVICE AND SEWER SERVICE

In order to protect the buyer, the agreement of sale should contain a warranty by the seller that the premises have direct access to designated public thoroughfares, or the agreement to provide access to public thoroughfares over private roads or other easements. The purchaser will also need a representation or warranty from the seller as to the present availability of water service, storm and sanitary sewer service, and perhaps gas service, at the boundaries of the premises. Such warranty or representation should include a statement that these facilities will be adequate for purchaser's intended use of the property and should specify what "tap in" or connection charges, if any, are payable in order to make use of these facilities and which party is to bear the expense.

C. RIGHT TO INSPECT PREMISES AND MAKE TESTS THEREON

Land upon which improvements are to be constructed must have certain support characteristics lest the cost of construction be prohibitive. A purchaser will want to have the right to test the land for these characteristics and will want to condition settlement upon their presence.

"Seller hereby grants to Purchaser, and persons designated by Purchaser, the right and permission at any time after execution of the agreement, and from time to time, to enter upon the Premises to inspect, appraise and make surveys of the Premises and to make borings, drive test piles and make soil bearing or other tests to determine the suitability of the Premises for building foundations and other improvements which Purchaser may wish to make for the purpose of constructing or erecting a ten story concrete office building on the Premises; provided, however, that said tests shall not be so conducted as to damage materially Seller's property or substantially interfere with Seller's use of the Premises. Purchaser shall have the right, at any time prior to the time of settlement, to terminate this agreement by giving written notice to Seller in the event that such tests indicate the presence of rock or other adverse conditions which, in Purchaser's judgment, will preclude the economic installation of building foundations or other improvements, or both, on or in the Premises."

D. BUILDING PERMITS

Before a builder can commence construction of buildings and improvements upon real property, most jurisdictions require him to obtain building permits or approvals of his plans from the appropriate county or municipal authorities.

PROBLEM

Using the formats previously discussed in sections II(M) and V(A) of this chapter, prepare a provision making the agreement of sale contingent upon purchaser obtaining necessary building permits for a 10 story office building.

VI. TYPICAL ADDITIONAL PROVISIONS OF AGREEMENTS OF SALE FOR COMMERCIAL IMPROVED REAL ESTATE

Commercial improved real estate is usually acquired either as an investment or for use in the purchaser's business, or both. There are additional provisions which are appropriate in an agreement of sale for the purchase of commercial improved real estate.

A. DESCRIPTION OF FIXTURES AND PERSONALTY INCLUDED IN THE SALE

You will recall from section III(E) of this chapter that it is important to list the fixtures and personalty to be included in a sale. For several reasons, it is even more important in a commercial transaction. One is that the purchaser may be purchasing an on-going business together with the real estate and also together with most, or even all, items of furniture, inventory, machinery and equipment. This contrasts with the typical residential transaction, in which it is unusual for much personalty to remain. A second reason is that the seller of a commercial building may not be the owner of everything contained in the building. He may himself lease equipment or it may be that most non-fixture items belong to tenants of the building. Thus, if the parties are not more specific, the purchaser might be unpleasantly surprised by a general reference to "the premises and all of Seller's property located therein". A third reason is simply the magnitude of the sums involved. A $50,000 house is likely to retain its value even though an attractive lighting fixture is removed. However, the personalty involved in a commercial transaction can represent a substantial portion of the value of the property. A provision similar to that discussed in section III(E) is suitable. However, some further protections are useful:

> "Seller hereby represents and warrants to Buyer that, at the time of settlement, Seller will have clear title to all of the aforesaid fixtures, machinery, apparatus and equipment, that Seller shall have full power, right and authority to sell the same to Buyer and that the same shall be delivered to Buyer in the same condition as they now are, ordinary wear and tear alone excepted, and free and clear of all liens, encumbrances, security interests and rights of possession of others therein."

B. POSSESSION

Because all or part of the property may be occupied by tenants at the time of the conveyance, a provision of the following type dealing with the problem of delivery of possession may be appropriate:

> "Possession of the Premises shall be given by Seller to Purchaser by delivery of a special warranty deed and keys to the Premises, subject to the existing leases as listed in Exhibit 'B' and any leases given by Seller between the date hereof and the time of settlement and approved by Purchaser in accordance with the provisions of this agreement. All unrented parts of the building on the Premises shall be delivered at settlement in broom clean condition and free of all personal property not conveyed to Buyer under this agreement."

C. ZONING AND LICENSING

The provisions relating to zoning and licensing earlier discussed in this chapter are also applicable in the case of commercial real estate. In addition, items such as the adequacy of off-street parking should be investigated, if such items are relevant to the purchaser's intended use of the property. In those parts of the country where municipal authorities issue certificates of occupancy or other documents certifying that the buildings on the property have been built in accordance with the plans and specifications approved at the time the building permits were issued, the seller should be required to produce that document at settlement. Similarly, where the agreement covers land in a municipality which issues certificates to the effect that a specified use of the property conforms to its zoning classification, the purchaser should request a provision in the agreement requiring the seller to furnish such a certificate at settlement.

D. EXISTING LEASES

If all or part of the property is leased to tenants and the parties intend that these leases will continue in effect after the conveyance to buyer, the purchaser will be concerned about the terms of the various leases. The purchaser's attorney should inspect the leases prior to execution of the agreement of sale in order to ascertain the terms of the leases, including the anticipated rental income from the property and the obligations the purchaser will assume as landlord (such as return of security deposits). In addition to inspecting the leases, the purchaser will want assurance that the leases inspected are true and correct copies of all of the leases, and that no changes in the leases will be made prior to settlement, without the consent of the purchaser.

PROBLEMS

Analyze the following provisions which a purchaser's attorney has prepared, including the reasons for them. Suggest changes in these provisions that a seller would request.

"(a) *Lease Provisions.* Various parts of the Premises are presently occupied under written leases. Seller warrants that Exhibit 'C' represents a complete schedule of all leases in effect at the date hereof accurately showing, for each such lease, inter alia, the name of the tenant, the date of the lease, the space leased, the rental, any security deposited by the tenant, the commencement date of the term, the length of the term or the expiration date thereof, the provisions with respect to renewal or extension of the term, the right if any, of the tenant to assign his lease and sublet the space he leases, and the right, if any, of the tenant to purchase the Premises or any part thereof. Seller and Purchaser have this day initialled Seller's copies of said leases. Seller warrants that there is no right of possession to any part or all of the Premises which is not set out in the leases described in Exhibit 'C.'

"(b) *Covenants, Representations and Warranties.* Seller, covenants, represents and warrants with, and to, Purchaser with respect to the leases listed in Exhibit 'C' that, as of the date hereof and as of the time of settlement:

(i) Said leases are in full force and effect and are the only leases affecting the Premises;

(ii) Neither the landlord nor the tenant is in default under any of the provisions of any of the leases;

(iii) The information relating to said leases as set forth in Exhibit 'C' is accurate;

(iv) No amendments, oral or written, have been made with respect to said leases other than those listed in Exhibit 'C,' and all of the terms of each of said leases are in writing;

(v) None of the tenants under said leases have made any security deposits thereunder other than as set forth in Exhibit

'C,' or prepayments of rent, and there are no sums to be credited to the tenants by reason of alterations, or other rental allowances, reductions in rent, or for free rental periods;

(vi) There are no rights of use or occupancy for any portions of the Premises now in effect or hereafter to come into effect except the tenancies under the leases listed in Exhibit 'C;'

(vii) No notices have been given to or by any of the tenants under said leases; and

(viii) No claim of any nature has been made by any tenant under any of said leases.

"(c) *Seller's Inability to Make Covenants, Representations and Warranties as at Time of Settlement.* In the event that Seller is unable to make all of the foregoing covenants, representations and warranties as at the time of settlement and Purchaser has not theretofore given written approval of whatever action, if any, Seller may have taken in connection with the cause of Seller's inability so to covenant, represent and warrant, Purchaser shall have the right to cancel and terminate this Agreement.

"(d) *Execution of Leases Prior to Settlement.* Seller agrees that, after the execution of this Agreement, no additional leases, licenses, easements or rights will be executed or given for any portion or portions of the Premises, nor will any existing leases be extended, cancelled, modified, added to or amended in any respect, or any assignment or subletting approved for any leases, without in each instance first obtaining the written approval of Purchaser.

"(e) *Termination of Leases Prior to Settlement.* Seller agrees that, after the execution of this Agreement, no action will be taken with respect to the termination of any of said leases without having obtained the prior written approval of Purchaser.

"(f) *Performance of Landlord's Obligations.* Seller agrees that all of the obligations of the landlord under said leases accruing to the date of settlement or arising from conditions existing prior thereto will be performed by Seller, and Seller hereby indemnifies and agrees to hold Purchaser harmless of from and against any claims, losses, damages, set-offs or counterclaims arising from the failure of Seller to fulfill said obligations.

"(g) *Assignment of Security Deposits.* The total sum of all security deposits, as listed in Exhibit 'C,' shall be given as a credit to Purchaser at settlement.

"(h) *Assignment of Landlord's Interest in Leases.* Seller agrees that at settlement Seller will, in a writing satisfactory to counsel for Purchaser, assign, transfer and set over to Purchaser all of Seller's right, title and interest in and to the leases listed in Exhibit 'C' and such other leases as shall hereafter be entered into with the approval of Buyer as aforesaid, and to deliver to Buyer Seller's fully executed copy of each of said leases. The said assignment of leases shall be free and clear of any right, title or interest of real estate brokers or other persons in the rents, whether or not such brokers or other persons negotiated the said leases or have contracted with Seller, or anyone else, for the collection of said rents. At or before settlement, Seller will pay the balance of the compensation in full owing to all brokers who negotiated or obtained leases for any part of the Premises, and will produce releases to that effect at settlement. The aforesaid assignment of leases shall contain Seller's warranty of title to said leases and shall contain an assumption of all of Seller's duties and obligations thereunder by Purchaser.

"(i) *Notifying Tenants of Lease Assignments.* Seller agrees to execute at settlement letters to be prepared by Purchaser for transmission to the tenants of the Premises informing said tenants of the assignment of said leases to Purchaser.

"(j) *Collection of Rents After Settlement.* Except as set forth in paragraph hereof, all rents and other sums collected by Purchaser, after settlement, up to the respective amounts currently due Purchaser from time to time, will be retained and applied by Purchaser on account of the rents and other sums to become due to Purchaser, notwithstanding that there may be rents and other sums due to Seller for any period prior to settlement. If and when any tenant shall pay to Purchaser a sum in excess of all rents and other sums which have accrued to Purchaser, and which sums are on account of arrearages which became due prior to settlement, Purchaser will remit such excess to Seller to be applied on account of the indebtedness due to Seller. Purchaser assumes no obligation to collect or enforce the payment of any such moneys which may be owing to Seller. Any broker collecting rents for the Premises shall have the right to deduct and retain from Seller's share of such rent and other sums, compensation at the same rate payable to such broker in connection with rents collected from similar space in the Premises.

"(k) *Survival.* All of the provisions of this Section shall survive and continue after settlement and shall not merge therein."

The student should recognize that paragraph (j) touches on several problems. If a tenant's rent is in arrears at the time of settlement, paragraph (j) makes clear that the purchaser will not apply future rental payments to the arrearage (which would be rightfully the seller's money) until the tenant has first paid the purchaser all sums which have accrued after settlement. The paragraph leaves open the question of the treatment of rental payments which relate to periods prior to settlement but which are not due as of the date of settlement. Since rent is normally prepaid, this problem should not occur with respect to rent. However, it will commonly arise in regard to items of additional rent such as increased taxes or sums due because of an escalator provision relating to operating expenses. These items are normally billed to the tenant at the end of a rental or calendar period. The provision does not deal with apportionment of rent already paid to seller for periods which extend beyond the date of settlement. That item is normally handled in a separate provision devoted to all types of apportionments.

E. WARRANTY AS TO INCOME AND EXPENSES GENERATED BY PREMISES

If the property is being acquired solely or partially for investment purposes, the purchaser will want an accurate financial history of the premises in order to make projections as to what kind of income the property will generate in the future. Therefore, he will want to require seller to produce, and warrant the accuracy of, financial statements relating to the operation of the property and to permit inspection of books and records containing the relevant financial data.

F. SERVICE CONTRACTS

The operation of most commercial or industrial buildings requires various kinds of management and service contracts. For example, janitorial service may be supplied by an independent contractor, rather than being performed by employees of the owner of the building. It is desirable that there be no interruption in the services at settlement. Provisions dealing with the care of assignment of various service and management contracts (which are usually assignable to succeeding owners of the property) are similar in form and nature to the foregoing provisions dealing with leases.

PROBLEM

Prepare proper provisions dealing with service contracts, including contracts for janitorial services and for servicing the heating and air-conditioning system.

G. APPORTIONMENTS

In addition to the usual apportionments which should be covered in an agreement of sale, a commercial transaction may involve apportionment of percentage rentals, payment under maintenance and service contracts and commissions for lease brokerage and managing agents, and others, depending upon the particular situation presented.

1. Percentage Rentals

Many leases of commercial property provide, in addition to a fixed rental payment known as "minimum rent," that the tenant will share with the landlord a percentage of the receipts or profits the tenant derives from his business. This latter payment, usually referred to as "percentage rental", is usually calculated by a method or formula contained in the lease.[22] Whether and how much percentage rent is payable depend upon the volume of tenant's business during a specified period for which the percentage rent is payable. The percentage

---

22. Percentage rental is discussed in detail in Chapter 9 of these materials.

rent is either payable on estimated installments, with an adjustment made at the end of its lease year, or no installments are made and the computation of percentage rent due is made at the end of the lease year.

If a lease of all or part of the property to be sold has a percentage rent provision, the purchaser and seller would normally agree upon a method for apportionment of the percentage rent. Since the total percentage rent to be paid will usually not be determined or collected until after settlement, the parties must anticipate making a post-settlement adjustment. Normally, the purchaser will receive the money from the tenant and account to seller for the seller's share. If, however, the seller does not trust the purchaser, or the seller is worried about the financial condition of the purchaser, payment could be made to an escrowee. Note that if in any situation tenant is to pay percentage rent directly to an escrowee, the seller will have to notify tenant, in writing, that payment of percentage rent should be made to the escrowee through the balance of the current lease year and thereafter to the purchaser.

2. Maintenance and Service Contracts, Etc.

In those instances where the owners of a commercial building have entered into employment contracts with personnel who operate the building and contracts for cleaning, elevator maintenance, burglar alarm service and the like, the contracts will frequently be assigned to the buyer. If so, a method of apportioning the credits due or amounts owing under these contracts should be specified in the agreement of sale. An apportionment may also be necessary with respect to vacation and other fringe benefits under employment contracts. A sample of a provision relating to the above mentioned apportionments follows:

> "At settlement, in accordance with paragraph _____ hereof, Seller shall assign to Purchaser certain contracts concerning maintenance, personnel and supplies used in operating the premises. Any pre-payment made by Seller pursuant to said contracts, as well as any payments which will be made by Purchaser, part of which will apply to periods prior to the settlement, shall be apportioned by the parties. An apportionment shall also be made with respect to wage and vacation pay, for the year in which the Premises are conveyed to Purchaser, due or paid to personnel directly employed by Seller for work on the Premises."

3. Lease Brokerage and Managing Agent's Commission

Often, when a real estate broker is entitled to a commission for obtaining a tenant and negotiating a lease, the broker's commission will be a certain percentage of the rents to be paid to the broker as rent is paid by the tenant. This type of arrangement is common where the broker is also the collection agent for the landlord. Frequently the agreement with the agent will contain a provision for a lump sum payment of the balance of the commission if the collection arrangement is terminated.   The seller would want the agreement to provide that the purchaser will indemnify and save the seller harmless against all lease brokerage claims accruing after settlement and against any liability for the lump sum payment due if the broker's rent collection authority is terminated.

VII. CONDOMINIUMS

The word "condominium" is derived from Latin and means "owning together." As used in modern real estate parlance, a condominium is essentially a form of ownership of real property which involves two elements: (a) a private "unit"—an apartment, store, office, floor or section of a building—to which an owner has fee title and a right of exclusive possession and control; and (b) public or common areas, which are owned by all of the unit owners in common and for which expenses are shared by all unit owners. The public or common areas may include structural elements of the building or buildings, lobbies and halls, utility systems, the land itself, recreational facilities, parking areas, elevators, roads and drives and everything else in the condominium except for the actual private unit.

For simplicity and ease of reference, we will refer primarily to apartment building condominiums, which are by far the most common form of condominums in the United States at this time. However, it is important to realize that most of the observations and conclusions set forth in these materials are equally applicable to commercial and industrial properties such as office buildings, shopping centers and factories.

A. THE LEGAL BASIS OF CONDOMINIUM OWNERSHIP

The condominium concept is an ancient one, known in Rome and commonly used for many years in Europe. When the concept was imported to the United States in the early 1960's, many lawyers believed that the common law provided the necessary tools to organize and govern condominiums and that no additional legislation was required. However, there were substantial areas of doubt, and to resolve the matter various state legislatures passed statutes authorizing creation of condominiums and setting forth the requirements, rights and obligations of condominium ownership. It is important to note that there is no uniformity to these statutes, and in analyzing the legal aspects of any condominium project, one must consult the statute of the state in which the condominium is located. However, there are certain features which are common to virtually all residential condominiums.

1. Declaration

The declaration of condominium (also known as master deed) is similar to a constitution. Its purpose is to set forth the basic rights and obligations of those who will be governed by it, the unit owners. The declaration establishes that a building is a condominium and sets out certain other basic information, usually including the following:

(a) General Information

The declaration usually begins with a description of the property. This will include not only a metes and bounds description such as one would expect to find in a deed, but also rather full description of any building on the property including permanent fixtures such as heating and cooling systems, elevators, and the like. The declaration will also set forth the designation of the various units (e. g., Apartment 1A, 1B, etc. or Apartment 101, 201, etc.). In addition, the declaration may contain any restrictions placed upon use. For example, there may be a provision requiring that the apartments be used only for residential purposes.

(b) Units and Common Elements

The declaration will provide a definition of what constitutes the common property (often known as "common elements") and what constitutes the unit. The definition is usually very precise. A unit may only include, for example, the interior space from the interior face of walls and ceilings. Anything which is near the boundaries of the unit must be defined in terms of whether it is a part of the unit or the common elements, including windows, window and door frames, sub-floors, plumbing and the like. The declaration will also specify the percentage ownership interest of the common elements which is allocable to each unit, and, if different, the percentage share of common expenses which must be borne by the owner of that unit. Common expenses are defined in the declaration and include the cost of operating and maintaining the common elements and the administrative costs of the condominium itself.

(c) Managing Body

The declaration also provides for establishment of a managing body known as a council, board of managers or board of directors. (For purposes of these materials we shall refer to this governing body as a "Council".) The Council is very similar to the board of directors of a business corporation. The Council is responsible for the overall management and operation of the condominium although it may engage agents to assume day-to-day managerial responsibilites. The Council's function includes preparation and adoption of a budget and assessment of common charges against individual owners. The declaration or the by-laws (discussed below) will provide for the initial term of office and procedures for electing a new Council.

The declaration is normally recorded in a place of public record. Each unit owner is charged with knowledge of the contents of the recorded declaration even if he has not read it.

(d) Plans

Generally a set of plans prepared by an architect or engineer either accompanies or is included in the declaration. The plans depict the perimeter of the property, the layout of each floor and of the common areas, and floor plans for each unit. These plans are similar to a survey; they are a graphic two-dimensional representation of the verbal description of the units and common elements.

2. By-Laws or Code of Regulations

Just as a corporation will adopt a set of by-laws setting forth the procedures for administration of its affairs, a condominium requires a set of rules and regulations for the conduct of its affairs. Some of the items normally covered in the code are the following: (a) time and place of regular and special meetings of unit owners; quorum and voting procedures at such meetings; (b) number and qualification of members of the Council, their term of office, and time and place of their meetings; (c) officers and their qualifications, terms of office and times and places of their regular and special meetings; (d) method of determination and assessment of common expenses; (e) procedures for collection of delinquent assessments; (f) restrictions on use of the property; (g) procedures for maintenance and repair of common elements; (h) restrictions, if any, on additions, alterations and improvements to any individual units; (i) insurance matters, such as the type and amount of insurance and application of insurance proceeds; (j) restrictions, if any, on sale, leasing and mortgaging units; and (k) the keeping of books and records and other management matters.

The code is often also recorded, and any purchaser, tenant or mortgagee is charged with notice of all of the provisions of the code and is bound to comply with them to the extent applicable.

3. Management Contract

Often, the sponsor or developer of a condominium property will remain in charge of management until all units are sold and for some time thereafter. The sponsor wants to do this to assure the success of the property and in some cases to earn management fees. Purchasers are generally eager to have the sponsor remain with the building at least for a limited amount of time, to assure continuity of management. This is particularly true in the conversion of rented buildings to condominium buildings. In such cases the Council will normally enter into a contract with the sponsor pursuant to which the sponsor will agree to perform normal management functions such as billing and collecting the monthly charges for common expenses, hiring and supervising employees and overseeing maintenance repairs. The contract will be for a specific period of time and will stipulate the amount payable to the manager, the time or times at which such payments are to be made and the management functions to be performed.

4. Prospectus

Although a condominium is generally considered to be real estate for all purposes, some state securities commissions have taken the position that the sale of condominium units is tantamount to a sale of securities and is, therefore, subject to all the strictures placed upon a sale of securities under the laws of that state. In addition, some states have enacted statutes specifically dealing with the sale of condominiums. In general, these laws require that the sponsor furnish each prospective purchaser with a prospectus which discloses the significant features of the condominium including the cost of purchase and maintenance, the estimated cost of taxes, the cost of mortgage financing, settlement charges, information concerning management and any other items which a purchaser ought to know.

B.   FIRE INSURANCE

Fire insurance presents an unusual problem which merits special attention. In a condominium, each owner has an interest in seeing that all portions of the building are covered by insurance and that the insurance proceeds will be available for repair or reconstruction in the event of damage or destruction. As a result, many high-rise condominiums obtain a single insurance policy naming all of the unit owners as insureds, with mortgagee clauses in favor of their respective mortgagees. The policy is held by the Council and the premiums are paid by the Council as a common expense. It is important to note that insurance obtained for the whole building will not normally cover contents of an apartment against loss by fire or theft. Therefore, each unit owner will have to maintain his own insurance on the contents of his apartment. Each unit owner may also want to insure separately for any major improvements which he makes to his unit.

Many statutes and many condominium documents provide that in the event the property is totally destroyed, the unit owners will decide collectively whether or not to rebuild. Usually the statute or the condominium documents specify that the insurance proceeds must be used for reconstruction unless a high percentage (perhaps 75%) of the unit owners vote not to rebuild. If the unit owners vote not to rebuild, the land and the remains of the building, if any, will be sold, and the proceeds of the sale plus insurance proceeds will be allocated among the unit owners in accordance with their percentage interests in the common elements. The unit owners will then apply their individual proceeds first to the repayment of any mortgages and other liens on their respective units, and will retain any balance for their own use.

C. REPRESENTING A CONDOMINIUM PURCHASER

In representing a prospective purchaser of a condominium, there are several areas of concern to the purchaser.

1. The Condominium Documents

One must read the condominium documents carefully to ascertain that they will provide a practical, as well as legally correct, set of procedures for operation of the property. Voting rights, procedures for election of members to the Council, and procedures for establishing the budget and assessing and collecting common charges must be carefully analyzed to be sure that they are responsible and fair to the prospective purchaser and, at the same time, provide adequate means for assessing and collecting common expenses from all of the purchasers. The proposed management arrangements must be carefully considered, and fire insurance problems must also be carefully analyzed.

2. The Common Expenses

In connection with the common expenses, the purchaser will want to know what the estimated expenses will be, how and by whom the estimates have been prepared, and on what experience the estimates are based. The purchaser will also want to know on what basis the proportionate interests in the common elements have been allocated. For example, one would want to know whether all apartments of the same size and type have the same interest in the common elements, whether percentages have been allocated on the basis of square footage, on the basis of value of amenities within the apartment, or some combination of these items. The purchaser will also want to know what guarantees, if any, the seller is prepared to make with respect to the common expenses. In some instances, sellers will agree to make good the difference between estimated common expenses and actual common expenses if actual expenses are higher than estimated. In some cases, the sellers will agree to buy back the apartment within a specified period of time (usually one or two years) at the same price as the original sale, as a part of guarantee with respect to expenses. Without such guarantees, or some reasonable assurance that the estimates are correct, the purchaser may find that the monthly charges are far in excess of what he originally anticipated.

3. Reserved Rights of Developer

The purchaser's attorney should also scrutinize the documents carefully (especially the proposed Agreement of Sale) to be sure that the developer has not reserved the right to amend the condominium documents after the purchaser has signed an Agreement of Sale, except for minor amendments which do not in any way increase the liability or obligation of the purchaser or in any way adversely affect him. Under no circumstances should the seller have the right to change the proportionate interests in the common elements, since this could result in a substantial increase in the purchaser's obligations for common expenses. Conversely, a reduction in the purchaser's proportionate interest could adversely affect him in the event of a total destruction by fire since his share of the total insurance proceeds is based on his percentage interest.

4. Ownership of Common Elements

In some states, the common elements, or the recreation areas, or both, may be owned by a separate, non-profit corporation, in which each purchaser may hold membership. However, the problems outlined above will be the same in principle regardless of whether the "condominium association" is an unincorporated body governed by an elected council or a non-profit corporation governed by a board of directors elected by the property owners.

VIII. DISCUSSION OF OTHER TYPES OF REAL ESTATE AGREEMENTS OF SALE

A. OPTION AGREEMENTS

An option is a contract, whereby the owner of property (the "optionor") binds himself to sell the property on specified terms to the purchaser (the "optionee"), but the purchaser has no corresponding obligation to purchase the property unless he exercises the option by electing to make the purchase on the terms set forth in the option agreement. The optionee normally pays a price to obtain the option (the "option price"). The option price might vary from one dollar to thousands of dollars depending upon the value of the option and the amount of time the optionee has to exercise his option. Upon the exercise of his option, the optionee is deemed to have the same interest in the property as a purchaser who has signed an agreement of sale for the property on the date the option was granted.

Since the option becomes a full-fledged agreement of sale once the option is exercised, and since neither party thereafter has any unilateral right to change the terms of the agreement, it is important that the option agreement contain the same essential provisions as an agreement of sale, in addition to the grant of the option and the provision dealing with the procedure for exercise of the option. One way of preparing an option agreement would be to prepare a simple document setting forth the terms of the option with an agreement of sale attached as an exhibit.

The option should state that the notice of exercise of the option will be in writing and should set out in detail the manner and place of delivery and even the exact text of the notice. Unless the optionee has already paid a substantial amount of money as consideration for the option, he should be required, upon exercise of the option, to pay a sum of money as a deposit. Option agreements usually provide that the consideration for the option will be retained by the optionor in the event the option is not exercised, but that, if it is exercised, the consideration will be credited to the optionee on account of the purchase price. It is not uncommon, however, for the optionor to receive a substantial sum of money merely as the price of the option and in such a case there is no credit towards the purchase price. Often, as discussed in Chapter 9, an option to purchase is granted to a tenant in his lease.

B. INSTALLMENT SALE AGREEMENTS

An installment sale agreement is one method of financing a purchase of property in lieu of obtaining a mortgage loan. The instrument itself is really a combination of an agreement of sale and a purchase money mortgage. It contains all of the essential provisions of a typical agreement of sale plus many typical mortgage provisions, such as the payment terms and the rights and remedies of the installment seller in the event of a breach of the agreement by the purchaser. Unlike the usual methods of financing a purchase, however, legal title to the property does not pass to the purchaser until all installment payments have been made.

C. SALE—LEASE BACK AGREEMENTS

The sale-lease back transaction is a financing technique whereby an owner of real estate can retain possession and use of the property while freeing his investment in the property for other use. The transaction itself consists of a sale of the premises by the owner to another entity for a specified purchase price, followed immediately by a lease of the property from the purchaser to the seller. Consequently, agreements relating to the future sale and lease-back of a piece of real estate usually take the form of an agreement of sale containing all the usual provisions for the particular type of real estate to be conveyed, to which is added one or more provisions obligating the parties to enter into a lease of the premises. A sample of such a provision follows:

> "This agreement, and the obligation of the parties to complete settlement hereunder, is expressly conditioned upon the parties executing the lease attached hereto as Exhibit 'A' and executing and acknowledging the memorandum of lease attached hereto as Exhibit 'B', both of which are hereby made part hereof."

The principal provisions of the lease should be agreed upon prior to the execution of the "agreement of sale" and they should either be set out verbatim in the agreement or, as provided in the above sample provision, a completed but unsigned copy of the lease should be attached to the "agreement of sale" as an exhibit. A discussion of the leasing aspects of sale-leaseback may be found in Chapter Nine of these materials.

Chapter Three

RECORDING STATUTES

I. INTRODUCTION

In the United States the methods of proving ownership of land and of conveying interests in land are based upon a system of recording in a public place all deeds and other written documents and instruments which evidence ownership of, or some other interest in, any parcel of land. The basic purpose of the public recording of documents which evidence ownership of an interest in land is to provide a reliable and predictable system whereby persons may have ready access to necessary information concerning ownership of interests in land, in order to make informed decisions with respect to buying, selling, taking mortgages and using real property. To that end, the states have enacted recording statutes which penalize those who fail to record interests and which protect people who comply with the statute, especially from transactions which are not made public through proper recordation and which affect the parcel in which they have an interest.

There are variations from state to state with respect to (a) which instruments are recordable, (b) what the recording requirements are, and (c) which persons and interests are protected by the statutes. However, all of the states attempt to establish rules for determining the relative order and priority [1] of rights among competing claims to a parcel of land, based on a variety of considerations, including the time the claim was first established, the time the claim was first recorded, the nature of the claim, whether or not something of value was given for the claim and the "innocence" of each claimant.

Our system is neither historically nor logically the only possible system to provide stability and predictability in land ownership. For example, in England an owner was once required to prove his title by producing the original deeds in his chain of title. This system has obvious disadvantages: deeds may be stolen, lost or forged and they are not accessible to the general public for inspection. Consequently, this procedure is no longer used in England or in the United States.

---

1. A claim which is given precedence over another claim is said to be superior, and the lessor claim is said to be subordinate. The word "priority" is sometimes used to mean superior, but at other times is simply used to mean that the prior claim was established before the claim to which it is being compared. Although a claim which is "prior in time" is sometimes also "prior in right", this is not always the case. For purposes of this chapter, assume that the word "prior" refers to priority of time, unless the text specifically refers to priority of rights.

The discussion which follows is intended to familiarize you with the fundamentals of recording interests in real estate under the various systems in use in the United States today.

II. RECORDING SYSTEMS

In general terms there are two land-title systems in use in the United States today, one of which is supplemental to the other.   All the states use a recording system which requires those having an interest in real estate to make a public record of that interest.   The system itself does not discriminate between various interests or make judgments as to the merits of the documents recorded.   Any such judgments must be made by those using the records.

Several states, in addition to the above recording system, have adopted the "Torrens System" of land registration.   That system results in a registration of each interest in a parcel of land.   The registration process in the Torrens System involves an evaluation by a court, at least in the initial registration, of each interest claimed.   The Torrens System will be discussed in greater detail below.

A. RECORDING STATUTES

The recording laws provide evidence of an interest of a person or entity in a particular parcel of real estate.   While the laws themselves vary among the states, the basic theory behind each of them is similar.   A place for public recording and a system for recording and retrieving information are provided.   Their use is encouraged by granting certain protections to those who use them and by withholding protections from those who fail to use them.

The recording acts vary in terms of the priority of rights given to instruments recorded and unrecorded and in terms of the penalties for not recording.   There are three general types of recording statutes.

1. "Race" Statutes

Race statutes provide that interests in real estate receive their priority of right based solely on the time of recording.   The actual date on which an interest was obtained is irrelevant.   The race statute puts a premium on adherence to the system.   The use of the word "race" in connection with such statutes refers to the possibility that there might be a race to the recording office to record a document when there are two parties with conflicting rights.   The first person to record his interest will receive priority of right, notwithstanding that he may actually know of the interest another party has in the land.

Because of the unfair results often caused by application of race statutes, they are rarely used today with respect to deeds, although several states have race statutes that apply to mortgages. An example is the Pennsylvania law governing priority of mortgages:

> "From and after the passage of this act, all mortgages, or defeasible deeds in the nature of mortgages, made or to be made or executed for any lands, tenements, or hereditaments within this Commonwealth, shall have priority according to the date of recording the same, without regard to the time of making or executing such deeds; and it shall be the duty of the recorder to endorse the time upon the mortgages or defeasible deeds, when left for record, and to number the same according to the time they are left for record, and if two or more are left upon the same day, they shall have priority according to the time they are left at the office for record. No mortgage, or defeasible deed in the nature of a mortgage, shall be a lien, until such mortgage or defeasible deed shall have been recorded, or left for record, as aforesaid."

[Act of April 27, 1927, P.L. 440, § 1]

The Pennsylvania mortgage race statute has a significant feature which is common to mortgage race statutes. Mortgages taken by the seller of a property to secure payment of the balance of the purchase price ("purchase money mortgages"), and mortgages created to pay the purchase price which are expressly stated to be purchase money mortgages receive special treatment under the Pennsylvania race statute. So long as such mortgages are recorded within ten days of their delivery, the lien dates back to the date of creation. Therefore, these types of mortgages are not really subject to the race effect of the statute until ten days have elapsed.

EXAMPLE:

> Purchaser purchased land from Seller on July 15 and financed the purchase with a mortgage loan from First Mortgage Bank. On July 20, Purchaser borrowed money from Friendly Finance Co. and secured the loan by granting Friendly Finance a mortgage on the same piece of real property. If First Mortgage records its mortgage by the 25th of July it will have the superior lien even if Friendly Finance has previously recorded its mortgage. After the expiration of the 10-day period on July 25, the priority of right of these mortgages will depend on the first to record. Friendly Finance is in a very unfavorable position. Notwithstanding its ignorance of First Mortgage's mortgage, even after checking the records, the lien of its mortgage will be subordinate to that of the First Mortgage mortgage if First Mortgage records by July 25.

2. "Notice" Statutes

The theory of a notice statute is that a person who records his interest should be protected from later claimants, whereas one who fails to record his interest should lose his priority of right to another party whose interest is subsequently created, *provided* the latter party had no knowledge of the unrecorded interest. The theory is implemented by creating the legal presumption that the recording of a document in the proper place of public record is tantamount to giving actual notice of the contents of the document to every person who might later claim an interest in the property in question. Every such person is presumed to have checked the public records before acquiring any such interest. Whether or not the person has done so, the later claimant is said to have "constructive notice" of any such recorded documents. However, if the original claimant in a notice state fails to record an instrument, he cannot retain his priority just by beating the owner of a subsequently created interest to the recorder's office. He loses his unrecorded priority once the subsequent interest is *created*.

An example of a "notice" statute is the Massachusetts statute reproduced below:

> "A conveyance of an estate in fee simple, fee tail or for life, or a lease for more than seven years from the making thereof, shall not be valid as against any person, except the grantor or lessor, his heirs and devisees and persons having actual notice of it, unless it . . . is recorded in the registry of deeds for the county or district in which the land to which it relates lies."

[Massachusetts Laws Ch. 183, § 4 (1947)]

A party who is without actual or constructive notice of a prior deed is called an "innocent" purchaser. An innocent purchaser who receives a deed is immediately protected against a prior deed which is unrecorded on that date. It makes no difference if the prior purchaser records thereafter and before the recording of the subsequent deed. To illustrate the operation of a notice statute, assume Appley conveys to Bendix, who does not record the deed. Subsequently Appley conveys to Cutter, who is without actual or constructive notice of the deed to Bendix, and who has paid money to Appley in exchange for the conveyance.[2] Cutter's right is superior to Bendix's, even if Bendix records before Cutter does, and whether or not Cutter ever records. Bendix is penalized for not recording and for not recording immediately. Approximately two-thirds of the states have "notice" recording statutes similar to the Massachusetts statute reprinted above.

3. "Notice-Race" Statutes

The notice-race statute is very similar to, and far more common than, the race statute. Basically, it works exactly like a race statute

---

2. It is not necessary for a grantee or assignee of an interest in property to pay money in order to achieve a favored status, but if money is not paid then some legal equivalent must be given, such as a promise to do something, the forgiveness of a debt or the payment of some property other than money. The favored status is referred to as a "purchaser for value", and excludes the recipient of a gift. If the transfer was not a sham or a fraud, then the purchaser attains the most favored status of a "bona fide purchaser for value" which is often referred to just as a "bona fide purchaser" or "b.f.p.".

except when the party trying to claim priority of interest had actual or constructive notice of the prior unrecorded interest. A pure race statute disregards actual or constructive notice, whereas a notice-race statute grants no priority of right to the owner of the subsequent interest, if such subsequent owner had actual or constructive knowledge of the prior interest, and no matter which party records first.

An example of this kind of statute is the recording act in Pennsylvania concerning deeds and other conveyances (but not mortgages):

"All deeds, conveyances, contracts, and other instruments or writing wherein it shall be the intention of the parties executing the same to grant, bargain, sell, and convey any lands, tenements, or hereditaments situate in this Commonwealth, upon being acknowledged by the parties executing the same or proved in the manner provided by the laws of this Commonwealth, shall be recorded in the office for the recording of deeds in the county where such lands, tenements, and hereditaments are situate. Every such deed, conveyance, contract, or other instrument of writing which shall not be acknowledged or proved and recorded, as aforesaid, shall be adjudged fraudulent and void as to any subsequent bona fide purchaser [3] or mortgagee or holder of any judgment, duly entered in the prothonotary's [4] office of the county in which the lands, tenements, or hereditaments are situate, without actual or constructive notice unless such deed, conveyance, contract, or instrument of writing shall be recorded, as aforesaid, before the recording of the deed or conveyance or the entry of the judgment under which such subsequent purchaser, mortgagee, or judgment creditor shall claim. Nothing contained in this act shall be construed to repeal or modify any law providing for the lien of purchase-money mortgages."

[Act of May 12, 1925, P.L. 613 § 1]

The notice-race statute, unlike the typical notice statute, protects the subsequent bona fide purchaser for value without notice only in the event he records the deed before the prior unrecorded deed is recorded. To illustrate, assume Appley conveys property to Bendix. Subsequently Appley also conveys the same property to Cutter who searches the record and, because Bendix has yet to record his deed, finds nothing inconsistent on the record with Appley's title. Bendix then records his interest. Subsequently Cutter records his deed. Title belongs to Bendix under the above statute. Although Cutter had no record notice, he is penalized for not recording immediately.

---

3. See footnote 2 regarding bona fide purchasers.

4. In Pennsylvania the chief clerk of a trial-level court is called a prothonotary.

B. OTHER TIME LIMITS UNDER THE RECORDING SYSTEMS

Many states have provisions in their recording statutes which make certain recordable interests void against all third parties, if these interests are not recorded within a specified time period.

In Pennsylvania, for example, deeds and other instruments of conveyance executed within the Commonwealth must be recorded within ninety days of their delivery. Those executed outside of the Commonwealth must be recorded within six months from their execution. The failure to record deeds in accordance with the stated time limits makes the deed or conveyance fraudulent and void against subsequent purchasers or mortgagees for a valuable consideration, and against creditors of the grantor, whether or not the subsequent purchaser records the deed, the mortgagee records the mortgage, or the creditor enters a judgment.

Similarly, a mortgage which encumbers Pennsylvania real estate will be effective between the parties but will not be a valid security instrument on the real property unless recorded within six months from the date of execution.

PROBLEMS

Is your state a race, notice or race-notice jurisdiction as to deeds? As to mortgages? What time restrictions are there on effective recording of deeds? Of mortgages?

C. WHAT CLASSES OF PERSONS ARE PROTECTED BY RECORDING ACTS

In a few states the priorities established through recording benefit all third parties (i. e., anyone other than the original owner and the party whose interest is evidenced by a recordable instrument). In other states, only purchasers and mortgagees are benefited. In still other states, certain creditors of the grantor of an unrecorded deed are benefited.

Whether a purchaser or creditor is protected from an unrecorded instrument in some states may depend on whether he has notice. A party may have actual knowledge of the unrecorded instrument or constructive notice. Constructive notice may be, for example, the presence of a party in possession of the land in question. The theory of constructive notice is that certain facts should alert a reasonable person to the possibility that there may be an adverse claim to the property and lead him to make further inquiry as to the state of the title.

In general, the recording statutes attempt to protect a party if he is a bona fide purchaser, mortgagee, or creditor without actual or constructive notice of the prior unrecorded instrument.

D. THE TORRENS SYSTEM

Under the recording acts system, the evidence of ownership or title is made public for the prudent purchaser or creditor to examine and to draw his own conclusions.

In the mid-nineteenth century an alternative recording system was developed by an Australian, Sir Robert Torrens, and bears his name, the Torrens System. Torrens suggested a system whereby a purchaser of property could go to a court and have his title officially determined. As a result of the proceeding the purchaser would receive a certificate declaring his ownership, and a duplicate of the certificate would be registered in the Torrens section of the public land records. The certificate would have noted on it any mortgages, liens or other interests in the property. When the owner subsequently sold the land it would not be necessary to search his chain of title since the certificate of title would serve as conclusive proof of his ownership. The Torrens registration officer would simply search his records to confirm that the seller has not already conveyed the property and that no liens exist other than those noted on the owner's certificate. In due course, the registration officer would then issue a new owner's Torrens registration certificate to the new buyer. By using the Torrens System the need for title insurance (to be discussed in Chapter Four) is theoretically obviated. In practice, many banks and other mortgagees are unwilling to rely on the Torrens certificate alone and require either title insurance or other proof of title.

Presently twelve American states, Colorado, Georgia, Hawaii, Illinois, Massachusetts, Minnesota, New York, North Carolina, Ohio, Oregon, Washington and Virginia have Torrens registration statutes. In each state the Torrens system is voluntary and exists side by side with a recording system. Because of the expense of the court proceeding required for initial registration, the Torrens system is not widely used in any state.

III. WHAT INSTRUMENTS MAY BE RECORDED

A. GENERAL LIST

The modern recording statutes embrace practically all instruments which may affect legal or equitable title to land, including, in some cases, leases. The following are instruments which may be recorded in one or more states:

1. Deed.
2. Mortgage.
3. Agreement of Sale or Memorandum of Agreement of Sale.
4. Assignment of Mortgage.
5. Certificate of Bankruptcy.
6. Conveyance of Permanent Rights or Privileges.
7. Decree of the Court.

8. Judgment.
9. Lease or Memorandum of Lease.
10. Map or Plan of Sub-Division in Lots.
11. Power of Attorney Relating to Real Property.
12. Purchase-Money Mortgage.
13. Release or Satisfaction of Mortgage Lien.
14. Sheriff or Marshall's Deed.
15. Trust Deed.
16. Condominium Documents.
17. Homeowner's Association Documents.
18. Option or Memorandum of Option.
19. Assignment of Leases.
20. Assignments of other Interests in Real Property.
21. Security Agreements.
22. Financing Statements.
23. Trust Agreements.

B. RECORDING CERTAIN INSTRUMENTS

The following section is intended to familiarize you with the recording of various instruments other than deeds and mortgages which will be covered in detail in succeeding chapters of these materials.

1. Judgments and Judgment Notes

A judgment is a decision by a judge or jury or a written admission (in recordable form) that one party owes a particular sum of money to another. Judgments are recorded in an index generally referred to as the "judgment index". Once it is entered in the appropriate index, a judgment creates a lien on all real property of the judgment debtor in the jurisdiction (usually the county) in which the judgment is recorded. A judgment obtained in states which use counties as the basis for court jurisdiction may be transferred from the county in which it is obtained to other counties in the same state or may even be transferable to other states. Once transferred, the judgment will create a lien on all property of the debtor in the county to which the judgment is transferred as well as the county from which it was transferred.

Prior to execution on a judgment, however, the judgment holder possesses a lien (as of the date of recording) which attaches to all the debtor's real property in the county in which the judgment is recorded. Thereafter, if the debtor conveys a portion of his property to a third party, the third party will take the property subject to the lien of the judgment, so that when the judgment holder executes on his judgment, he may order the sheriff to sell the portion of the third party's land formerly owned by the debtor. The third party will have record (constructive) notice of the judgment lien from the fact that the judgment is recorded against the debtor in the judgment index. Thus, the lien of the judgment is similar to the lien of a mortgage.

2. Lis Pendens

A complaint, which is a document used to initiate a lawsuit, may be recorded in certain instances. When there is a dispute between parties affecting title to land the party asserting the claim to ownership will want his interest recorded so that the record owner cannot sell or transfer the property to an innocent third party. This situation might arise, for example, if a seller refuses to transfer title to property to a purchaser because he believes the purchaser breached the terms of the agreement of sale. If the purchaser is not in breach, he may bring a lawsuit in a court of equity to compel the seller to convey the property to him. This action does not, however, prevent the seller from conveying good title to a third party where the agreement of sale is not recorded. In order to protect his interest in the land, the purchaser can have the pendency of the lawsuit noted in the office of the prothonotary or court clerk in the judgment index. This entry of a "lis pendens" (pending lawsuit) constitutes constructive notice to the public of the claims contained in the pleadings of the purchaser's lawsuit. If another purchaser purchases the land in question after the lis pendens is recorded, he takes title subject to the outcome of the lawsuit. If the plaintiff-purchaser wins the lawsuit, he will have the right to purchase the property in preference to whatever rights the second purchaser has in the property. The lis pendens is available only when the lawsuit affects title to the land.

3. Agreements of Sale

An agreement of sale need not be recorded in order to make it effective between the parties. However, unless the purchaser is in possession of the premises (thereby giving constructive notice to third persons of the purchaser's interest), the purchaser is exposed to the risk that third parties, such as bona fide purchasers and lienors of the seller, may acquire rights superior to the purchaser's. Therefore, it would appear to be in the purchaser's best interest to record the agreement of sale. However, in most areas agreements of sale are customarily not recorded and the seller typically requires that the agreement of sale not be recorded. The reason that sellers take this attitude is that if the purchaser should default under the agreement of sale, the seller would be unable to convey title to another purchaser unless the agreement is cancelled or in some way stricken from the record. Unless the defaulting purchaser cooperates, the process for accomplishing either result is expensive and time consuming.

4. Leases and Memoranda of Leases

Leases of real property create rights of possession in the tenant, as well as other rights. Under certain circumstances they should be recorded. For example, where the owner has agreed to lease a store which is not yet built, the tenant will not have immediate possession. The tenant can establish a priority for his rights under the lease by recording the lease or, more typically, a memorandum of the lease.[5] Similarly, where the tenant is not taking immediate possession and a mortgage will be created before he takes possession, it is often desired by all the parties (tenant, mortgagee and owner) that the lease should be prior to the mortgage. This can be accomplished by recording the lease before the mortgage. The desirability of the prior recorded lease is discussed in greater detail in Chapter Nine of these materials. Additionally, a lease which grants the tenant special rights in the property, such as an option to purchase the premises, should be recorded to protect the tenant from bona fide purchasers who, while they might have had constructive notice of the possessory rights in the lease, due to tenant's possession, would not have had notice of the tenant's right to purchase.

There are circumstances where it will not be desirable to record the entire lease, usually either because of its length or the fact that the lease contains certain matters which the parties do not wish to be of public knowledge. The law in many states recognizes this possibility and permits the recording of a memorandum of lease which has the same effect as if the lease were recorded. The content of the memorandum of lease is dictated by the recording statute and the desires of the parties. Generally, however, the memorandum must at least set forth (a) the names of the parties, (b) a description of the premises, and (c) the term of the lease. The Pennsylvania statute requires at least the following information to be contained in a memorandum of lease:

"(1) The name of the lessor in such lease, sublease or agreement;

(2) The name of the lessee therein;

(3) The addresses, if any, set forth therein as addresses of such parties;

(4) A reference to the date thereof;

(5) The description of the demised premises in the form set forth therein;

(6) The date of commencement of the term of the lease, if a fixed date, and if not the full provision or provisions thereof pursuant to which such date of commencement is to be fixed;

(7) The term of the lease;

---

5. Most states (but not all), permit the recording of memoranda or short forms of agreements in lieu of recording the entire agreement.

(8) If the lessee has a right of extension or renewal, the date of expiration of the final period for which such right is given;

(9) If the lessee has a right of purchase of or refusal on the demised premises or any part thereof, a statement of the term during which said right is exercisable."

[Act of June 2, 1959, P.L. 454, § 2]

Leases, subleases, and memoranda of leases are indexed by the recording officer in the grantor index against the lessor and in the grantee index against the lessee.

5. Assignments of Mortgages

Often the holder of a mortgage wishes to sell his interest to another in order to recover all or a portion of the debt owed him without waiting for the full term of the mortgage to expire.[6] This is accomplished by assigning the mortgage to the purchaser of the original mortgagee's interest. Such assignments of mortgages are recorded in order to protect the interests of the assignee. If the assignee's interest were not recorded, a satisfaction or release of the mortgage given by the original mortgagee would be binding upon the assignee in relation to any party or prospective claimant without actual knowledge of the assignment. Assignments are recorded in a separate assignment of mortgage book. In addition, the assignment will be noted on the margin of the mortgagor-mortgagee index where the original is set out, together with the book and page where the assignment of mortgage is recorded, and the date of the assignment.

6. Satisfaction of Mortgages

After a mortgage debt has been paid, the mortgagee must execute a "satisfaction piece" indicating that the terms of the mortgage have been fulfilled and the mortgagee has no further interest in the property. The mortgagee, at the request of the mortgagor or owner of the mortgaged premises, must enter the satisfaction piece of record in the office where the mortgage is recorded.[7] The satisfaction piece constitutes a discharge of the mortgage debt and a release of the lien of the mortgage, and its recording is essential to clear the title to the land from the mortgage encumbrance.

The recording officer indexes the satisfaction piece against the name of the mortgagee or the last assignee of the mortgage and also indicates the recording of the satisfaction piece beside the original mortgage record.

6. This has been especially true from the time that the government commenced efforts to develop a secondary market in mortgages by the creation of the Federal National Mortgage Association ("FNMA"), the Government National Mortgage Association ("GNMA") and the Federal Home Loan Mortgage Corporation ("FHLMC"), all of which will be discussed in Chapter Eight.

7. Some jurisdictions impose penalties upon a mortgagee who, having been fully repaid, refuses to execute a proper mortgage satisfaction.

IV. HOW TO RECORD DOCUMENTS

Having reviewed the common types of recording systems and some of the documents which may be recorded, we shall turn briefly to a discussion of the mechanics of recording an instrument.

Recording is effected by taking the document, in an approved form, properly executed and acknowledged, and presenting it to the office of the public official charged with the responsibility of recording such instruments in the county in which the real estate involved is located.[8] The public official usually immediately stamps the document with a time-date stamp to indicate the time and date deposited.

An instrument is deemed to be recorded at the time and date it is deposited with the proper official. Subsequently, the instrument is entered into the appropriate record book either by photocopy or by microfilming. The original instrument is then returned to the owner of the instrument.

A. THE INDEX

The recording system would be unmanageable and ineffective without an index to title records. Two methods of indexing are generally used.

1. Tract Indices

If a state has instituted a system where all the land has been officially surveyed and the parcels or tracts assigned numerical designations,[9] the index is subdivided numerically to coincide with the tract designations. A portion of such an index is set aside for each tract of land and contains recording references to the books and pages of the records that have documents relating to that tract. Indices may, in addition, provide information describing the character of the instruments listed and noting date, date of recording, and the names of the parties. Such indices are known as "abstract books". In several states tract indices or abstract books are part of the recording system and are matters of public record. In other states they are not part of the recording system and either do not exist or are privately maintained.

2. Name Indices

Name indices are based upon the names of the parties to the instrument. The names of the parties granting an interest in real estate, as grantor, mortgagor, vendor, lessor, optionor or assignor, are entered in pages of the record books or in separate books used

---

8. If the real estate is located in more than one county, the document must be recorded in each of the counties involved.

9. The process is generally known as "platting" and the surveys are known as "plats".

for indexing purposes only. As each instrument is recorded, the name of the granting party is written in the page or book corresponding to the alphabetical index of his name, together with the name of the other party to the instrument, the book and page in which the instrument is recorded, relevant dates and a description of the property. At the same time, in either the same index or in a separate index maintained for this purpose, the name of the party receiving the interest, as grantee, mortgagee, vendee, lessee, optionee or assignee, is recorded alphabetically, together with the same sort of relevant information concerning the instrument.

We speak of these indices as the "grantor index" and "grantee index" respectively. In some states, mortgage information is separately indexed in a "mortgagor index" and "mortgagee index". These indices also may be divided into separate sheets of books for different years. There may also be separate indices for judgments, liens and miscellaneous documents.

The value of the name indices is that they permit a title "searcher" to search the prior title history from the present owner, whose name may be found in the grantee index, by finding his immediate grantor, tracing back that grantor's grantor from the grantee index, and so on, until the original conveyance from the sovereign, such as the English King, Spanish King, federal or state government.

Then, in order to ascertain the existence of mortgages or other encumbrances upon the property, the relevant indices (e. g., mortgage or judgment) must be examined. To be reliable, the examination must cover the period during which a particular grantor and all predecessors in title owned the property. Use of the indices will be discussed in more detail in Chapter Four.

B. ACKNOWLEDGEMENTS

Any instrument presented for recording must be acknowledged. An acknowledgement is an affidavit by an authorized state or local official that the person whose signature appears on the instrument personally appeared before the official and "acknowledged" executing the instrument with full knowledge of its contents and purpose. The Uniform Acknowledgement Act provides that acknowledgements may be taken by the following individuals:

1. Judge of a Court of Record.
2. A clerk or deputy clerk of a court having a seal.
3. Commissioner or register (or recorder) of deeds.
4. Notary public.
5. Justice of the Peace.
6. Certain officials in a Chancery Court.
7. A duly licensed attorney at law.

An instrument executed by a corporation is signed by an authorized officer of the corporation and the secretary or assistant secretary who attests to the other officer's signature. The authorized officer then appears before the appropriate official and acknowledges that he is in fact the officer whose name appears as an officer in the instrument.

An acknowledgement taken in the United States, but not in the state in which the instrument is being offered for recording, must generally, in accordance with the Uniform Acknowledgement Act, be authenticated by a certificate which verifies the authority of the state or local official who made the acknowledgement. If the acknowledgement is taken by the clerk or deputy clerk of a court, the presiding judge of the court must execute the authentication. If the acknowledgement is taken by a notary public, or any other authorized person, the authentication must be made by a clerk of any court of record of the county in which the acknowledgement is taken.

Laws and local practices regarding acknowledgements vary widely from jurisdiction to jurisdiction. Some states do not accept acknowledgements made by an attorney. Some states accept a rubber stamp of the acknowledging official whereas other states require a seal which is embossed upon the document leaving a permanent impression. The language of the form of acknowledgement varies. Also, notwithstanding that the Uniform Acknowledgement Act requires only that the signatory acknowledge that a signature is his, local laws or practices may dictate that the signatory actually sign the document while the party taking the acknowledgement looks on, and in such areas an attempt by a signatory to have a previously made signature acknowledged will be unsuccessful. The best practice, especially when the document concerned is to be recorded outside your usual locale, is to consult a local attorney or the public official who will be receiving the document for recording and to inquire as to the local requirements.

C. RECORDING COSTS

In all states and counties a person who submits a document to a local official for recording must pay certain fees and charges.

1. Filing Fees

Generally the fee is collected by the official who accepts instruments for recording. The fee is normally computed from a published schedule, and is usually based on the type of document presented for recording and the number of pages that the document contains. The filing fee can be viewed as a type of handling charge collected by the local recorder to help defray the costs of maintaining an index system.

2.　Transfer, Recording and Intangible Taxes

In addition to filing fees, most state and/or local governments impose a tax on certain transactions or upon the documents effecting the transaction. Such taxes are usually assessed upon a transfer of title or a mortgage, but may include other transactions.

It is important to know whether the recording of a particular deed or any other particular instrument is taxable under state and/or local law or ordinance.[10] Realty transfer taxes and recording taxes are quite popular sources of revenue because they are easily administered and cannot be avoided except at the risk of losing the benefits of the recording system. Evidence that the taxes have been paid is generally a condition to acceptance of an instrument for recording. The taxes are often substantial and in some states can represent one of the major costs of settlement for the seller or the purchaser, or both.

Usually the amount of the tax is based upon the dollar amount of the transaction. If the document does not set forth the true consideration for the transaction or if the transfer is claimed to be exempt from tax,[11] it is usually necessary to insert at the end of the deed, or to attach to the deed, an affidavit stating the true consideration or reason for exemption.

V.　SUMMARY

A legal assistant needs to know how to use the recording system, in terms of getting documents recorded and retrieving information. A legal assistant should also be aware of the theory behind the local system. This understanding is useful in many aspects of real estate, and is especially useful in working with title abstracts and title insurance reports, which are the subjects of the next chapter.

---

10. Until recently the federal government imposed a stamp tax on such transfers. That tax is no longer in effect.

11. Intra-family transfers are an example of a class of transactions that might be exempted from a transfer tax.

Chapter Four

TITLE ABSTRACTING AND TITLE INSURANCE

I. INTRODUCTION

A. GENERAL INTRODUCTION

In Chapter Three we discussed recording systems and statutes. As we saw there, the philosophy behind recording statutes is to promote certainty with respect to interests in real property. The systems reinforce the claims of those who comply with the requirements of public recording, and deny support to those who fail to comply.

We will discuss briefly in this chapter the concepts of "title" and "good and marketable title". When used in connection with real estate, the word "title" means the ownership of an interest, and usually a fee interest, in real property.

Title abstracting is simply the gathering of information from various public records concerning the title to particular real property. Traditionally, title abstracting has been performed by lawyers, who then render opinions as to title. An opinion is neither a guaranty nor an insurance of title. Increasingly since 1876,[1] purchasers and lenders have instead sought insurance of title from title insurance companies. This has particularly been so in certain large metropolitan areas, and in large commercial transactions throughout the country.

The purpose of this chapter is to teach the student how to understand and work with title insurance reports and policies. To understand properly how to deal with title insurance reports, a paralegal must have some understanding of the abstracting procedure. This chapter offers that understanding but does not purport to train the student to be an abstracter.

B. MARKETABILITY OF TITLE

The goal of an examination of title is to determine whether the title is "marketable". A marketable title is one which is free from all reasonable doubt or controversy, free from liens and unencumbered.[2] Conversely, an unmarketable title is one which is encumbered, is subject to liens or has such serious defects that there is a

---

1. Commonwealth Land Title Insurance Company, which is headquartered in Philadelphia, was founded in 1876 and claims to be the oldest title insurance company in America.

2. Examples of encumbrances are liens, mortgages and leases.

reasonable chance it would subject a buyer to the hazards of adverse claims or litigation.

There are many defects in title which may come to light in the examination. Some of these defects are serious and some are not. The ultimate determination is not whether title is free of all defects and doubt, but whether the apparent defects affect marketability. The trend in modern real estate transactions seems to be that a marketable title is one which is unencumbered, is not subject to liens and will enable a purchaser to hold it during his period of ownership peacefully, that is, without any legitimate adverse claims.

Obviously, it is difficult to apply the vague notion of marketability to every case. Some titles appear to be marketable from the public land records, and yet may not be marketable because a grantor's signature in one deed in the chain of title may have been forged. Marketability is sometimes a question of law, sometimes a question of fact and sometimes an issue of both law and fact. If a will or a deed in the chain of title has to be interpreted by a court, then marketability is a question of law. If a party claims title by adverse possession, then marketability is often a question of fact (e. g., did the claimant have possession or use for the required period) or a mixed question of fact and law (e. g., was the possession or use of a kind that is adverse).

In order to determine whether a title is marketable, the history of the title must be summarized. An examination of the complete history should then reveal whether the chain of title to the present owner is clear and unbroken. The history of a title which is compiled by a title examiner is called an "abstract". The abstract contains a complete summary, including recording and docket information, of all documents and entries in the public records pertaining to the property.

C.   TYPES OF TITLE EXAMINATION

There are several types of title examinations: the attorney direct search and opinion, the abstract and opinion, the Torrens registration and title insurance. The choice in any case usually relates to the custom in effect in the area in which the property is located, and the type of transaction in question.

1.   Attorney Direct Search with Opinion

Under the direct search system, an attorney usually makes a title examination directly from the records at the recorder's office. After compiling a brief of title, the attorney will analyze it and render an opinion as to whether or not the title is marketable. The formal opinion sets forth all pertinent items and also may call for additional information in order to clear up possible clouds or encumbrances. The attorney search and opinion system is still in wide use throughout the United States, especially outside of metropolitan areas. The purchaser of property relies on the skill and integrity of the lawyer who examines the title. In the event the lawyer has made a mistake and the title turns out to be defective, the purchaser may sue the lawyer. Lawyers who render .title opinions generally carry insurance against this risk well in excess of their normal malpractice coverage.

2. Abstract and Opinion

Under the abstract system, a search is made by an abstracter who then prepares an abstract showing all recorded instruments affecting the land in question. The abstracter certifies that the abstract is a complete and accurate copy of all record items. The abstract is kept up to date by a further search at the time of each transfer of ownership and is delivered to each new owner. The purchaser's attorney reviews the abstract and renders an opinion after completing an examination of the abstract. This method of title examination is used primarily in certain western states and in Florida.

3. Torrens System

As mentioned in Chapter Three, under the Torrens or land registration system, the applicant files a request for registration of land with a court in the county where the land is located. If the court finds that the applicant has good title, it issues a certificate of title to the county land registrar and the owner. The certificate of registration contains all pertinent data as to the particular parcel of land, such as the names of the owners, description of the property, mortgages, liens, easements or other encumbrances and any other facts pertinent to the title. Every time there is a transfer of title (or a change in title ordered by a court decree), the registrar will cancel the old certificate of registration and issue a new one. To determine the validity of each registration, a search can be made in the Torrens registrar's office of all the facts endorsed on the owner's certificate. At the present time, the Torrens system of land registration procedure is in force only in 12 states: Colorado, Georgia, Hawaii, Illinois, Massachusetts, Minnesota, New York, North Carolina, Ohio, Oregon, Virginia and Washington.

4. Title Insurance

Title insurance companies are specifically incorporated as such, and are regulated by the insurance departments of the various states.[3] One way in which they operate is to have employees or agents prepare abstracts in the usual manner. The company then issues a title insurance policy on the basis of the abstract.

3. All states except Iowa permit title insurance companies to operate and is-sue title policies respecting real estate within their respective borders.

In certain areas, however, title companies do not rely wholly on abstracts from the public records. Instead, the title companies maintain their own separate system of records, often using a tract index system rather than the grantor/grantee system maintained in the public records. The title insurance company can conduct a search of these files at its own facilities. However, it will have to search the public records for the period of time between the last transfer on the title company's records and the date of the report.[4] A report of title is then issued based upon the search.

II. RECORDING SYSTEMS

A. IN GENERAL

The recording system, as it exists with variations from state to state, establishes a public repository for transcriptions (or copies) of original documents which have a bearing on land titles. All states have laws known generically as the "Statute of Frauds", which, among other things requires documents transferring title to real estate to be in writing. The written document, which is then "recorded", preserves evidence of ownership and gives notice to all persons who may wish to acquire an interest in the property. The public land records should be examined before land is purchased or a loan is made on the security of land. In addition, the records should sometimes be examined before land is leased.

As mentioned in Chapter Three, recording acts are now in force in all states. The purposes of these acts have been stated to be (a) a prompt recordation of all conveyances by according protection to a claimant who properly and timely records, (b) protection of subsequent purchasers against secret or unknown conveyances, and (c) preservation of accessible histories of each title so that any one needing information may find it and rely upon it.

In order to accomplish the purposes of recording, land records are required to be maintained in the county where the land is located, in the county courthouse building. Therefore, an examination of the title to a particular property begins in the county in which the land is situated. Sometimes, however, records in the state capital and federal courthouse must also be examined.

Access to the various documents on record is dependent on an index system. The abstracter must consult the index to locate the instruments so that he can examine and appraise them and evaluate the title.

B. THE INDEX SYSTEMS

There are basically two kinds of index systems: the grantor-grantee index which indexes by the names of the parties; and the tract index, which indexes by reference to parcels of land.

---

4. The search for information appearing on the public records since the title company's last entry is called a "bringdown".

1. The Grantor-Grantee Index

In the grantor-grantee index, each deed or instrument is indexed both under the name of the grantor and under the name of the grantee.[5]

The theory of a recording system is that a purchaser is chargeable with notice of all matters affecting the title which are expressly set forth in any instrument or proceeding forming an essential link in the title. The grantor-grantee index system is based on the "chain of title" theory which states that all recorded instruments outside the chain of title to a particular parcel are irrelevant to the examination and do not give constructive notice of an interest to the prospective purchaser. The recording acts extend the doctrine of notice to title records, with the result that a purchaser is bound by all facts which can be disclosed from an examination of all instruments in his chain of title.

In the grantor-grantee index system of some states there is the practice of using a separate set of books and separate indices for recording deeds, mortgages, judgments, attachments, mechanics liens, tax liens and various other miscellaneous documents. Furthermore, some records outside the recorder's office may have to be consulted. For example, probate court records must be searched for devolution of title through decedents, assessor's records must be reviewed for tax information, federal court records for bankruptcies and state offices for corporate tax information.

2. The Tract Index

The tract index is compiled by parcels of land rather than by the parties to the instrument of conveyance. Tracts vary in size from government survey system sections or quarter sections to a city block or lots of a subdivision. Instruments affecting property in a particular tract are indexed on the pages assigned to that tract. In order to use a tract index you first locate the parcel of land on the recorder's map. The map will show an identification number for each parcel. The starting point is normally a series of large maps which break a city or town into large sections using separate identification numbers for each section. Depending on the size of the parcel and the refinement of the system in that area, there might be further references to maps showing an even smaller, and therefore more detailed area. Eventually, an identification number is obtained, and that number will lead to all instruments relevant to that parcel, whenever and by whomever filed.

---

5. If leases, mortgages and other documents are included in the same books, then the grantor index will include the other "or" words, such as "mortgagor" and "lessor." The "or" search will tell you what someone who has an interest in the land is doing to the land, such as leasing it, mortgaging it or deeding it.

C.   DIFFERENCES

The major difference between the two systems is that a tract index gives the title searcher all of the relevant instruments by one reference number. The searcher then must arrange the instruments and try to complete a chain of title. In searching a grantor-grantee index, the examiner first searches backwards from the present title holder to some certain source of title (such as the U.S. Government) and then searches forward along the chain to discover all relevant documents.

III.   THE ABSTRACT

A.   IN GENERAL

An abstract has two basic components. The first component is the chain of title to the present owner. The second is the discovery of encumbrances which relate to the property being abstracted.

B.   CHAIN OF TITLE

Following the caption which contains a description and a survey reference, the first part of an abstract is the compilation of all recorded instruments to form the chain of title. This compilation is done in chronological order from the first deed in the abstract down to the most current. The abstract will contain a summary of the important facts from each recorded instrument.

The synopsis of each deed in the chain of title should contain the following:

(a) Full names of grantors and their marital status (if individuals).

(b) Full names of grantees and their marital status (if individuals).

(c) Date of Deed.

(d) Consideration stated in deed.

(e) Date of acknowledgement.

(f) Date of recording.

(g) Deed book volume and page references.

(h) Reference to payment of any documentary stamps or transfer taxes.

(i) Statement of whether the description in the deed corresponds to the description in the caption to the abstract.

(j) Recitation of the preceding deed or other facts in the preceding title.

(k) Recitation of all exceptions, reservations, restrictions, conditions, covenants, encumbrances or any other pertinent fact affecting title.

The purpose of compiling the information is to establish an unbroken chain of valid transfers of title from the last indisputable holder of title to the current holder. As we shall see, a title report will sometimes require certain documents or other proofs to be produced in order to verify or complete the unbroken chain.

C. SEARCH FOR ADVERSE CONVEYANCES AND ENCUMBRANCES

The search for adverse conveyances and encumbrances is begun by placing all of the names of the parties in chronological order. The examiner must check the index for the names of all the parties in the chain of title. As to adverse conveyances and creation of mortgages, each party need only be checked for the period of time during which he owned the property. Judgments against a particular party must be checked for the period prior to ownership as well as the time during which a party held title to the property.[6]

1. Adverse Conveyances

The examiner must check the name of each party in the grantor index. If there was a conveyance during the party's ownership of the subject property, other than the conveyance to the next party in the chain of title, the examiner must review the conveyance in order to determine whether it purported to convey any part of or interest in the subject property. There might be conveyances granting easements and these would be indicated in the abstract.

2. Mortgages

The examiner must go to the mortgagor index and determine if any mortgages were created by any of the named parties during their period of ownership of the property. If they were, the examiner must check the terms of each such mortgage and determine whether it affected the subject property. If a mortgage was created which affected the subject property, the examiner must look at the record to determine whether the mortgage has been satisfied. If the mortgage has been satisfied then the examiner makes note of that fact and can disregard the mortgage. If the mortgage has not been satisfied, it will appear as a lien or encumbrance on the abstract.

3. Judgments

A judgment which is recorded is a lien against all of the judgment debtor's real estate in the county where the judgment is recorded. Judgments only last for a specified period of time in each jurisdiction, after which they may be renewed for a fixed period of time and in that manner renewed again and again. The examiner

6. This is because judgments are usually a lien upon property acquired after the date of the judgment.

must check the judgment indexes for each of the parties who held title to the real estate during the appropriate period while judgments could still be effective. If any party had a judgment on record against him during the period while he was in title, that judgment will be a lien against the subject property unless the examiner can determine that the judgment has been satisfied or has expired, or the lien has been released.

4. Tax Liens

Local real estate taxes and water and sewer rents which are unpaid are liens against the real estate against which they are assessed. The tax lien records are normally indexed by reference to the premises rather than the owner. Therefore, the examiner need only search the subject property in the tax lien records.

5. Federal Search

In addition to the search which is made at the county land records and courthouse, a search must be made of the records in the federal courthouse in the judicial district in which the land is located. This search is to determine whether any judgments and federal tax liens which could still be effective have been filed and to see if the grantor has been adjudged a bankrupt (in which case he may not be able to transfer the property without leave of court).

IV.   TITLE REPORT

A.   IN GENERAL

If a title insurance company is involved, then the results of the abstract will be in the form of a title report. The format and layout of the report will vary from company to company. All reports, however, will contain certain basics. A blank report of the Commonwealth Land Title Insurance Company has been reprinted at the end of this chapter, and reference will be made to it for an analysis of the basic portions of the report.

B.   ANALYSIS OF TITLE REPORT

1. Caption and Title Report Number

The heading of the title report contains the title number and the date of the report. The title company maintains its internal records by reference to the title report number. The number can be used as a reliable shorthand reference to the policy in drafting corporate resolutions or agreements of sales. The date is important because if the title report is revised for some reason, the report number remains the same, and only the date changes (e. g., "revised July 21, 1977").

The caption just below the heading gives a brief description of the transaction to be insured. If the transaction is a purchase being financed by a mortgage loan, then the caption will indicate that the instruments to be produced include a deed from the seller to the purchaser and a mortgage from the purchaser to the lender. The caption should be reviewed immediately upon receipt of a report to ensure that the full transaction is included and that all the parties are correctly scheduled. The caption is where most errors are made and any discrepancies should be quickly reported.

The recital section of the caption is a summary of the relevant information concerning the most recent recorded conveyance of the property in question. Inclusion of recitals in deeds and mortgages will be of great assistance to future title searchers attempting to trace a chain of title.[7]

2. Taxes, Sewer and Water Rents

In most states, unpaid local real estate taxes impose a statutory lien upon real property, in some cases a first lien ahead even of a mortgage. The title company will list as a requirement of closing that tax receipts be produced so that the title insurer can be certain that real estate taxes then due have been paid. The title insurance company will then insure title against the lien of past real estate taxes. It will not, of course, insure title against the lien of future real estate taxes, as payment of those taxes is in the control of the owner and not the title insurer.

Sewer and water charges, where they are supplied by municipal authorities, are treated in the same manner as real estate taxes, and for the same reason.

3. Mechanics and Municipal Liens

A mechanics lien is a statutorily created remedy which gives laborers and suppliers of materials a right to create a special priority lien upon real estate which their labors or materials have improved. Mechanics liens laws vary, but often the state law permits the priority of the lien to "relate back" (i. e., to become effective) to a time earlier than the filing of the lien, and usually from the commencement of the work. Thus, the section marked "Mechanics and Municipal Claims" might or might not have actual filed claims listed, but in either event it will also have an exception for *unfiled* claims. This objection may sometimes be removed by an affidavit from the owner that no work has been performed by any contractors within a specified period of time. The problem of title insurance respecting mechanics liens when work *has* been recently done is a very difficult one that has received considerable attention from large lenders and from the title insurance industry. As a legal assistant, you need only recognize that the problem exists.

7. See Chapter Ten, *Deeds of Conveyance.*

4. Mortgages and Judgments

The next section will list the necessary reference data for mortgages and judgments that appear in the public record. Most title companies list any judgments found in the county in which the property is located docketed against anyone with a similar name. If a judgment is against someone other than the owner, then the judgment may be removed as an objection. In the case of a mortgage upon the property or a judgment that is really against the owner, the lawyer or paralegal for the owner will have to have the judgment and mortgage satisfied, either prior to or at settlement. If the judgment or mortgage is to be paid out of the proceeds of settlement, then usually all that is needed is a form of pay-off statement from the mortgagee or judgment creditor stating that the mortgage or judgment will be satisfied upon payment of a certain sum.

5. Objections

The remainder of the report is given over to various objections. These may be classified as follows.

(a) General Standard Objections

Title companies often have already printed on their reports certain objections, that are exceptions to its title insurance coverage, which are standard for every transaction, no matter what the property is or who the parties are. Standard objections are not completely standard throughout the nation or from company to company, but they generally include an exclusion for tenants under unrecorded lease and an exclusion against any easements or encroachments that would be visible from an inspection of the property or that a proper survey would disclose. Standard objections are sometimes removed and sometimes not, depending on the particular transaction.

(b) Property-Specific Objections

Certain objections are added for specific properties. These objections might be standard for the type of property, e. g., property abutting a canal, or might be specific easements, restrictions and rights of way that have been shown to affect the property. These objections would also include recorded leases or other rights that have also been shown to affect the property. These objections normally remain unless something affirmative is done, such as producing a termination of a lease.

(c) Party-Specific Objections

Certain objections appear because of the nature of the parties involved or because of peculiarities in the chain of title. Again, some of these objections are standard for certain parties, e. g., a corporate seller must usually show that the Board of Directors authorized the transaction, and an estate must show that proper letters testamentary were filed and that federal and state estate and inheritance taxes have been taken care of. Other objections are included because of a need to fill gaps in the chain of title. Let us suppose, for example, that the last recorded deed for a parcel shows title to have been conveyed to Diogenes Corp., in 1958. In 1967, Diogenes Corp. merged with Lampco, Inc., and Lampco, Inc. was the survivor corporation. No deed was recorded, and the title passed to Lampco, Inc. by operation of law. In 1976, Lampco, Inc. dissolved, at a time when its sole shareholders were Xerxes and Darius, each owning 5,000 shares of stock. No deed was recorded, and the title passed to Xerxes and Darius as tenants in common, by operation of law. A title company would want satisfactory evidence of all this, including at least a certificate of merger from the state corporate bureau respecting the 1967 merger and a certificate of dissolution for the 1976 dissolution. Additionally, the title company might require corporate resolutions showing that the merger and the dissolution were both duly authorized.

V. SUMMARY AND CONCLUSION

A major source of conceptual confusion respecting title insurance is the word "insurance" itself. Most of us think of insurance as a means of obtaining a measure of protection against financial loss for future events. Title insurance insures against financial loss only for future events based on claims that derive from the *past*, and not against claims that arise out of future events. The title insurance policy is really a financially-backed opinion of the state of title as it stands immediately after recordation of the instrument involved in the transaction being insured. Thus, the main impetus of title insurance underwriting is to establish firmly what has happened in the past, up through and including settlement. To the greatest extent possible, the title insurance company will try to establish a complete chain of title, fully documented, without gaps and deficiencies.

In minimizing the risks of issuing title insurance policies, title companies perform services and functions which overlap the traditional functions of a lawyer in a real estate transaction. An attorney representing a client purchasing from a corporation would want to make sure that the corporation was authorized to convey the property. The title company has the same concern, and is likely to seek the same proof—certified resolutions of the Board of Directors (and, in some instances, of the shareholders as well).

The role of the title insurer, and the measures that the company takes to minimize its risks, shape the format and function of the title report itself. Thus the report states what a search of the public records has disclosed about the status of title as it relates to the contemplated transaction, and further describes what gaps must be filled in, and what documents and proofs must be produced, in order for the title insurer to be able to issue a policy after settlement insuring that the title on that day is as stated therein. The policy is not prospective or predictive, it is just a description of title as of one fixed moment in time.

The function of the title report shapes its utility. As a legal assistant, you can use the title report as a guide to the agenda of documents that must be produced in order to complete a settlement. The title report gives advance notice of certain problems, and an opportunity for the parties to allocate responsibility for solving the problems.

The following documents are a title report prepared for a specific transaction, and the title policy issued to the owner of the property following the transaction.

EXAMPLE:

NO.   DATE

TITLE·REPORT

Commonwealth Land Title Insurance Company

Home Office: 1510 Walnut Street, Philadelphia, Pennsylvania 19102

COMPANY WILL ISSUE ITS CURRENT A.L.T.A. POLICY OF TITLE INSURANCE WITH RESPECT TO THE PREMISES ENDORSED HEREON, UPON SETTLEMENT OF THE TRANSACTION, RECORDATION OF THE INSTRUMENTS AND COMPLIANCE WITH ALL OF THE REQUIREMENTS SET FORTH HEREIN, IN CONFORMITY WITH THIS TITLE REPORT.

AMOUNT OF POLICY

Alfred L. Mackler
Asst. Vice President

MORTGAGEE $ _____ OWNER $ _____

SCHEDULE A INSTRUMENTS TO BE PRODUCED AND RECORDED	*See Last Page for description and recital as to premises:–* 810 South 9th Street, Darby Boro. Del. Co DEED: James Freeport and Dorothy Freeport, his wife TO: John Hannahan and Thelma M. Hannahan DATED RECORDED MORTGAGE: $ _____ John Hannahan and Thelma M. Hannahan TO: Sharon Federal Savings and Loan Association DATED RECORDED
SCHEDULE B-1	*UPON SATISFACTORY EVIDENCE OF DISCHARGE, SATISFACTION OR COMPLIANCE WITH THE FOLLOWING ITEMS AFFECTING TITLE TO THE SUBJECT PREMISES, SUCH ITEMS WILL BE REMOVED AND THE POLICY WILL BE ISSUED WITHOUT EXCEPTION THEREFOR.* ADDITIONAL EXCEPTIONS BASED ON A CONTINUATION OF TITLE SEARCHES WILL BE ADDED IF NOT DISPOSED OF TO SATISFACTION OF COMPANY. Possible unfiled mechanics liens and municipal claims. Terms of any unrecorded lease or rights of parties in possession. Proof that all natural persons in this transaction are of full age and legally competent. Proof of identity of parties as set forth in Recital. Payment of State and local Real Estate Transfer Taxes, if required. Possible additional assessments for taxes for new construction or for any major improvements pursuant to provisions of Acts of Assembly relating thereto.
TAXES	Receipts for all taxes for the years 1973 to 1975 inclusive to be produced. Due for current year 1976.
WATER RENTS	Receipts to be produced for years 1971 to 1975 inclusive. Due for current year 1976. Possible charge for water pipe installation and connection.
SEWER RENTS	Receipts to be produced for years 1971 to 1975 inclusive. Due for current year 1976. Possible charge for sewer installation and connection.
MECHANICS AND MUNICIPAL CLAIMS	NONE
MORTGAGES	$9,200.00 James Freeport and Dorothy Freeport, his wife to Sharon Savings and Loan Association dated February 29th, 1968 and recorded March 1st, 1968 in Mortgage Book 2749 page 942.
JUDGMENTS	Public Consumer Discount Company vs James Freeport and Dorothy Freeport, C.P. 72-1489 filed 4-1-1972 DSB $4,000.00 Docket 369 page 542

[R6965]

SCHEDULE B-II *THE PREMISES ENDORSED HEREON ARE SUBJECT TO THE FOLLOWING ITEMS WHICH, TOGETHER WITH ITEMS NOT REMOVED IN SCHEDULE B-I, WILL BE EXCEPTED IN THE POLICY. ITEMS MARKED "SUBORDINATE" WILL APPEAR IN THE POLICY BUT COMPANY WILL INSURE THAT SUCH ITEMS ARE SUBORDINATE TO THE INSURED MORTGAGE (MORTGAGE POLICY ONLY).*

EXCEPTIONS

1. Discrepancies or conflicts in boundary lines, easements, encroachments or area content which a satisfactory survey would disclose.

2. Possible additional assessments for taxes for new construction or for any major improvements pursuant to provisions of Acts of Assembly relating thereto.

3. Easement of 9 feet wide driveway on Southwest, and subject to the proportionate part of keeping said driveway in good order and repair.

4. Restrictions affecting title as in Deed Book K-6 page 542 and Deed Book 2483 page 601.

5. Rights granted to the Philadelphia Electric Company and Bell Telephone Company in Deed Book 1243 page 609.

ENDORSEMENTS   The following endorsements will appear in Policy if indicated.

Endorsement Pa. 300   Endorsement_____ Endorsement _____ _____

[B8988]

TITLE INSURANCE SERVICES AVAILABLE

THROUGH THIS COMPANY, ITS SUBSIDIARIES, AGENTS, & APPROVED ATTORNEYS, IN:

Alaska	Kansas		New Jersey	Utah
Alabama	Kentucky		New Mexico	Vermont
Arizona	Louisiana		New York	Virginia
Arkansas	Maine		North Carolina	West Virginia
California	Maryland		North Dakota	Wisconsin
Colorado	Massachusetts		Ohio	Wyoming
Connecticut	Michigan		Oklahoma	
Delaware	Minnesota		Oregon	◆
Florida	Mississippi		Pennsylvania	
Georgia	Missouri		Rhode Island	
Hawaii	Montana		South Carolina	Bahamas
Idaho	Nebraska		South Dakota	District of Columbia
Illinois	Nevada		Tennessee	Puerto Rico
Indiana	New Hampshire		Texas	Virgin Islands

DESCRIPTION and RECITAL

ALL THAT CERTAIN brick messuage and lot or piece of land SITUATE on the Northwesterly side of Ninth Street, in the Borough of Darby, County of Delaware and State of Pennsylvania, and described as Lot No. 12, according to a certain survey and plan made by Alonzo H. Yocum, Surveyor, dated the 27th day of May A.D. 1922 and recorded in the Office for the Recording of Deeds, &c., in and for the County of Delaware aforesaid, in Deed Book 701 page 462 &c. as follows:

BEGINNING at a point in the Northwesterly side of Ninth Street at the distance of 208.84 feet Southwestwardly from a point in the corner formed by the intersection of the Southwesterly side of Willow Street and the Northwesterly side of Ninth Street; thence extending South 22 degrees 6 minutes West 22 feet to a point; thence extending North 67 degrees 46 minutes West 108 feet to a point; thence extending North 22 degrees 6 minutes East 22 feet to a point; thence extending South 67 degrees 46 minutes East passing through the center of the party wall of the messuage hereby conveyed and the messuage adjoining on the Northeast 108 feet to a point in the Northwesterly side of Ninth Street, the first mentioned point and place of beginning.

BEING No. 810 South Ninth Street.

TOGETHER with the right and subject to a corresponding right in the owner or owners of the adjoining property on the Southwest of using as and for a passageway and driveway forever, a certain 9 feet wide driveway and extending in length 88 feet and shown on said plan and laid out half on the property hereby conveyed and half on the property adjoining on the Southwest for the common use and benefit of each of the said properties.

BEING the same premises which Howard J. Elkins and Mildred E. Elkins, his wife by Deed dated February 29, 1968 and recorded in Deed Book 2849 page 180 conveyed unto James Freeport and Dorothy Freeport, his wife, in fee.

[B8967]

PA 10 ALTA Owner's Policy
1970-Form B (Amended 10/17/70)

SPECIMEN

POLICY
OF
TITLE
INSURANCE

Issued by

COMMONWEALTH LAND
TITLE INSURANCE COMPANY

Title Insurance Since 1876

HOME OFFICE
1510 WALNUT STREET
PHILADELPHIA, PA. 19102

POLICY OF TITLE INSURANCE

COMMONWEALTH LAND
TITLE INSURANCE COMPANY

(a stock company)
PHILADELPHIA, PENNSYLVANIA

SCHEDULE A

POLICY NO. C-842-785-D	**DATE OF POLICY:** *The date shown below or the date of recording of the instrument referred to in Item 3 whichever is the later.*	**AMOUNT OF INSURANCE** $40,000

1. Name of insured: John Hannahan and Thelma M. Hannahan, Husband and Wife

2. The estate or interest in the land described herein and which is covered by this policy is:

Owners in fee.

3. The estate or interest referred to herein is at Date of Policy vested in:

insured, by deed from James Freeport and wife to insured, dated January 28, 1976 and recorded January 29, 1976 in Deed Book 4216 page 379 at Media, Pennsylvania

4. The land referred to in this policy is described in the said instrument and identified as follows:

ALL THAT CERTAIN brick messuage and lot or piece of land SITUATE on the Northwesterly side of Ninth Street, in the Borough of Darby, County of Delaware and State of Pennsylvania, and described as Lot No. 12, according to a certain survey and plan made by Alonzo H. Yocum, Surveyor, dated the 27th day of May A.D. 1922 and recorded in the Office for the Recording of Deeds, &c., in and for the County of Delaware aforesaid, in Deed Book 701 page 462 &c. as follows:

SPECIMEN

Countersigned:

....
Authorized Officer or Agent

[handwritten marginalia: "recording date", "right-of-way."]

COMMONWEALTH LAND
TITLE INSURANCE COMPANY

OWNER'S TITLE INSURANCE POLICY

SUBJECT TO THE EXCLUSIONS FROM COVERAGE, THE EXCEPTIONS CONTAINED IN SCHEDULE B AND THE PROVISIONS OF THE CONDITIONS AND STIPULATIONS HEREOF, COMMONWEALTH LAND TITLE INSURANCE COMPANY, a Pennsylvania corporation, herein called the Company, insures, as of Date of Policy shown in Schedule A, against loss or damage, not exceeding the amount of insurance stated in Schedule A, and costs, attorneys' fees and expenses which the Company may become obligated to pay hereunder, sustained or incurred by the insured by reason of:

1. Title to the estate or interest described in Schedule A being vested otherwise than as stated therein;

2. Any defect in or lien or encumbrance on such title; *[handwritten: i.e. forgery [a][k][a]]*

3. Lack of a right of access to and from the land; or *[handwritten: virtual omtg foreclosure - easement - did it cause a loss]*

4. Unmarketability of such title; *[handwritten: landlocked]*

IN WITNESS WHEREOF the Company has caused this Policy to be signed and sealed, to be valid when Schedule A is countersigned by an authorized officer or agent of the Company, all in accordance with its By-Laws.

COMMONWEALTH LAND TITLE INSURANCE COMPANY

By _____ President

Attest: _____ Secretary

[SPECIMEN overprint; corporate seal at left]

EXCLUSIONS FROM COVERAGE

[handwritten: specifically excluded]

The following matters are expressly excluded from the coverage of this policy:

1. Any law, ordinance or governmental regulation (including but not limited to building and zoning ordinances) restricting or regulating or prohibiting the occupancy, use or enjoyment of the land, or regulating the character, dimensions or location of any improvement now or hereafter erected on the land, or prohibiting a separation in ownership or a reduction in the dimensions or area of the land, or the effect of any violation of any such law, ordinance or governmental regulation.

2. Rights of eminent domain or governmental rights of police power unless notice of the exercise of such rights appears in the public records at Date of Policy.

3. Defects, liens, encumbrances, adverse claims, or other matters (a) created, suffered, assumed or agreed to by the insured claimant; (b) not known to the Company and not shown by the public records but known to the insured claimant either at Date of Policy or at the date such claimant acquired an estate or interest insured by this policy and not disclosed in writing by the insured claimant to the Company prior to the date such insured claimant became an insured hereunder; (c) resulting in no loss or damage to the insured claimant; (d) attaching or created subsequent to Date of Policy; or (e) resulting in loss or damage which would not have been sustained if the insured claimant had paid value for the estate or interest insured by this policy.

[B7790]

[handwritten at bottom: "Exclusions from coverage" "Broken down in notes dated." "1) 2) 3)" "3-1-04"]

SCHEDULE B

Policy No._____

This policy does not insure against loss or damage by reason of the following:

1. Discrepancies or conflicts in boundary lines, easements, encroachments or area content which a satisfactory survey would disclose.

2. Possible additional assessments for taxes for new construction or for any major improvements pursuant to provisions of Acts of Assembly relating thereto.

3. Easement of 9 feet wide driveway on Southwest, and subject to the proportionate part of keeping said driveway in good order and repair.

4. Restrictions affecting title as in Deed Book K-6 page 542 and Deed Book 2483 page 601.

5. Rights granted to the Philadelphia Electric Company and Bell Telephone Company in Deed Book 1248 page 609.

SPECIMEN

American Land Title Association Owner's Policy - 1970 - Form B (Amended 10/17/70)
810-35-1351

Sched. B
[B7792]

SPECIMEN

CONDITIONS AND STIPULATIONS

1. DEFINITION OF TERMS

The following terms when used in this policy mean:

(a) "insured": the insured named in Schedule A, and, subject to any rights or defenses the Company may have had against the named insured, those who succeed to the interest of such insured by operation of law as distinguished from purchase including, but not limited to, heirs, distributees, devisees, survivors, personal representatives, next of kin, or corporate or fiduciary successors.

(b) "insured claimant": an insured claiming loss or damage hereunder.

(c) "knowledge": actual knowledge, not constructive knowledge or notice which may be imputed to an insured by reason of any public records.

(d) "land": the land described, specifically or by reference in Schedule A, and improvements affixed thereto which by law constitute real property; provided, however, the term "land" does not include any property beyond the lines of the area specifically described or referred to in Schedule A, nor any right, title, interest, estate or easement in abutting streets, roads, avenues, alleys, lanes, ways or waterways, but nothing herein shall modify or limit the extent to which a right of access to and from the land is insured by this policy.

(e) "mortgage": mortgage, deed of trust, trust deed, or other security instrument.

(f) "public records": those records which by law impart constructive notice of matters relating to said land.

2. CONTINUATION OF INSURANCE AFTER CONVEYANCE OF TITLE

The coverage of this policy shall continue in force as of Date of Policy in favor of an insured so long as such insured retains an estate or interest in the land, or holds an indebtedness secured by a purchase money mortgage given by a purchaser from such insured, or so long as such insured shall have liability by reason of covenants of warranty made by such insured in any transfer or conveyance of such estate or interest; provided, however, this policy shall not continue in force in favor of any purchaser from such insured of either said estate or interest or the indebtedness secured by a purchase money mortgage given to such insured.

3. DEFENSE AND PROSECUTION OF ACTIONS—NOTICE OF CLAIM TO BE GIVEN BY AN INSURED CLAIMANT.

(a) The Company, at its own cost and without undue delay, shall provide for the defense of an insured in all litigation consisting of actions or proceedings commenced against such insured, or a defense interposed against an insured in an action to enforce a contract for a sale of the estate or interest in said land, to the extent that such litigation is founded upon an alleged defect, lien, encumbrance, or other matter insured against by this policy.

(b) The insured shall notify the Company promptly in writing (i) in case any action or proceeding is begun or defense is interposed as set forth in (a) above, (ii) in case knowledge shall come to an insured hereunder of any claim of title or interest which is adverse to the title to the estate or interest, as insured, and which might cause loss or damage for which the Company may be liable by virtue of this policy, or (iii) if title to the estate or interest, as insured, is rejected as unmarketable. If such prompt notice shall not be given to the Company, then as to such insured all liability of the Company shall cease and terminate in regard to the matter or matters for which such prompt notice is required; provided, however, that failure to notify shall in no case prejudice the rights of any such insured under this policy unless the Company shall be prejudiced by such failure and then only to the extent of such prejudice.

(c) The Company shall have the right at its own cost to institute and without undue delay prosecute any action or proceeding or to do any other act which in its opinion may be necessary or desirable to establish the title to the estate or interest as insured, and the Company may take any appropriate action under the terms of this policy, whether or not it shall be liable thereunder, and shall not thereby concede liability or waive any provision of this policy.

(d) Whenever the Company shall have brought any action or interposed a defense as required or permitted by the provisions of this policy, the Company may pursue any such litigation to final determination by a court of competent jurisdiction and expressly reserves the right, in its sole discretion, to appeal from any adverse judgment or order.

(e) In all cases where this policy permits or requires the Company to prosecute or provide for the defense of any action or proceeding, the insured hereunder shall secure to the Company the right to so prosecute or provide defense in such action or proceeding, and all appeals therein, and permit the Company to use, at its option, the name of such insured for such purpose. Whenever requested by the Company, such insured shall give the Company all reasonable aid in any such action or proceeding, in effecting settlement, securing evidence, obtaining witnesses, or prosecuting or defending such action or proceeding, and the Company shall reimburse such insured for any expense so incurred.

4. NOTICE OF LOSS—LIMITATION OF ACTION

In addition to the notices required under paragraph 3(b) of these Conditions and Stipulations, a statement in writing of any loss or damage for which it is claimed the Company is liable under this policy shall be furnished to the Company within 90 days after such loss or damage shall have been determined and no right of action shall accrue to an insured claimant until 30 days after such statement shall have been furnished. Failure to furnish such statement of loss or damage shall terminate any liability of the Company under this policy as to such loss or damage.

5. OPTIONS TO PAY OR OTHERWISE SETTLE CLAIMS

The Company shall have the option to pay or otherwise settle for or in the name of an insured claimant any claim insured against or to terminate all liability and obligations of the Company hereunder by paying or tendering payment of the amount of insurance under this policy together with any costs, attorneys' fees and expenses incurred up to the time of such payment or tender of payment, by the insured claimant and authorized by the Company.

6. DETERMINATION AND PAYMENT OF LOSS

(a) The liability of the Company under this policy shall in no case exceed the least of:

(i) the actual loss of the insured claimant; or
(ii) the amount of insurance stated in Schedule A

(b) The Company will pay, in addition to any loss insured against by this policy, all costs imposed upon an insured in litigation carried on by the Company for such insured, and all costs, attorneys' fees and expenses in litigation carried on by such insured with the written authorization of the Company.

(c) When liability has been definitely fixed in accordance with the conditions of this policy, the loss or damage shall be payable within 30 days thereafter.

Conditions and Stipulations Continued on Cover

[B7793]

SPECIMEN

CONDITIONS AND STIPULATIONS

(Continued)

7. LIMITATION OF LIABILITY

No claim shall arise or be maintainable under this policy (a) if the Company, after having received notice of an alleged defect, lien or encumbrance insured against hereunder, by litigation or otherwise, removes such defect, lien or encumbrance or establishes the title, as insured, within a reasonable time after receipt of such notice; (b) in the event of litigation until there has been a final determination by a court of competent jurisdiction, and disposition of all appeals therefrom, adverse to the title, as insured, as provided in paragraph 3 hereof; or (c) for liability voluntarily assumed by an insured in settling any claim or suit without prior written consent of the Company.

8. REDUCTION OF LIABILITY

All payments under this policy, except payments made for costs, attorneys' fees and expenses, shall reduce the amount of the insurance pro tanto. No payment shall be made without producing this policy for endorsement of such payment unless the policy be lost or destroyed, in which case proof of such loss or destruction shall be furnished to the satisfaction of the Company.

9. LIABILITY NONCUMULATIVE

It is expressly understood that the amount of insurance under this policy shall be reduced by any amount the Company may pay under any policy insuring either (a) a mortgage shown or referred to in Schedule B hereof which is a lien on the estate or interest covered by this policy, or (b) a mortgage hereafter executed by an insured which is a charge or lien on the estate or interest described or referred to in Schedule A, and the amount so paid shall be deemed a payment under this policy. The Company shall have the option to apply to the payment of any such mortgages any amount that otherwise would be payable hereunder to the insured owner of the estate or interest covered by this policy and the amount so paid shall be deemed a payment under this policy to said insured owner.

10. APPORTIONMENT

If the land described in Schedule A consists of two or more parcels which are not used as a single site, and a loss is established affecting one or more of said parcels but not all, the loss shall be computed and settled on a pro rata basis as if the amount of insurance under this policy was divided pro rata as to the value on Date of Policy of each separate parcel to the whole, exclusive of any improvements made subsequent to Date of Policy, unless a liability or value has otherwise been agreed upon as to each such parcel by the Company and the insured at the time of the issuance of this policy and shown by an express statement herein or by an endorsement attached hereto.

11. SUBROGATION UPON PAYMENT OR SETTLEMENT

Whenever the Company shall have settled a claim under this policy, all right of subrogation shall vest in the Company unaffected by any act of the insured claimant. The Company shall be subrogated to and be entitled to all rights and remedies which such insured claimant would have had against any person or property in respect to such claim had this policy not been issued, and if requested by the Company, such insured claimant shall transfer to the Company all rights and remedies against any person or property necessary in order to perfect such right of subrogation and shall permit the Company to use the name of such insured claimant in any transaction or litigation involving such rights or remedies. If the payment does not cover the loss of such insured claimant, the Company shall be subrogated to such rights and remedies in the proportion which said payment bears to the amount of said loss. If loss should result from any act of such insured claimant, such act shall not void this policy, but the Company, in that event, shall be required to pay only that part of any losses insured against hereunder which shall exceed the amount, if any, lost to the Company by reason of the impairment of the right of subrogation.

12. LIABILITY LIMITED TO THIS POLICY

This instrument together with all endorsements and other instruments, if any, attached hereto by the Company is the entire policy and contract between the insured and the Company.

Any claim of loss or damage, whether or not based on negligence, and which arises out of the status of the title to the estate or interest covered hereby or any action asserting such claim, shall be restricted to the provisions and conditions and stipulations of this policy.

No amendment of or endorsement to this policy can be made except by writing endorsed hereon or attached hereto signed by either the President, a Vice President, the Secretary, an Assistant Secretary, or validating officer or authorized signatory of the Company.

13. NOTICES, WHERE SENT

All notices required to be given the Company and any statement in writing required to be furnished the Company shall be addressed to its Home Office, 1510 Walnut St., Phila., Pa. 19102.

—Valid Only If Schedules A and B Are Attached

PA 10 ALTA Owner's Policy - 1970 - Form B (Amended 10/17/70)
295-00-1352   [B7788]

Chapter Five

SURVEYS AND LEGAL DESCRIPTIONS

I. INTRODUCTION

A real estate transaction concerns a particular parcel of land. "Surveys" and "legal descriptions" are used in defining parcels of land. A survey is a graphic representation of the property, similar to a map. Like a map, a survey can simply show the boundaries of the property, or may show a variety of other facts concerning the property, such as the existence and location of buildings and other improvements, easements, encroachments or improvements to be built. A survey is not normally a part of most real estate related documents, such as deeds or mortgages. Surveys are often made a part of documents relating to the first division of a large tract or to a legal scheme affecting a large tract, examples being a subdivision plan,[1] a declaration of condominium,[2] a declaration of easement,[3] or a declaration of covenants, easements and restrictions.[4]

A legal description is simply a written description that is deemed to be legally sufficient to define a parcel of real estate in connection with a particular transaction. The English and American courts have often found very untechnical descriptions to be legally sufficient, such as a reference to the south forty acres. A legal description, usually means a much more technical description.

The purpose of this chapter is to teach the student how to read a survey and a legal description and how to compare the two in order to find any inconsistencies. In addition, a legal assistant should be able to prepare a legal description from a survey and to sketch out a rough survey from a legal description.

---

1. The subdivision (dividing up) of a larger tract often requires local approval, and is often accomplished by recording an approved survey as a subdivision plan.

2. Many state condominium statutes require the recording of a form of survey showing the location of the units and common elements of the condominium.

3. It is fairly common to record a declaration of easements in connection with a tract which is to be developed in stages, and perhaps for multiple use, and which is to have certain common areas and cross-easements. Such a declaration of easements often contains, or refers to, a recorded survey.

4. A declaration of covenants, easements and restrictions is often used to establish a mandatory home owners association and may contain, or refer to, a recorded survey.

II. SURVEYS

A. BACKGROUND

A surveyor [5] is an individual who, by the use of a transit and other land measurement instruments, is able to locate and measure land and thereafter to draw a map-like diagram of a parcel of land. In jurisdictions where surveyors are officials of the local government, only those surveys produced by the official surveyor will be acceptable for some purposes.

For historical, geographical, economic and topological reasons, there are very different practices with respect to surveys in different areas of the country. Even within an area, practices have changed as different uses have been made of the land. As you read this chapter, you should consider the different surveying needs and practices in various areas, such as an urban area, a new suburban development, a farming district and a mineral-rich mountain region.

While it is always useful to have a survey made when one is buying, leasing or taking a mortgage on land, it is not always economically feasible or worthwhile. This is particularly true when a legal description of the land exists and it is located in an urban area where boundary lines are easily identified.

B. MECHANICS OF THE SURVEY

1. Point of Reference

Surveys must have a starting point, preferably one which relates to some identifiable physical object, often called a monument. A monument might be a street, a body of water, a rock, or a tree. The more permanent a monument is, both as to time and as to location, the more useful it is for purposes of a survey. A stream whose course shifts from time to time, for example, is not a good reference point.

2. Metes and Bounds Survey

After locating a point of reference, the surveyor will choose a starting point along the boundary of the property to be surveyed by going along one or more lines from the point of reference, and from there the surveyor will describe the boundary itself as consisting of several lines. There are two things that must be known about any line shown on a survey: (i) the direction in which the line runs (its "bound") and (ii) the length of the line in that direction (its "mete"). The mete can be precisely determined by use of a tape measure. In order to determine the bound the surveyor uses a transit, which is a sophisticated compass. The compass is divided into 360 degrees

---

5. George Washington was a surveyor, as were Mason and Dixon, whose sur-vey settled a boundary dispute between Pennsylvania and Virginia.

(360°); each degree is divided into 60 minutes (60'); and each minute is divided into 60 seconds (60''). A bearing will therefore include degrees, minutes and seconds in a given direction. (For example, South 56° 4' 10'' West.) Figure 1, below, represents the face of a compass. The face of the compass is divided in half from left to right, the upper half is north and the lower half is south. The first direction mentioned indicates whether, as the surveyor sights along a line, the compass needle points somewhere in the upper half (north) or lower half (south). The numbers that follow indicate how far from due north or due south the line crosses the compass. Rather than using 360°, the surveyor divides the compass into 90° quadrants (see Figure 1). Therefore, South 18° 20' 3'' indicates that the line crosses the south half of the compass 18° 20' 3'' to the east or west (right or left) of due South. The addition of the direction "East" (South 18° 20' 3'' East) indicates the line crosses to the east (right). It would appear on the compass as follows:

Figure 1

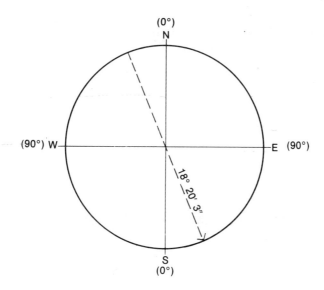

[B7796]

Of course, if the surveyor had started from the other end of the line it would be equally accurate to say the line is North 18 degrees (18°), 20 minutes (20'), 3 seconds (3'') West.

Therefore, a metes and bounds survey consists of defining the boundaries in terms of their compass direction and length.

3. Government or Rectangular Survey Systems

(a) Background

In 1785, the federal government recognized the difficulty of locating a beginning point for a metes and bounds description in most rural areas and the then unexplored regions of the west. In that year, the rectangular survey system was adopted. It applied to all lands other than the original 13 states. Today the system is used in 30 states, including all those west of the Mississippi River except Texas, and all states, (except for the original 13) north of the Ohio River, including Alaska. In addition, the system is used in Mississippi, Alabama and Florida.

Even states using the rectangular survey system have need of a metes and bounds description, as many of the original parcels have been divided or sold in smaller units. The rectangular survey system, in that event, is used merely to fix the starting point for a metes and bounds description, especially in some of the more densely populated areas of states using the rectangular survey system. The system provides very precise fixed beginning points.

(b) Mechanics of the System

The rectangular survey system is based on "Meridians" which are imaginary surveying lines running north and south and "Base Lines" which are imaginary surveying lines running east and west. The Principal Meridians and Base Lines are fixed by a government survey. They relate to longitude and latitude measurement. Thirty-four Principal Meridians have been established, and are identified by number. At intervals of 24 miles on each side of Principal Meridians "Guide Meridians" have been established. They are referred to as "First Guide Meridian East", "Third Guide Meridian West", etc. Similarly, every 24 miles north of a Base Line, "standard parallels" have been fixed.

The area bounded by two meridians (one Principal Meridian and one Guide Meridian) and two base lines (one Base Line and one standard parallel or two standard parallels) is a square block consisting of 24 miles on each side of the square. Each 24-mile square block is further divided into 16 square blocks which are called Townships. Each township is six miles on every side of the square. A line of townships running north and south is a called a Range. Each range is assigned a number (1, 2, 3, 4, and so on) based on its position in relation to the nearest Principal Meridian. A line of townships running east and west is called a Tier and is assigned a number (1, 2, 3, 4, and so on) based on its position in relation to the nearest Base Line. Therefore, the diagonally marked township on the following diagram would be known as Township tier 6 north (i. e. north of the base line) range 2 west of the 2nd Principal Meridian (Township T. 6N. Rge. 2W of 2nd P.M.). The cross-hatched township would be Township T. 6N. Rge. 2E of 2nd P.M.

Figure 2

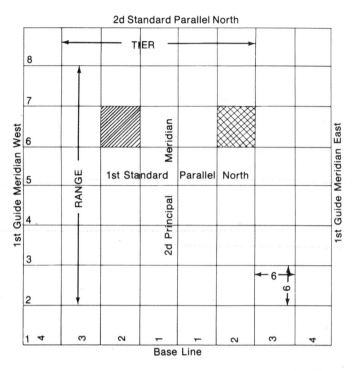

[B7795]

Each township is further divided into 36 square blocks which are called Sections. Sections are squares of one mile on each side. They are numbered consecutively starting with the upper right hand section of the township and continuing first right to left, then left to right and so on until all the sections are numbered.

Figure 3

6	5	4	3	2	1
7	8	9	10	11	12
18	17	16	15	14	13
19	20	21	22	23	24
30	29	28	27	26	25
31	32	33	34	35	36

[B7294]

With this system, the section in the uppermost right hand corner of the cross-hatched township of Figure 2 would be known as Section 1, Township tier 6 north, range 2 east of the 2nd Principal Meridian or by shorthand, Section 1 Township T. 6N. Rge. 2E. 2nd P. M. Finally, each section can be divided into even smaller parcels.

Figure 4

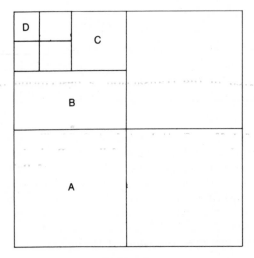

Section 1

[B7295]

The parcel delineated as A on Figure 4 would be called the Southwest (or SW) ¼ of Section 1; B would be the South (or S) ½ of the Northwest (or N.W.) ¼ of Section 1; C would be the NE ¼ of the NW ¼ of Section 1; while D is the NW ¼ of the NW ¼ of the NW ¼ of Section 1. The full description of parcel D of Section 1 would be: NW ¼ of the NW ¼ of the NW ¼ of Section 1, Township T. 6N, Rge. 2E. of 2nd P.M.

(c) Reference Points

It would be possible to use the governmental survey system to arrive at a corner of a government unit and to use that corner, or a point which can be defined in relation to that corner, as the starting point for a metes and bounds survey.

III. TYPES OF LEGAL DESCRIPTIONS

A. STREET NUMBER OR NAME

Property may be described merely by referring to the name and number of the street on which it is located, or by its name in the case of a farm or estate (e. g. "Forsyth Manor"). Although such descriptions are adequate for most nonlegal purposes they are the poorest form of legal description since boundaries of the property are omitted. The use of a street number may clearly designate a particular structure, but it would not make clear the boundaries of the lot on which the structure is located. Street numbers or property names should never be used as the sole legal description in deeds or mortgages,[6] although for purposes of leasing property in urban areas or for agreements of sale where no legal description is yet available, reference to land by street number may be justified.

B. MONUMENTS

In areas and transactions where the cost of a survey necessary for an accurate description would be out of proportion to the amount of money involved in the transaction, a description by monuments alone may be warranted. An example of this type of description follows:

> The farm of Jeffrey Scott located at Childsville, Potter County, Alabama, bounded and described as follows: Beginning at the large dead oak tree on Lee Road where the farms of Brian Alan and Jeffrey Scott are divided by a fence. Then along Lee Road to the point where Lee Road meets Roberta Creek. Then along Roberta Creek to a point where the creek is met by the fence dividing the farms of Brian Alan and Jeffrey Scott. Then along said fence to the large dead oak tree, the point of beginning.

The difficulties of such a description are obvious. Fences are not permanent and creeks shift courses and dry up. Therefore, whenever possible and financially feasible, descriptions based on a survey should be utilized.

C. SUBDIVISION PLOT PLAN

In most instances, a builder or real estate developer will buy a parcel of land with the idea of dividing it into smaller parcels and erecting homes or other buildings on these smaller parcels, a process known as subdivision. The builder cannot do this without receiving consent from the appropriate local authorities. In order to have the authorities consider the application for subdivision, the builder must provide them with a subdivision plot plan in the form of a map which is a survey of the entire subdivision. In addition the plan will depict every lot and will contain measurements so that subsequently the location of the lots can be determined. Each lot will be assigned a reference number.

---

6. Despite the admonition, it is nevertheless true that a deed or mortgage with a bare street number or property name may be a legally effective conveyance or encumbrance. However, the inherent uncertainty breeds lawsuits and disputes.

The legal description for any one lot may be obtained by referring to the plot plan and then to the particular lot by number. An example of such a description is as follows:

> All that certain lot, piece or parcel of land, shown upon a map or plot plan of land at Lyndora, Butler County, Pennsylvania, surveyed by John Doe, dated July 8, 1943; as and by the lot number 205.

Since the plot plan is on file with the recorder of deeds in Butler County the exact location of the lot referred to can always be determined.

D. METES AND BOUNDS

Metes and bounds is the most accurate method of legal description. Such a description is created from a survey of the land and merely reproduces in words the lengths of boundaries and compass directions. A description by metes and bounds, however, is only valuable if the starting point of the description is readily and permanently ascertainable. This means that a metes and bounds description is more useful in urban and suburban areas where starting points such as the intersections of streets can be located with accuracy.

1. No Compass Reference Necessary

Metes and bounds descriptions can be relatively simple or extremely complicated, depending on how regular the lot is, whether there are any curved lines, and whether or not the land is located in an area where there is easy reference to streets or other physical monuments. For example, if the area surveyed is bounded by fronting and intersecting streets, the metes and bounds description is relatively uncomplicated as the following survey and legal description indicate.

Figure 6

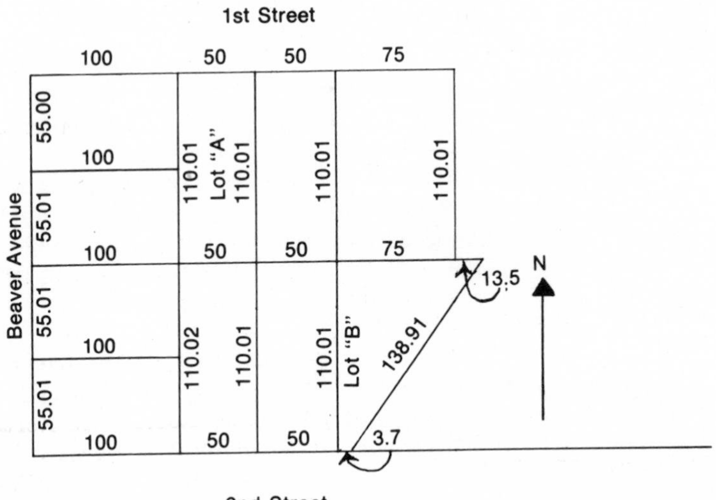

2nd Street

[B7298]

A description of lot "A", a perfectly rectangular or "regular lot", would read as follows:

> Beginning at a point on the southerly side of First Street, 100 feet in an easterly direction from the intersection of the southerly side of First Street and the easterly side of Beaver Avenue; thence along the southerly side of First Street, 50 feet; thence southerly parallel to the easterly side of Beaver Avenue, 110.01 feet; thence westerly parallel to the southerly side of First Street, 50 feet; thence northerly parallel to the easterly side of Beaver Avenue, 110.01 to the point and place of beginning.

A description of the "irregular lot", "B", is not much more complicated:

> Beginning at a point on the northerly side of Second Street, 200 feet easterly from the intersection of the easterly side of Beaver Avenue and the northerly side of Second Street; running thence northerly and parallel to the easterly side of Beaver Avenue, 110.02 feet; thence easterly parallel to the northerly side of Second Street, 88.50 feet; thence southwesterly, 138.91 feet to a point on the northerly side of Second Street, which point is 3.70 feet easterly from the point or place of beginning; and thence westerly along the northerly side of Second Street, 3.70 feet to the point or place of beginning.

2. Compass References Necessary

Where there are no fronting or intersecting streets, or the side lines are not parallel, it is necessary to refer to compass directions. An example of a lot where compass directions are necessary is set forth in the following survey:

A description of this parcel of land would read as follows (note the difficulty in locating a "good" starting point):

> All that tract or parcel of land beginning at the junction of the westerly line of the land now or late of William Smith and the southerly side of Upper Lane and running thence along the land of said William Smith, South 18 degrees, 17 minutes 30 seconds East 430.05 feet; thence along the land of said William Smith North 71 degrees, 42 minutes, 30 seconds East 383.52 feet to a point where the land of the said William Smith intersects with the land now or late of Peter Jones; thence along the land of said Peter Jones South 21 degrees 36 minutes 30 seconds East 1585.13 feet to the intersection of the land of Peter Jones and Lower Avenue; thence along said Lower Avenue South 72 degrees 42 minutes 40 seconds West 1387.50 feet; thence continuing along said Lower Avenue South 76 degrees, 52 minutes 40 seconds West, 264.80 feet to the point of intersection of Lower Avenue and the land now or late of Robert Roe; thence along the land of said Robert Roe North 17 degrees 33 minutes 40 seconds West 1297.28 feet; thence North 71 degrees 15 minutes 10 seconds East 4 feet; thence continuing

Figure 7

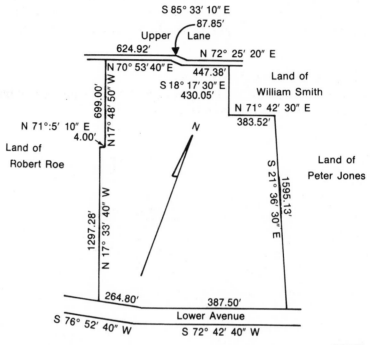

[B7646]

along the land of said Robert Roe North 17 degrees, 48 minutes, 50 seconds West a distance of 699 feet to the intersection of the land of said Robert Roe and Upper Lane; thence along Upper Lane North 70 degrees 3 minutes 40 seconds East 624.92 feet; thence continuing along said Upper Lane South 85 degrees 33 minutes 20 seconds East 87.85 feet; thence continuing along said Upper Lane North 72 degrees 25 minutes 20 seconds East 447.38 feet to the point or place of beginning.

Notice that the description runs clockwise around the lot. It is customary that a legal description name the boundaries in a consistent manner, whether it be clockwise or counter-clockwise. Sometimes a surveyor is not consistent. In that event the person writing the legal description should reverse the bearings where necessary, so that the description reads consistently clockwise or counter-clockwise. In the survey, for example, the surveyor may have first surveyed the Lower Avenue boundary starting from the west and continuing in an easterly direction along Lower Avenue. The first bearing along Lower Avenue would then have read N 76° 52' 40" E. If a person prepared a legal description without reversing the Lower Avenue description or, alternatively, all other bearings, the description would not be consistently clockwise or counter-clockwise. In order to reverse a bearing one simply imagines that the line runs in the opposite direction on a compass face. Therefore, a line which is North 85° East becomes South 85° West; a line which is South 18° 20′ 3″ East is, from the other vantage point, North 18° 20′ 3″ West (See Figure 1.)

3. Surveys Containing Curved Lines

A complication which one might encounter in a metes and bounds survey is a lot that has curved boundaries.

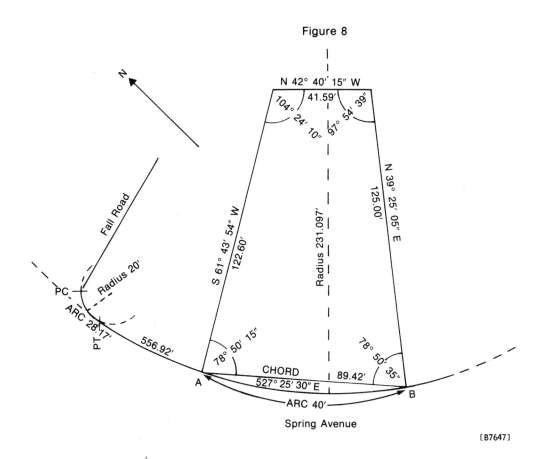

Figure 8

[B7647]

In order to describe a curve one must become familiar with several basic terms; (a) the "arc" is the length of the curving line which is part of the lot description (the distance between A and B on the curved line); (b) the "chord" is the length of a straight line drawn from the start of the arc to the end of the arc (the distance between A and B on a straight line); and (c) the "radius" is the length of an imaginary line drawn from any point on the curved line to the center of an imaginary circle which would be formed by extending the curved line all the way around until it closed.

IV. CHECKING THE LEGAL DESCRIPTION FOR ACCURACY
A. SURVEY

Where there is a survey, one may verify the accuracy of a legal description comparing the metes and bounds to those shown on the survey.

B. WHERE THERE IS NO SURVEY

If no survey exists and it is not feasible to obtain a new one, a cursory check of the accuracy of a legal description is still possible. This is done by drawing, in scale, the boundary lines described in the legal description to see if they start and end at the same point.

If, for example, you prepare a drawing of the following legal description you would find that the description is incorrect:

> Beginning at a point on the southerly side of Well Avenue 25 feet easterly from the corner formed by the intersection of the southerly side of Well Avenue and the easterly side of Pine Street; thence southerly parallel to the easterly side of Pine Street 76.50 feet; thence easterly parallel to the southerly side of Well Avenue, 37.25 feet; thence northerly parallel to the easterly side of Pine Street, 75.00 feet to the southerly side of Well Avenue; thence westerly along the southerly side of Well Avenue, 33.36 feet to the point or place of beginning.

Under these circumstances it would be necessary to have a survey made so that a correct legal description could be prepared. Absent such a survey there is no way of knowing the size of the lot.

V. INTERPRETATION OF LEGAL DESCRIPTIONS
A. WIDTH OF BOUNDARIES

Legal descriptions often refer to streets, streams, railroad rights of way or other natural boundaries. Such monuments have a certain width. It is important to know, therefore, if the land being described extends only to the nearer edge, the middle or the more distant edge of the boundary. This issue is sometimes resolved by a clear cut statement in the instrument itself. However, if no such statement exists, the usual rule is that the land described extends to the middle of the boundary.

Figure 9

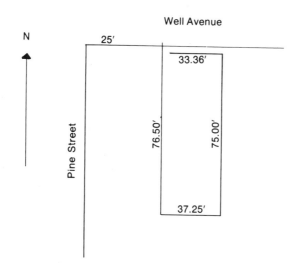

[B7296]

B. INCONSISTENCY IN THE DESCRIPTION

On occasion, a legal description will contain more than one descriptive reference. For example, a particular metes and bounds description may read in part, ". . . 365.50 feet to a point where an iron fence meets Wilson Road". If upon survey it turns out that the point of intersection of the fence and road is really 372.60 feet, there is an internal inconsistency in the description which must be resolved. Another fairly common inconsistency, particularly with large tracts, is between a metes and bounds description and quantity statements (e. g. "containing 64 acres").

Although every jurisdiction has its own rules of construction in cases of inconsistency, points of reference are generally considered reliable, and as a consequence determine the size and legal description of the lot, in the following order of priority:

1. Monuments
2. Map References (e. g. meridians)
3. Metes and Bounds
4. Quantity Statements (containing 64 acres)
5. Lot Numbers

A monument which is referred to in a legal description will generally prevail as a boundary marker rather than a stated distance. The paramount importance and interpretive priority given to monuments by the law, plus the fact that people often think of what they own or will buy by reference to monuments, have caused lawyers and surveyors to make common mention of monuments in surveys and legal descriptions.

VI. CONCLUSIONS

Very likely you will not be called upon to prepare a survey, or perhaps even a legal description. However, a paralegal must be able to compare a survey with a legal description and to ascertain whether there are any inconsistencies.

Chapter Six

TITLE HOLDERS

Part One

INTRODUCTION TO TITLE HOLDERS

I. INTRODUCTION

Every time real property is to be conveyed from one person or entity to another, a decision must be made by the new owner as to the nature of the entity which will hold the title. Title might be held by one or two individuals, by a group of individuals, as individuals or as a partnership, or by a corporation. The choice is usually determined on the basis of the following considerations: (a) the purpose for which the property will be used; (b) the liabilities incurred upon acquisition by the new ownership entity; (c) the ease of transferring or selling the property; (d) possible costs of acquisition and of transfer or sale of the property; (e) the imposition of tax on income derived from the property; and, (f) inheritance and estate tax implications. The purpose of this Chapter is to explore the different legal forms in which title may be held and the considerations involved in choosing a particular form.

II. TITLE IN THE NAME OF AN INDIVIDUAL

Taking title in the name of one individual does not generally raise any problems or require extensive documentation. The individual title holder is entitled to all of the rents and profits and need have no agreement with anyone else with respect to the use and operation of the real estate, unless, of course, he leases it or grants rights to use it to others. The individual title holder will be personally liable for claims arising out of ownership and operation of the real estate. The individual owner is taxed upon the income from the property and may deduct from his income tax any loss generated by the property. In the event he wishes to convey the title, he needs no one's consent or joinder, unless he is married, in which case he must usually obtain the joinder of the spouse.[1]

III. TITLE IN JOINT NAMES

Property may be held in the names of several individuals or entities. In practice, the choice of an appropriate form of joint owner-

---

1. See Chapter One for a discussion of rights of dower and curtesy.

135

ship is sometimes difficult and usually requires careful analysis. The principal forms of joint ownership are tenancy in common, joint tenancy and tenancy by entireties.

A.   TENANTS IN COMMON

A tenancy in common exists where two or more persons each own an undivided interest in the entire property. This means that while there is more than one owner of the property, the interests are not physically distinct but are fractional interests in the whole.

Under the law of most states, a tenancy in common exists when two or more persons [2] own an interest in property and the deed or other document conveying the ownership interest to them does not clearly indicate the form of ownership. For example, if the property were owned by "James Large and Martin Jones" without any additional words indicating the type of interest owned by the parties, they would be deemed to be tenants in common in most states. Also, in most jurisdictions, tenants in common are presumed to own equal undivided interests in the property (except that spouses, if so named, are often treated as one co-owner) unless the deed(s) establishing their interest provide otherwise. If co-tenants are to have disproportionate interests, this should be specified in the granting clause of the deed, as shown in Chapter Ten.

Tenants in common should establish among themselves, by written agreement if possible, the precise nature of their relationship with each other. The agreement should set forth the relative rights and obligations of the co-owners with respect to rents, profits, losses and liabilities arising from the ownership and operation of the real property as well as setting forth the rights of the co-owners with respect to management, control and use of the real property. A tenant in common may convey, mortgage or devise his undivided interest without the consent of his co-tenants, unless, of course, the co-owners have agreed to the contrary. His interest passes to his heirs, or personal representatives if he dies intestate; it does not pass to the surviving co-tenants. Unless otherwise agreed, a tenant in common who takes possession of the entire property to the exclusion of his co-tenants must pay his co-tenants their proportionate shares of the rents and profits. A tenant in common must obtain the joinder of his or her spouse, if any, in order to make a transfer or conveyance which is free and clear of dower or curtesy interests (or other statutory rights in lieu of dower or curtesy). All of the co-tenants (or an agent authorized by all of them) must sign leases as joint lessors, if the proposed tenant is to have the exclusive right to possession of the real estate.

---

2. The tenants in common are often referred to as "co-tenants" or "co-owners".

B. JOINT TENANTS

A joint tenancy is similar to a tenancy in common in that two or more owners possess an undivided interest in the property. The primary distinction between a tenancy in common and a joint tenancy is that a joint tenancy involves a right of survivorship. This means that if one of the joint tenants dies, the ownership of the entire property automatically passes to the surviving joint tenant or tenants without the necessity of any payment by the surviving joint tenant. Because of this survivorship feature, a joint tenancy will not be presumed. The joint tenancy must be specifically spelled out in the deed or other instrument conveying the property. Accordingly, the deed for a property which was owned jointly by two or more persons would indicate that the property had been conveyed to "James Large and Martin Jones as joint tenants with right of survivorship". At English common law, and still in most jurisdictions, a joint tenancy with right of survivorship can only be created if all of the parties have an identity of interest in that they have received their interest in the property at the same time, by the same document, from the same grantor and in equal shares.[3] As with tenants in common, in most jurisdictions it is presumed that joint tenants have equal rights among themselves, regardless of the amount each actually contributed to the acquisition of the real estate.

Because of the fellow joint tenant's right of survivorship, a joint tenant cannot dispose of his or her interest by will. However, during lifetime, a joint tenant may break the "jointure" and may convey the interest to a third party or mortgage or assign the interest. Even without consent, the joint tenant's interest may be sold pursuant to a judgment obtained by creditors, which will also serve to break the jointure. In any of the preceding cases the joint tenancy (the "jointure") ends (is "broken") as between the new owner and the remaining joint tenant. The new owner becomes a tenant in common with the other former joint tenant or tenants. Thus, if Appley, Bendix and Cutter all hold as joint tenants, and Appley sells her interest to Davenport, then Bendix and Cutter are still joint tenants between themselves with respect to their interest, although they are tenants in common with respect to Davenport.

Joint tenants are often given special treatment under transfer, estate and inheritance tax laws because of the right of survivorship. The establishment of a joint tenancy does not of itself create a new

---

3. Suppose Fred Stolz, widower, owned real property in his own name and decided to create a joint tenancy with his daughter Frieda, who is unmarried. At English common law he could not do so by conveying a one-half interest to her, because the tenancy created would not meet the identity of interest test, in that they did not receive their interests at the same time and from the same grantor. Consider the use of an intermediate third party grantee who would act as a common grantor, thus establishing the necessary identity of interest.

entity, and thus does not have any effect respecting income tax or personal liability for debts which arise in connection with the property.

C. TENANTS BY ENTIRETY

With one significant difference, a tenancy by the entireties is a joint tenancy where the owners of the property are husband and wife. In many jurisdictions, the conveyance of real property to a husband and wife automatically creates in them a tenancy by entirety, rather than a joint tenancy or tenancy in common. This is because, at common law, husband and wife were considered to be one legal entity, even though that entity consisted of two natural persons. The law treated them as though they could not acquire individual, undivided interests but only a single interest in the entire estate. Accordingly, they could not be deemed tenants in common or joint tenants.

The fundamental difference between tenants by entirety and joint tenants arises from the fact that neither tenant by entirety owns an undivided share. The notable feature of a joint tenancy is the ease with which the jointure may be broken, either voluntarily by one joint tenant, even without the consent of the other, or involuntarily by the actions of a creditor of one of the joint tenants. A tenancy by the entireties may not be broken by either spouse without the consent of the other. In most of the jurisdictions which recognize the entirety estate, a creditor of only one spouse may not execute upon the property, since in legal theory the debtor spouse has no individual interest in the property, present or future. Rather the property is owned by the legal entity of husband and wife. Similarly, neither spouse alone may transfer or mortgage any interest in the property since neither has any legal interest to convey or mortgage. Divorce has the legal effect of converting the status of tenants by entirety to tenants in common.

Another difference is that tenants by entirety do not have to account to each other for rents from the real property. It is presumed that such rents will be used for the benefit of both.

As in the case of joint tenancy, at the death of one of the tenants by entirety the surviving tenant becomes the sole owner of the entire estate.

There are two principal benefits gained by holding property as tenants by the entirety. Creditors of one spouse cannot claim such property while both spouses are alive. Furthermore, in many states, state inheritance taxes are not imposed upon property held by entirety when the first spouse dies. However, property held by entirety may be subject to the federal estate tax on the estate of the first spouse to die. Income tax and personal liability are imposed as in the case of other property interests owned by individuals. In practice, tenancies by entirety are not often created, except with respect to family residences. Other forms of joint ownership involving husbands and wives are usually more useful and convenient where commercial property is involved.

D. COMMERCIAL PRACTICES REGARDING TITLE IN JOINT NAMES

For various reasons, it is relatively uncommon for a group of individuals to take title to commercial real estate in joint names as tenants in common, joint tenants or tenants by the entireties. Joint tenancies are rare in a commercial setting both because the jointure is so easy to break that it is ineffective and because the joint tenancy, if not broken, may result in depriving the estate and the heirs of a deceased joint tenant of a valuable asset while granting the surviving joint tenant a total windfall.

The only fairly common situation in which tenancy in common is used is for a joint venture, which will be discussed in greater detail below. You should understand that joint venturers will not rely upon the common law regarding tenants in common to govern their relationship. The common law principles regarding tenancy in common arose in the context of English agricultural life, and those principles would be insufficient, and oft-times incorrect, if applied as the sole guiding force in the typical commercial joint venture situation. Thus, in practice, tenants in common will enter into an extensive co-owners' agreement or joint venture agreement. The result is that a joint venture is more like a partnership in terms of the economic relationships among the parties, and joint ventures will be discussed together with partnerships.

IV. PARTNERSHIPS AND JOINT VENTURES

The most common choice to be made by a group of individuals about to acquire real property for business purposes is whether to form a corporation to take title or whether to form a partnership or joint venture to take title.[4] The subject of partnerships and joint ventures, and the agreements used to create these entities, will be considered in greater detail in Chapter Seven of these materials. The following discussion is intended only to familiarize the student with the general characteristics of partnerships and joint ventures, and to discuss the relative advantages of each form.

A. GENERAL PARTNERSHIPS

1. Nature of a Partner's Interest

An interest in a partnership is personal property. It is the partnership entity which holds title to the real property, not the individual

---

4. As indicated above, it is incorrect to say that the joint venture takes title. The joint venturers take title as tenants in common.

partners. The partners have no separate interest in the real property itself. Real estate acquired with partnership funds is deemed to be partnership property, unless a contrary intent is specified.

Since an interest in a partnership is personal property, the spouse of a partner has no dower right or other interest in partnership property acquired with partnership funds. Accordingly, a spouse need not join in any deed to be executed by the partnership. Similarly, a creditor having a judgment against one partner cannot enforce it against any partnership property per se. The creditor can only enforce the judgment against the partner's interest in the partnership, which, if the partnership were dissolved and liquidated, would entitle the creditor to the debtor partner's share in the assets of the partnership remaining after all partnership debts have been paid.

2. General Characteristics of a Partnership

Although the law may differ from state to state, partnership property may generally be conveyed on behalf of the partnership by any general partner. In the event a partnership dissolves without being reformed,[5] the former partners become tenants in common in the real property previously owned by the partnership.

(a) Personal Liability

Partners have unlimited personal liability as individuals for the debts and obligations of the partnership. If the partnership incurs debts or liabilities which exceed the value of the property owned by the partnership, the assets of the individual partners are subject to claims by creditors. Partners will be required to meet these claims out of their personal assets without regard to the proportion of capital which each contributed to the partnership or to the proportion of their partnership interest.

(b) Control

All partners have a legal right to take part in the management of the partnership. Partners can, however, give up this right or limit it in a partnership agreement signed by all the partners.

(c) Tax Implications

Federal income tax considerations will be discussed in Part Two of this Chapter.

---

5. As will be discussed in Chapter Seven, a partnership may be technically dissolved and immediately reformed upon the happening of certain events. Usually when businessmen, and many lawyers, speak of a partnership dissolving, they are referring to a decision to terminate the partnership form, and not to a technical dissolution.

3. Form in Which Title is Held

If title to real property is to be held by a partnership, it is necessary to determine whether title will be taken in the name of the partnership itself, (e. g., "Bluestone Company, a co-partnership") or in the names of the individual partners, (e. g., "Adam Bell and Ella Johnson, co-partners trading as Bluestone Company, for the uses and purposes of such partnership"). If there is a transfer tax imposed upon the recording of deeds reflecting changes in the membership of the partnership, it may be preferable to keep title in the name of the partnership entity rather than in the names of the individual partners so that transfers of individual partnership interests (which are personal property) will not require the recording of deeds. The important thing to understand is that even if title is taken in the names of the individual partners, as partners, the real property is owned by the partnership as an entity and not by the partners in their individual capacity.

B. LIMITED PARTNERSHIPS

Limited partnerships are quite similar to general partnerships with the following exceptions:

1. Classes of Partners

Limited partnerships consist of at least one general partner and at least one limited partner. The general partner (or general partners) is responsible for the management of the partnership.

2. Liability

While the general partner is personally liable for partnership debts (as are all the partners in a "general" partnership), the liability of a limited partner is limited to his investment (which is called his capital contribution) in the partnership. It is this limitation on the limited partner's liability which gives this form of partnership its name.

3. Control

The other major distinguishing characteristic of a limited partnership is that only the general partners have the legal right to manage the partnership. The limited partners have no management authority.

In all other regards, for purposes of this chapter, you may consider general partnerships and limited partnerships to be identical.

C. JOINT VENTURES

The use of joint ventures is considered to be an alternative to the use of partnerships or corporations. A joint venture has been called a kind of partnership that was established for a single business venture (usually not the only business venture of the joint venturers) rather than a partnership which encompasses all or most of the business ventures of the partners. The joint venturers normally agree upon the rules for ownership and operation of the real property to be owned by the joint venture, including the formula for sharing the profits and losses, and set forth their decision in a joint venture agreement. Although case law may vary from state to state, the individual joint venturers are generally deemed to be tenants in common with respect to the real estate, and the joint venture is not considered to be an entity which can hold title itself. Accordingly, the venturer's spouses must sign the deed in order to convey the real estate, and a judgment against one joint venturer will be a lien against his undivided interest in the real property.

The usual reason for electing to form a joint venture rather than a general partnership is that the venturers desire to insulate themselves as much as possible from the open-ended liability of a general partnership. As you shall see in Chapter Seven, a partner of a general partnership has very broad powers to bind the partnership to various contractual relationships, even though the other partners do not consent and even though the contract may be outside of intended scope of the partnership. By use of the joint venture form, the investors hope that they will not be liable for any contract that one of the venturers has signed on behalf of the venture, but which they have not signed, or at least that they will not be liable unless the contract in question is clearly within the scope of the single business of the venture.

V. CORPORATIONS

A. GENERAL CHARACTERISTICS OF CORPORATE OWNERSHIP

In many situations title to real estate must be taken in the name of a corporation because corporate assets are used to make the purchase. Corporations are entities which are formed pursuant to a specific state (or federal) statute. There is no such thing as a common law corporation and one cannot be formed in the absence of an enabling statute. The major characteristics of a corporation are that it is considered to be a separate person (but not an individual) distinct from its directors, officers and shareholders; that it may have perpetual existence; that it has centralized control and management; that the interests in the corporation are transferrable; and that the shareholders have limited liability.

B. ADVANTAGES OF CORPORATE OWNERSHIP

There are several benefits of corporate ownership. The stockholders will have no personal liability with respect to corporate debts, contracts or other liabilities. Because a corporation's life is perpetual, the corporation and the surviving shareholders do not incur any federal estate tax, local inheritance tax, or real estate transfer taxes upon the death of a stockholder. The shareholders do not have any direct interest in the real property of the corporation, and therefore there are no problems with rights of dower or curtesy. Also, property owned by a corporation may be conveyed by action of the board of directors and officers without the necessity of having a deed executed by all of the shareholders.

C. DISADVANTAGES OF CORPORATE OWNERSHIP

Some factors (other than federal income tax factors) to consider in using the corporate entity as a title holder are the additional expenses of forming and maintaining the corporation; additional taxes or higher tax rates imposed on the corporation by state and/or local authorities; the need to qualify to do business in the jurisdiction in which the real estate is located if the corporation is not organized under the laws of that state; and the possible requirement of special approval by the stockholders of the corporation, in addition to the usual authority from the board of directors, to sell real estate owned by a corporation if it is the principal asset or only asset of the corporation.

Part Two

INCOME TAX CONSEQUENCES OF PARTNERSHIP vs. CORPORATION

I. INTRODUCTION TO FEDERAL INCOME TAXES

As you probably know, the Federal government through the Internal Revenue Service (IRS) imposes a tax on net income earned by all taxable individuals and entities in the United States. This means that each individual or taxable entity must add up all of its income which is subject to tax (gross taxable income), subtract all items that the Internal Revenue Code permits it to deduct (tax deductions) and then pay tax on the remaining amount (net taxable income). For individuals, this net taxable income is taxed on the basis of a progressive rate. That is, a certain level of net taxable income is taxed at the lowest rate (e. g., the first $500 is taxed at 14% for single taxpayers)[6] and the next level is taxed at a higher rate (e. g., from $500 to $1,000 is taxed at 15% and so on until at $100,000 and above, a 70% tax is reached. With regard to corpora-

---

6. Tax rates and other tax information are all as of October 1, 1977. The information and discussion are greatly simplified and should not be considered as instructions for completing tax returns.

tions, however, net taxable income is taxed in only two steps. Presently, that is 22% on the first $25,000 of net taxable income and 48% on any amount over $25,000.

II. THE CONCEPT OF TAX DEDUCTIONS

A. GENERALLY

Anyone who has filled out a personal tax return is familiar with the fact that only a very limited number of expenses qualify as tax deductions (e. g., interest, certain medical expenses, certain state and local taxes and charitable contributions). The more payments a taxpayer makes that can qualify as tax deductions the lower will be the net taxable income and, thus the lower the tax. For example, assume a taxpayer has gross taxable income of $20,000. Of that $20,-000 the taxpayer spends over the course of a year $15,000 and saves $5,000. If all of the money the taxpayer spent was also a tax deduction, he would only have $5,000 of net taxable income and as a single taxpayer would pay approximately $900 in taxes. However, most of a taxpayer's living expenses, such as food, clothing, rent and household goods, are not tax deductions. For our hypothetical single taxpayer, if only $6,000 of the $15,000 the taxpayer had spent qualified as a tax deduction, he would have net taxable income of $14,-000 ($20,000—$6,000) on which he would pay a tax of $3,210.

If a taxpayer is operating a business, however, almost all of the business related goods and services for which the taxpayer spends money are tax deductions. The rationale for this is that since all of the income derived from the business is part of gross taxable income, all of the costs of making that money ought to be deductible so that the taxpayer pays only on the net amount earned.

B. DEPRECIATION

Depreciation is a special kind of tax deduction. Most of the business expenses a taxpayer incurs are for items or services used up either immediately or within a short time. For example, if a taxpayer pays wages, it is for work already performed; if cleaning supplies are purchased, they will be used up quickly. However, some items are intended to be used over a long period of time. For example, a taxpayer who operates a shoe business may purchase a cash register. One would expect the register to last perhaps 10 years. If the taxpayer could take a tax deduction for the full cost of the cash register in the year he purchased it, that would not be a true reflection of the costs of doing business in that year. For example, assume the cash register costs $1,000. At the end of the first year of use the cash register may have lost only $100 of value and still be worth $900. Thus the true cost of the cash register for that year is only $100, and that is all that should be allowed as a tax deduction. Of course, as the cash register loses value in the ensuing years, the taxpayer can take a tax deduction for those costs. This loss of value each year is called depreciation.

It would be time consuming and difficult to attempt to determine what the true economic depreciation of an item is for any one year. Hence, the IRS allows depreciation deductions to be computed by set formulas. There are a number of such formulas, most of which are beyond the scope of this book. The easiest one to understand and the one most often used is called the straight line method. To compute the depreciation deduction for any one year using the straight line method, a taxpayer takes the cost of the item (called the "basis") subtracts the scrap value (called the "salvage value"), if any, of the item when it no longer will be useful to the taxpayer and divides the resulting number by the number of years of use (called the "useful life") the taxpayer expects to get from the item. This formula would be:

$$\frac{\text{Basis} - \text{Salvage Value}}{\text{Useful Life}} = \text{Annual Depreciation Deduction}$$

IM–444

In our cash register example, assuming a salvage value of $50, the formula would be:

$$\frac{\$1,000 - \$50}{10} = \$95$$

IM–445

The depreciation deduction to which the taxpayer would be entitled for each of the 10 years would be $95 per year. Notice, the actual expenditure of money only occurs in the first year. In each succeeding year the depreciation deduction is taken without any further expenditure of money. That is why depreciation is often called a "non-cash" deduction. Also notice that a taxpayer gets the deduction without having to prove the actual loss in value. Hence the depreciation deduction can be taken even if the asset is actually *increasing* in value as is often the case with buildings and other improvements to real estate.

One final note on depreciation. A taxpayer can take a depreciation deduction only if the item can lose value from *use*. That is, the item must be susceptible to wearing out. Thus a share of stock owned by a business (only business assets may be depreciated) may lose value, but it cannot be depreciated because it does not lose value by use. So too, if a taxpayer owns real estate, only the building can be depreciated since land theoretically does not wear out.[7]

---

7. A taxpayer who farms the land or takes the minerals out of it is entitled to a different deduction for this loss in value which is called "depletion".

III. CONCEPT OF TAX LOSS AND TAX SHELTER

As has been discussed above, a taxpayer computes his net taxable income by subtracting his tax deductions, including depreciation, from his gross taxable income. It should be noted at this point, that a taxpayer must compute his net taxable income (or loss) derived from each and every business in which he has an interest. For example, assume a taxpayer, Mr. X, has a job from which he earns a wage, receives interest from bank accounts and dividends from shares of stock he owns. In addition, the taxpayer has an antique business and owns a small apartment building. When the taxpayer prepares his tax return he first segregates his personal income (wages, interest and dividends) and subtracts from that his personal tax deductions (such as medical, interest paid, state and local taxes, contributions) to get his net taxable personal income. The taxpayer then does the same thing for each of his businesses. At that point he combines all net taxable incomes to determine his total net taxable income. The major reason tax returns are set up that way is to make it easier for the IRS to understand and check on the items reported.

In computing the net taxable income for a business, it is not at all unusual for the tax deductions to exceed the gross taxable income. When this occurs, the taxpayer is said to have suffered a tax loss, which is the opposite of net taxable income. In some cases this results from actually paying out in wages and other costs of doing business, more than the taxpayer takes in.[8] In many cases, however, particularly where the business has substantial depreciable property, the taxpayer actually takes in more than his cash expenses but he has a tax loss because of his non-cash depreciation deduction.

A brief example may make this clearer. Assume that a taxpayer owns a small apartment building from which he has collected $10,000 of rent in a given year. In that same year he paid out $2,500 in real estate taxes, $3,000 interest on the mortgage and another $2,500 for maintenance of the property and other miscellaneous expenses (e. g. repairs, cleaning, wages, utilities, accounting fees). If the taxpayer computed his net taxable income at this point it would look like the following:

Gross Taxable Income	
Rents	$10,000
Tax Deductions	
Real Estate Taxes $2,500	
Interest on Mortgage $3,000	
Maintenance and Miscellaneous Expenses $2,500	$ 8,000
Net Taxable Income	$ 2,000

IM–447

---

8. Even a business that is actually losing money may be generating some cash, because loans to the business are not counted as income.

However, the taxpayer has a depreciable asset, his apartment building. Assume it cost him $90,000 for the land and building. Also assume that the building has a useful life of 25 years and that there is no salvage value. Finally, assume that the taxpayer reasonably allocates the $90,000 between land and building as follows: $15,000 to land value and $75,000 to the value of the building. (Remember only the building can be depreciated and not the land.) The depreciation deduction can be computed as follows:

$$\frac{\$75,000 - 0}{25 \text{ years}} = \$3,000 \text{ per year}$$

IM–448

If the taxpayer takes into account this $3,000 depreciation deduction, his business tax computation would be as follows:

Gross Taxable Income		
Rents		$10,000
Tax Deductions		
Real Estate Taxes	$2,500	
Interest on Mortgage	$3,000	
Maintenance and Miscellaneous Expenses	$2,500	
Depreciation Deduction	$3,000	
		$11,000
Tax Loss		($ 1,000)

IM–449

Notice that the taxpayer has a tax loss and thus has no tax liability from this business even though he actually has $2,000 in cash left over at the end of the year. We say that the depreciation has given the taxpayer a "tax shelter". In other words, it has sheltered the $2,000 from being taxed and thus the taxpayer can keep all $2,000 for his own use rather than pay some of it in taxes. But, also notice that our taxpayer has an additional advantage. In our example, the depreciation deduction sheltered the remaining $2,000 of gross taxable income from the apartment house business. However, there is an additional $1,000 of loss that was not used in sheltering the income from this business. This amount, which is shown above as being a tax loss, is excess tax shelter. When the taxpayer combines his personal tax computations with his business tax computations, the $1,000 tax loss from the apartment house business will be used to shelter from taxes $1,000 of income from other sources which otherwise would have been taxed. This excess tax shelter is the main attraction for many investors in real estate.

IV. COMPARISON OF PARTNERSHIPS AND CORPORATIONS

A. TAXATION OF PARTNERSHIPS

Partnerships, while entities for purposes of holding title to real estate are not considered to be entities for purposes of paying taxes. That is, a partnership pays no federal income tax. Any net taxable income or tax loss that a partnership has is divided among the partners, according to the percentage interest each owns in the partnership, and accounted for on the individual tax return of each partner. Being a partner in a partnership is identical for tax purposes to the operation by a single taxpayer of a business in our prior discussion. For example, assume that two taxpayers form a 50–50 partnership to own the apartment building used as an example in the preceding section. Each year the net taxable income or tax loss of the partnership would be computed and divided between them. Thus if there were $1,000 of net taxable income each taxpayer would show an additional $500 of net taxable income on his personal tax return. If, however, there were a $1,000 tax loss each taxpayer would have $500 to use to shelter other taxable income on his personal tax return.

B. TAXATION OF A CORPORATION

Corporations are different from partnerships in that they are taxable entities as well as title holding entities. This means that corporations must directly and separately account to the IRS for any net taxable income or tax loss. Assume again two taxpayers who form a corporation to hold the apartment building. If the corporation has net taxable income it is taxed at the corporation rate (22% on the first $25,000 and 48% thereafter). If the shareholder taxpayers are to get any of this money however, the corporation would have to pay it to them as dividends. When each shareholder taxpayer receives the dividends they are taxable income to him. This means that to get income to a shareholder it must be taxed twice, once on the corporate level and once again to the shareholder when he receives it as a dividend. This is the first major tax disadvantage of a corporation as opposed to a partnership. Partnership income to each partner is only taxed once on the individual partner level while corporate income to each shareholder is taxed twice.

The other major tax advantage of the partnership over the corporation occurs when the entity holding the real estate has a tax loss or excess tax shelter created by the depreciation deduction. If the entity is a partnership, each partner can use his proportionate share of the tax loss to shelter other personal income. However, if the title holding entity is a corporation, the tax loss belongs to the corporation in its capacity as a taxable entity and there is no way to pass through any of the loss to the shareholders. This results from the corporation's tax entity status. Thus, there is no way a shareholder can use the excess tax shelter to shelter other personal income. The corporation must retain the loss and can make use of it only by carrying it forward to succeeding years to shelter taxable income of the corporation, if any, in those years. Using the same assumptions as to revenue and deductible items set forth under III above, a corporation which owned the property would realize the same $2000 of "sheltered" income and $1,000 of "excess" tax shelter as would an individual or partnership. In order to benefit its shareholders directly, however, the corporation must pay a dividend, which is taxable. Assuming the shareholders pay 50% of their income in taxes, the $2,000 cash generated would yield a total of $1,000 to the shareholders after payment of the dividend. The "excess" shelter has no direct value to the shareholders. By way of comparison, the partners of the partnership could not only receive the $2,000 tax free, they also receive the benefit of the $1,000 excess shelter directly. If the partners are in the 50% tax bracket, the excess shelter will save them $500 in taxes on other income. Thus it may be said that the partners would benefit directly by the sum of $2,500, while the shareholders' direct benefit from the same investment is only $1,000.

V.   CHOICE OF ENTITY

In the overwhelming majority of cases the use of a partnership to own income producing real estate is preferable to the use of the corporation. This is particularly true since the limited partnership can be used to get the limited liability characteristic of the corporation, at least for the limited partners. There are situations where it would be advantageous from a tax point of view to use a corporation as the title holding entity rather than a partnership. These situations occur generally where the following three characteristics exist:

(1) The entity will show a net taxable income rather than a tax loss.

(2) The net taxable income is intended to be reinvested in the property. That is it will remain in the entity and is not to be paid out to the owners of the entity.

(3) The owners of the entity would pay taxes at a higher individual rate than the corporate rate on the same amount of net taxable income.

Part Three

STRAW PARTIES

I. INTRODUCTION

A straw party or nominee is one who holds title to property on behalf of the actual or beneficial owner. It is sometimes desirable to have title to real estate and related personal property held in the name of a straw party or nominee. Some of the reasons follow:

A. USE OF A STRAW PARTY SIMPLIFIES THE TRANSFER OF TITLE

When real estate will be owned by a relatively large group of people as tenants in common, joint tenants or partners, it will often be time consuming and difficult to locate all of those needed to sign deeds, leases and other legal documents on behalf of all of the real owners. One solution is to have title held by an agent (called a "straw party") for all of the real owners, having the authority to sign specific documents such as mortgages and leases on behalf and at the direction of the real owners.

B. USE OF A STRAW PARTY MAY AVOID POSSIBLE TITLE PROBLEMS

When the beneficial owners of property are individuals and one of them dies, there is a "cloud" on title until the administration of the deceased owner's estate is begun. In the interim it would be very difficult to sell, lease or mortgage the property.

C. USE OF A STRAW PARTY MAY SECURE ANONYMITY OF OWNERSHIP

In various circumstances the owners of real estate do not want the general public to know that they have acquired the property. This occurs frequently when a well known individual, partnership, corporation or other institution seeks to assemble numerous small parcels of real estate. If the developer's intention becomes public, the owner of each small parcel needed to assemble the project may try to hold out for a greater price.

D. USE OF A STRAW PARTY MAY AVOID PERSONAL LIABILITY ON MORTGAGE OBLIGATIONS

In some jurisdictions the beneficial owner of the real estate will not be personally liable on a mortgage note or bond executed by his agent if the beneficial owner is an undisclosed principal. Therefore, if a straw party executes a mortgage and note, then the liability of the real owners under the note will be limited to the land. Straw parties selected with this purpose in mind are, of course, people without property of their own since they will technically have unlimited liability for the full amount of a note or bond.

II. INDIVIDUALS AS NOMINEES OR STRAW PARTIES

A. COMMON PRACTICE

It has long been customary for individuals to act as straw parties. Real estate brokers often sign agreements to purchase land on behalf of undisclosed principals, particularly where anonymity is important. Some individuals serve as professional nominees, and, for a fee, will sign mortgage notes and mortgages for beneficial owners who wish to avoid personal liability. The documents used in such cases are prepared in exactly the same form as they would be if the straw party were the real owner or mortgagor of the real property.

B. DECLARATION OF TRUST

There should always be written evidence of the agency or trust relationship between the beneficial owner and his nominee. Such an agreement should be signed by the parties prior to, or simultaneously with, the acquisition of record title by the straw party. In most cases it is sufficient for the straw party to execute a statement acknowledging that he holds title merely as trustee, nominee or agent for the specifically named beneficial owner. It is advisable to have such a document acknowledged by the signing parties so that it can be recorded, thereby giving constructive notice of the agency relationship either simultaneously with the conveyance of record title to the straw party or at some later time if the beneficial owner so desires. Without such an agreement, the heirs or successors of the individual straw party may claim that the straw party was, in fact, the real owner of the real estate. A declaration of trust will always contain a statement by the straw party (trustee) to the effect that the straw party is holding title for another and will deed the property to the beneficial owner, or do any other act with regard to the property, upon the request of the beneficial owner.

C. CONTROL OF NOMINEE REQUIRED

Needless to say, the real owner's choice of an individual straw depends to a great extent upon the confidence the real owner has in its ability to control the activity of the straw party in connection with the real estate. The real owner must be sure that the straw party will not (a) violate the agency relationship and disclose the identity of the real owner, (b) sign documents without authority, or (c) convey record title to another person. The owner must also be able to obtain from the straw party, upon request, a deed conveying the real estate to him or to someone else, at his direction. The straw party must be readily available to sign, at the real owner's request, those documents which must be signed by the holder of record title, such as deeds to parts of the real estate, leases and other agreements. It is a wise practice to obtain from the straw party, simultaneously with the conveyance of nominal title to the straw party, a signed and acknowledged deed conveying the real estate to the real owner. Such a deed can then be held by the real owner and used when the occasion for its need arises.

D. PROBLEMS CREATED BY THE USE OF INDIVIDUALS AS NOMINEES

While it has been customary to use individuals as straw parties, this practice sometimes results in problems. For example, the straw party may die while holding title to the real estate. In that case it would be necessary to subject the property to the administration of the straw title holder's estate until such time as the personal representative is willing to execute a deed to a new straw or the real owner. In addition, the personal representative may be unwilling to sign documents on behalf of the real owners at least until he is fully aware of the obligations of the deceased straw title holder.

Although in some jurisdictions use of an individual nominee may protect the real owner from personal liability on mortgage notes, bonds or contracts, the straw party incurs this very same liability. Accordingly, the straw party must be and remain "judgment proof" or impecunious. An individual straw party should hold title only to a single piece of property at any one time, since judgments against the straw party will be record liens against all properties of which the straw party is the title holder of record. In addition, individual nominees should be single persons who have never married. Otherwise, future grantees and others will require proof that it is not necessary to have the straw party's spouse join in the conveyance or other instrument.

III. CORPORATIONS AS NOMINEES

A. BENEFITS OF USING CORPORATE NOMINEES

The problems which may arise out of the use of an individual as a nominee are eliminated when the straw party is a corporation. A corporation can have perpetual existence. A new and different corporation can be used as a straw for each different parcel of real estate, thereby insulating each property from the liabilities of others. A corporation can be easily and quickly formed, and can be controlled by individuals whom the real owner trusts such as attorneys, accountants, or brokers. A corporation can be kept judgment proof and impecunious simply by keeping its assets at a nominal level. Finally, a corporation acts through its officers and it may have as many authorized officers as the board of directors determines, thus making it relatively easy to have documents signed.

B. INCOME TAX PROBLEMS CREATED BY THE USE OF CORPORATE NOMINEES

There should be no conceptual difference between the use of an individual as a nominee and agent for a real owner and the use of a corporation as a nominee and agent. However, the case law dealing with income tax issues in this area has created a confusing situation. If nominal title to real estate is held in the name of an individual straw, there is no doubt that it is the real owner who is taxable on the income from the real estate and not the straw party. For example, assume a real estate broker, Jane Smith, signs an agreement of sale and takes nominal title to an income producing property on behalf of her principal, the real owner, pursuant to a declaration of trust requiring her to forward all rents and other income from the property to the real owner. The burden of the income tax (and all other taxes and carrying costs) should and does fall upon the real owner, the one who receives the benefit of such income. The real estate broker, who is merely a straw party and conduit for transmittal of the funds, is only the agent of the real owner. In such cases the Internal Revenue Service looks to the real owner to pay the applicable tax on the income from the property even though record title is in Jane Smith's name.

Unfortunately, in several cases involving corporate agents as straw parties, the Internal Revenue Service has persuaded the tax courts to impose an income tax on the corporate straw on the theory that the corporate straw itself is the real owner, since it was formed and organized for the sole purpose of serving as a vehicle for the acquisition of title for its shareholders (who are sometimes the real owners). In fact, some courts have held that, for tax purposes at least, since the corporation is an entity set up for the benefit of the real owner and owned by the real owner, it must be deemed an independent entity, rather than a mere agent and nominee, and therefore the real recipient of the income from the property. Such cases often allow the Internal Revenue Service to tax the corporate straw on the income at corporate rates and then impose a second tax on the income distributed by the straw corporation to its shareholders as dividends paid by the straw corporation.

Contrary to the position of the Internal Revenue Service, many tax lawyers argue that the corporate straw is no different from the individual straw. The corporation is in the business of acting as an agent and nominee and is not in the business of owning real estate for its own benefit. However, to prove that the corporation is merely an agent of the real owner and not a real owner itself, it becomes imperative that the underlying documentation of the relationship corroborate the agency theory. It is also important to maintain the independent nature of the corporate straw during the entire period when the straw is in title. The documents involved must be carefully drafted and the corporate straw must operate strictly in accordance with the applicable rules of agency law. The following section outlines the corporate procedure and documentation for a straw corporation.

C. BASIC RULES FOR THE USE OF CORPORATE NOMINEES

In order to have any chance that the straw will not be taxed as the real owner, it is necessary to follow the following rules when forming a corporation to be used as an agent and straw party:

1. Articles of Incorporation

The corporation's Articles of Incorporation should clearly state that its corporate powers are limited to "holding title to real and personal property only on behalf of others and not for its own account".

2. Capitalization

The amount of the corporation's authorized stock should be minimal and very little need actually be issued. Several hundred dollars worth, for example, should be sufficient for the corporation to purchase a minute book, stock book and corporate seal and to pay the advertising fees, attorney's fees and other costs of incorporation.

3. Shareholders

The shareholders of the straw corporation must be different from the real owners of the property. The straw corporation must be established not by the real owners, but by an independent person, such as an attorney or a professional straw party corporation shareholder.

4. Directors and Officers

The directors and officers, who may be the same persons as the stockholders, should be different from the real owners of the property. For example, when a law firm establishes its own straw corporations to act as agents for the lawyers' clients, the officers and directors of the straw corporations are usually the lawyers of the firm.

5. Organization

The straw corporation must be organized as a corporation, the sole business activity of which is acting as a nominee for others. Accordingly, the straw corporation must have its own bank account into which the stockholders deposit the cash paid for the stock of the straw corporation and the service fees paid to the straw corporation by the real owners for the services of the straw corporation as a nominee and straw. The organization minutes of the Board of Directors will be similar to organization minutes of ordinary corporations.

6. Straw Party Agreement

The real owners should formally enter into a straw party agreement with the corporate straw, by which the corporate straw agrees for a fee to act as their agent and perform the service of holding nominal title.

7. Declaration of Trust

The straw corporation should execute a formal agreement in recordable form, in favor of the real owners, establishing the agency relationship and setting forth all of its terms. As in the case of an individual straw party, such an agreement is called a "declaration of trust" or "certificate of nominal title holder". The agreement should express the underlying basis of the agency relationship, and establish that the straw corporation has no discretionary authority to act with respect to the property held in its name, but may act only upon the written directions of the real owners. It should include representations that the straw corporation has not advanced any funds of its own to acquire the property to which it will hold nominal title, that it will not be required to advance any funds in connection with the ownership or operation of the property, and that it will not receive any of the benefits derived from ownership or operation of the property. The straw corporation should agree to reconvey the property to the real owners, or to any other person or persons selected by the real owners, at any time, merely upon the request of the real owners, at no cost to the real owners except the cost of preparing and recording the necessary deed. The certificate should also contain the straw corporation's agreement not to encumber the premises or subject the title to any liens other than those created at the express written direction of the real owners.

8. Income and Expenses

It is crucial that all income and expenses with respect to the real estate are paid to and from the real owners' bank account and not the bank account of the corporate straw. The only funds to be deposited in the corporate straw's bank account should be the nominal capital contributions from its own stockholders and the service fees it receives for acting as nominal title holder. Its only expenses should be federal, state, and local taxes, the cost of the minute book, stock book and seal; fees payable to the corporation's lawyer for organizing the corporation; fees payable to its accountant for preparing its state and federal income tax returns; and fees payable to those who prepare the certificate of nominal title holder and corporate minutes, if they are not prepared by the straw corporation's own officers. If the stockholders of the straw corporation are not also its officers and directors, it may be necessary for the corporation to pay nominal salaries to its officers.

If a lease is to be signed by a straw corporation on behalf of the real owners of the leased real estate, it is important to provide that the rent is not made payable to the straw corporation. The simplest way to handle this problem is to be sure that the real owners have included in the lease a requirement that the rent be paid either to the real estate broker who acts as an agent for the real owners in managing the property and collecting the rents, or to the real owners themselves, but under a registered fictitious name. If, for any reason, checks are made payable to the corporate straw for sums which belong to the real owners, such as mortgage loan proceeds, rents, insurance or condemnation proceeds, such checks should be endorsed over to the real owners and not deposited in the bank account of the corporate straw. Finally, if the straw corporation proves to be a profit-making enterprise because its annual service fees exceed its annual expenses, dividends may be declared and paid to its shareholders.

Chapter Seven

PARTNERSHIP AGREEMENTS

I. INTRODUCTION

As we discussed in Chapter Six, in many real estate transactions there are substantial federal income tax advantages which can be realized by placing title to real property in a partnership rather than in a corporation. For tax purposes, a partnership is merely a "conduit". The profits [1] of the entity are taxable directly to the various partners, whereas a corporation pays a tax itself on profits, and the shareholders then pay individual taxes on any dividends distributed by the corporation. The result is a double tax on the profits distributed on dividends. Similarly, losses of the partnership entity "pass through" to the partners who may each deduct an appropriate share of a partnership loss against their personal income. Real estate ventures frequently generate substantial "paper" losses resulting from large deductions for depreciation of a building which, in a rising real estate market, may actually be appreciating in value. The desire to make use of the deductions on individual tax returns is often the major factor which causes the owners of a real estate venture to hold title in a partnership.

When several individuals form a corporation, many of the rights and obligations they owe to each other, to the corporation itself and to creditors are clearly defined by the applicable business corporation law. Other rights and obligations are controlled by the basic corporate documents, such as the articles of incorporation and the bylaws, or by agreements among the shareholders. Although there are statutes applicable to partnerships, the rights and obligations of partners among themselves and as to third parties are to a much greater extent controlled by contract among the partners, usually in the form of one basic document, the partnership agreement. In addition, the rules and regulations which govern the conduct of a partnership business, and which relate to matters such as the time and place of meetings, performance of management functions, bank accounts, capital structure and the like, are usually set forth in that same basic document, the partnership agreement, rather than by a series of documents, such as articles, bylaws, charters and the like. Partnership agreements also include provisions which in the context of a corporation would

---

1. The terms "profits" and "losses" are used in their tax accounting sense. There may well be "profits" upon which a tax must be paid even though there has been no cash generated which can be distributed to the partners to help pay that tax. Conversely, there can be "losses" at a time when the partnership is making money from a cash flow point of view and has cash available to distribute to the partners. Distributions of cash made by a partnership then showing tax losses are not taxed as income to the partners.

157

normally be embodied in shareholders' agreements, such as the rights and obligations of the parties upon the death of a party or in the event one wishes to sell an interest during his lifetime. Moreover, just as the capital structure of a corporation can become complicated by issuance of classes of stock (such as preferred or common) which may in turn be subdivided into series, owners of partnership interests may have differing rights vis-a-vis each other. Such differences in treatment of partners must be specifically embodied in the partnership agreement.[2]

The two basic types of partnerships commonly used in real estate transactions are discussed below.

A. GENERAL PARTNERSHIPS

General partnerships are governed by the Uniform Partnership Act (hereafter "UPA") some form of which has been adopted in virtually every state.

In a general partnership, a group of individuals or entities join together to carry on a business. Each partner is an agent for the others in all matters within the scope of the partnership business, and each partner is personally liable[3] to creditors *without limit* for partnership debts. Accordingly, if one of three partners enters into a contract on behalf of the partnership and the contract is within the normal scope of the partnership business, each partner will be personally liable for performance of that contract. If the partnership defaults, each partner's personal assets may be sold to satisfy any resulting judgment entered against the partnership which cannot be satisfied out of partnership assets.

Even this brief description of a general partnership will make immediately apparent the fact that this is not an entity which can be used unless the parties know each other well and have full confidence in one another's integrity and business judgment. However, in many real estate transactions, some of the partners may be merely passive investors who are willing to invest money in a venture just as they are willing to purchase stock in a company traded on the New York Stock Exchange. Although they are prepared to lose their investment, they are unwilling to expose their personal assets to the good faith and business judgment of others involved in the venture. In such a case, the investors may form a limited partnership pursuant to the Uniform Limited Partnership Act.

2. As we shall see, partnership agreements may be oral, or even may never have been verbalized but may be surmised from the course of dealings of the parties.

3. See Chapter Two, for discussion of what is meant by "personal" liability.

B. LIMITED PARTNERSHIPS

Under the Uniform Limited Partnership Act (hereafter "UL PA"), the partners are divided into two classes, general and limited.[4] A general partner has unlimited power to act for the partnership and has unlimited liability to creditors, just as he would in a general partnership. However, a limited partner's liability to creditors is limited to the amount he or she has contributed, or has agreed to contribute, to the partnership. A limited partner who is not also a general partner has no right to participate in the management and control of the business of the partnership. A limited partner will lose limited liability status if he or she does take part in management, although a limited partner is permitted to take part in certain basic decisions, such as sale of all the partnership property. Thus, limited partners surrender the right to participate in management and control of the partnership business, and receive in exchange protection from liability to creditors in the event the business is unsuccessful.

The federal income tax advantages of a general partner also accrue to a limited partner with certain minor exceptions which are beyond the scope of this book.

Most real estate "syndications" are in fact limited partnerships in which a promoter or developer acts as general partner and then sells limited partnership shares to investors to raise money, just as a corporation might sell its stock to investors to raise the capital it needs to acquire assets and operate its business.

C. THE PURPOSES OF THIS CHAPTER

The text which follows will consider the drafting of partnership agreements. The text will focus on matters which are common to nearly all partnership transactions, and will attempt to suggest, by use of specimen clauses, one or more ways in which a particular matter can be treated. You should recognize that these provisions do not represent the only way of treating a problem, or even the best way. Each partnership will have its own peculiarities and each group of partners will have its own ideas as to how the partnership should operate. However, this text should be helpful in suggesting the nature of the most common problems and several common solutions.

II. DRAFTING GENERAL PARTNERSHIP AGREEMENTS

Neither the UPA nor common law require that a partnership agreement be in writing, or even that there be any partnership agreement at all, written or oral. There are many cases in various American jurisdictions in which a major issue is whether or not certain

---

4. A person may be both a general and a limited partner. However, in order to have an effective partnership, there must be at least two different persons who are partners.

persons are partners at all. One reason for the existence of a written partnership agreement is to resolve this issue by establishing that the parties in fact intend that they be partners. A clear expression of the intent of the parties is normally decisive for purposes of state law,[5] although there have been numerous cases in which the persons having an economic relationship have denied in written agreements that they are partners only to have a court determine that, at least for some purposes, they are partners.

A second reason for having a written agreement is that the UPA and the common law of partnerships are sketchy and incomplete in filling out the details of the respective rights and obligations of the partners. It is likely that the relationship between the parties is considerably more complex. If a dispute arises, it is much easier to prove what that relationship was if there is a written agreement which accurately describes that relationship.

Another reason for having a written partnership agreement is that the act of drafting the agreement raises questions and issues which the partners might not otherwise consider. It is often the case that relatively unsophisticated clients have not comprehended the implications of entering into a partnership arrangement, and the process of preparing the agreement helps to force the parties to consider the implications of the arrangement and possibly to realize that certain very basic decisions have yet to be made as to what the arrangement between the parties really is.

In order to aid your understanding of these materials, we have included at the end of the chapter a sample partnership agreement, and a sample limited partnership agreement. As you read the various sections of this Chapter, you should review the sample agreements and study their provisions carefully in order to determine whether you understand the meaning and purpose of each clause.

A. EFFECTIVE DATE OF AGREEMENT AND NAMES OF PARTIES

Like most agreements, partnership agreements usually begin with a reference to the date of the agreement and a statement of the identity of the parties to the agreement.

1. Date

In many cases the parties have actually formed a partnership before they commit their agreement to writing and it may be useful to refer in the agreement not only to the date on which it is signed, but also to the date as of which the parties considered themselves to have become partners.

5. The determination of whether persons are partners for federal income tax purposes is a separate determination independent of state law and emphasizing distinctly different tests and criteria.

2. Names of Partners

The names of all the individuals [6] and entities who are to be partners should be listed, as well as their status (e. g., executors and trustees). In some states it is improper for a corporation to be a general partner in a partnership. That position is based on the theory that the Board of Directors is charged with managing the corporation as fiduciary for the shareholders. If the corporation were a general partner, it might be committed by another general partner to an obligation not specifically approved by its Board of Directors. Therefore, the Board of Directors may be considered to have abdicated its responsibility to its shareholders. However, in several states, such as Delaware and states that have adopted variations of the Model Business Code, the corporation statute has been amended specifically to allow a corporation to be a general partner in a partnership, and this appears to be the modern trend.

It is generally a good practice to include an address for each partner for ease of reference, although it is not necessary.

An example of a provision setting forth the date of the agreement and the names of the parties follows:

"THIS AGREEMENT made as of the _____ day of _____, 19___ by and among _____ (hereinafter sometimes collectively referred to as the 'Partners')."

B. RECITALS

Recitals set forth the background to an agreement. Although recitals are not a necessary part of a partnership agreement, they may be helpful to a future reader of the agreement (such as a judge) in providing a general understanding of the agreement. An example of a simple recital is set forth on page 193.

C. CREATION OF PARTNERSHIP

A provision should be included stating the specific intention of the parties to form a partnership:

"The Partners hereby confirm the formation of a partnership (the 'Partnership') to be governed, except as herein otherwise provided, by the provisions of the Uniform Partnership Act of the State of New York."

D. PURPOSE OF THE PARTNERSHIP

Section 9 of the UPA provides:

"(1) Every partner is an agent of the partnership for the purpose of its business, and the act of every partner, including the execution in the partnership name of any instrument, for appar-

---

6. Please remember that the term "person" may include natural persons and entities, while the term "individual" only refers to natural persons.

ently carrying on in the usual way the business of the partnership of which he is a member binds the partnership, unless the partner so acting has in fact no authority to act for the partnership in the particular matter, and the person with whom he is dealing has knowledge of the fact that he has no such authority.

(a) An act of a partner which is not apparently for the carrying on of the business of the partnership in the usual way does not bind the partnership unless authorized by the other partners.

.　.　.

(3) Unless authorized by the other partners or unless they have abandoned the business, one or more but less than all the partners have authority to:

(a) Assign the partnership property in trust for creditors or on the assignee's promise to pay the debts of the partnership,

(b) Dispose of the good-will of the business,

(c) Do any other act which would make it impossible to carry on the ordinary business of a partnership,

(d) Confess a judgment,

(e) Submit a partnership claim or liability to arbitration or reference.

(4) No act of a partner in contravention of a restriction on authority shall bind the partnership to persons having knowledge of the restriction."

A reading of Section 9 of the UPA should demonstrate the importance of a provision setting forth the purpose of the partnership, which provision is sometimes combined with the provision creating the partnership:

"The Partners hereby form a partnership to be governed by the Uniform Partnership Act of the State of Texas, except as herein otherwise provided, for the sole purpose of owning and operating 'Happy Gardens Apartment', and for no other purpose."

The clause set forth above shows such a combination of the purpose clause with the clause confirming the formation of the partnership. As a matter of style, many people prefer to include a separate clause on purposes of the partnership, particularly in those cases where there may be reason to spell out the purposes of the partnership in much greater detail than we have above.

The draftsman should always consider whether the purpose should be broadly or narrowly described. It may be convenient to include a broad purpose clause, as one commonly does when forming a corporation, to give the partnership maximum flexibility in connection with its operations. On the other hand, the Uniform Partnership Act specifies that every partner is an agent of the partnership for the purpose of its business. Therefore, any act of a partner which appears to bear some relationship to the business purposes of the partnership binds the partnership unless the partner so acting in fact has no authority to act for the partnership in the particular matter, and the person with whom he is dealing knows that the partner has no such authority. It follows that if any partner has reservations about any other partners, the clause should be narrow and the purpose clearly defined.

E. NAME

The UPA makes no reference to partnership names, and there is no legal requirement that a partnership use any name other than the names of its partners. Accordingly, John Jones and Thomas Smith may trade as Jones & Smith, or John Jones and Thomas Smith co-partners, or Jones & Smith, a partnership. Often, however, the partners will desire to operate under a name other than their own surnames:

> "The name of the Partnership shall be Happy Gardens Associates. The aforesaid name will be registered in the appropriate public office as the assumed or fictitious name of this Partnership."

In most jurisdictions, if the partners are going to use a name other than the surnames of the various partners, the partnership will be considered to be a business firm trading under a fictitious name. In most, if not all, jurisdictions in order to operate under a fictitious name it is necessary to file documents with the county clerk or in some other public place, setting forth the names and addresses of the partners together with a statement of the proposed fictitious name. The purpose of fictitious names registration statutes is to protect creditors and other people who may deal with the partnership, or who may have some claim against the partnership (as for example, a person injured by some condition on the partnership property) and who might not otherwise be able to ascertain who the partners really are and where they may be found and served with legal process. In many jurisdictions, failure to register is a misdemeanor, which is punishable by a fine, or imprisonment, or both. In addition, failure to register may be a bar to bringing any lawsuit in the courts of the state in which the partnership is doing business without having registered. However, failure to register will not affect the existence of the partnership nor the rights and obligations of the partners among themselves.

F. PLACE OF BUSINESS

Although it is not necessary, generally a clause is included giving the partnership a particular office or address for purposes of serving notices, service of process and the like. The UPA does not require the partnership to have a specific office or place of business apart from the partners' respective residences. A provision concerning a partnership address is set forth below:

> "The Partnership's mailing address shall be at 62 Edgewater Avenue, Plainville, Connecticut, or such other address as all of the Partners may from time to time determine."

G. FISCAL YEAR

The partnership agreement should specifically dictate the fiscal year to be used by the partnership for accounting purposes especially if the partnership year is to be other than the calendar year. It should be noted, however, that there are significant restrictions on the right of a partnership to elect to use, for tax purposes, a fiscal year different from the calendar year.

H. PARTNERSHIP INTEREST

Each shareholder in a corporation holds a certain number of shares. The shareholder's interest in the corporation can be expressed by the ratio of the number of shares owned by the shareholder to the total outstanding number of shares of the corporation, and that ratio can be expressed as a percentage. For a corporation having only one class of shares, and absent any contrary agreement among the shareholders, a shareholder's percentage interest in the corporation will correspond precisely to the entitlement of that shareholder to any distributions and dividends which the corporation makes and to the assets of the corporation in a dissolution.

Partners in a partnership typically do not own shares. It is customary, however, for some designation to be made of the respective percentage interest which each partner has in the partnership, using some sort of provision similar to the following:

Section 3.1 Partnership Interests

> "Each Partner's respective percentage interest (hereinafter referred to as 'Partnership Interest') in the Partnership shall be as set forth beside that Partner's name:

Partner	Partnership Interest
Frederica Garcia	40%
Ricardo Lopez	30%
Samuel Downby	30%"

In the absence of a provision ascribing a partnership interest, the UPA provides that all partners shall be equal and shall share equally in all profits, losses and distributions, including distributions upon dissolution. Thus it is essential to specify partnership interests if the partners intend not to be completely equal partners.

It is often difficult to determine the partnership interest of each partner because there are often several aspects of the partnership concerning each of which the partners participate in different ratios from the other aspects. Thus, in the case of G.L.D. Associates, let us suppose that Garcia is the financial backer, Downby is supplying the land and Lopez is the developer who will provide his services. In terms of contributions to the capital, Garcia may be contributing $450,000 in cash, Downby may be contributing land worth $250,000 and Lopez may only be contributing $20,000 in cash and his services and expertise. The partners may have agreed that for tax accounting purposes they shall share profits and losses in the ratio of Garcia 40%, Lopez 30% and Downby 30%. Distributions of cash flow may be in terms of a cumulative annual first preferential distribution to Garcia of $45,000, a cumulative annual second preferential distribution to Downby of $35,000, a non-cumulative annual third preferential distribution to Lopez of $20,000 and a distribution thereafter to each partner in the ratio of Garcia 40%, Lopez 30% and Downby 30%. Distributions on sale of the property might require other priorities and preferences. Thus, the designation of a partnership interest in G.L.D. Associates is not going to produce one ratio which will carry throughout all these factors. The following sections will review these factors individually.

I. CAPITAL AND FINANCING

A partnership, like a corporation or any other business entity, generally requires funds in order to commence business. These funds are raised either through borrowing or through capital investments made by parties interested in the business. In a partnership, the parties decide how much capital, in the form of money or other property, will be required, how much of that capital each one will contribute and in what form. Normally, for partnership bookkeeping purposes, a capital account is maintained for each partner which shows at any given time that partner's interest in the business, in dollars, (not in percentage of total ownership) in relation to the dollar value of the interest of all other partners.

If all the partners of a partnership are to contribute equally to capital and are to share equally in all profits, losses and distributions, then the maintenance of a capital account in accordance with normal accounting practices will be a sufficient and proper way to determine the respective obligations and entitlements of the partners. Accounting procedures dictate that the capital account of each partner be increased by any further capital contributions made to the partnership and by the partner's respective share of any profits of the partnership, and decreased by distributions to the partner and by the partner's respective share of any losses of the partnership.[7] Unless

---

7. Remember that profits and losses are calculated to take into account such items as depreciation and principal amortization, and may have nothing to do with cash available for distribution.

the partnership agreement provides otherwise, upon dissolution of the partnership the assets of the partnership first are used to pay each partner his respective capital account and then are distributed to each partner in accordance with the partner's respective interest in the partnership. Thus, if everyone is equal and contributes and receives distributions equally, letting the UPA and the capital account control is reasonable.

However, as we have set forth with the description of G.L.D. Associates, often the partners are not equal and have negotiated specific terms respecting contributions and distributions. In drafting the provisions respecting capital accounts, capital contributions and distributions for such a partnership as G.L.D. Associates, one must be careful not to let the capital accounts as kept in accordance with accounting principles control distributions, especially distributions upon dissolution.

A technique which is sometimes useful in drafting a partnership agreement for a partnership like G.L.D. Associates is the creation of "capital balances" for each partner, which are distinct from capital accounts and are maintained and computed differently from capital accounts. For example, Garcia may really see herself as a more of a financial investor than a partner. She is investing $450,000 and expects to earn 10% annually on it. It is for that reason that she gets a first preferential annual cumulative distribution of $45,000, if the money is available for distribution. Under capital account accounting principles, the annual distributions of $45,000 are a return of capital and they reduce her capital account. For Garcia, that annual distribution is a return *on* not a return *of* her $450,000 and she would expect upon a dissolution to get her entire $450,000 back before any other partner received anything. Thus, we may consider that Garcia has a capital balance of $450,000, Downby has a capital balance of $250,000 and Lopez has a capital balance of $200,000 none of which capital balances shall be reduced or increased except as specifically stated in the agreement. We shall follow this concept through our discussion and see whether it might be useful.

J. ADDITIONAL CONTRIBUTIONS TO CAPITAL

Frequently in new business ventures the entrepreneurs do not fully anticipate the amount of equity capital they will need to get the business started. When this happens in the case of a corporation, the corporation may attempt to sell additional stock in order to raise additional funds. Similarly, a partnership may attempt to find new partners to make additional contributions, and then adjust their percentage interest accordingly. A simpler approach would be for each partner to contribute additional capital. However, the situation may be complicated if some, but not all partners, are in a position to put in additional funds. Can those who wish to contribute do so, or must the partnership dissolve? If those who are in a position to contribute additional funds do so not only for themselves but also for the insolvent or recalcitrant partners, what remedy will they have against those who have not contributed? Conversely, each partner wants to be certain that in the event he or she is unable or unwilling to make a pro rata contribution he or she cannot be summarily discharged from the partnership and the investment wiped out. There are many different ways of resolving these conflicting interests and demands. The answers furnished by the UPA are either incomplete or unsatisfactory in most real estate transactions involving investors on the one hand and developers, or promoters, and builders on the other. Consider the following portions of Section 18 of the UPA, in light of the comments set forth above:

"The rights and duties of the partners in relation to the partnership shall be determined, subject to any agreement between them, by the following rules:

(a) Each partner shall be repaid his contributions, whether by way of capital or advances to the partnership property and share equally in the profits and surplus remaining after all liabilities, including those to partners, are satisfied; and must contribute towards the losses, whether of capital or otherwise, sustained by the partnership according to his share in the profits.

. . .

(c) A partner, who in aid of the partnership makes any payment or advance beyond the amount of capital which he agreed to contribute, shall be paid interest from the date of the payment or advance.

(d) A partner shall receive interest on the capital contributed by him only from the date when repayment should be made.

. . .

(g) No person can become a member of a partnership without the consent of all the partners.

(h) Any difference arising as to ordinary matters connected with the partnership business may be decided by a majority of the parners; but no act in contravention of any agreement between the partners may be done rightfully without the consent of all the partners."

For one example of a way in which these conflicting demands might be resolved, review Article 7 of Form on page 194.

K. PROFITS AND LOSSES AND TAX RETURNS

As we have previously indicated, in the absence of agreement to the contrary, the UPA provides that the partners shall share profits and losses equally. Profits and losses are basically accounting and tax concepts and do not correlate with the economic factor of whether any cash is available for distribution and if so, how much.

However, some allocation must be made of profits and losses because they are tax concepts with tax consequences, and because each partner must report on his individual return his respective share of the profits and losses of the partnership. Usually, for a general partnership, the allocation of profits and losses reflects most closely the percentage interest of each partner in the partnership, and this would be the case even with G.L.D. Associates.

As we have previously discussed, the primary reason that profit and loss do not necessarily correlate with cash available for distribution is the effect of depreciation and mortgage payments. For a corporation or partnership that operates an active business, profit and loss are fairly accurate indicators of how the business is doing. Real estate partnerships are different in that the major asset of the partnership, being the buildings and improvements owned by the partnership, are depreciable assets, and in that real property is usually highly mortgaged, so that one of the major expenses of the partnership is debt service. The effect of depreciation is that a certain amount of money is deducted as if it were spent by the partnership for business purposes, whereas in fact no money was spent. The effect of self-amortizing mortgages is that in the later years of the mortgage, as a greater portion of the regular monthly installments consists of principal repayment (which may not be deducted as a business expense) rather than interest (which can be deducted), the partnership comes into the position of paying out dollars without being able to deduct all of those dollars from income and thus forcing the partners to pay income tax on some portion of those dollars even though the dollars on which the partners are paying income tax are not available for distribution to them.

L. CASH FLOW AND DISTRIBUTIONS

As we have discussed above, profits and losses may not be an accurate measure of the economic realities of what cash is available to the partnership; that is, what amount of money is left over after all expenses have been paid. Usually, if a partnership agreement does contain a separate provision regarding distributions, that provision will contain some definition of available cash, which is usually referred to as the "cash flow" or "net profits". The following is an example of how the partnership agreement for G.L.D. Associates might deal with the question of distributions of cash flow based upon the business deal for G.L.D. Associates as previously described. There are also included comments and questions concerning the reason for the inclusion of specific provisions:

ARTICLE VI: *Cash Flow, Distributions and Extraordinary Distributions*

§ 601. *Cash Flow Defined.* For purposes of this Agreement the term 'cash flow' shall mean the profits or losses of the Partnership, (exclusive of any items arising from Extraordinary Events, as hereinafter defined in Sections 603 and 604) ascertained in accordance with generally accepted accounting practices consistently applied, except that in determining cash flow the following adjustments shall be made to the current year's profit and loss:

(a) There shall be added back depreciation of buildings, improvements and personalty; and

(b) There shall be deducted mortgage amortization, repayment of authorized loans of the Partnership, capital expenditures, prepaid expenses, and reasonable reserves for working capital and other contingencies established by the Managing Partner including reserves necessary for capital expenditures, and other items not expensed for accounting purposes paid by the Partnership.

§ 602. *Distributions of Cash Flow.* The Partnership shall distribute to each Partner entitled thereto, at such times as the Managing Partner shall determine, the Cash Flow of the Partnership in the following manner, order and priority:

(i) First: An amount equal to ten (10%) percent per annum of Garcia's Capital Balance from time to time during the fiscal year in question shall be distributed to Garcia.

(ii) Second: To the extent that Garcia has not received the sums to which she would have been entitled under Section 602(i) hereof for any previous fiscal year or years, such deficiency shall be distributed to Garcia.

[Comment: **This provision is necessitated by the cumulative aspect of Garcia's preference**]

(iii) Third: An amount equal to ten (10%) percent per annum of Downby's Capital Balance from time to time during the fiscal year in question shall be distributed to Downby.

(iv) Fourth: To the extent that Downby has not received the sums to which he would have been entitled under Section 603(iii) hereof for any previous fiscal year or years, such deficiency shall be distributed to Downby.

(v) Fifth: An amount equal to ten (10%) percent per annum of Lopez' Capital Balance from time to time during the fiscal year in question shall be distributed to Lopez.

(vi) Sixth: Any remaining Cash Flow shall be distributed to all Partners in proportion to their respective interests in the Partnership.

PROBLEM

Why is the sixth level of distribution to all partners and not to Lopez to the extent he has not received distributions in prior years?

Comment and Discussion: Rather than state the preferential returns as a percentage of Capital Balance, they could have been stated as fixed sums, being $45,000; $25,000 and $20,000. As you review

Sections 603 and 604 consider the reasons for establishing a Capital Balance and drafting the distribution language in terms of the Capital Balances. The reference to Out Parcels means those portions of land outside of the major first-phase development, which may be developed by the partnership for related uses or may be sold separately.

§ 603. *Qualified Extraordinary Disposition.* A Qualified Extraordinary Disposition shall mean and refer to any sale or other disposition (other than a lease) of one or more of the Out Parcels or any part thereof including any sale or other disposition thereof accomplished by condemnation, deed in lieu of condemnation or other means of taking for a public purpose, but not in connection with the sale or other disposition of the entire Property. All net proceeds from time to time derived from any Qualified Extraordinary Disposition shall to the extent available be distributed by the Partnership as follows:

(i) First: To Garcia to the extent and in reduction of her Capital Balance.

(ii) Second: After Garcia's Capital Balance has been reduced to zero, then to Downby, to the extent of and in reduction of his Capital Balance.

(iii) Third: After Downby's Capital Balance has been reduced to zero, then to Lopez, to the extent of and in reduction of his Capital Balance.

(iv) Fourth: After Lopez' Capital Balance has been reduced to zero, then to all Partners in the same proportion as their respective Partnership Interests.

§ 605. *Extraordinary Dispositions.* An Extraordinary Disposition shall mean and refer to any of:

(a) Sale, conversion (voluntary or involuntary) or other disposition (other than a lease) or all or any portion of the Partnership Property, other than a sale or other disposition solely of all or any part of one or more of the Out Parcels, and including any such sale or other disposition by condemnation, deed in lieu of condemnation or other means of taking for a public purpose.

(b) Refinancing of all or any portion of the Property.

(c) Fire or other insured casualty. To the extent that there are net proceeds from time to time derived from any Extraordinary Disposition in excess of accounts actually expended in the restoration or repair of the Partnership Property or applied to Partnership obligations, then such proceeds shall be distributed to the extent available from time to time, in the following order and priority:

(i) First: As cash flow in accordance with Section 602(i) hereof, to the extent to which rights have accrued thereunder during the fiscal year.

Comment: Remember that the preference is in terms of a certain percentage per annum and can be considered to be accruing daily in a manner similar to the accrual of interest.

(ii) Second: As cash flow in accordance with Section 602(ii) hereof.

(iii) Third: As cash flow in accordance with Section 602(iii), to the extent rights have accrued thereunder during the fiscal year of such distribution.

(iv) Fourth: As cash flow in accordance with Section 602(iv) hereof.

(v) Fifth: As cash flow in accordance with Section 602(v) hereof, to the extent rights have accrued thereunder during the fiscal year of such distribution.

(vi) Sixth: To Garcia to the extent and in reduction of her Capital Balance.

(vii) Seventh: To Downby to the extent and in reduction of his Capital Balance.

(viii) Eighth: To Lopez to the extent and in reduction of his Capital Balance.

(ix) Ninth: To all Partners in the same proportion as their respective Partnership Interests.

M.　CONTROL—MANAGEMENT

Control and management, like other areas of the agreement, can be handled in a variety of ways. In the absence of an agreement, UPA Section 18(e) provides that each partner has an equal right to participate in management and conduct of the partnership business. Moreover, under UPA Section 9(i) each partner has the apparent authority to bind the partnership to contracts within the scope of the partnership's business. The following questions must be considered:

(a) As to major policy decisions, such as the sale or mortgaging of substantially all of the partnership's real estate, will unanimous consent be required? If not, will a majority in number be required or a majority in interest?

(b) Will day-to-day decisions on operations require approval of only one partner, two partners, a majority or will these decisions also require approval of all the partners? In many real estate ventures, such as ownership of an apartment building, it is not practical to have all partners participate in day-to-day decisions, such as whether to lease a particular apartment to a particular tenant or whether to permit a tenant to break a lease upon forfeiting his security deposit.

(c) Will there be a managing partner, and if so what will be his or her duties? What will be the extent of his or her authority? How much time will he be required to spend on partnership business?

Will he receive any salary or other compensation in addition to the partnership draw for serving as managing partner?

Consider Article 9 of the Form on page 197 Partnership Agreement as an alternative for a fairly simple real estate partnership which does not operate an active business.

N. PROHIBITED ACTS

1. General Matters

It is common to include in a partnership agreement a section covering certain acts which the partners are specifically prohibited from doing on behalf of the partnership. Among those which should be considered are the following:

(a) Lending the firm's money and/or credit, or pledging the firm's assets.

(b) Competing with the partnership.

If a partner is not to compete with the partnership, the clause is more likely to be enforceable if there are limits as to time and place. For example, one may provide that no partner will compete with the partnership while he is associated with the partnership and for a period of two years thereafter and/or that he will not compete within a radius of five miles from the partnership property. If a partner is to be permitted to compete with the partnership, then this understanding must be specifically set forth, since otherwise a partner who competes with the partnership is guilty of a breach of his fiduciary duty to the partnership and to the other partners and will be required to account to the partners for any profits made from the competing venture.

A specimen provision relating to some of the above matters is as follows:

"No partner shall, without the consent of the others:

(a) Endorse or guarantee for or on behalf of the partnership any commercial paper, note or other obligation, or act as an accommodation party, or otherwise become surety for any person, firm or corporation.

(b) On behalf of the partnership, borrow or lend money, or make, deliver or accept any commercial paper, or execute any mortgage, bond or lease, or purchase or contract to purchase, or sell or contract to sell any property for or of the partnership other than the type of property bought and sold in the regular course of its business, or compromise or release any debts due the partnership except upon full payment thereof."

In the absence of prohibitive clauses, UPA Sections 9(2) and 9(3) apply. They are as follows:

> "(2) An act of a partner which is not apparently for the carrying on of the business of the partnership in the usual way does not bind the partnership unless authorized by the other partners.
>
> (3) Unless authorized by the other partners or unless they have abandoned the business, one or more but less than all the partners have no authority to:
>
> (a) Assign the partnership property in trust for creditors or on the assignee's promise to pay the debts of the partnership,
>
> (b) Dispose of the good-will of the business,
>
> (c) Do any other act which would make it impossible to carry on the ordinary business of a partnership,
>
> (d) Confess a judgment,
>
> (e) Submit a partnership claim or liability to arbitration or reference."

2. Conveyance of the Partnership's Real Estate

As in the sample provision above, it is important to prohibit specifically the conveyance of partnership real estate by one partner, if that is the desire of the partners. That is because with respect to a transfer of real estate, the UPA provides that any partner may convey title by a deed executed in the partnership name. The partnership is bound by the conveyance if the conveyance actually was, or appeared to be, in the normal course of the partnership's business, unless in fact the partner so conveying had no authority to make the conveyance and unless the grantee knew that fact. However, if the grantee is a bona fide purchaser for value without knowledge of any restriction, or even if the grantee is not a bona fide purchaser for value without notice, but subsequently conveys to a bona fide purchaser for value without knowledge of any restriction, the partnership is bound by the conveyance even if the partner who delivered the deed had no actual authority to do so. Section 10 of the UPA is as follows:

> "(1) Where title to real property is in the partnership name, any partner may convey title to such property by a conveyance executed in the partnership name; but the partnership may recover such property unless the partner's act binds the partnership under the provisions of paragraph (1) of section 9, or unless such property has been conveyed by the grantee or a person claiming through such grantee to a holder for value without knowledge that the partner, in making the conveyance, has exceeded his authority.
>
> (2) Where title to real property is in the name of the partnership, a conveyance executed by a partner, in his own name, passes the equitable interest of the partnership, provided the act is one within the authority of the partner under the provisions of paragraph (1) of section 9.

(3) Where title to real property is in the name of one or more but not all the partners, and the record does not disclose the right of the partnership, the partners in whose name the title stands may convey title to such property, but the partnership may recover such property if the partners' act does not bind the partnership under the provisions of paragraph (1) of section 9, unless the purchaser or his assignee, is a holder for value, without knowledge.

(4) Where the title to real property is in the name of one or more of all the partners, or in a third person in trust for the partnership, a conveyance executed by a partner in the partnership name, or in his own name, passes the equitable interest of the partnership, provided the act is one within the authority of the partner under the provisions of paragraph (1) of section 9.

(5) Where the title to real property is in the names of all the partners, a conveyance executed by all the partners passes all their rights in such property."

In order to avoid the question of authority, a purchaser will generally require signatures of all partners and an affidavit or other proof that the signatories are in fact all the partners of the partnership.

O. TRANSFERS OF PARTNERSHIP INTEREST

There are two ways in which a partnership interest may be transferred: Voluntarily, by an instrument of assignment, as would normally happen in the case of a gift, sale, or pledge; and involuntarily, as in the case of a bankruptcy, imposition of a charging lien, foreclosure on an encumbrance or death.

1. Voluntary Assignment

In the absence of any agreement by the other partners, an assignment by a partner of his interest in a partnership does not give the assignee a right to participate in the management or administration of the partnership business or affairs, or to require any information or account of partnership transactions, or to inspect the partnership books. An assignment merely entitles the assignee to receive the profits to which the assigning partner would otherwise be entitled. Furthermore, on dissolution the assignee will receive the assigning partner's interest. In other words, the assignee does not become a partner although he does succeed to his assignor's right to receive distributions from the firm. If the non-assigning partners object to the assignee, even with his limited rights, they may dissolve the partnership. However, an assignee may become a full-fledged partner if all the other partners agree.

It is important to distinguish between assignment of a partnership interest and assignment of an interest in specific partnership property. The UPA (Section 25(2)) provides that a partner's right in specific partnership property is not assignable except in connection with an assignment of the rights of all partners in the same property. To illustrate, suppose A and B, as partners, own two identical apartment buildings, each of equal value. A may assign to C his partnership interest in the firm of AB. C will then be entitled to receive A's share of profits as set forth above. However, A may not in his own name sell to C one of the buildings or an undivided one-half interest in either building. The UPA and common law consider the partnership as an entity separate and apart from the partners for purposes of ascertaining property rights in partnership property. To this extent the partnership is analogous to a corporation.

In connection with voluntary transfers, the parties almost always want to impose some restriction on a partner's right to "alienate" (sell, give or pledge) a partnership interest. In some cases, especially those involving partnerships that operate an active business, there may be an absolute prohibition on voluntary transfers. However, in real estate ventures the parties are often investors in a partnership, rather than a corporation, solely because of the federal income tax advantages of the partnership form. In such partnerships it is more common to provide a right of first refusal rather than an absolute prohibition. That is, if a partner wishes to sell his interest, he may obtain an offer from an outsider, but before he can accept the offer, he must first offer the interest he wishes to sell to his partners on the same terms and conditions as contained in the outsider's offer. If the partners do not wish to purchase the interest, it can then be sold to the outsider.

PROBLEM

Consider the relationships between the provisions dealing with restrictions upon transfer and the provisions dealing with management and control.

2. Involuntary Assignments

(a) Death or Bankruptcy

Death or bankruptcy of a partner causes a dissolution of the partnership. (See UPA Section 31(a)). Dissolution is the time when the partners cease to carry on the business *together* [8] and is generally followed by liquidation of the partnership's assets, payment of debts and finally termination of the partnership. Obviously, the surviving partners may not want to liquidate the business on the happening of an unforeseen event. As a result, almost every partnership agreement provides for continuation of the partnership business on the

---

8. "Dissolution" is a highly technical term, and it and "termination" often have different meanings under state law and under federal tax law. The word "together" is emphasized be- cause in the case of death the business is still operating, but all of the partners are no longer operating it, as one has died. The death effects an instantaneous technical dissolution.

death of a partner. The partnership could continue with the heirs of the decedent as a new partner or the surviving partners may continue alone. In the latter case it is desirable to spell out the terms of any payment to be made to the decedent's estate since the UPA is silent on this subject.

There are many alternative provisions which may be drafted to cover the event of death of a partner. The agreement may provide that the interest of a partner who dies will be transferred to his or her personal representative and ultimately to the surviving spouse or children or to whomever he may have left the interest by will. On the other hand, the parties may prefer to have the surviving partner or partners purchase the interest of the deceased partner. However, a possible purchase raises several questions: Should the purchase be at the option of the survivor, or should it be mandatory? In either event, how should the price be determined? Should there be a specific agreement on price or should it be determined by some formula? If the price will be determined by formula, what should the formula be? What should the method of payment be? Should the surviving partner be required to pay cash, or may part of the price be paid by notes? If part of the price is to be deferred, over what period, and with what interest on unpaid sums? Should the parties purchase insurance on each others' lives to fund this kind of purchase?

(b) Creditor

It follows from what has been said above concerning the existence of the partnership as an entity analogous to a corporation that a creditor of an individual partner may not execute upon a partner's interest in specific partnership property, although he may be able to execute upon the debtor's interest in the partnership itself. In the illustration given above, creditors of the AB partnership might reach both apartment buildings, but creditors of A alone or B alone could not. However, creditors of A alone may, if they obtain a judgment, apply for a "charging order" against A's partnership interest. The holder of a charging order is in a position similar to that of an assignee. He is entitled to receive A's share of profits and other distributions but he may not participate in the management of the firm. It is in effect an involuntary assignment. There is some authority for the proposition that the holder of a charging order may foreclose on the order and become an "owner". However, there is also some authority to the effect that the other partners may then "redeem" the charged interest by paying the debt with interest. The UPA is silent on these points and the authorities are scattered and in most states these points have never been specifically adjudicated.

In the case of involuntary transfers (other than in the case of death) it is common to include a clause which attempts to give the other partners the same rights that they would have in the case of a voluntary transfer. However, since there is no outside offer to determine the price, and since the assignee is probably entitled as a matter of law to the value of the asset (or the amount of the debt, if it is less than the value of the asset), the price is normally the fair market value of the property.

Review Articles 10, 11 and 12 of the Form Partnership Agreement beginning on page 197 for one example of a resolution of some of the above. It should also be noted that the parties might consider a liquidation of the partnership in the event of death of a partner. However, this is not common in real estate partnerships involving an existing established building, because generally the services of any one partner are not required to keep the business going. Furthermore, it may be undesirable to agree to offer a property for sale at some future time which will be determined entirely fortuitously, without any regard to the then current status of the market, availability of mortgage financing for prospective purchasers, and the like.

P.   TERM AND TERMINATION

The partnership agreement should set forth the events which will cause a termination of the partnership and the consequences which will flow from a termination. The following might be suitable for a simple partnership:

> "This Partnership shall continue until the earlier of December 31, 2025 and the termination by (i) the sale or other disposition of all or substantially all of the Partnership property, or (ii) the agreement of 66⅔% in interest of the Partners. Upon termination, the assets of the Partnership shall be liquidated and distributed in the following order: (A) sums owing to mortgagees and other creditors of the Partnership other than Partners; (B) sums, if any, owing to Partners other than for capital and profit; (C) sums owing to Partners in respect of capital; and (D) the balance, if any, shall be distributed to the Partners in accordance with their respective interests."

The distribution on liquidation set forth above follows the pattern of the Uniform Partnership Act (see UPA Section 40). In the absence of the first sentence, the partnership can be dissolved with impunity by any partner at any time, since the relationship is entirely consensual. Even with the above provision, any partner can still dissolve the partnership at any time. However, such a dissolution would be in breach of the contract and the dissolving party would be liable for damages caused by the breach. In addition, the other partners could continue the business (as a new partnership) without the breaching partner, rather than winding up and terminating the business.

PROBLEM

Why would the above provision not be suitable for G.L.D. Associates?

Q. GOVERNING LAW—INTERPRETATION

Especially if the partners live in different states from each other or the partnership property, the partners will often desire the agreement to contain a provision stating which state's law will govern the partnership and will be used to interpret ambiguities in the agreement. The choice of law clause can avoid arguments at a subsequent date as to which state's law applies. Normally, the law of the state in which the real estate lies will apply to questions pertaining to the real estate. If the partners are residents of another state, and the agreement has been negotiated, signed and is to be carried out in that other state, the law of the other state may apply to the relationship of the partners among themselves. Although the UPA has been widely adopted, courts in the various states have not always been consistent in their interpretation of the Act. Therefore, the parties may wish to designate whose law will apply even where all of the states whose law might be controlling have adopted the UPA. A provision concerning choice of law follows:

> "(a) The Partners acknowledge that this Partnership Agreement has been made with reference to the laws of Illinois and accordingly this Agreement shall be construed in accordance with the laws of Illinois."

R. NOTICES

A provision should be included setting forth the method of giving notice to the parties.

S. ARBITRATION

In the event of a dispute between the parties, any party would normally be entitled to seek a court decision resolving the dispute. However, some attorneys prefer arbitration as a method of resolving disputes because it is generally quicker and less expensive than litigation through the courts. Other attorneys prefer to use the courts, notwithstanding the delay and expense, because they believe they are more likely to achieve an equitable result before a judge than before an arbitration panel. Although arbitration awards may be appealed to a court of law, in some states the courts have indicated that they will give great weight to the arbitrators' findings, reversing them only when the arbitrators have clearly acted improperly. If the parties wish to provide for resolution of disputes by arbitration, a provision such as the following would be inserted in the agreement:

> "Any deadlock, controversy or claim arising out of or in connection with this Agreement, or the breach thereof, shall be settled by sub-

mission to arbitration in the City of Chicago in accordance with the rules of the American Arbitration Association then obtaining and the award of the arbitrator or arbitrators shall be final and binding upon the parties. Judgment may be entered upon such award in any court of competent jurisdiction, and no appeal shall be taken therefrom."

T. MISCELLANEOUS AND BOILERPLATE PROVISIONS

In addition to the various provisions discussed above, some or all of the following items, many of which you have encountered in other agreements, are typically included in a partnership agreement:

1. Partner in Default

"So long as any Partner shall be in default hereunder, he shall have no right to participate in the management of the Partnership, and any distributions of Partnership funds during such period shall be made solely to the non-defaulting Partners."

2. Death of a Partner

"In the event of the death of a Partner, the business of the Partnership shall not terminate, but shall be continued by the surviving Partners, subject to all of the terms, covenants and conditions of this Agreement."

3. Cumulative Remedies

"The remedies provided in this Agreement are in addition to and not in limitation of any remedy which the non-defaulting Partners may have at law or in equity, or by statute all of such rights and remedies being herein specifically reserved."

4. Severability of Provisions

"If any provision of this Agreement is held to be invalid, the remaining provisions of this Agreement shall not be affected thereby, but shall continue in full force and effect."

5. Entire Agreement

"This Agreement sets forth the entire understanding and agreement of the parties with respect to the subject matter of this Agreement, and there are no other promises, warranties, or understandings, oral or written, of any kind or nature whatsoever among them."

6. Number and Gender

"For purposes of this Agreement, the masculine shall include the neuter and the feminine, and the singular shall include the plural, as the context may require."

7. Successors and Assigns

"Subject to the restrictions herein contained pertaining to assignment, this Agreement shall inure to the benefit of, and be binding upon, the parties hereto and their respective heirs, personal representatives and assigns."

8. Captions

"The captions contained herein are only for the convenience of the parties. They are not a part of this Agreement and they do not modify, amplify or give full notice of the terms hereof."

U. SIGNATURES

A place at the end of the agreement should be provided for the signatures of the parties:

"IN WITNESS WHEREOF, the parties hereto have hereunto set their respective hands and seals the day and year first above written.

_____ [*Seal*]
Name
Address:

_____ [*Seal*]
Name
Address:

_____ [*Seal*]
Name
Address: "

III. LIMITED PARTNERSHIP AGREEMENTS

We have previously noted that there are two types of partnerships in common use, the general partnership, discussed in the preceding materials, and the limited partnership, which is discussed below.

The outstanding characteristics of a limited partnership which distinguish it from a general partnership are as follows:

A. CLASSES OF PARTNERS—LIABILITY FOR DEBTS

A limited partnership consists of two classes of partners: general partners, who are fully responsible to creditors of the partnership, and limited partners, whose liability to creditors of the partnership is limited to their respective contributions to the capital of the partnership. A general partner exposes all of his or her assets to claims of creditors of the partnership, to the extent that the partnership assets are insufficient to pay the partnership creditors. If the business fails, he may lose not only what he has invested in the partnership, but also such other assets as he may own. In contrast, a limited partner, if the business fails, cannot lose more than the amount he has contributed or has agreed to contribute, to the partnership. Thus, a limited partner is treated more as a passive investor, analogous to a minority shareholder of a corporation.

B. MANAGEMENT

It follows logically from the differing obligations of the partners to creditors, and the theory of the limited partner as passive investor, that the general partners will be in charge of management of the partnership business. A limited partner should not be in a position to manage the partnership business, since this may result in incurring partnership debts for which the general partner would ultimately be liable. However, a limited partner does have the same rights as a general partner to have the partnership books kept at the principal place of business of the partnership, to inspect and copy the books, to have full information on all partnership affairs, to have the partnership dissolved by decree of court, to receive a share of profits realized on operations and to receive back his contribution to capital, to the extent it is available, if and when the partnership is dissolved. A limited partner also will not lose his status as a limited partner by reason of having a right to participate in certain basic partnership decisions, such as sale of all the partnership property.

C. CERTIFICATE OF LIMITED PARTNERSHIP

Another distinguishing characteristic of a limited partners is that it, like a corporation, is completely a creature of the sta statute. There were general partnerships before the UPA, and formalities are necessary to create a general partnership. Th were no limited partnerships before the ULPA and in order to cr an effective limited partnership (that is, one in which the lim partners have limited liability), it is necessary to comply with formalities of the ULPA. Among these formalities is that all partners must sign and swear to a certificate, commonly known Certificate of Limited Partnership, which sets forth (i) the n and addresses of the partners; (ii) identifies partners as gener limited; (iii) indicates the contribution made by each partner the additional amounts if any, which each partner has agreed to tribute to the partnership; and (iv) various other matters are required by the Uniform Limited Partnership Act.

The Certificate must be recorded in the designated pla public recording, which varies from state to state. Public fili the Certificate enables any prospective creditor, or any other who may have dealings with the partnership, to find out wh partners are, which of them are general and which are limite the amounts which the limited partners have contributed o agreed to contribute. The obvious purpose for filing such a cert in a public place is to protect creditors who might otherwise be they are dealing with a general partnership in which all parties are responsible for amounts due the creditor, whereas, in fact, all or most of the wealthiest partners have limited liability. The result is to encourage investing by parties who have capital, but who will not participate in detailed operation of the partnership business. Again, remember that the entity chosen is in a partnership form for tax reasons. Without those tax considerations, the normal form of investment for limited partners would be as corporate shareholders.

Limited partnerships provide for the investor most of the advantages of a corporation, including: limited liability, centralized management, and fairly transferrable interests. At the same time, this entity will be considered, for federal income tax purposes, as a partnership. Therefore, it is not surprising that many, if not most, large syndicated real estate transactions are in fact limited partnerships.[9]

IV. DRAFTING LIMITED PARTNERSHIP AGREEMENTS

Like the Uniform Partnership Act, the Uniform Limited Partnership Act sets out in broad outline the rights, liabilities and obligations of the partners among themselves and vis-a-vis third parties, but leaves a great deal of flexibility for variation by agreement. Since no two real estate transactions are exactly alike, limited partnership agreements vary greatly. The provisions which are discussed below may be considered as fairly typical, although there are many possible variations in the way any given subject may be handled. A sample limited partnership agreement is appended at the end of this Chapter.

A. FORMATION OF PARTNERSHIP

As in the case of a general partnership, the introductory provision should name the parties, state their intention to create a partnership and set forth the date of the agreement.

It may be convenient, if there are many limited partners, to refer to them at the outset only as "the parties whose signatures appear at the end of this agreement" rather than naming them, as was done in Form VII–2. This is purely a matter of style and convenience.

B. NAME AND ADDRESS

"The name of the Partnership shall be Ten Mile River Mall, Ltd.
a limited partnership, and its principal office shall be at (_____)

---

9. Although a full discussion of the federal income tax aspects of partnerships is beyond the scope of these materials, the student should be aware that there are some instances in which limited partnerships may not be able to obtain the tax advantages of the partnership form. Presumably this will have been considered by the attorney before he asks you to draft a limited partnership agreement.

or such other place as the General Partner may designate upon ten days written notice to the Limited Partners."

The ULPA provides that the surname of a limited partner shall not appear in the partnership name and that a limited partner whose name does appear is liable as a general partner to partnership creditors who extend credit to the partnership without actual knowledge (not just constructive knowledge) that the named partner is not a general partner.

C. PURPOSE

If the partnership is being formed for the purpose of acquiring only one property or one group of properties, the property should be identified and the purpose limited to that identified property. Usually the purpose clause in a limited partnership agreement is drafted more narrowly than for a general partnership. The limited partners have no voice in partnership decisions and they want to make sure that the general partner cannot, for example, sell all the partnership real estate and purchase an auto agency.

The ULPA provides that a limited partnership may carry on any business which a partnership without limited partners may carry on. Several states have adopted variations on this provision, specifying, for example, that a limited partnership may not engage in the banking business, insurance business, railroad business, trust business, and a few others.

D. TERM

The Uniform Limited Partnership Act requires that the Certificate of Limited Partnership state the "term for which the partnership is to exist". Therefore, a term is generally included in the limited partnership agreement. Unless all of the partners are corporations, the term of the partnership cannot be perpetual, although it can be indefinite. Generally the partners will pick a period of from 25 to 35 years in a real estate transaction, on the theory that the property will probably be sold and the partnership liquidated before that time. An example of a provision relating to the term of a limited partnership is set forth below:

"This Partnership shall commence as of the date hereof and shall continue for a period of 30 years unless sooner terminated pursuant to the provision hereof."

E. CAPITAL CONTRIBUTIONS

As in the case of a general partnership, a provision should be included describing the capital contributions of the various partners. Often in the case of a limited partnership, the partners will not make cash capital contributions in the same proportions as their interest in the partnership. Generally the people making lesser cash contributions are general partners. For example, a general partner who developed the idea for a transaction and then did the necessary work (such as acquiring title and obtaining financing and investors) to bring it to fruition, may receive a 10% interest in profits of the partnership in consideration for his efforts, although he may make no cash contribution to capital. The ULPA provides that contributions of a *limited* partner may be cash or other property, but not services. By implication this seems to recognize that the contribution of the general partners may be wholly or partly by services.

F. PARTNERSHIP INTERESTS; PROFITS AND LOSSES; CASH FLOW AND DISTRIBUTIONS

The areas of partnership interests, profits and losses, and cash flow and distributions are substantially the same with respect to limited partnerships as with respect to general partnerships. Indeed, G.L.D. Associates could well have been a limited partnership, with Garcia, and possibly Downby, being a limited partner. Because of the prevalence of limited partnerships in transactions that are heavily tax-oriented [10], there are some aspects which should be further discussed.

The ULPA makes no reference to allocation of depreciation. However, it is possible to allocate depreciation and other loss items in a manner which is not proportionate to percentage interest. For example, a partner having a 20% interest in the profits and losses may be charged with 50% of the depreciation and receive the resulting deduction for federal income tax purposes. However, the Treasury will accept that allocation only if there is "substantial economic justification" for a disproportionate allocation of depreciation, or any other item of loss. There has been a great deal of discussion among lawyers as to what constitutes "substantial economic justification". This is an area in which the assistance of tax specialists, attorneys and accountants, is often required.

G. BOOKS AND RECORDS

The agreement should set forth information concerning the location of the partnership books of account and the rights of access of the partners. Usually, as part of his management functions, the general partner will keep all the books and records, and prepare tax returns, financial statements and the like. A provision concerning these matters is set forth below:

> "The Partnership shall maintain full and accurate books at its principal place of business, or such other place as shall be designated

---

10. Changes in the tax laws since the 1960's and most recently in the 1976 Tax Reform Act, have cut down on the usefulness of tax-shelter deals that offered artificial tax losses and which often had no other economic justification. Despite the changes, tax considerations still have substantial weight in the area of real estate partnerships.

for such purposes by the General Partner, and all Partners shall have the right to inspect and examine such books at reasonable times. The books shall be closed and balanced at the end of each fiscal year. The General Partner agrees to deliver to the Limited Partners, after the expiration of each fiscal year of the Partnership, a balance sheet and profit and loss statement, together with a statement showing the capital accounts of each Partner, the distributions to each Partner, and the amount thereof reportable for federal tax purposes and for any state or local tax purposes."

In the absence of a provision in the partnership agreement, it is not clear the extent to which a general partner would be required to deliver the detailed financial information required in the clause set forth above. The ULPA provides only that a limited partner has "the same rights as a general partner" to have partnership books kept at the principal place of business of the partnership, to inspect and copy them, to have full information on all things affecting the partnership and to receive a formal account of partnership affairs under proper circumstances.

H. BANK ACCOUNTS

The ULPA makes no specific reference to the keeping of bank accounts. To avoid any question, the following provision is normally found in a limited partnership agreement:

"All funds of the Partnership are to be deposited in the Partnership name, in such bank account or accounts as shall be designated by the General Partner. Withdrawals from any such bank account or accounts shall be made upon such signature or signatures as the General Partner shall designate in writing."

I. MANAGEMENT, RIGHTS, DUTIES AND OBLIGATIONS OF THE PARTIES

Section 9 of the ULPA provides that a general partner has all the rights and powers, and is subject to all the restrictions and liabilities of a partner in a general partnership. However, the ULPA further specifies certain things the general partner cannot do without the consent of the limited partners. For example, the general partner may not do any act which would make it impossible to carry on the business of the partnership; he may not confess a judgment against the partnership; and he may not admit another person as a general partner. It is, therefore, generally desirable to spell out the rights and powers of a general partner to manage the partnership business in greater detail than the statute does. In Article 11 of the Limited Partnership Agreement, the general partner is given broad powers, including powers beyond those set forth in or implied by the ULPA. In some cases it may be desirable to limit the powers of the general partner so that he has less power than a partner in a general partnership. Subparagraph (b) of Article 11 may appear at first reading to be superfluous. However, Section 7 of the ULPA, which provides that a limited partner will not become liable as a general partner unless he takes part in the control of the business, raises the possible inference that a limited partner who is willing to risk limited liability status may become involved in management and control. Accordingly, it is common for a general partner to include a section such as subparagraph (b) in the agreement.

J. ASSIGNMENT OF PARTNER'S INTEREST

1. General Partner

The limited partners, as passive investors, are relying on the skill of the general partner in managing the partnership business. Therefore, the agreement will normally provide that a general partner may not assign his or her interest to another party:

> "The General Partner shall not assign, pledge, encumber, sell or otherwise dispose of any portion of his interest as General Partner in this Partnership."

If the general partner attempts to dispose of part of his interest in the partnership, he will be liable to the limited partners for the breach of the foregoing agreement.

2. Limited Partner

It is more common for a limited partner to be permitted to assign his interest to another investor. In fact, the ability to transfer the interest freely may be one of the attractions to induce the limited partner to invest. In the absence of any specific clause in the agreement, Section 19 of the ULPA provides as follows:

> "(1) A limited partner's interest is assignable.
>
> (2) A substituted limited partner is a person admitted to all the rights of a limited partner who has died or has assigned his interest in a partnership.
>
> (3) An assignee, who does not become a substituted limited partner, has no right to require any information or account of the partnership transactions or to inspect the partnership books; he is only entitled to receive the share of the profits or other compensation by way of income, or the return of his contribution, to which his assignor would otherwise be entitled.
>
> (4) An assignee shall have the right to become a substituted limited partner if all the members (except the assignor) consent thereto or if the assignor, being thereunto empowered by the certificate, gives the assignee that right.
>
> (5) An assignee becomes a substituted limited partner when the certificate is appropriately amended in accordance with Section 25.
>
> (6) The substituted limited partner has all the rights and powers, and is subject to all the restrictions and liabilities of his assignor, except those liabilities of which he was ignorant at the time he

became a limited partner and which could not be ascertained from the certificate.

(7) The substitution of the assignee as a limited partner does not release the assignor from liability to the partnership under Sections 6 and 17."

The sample provision which follows effectively allows the limited partners to assign their interests with the permission of the general partner: [11]

"No assignee, legatee or distributee of the whole or any portion of a Limited Partner's interest in the partnership shall have the right to become a Substitute Limited Partner in place of his predecessor in interest with respect to the whole or any portion of said interest without the written consent of the General Partner, whose consent shall be binding and conclusive. The consent or approval of any of the Limited Partners shall not be required.

As a condition to admission as a Substitute Limited Partner with respect to the whole or any portion of the interest of any Limited Partner, each such assignee, legatee or distributee shall execute and acknowledge such instruments, in form and substance reasonably satisfactory to the General Partner, as the General Partner shall deem necessary or desirable to effectuate such admission and to confirm the agreement of the person being admitted as such Substitute Limited Partner to be bound by all of the terms and provisions of this agreement, as the same may have been amended, with respect to the interest or portion of interest acquired from or through said predecessor in interest; such assignee, legatee or distributee shall pay all reasonable expenses in connection with such admission as a Substitute Limited Partner, including, but not limited to, the cost of the preparation, filing and publishing of any amendment of the Certificate of Limited Partnership necessary or desirable in connection with the admission of such assignee, legatee or distributee."

K. DEATH, RETIREMENT OR INCOMPETENCE
OF A PARTNER

1. General Partner

It is typical for a limited partnership agreement to deal with the possibility of the inability of a general partner to serve, whether due to death, incompetence, retirement or other cause. In the ab-

---

11. The only real concerns of the general partner regarding transfers by limited partners of their interests are the effects of such transfers upon the relevant securities laws and the tax laws. Too many transfers in a year may cause a termination of the partnership for tax purposes. The lack of restrictions upon transfer may cause the syndication of the partnership to lose whatever exemptions it may have from securities laws registrations and may lead to various kinds of liability for the promoter and/or general partner.

sence of an agreement, ULPA Section 20 would apply.   That section provides as follows:

> "The retirement, death or insanity of a general partner dissolves the partnership, unless the business is continued by the remaining general partners
>
> (a) Under a right so to do stated in the certificate, or
>
> (b) With the consent of all members."

It is important to remember the distinction between "dissolution" and "termination."   Dissolution is the change in the relationship of the partners caused by any partner ceasing to be associated in the carrying on of the business (see UPA Section 29).   Even after dissolution, a partnership is not terminated but continues to exist until the winding up of partnership affairs is completed.   In fact, the UPA specifies that the authority of partners to act for the partnership continues in winding up partnership affairs and completing transactions begun but not yet finished at the time of dissolution.   This would seem equally applicable to limited partnerships, except that the representative of the general partner (such as an executor), rather than the limited partners, would complete the winding up and termination.   There is no specific authority in the ULPA for the remaining general partners, if any, to continue the business of the partnership, in the absence of an agreement to that effect, nor is there any authority for the limited partners to elect a new general partner in the absence of a specific agreement.   A provision, dealing with the problem of the inability of a general partner to serve, is set forth below.[12]

> "(a) In the event of the death, retirement or adjudication of insanity or incompetency of a General Partner, the Partnership shall be dissolved but the business of the Partnership may be continued and the Partnership reinstated upon election of all of the Partners, General and Limited, within thirty (30) days after the occurrence of such death, retirement or adjudication of insanity or incompetency and written notice of such election to all partners hereunder. Upon the failure to so elect, the Partnership shall forthwith be dissolved and terminated and, upon such termination of the Partnership, a notice of dissolution, as required by law, shall be filed.
>
> (b) In the event of the death, retirement or adjudication of insanity or incompetency of a General Partner and the continuation of the Partnership business, pursuant to the provisions of subparagraph (a) hereof, the General Partner who has died, retired or been adjudicated insane or incompetent shall be released of obligations hereunder which have not previous thereto become fixed or accrued.   Such partner or his representatives shall thereafter

---

12.   Again, for tax purposes this is a very sensitive section. Mistakes in drafting this section could lead to the limited partnership being taxed as if it were a corporation, which would usually be a disastrous result. Expert tax advice is needed here.

have the status of a Limited Partner with no right to participate in the management of the Partnership business, but shall continue to be entitled to the share in profits and distributions which he originally held under this agreement.

(c) If a Limited Partner shall die, his executors or administrators (or if he shall be adjudicated insane or incompetent, his committee or representative) shall have the same rights that such Limited Partner would have had if he had not died or had not become insane or incompetent and the share of such Limited Partner in the assets of the Partnership shall, until the termination of the Partnership, be subject to the terms, provisions and conditions of this agreement as if such Limited Partner had not died or become insane or incompetent."

With reference to general partners, the foregoing clause is designed to cover a situation in which there is more than one general partner. In the event there is only one general partner the parties may wish to revise subparagraph (a) above so that the limited partners have the right within a specified time period to elect a successor general partner from their number to continue the business of the partnership. On the other hand, they may simply wish to provide for dissolution and termination of the partnership by the executor of the general partner, or by the limited partners or by a liquidating trustee.

2. Limited Partner

Death of a limited partner should not create the same problems as death of a general partner. Section 21 of the ULPA provides the following:

"(1) On the death of a limited partner his executor or administrator shall have all the rights of a limited partner for the purpose of settling his estate, and such power as the deceased had to constitute his assignee a substituted limited partner.

(2) The estate of a deceased limited partner shall be liable for all his liabilities as a limited partner."

The quoted provision indicates that the death of a limited partner would not cause the dissolution of a partnership. The personal representative of a limited partner would appear to have the right to transfer only the decedent's right to distributions, and the purchaser may not have the right to become a substitute limited partner without the consent of all the partners, depending upon the partnership agreement. Note that subparagraph (c) in the clause set forth above respecting the death of a partner would permit the executor, without the consent of the general partner or any other limited partners, to become, in effect, a substitute limited partner.

L. DISTRIBUTION OF ASSETS ON LIQUIDATION

Distribution of assets upon liquidation is typically governed by the partnership agreement. In the absence of an agreement, Section 23 of the ULPA controls:

"(1) In settling accounts after dissolution the liabilities of the partnership shall be entitled to payment in the following order:

(a) Those to creditors, in the order of priority as provided by law, except those to limited partners on account of their contributions, and to general partners.

(b) Those to limited partners in respect to their share of the profits and other compensation by way of income on their contributions.

(c) Those to limited partners in respect to the capital of their contributions.

(d) Those to general partners other than for capital and profits.

(e) Those to general partners in respect to profits.

(f) Those to general partners in respect to capital.

(2) Subject to any statement in the certificate or to subsequent agreement, limited partners shall share in the partnership assets in respect to their claims for capital, and in respect to their claims for profits or for compensation by way of income on their contributions respectively, in proportion to the respective amounts of such claims."

The pattern of distribution is similar to that in the UPA except limited partners are prior to general partners and amounts due partners for profits precede capital contributions.

The partnership agreement will usually provide for a different distribution upon liquidation, which may be as set forth in Article 16 at page 209 or as contained in § 604 of the G.L.D. Associates partnership agreement.

The ULPA makes no reference to any particular time for winding up partnership affairs. In any given partnership it may or may not be desirable to include a specific period.

The ULPA does not make the general partners personally liable for the return of the capital contributions of the limited partner nor does it specifically require the general partner to pay to the partnership any deficit in the general partner's capital account. However, provisions leading to the same result are inserted for the benefit of the general partner since the act does not specifically negate such liabilities.

M. MISCELLANEOUS AND BOILERPLATE PROVISIONS

As in the case of general partnership agreements, there are a number of so-called "boilerplate" clauses which generally appear in limited partnership agreements. The clauses are virtually identical in the two types of agreement.

N. SIGNATURES

As in the case of the general partnership agreement, the signatures appear at the end of the document. However, as indicated below, the limited partners often sign at a different place than the general partners:

"IN WITNESS WHEREOF, the undersigned have executed this Agreement as of the day and year first above written.

> _____ [*Seal*]
> General Partner
> Address:
> (Signatures of Limited Partners
> appear on attached Schedule 'A') "

O. SCHEDULES

Often the agreement will refer to a schedule which is a list of partners, their contributions, and their percentage interests. A specimen schedule is as follows:

Name	Limited or General Partner	Capital Contribution	Percentage Interest
John Jones	General	$1,000.	25%
_____ [*Seal*] Jennifer Lake 135 Lark Lane Parkview, Pa.	Limited	10,000.	25%
_____ [*Seal*] Jason Smith 153 Primrose Lane Centerville, Pa.	Limited	10,000.	25%
_____ [*Seal*] Elaine Coffee 2154 Disston St. Phila., Pa.	Limited	10,000.	25%

V. JOINT VENTURES

A joint venture is an entity which is virtually indistinguishable from a partnership. It can be loosely defined as a collection of individuals and/or entities who form a group (a joint venture) for the purpose of carrying on a single business enterprise. Technically, a joint venture is not a partnership and should not be governed by the UPA or other partnership act in effect in a particular state. However, the courts of many states have applied all or portions of the state's partnership law to joint ventures. While a joint venture agreement may be identical to a partnership agreement, the draftsman must keep in mind that omissions may be particularly harmful, as one cannot count on the state's partnership law governing any situation which is left open.

A. ADVANTAGES OF JOINT VENTURE FORM

The joint venture is viewed by lawyers as a vehicle to be used for single transactions. Whereas a partnership might appropriately develop and own several shopping centers, a joint venture would probably develop and own only one. If the same venturers developed several shopping centers they would normally create a new joint venture for each.

Because of the limited scope of activity of a joint venture, many lawyers feel that it is more difficult than in the case of a partnership for one venturer to incur obligations for which all venturers would be responsible. The theory rests on the view that the limited scope of a joint venture is more obvious to third parties than the limited scope of a particular partnership. Therefore, the courts are less likely to bind a joint venture to obligations incurred outside the scope of the venture's purpose. Weighed against this advantage are several disadvantages.

B. DISADVANTAGES OF JOINT VENTURE FORM

1. Inability to Limit Liability

The ULPA does not apply to joint ventures. In addition, no other statute granting limited liability to participants applies. Therefore, it is presently impossible to create a joint venture with the limited liability advantages of a limited partnership. Limited liability could be obtained, however, by creating corporations to act as joint venturers.

2. Interest in Joint Venture is Real Property

It was previously mentioned that a partner's interest in a partnership which owns real estate is viewed by the law as personal property. That means that the partner may transfer his interest without being concerned about dower, curtesy or any other rights of a spouse which automatically attach to real property. In addition, a judgment against a partner would not create a lien on the partnership's real estate.

The interest of a joint venturer, on the other hand, is usually considered a direct interest in real estate. The joint venturer is considered a tenant in common with the other venturers in each piece of real property owned by the venture. Therefore, the spouses and judgment creditors of the respective venturers obtain rights in the property owned by the joint venture. As a practical matter, that at least means the spouses will have to join in all deeds granting real property of the venture.

Another disadvantage of the joint venture is that in most states it is unclear whether property can be owned in the name of the venture. If all of the participants in a partnership or venture are named as grantees in a deed, changes in partners or venturers will require recording of a new deed, which may result in assessment of a transfer or recording tax.

Finally, because the venturers are considered tenants in common, it is possible for any venturer to bring a "partition" action in court, forcing the venture to sell its real estate and divide the proceeds. This disadvantage can be easily overcome by providing in the joint venture agreement that all venturers waive their right of partition.

Notwithstanding the disadvantages, many real estate developers now use the joint venture format.

VI.   CONCLUSION

The preparation of partnership agreements challenges all of a draftsman's skills. The issues are complex and interwoven. Tax and securities law considerations are just as important as the normal real estate concerns.

General Partnership Agreement

EXAMPLE:

THIS AGREEMENT made as of the ___ day of _____, 19__ by and among _____ and _____.

(hereinafter sometimes collectively referred to as the "Partners".)

WITNESSETH:

A. The Partners desire to form a partnership for the purpose of acquiring certain premises shown as _____, on the _____, _____, consisting of approximately _____ acres along _____, _____, _____ (the "Premises".)

B. The parties hereto are entering into this Agreement for the purpose of confirming their respective rights and obligations in connection with the Partnership.

NOW, THEREFORE, the parties hereto, intending to be legally bound hereby, agree as follows:

1. *Formation—Parties.* The Partners hereby confirm the formation of a partnership (the "Partnership") to be governed, except as herein otherwise provided, by the

provisions of the Uniform Partnership Act of the State of
————. The sole purpose of the Partnership shall be acquisition, improvement, development, ownership and operation of the Premises; the Partnership shall have no other purpose or purposes whatsoever.

Notwithstanding the Uniform Partnership Act of the State of ———— no Partner shall be considered an agent of the Partnership, and no act or signature of any Partner, whether or not for apparently carrying on in the usual way the business of the Partnership, shall bind the Partnership, unless the Partner so acting has in fact received authority pursuant to this Agreement to act for the Partnership in the particular matter involved.

2. *Name.* The name of the Partnership shall be ————. The aforesaid name will be registered in the appropriate public office as the assumed or fictitious name of this Partnership.

3. *Place of Business.* The Partnership's mailing address shall be at ———— or such other address as all of the Partners may from time to time determine.

4. *Fiscal Year.* The Partnership's fiscal year shall be the calendar year.

5. *Participation in Partnership.* Each Partner shall have a 33⅓% interest in the Partnership, and in the profits, losses and distributions thereof. All references in this Agreement to a Partner's percentage interest or his proportionate or pro rata share shall, unless otherwise stated, refer to such Partner's percentage participation in the Partnership as stated herein.

6. *Initial Capital.*

(a) An individual capital account shall be maintained for each Partner, to which contributions and profits shall be credited and withdrawals and losses debited.

(b) The initial capital of the Partnership shall be the amount required (in addition to mortgage loans) to complete settlement on the Premises, which shall be contributed by the Partners pro rata promptly upon execution of this Agreement. The Partners acknowledge that each of them has heretofore contributed ———— towards this amount.

7. *Additional Contributions to Capital.* If and to the extent the Partnership requires funds in addition to the capital contributions which are referred to above, and such other funds as the Partnership may borrow from banks or other financial institutions, each of the Partners shall be obligated to contribute his pro rata share of such additional

sums. The determination of whether such sums are required for the business of the Partnership, and the amount thereof, shall be made by 66⅔% in interest of the Partners and such Partners shall also determine the time and method of payment of such funds. Each Partner agrees to make such payments in the manner and upon the dates so designated, provided at least 30 days prior written notice shall have been given of the amount required and the manner and time and place of payment. If any Partner shall fail to make any such payment in accordance with such notice, there shall be the following consequences:

(a) Any non-defaulting Partner may elect to advance the amount required of the defaulting Partner as a loan to the defaulting Partner which shall be due and payable upon demand, with interest at the prime rate from time to time charged by _____. The Partner or Partners who shall have made such a loan shall have the right to deduct the amount thereof (with interest accrued thereon) from the defaulting Partner's share of the profits and/or any other money due or to become due him with respect to the Partnership, but this shall not be their only remedy for collection of the debt. The defaulting Partner's interest in the Partnership shall be security for such a loan with the same force and effect as though a court of competent jurisdiction had upon proper application charged the interest of the debtor Partner with payment of the amount of such debt (with interest as aforesaid) pursuant to the applicable provision of the Uniform Partnership Act. If more than one non-defaulting Partner wishes to make such a loan, each such non-defaulting Partner may make a loan in the proportion that his percentage interest bears to the total percentage interests of all non-defaulting Partners who wish to make the loan.

(b) If no Partner desires to advance a loan as aforesaid, any non-defaulting Partner may advance the amount required and the advance shall, at his option, be considered a contribution to the capital of the Partnership. In that event, the Partner making such contribution shall have the right to acquire a fraction of the defaulting Partner's interest in the Partnership; the numerator of such fraction shall be the amount of the defaulting Partner's assessment which the non-defaulting Partner contributes, and the denominator shall be the initial capital contribution of the defaulting Partner, as set forth above, plus the amount of all additional capital contributions made by and/or assessed against the defaulting Partner, including assessments then in default. Upon payment by the non-defaulting Partner of the contribution referred to in the preceding sentence, the percentage interest of the non-defaulting Partner shall be deemed increased and the percentage interest of the defaulting Partner shall be deemed decreased as aforesaid. Thereafter, to that extent, the default shall be deemed cured; provided, however, the defaulting Partner shall deliver to the acquiring Partner any instruments he may reasonably request to perfect such transfer of ownership. If more than one Partner desires to make an advance pursuant to this subparagraph, each such Partner may make advances in the proportion that his percentage interest bears to the total percentage interests of the non-defaulting Partners, and each shall be entitled to acquire a corresponding portion of the Partnership interest available for acquisition by reason of the default.

(c) The defaulting Partner shall have the right, within a period ending one year after a contribution to capital shall have been made by another Partner pursuant to subparagraph (b) above, to reacquire 80% of that portion of his Partnership interest which has been acquired by the non-defaulting Partner (or Partners, as the case may be), upon payment of the amount advanced by the non-defaulting Partner or Partners, together with interest thereon at the prime rate charged by _____ for the period from the date of advance to the date of reacquisition.

(d) If the non-defaulting Partners do not wish to make a loan pursuant to subparagraph (a) above, or a contribution to capital pursuant to subparagraph (b) above, then the defaulting Partner may pledge his percentage interest to a bank or other institutional lender as collateral for a loan not greater than the assessment, provided, such a loan is effected and the assessment paid within 60 days after the date of the assessment and provided further that the lender agrees in writing to give the other Partners written notice of and a reasonable opportunity to cure any default; otherwise the non-defaulting Partners may, at their option, sell to any third party the same portion of the interest of the defaulting Partner as they might have acquired pursuant to subparagraph (b) above on such terms and conditions as they may deem proper and the defaulting Partner shall have no right to repurchase such Partnership interest. The defaulting Partner agrees to deliver to such third party such documents as may reasonably be required to evidence and confirm the transfer, and if he fails to do so, the non-defaulting Partners, or any of them, may do so on his behalf as his attorney-in-fact.

(e) The proceeds of sale pursuant to subparagraph (d) shall be applied in the following order of priorities: (i) to the amount owed to the Partnership by the defaulting Partner on account of the assessment for which his Partnership interest has been sold, together with interest at the prime rate charged by _____ from the date of default to the date the funds are received from the purchaser; (ii) to any other amounts the defaulting Partner may owe to the Partnership for capital contributions in default, outstanding loans, or otherwise; (iii) to the defaulting Partner, but only to the extent of capital contributions actually made by him while a Partner, without interest; and (iv) the excess, if any, shall belong to the Partnership and shall be Partnership property as compensation for time, effort, and expense in finding the buyer and completing the transfer.

8. *Computation of Profits and Losses—Distributions.* The Partnership shall engage an independent certified public accountant satisfactory to 66⅔% in interest of the Partners to keep the Partnership books and records. The Partnership's net profits and losses shall be determined annually by such accountant in accordance with the accounting methods used by the Partnership for federal income tax purposes. Distributions shall be made to all Partners in accordance with their respective percentage interests in the Partnership, as soon as possible after the close of each Partnership fiscal year, or such other times as 66⅔% in interest of the Partners may determine.

9. *Control—Management.*

All major policy decisions affecting the business of the Partnership, including, without limitation thereto, the time and place of distributions, expenditures in excess of $500., the time and amount of additional capital contributions or other cash calls, if any, and decisions involving development, construction, loans, mortgages or other financing or refinancing, leases for all or substantially all of the Premises or substantially all of the improvements, and sale or other disposition of the Premises or any part thereof, shall require the approval of 66⅔% in interest of the Partners and action may be taken on behalf of the Partnership only upon such approval.

10. *Disposition of Partnership Interests.*

(a) With the exception of transfers from a Partner, by inter vivos gift, or by bequest or intestacy, to one or more persons consisting of his executor or administrator, spouse, child, child jointly with the spouse of such child, grandchild, or to a trustee for his spouse, child, child jointly with the spouse of such child, or grandchild, (subject to

compliance by each such transferee with paragraph (a)
(iii) of this Article), and except as otherwise provided in
Article 7(d), no Partner without the consent of all other
Partners, may convey, sell, assign, give, donate, pledge,
deposit or otherwise dispose of or encumber his interest,
or any part thereof except in accordance with the following
conditions:

(i) If any Partner shall desire to dispose of his interest in the Partnership other than as he is specifically permitted to do, he must first offer his interest to the remaining Partners, in writing, which offer shall state all the relevant terms including the terms of payment. Thereupon, the
remaining Partners shall have the right to acquire all,
but not less than all, of the interest being offered to them
in whatever proportions they may agree upon among themselves. Such offer may be accepted only by written notice
to the offering Partner, postmarked not later than midnight
on the 30th day after the date on which the offer has been
submitted by the offering Partner. In the event the remaining Partners fail or refuse to purchase the offering Partner's interest, the offering Partner shall have the right to
sell all (but not less than all) of his interest to any person
or group of persons of his choice for a period of three months
commencing at the expiration of the 30 day period referred
to above; provided, however, that the offering Partner may
not sell or otherwise dispose of his interest to any person
upon any terms more favorable to the prospective purchaser
than the terms previously offered the remaining Partners.
The terms referred to in the preceding sentence shall include only the aggregate price, the aggregate amount of
deferred payments (if any), the interest rate on any deferred payment, the length of time over which any deferred
payment may be made, and the time within which the purchaser may settle.

(ii) If during the aforesaid three month period the
offering Partner shall obtain a bona fide offer upon terms
more favorable to the prospective purchaser than the terms
previously offered to the remaining Partners, the offering
Partner, upon receiving such a bona fide written offer
from the prospective purchaser, shall, if he wishes to accept such offer, first offer the interest for sale to the remaining Partners on the same terms and conditions, and
the remaining Partners shall thereupon have the right to
acquire such interest by accepting such offer within a period
of 15 days from the date on which the offer is communi-
cated to them. If the remaining Partners fail or refuse to
accept such offer, the offering Partner shall have the right

to accept the offer of the prospective purchaser within a further period of 15 days thereafter. If the interest is not sold within the period provided herein, the terms and provisions of this Agreement, including subparagraphs (a)(i) and (a)(ii) of this Article shall continue to apply with respect to the said interest.

(iii) Each and every transfer shall be subject to the terms and conditions of this Agreement and any amendment or modification thereof with the same force and effect as if the transferee had originally been a party to this Agreement with all the rights and obligations of his transferor.

(iv) Before any transfer shall be valid, the transferee shall deliver to the other Partners a statement acknowledging that the transferee has read the provisions of this Agreement and intends to be legally bound by all the terms and conditions of this Agreement and any amendments or modifications thereof.

(b) Any person who shall succeed to the interest of a Partner by inter vivos gift or by bequest or intestacy, and any guardian or personal representative of any Partner who is deceased or adjudicated incompetent, shall not have any right to vote on any aspect of the Partnership business nor shall such person's consent be required for any Partnership decision which otherwise requires approval of all or some of the Partners. Wherever in this Agreement 66⅔% in interest of the Partners is required for any Partnership action, it shall mean 66⅔% of those eligible to participate in management.

11. *Involuntary Dispositions.* In the event of any application to a competent court by any judgment creditor of a Partner to charge the interest of the debtor Partner with payment of the unsatisfied amount of such judgment debt, or for appointment of a receiver for the debtor Partner's share of the profits, or in the event of any other form of legal proceeding or process by which the interest of any partner may be sold either voluntarily or involuntarily, including, without limitation thereto, the filing of any petition by or against any Partner under the Bankruptcy Act or any other state or federal law pertaining to insolvency, the other Partners shall have the right (unless said proceeding is discharged with prejudice within ninety days) to purchase the interest of such Partner or the Partner's personal representative or transferee. The other Partners shall have fifteen days after receipt of notice of any such occurrence within which to give written notice to the selling Partner or his personal representative or transferee of their election

to purchase the interest. Those Partners who elect to purchase shall do so in proportion to their relative interests in the Partnership.

The purchase price to be paid for such interest shall be the selling Partner's pro rata share of the fair market value of the Partnership assets on the date of institution of the proceedings giving rise to the transfer, less liabilities of the Partnership or liabilities to which property of the Partnership is subject on such date. Any amounts owed by the selling Partner pursuant to Article 7 shall be deducted from the purchase price. In the event of disagreement among the parties as to the fair market value, it shall be determined by an appraisal by a qualified real estate expert selected by the parties, and the opinion of the expert so chosen shall be final. In the event the parties are unable to agree upon an expert, fair market value shall be determined by an arbitrator in accordance with the rules of the American Arbitration Association then in force and the decision of such arbitrator shall be final and binding on all parties. One-half the costs of appraisal or arbitration shall be paid by the selling Partner and the other one-half shall be paid by the purchasing Partner or Partners.

12. *Term and Termination.*

(a) This Partnership shall continue until terminated by (i) the sale or other disposition of all or substantially all of the Partnership property, or (ii) the agreement of 66⅔% in interest of the Partners. Upon termination, the assets of the Partnership shall be liquidated and distributed in the following order: (A) sums owing to mortgagees and other creditors of the Partnership other than Partners; (B) sums, if any, owing to Partners other than for capital and profit; (C) sums owing to Partners in respect of capital; and (D) the balance, if any, shall be distributed to the Partners in accordance with their respective percentage interests.

13. *Banking.* The Partnership shall, promptly after execution hereof, open a bank account in the Partnership name in a commercial bank in the area of _____, _____. Checks written on the Partnership account shall require the signature of any two Partners. The Partnership will open and maintain such other bank accounts as the Partners may designate.

14. *Other Properties.* _____ hereby assigns to this Partnership all of his right, title and interest as Buyer in, to and under a certain Agreement of Sale dated _____ with _____ with respect to the Premises. The Partner-

ship hereby accepts such assignment and assumes _____ obligations under the said Agreement and agrees to indemnify him and hold him harmless from and against any loss, liability or damage thereunder. All of the Partners acknowledge that _____ is the equitable owner of two other tracts of land on _____ located adjacent to or near the Premises; nothing contained in this Agreement shall be construed to require _____ to assign his rights in the aforesaid two tracts to this Partnership. _____ may acquire legal title to the said two other tracts, or either of them, and develop, improve, lease, convey and otherwise deal with said tracts, or either of them, solely for his own account.

15. *Governing Law—Interpretation.*

(a) The Partners acknowledge that this Partnership Agreement has been made with reference to the laws of the State of _____ and accordingly this Agreement shall be construed in accordance with the laws of the State of _____.

(b) If any provision of this Agreement is held to be invalid, the remaining provisions of this Agreement shall not be affected thereby, but shall continue in full force and effect.

16. *Notices.* All notices, approvals and other communications required or permitted under the terms hereof, shall be in writing and delivered by registered or certified U.S. mail, postage prepaid, return receipt requested, to the address of the party to be charged with such notice set forth beside his signature on the final page hereof, or to such other address as the party to be charged with such notice may designate from time to time in the aforesaid manner.

17. *Entire Agreement.* This Agreement sets forth the entire understanding and agreement of the parties with respect to the subject matter of this Agreement, and there are no other promises, warranties, or understandings, oral or written, of any kind or nature whatsoever among them.

18. *Number of Gender.* For purposes of this Agreement, the masculine shall include the neuter and the feminine, and the singular shall include the plural, as the context may require.

19. *Successors and Assigns.* Subject to Article 10 hereof, this Agreement shall inure to the benefit of, and be binding upon, the parties hereto and their respective heirs, personal representatives and assigns.

20. *Miscellaneous.*

(a) So long as any Partner shall be in default hereunder, he shall have no right to participate in the management of the Partnership, and any distributions of Partnership funds during such period shall be made solely to the non-defaulting Partners.

(b) The remedies provided in this **Agreement** are in addition to and not in limitation of any remedy which the non-defaulting Partners may have at law or in equity, or by statute all of such rights and remedies being herein specifically reserved.

(c) In the event of the death of a Partner, the business of the Partnership shall not terminate, but shall be continued by the surviving Partners, subject to all of the terms, covenants and conditions of this Agreement.

21. *Captions.* The captions contained herein are only for the convenience of the parties. They are not a part of this Agreement and they do not modify, amplify or give full notice of the terms hereof.

IN WITNESS WHEREOF, the undersigned have hereunto affixed their hands and seals the day and year first above written.

—————————— [*Seal*]

ADDRESS:

—————————— [*Seal*]

ADDRESS:

By ———————— [*Seal*]

Attest ————————

ADDRESS

Limited Partnership Agreement
EXAMPLE

THIS AGREEMENT made as of the ———— day of ————, 19— in ———— Pennsylvania, by and among ———— a co-partnership formed under agreement dated February 11, 1965, which has its principal office at ————.

Pennsylvania (hereinafter referred to as the "General Partner") and the parties whose names appear on Schedule "A" attached to this Agreement and hereby made a part hereof (hereinafter referred to as the "Limited Partners") [the General Partner and the Limited Partners are sometimes hereinafter referred to collectively as the "Partners"].

WITNESSETH:

1. *Formation of Limited Partnership.* The parties hereto hereby form a limited partnership (sometimes hereinafter referred to as the "Partnership"), pursuant to the Uniform Limited Partnership Act of the Commonwealth of Pennsylvania, and agree to execute all instruments and documents in addition to this agreement which may be necessary to comply with the requirements of said Act.

2. *Name and Address.* The name of the Partnership shall be _____ LIMITED PARTNERSHIP, and its principal office shall be at _____ or such other place as the General Partner may designate upon ten days written notice to the Limited Partners.

3. *Purpose.* The sole purpose of this Partnership is to acquire for investment the property known as Philadelphia, Pennsylvania (the "Partnership Property").

4. *Term.* This Partnership shall commence as of the date hereof and shall continue for a period of 30 years unless sooner terminated pursuant to the provisions hereof.

5. *Capital Contributions.*

(a) The captialization of the partnership shall be $_____, which shall be contributed by the Limited Partners and by the General Partner as follows:

(b) The Limited Partners shall contribute as capital, in the aggregate, $_____, in cash; each Limited Partner shall contribute the portion thereof set forth next to his name on Schedule A, all of which has been received by the Partnership.

(c) The capital contribution of the General Partner, which shall be valued at $_____, shall be equitable title to the Partnership Property and any cash required to satisfy costs incurred in connection with the acquisition and improvement of the Partnership Property which shall not have been satisfied by the cash capital contributions of the Limited Partners and the proceeds of any mortgage to which the Partnership Property will be subject.

(d) The Limited Partners shall not be required to make any payments to the Partnership, or to any of its creditors, in money or in property, as loans, capital, or otherwise, except the capital contributions referred to above.

6. *Profits and Losses.*

(a) Except as provided in subparagraph (e) below the net profits of the Partnership (as hereinafter defined) shall be divided, and any losses shall be borne, by the Partners in accordance with their respective percentage interests in the Partnership set forth next to their names on Schedule A. All references in this agreement to a Partner's percentage interest or his pro rata share shall mean the percentage interest in the profits and losses set forth next to his name as aforesaid.

(b) For purposes of this agreement, the term "net profit" shall mean net profits derived from the Partnership Property, as determined in accordance with generally accepted accounting principles by the independent certified public accountants regularly engaged by the Partnership, except that in making such determination such accountants:

(i) shall not deduct any amounts for depreciation or amortization;

(ii) shall deduct all amounts (including interest and principal) paid on account of mortgages or other loans; and

(iii) if the General Partner, in its discretion, sets aside amounts as reserves for future capital needs, improvements, or contingencies, or if the General Partner pays for any such items from current income, the amounts set aside or paid, as the case may be, shall also be deducted.

(c) The net profits of the Partnership, as hereinabove defined, shall be distributed among all Partners in accordance with their respective percentage interests in the Partnership semi-annually, or more often at the discretion of the General Partner.

(d) All depreciation shall be allocated among the General and Limited Partners in accordance with their respective percentage interests in the Partnership.

(e) Notwithstanding anything to the contrary herein contained, the liability of the Limited Partners to creditors of the Partnership for the losses of the Partnership shall in no event exceed the aggregate amount of their respective capital contributions. Any such liabilities in excess of such contributions shall be the responsibility of the General Partner alone.

7. *Distribution of Proceeds of Mortgage Loans, Condemnation, Etc.*

All funds received by the Partnership by reason of the proceeds of mortgage loans, or from condemnation awards, or insurance covering destruction in whole or in part of the Partnership Property (except to the extent such funds are used to pay off existing mortgages or liens, or are expended for additions to or repair or restoration of the Partnership Property) shall, after the establishment of such reserves as the General Partner in its discretion may deem necessary, be divided among all the Partners in accordance with their respective percentage interests.

8. *Sale of Assets.* Notwithstanding anything to the contrary contained in Article 6 hereof, in the event of any sale or assignment of all or any portion of the Partnership Property (other than a sale or assignment as security for a loan to the Partnership) the net proceeds realized from such sale or assignment shall be allocated and distributed in the following order of priorities:

(a) Each Partner shall receive an amount equal to his cash capital contribution, reduced by any amounts he may previously have received pursuant to Article 7 above. If the funds available for distribution are less than the aggregate amount of Partners' capital contributions (reduced as set forth in the preceding sentence) the funds available shall be distributed among the Partners in proportion to their respective cash capital contributions.

(b) After the distribution referred to in subparagraph (a) above, there shall be distributed to the General Partner an amount equal to the difference between (i) the capitalization of the Partnership as set forth in Article 5(a) above, and (ii) the total of the original cash contributions of the General Partner and the Limited Partners (less the amount, if any, received by the General Partner pursuant to Article 7 above).

(c) The remainder, if any, shall be distributed among the Partners in proportion to their respective percentage interests in the Partnership.

9. *Bank Accounts.*

(a) All funds of the Partnership shall be deposited in such bank or banks as may from time to time be selected by _____ or a successor to _____ designated by the General Partner, in such account or accounts, and under such designations, as _____ or his successor may determine.

(b) Items for deposit, collection or discount belonging to the Partnership shall be deposited in the aforesaid accounts. Endorsement for deposit may be made by any person or persons authorized to sign checks as specified below, and such endorsement may be made in writing or by a stamp, with or without designation of the person so endorsing, or by a bank stamp endorsement.

(c) Checks, drafts, or other withdrawal orders for the payment of money out of Partnership bank accounts shall be signed by _____ or his successor, or by such person or persons as he shall, from time to time, authorize in writing to sign checks, drafts or orders upon such account, and any bank in which such an account is maintained is hereby authorized to honor instruments signed in accordance with this paragraph, regardless of the payee named in such check, draft or withdrawal order. _____ or his successor, is further authorized to cause checks for the payment of money out of any such account to be executed by means of a mechanical check signer, and in any such case, the bank in which an account is maintained on behalf of this Partnership is hereby authorized and directed to accept and pay out of moneys on deposit with it any and all checks bearing a facsimile signature of _____ or his successor, no matter by whom or how the said facsimile signature or signatures shall have been impressed thereon, the said facsimile signature or signatures to be in the form of a specimen furnished to the bank in which said account is maintained.

10. *Books and Records.* The Partnership shall maintain full and accurate books at _____ Pennsylvania, or such other place as shall be designated for such purposes by the General Partner, and all Partners shall have the right to inspect and examine such books at reasonable times. The books shall be closed and balanced at the end of each fiscal year. The General Partner agrees to deliver to the Limited Partners, after the expiration of each fiscal year of the Partnership, a balance sheet and profit and loss statement, together with a statement showing the capital accounts of each Partner, the distributions to each Partner, and the amount thereof reportable for federal tax purposes and for any state or local tax purposes.

11. *Management, Rights, Duties and Obligations of Partners.*

(a) *General Partner*: The General Partner shall manage the Partnership business and shall devote such time to the Partnership as shall be necessary to conduct the Partnership business in an efficient manner, and it shall be reimbursed by the Partnership for all costs expended and shall be entitled to make a reasonable charge for services rendered to this Partnership by the General Partner or any member of the General Partner. The General Partner shall have full charge of the management, conduct and operation of the Partnership business in all respects and in all matters, and in its absolute discretion shall have the power on behalf of the Partnership to do all of the following, upon such terms as the General Partner in its absolute discretion may deem proper:

(i) Deal in any Partnership assets, whether real estate or personalty, including, without limitation, sell, assign, exchange, or convey title to, and grant options for the sale of all or any portion of the Partnership Property, including any mortgage or leasehold interest or other realty or personalty which may be acquired by the Partnership; hold title to the Partnership Property in its own name, or the name of any member of the General Partner or any other party the General Partner may designate, as the nominee of this Limited Partnership; lease, or sublease, as the case may be, all or any portion of the Partnership Property without limit as to the term thereof, whether or not such term (including renewals and extensions thereof) extends beyond the date of the termination of the Partnership; borrow money and as security therefor encumber all or any part of the Partnership Property; obtain refinancing of any mortgage or mortgages or any deed of trust or deeds of trust placed on the Partnership Property, or repay them in whole or in part; increase, modify, consolidate or extend any mortgage or mortgages or deed of trust or deeds of trust placed on the property; and invest any surplus or reserve funds of the Partnership.

(ii) Employ from time to time persons, firms, or corporations for the operation and management of the Partnership Property, including without limitation, rental agents, accountants and attorneys on such terms and for such compensation as the General Partner shall determine, notwithstanding the General Partner or any partner of the General Partner, or members of their families or corporations in which they have an interest, may have a financial interest in such firms or corporations;

(iii) Execute, acknowledge and deliver any and all instruments to effectuate the foregoing, including, without limitation, deeds, assignments, mortgages, bills of sale, leases, and other contracts;

(iv) Possess, without limitation, all of the powers and rights of General Partners in a partnership formed under the Limited Partnership Act of the Commonwealth of Pennsylvania.

(v) The General Partner shall in no event be liable to the Limited Partners for any act or omission performed or omitted by it in pursuance of the authority granted to it by this agreement, except in case of fraud or gross negligence.

(b) *Limited Partners*: The Limited Partners shall take no part in, or interfere in any manner with the management, conduct or control of the Partnership business or the sale, leasing or refinancing of its assets and shall have no right or authority to act for or bind the Partnership.

12. *Assignment of General Partner's Interest.* The General Partner shall not assign, pledge, encumber, sell or otherwise dispose of all or any portion of its interest as General Partner in the Partnership.

13. *Assignment of Limited Partners' Interest.* No Limited Partner shall have the right to substitute an assignee, legatee or distributee in his place, except on the following terms and conditions:

(a) No assignee, legatee or distributee of the whole or any portion of a Limited Partner's interest in the Partnership shall have the right to become a Substitute Limited Partner in a place of his predecessor in interest with respect to the whole or any portion of said interest without the written consent of the General Partner, which shall not be unreasonably withheld.

(b) As a condition to his or her admission as a Substitute Limited Partner with respect to the whole or any portion of the interest of his predecessor in interest, such assignee, legatee, or distributee shall execute and acknowledge such instruments, in form and substance satisfactory to the General Partner, as the General Partner shall deem necessary or desirable to effectuate such admission and to confirm the agreement of the Substitute Limited Partner to be bound by all of the terms and provisions of this agreement and any amendments hereto. Such assignee, legatee or distributee shall pay all reasonable expenses in connection with such admission as a Substitute Limited Partner, including, without limitation, legal fees and the cost of the preparation, filing and publishing any amendment to the Certificate of Limited Partnership if necessary or desirable in connection therewith.

14. *Bankruptcy, Insolvency or Assignment for Benefit of Creditors for the Limited Partner.*

If any Limited Partner shall take advantage of any bankruptcy or insolvency act, or if any insolvency petition shall be filed against any Limited Partner and final adjudication of insolvency or bankruptcy entered thereon, or if any Limited Partner shall make an assignment for the benefit of his creditors, then within thirty (30) days after any such adjudication or assignment, the General Partner may, at its option, purchase such Limited Partner's interest in the Partnership at a price equal to that Limited Partner's pro rata share of the fair market value of (a) the Partnership Property, less (b) obligations of the Partnership or obligations to which the Partnership Property is subject, as of the date such person is adjudicated a bankrupt or insolvent, or the date of the assignment for the benefit of creditors, as the case may be. The Limited Partner's trustee in bankruptcy or other legal representative shall execute such documents, in form satisfactory to the General Partner, as may be necessary to evidence and effect such transfer. If such trustee or legal representative fails or refuses to execute such documents, the General Partner is hereby irrevocably authorized to execute them in the name of, and on behalf of the Limited Partner, as the attorney-in-fact for such Limited Partner. Purchase of the Limited Partner's interest as aforesaid shall be consummated for cash within sixty (60) days after the General Partner has exercised its option by notice in writing to the Limited Partner or his trustee or personal representative. In the event of disagreement as to the fair market value of the Partnership Property, the matter shall be submitted to a mutually acceptable M.A.I. appraiser having a place of business in the county in which the Partnership Property is situate, and his decision shall be final and binding. The cost of appraisal shall be divided equally between the seller and the General Partner.

15. *Termination.* The Partnership may be terminated by the General Partner prior to the end of its term, upon at least thirty (30) days prior written notice by the General Partner to the Limited Partners. In such event, the General Partner shall wind up and liquidate the business of this Partnership by selling the Partnership's assets and distributing the net proceeds therefrom, after the payment of Partnership's liabilities, in accordance with the following Article.

16. *Distributions on Liquidation.*

(a) On liquidation, the Partnership assets shall be distributed in payment of the liabilities of the Partnership in the following order:

(i) To the payment of the debts and liabilities of the Partnership and the expenses of liquidation, including a sales commission to the selling agent, if any.

(ii) To the setting up of any reserves which the General Partner deems reasonably necessary for any contingent or unforeseen liabilities or obligations of the Partnership or of the General Partner arising out of or in connection with the Partnership. At the expiration of such period as the General Partner shall deem advisable, the balance thereof, if any, shall be distributed in the manner provided in this Article, and in the order named.

(iii) To the payment of the Partners in the same manner as set forth in Article 8.

(b) A reasonable time, as determined by the General Partner, not to exceed one year, shall be allowed for the orderly liquidation of the assets of the Partnership and the discharge of liabilities to creditors so as to enable the General Partner to minimize any losses attendant upon liquidation.

(c) Anything in this Agreement to the contrary notwithstanding, the General Partner shall not be personally liable for the return of the capital contributions of the Limited Partners, or any portion thereof; it is expressly understood that any such return shall be made solely from Partnership assets. Without limitation of the foregoing, the General Partner shall not be required to pay to the Partnership or the Limited Partners any deficit in the General Partner's capital account upon dissolution or otherwise. The Limited Partners shall not have the right to demand or receive any property other than cash in connection with termination and liquidation of the Partnership.

17. *Notices.* All notices required or permitted to be given pursuant to this agreement shall be in writing and shall be sent by registered or certified mail, return receipt requested, to each Limited Partner at the address set forth on Schedule A, or to such other place as the person to be charged with such notice may direct in the aforesaid manner. Notices to the Partnership or to the General Partner shall be sent to the principal office of the General Partner.

Chapter Eight

REAL ESTATE MORTGAGES

Part One

RESIDENTIAL MORTGAGES

I. INTRODUCTION

A mortgage is a means by which a creditor can obtain an interest in a debtor's real property. The use of mortgages as a security device in connection with the lending of money began with the break-up of the feudal system and the inception of a money economy in England. Pursuant to the earliest known form of a mortgage, a creditor (the "mortgagee") was granted possession of the land of his debtor (the "mortgagor") and was permitted to keep any rents or profits without applying them to the reduction of the debt. The rents or profits took the place of interest[1] on the debt and the mortgagor was expected to repay the debt out of his other resources. Mortgages in their modern form became more common as the capitalist system began to develop between 1200 and 1450. Under the modern form of mortgage, the mortgagor retains possession and use of the property.

For the present purposes, a mortgage may be defined as "any form of written instrument whereby a lien is created upon real estate or whereby title to real estate is reserved or conveyed as security for the payment of a debt or fulfillment of other obligations". Some states adhere to a "title theory" of mortgages. In such states, a mortgage is considered to be a technical conveyance or transfer of real estate by the mortgagor to the mortgagee, given to secure performance of an obligation, most commonly repayment of a debt. If and when the debt has been paid the conveyance becomes null and void and the property reverts to the debtor. In other states, known as "lien theory" states, the creation of the mortgage does not constitute a technical conveyance, but simply creates an immediate lien against the mortgaged real estate. The practical differences between the two theories are of little significance. In either case, the mortgagee holds an interest in the land only as security for the debt and must surrender that interest when the debt has been repaid.

---

1. Interest in the form of money was considered usury during that era and was unlawful.

211

In some states, particularly in the South and the West, deeds of trust are used instead of mortgages. There are several technical differences of form between a mortgage and a deed of trust. However, the purposes of the two instruments are the same. Under a deed of trust, the debtor transfers the property to a trustee who holds title to the real estate in trust until the debt is paid, whereupon the trustee reconveys the property to the debtor. If the debt is not repaid in accordance with its terms, the trustee will either sell the property and pay the proceeds to the creditor, or transfer title to the creditor.

If the debtor's obligations are not discharged, the mortgagee may obtain title to the real estate [2] or sell it to others. Nevertheless, to protect debtors from the loss of their lands because of technical or insignificant defaults, English courts of equity from an early date intervened on behalf of debtors. To redress the harsh and technical treatment sometimes imposed by creditors, courts of equity began to force reconveyance by the creditors even when the debtor had failed to perform completely or promptly. The equity courts gradually developed as a remedy for debtors a right to reacquire or "redeem" the real estate, notwithstanding incomplete or imperfect performance. Even now a mortgagor's rights in mortgaged real estate are referred to as the "equity" or "equity of redemption".

Although a mortgagor is entitled to protection against harsh and unreasonable remedies, the mortgagee must be able at some point to extinguish or "foreclose" the mortgagor's right to redeem his "equity of redemption". The practice developed whereby a mortgagee, after a default had occurred, would file suit in a court of equity to obtain a decree foreclosing the mortgagor's right to redeem the property. Once that decree had been entered, the mortgagee was free to sell the property to anyone it might choose. The foreclosure sale is the direct lineal descendant of the English decree in equity foreclosing the borrower's right to redeem.

The purpose of the following sections of these materials is to outline for the student the basic transactions and situations for which mortgages are created, and to review the documentation and activity involved in different kinds of mortgage transactions. The basic mortgage documents for residential, industrial-commercial and construction mortgages have many similarities, but they also each have many distinguishing characteristics. The greater risks in commercial and construction mortgages result in more complex documentation of the transactions. In this chapter we will discuss residential, commercial-industrial, construction and industrial development authority mortgages, and also the subject of foreclosure.

---

2. In a title theory state the mortgagee technically has title from the outset.

II. RESIDENTIAL MORTGAGES

The purchase of a home is the largest single investment most people ever make. It is not surprising to find that in most cases the buyer of a home does not have all of the funds required to complete the purchase. Normally he will have to finance part of the cost by borrowing the money, usually from a bank, insurance company or savings and loan association. Accordingly, most home buyers will insist that the agreement under which they purchase a home contain a provision which makes their obligation to purchase contingent on being able to obtain a satisfactory mortgage loan. Such mortgage contingency clauses were discussed in Chapter Two of these materials.

A. METHODS OF REPAYMENT

1. Interest

When a borrower borrows money to finance the purchase of real property, he must repay the amount of money borrowed, usually called the "principal", and pay the lender an amount, usually known as "interest", for use of the money for the period of time that it has been borrowed. The total dollar amount of interest which will be paid by the borrower over the life of a loan is dependent upon the rate of interest and the length of time for which the money is borrowed, as well as the amount of the loan.

The interest rate charged by a lender is traditionally stated as a percentage charge for use of money for a period of one year. Therefore, if one borrows $1,000 at 9% interest, he would pay $90 per year in interest (.09 × $1,000). If he were to repay the loan in six months he would pay $45 interest (.09 × 6/12 × $1,000). The interest is stated on an annual basis, but is recalculated for shorter time periods. The interest can be calculated on a monthly basis by multiplying the rate by 1/12 or on a daily basis by multiplying by 1/365.[3]

PROBLEMS

1. What is the interest on $1,500 at 8% for one year?

2. What is the interest on $2,500 at 6% for nine months?

2. Principal

It is possible to borrow money for a specified period of time (the "term" of the loan) and repay the principal as a lump sum at the end of the term of the loan. Such a loan is said to have a "bal-

---

3. Because of the varying lengths of months and also because of leap year certain conventions have been generally adopted concerning the calculation of interest. Often, for example, the year is treated as if it consisted of 12 months of 30 days each, and banks often charge daily interest by multiplying annual interest by 1/360 rather than by 1/365. A 360 day year is often called a "banker's year".

loon payment" at the end, because the final payment is so much larger than the period payments of interest only that it is like a balloon on the end of a string. Interest-only balloon loans [4] were the usual type of mortgage loan, both residential and commercial, until the Depression. Many lenders found during the Depression that balloon loans did not afford them sufficient security upon default, especially in a time of declining real estate values, since they had to look to the mortgaged property for recovery of the entire principal sum of the loan. Therefore, lenders sought a form of loan which would involve gradual repayment of principal during the term of the loan, thus reducing their dependence on the value of the mortgaged property as the loan was paid off. Presently, full or partial balloon loans are used almost exclusively in a commercial context. Residential mortgages are structured to include periodic payments of portions of the borrowed principal as well as interest.

There are many possible methods of repaying principal. For example, the same amount of principal could be repaid with each installment. A twenty year loan of $24,000 could be repaid in 240 monthly installments of $100 each plus interest on the then outstanding principal balance. With this method of payment the interest payments will change each month and payments will be large in early years and decline in later years. For homeowners, that is often a serious problem if earnings are expected to rise in the future. In order to illustrate the problem there is a chart set forth below indicating several monthly payments on a 9% loan of $24,000 for 20 years:

Time of Payment	Principal Unpaid	Principal	Interest	Total Amount Of Payment
Month # 1	24,000	100	180	280
Month # 2	23,900	100	179.25	279.25
Month # 3	23,800	100	178.50	278.50
*	*	*	*	*
Month # 100	14,000	100	105	205
Month # 200	4,000	100	30	130
Month # 240	100	100	0.75	100.75

Most homeowners would prefer to make a constant monthly payment of principal and interest combined over the life of a loan. In order to accommodate that desire, financial institutions have developed the "level payment" loan. Other names such as "level monthly payment", "self-amortizing" or "self-liquidating" loan are often used to describe this loan. The amount of the level payment is calculated so that if the payment is first applied to interest with the re-

---

4. Also known as "standing" loans, since the principal stands the same throughout the term of the loan.

mainder reducing principal, the loan will reduce to $0 by 240 equal payments. For example, the level payment necessary to repay a $24,000 loan at 9% per annum interest over 20 years is $215.93 per month. That portion of the $215.93 payment which is necessary to cover the interest for the prior month is paid first and the balance is applied to the principal. As noted above, the interest due after the first month of this loan was $180 ($24,000 × .09 = $2,160; $2,-160 ÷ 12 = $180.) Thus, the first month's payment will be applied $180 to interest and $35.93 in principal. In the second month the borrower will have an outstanding principal balance of $23,964.07 ($24,000 − $35.93). The interest due for this month is $179.73 ($23,-964.07 × .09 = $2,156.75; $2,156.75 ÷ 12 = $179.73). The $179.73 is paid first and $36.20 is applied to principal. Each month the interest portion of the payment decreases and the principal portion increases. By the end of the term of the loan the interest portion is very small and the principal portion is almost the whole level payment.

The following amortization table shows the portion of each installment payment that is applied to principal and interest during the life of a 20 year, $24,000 mortgage at 9%. See pages 216–217.

B. THE APPLICATION FOR A MORTGAGE

Once the purchaser and seller have signed a residential agreement of sale, the purchaser will apply to a lending institution for a loan. The lender will insist upon obtaining certain information from the purchaser before considering the request for a loan, including: the purchase price of the property; the percentage of the purchase price that the purchaser desires to borrow; the purchaser's income (to determine whether it is sufficient to pay the normal expenses and make the monthly payment on the mortgage); the purchaser's reputation and credit standing in the community; and the borrower's other financial resources. The lender will require the purchaser to complete an application form, and, usually, to pay fees for a credit report and for an appraisal of the property.

Upon receipt of an application, the lender will obtain a report on the borrower's credit from an independent credit investigating agency, and will have an appraisal made to ascertain the approximate fair market value of the property. The lender will also require a signed copy of the agreement of sale to confirm the existence and terms of the agreement of sale.

In most conventional residential mortgage loan situations, the purchaser wishes to borrow from 50% to 80% of the purchase price. However, there are cases in which the buyer finds it necessary to borrow as much as 95% of the purchase price. Obviously, the less "equi-

EXAMPLE: Schedule of Direct Reduction Loan

Amortization Schedule

ANNUAL % RATE	PAYMENT $	LOAN $	TERM: YEARS	MONTHS	PERIODS
9.000	215.94	24,000.00	20		240

PAY'T NO.	INTEREST PAYMENT	PRINCIPAL PAYMENT	BALANCE OF LOAN	PAY'T NO.	INTEREST PAYMENT	PRINCIPAL PAYMENT	BALANCE OF LOAN
1	180.00	35.94	23,964.06	61	159.67	56.27	21,233.02
2	179.73	36.21	23,927.85	62	159.25	56.69	21,176.33
3	179.46	36.48	23,891.37	63	158.82	57.12	21,119.21
4	179.19	36.75	23,854.62	64	158.39	57.55	21,061.66
5	178.91	37.03	23,817.59	65	157.96	57.98	21,003.68
6	178.63	37.31	23,780.28	66	157.53	58.41	20,945.27
7	178.35	37.59	23,742.69	67	157.09	58.85	20,886.42
8	178.07	37.87	23,704.82	68	156.65	59.29	20,827.13
9	177.79	38.15	23,666.67	69	156.20	59.74	20,767.39
10	177.50	38.44	23,628.23	70	155.76	60.18	20,707.21
11	177.21	38.73	23,589.50	71	155.30	60.64	20,646.57
12	176.92	39.02	23,550.48	72	154.85	61.09	20,585.48
13	176.63	39.31	23,511.17	73	154.39	61.55	20,523.93
14	176.33	39.61	23,471.56	74	153.93	62.01	20,461.92
15	176.04	39.90	23,431.66	75	153.46	62.48	20,399.44
16	175.74	40.20	23,391.45	76	153.00	62.94	20,336.50
17	175.44	40.50	23,350.95	77	152.52	63.42	20,273.08
18	175.13	40.81	23,310.15	78	152.05	63.89	20,209.19
19	174.83	41.11	23,269.04	79	151.57	64.37	20,144.82
20	174.52	41.42	23,227.62	80	151.09	64.85	20,079.97
21	174.21	41.73	23,185.89	81	150.60	65.34	20,014.63
22	173.89	42.05	23,143.84	82	150.11	65.83	19,948.80
23	173.58	42.36	23,101.48	83	149.62	66.32	19,882.48
24	173.26	42.68	23,058.80	84	149.12	66.82	19,815.66
25	172.94	43.00	23,015.80	85	148.62	67.32	19,748.34
26	172.62	43.32	22,972.48	86	148.11	67.83	19,680.51
27	172.29	43.65	22,928.83	87	147.60	68.34	19,612.17
28	171.97	43.97	22,884.86	88	147.09	68.85	19,543.32
29	171.64	44.30	22,840.56	89	146.57	69.37	19,473.95
30	171.30	44.64	22,795.92	90	146.05	69.89	19,404.06
31	170.97	44.97	22,750.95	91	145.53	70.41	19,333.65
32	170.63	45.31	22,705.64	92	145.00	70.94	19,262.71
33	170.29	45.65	22,659.99	93	144.47	71.47	19,191.24
34	169.95	45.99	22,614.00	94	143.93	72.01	19,119.23
35	169.61	46.33	22,567.67	95	143.39	72.55	19,046.68
36	169.26	46.68	22,520.99	96	142.85	73.09	18,973.59
37	168.91	47.03	22,473.96	97	142.30	73.64	18,899.95
38	168.55	47.39	22,426.57	98	141.75	74.19	18,825.76
39	168.20	47.74	22,378.83	99	141.19	74.75	18,751.01
40	167.84	48.10	22,330.73	100	140.63	75.31	18,675.70
41	167.48	48.46	22,282.27	101	140.07	75.87	18,599.83
42	167.12	48.82	22,233.45	102	139.50	76.44	18,523.39
43	166.75	49.19	22,184.26	103	138.93	77.01	18,446.38
44	166.38	49.56	22,134.70	104	138.35	77.59	18,368.79
45	166.01	49.93	22,084.77	105	137.77	78.17	18,290.62
46	165.64	50.30	22,034.47	106	137.18	78.76	18,211.86
47	165.26	50.68	21,983.79	107	136.59	79.35	18,132.51
48	164.88	51.06	21,932.73	108	135.99	79.95	18,052.56
49	164.50	51.44	21,881.29	109	135.39	80.55	17,972.01
50	164.11	51.83	21,829.46	110	134.79	81.15	17,890.86
51	163.72	52.22	21,777.24	111	134.18	81.76	17,809.10
52	163.33	52.61	21,724.63	112	133.57	82.37	17,726.73
53	162.93	53.01	21,671.62	113	132.95	82.99	17,643.74
54	162.54	53.40	21,618.22	114	132.33	83.61	17,560.13
55	162.14	53.80	21,564.42	115	131.70	84.24	17,475.89
56	161.73	54.21	21,510.21	116	131.07	84.87	17,391.02
57	161.33	54.61	21,455.60	117	130.43	85.51	17,305.51
58	160.92	55.02	21,400.58	118	129.79	86.15	17,219.36
59	160.50	55.44	21,345.14	119	129.15	86.79	17,132.57
60	160.09	55.85	21,289.29	120	128.49	87.45	17,045.12

The final payment is usually somewhat different from the regular payment, and is shown starred on the last line.

[B7815]

ANNUAL % RATE	PAYMENT $	LOAN $	TERM: YEARS	MONTHS	PERIODS
9.000	215.94	24,000.00	20		240

PAY'T NO.	INTEREST PAYMENT	PRINCIPAL PAYMENT	BALANCE OF LOAN	PAY'T NO.	INTEREST PAYMENT	PRINCIPAL PAYMENT	BALANCE OF LOAN
121	127.84	88.10	16,957.02	181	78.00	137.94	10,262.19
122	127.18	88.76	16,868.26	182	76.97	138.97	10,123.22
123	126.51	89.43	16,778.83	183	75.92	140.02	9,983.20
124	125.84	90.10	16,688.73	184	74.87	141.07	9,842.13
125	125.17	90.77	16,597.96	185	73.82	142.12	9,700.01
126	124.48	91.46	16,506.50	186	72.75	143.19	9,556.82
127	123.80	92.14	16,414.36	187	71.68	144.26	9,412.56
128	123.11	92.83	16,321.53	188	70.59	145.35	9,267.21
129	122.41	93.53	16,228.00	189	69.50	146.44	9,120.77
130	121.71	94.23	16,133.77	190	68.41	147.53	8,973.24
131	121.00	94.94	16,038.83	191	67.30	148.64	8,824.60
132	120.29	95.65	15,943.18	192	66.18	149.76	8,674.84
133	119.57	96.37	15,846.81	193	65.06	150.88	8,523.96
134	118.85	97.09	15,749.72	194	63.93	152.01	8,371.95
135	118.12	97.82	15,651.90	195	62.79	153.15	8,218.80
136	117.39	98.55	15,553.35	196	61.64	154.30	8,064.50
137	116.65	99.29	15,454.06	197	60.48	155.46	7,909.04
138	115.91	100.03	15,354.03	198	59.32	156.62	7,752.42
139	115.16	100.78	15,253.25	199	58.14	157.80	7,594.62
140	114.40	101.54	15,151.71	200	56.96	158.98	7,435.64
141	113.64	102.30	15,049.41	201	55.77	160.17	7,275.47
142	112.87	103.07	14,946.34	202	54.57	161.37	7,114.10
143	112.10	103.84	14,842.50	203	53.36	162.58	6,951.52
144	111.32	104.62	14,737.88	204	52.14	163.80	6,787.72
145	110.53	105.41	14,632.47	205	50.91	165.03	6,622.69
146	109.74	106.20	14,526.27	206	49.67	166.27	6,456.42
147	108.95	106.99	14,419.28	207	48.42	167.52	6,288.90
148	108.14	107.80	14,311.48	208	47.17	168.77	6,120.13
149	107.34	108.60	14,202.88	209	45.90	170.04	5,950.09
150	106.52	109.42	14,093.46	210	44.63	171.31	5,778.78
151	105.70	110.24	13,983.22	211	43.34	172.60	5,606.18
152	104.87	111.07	13,872.15	212	42.05	173.89	5,432.29
153	104.04	111.90	13,760.25	213	40.74	175.20	5,257.09
154	103.20	112.74	13,647.51	214	39.43	176.51	5,080.58
155	102.36	113.58	13,533.93	215	38.10	177.84	4,902.74
156	101.50	114.44	13,419.49	216	36.77	179.17	4,723.57
157	100.65	115.29	13,304.20	217	35.43	180.51	4,543.06
158	99.78	116.16	13,188.04	218	34.07	181.87	4,361.19
159	98.91	117.03	13,071.01	219	32.71	183.23	4,177.96
160	98.03	117.91	12,953.10	220	31.33	184.61	3,993.35
161	97.15	118.79	12,834.31	221	29.95	185.99	3,807.36
162	96.26	119.68	12,714.63	222	28.56	187.38	3,619.98
163	95.36	120.58	12,594.05	223	27.15	188.79	3,431.19
164	94.46	121.48	12,472.57	224	25.73	190.21	3,240.98
165	93.54	122.40	12,350.17	225	24.31	191.63	3,049.35
166	92.63	123.31	12,226.85	226	22.87	193.07	2,856.28
167	91.70	124.24	12,102.62	227	21.42	194.52	2,661.76
168	90.77	125.17	11,977.45	228	19.96	195.98	2,465.78
169	89.83	126.11	11,851.34	229	18.49	197.45	2,268.33
170	88.89	127.05	11,724.29	230	17.01	198.93	2,069.40
171	87.93	128.01	11,596.28	231	15.52	200.42	1,868.98
172	86.97	128.97	11,467.31	232	14.02	201.92	1,667.06
173	86.00	129.94	11,337.37	233	12.50	203.44	1,463.62
174	85.03	130.91	11,206.46	234	10.98	204.96	1,258.66
175	84.05	131.89	11,074.57	235	9.44	206.50	1,052.16
176	83.06	132.88	10,941.69	236	7.89	208.05	844.11
177	82.06	133.88	10,807.81	237	6.33	209.61	634.50
178	81.06	134.88	10,672.93	238	4.76	211.18	423.32
179	80.05	135.89	10,537.04	239	3.17	212.77	210.55
180	79.03	136.91	10,400.13	240	1.58	210.55	.00

FINAL PAYMENT: 212.13

The final payment is usually somewhat different from the regular payment, and is shown starred on the last line.

TOTAL INTEREST: 27821.79

TOTAL PRINCIPLE: 24000.00
SUM OF BALANCES: 3709572.82   21

[B7816]

ty"[5] in the purchase, the greater the lender's risk, because the lender has less assurance that it will be able to sell the property, in the event of a default, at a price which will pay all expenses of foreclosure, unpaid interest and the balance due on the loan.

To assist purchasers of modest means who lack funds for a substantial down payment, certain governmental or quasi-governmental agencies, such as the Federal Housing Administration (FHA) or the Veterans Administration (VA) will, under certain circumstances, issue a guarantee of repayment to the lender.[6] Upon application by a qualified borrower, the FHA or VA will agree to guarantee payment to a lender of substantially the entire amount of the loan. The credit backing of the United States government makes such loans much more attractive to institutional lenders, who might otherwise be prevented by regulation or banking policy from making such loans. You should be aware that, as a condition to issuing a guarantee, both the FHA and the VA impose certain requirements. For example, FHA and VA may insist that the real estate meet certain minimum standards pertaining to quality and safety of construction. VA and FHA also have qualifying requirements as to the maximum amount of money which an applicant may earn and the maximum amount of the loan. FHA and VA also require that the interest rate to be charged the borrower not exceed certain specific rates which the FHA and VA from time to time determine.[7] If the maximum interest rate FHA will allow on a mortgage is less than the then prevailing market rate of interest, the lender, as a condition for making the FHA insured loan, may require a lump sum payment at the outset in addition to the periodic payments of interest. Making a lump sum payment is referred to as paying "points". A point equals one per cent of the amount of the mortgage.[8] The points are calculated to provide the lender with the same "yield" or income on the loan

5. When mortgage lenders speak of "equity" they mean the difference between the value of the property and the principal sum of the mortgage. If the mortgaged property has a value equal to the purchase price, then the purchaser's equity will initially be that portion of the purchase price that the purchaser pays out of his or her own pocket.

6. The programs of other agencies, such as the Federal National Mortgage Association ("FNMA" or "Fanny Mae"), the Government National Mortgage Association ("GNMA" or "Ginny Mae") and the Federal Home Loan Mortgage Corporation ("FHLMC" or "Freddy Mac") are usually programs by which the agencies agree to purchase mortgages that are not in default rather than to insure mortgages.

7. State laws regulating interest rates typically exempt VA and FHA loans.

8. A $900 lump sum payment on a $30,-000 mortgage is a payment of 3 points. Even in a conventionally financed transaction, a lender may require a payment of a "placement fee" or "origination fee" as a consideration for making the loan. Lawyers often refer to such fees as points. Ostensibly, these fees are intended to cover the expenses of the lender in considering the application. In fact, in many cases the charging of a placement fee is simply a way of increasing the net income which the lender will realize upon the transaction.

which he would have received over the period of the loan if the loan had been made at the market rate of interest rather than the FHA rate. The applicable law usually provides that points must be paid by the seller rather than the purchaser, because the points are additional interest and, if the purchaser were to pay them, the loan would be in violation of the legally permitted limit. As a result, the seller who is selling his property under an FHA insured loan will seek a somewhat higher price to offset the points the seller will have to pay.

The FHA and VA guarantee is like an insurance policy for the lender. The borrower pays a premium equal to an extra $\frac{1}{2}\%$ in interest per year which goes to the FHA or VA to finance the program. Of late, private companies have entered the field of mortgage insurance. These companies operate in similar fashion to the FHA or VA. However, they do not require that the property meet the same sort of standards, nor do they limit the amount of interest that may be charged by the lender. In many cases the private mortgage insurance only applies until the borrower has repaid a portion of the loan. Normally this point is reached when the borrower has paid principal in an amount so that the remaining principal balance is equal to or less than 80% of the purchae price of the property.

C. ISSUANCE OF COMMITMENT LETTER

If the lender is satisfied with the property and with the credit standing of the borrower, and if the lender is willing to make the loan on the terms contained in the application, it will issue to the borrower a letter, commonly known as a "commitment letter". In the commitment letter the lender will agree to lend a specific amount of money to the borrower on terms and conditions set out in the commitment letter. A commitment letter is technically an offer to make a loan on the conditions set forth in the letter. The lender will require the buyer to countersign the commitment letter and return a copy to the lender, indicating the borrower's acceptance of the offer. Once the offer has been accepted, the commitment constitutes a contract to lend and borrow between lender and borrower, provided the conditions imposed on the borrower are met. Those conditions are discussed in Section D below. See **Example: Commitment Letter (Residential Mortgage)** on page 224.

D. PREPARATION FOR SETTLEMENT

Having received the commitment letter, the borrower and his or her attorney must begin to prepare for settlement. As we discussed in Chapter Two, the settlement is the time when the purchaser will acquire the new home, partially with funds obtained from the lender. It will often be the task of the legal assistant to prepare for settlement in accordance with the commitment letter, and also in accordance with the agreement of sale. Some of the usual requirements of the commitment are as follows:

1. Mortgage Documents

In connection with a mortgage loan it is usually necessary to create two documents. The first is a mortgage note, or bond, which evidences and creates the debt and which sets forth the terms for repayment. The second is a mortgage which grants a security interest in the mortgaged property in case the debt is not repaid. In most instances, the mortgage documents are prepared by the lender on its own forms. In some localities, it is customary for the borrower's attorney to prepare the mortgage documents, but normally they are prepared upon forms furnished or approved by the lender. The form and content of the mortgage documents are considered more fully in Section VI of this chapter.

2. Title Search

The lender will require that a competent person, who may be an abstractor or conveyancer, a title company, or an attorney, search the public records to ascertain who now owns the property and what persons, if any, other than the record owner, have any rights in the property. In this manner, the lender will be assured that at settlement the borrower can properly create a mortgage which will constitute a first lien on the property. In many localities, lenders require that the borrower purchase title insurance. Under this procedure, an insurance company issues an insurance policy to the lender, not insuring repayment of the mortgage loan, but insuring the validity and priority of the mortgage lien. If the borrower does not own the property because of some technical defect in title or if the mortgage is defective and cannot be foreclosed because of a defect in the execution or recording of the mortgage instrument, the title insurance company will protect the mortgagee against economic loss.

In the typical residential transaction the seller has the legal obligation to convey good and marketable title, and thus has the burden of clearing title. This involves presenting to the lender or to the title company, as the case may be, various documents required to remove from the public records any lien for judgments, unpaid taxes, unpaid water or sewer rent, prior mortgages, and the like, which might take priority over the lien of the mortgage being created.

3. Termite and Other Certificates

In some instances, particularly in an FHA insured mortgage, the lender may require the borrower to produce a certificate with respect to the condition of the premises being purchased, such as the roof, the plumbing or the electrical work. Such certificates may be obtained, for a fee, from reputable roofers, plumbers and electricians. The lender may also require the borrower to produce a certificate from a termite exterminating company to the effect that the premises are free of termites and other wood-boring insects and free of damage that was caused by such insects.

4. Insurance

Since the lender is depending to a large extent upon the value of the real estate as security for repayment of the debt, the lender will want to be protected in the event any buildings on the property are destroyed or damaged by fire, wind, or other casualty. Accordingly, the lender will normally require that the borrower deliver at settlement a fire insurance policy, in a form and with a company approved by the lender, in an amount not less than the amount of the mortgage loan. The lender will also require that the policy have a "mortgagee endorsement", the effect of which is to require the insurance company, in the event of loss, to prepare its check for the amount of the loss to the order of both the borrower and the lender. This insurance fund, at least temporarily, takes the place of the destroyed structure as security for the loan. The mortgage documents will normally contain provisions for the disbursement of the insurance funds once they are received from the insurance company. The insurance company is also required to give notice to the lender in the event the policy is to be cancelled.

5. Closing

If the borrower is using borrowed funds to purchase real estate, the closing [9] on the mortgage loan will usually take place at the same time as the closing on the purchase of the real estate. This combined closing will be discussed in detail in Chapter Eleven. At closing, the borrower will sign the note and the mortgage and deliver them to the lender, together with the fire insurance policy and any required certificates concerning the condition of the property. The lender will in turn deliver its check to the borrower, or to the title company which is going to insure the borrower's title and the lender's lien, for disbursement to the seller. The title company, or the attorney, if no title company is employed, will then make up a settlement sheet showing the amount advanced by the lender and the charges due the lender. In connection with this, the lender will sometimes require that the following sums be paid at the closing:

(a) Interest to the First Day of the First Regular Interest Period

Occasionally, lenders charge interest in advance so that interest paid May 1 will be for the period May 1 to May 31. Most lenders, however, charge interest in arrears, so that interest paid on May 1 will be for the period April 1 to April 30. Most lenders have a standard due date for all their loans, usually on the first or the fifteenth

---

9. Remember that "closing" and "settlement" are synonymous.

of each month, regardless of the day that closing takes place. Each of the monthly payments, including the first, is equal to all the others. It is therefore usually necessary at settlement to collect a certain amount of interest in advance in order to reconcile all of the above. For example, suppose a lender charges interest in arrears and requires payment on the first of each month. If settlement takes place on March 20, the first payment will be due May 1 and will include interest for the month of April. Thus, at settlement, the lender collects interest for the 11 days from (and including) March 20 to (and including) March 31. Thus, even a lender who normally charges in arrears will typically make the one charge of advance interest payable at settlement.

PROBLEM

Assume that a lender charges interest in advance and requires payment on the fifteenth of each month. Settlement takes place on October 20 and the first payment is due November 15. If the loan is for $20,000 at the interest rate of 8% per annum, what interest charge will be made at settlement?

(b) Escrow Funds

(i) Real Estate Taxes

In some jurisdictions, unpaid real estate taxes, and in some cases other municipal charges such as sewer rent, will become a lien on property which is prior to the lien of the mortgage. Normally, liens only take priority from the time that they are recorded in a public place. However, there are exceptions to this rule, and real estate taxes are often among the exceptions. These taxes may become a first lien on the property, ahead of all mortgages, even though the taxes arise in years subsequent to the year in which the mortgage was created and recorded. To prevent a loss of priority to unpaid real estate taxes, the lender may require the borrower to pay to the lender with each monthly mortgage payment an amount equal to $\frac{1}{12}$th of the annual tax payment, as estimated by the mortgagee. The tax fund accumulated is held by the mortgagee in escrow. We have discussed the escrow concept in previous chapters. In this context it means that the mortgagee does not own the money but is merely holding it for distribution to a third party, the tax collector. The mortgagee will apply the escrow fund each year to pay the real estate taxes due on the property. Normally the buyer will readily agree to this because it is a convenient way for him to pay real estate taxes. However, unless the first mortgage payment is due on the first day of the tax year, the taxes will be due before borrower has made 12 payments. Accordingly, the lender will not have collected enough money out of the monthly payments to pay the full tax bill. To prevent this, the lender will require that the borrower pay in advance at closing a sum of money which, when added to the regular tax payments made during the remainder of the year, will be sufficient to pay the tax bill.

(ii) Insurance Premiums

Some lenders will also require that the amount required to pay fire insurance premiums on the mortgaged property be paid into escrow with each monthly payment. Therefore, it may be necessary to pay an initial amount into escrow for insurance premiums at settlement, just as in the case of taxes. However, this is far less common, since insurance premiums are normally paid one year in advance at the time the policy is purchased, which should be near the time of settlement. Accordingly, if the lender collects ½th of the annual premium commencing with the first payment, it will have the right amount for the next year's premium at the time it is due.

(c) Miscellaneous Charges

The mortgagee will collect at settlement any sums still due it for a credit report, appraisal fees, mortgage placement fees, "points" or the like.

Normally, the representative of the lender will take from the closing the original note or bond and warrant, a copy of the mortgage, a settlement sheet and checks for any amounts due the lender as set forth above. The original mortgage will remain with the title insurance company or the lender's attorney, who will immediately have it recorded in the recording office in the county (or other proper jurisdiction) in which the real estate is located. The borrower will normally take from closing a copy of the note, a copy of the mortgage and a copy of the settlement sheet. If the closing is also to purchase real estate, the proceeds of the loan will be used to pay the seller. If the loan is for some other purpose and the borrower is using already owned real estate as security, the proceeds will be given to the borrower.

E.　POST CLOSING

After the recorder has made a copy of the mortgage and entered the name of the mortgagor and the mortgagee in the appropriate indices in his office, the original will be returned to the title company or the lender's attorney for forwarding to the lender, to be kept in its vault until the mortgage has been paid, assigned,[10] or foreclosed. Anyone subsequently searching title to the real estate will find that the owner has subjected it to the lien of this particular mortgage, and will find a copy of the mortgage.

10.　Assignment of mortgages will be discussed in Chapter 11.

EXAMPLE: Commitment Letter (Residential Mortgage)

XYZ Bank
12 S. Broad Street
Philadelphia, Pa. 19103

CONVENTIONAL MORTGAGE
March 1, 1977

Premises:

Mortgagor:

Amount: $ Int. Rate: % Term: years   Monthly Payment
                                                            Int. & Prin.
                                                            $

Philadelphia, Pennsylvania 19116

Dear

Your application for a first mortgage loan on the terms outlined above has been approved subject to the following provisions.

The following must be submitted to this office <u>at least five working days before settlement</u>.

1. The prepared mortgage papers on the enclosed forms.

2. A "marked-up" report of title issued by a title insurance company approved by XYZ indicating that the mortgage will be insured as a first lien, free and clear of all encumbrances, subject only to such objections as meet with our approval. The title report must include copies or abstracts of all recorded public utility agreements, restrictions and easements.

Please direct the mortgage papers to our SETTLEMENT SUPERVISOR and inform him of the settlement date with the Title Company. The approved papers will then be forwarded directly to the Title Company, together with **our** check and letter of instructions.

At settlement, we must be furnished a fire insurance policy (not a binder) with extended coverage in the full amount of the loan. The policy shall be for a term of not less than three years in a company acceptable to XYZ and include a standard mortgagee clause in favor of The XYZ Bank.

Our commitment to make this loan will expire May 31, 1977.

[B7817]

If the property to be mortgaged is located in New Jersey a new survey must be submitted and fire insurance coverage must specifically protect outbuildings and garages (if any). Settlement for New Jersey properties must be held in Pennsylvania.

If you decide to accept this commitment, you may do so only by signing and returning one copy of the enclosed DISCLOSURE STATEMENT REQUIRED BY FEDERAL LAW so that it is received by XYZ, Mortgage Department, 12 South Broad Street, Philadelphia, Pennsylvania, 19107, within 10 days of the date of this letter, in which case the commitment will become a contract binding both on you and on XYZ in accordance with its terms. If you do not sign and return the Statement, this commitment will lapse.

Prepayment of the principal balance may be made in whole or in part at any time without penalty.

At the time of settlement a fee of $100.00 will be charged the purchaser representing the balance of our 1% service charge for this loan.

Sincerely,

Assistant Mortgage Officer   [B7818]

Part Two

COMMERCIAL–INDUSTRIAL MORTGAGES

Now let us consider the use of mortgage loans for the financing of a commercial development (e. g. a shopping center) or an industrial building (e. g. a factory). In this chapter, we will consider a situation in which the prospective borrower owns a fully improved piece of real estate, that is, one on which a completed building has been constructed. We will also assume that the building is about to be leased to a business tenant. We will consider in a later chapter the special problems which arise when an owner of undeveloped land wishes to use a mortgage loan to finance the construction of a new building for his own use or for the use of a tenant.

I. THE APPLICATION FOR A COMMERCIAL–INDUSTRIAL MORTGAGE

A. THE MORTGAGEE'S CONCERNS

As in the case of a residence, the mortgage transaction begins with the borrower's application for a loan to the mortgage lender. In this case, the mortgagee is concerned not only with the integrity and credit rating of the borrower, and the value of the real estate offered for security, but also with the credit rating and integrity of the tenant and with the amount of rent to be paid by the tenant. The reason for this should be apparent; the building will be occupied by the tenant and the rents will provide the owner with the primary source of funds required to pay principal and interest on the mortgage,[1] as well as taxes, insurance and maintenance. The mortgagee, therefore, wants to know (a) that the tenant is in possession and prepared to pay rent; (b) that the tenant has no legal claim against the landlord or anyone else which would permit the tenant to refuse to pay rent; (c) that the amount of the rent is sufficient to pay the debt service and other operating costs; (d) that the tenant has a good credit rating and is likely to pay the rent; and (e) the term of the lease.

In many commercial-industrial transactions, the amount of the loan is so substantial that the mortgagee realistically cannot expect to receive payment from the borrower and/or the borrower's own assets. Therefore, the mortgagee is very much concerned with the quality and condition of the real estate and the quality of the tenant and terms of the lease because it is from these sources, rather than from the borrower's other income and assets, that the mortgage payments will come. Indeed, as we shall see, there are many commercial mortgages in which the mortgagor's liability is limited to his interest in the mortgaged property, and the mortgagee is not permitted to look to the mortgagor's other income and assets.

Before making the loan, the lender wants to know what the operating costs are, including the taxes, the insurance costs, the maintenance and repair costs, and the water and sewer and utility charges, and it also wants to know whether it is the owner or the tenant who has the responsibility to pay them. Finally, it also wants to know that after payment of all these charges (whether by the owner or the tenant) and after debt service, there will be sufficient funds from the rent to provide some kind of profit, generally referred to as "cash flow" for the owner. Unless there is some cash flow for the borrower, the borrower may lose interest in the project and let the property run down, and may even default under the mortgage. Conversely, if there is substantial cash flow, the borrower is going to work very hard to avoid any possible default under the mortgage through which he could lose the entire project.

The following is an example of the contents of an application for a commercial or industrial mortgage.

---

1. Annual payments of principal and interest due on a mortgage loan are sometimes referred to as "debt service".

EXAMPLE: Mortgage Application (Commercial or Industrial)

Name of Bank _____ Account Officer _____ Address & Branch of Bank

LOCATION AND PHYSICAL DESCRIPTION OF SECURITY

Street Address

between what major cross streets

City   County   State

LAND: Dimensions   Sq. Ft. Area

BUILDING: Type, Use, Size and Stories:

YEAR BUILT: REMODELED (YR. & COST):

(The property is to be insured as required by New York Life Insurance Company and the policies will be delivered to the Company with mortgagee loss clauses attached.)

MORTGAGOR'S STATEMENT OF COST

Existing construction: Date purchased   Cost $

Proposed construction: Starting date   Est. completion date   Cost $

Land: Date purchased or optioned   Purchase price $

Est. Current Value: Land $ Improvements $ Total $

Are there any mortgages against the property at this time? If none, so state. If so, give mortgagee, interest rate, maturity, loan balance, payments and prepayment options.

Are there any other mortgage application(s) or mortgage loan commitment(s) presently outstanding against this security; (If none, so state):

ATTACHMENTS: ☐ Legal Description and Survey showing location and description of all easements. ☐ Plot Plan. ☐ Building Plans and Specifications. ☐ Owner's Financial Statements. ☐ Operating Statements. ☐ Pro-Forma Statements. ☐ Photos. ☐ Cost Breakdown. ☐ Owner's Detailed Statement of Equity Source. ☐ Copy of Ground Lease. ☐ Rent Roll showing name of tenant, designation of space, square foot area, minimum annual rental, renewal options, date of lease, dates of commencement and expiration and conditions which permit tenant to cancel for any reason other than landlord's breach. ☐ Copies of principal Leases.

Accompanying this application is check of the undersigned in the amount of $ It is agreed that if you issue a commitment for the loan (or the purchase thereof) as applied for herein and such commitment is not accepted in writing within 10 days from the date of such commitment, you will retain $ as an application fee, and return the balance (if any) of the above amount. It is further agreed that upon the acceptance of such commitment, the above amount (first mentioned) shall be applied toward the required commitment fee and/or security deposit.

Concurrently, with the acceptance of your commitment as applied for, the undersigned will deposit with Life Insurance Company, an additional $ as a security deposit on account of liquidated damages, which deposit shall not bear interest. If and when the loan is funded,   Life will refund the security deposit.

The undersigned further agrees that the form and substance of each and every document evidencing the loan or the purchase thereof and the security therefor and title and evidence thereof must be satisfactory to the Company, and any and all obligations incurred by the Company by reason of commitment issued for the loan shall be subject to such approval. The undersigned further agrees to pay all fees and expenses incurred in connection with closing the loan or purchase thereof including fees and expenses of local counsel, if any, employed by the Company in connection therewith, title insurance charges, cost of survey, recording and filing fees, documentary stamps and other taxes payable in connection with the closing of the loan. The undersigned will arrange with the occupants of the premises for full inspection by the Company's appraisers.

_____ Broker's Signature   _____ Signature of individual, partnership, corporation, etc. to whom commitment is to be issued.

Address   Address

Date   Date   (B7819)

EXAMPLE: Mortgage Loan Application

**MORTGAGE
LOAN APPLICATION**
(INCOME PROPERTY)

LIFE INSURANCE COMPANY

Please sign and submit in triplicate. All questions must be answered.

The undersigned hereby applies for: ☐ a direct loan from   Life Insurance Company or ☐ a loan to be purchased by assignment by   Life Insurance Company upon the terms and conditions set forth below,

To be secured by:

     ☐ a first mortgage or deed of trust on the marketable fee simple title to the property described below:

     ☐ a first mortgage or deed of trust on the lessee's interest in the following leasehold estate:
        (Give lessor, lessee, annual ground rent, initial term, renewal options, lease maturity date, contingent rental)

and on the easements appurtenant thereto and on all improvements to the property, free of prior mechanics, or materialmen's liens or special assessments for work completed or under construction on the date of the closing, and, if the Company requires, as additional security, it shall receive a chattel first mortgage (free of title retention agreements) on all fixtures and articles of personal property now or hereafter attached to or used in connection with the management, maintenance, and operation of the property, and an assignment of the lessor's interest in each occupancy lease of or affecting any part of the said property as additional security for the loan, which assignment shall be recorded and copy of which shall be served on the tenant; as to each lease to be assigned, the lease shall be in full force and effect, there shall be no offsets or defenses to enforcement of the lease, the tenant shall have accepted its premises, confirmed the commencement of its lease term, be in occupancy and paying rent on a current basis, evidence of which shall be furnished the Company.

LOAN

Amount: $ Interest Rate: %   Term

Repayable in monthly installments of $ due on the 10th of the month to be applied first to interest and then to principal, and monthly deposits for real estate taxes and hazard insurance.

Additional compensation to   Life:

Non-refundable commitment fee:

Rental requirement for loan advance(s):

Prepayment Privilege:

Estimated Funding Date:

Liquidated Damages: $ to be paid to   Life, if, after acceptance of the commitment, the loan fails to close for any reason whatsoever except default by   Life.

MORTGAGOR

Give name and address of borrower, (if borrower is a partnership or a corporation, give name and addresses of partners or stockholders and their respective interests. If borrower is a trust, give full designation thereof, and identify beneficiary(s) with address(es).

[B7820]

B. THE MORTGAGOR'S CONCERNS

There are also items which are of special concern to a mortgagor in addition to those involved in a residential transaction. If the value of the building is substantially in excess of the amount which the borrower seeks, the rent is sufficient to pay debt service and all expenses and carrying charges, and the tenant is a large substantial company with excellent credit (sometimes referred to as a "triple A" tenant) the borrower may ask the lender not to look to the borrower at all for repayment, but to rely entirely upon the value of the real estate and the lease. As discussed in Chapter Six, this can be accomplished through the use of a "straw" to make the application and sign the mortgage documents. Another method of accomplishing the same result is simply to insert in the mortgage documents a statement to the effect that liability under the documents will be enforced only out of the real estate. Specific clauses "limiting liability to the land" are considered in section VI of this chapter.

Frequently, the mortgagor may own more property than he wishes to subject to the lien of the mortgage. For example, a mortgagor may have a shopping center and parking area, with an adjacent tract of undeveloped ground. Mortgagor may not wish to subject the undeveloped ground to the lien of the mortgage, because he may wish to sell it or build on it at a later time. In connection with any such later construction, he might have to create a mortgage in favor of another lender. If he should sell the underdeveloped land he would have to pay off any mortgage in order to deliver clear title to the buyer. Accordingly, it is important to consider precisely what area is to be mortgaged in preparing the mortgage application. If less than all of the area owned by the borrower is going to be covered by the mortgage, the mortgagor needs to consider the advisability of creating cross-easement rights between the tracts which will be superior in right to the mortgage.

II. ISSUANCE OF COMMITMENT

Assuming the borrower's mortgage application is approved, a commitment will be issued by the lender. Although the terms and conditions of the commitment are often quite complicated, the effect is the same as in the case of a residential mortgage. In many instances, because of the expense incurred by the lender in analyzing an application for a commercial or industrial mortgage, a substantial commitment fee will be charged.

Once accepted by the borrower, along with the payment of any fee which may be due, the commitment letter forms a contract pursuant to which the mortgagee is legally bound to make the loan and the borrower is legally bound to borrow the money on the terms and conditions set forth in the commitment letter.

The commitment letter indicates some of the primary concerns of the mortgagee.

A. TITLE AND TITLE INSURANCE

In the usual case, the mortgagee expects a first lien for the mortgage. Moreover, as in the case of a residential mortgage, the mortgagee will want a title insurance policy insuring that the mortgagee's lien is a valid lien (not subject to attack for forgery, improper recording, defective title in the borrower, or the like) and that it is a first lien. A first lien means that, in the event of a judicial sale of the property, the first funds payable from the proceeds of sale (after real estate taxes and certain expenses of sale) will be payable to the mortgagee up to the full amount of the mortgage debt plus interest and costs incurred by the mortgagee. Because of the large dollar amount of the insurance, a complication concerning title insurance may arise in the case of a large commercial—industrial transaction. Many institutional lenders are reluctant, in the case of very large mortgages, to have only one title insurance company underwrite the entire risk of a defective title because the title insurance company itself may not have sufficient financial strength to assure that it will be able to pay such a large potential loss. Customarily, title insurance companies reinsure such risks; that is, they will take part of the risk, for example, the first $500,000., and then they will in turn reinsure the balance of the risk with another company or companies. If the lender is concerned with this problem there are various ways in which the problem might be covered in the commitment letter. For example, the lender may insist on the right to approve the title insurance company, the right to require reinsurance with acceptable companies, and the delivery of copies of the reinsurance agreements at closing.

B. LEASE ON PREMISES

1. Rights of Tenant versus Mortgagee

If the lender is depending upon rental from the lease for repayment of the debt, it may also require in the commitment letter that the lease be either presently or collaterally assigned to it as additional security for the loan. A present assignment requires the landlord-borrower to transfer to the lender the landlord's right to collect rents due under the lease. To the extent the periodic rent exceeds the mortgage payment, the excess will be turned over to the landlord by the mortgagee. In most instances, the lender will accept a collateral assignment, which means that, so long as the borrower is not in default of the loan, the borrower will collect the rents and remit the amount required for debt service. Only upon default would the lender exercise its rights to require that rents be paid directly to it.

An important question arises with respect to the relative priorities of the lease and the mortgage. For example, if the mortgagee forecloses or takes possession, can the mortgagee terminate the lease, in the belief that the property would be more valuable without being burdened by the lease? On the other hand, can the tenant terminate the lease by reason of the mortgagee foreclosing? According to the Common Law and the laws of most jurisdictions, the answers to these two questions depended upon whether the mortgage or the lease came first in time. The answers were rooted in the title theory of mortgages. The courts reasoned that once a borrower has leased the property to a tenant, the borrower's rights in the property are limited to the right to regain possession of the property at some future time (upon expiration or termination of the lease) and the right to collect rent in the interim. Since the borrower cannot transfer to the mortgagee any greater rights than the borrower has, the borrower can transfer to the mortgagee only the right to get the property back at some future time and the right to collect rent in the interim. Accordingly, if the mortgagee had legal notice of the existence of the lease before the mortgage was created,[2] then, in the event of a foreclosure, the mortgagee (or any other purchaser at the Sheriff's sale) acquires title subject to the rights of the tenant. The purchaser at a foreclosure sale can purchase only what the mortgagee has to sell: a lien on the borrower's rights to get the property back at some future time and to collect rents in the interim. So long as the tenant fulfills his obligations under the lease, the purchaser cannot dispossess the tenant, increase the rent, or change any of the terms and conditions of the lease. Likewise the tenant's condition is unaffected by activity respecting an inferior interest in the property. The tenant, therefore, has no right to claim a default in the lease or otherwise to terminate the lease simply by reason of the foreclosure.

Conversely, once the mortgage has been signed, acknowledged and recorded, all the borrower has left is a right to get the property back from the mortgagee at some future time, if and when he pays the mortgage debt. Technically, the mortgagor does not have even the right to possession of the premises. The mortgagee has the right to possession, although such right is rarely, if ever, exercised in the absence of a default. It follows that a tenant whose lease begins after the mortgage transaction can obtain his right to possession only subject to the prior right of possession of the mortgagee. In such a case, the mortgagee (or any other purchaser at a foreclosure sale) will acquire the property free of the lease. Another way of expressing this is that once the mortgagee's rights (including its unexercised right to possession) have become fixed, such rights cannot be diminished by a subsequent act of the landlord and a third

---

2. As you will recall from Chapter Three, the mortgagee will have the legal notice of the existence of the lease if (a) it actually knows of the existence of the lease, (b) the tenant is in possession of the premises, or (c) the lease (or a memorandum of the lease) has been recorded.

party, the tenant. In such a case, the tenant's rights have been cut off by the foreclosure, and the tenant therefore no longer has any obligations under the lease. Thus, upon a foreclosure of a superior mortgage, a tenant is free to vacate the property and cease paying rent and will have no further obligation on account of the lease. This may be a desirable result for a tenant if, as is often the case, the reason that the mortgagor defaulted was that the project (for example, a shopping center) is an economic failure.

2. Attornment and Non-Disturbance

In a case in which the mortgage is prior in right to the lease, a foreclosure will terminate the rights of the tenant. This occurs because the tenant's rights depended on the rights of the landlord, which were extinguished by the foreclosure sale. This could be a problem for the mortgagee. For example, in a shopping center in which the mortgagee is depending upon rental payments pursuant to a lease signed by a good tenant, the tenant might now like to avoid the terms of the lease. In the event of foreclosure on a prior mortgage, the inadvertent extinguishment of the lease would allow the tenant to leave the premises with no further obligations under the lease. The mortgagee will want to be certain that such a lease will not be extinguished by a foreclosure.

The mortgagee's problem can most easily be avoided if the tenant is in possession of the premises prior to the mortgage or if the lease is recorded prior to the mortgage. However, even if the lease came before the mortgage, it may have provided that it is subordinate to any mortgage, no matter when created. In addition, some mortgagees may require the tenant to execute a subordination agreement[3] declaring the lease subordinate to the mortgage, because they want it clear that their mortgage has priority over all other recorded interests.

Where the lease is subordinate, or is subordinated, the mortgagee may require the borrower to obtain a separate agreement with the tenant requiring the tenant to "attorn"[4] to the mortgagee. In practical terms, this means that the tenant agrees that in the event of a foreclosure, the lease will not be extinguished but will continue as a lease between mortgagee and tenant, and that the tenant will thereupon pay rent directly to the mortgagee.

Where the lease is subordinate, the tenant is concerned that, even though he may pay rent promptly, the landlord may for one

3. A subordination agreement is an agreement by which a party having a superior right of some sort agrees with someone having an inferior right that, as between the two of them, the inferior right shall be treated as if it were superior.

4. To "attorn" is to agree to recognize that another party, who would not otherwise have privity, may enforce a contract as though it were originally a beneficiary of the contract.

reason or another fail to comply with the terms of the mortgage, resulting in a foreclosure which could extinguish the lease. The risk of premature termination of the lease is particularly threatening when the tenant is investing substantial amounts of money in improvements which become part of the real estate, such as air conditioning, heating systems, and other types of fixtures which would be difficult and expensive to remove. To protect himself from this problem, the tenant will want to have an agreement from the mortgagee, called a "non-disturbance agreement".[5] A non-disturbance agreement contains the agreement of the mortgagee that, in the event of foreclosure, the tenant may remain on the property so long as he continues to comply with the terms of the lease. Mortgagees are frequently willing to give such agreements. However, a mortgagee may be concerned that rent may be paid far in advance, leaving the mortgagee with a tenant who cannot be dispossessed and who has already paid rent to the defaulting mortgagor, who is probably completely insolvent. To prevent such a problem, the non-disturbance agreement may include a provision prohibiting the tenant from making advance rental payments.

C. COMPLIANCE WITH LAWS

In a commercial—industrial situation, the mortgagee will frequently want to be certain that the premises are in compliance with the myriad laws and regulations pertaining to building safety, fire, health, zoning, subdivision and the like. The mortgagee may require evidence of such compliance at settlement. Mortgagees are more concerned about this in a commercial context than a residential context because: (a) larger amounts of money are involved; (b) the regulations and ordinances pertaining to commercial—industrial buildings are more complex and often stricter than those applied to single-family residential properties; and (c) the ordinances and regulations are frequently more stringently enforced respecting commercial and industrial properties. The mortgagee must look at the property as though to purchase it. A mortgagee would probably not want to purchase a property in which it may have to invest substantial additional funds to effect compliance with local codes.

D. EASEMENTS

The mortgagee will want to be sure that the property has the benefit of easements for access to public roads, and that the mortgaged premises are served by water, sewer, electric, gas and other utilities. The borrower may have to create these easements over other property which it owns. If the property which would provide access is itself subject to another mortgage, then the other mortgagee will

---

5. Usually a non-disturbance agreement is the quid pro quo for an attornment agreement and they are frequently combined into one document.

have to consent in writing to the easements to avoid the possibility that the easements will be extinguished by a foreclosure on the other mortgage.

III. PREPARATION OF DOCUMENTS

Frequently in a commercial—industrial transaction, the responsibility for the preparation of documents will be divided between counsel for the borrower and counsel for the lender. The lender's council will want to examine the lease and to prepare the note, mortgage and assignment of lease on forms satisfactory to the lender. Lender's counsel will also want to examine the title report to make sure there are no easements, liens or other title objections which could adversely affect the value of the property and/or the priority or validity of the lien. It will be the burden of the borrower's counsel, generally, to review the documents prepared by the lender's counsel and to furnish surveys, corporate resolutions authorizing the loan (if the borrower is a corporation), receipts evidencing payment of taxes, water charges and sewer rents. The borrower's counsel may also prepare subordination, attornment and/or non-disturbance agreements and any easement agreements which may be required.

IV. CLOSING

As in the case of the residential mortgage, at closing all the necessary papers referred to above will be executed, acknowledged before a notary public where necessary, and delivered to the appropriate parties. The documents which are to be recorded (which may include, in addition to the mortgage, an assignment of leases, a subordination, non-disturbance and attornment agreement and an easement agreement) will be delivered to the party responsible for recording them.

V. POST CLOSING

After closing, the documents which have been recorded will be returned to the mortgagee, or to the mortgagor in the case of any easement agreement. After the closing, both the mortgagor and the mortgagee will want a complete set of original or conformed closing documents showing the recording data of any recorded documents.

PROBLEM

It is often the task of a legal assistant to follow up on post closing requirements including the furnishing of copies of all documents to the client. What format might you follow as a paralegal after a commercial mortgage closing which included 23 documents executed or provided by your client?

Part Three

CONSTRUCTION MORTGAGES

I. INTRODUCTION

Now let us consider a situation in which a corporation decides to construct a new building and finance the construction through a mortgage. We will be considering construction financing in the context of the following fact situation:

SAMPLE FACT SITUATION.

Cen Tenn Realty Co., Inc. has purchased a shopping center, together with a large tract of adjacent vacant ground. The purchase price was $4 million which was paid partly in cash and partly by accepting title to the premises subject to an existing mortgage in favor of First Mortgagee Insurance Company. Cen Tenn would like to construct a large store on the adjacent vacant ground and lease that store to Xerxes Department Store Co., which is a well known operator of discount department stores across the United States. Being a well known chain, Xerxes will probably draw a great deal of extra traffic to the shopping center. If Cen Tenn can build that store, it believes that it can find tenants at favorable rents for the vacant stores, and also receive increased rents in existing stores (most of which pay rent based at least in part on a percentage of gross business).[1]

Cen Tenn approaches Xerxes and makes tentative arrangements for construction and leasing of a store containing 80,000 square feet of floor space at a rental of $160,000.00 per year, plus a certain amount for increases in taxes and maintenance. Cen Tenn must now ascertain the cost of building the store. It must also determine whether it can borrow the money required to construct the store, on terms that would make the rent payable by Xerxes sufficient to pay the interest and principal on the mortgage loan plus real estate taxes, insurance and miscellaneous expenses in connection with the building (to the extent that Xerxes has not agreed to pay these items) and leave some profit for Cen Tenn. Cen Tenn and Xerxes meet with their respective architects and engineers to decide on what kind of building

---

[1]. The concept of rent based on a percentage of gross business will be considered in detail in Chapter 9 of this book. At this point it is sufficient to understand that in addition to a fixed monthly amount, the rental will include a percentage of the dollar amount of the tenant's sales at the leased premises. Therefore, the higher the tenant's sales, the greater its rent.

will be required. This involves not only size and height, but building materials, store front, fixtures, air conditioning, electrical equipment and the like, all of which are important items of cost. After this, Cen Tenn approaches several general building contractors, and asks for bids based upon the preliminary plans and specifications prepared by the architects. It finds from the bids that the total cost of construction will be approximately $1 million. In addition, Cen Tenn will have to be prepared to pay certain fees to the construction lender (discussed below), legal fees, settlement costs, interest during the construction period (during which period no rent is collected from Xerxes), surveys, engineering, insurance, and miscellaneous costs. Cen Tenn computes these at approximately $100,000., making the aggregate cost of the new building $1.1 million.

II.   CONSTRUCTION LOANS AND PERMANENT LOANS

Lending institutions include commercial banks, savings banks, savings and loan associations, insurance companies, pension trusts and real estate investment trusts. Most lending institutions specialize in making either construction loans or permanent loans, to the general exclusion of the other. Commercial banks, as a rule, are most likely to make construction loans, and to have construction loan departments skilled in processing and supervising construction loans. Insurance companies are much more likely to make permanent loans. The following is a brief description of these two kinds of loans and the different risks attendant to them.

A.   THE PERMANENT LOAN

The application for a permanent mortgage for property to be constructed is substantially the same as in the case of any commercial— industrial mortgage.

The prospective permanent mortgagee will consider basically the same factors, including the value of the building, the financial standing of the tenant, and the integrity of the mortgagor. However, the permanent lender is agreeing to make a loan based on the security of a lease with a tenant who is not yet in possession for a building which is not yet constructed. The lender will want to make its obligation to lend the money contingent upon (i) the building being constructed in accordance with the plans and specifications presented to it with the application and (ii) the lease being in full force. If all the conditions are met, then the permanent loan will be funded and will be like any long-term mortgage. In our example, let us suppose that a commitment has been obtained from New Hampshire Mutual Life Insurance for a loan of $1,000,000 with interest at 9% per annum being a term of 25 years and being fully self-amortizing. Having obtained its permanent loan commitment, Cen Tenn must now seek a source of financing during the construction period.

B. THE CONSTRUCTION LOAN

New Hampshire Mutual is willing to lend on the condition that the improvements will be constructed according to the plans and specifications. However, New Hampshire Mutual, like many insurance companies and pension trusts, does not have the personnel or the knowledge to oversee the actual construction. Also the improvements are being constructed in a location far from the main office of New Hampshire Mutual. Therefore, New Hampshire is not willing to lend any money until the improvements are completed. However, Cen Tenn will need money to pay a general contractor periodically as the construction proceeds, which may take a year or more. The general contractor must pay its own workers, sub-contractors, and material costs as they are supplied. Since most developers do not maintain sufficient capital to finance the construction of large projects, the mortgagor needs to borrow money to meet these payments until the building is complete and it can receive funds from New Hampshire Mutual. The gap is filled by a construction lender, often a bank in the vicinity of the construction site. The construction lender, which, in our example, is The Second Centralia National Bank of Centralia, Tennessee, will lend the mortgagor up to $1,000,000, which will be advanced over a period of a year or two as the money is needed to meet payments on the construction. In our example the construction loan is for up to $1,000,000 for a term of one year, with monthly payments of interest only [2] during the term of the loan calculated on the basis of the outstanding principal from time to time advanced.

The Second Centralia either knows of or has on its own staff trained architects, engineers and inspectors who can check the construction and can verify that the bills for labor and materials are proper, that the value of the work is consistent with the amount of the bill, and that the plans and specifications, which have been approved by New Hampshire Mutual, are being followed. A construction lender will seldom advance 100% of the value of the work as it is done, preferring to advance a lesser percentage (often 90%) so that the value of the working plan, which is the security for the loan, will always exceed the amount outstanding on the loan. Second Centralia also has the bookkeeping facilities to keep track of how much has been advanced at any given time and to compute interest from month to month on the constantly changing principal. Because of the extra expense involved in construction lending, construction lenders will normally make a "supervision" or "inspection" charge, or

2. Why would you think the loan would be for interest only with no repayment of principal until the maturity date of the loan?

some other commitment fee or charge, of one to two percent of the total amount of the loan, payable at the settlement on the construction loan. In addition, the interest rate on construction loans will normally be higher than on permanent loans.

Second Centralia knows that Cen Tenn cannot possibly pay back $1,000,000 upon completion of construction out of its own funds. Second Centralia and Cen Tenn expect that the construction loan will be repaid out of the proceeds of the permanent loan. Indeed, as we shall see, often the actual technique used is to have the permanent lender purchase the construction loan from the construction lender for the full amount of the loan. In the jargon of the business it is said that the construction lender wishes to be "taken out" of the loan by the permanent lender. For this reason, the permanent loan commitment is often referred to as a "take-out".

The construction lender is also concerned with the financial stability and integrity of the general contractor. If the general contractor cannot live up to its commitment to build the improvements for $1,000,000., Second Centralia may be forced to hire another contractor, usually at a higher price, to complete the improvements in order to be in a position to satisfy the conditions of the permanent loan commitment. Even the "cushion" produced by paying less than 100% of each bill may not be enough to cover the extra expense of bringing in a new contractor. In addition, a construction lender must analyze the plans and specifications very carefully to ascertain whether the general contractor will be able to construct the building within the time allotted in the permanent loan commitment and for the amount of money available in the construction loan.

A construction lender is also concerned with the availability of water, sewer, curbs and other utilities, with access, and with zoning and building laws, since it wants to be sure that the building, when constructed, will be complete, usable and in compliance with law. Otherwise the tenant may refuse to take possession and the permanent lender may refuse to close the permanent loan.

To summarize, the construction lender must at every stage of construction consider what its situation would be if the borrower defaulted and it had to take over the borrower's position. In such a case, the construction lender would act as a developer and would coordinate and balance the requirements of the general contractor, the tenant and the permanent lender.

The following are examples of a permanent and construction loan commitment which might be used in the transaction described in the sample fact situation.

EXAMPLE: Construction Loan Commitment

SECOND CENTRALIA NATIONAL BANK

November 1, 1977

Cen Tenn Realty Co., Inc.
Centralia, Tennessee

> Re: Route 27 and Swamp Road
>   Centralia, Tennessee

Gentlemen:

Subject to acceptance of and compliance with the following terms and conditions, we have approved your request for a construction mortgage loan in an amount not to exceed One Million Dollars ($1,000,000.):

<u>Term</u>: Due and payable on or before December 15, 1978.

<u>Interest Rate</u>: 1% in excess of the Prime rate charged by us from time to time but in no event less than 9% per annum.

<u>Non-Refundable Service Charge</u>: $15,000., payable in from the proceeds of the initial disbursement of the loan.

<u>Documentation</u>: Prior to the initial disbursement of the loan, we shall be furnished with the following documents, which must be acceptable to us at our sole discretion:

1. Mortgage Note.

2. Mortgage.

3. Construction Loan Agreement.

4. Buy-Sell Agreement.

5. Schedule of Operation.

6. Lease between Cen Tenn Realty Co., Inc. and Xerxes Department Store Co.

7. Memorandum of Lease.

8. Assignment of Lease to us.

9. Report of Title.

10. Personal Guarantee of Daniel Developer.

[B7821]

11.   Declaration of Reciprocal Easements.

12.   Copy of Construction Contract with Best Builders, Inc. including trade payment breakdown.

13.   Final Working Plans and Specifications as approved by Borrower.

14.   Copy of Building Permit.

15.   Builder's Risk Insurance for the full amount of the loan with extended coverage, vandalism and malicious mischief protection.

16.   Approval from New Hampshire Mutual Life Insurance Company on the following items:

      A.   Mortgage Note.
      B.   Mortgage.
      C.   Lease.
      D.   Report of Title.
      E.   Declaration of Reciprocal Easements.

17.   Original accepted commitment of New Hampshire Mutual Life Insurance Company.

18.   Other documents which we may reasonably require.

Initial Disbursement: If the initial disbursement of the loan is not made on or before January 1, 1978, our approval will be automatically and fully terminated. The Construction Loan settlement must be held in Centralia.

Please indicate your acceptance hereof by executing and returning the enclosed copy of this letter on or before

                        Second Centralia National Bank

                 By_____
                     President

ACCEPTED:

By: _____

Date: _____

                                      [B7822]

EXAMPLE: Mortgage Commitment (Permanent Loan)

NEW HAMPSHIRE MUTUAL LIFE INSURANCE COMPANY

September 1, 1977

Cen Tenn Realty Co., Inc.
Centralia, Tennessee   Re: Route 27 and Swamp Road
                                           Centralia, Tennessee

Gentlemen:

     Your application for a mortgage loan covering property above
referred to, is approved in the amount of $1,000,000. for a term
of 25 years providing for constant payments of $8,392. each month
(10.08%) constant) which shall be applied first to interest at the
rate of 9% per annum and the balance in reduction of principal,
subject to the following terms and conditions:

1.   That either the Note, Mortgage or other suitable instrument
     shall provide that this company will participate in the annual
     gross income to the extent of 1% of the minimum rental income
     of $160,000. or 25% of the additional rental income as set
     forth in paragraph Art. 5A of the lease, whichever is the
     greater. You will furnish by March 15 of each year, a certi-
     fied statement for the preceding year, as submitted by the
     tenant and pay to us the amount due as herein set forth, as
     additional income.

2.   That you furnish to us by December 1, 1977, a complete set of
     plans and specifications and an M.A.I. appraisal which shall
     be satisfactory to us and indicate a value of not less than
     $1,350,000.

3.   The mortgage shall cover a plot of 3 acres, which is adjacent
     to and joining an existing shopping center known as Centraltown
     upon which 3 acre plot shall be erected a one story stell and
     masonry building having an area of 80,000 square feet.

4.   That a guaranteed survey of the subject property with the im-
     provements located thereon acceptable to our counsel be fur-
     nished at your expense.

5.   That a policy of title insurance issued by a title company accep-
     table to our counsel shall be furnished, which policy shall in-
     sure (Mortgagee) as owner and holder of a valid first mortgage
     lien on the subject premises.

6.   That fire insurance with extended coverage (minimum $50 deduc-
     tible) shall be furnished for the loan at the time of closing,
     in a company acceptable to us, properly endorsed in an amount
     to be determined by us upon receipt of appraisal as required
     under section #2 herein.   [B7823]

7.   The premises shall be in an undamaged condition at the time
      of closing.

8.   That the lease between you and Xerxes Department Store Co.
      expiring in 1999 providing for a minimum annual rent of
      $160,000. shall be in full force and effect.

9.   Upon acceptance of this commitment you will pay to us the sum
      of $20,000. which commitment fee shall be deemed earned by us
      by the issuance hereof and shall be non-refundable to you
      whether or not the loan contemplated hereby is actually made.
      However, should the loan close as herein agreed upon, we will
      refund the sum of $10,000. at the time of closing.

10.   That the building loan mortgagee agree not to assign their
      mortgage to any one other than to this company, and you will
      undertake to procure such agreement upon their issuance of a
      commitment.

11.   That upon closing of this loan an easement agreement will be
      delivered to us setting forth full parking privileges for the
      entire shopping center which shall remain in effect for the
      full term of our loan or any extension thereof.

12.   That either the Note, Mortgage or other suitable instrument
      provide that the loan cannot be prepaid during the first ten
      year period, that during the eleventh year the obligation
      may be prepaid upon payment of a penalty of 5%, thereafter
      the penalty shall reduce 1/2 of 1% each year until reduced
      to 2%.

13.   This commitment shall expire if the loan is not delivered to
      us as herein agreed upon by

14.   This commitment is subject to a satisfactory site inspection
      which shall be made by us within 10 days after our receipt
      of plans, specifications and M.A.I. appraisal. You will be
      advised within 5 days of our decision.

15.   In the event we are not satisfied with the M.A.I. appraisal
      or site inspection the commitment fee of $20,000. shall be
      returned to you within 5 days.

16.   All legal matters and documents shall be subject to the
      approval of our counsel.

17.   All costs and charges for title examination and issuance of
      policy, survey, mortgage tax, recording fees, revenue stamps
      and all other disbursements including legal fees ($1,000.)
      of our attorneys, in connection with the making of this
      mortgage loan shall be paid by you at the time of closing
      which shall take place at our office in Brooklyn, New York.

[B7824]

18.   The obligation shall be limited to the mortgage covering
the real estate and the lease with
There shall be no personal liability.

The terms of this letter may not be waived, modified or in
any other way, changed except as agreed to in writing and signed
by both parties.

If the terms and conditions of this commitment meet with
your approval, you will please so indicate by signing the acceptance below and returning to us a properly signed copy of this
letter.

This commitment shall become effective upon receipt of your
acceptance in Brooklyn, New York, within 5 days from the date
hereof, together with your check in the amount of $20,000.

                              Very truly yours,

                              New Hampshire Mutual Life
                              Insurance Company

                              By_____
                                 Vice-President

All the foregoing terms and
conditions are accepted

Cen Tenn Realty Co., Inc.

BY:_____

BY:_____

This   day of   , 1977   [B7825]

III. TITLE

A construction lender will take a different view of easements
and restrictions than will a mortgagee of property which has already
been developed. A mortgagee taking a mortgage upon an existing
building will often assume that any building restrictions or easements on the property do not adversely affect the building, particularly if the building has been there and in use for a number of years.
However, a construction lender taking a mortgage on vacant ground
has no such comfort from a fact situation that has survived the pas-

sage of time. The construction lender will, therefore, require that the title report contain the full text of any restrictions or easements (including utility company rights-of-way) and that such easements and restrictions be clearly located on a current survey of the property.

IV. PREPARATION OF DOCUMENTS

There are several parties who may be involved in a construction loan, including the developer, permanent lender, construction lender, general contractor and one or more major tenants. As a result, usually more documents are required than in the case of the other types of loans we have previously reviewed. Among the documents which may be necessary for a construction loan closing are the following:

A. CONSTRUCTION LOAN AGREEMENT

The basic understanding between the mortgagor and the construction lender, pursuant to which the construction lender agrees to advance the funds as they are needed for the project, is set forth in the construction loan agreement. The agreement is often prepared on forms supplied by the construction lender. For major transactions, the construction loan agreement will be thoroughly negotiated, as it is the single most important agreement between the borrower and the construction lender.

B. NOTE

Generally the note will be on the form of note used by the permanent lender. Using this form, the construction lender will include certain clauses outlining the construction loan arrangements. The considerations for a decision to include such clauses and examples of such clauses appear in section VI(A) of this chapter.

C. MORTGAGE

The mortgage will be similar to the mortgage required by the lender in the commercial—industrial situation. As in the case of the note, the construction lender will want certain clauses included to reflect the special construction loan arrangements. Drafting considerations for and examples of such clauses appear in section VI (B) of this chapter.

D. GENERAL CONSTRUCTION CONTRACT

The construction lender will want a copy of the contract between the borrower and the general contractor to be sure that the general contractor has obligated itself to construct the building within the time limit and for the amount of money the construction lender is depending upon. The latter concern may not be met by delivery of a copy of the contract, since many construction contracts are not for a fixed sum, but for cost plus a percentage of cost.

E. COMPLETION BOND

The general contractor has no direct obligation to the construction lender. Nevertheless, the construction lender wants to be sure it can enforce the construction contract directly against the general contractor in the event the construction lender takes the place of the borrower. Accordingly, the construction lender may require the general contractor to sign a bond guaranteeing that it will complete its obligation under the construction contract.

F. CORPORATE RESOLUTIONS

If the mortgagor is a corporation, the construction lender will want a copy of resolutions of the corporation's board of directors authorizing the loan. The copy should be certified by the secretary of the corporation.

G. INSURANCE

The construction lender will require insurance against destruction of the partially completed structure by fire and similar hazards. Such insurance will usually be on a "builder's risk" form which increases in value as the value of the construction increases. In addition, the construction lender will want the general contractor to carry liability insurance and workmen's compensation insurance.

H. SURVEY

As indicated above, a survey is extremely important to the construction lender in order to be sure that the proposed construction will not in any way interfere with any existing easements or rights of way or violate any existing enforceable building restrictions.

I. BUILDING PERMIT

The construction lender wants to be certain that the local municipal authority has issued a valid permit allowing the proposed construction. Generally, such a permit can be obtained only if the proposed building complies with the applicable building code as well as the zoning and sub-division ordinances.

J. BUY–SELL AGREEMENT

The permanent loan commitment is an agreement between the New Hampshire Mutual and Cen Tenn. Second Centralia, who is looking towards that permanent loan commitment to take it out, has no direct right to enforce that permanent loan commitment letter, because Second Centralia does not have privity of contract with New Hampshire Mutual. Similarly, New Hampshire Mutual has no control over the construction loan agreement and can neither directly enforce the construction loan agreement against Second Centralia nor require Second Centralia to sell the note to it upon completion of the project rather than to some other permanent lender. The only link between New Hampshire Mutual and Second Centralia is Cen Tenn, who may prove to be a weak link indeed, unable or unwilling to conclude the transaction as contemplated. A permanent lender and a construction lender generally forge a new, and direct, link between themselves by entering into a buy-sell agreement. This agreement, which creates the necessary privity of contract, includes the agreement of the permanent lender to purchase the note and mortgage from the construction lender in accordance with the terms of the permanent commitment letter, and the agreement of the construction lender to sell to the permanent lender. The permanent lender and construction lender each agree to attorn to the other in the event that the other takes over the position of the developer due to a default by the developer.

The buy-sell agreement is also usually signed by the developer. For the developer, it often serves as an opportunity to resolve some of the uncertainties of the permanent loan commitment. That commitment usually reserves the right of the permanent lender and its counsel to approve various aspects of the transaction. A developer often lacks the bargaining power to pin down the permanent lender further. The construction lender has the same need for certainty, and usually has the necessary bargaining power to gain a larger measure of certainty by getting the permanent lender to give its approval in the buy-sell agreement to a variety of items, such as the state of title and acceptability of exceptions to title.

The following Buy-Sell Agreement might be used in our sample fact situation.

EXAMPLE: Buy-Sell Agreement

Second Centralia National Bank
Centralia, Tennessee

December 1, 1977

New Hampshire Mutual Life Insurance Co.
Rocky Falls, New Hampshire

Gentlemen:

With reference to your commitment dated September 1, 1977 wherein you agree to make or purchase a first mortgage loan to Cen Tenn Realty Co., Inc. of not exceeding $1,000,000., we agree to make a construction loan up to that amount using papers to be submitted to and approved by you that will contain the terms of the permanent loan and be acceptable to you for later purchase.

In consideration of your agreeing to purchase such papers from us, without recourse, subject to the conditions of your commitment having been met, we agree to hold such papers available for such purchase and to cooperate with you in all reasonable ways, in connection therewith. The foregoing is subject to the following understanding becoming applicable in the event of default or expiration of your commitment.

We agree to take no action (by taking steps to enforce the terms of the papers or otherwise) which would give anyone the right to prepay the indebtedness nor to sell or assign the papers to others except with your prior written assent or unless within 20 days after receipt by you of notice from us specifying the nature of a default or advising of the expiration of your commitment you fail to purchase the papers, to extend the term of your commitment or the time for performance of a defaulted condition thereof for a reasonable period of time, to state that the default will not affect your agreement to purchase, or to make such reasonable change in the conditions of your commitment as will remove the default. In the event of default or expiration of your commitment, regarding which no notice as above is given by us, it is agreed that you shall have the right upon reasonable notice to us, to purchase such papers. Upon your request, any special collateral held by us solely in connection with the loan shall be assigned and delivered to you if you purchase said papers while a default exists or after the expiration of your commitment.

Very truly yours,

Second Centralia National Bank

By: _____

[B7766]

In consideration of your agreement in the above letter, we are pleased to accept the obligations imposed on us therein and agree to be bound thereby.

New Hampshire Mutual Life
Insurance Co.

By: _____

We hereby assign to Second Centralia National Bank all of our right, title, and interest in the aforesaid commitment and agree not to prepay the construction mortgage loan.

Cen Tenn Realty Co., Inc.

By: _____

[B7767]

K. DECLARATION OF CROSS EASEMENTS

In our hypothetical case the property was subject to an existing mortgage in favor of First Mortgagee Insurance Company. First Mortgagee Insurance Company has agreed that the new construction would enhance the over-all value of the shopping center. It will therefore release from the lien of its mortgage the area required to construct the new building for tenant. This will allow the mortgagor to create a first lien on that property in favor of Second Centralia. However, the fact that different portions of the shopping center will be subject to separate mortgages held by different mortgagees raises the possibility that at some future time, by foreclosure, the two portions of the shopping center might be vested in separate owners. Since the two portions together constitute a single integrated shopping center, each owner will need the right to go upon the property of the other for parking, access and possibly support. Accordingly, prior to recording of the new mortgage, the owner and the holder of the existing mortgage will execute a reciprocal easement agreement granting such easement rights to all present or future owners of either property. The agreement would normally consist of: (a) a recital of the relevant background; (b) the actual grant of the easement; (c) a provision concerning responsibility for the expense of maintaining the property subject to the easement; (d) a statement of the duration or term of the easement; and (e) a description of the property benefitted and burdened by the easement.

L. SECURITY AGREEMENT AND FINANCING STATEMENT

The construction lender may wish to obtain a security interest in the mortgagor's personal property at the premises, which will usually be in the form of a security agreement or a financing statement. Security agreements and financing statements, because they cover personal property rather than real property, are generally filed in the offices of the clerk of the local court for the county in which the real property to be mortgaged is located. In addition, one copy of the financing statement may have to be filed at the state capitol.

Example: Security Agreement and Financing Statement

SECURITY AGREEMENT made this 15th day of December, 1977, between Cen Tenn Realty Co., Inc., Centralia, Tennessee, a Tennessee corporation, ("DEBTOR"), and Second Centralia National Bank, 1 Central Plaza, Centralia, Tennessee ("SECURED PARTY");

W I T N E S S E T H :

On this date SECURED PARTY will lend to DEBTOR with interest, all as provided in and evidenced by a Mortgage Note ("Mortgage Note") of even date herewith, in the face amount of One Million Dollars ($1,000,000), and secured by a Mortgage ("Mortgage") also of even date upon the interest of DEBTOR in certain real estate situated in Central County, Tennessee, as more particularly described in said Mortgage.

NOW, THEREFORE, to induce the SECURED PARTY to lend the sum of $1,000,000 to DEBTOR, DEBTOR and SECURED PARTY, intending to be legally bound, hereby agree as follows:

1. DEBTOR hereby grants to SECURED PARTY a security interest in and mortgages to SECURED PARTY all of the interest of DEBTOR in the following described property, together with all parts, accessories, attachments and equipment at any time installed therein or affixed thereto and all accessories thereto and additions and replacements thereof and all proceeds of the foregoing (collectively referred to as "the collateral"):

All furniture, furnishings, fixtures, machinery and equipment and other tangible personal property of whatsoever kind and nature attached to or located on the real estate of debtor

[B7768]

located in Central County, Tennessee, containing in the aggregate

       acres, described in "Exhibit A", attached hereto and

hereby made a part hereof.

2.   This security interest is given as additional security

for the repayment of the aforementioned loan in accordance with the

terms of the Mortgage Note and the collateral shall be encumbered

in the same manner and on the same terms and conditions to which

the premises covered by the Mortgage are subjected. DEBTOR, for

itself and any subsequent owner, will at DEBTOR'S expense execute

and deliver for filing all financing and other statements and take

or join with SECURED PARTY in taking any other action requested by

SECURED PARTY to perfect and continue perfected SECURED PARTY'S

secured interest throughout the term of the Mortgage.

3.   All of the covenants and agreements in the Mortgage Note

and Mortgage to be performed by DEBTOR thereunder are incorporated

herein by reference, and all of the remedies provided for herein may

be exercised concurrently with the remedies provided for in the Mort-

gage Note and Mortgage.

4.   Until default DEBTOR shall be entitled to possession, use

and enjoyment of the collateral. A default under either the Mortgage

Note or Mortgage shall also constitute a default to this Agreement.

Under such circumstances, SECURED PARTY may exercise all rights and

remedies of a SECURED PARTY under the Uniform Commercial Code of

Tennessee.   [B7769]

IN WITNESS WHEREOF, the parties have executed this Agreement as of the day and year first above written.

Second Centralia National Bank   Cen Tenn Realty Co., Inc.

By _____   By _____

ATTEST: ATTEST:

_____   _____

(Corporate Seal)   (Corporate Seal)   [B7770]

Uniform Commercial Code—**FINANCING STATEMENT**—Form DSCB:UCC-1

PRINTED FOR AND SOLD BY JOHN C CLARK CO 1326 WALNUT ST , PHILADELPHIA PA 19107

IMPORTANT — Read instructions on back before filling out form

This FINANCING STATEMENT is presented to a Filing Officer for filing pursuant to the Uniform Commercial Code.	No. of Additional Sheets Presented:	Maturity Date 3. (optional):

1. Debtor(s) (Last Name First and Address(es):	2. Secured Party(ies): Name(s) and Address(es):	4. For Filing Officer: Date, Time, No.-Filing Office
Cen Tenn Realty Co., Inc. Centralia, Tennessee	Second Centralia National Bank 1 Central Plaza Centralia, Tennessee	

5. This Financing Statement covers the following types (or items) of property:	6. Assignee(s) of Secured Party and Address(es)
All furniture, fixtures, machinery and equipment and other tangible personal property of whatsoever kind and nature attached to or located on the real estate of debtor described below.	

7. ☐ The described crops are growing or to be grown on: *
☐ The described goods are or are to be affixed to: *
* (Describe Real Estate Below).

☐ Proceeds —   ☐ Products of the Collateral are also covered.

8. Describe Real Estate Here:	9. Name(s) of Record Owner(s):	
Parcel of ground located in Centralia, Tennessee as described in Exhibit A hereto		Cen Tenn Realty Co., Inc.

No. & Street	Town or City	County	Section	Block	Lot

10. This statement is filed without the debtor's signature to perfect a security interest in collateral (check appropriate box)

☐ already subject to a security interest in another jurisdiction when it was brought into this state, or

☐ which is proceeds of the original collateral described above in which a security interest was perfected:

Cen Tenn Realty Co., Inc.   Second Centralia National Bank

By _____   By _____
     Signature(s) of Debtor(s)   Signature(s) of Secured Party(ies)

(1) FILING OFFICER COPY - NUMERICAL

FORM DSCB:UCC-1 (Rev. 8-72)—Approved by Department of State of the Commonwealth of Pa.   [B7771]

V. PREPARATION FOR CLOSING

In addition to preparation of the documents set forth above, the construction lender will want to obtain the approval of the permanent lender as to (a) the form of the note and mortgage which the permanent lender will purchase by assignment upon completion of construction; (b) the form of lease to be used for the tenant or tenants of the property; and (c) the plans and specifications for the store. In many cases, the permanent lender either will prepare the note and mortgage, including the clauses concerning the construction loan, or will supply the forms of note and mortgage to be used by the construction lender.

VI. MECHANICS' LIENS

In any large construction project, the general contractor will purchase services and materials from other companies and tradesmen. These people are called subcontractors and materialmen. In the early 19th century, when the United States was expanding rapidly and it was considered socially useful to encourage people to go into the building trades and crafts, various states passed statutes giving artisans and mechanics a lien on any real property for which they had furnished labor or material. This lien is effective until the mechanic is paid, in full, for work on the property. The significant concept concerning mechanics' lien statutes is that they also benefit materialmen, mechanics and artisans who are subcontractors, and who therefore have no direct contractual relationship with the owner. Thus, even if the owner of the property has paid the general contractor for the work, if the general contractor did not pay the subcontractors, then the subcontractors were entitled to a lien upon the property. Like a mortgage, this lien could be executed upon to cause a judicial sale of the property, with the proceeds going to the holder of the mechanics' lien, among others. Ultimately, each state passed a mechanics' lien statute.

Mechanics' liens were unknown to the common law, and thus were not based on any common heritage brought here from England. There is considerable variety among the mechanics' lien laws of the several states. There is also substantial variation from state to state as to what an honest owner, who pays his general contractor, can do to protect himself against a mechanics' lien attaching to his property. The question of who should suffer the loss, if the general contractor, having been paid by the owner, is unable or unwilling to pay his subcontractor, is a particularly difficult one. The question has been resolved differently in different states. In a few states, a waiver by the general contractor of his right to file a mechanics' lien, also has the effect of waiving the rights of all subcontractors, provided the waiver is filed in a public place before any work begins. This is not true in most other states, where the question has basically been resolved in favor of subcontractors.

Mechanics' liens present an especially thorny problem for the construction lender and the title insurer. In some states, a mechanics' lien can be prior to the mortgage lien even if the mechanics' lien is actually filed or recorded after the mortgage, but the work began before the mortgage was recorded. The statutory scheme for priorities varies from state to state. A paralegal must be aware of the problem of mechanics' liens and learn the manner in which the problem is handled in the state in which the real estate is located.

VII. CLOSING

At closing for the construction loan, all of the various documents referred to above will be executed, acknowledged where appropriate, and delivered as in other mortgage settlements. Although there are many more documents than in the ordinary mortgage settlement, the procedure at settlement is basically the same.

VIII. POST CLOSING

After settlement, the owner and the construction lender will proceed in accordance with the construction loan agreement. Usually, the mortgagor or the general contractor will submit periodic requests for advances on account of the loan, on voucher forms supplied by the construction lender. The construction lender will send out its inspectors periodically to ascertain whether the work for which payment has been requested has actually been done and whether the value of the work is consistent with the amount of the payment requested. If the inspectors are satisfied, the construction lender will issue its check to the owner or the general contractor or, in some cases, directly to subcontractors.

IX. PERMANENT LOAN CLOSING

Closing on the permanent loan will be held some time after completion of the building and occupancy thereof by the tenant or tenants and before expiration of the term of the permanent commitment. At the closing on the permanent loan, the note and mortgage and collateral assignment of lease and any additional security documents (such as financing statements on personal property) will be assigned to the permanent lender, who will then issue its check to the construction lender. If the permanent lender's check exceeds the sum due the construction lender, the difference will be paid to the mortgagor as a final advance on the construction loan. The permanent lender will also require that the title search be continued down to the date of the permanent closing. This bring-down search will disclose any documents or liens which have been recorded subsequent to the mortgage which might in some way affect the validity or priority of the mortgage or which might indicate that there is some problem with payment of contractors or subcontractors. Interest for the final month of the construction loan will be apportioned and paid.

In some instances, the permanent lender may not purchase the existing documents by assignment but may simply lend the mortgagor the funds to pay the construction lender and then record a new mortgage. The advantage to assignment of the construction mortgage is that, for purposes of determining priority of interests, the lien held by the permanent lender will date back to the date of the construction loan closing.

There are three additional documents which are usually required by the permanent lender at the permanent loan closing.

A. DECLARATION OF NO SET-OFF

If the permanent lender is purchasing the note and mortgage from the construction lender, the permanent lender wants to be sure that the mortgagor does not have some defense to or counterclaim against the construction lender. The defense or counterclaim might arise out of a default by the construction lender in the construction loan agreement, or out of some transaction between the mortgagor and the construction lender completely separate from the loan being sold. To preclude such a problem, the permanent lender will require a statement from the mortgagor that the full amount of the loan is owing and that the mortgagor has no defenses, counterclaims or set-offs against the face amount of the note and mortgage. This estops the mortgagor from interposing any such defenses against the permanent lender at any time.

B. TENANT'S ESTOPPEL CERTIFICATE

Since the permanent lender is relying upon the rent payable by the tenant to pay interest and principal on the loan, the permanent lender wants to be sure (a) that the tenant has taken or is prepared to take possession of the building; (b) that the tenant agrees that the building as constructed complies with the terms of the lease; and (c) that the tenant at the time of settlement on the permanent loan has no defense to any claim for prepaid rent or other allowances. The permanent lender normally requires the mortgagor to obtain from each tenant a certificate or letter to that effect, which is called an "estoppel certificate".

C. CORPORATE RESOLUTIONS

As in the case of the construction loan closing, the permanent lender will want a certified copy of resolutions of the board of directors of a corporate mortgagor authorizing the officers of the corporation to execute the documents necessary to close the permanent loan.

Part Four

FEDERAL HOUSING ADMINISTRATION (FHA) MORTGAGES

The Federal Housing Administration (commonly called the "FHA") is an administrative part of the Department of Housing and Urban Development ("HUD"). The FHA is HUD's principal means of implementing HUD's various programs and policies in the housing field, as such programs and policies are determined by the President and the Congress. This chapter is only intended to familiarize the student with elementary FHA terminology and with the kind of programs that FHA has traditionally administered. The FHA mortgage programs are in a constant state of flux. New programs are adopted and old ones discarded, and new regulations and requirements are formulated continually for programs then being administered. The programs discussed below are examples of programs that have existed and, in one form or another, will very likely continue to exist for some time.

I. INTRODUCTION TO THE FHA

A. THE ROLE OF THE FHA

The FHA's principal business has traditionally been the insurance of mortgages on residential properties. It has also been assigned the responsibility of managing the Federal Government's programs of subsidizing mortgage payments so as to permit new and rehabilitated housing to be owned or rented by lower income occupants who would not otherwise be able to afford it. You should understand that the FHA does not act as the mortgagee, but rather insures the mortgagee against loss if there is a default on the mortgage. The insurance takes the form of an agreement by the FHA to purchase the mortgage loan from the holder, thus becoming the mortgage holder itself. Consequently, the owner or developer of an FHA-insured mortgage project must obtain mortgage commitments from lending institutions as if he were not using an FHA-insured mortgage, provided that the mortgagee or mortgagees must be approved by the FHA.

B. THE FUNCTION OF MORTGAGE INSURANCE

When the FHA, or any mortgage insurer,[1] insures a mortgage, it guarantees the mortgagee that if there is a default under the mort-

---

[1] Private insurance companies have come into existence which also insure all or part of mortgage loans. These companies operate for a profit. In-deed, the stock of the best known of them trade on national stock exchanges.

gage, the mortgagee will have the right to assign a mortgage in default to the FHA in consideration for the FHA's payment to the mortgagee of the outstanding principal and interest then owed on the mortgage. It is then up to the FHA either to foreclose the mortgage, to obtain a purchaser of the mortgaged property who will attempt to rescue the project, to refinance the mortgage, or otherwise to assist the mortgagor in carrying the property.

This kind of additional security for the mortgagee's loan is obviously beneficial to the mortgagee because it reduces its risk in making the loan. It is also beneficial to the mortgagor because the reduced risk to the mortgagee will permit the mortgagee to make loans which it would not otherwise make. The interest rate for an FHA-insured loan may be lower than the interest rate for a comparable non-insured mortgage because of the lower risk to the mortgagee. Another way in which FHA involvement benefits a borrower is in the amount of the total project cost which can be borrowed through an FHA-insured mortgage loan. Such a mortgage will frequently be made at a higher loan-to-value ratio than the mortgagee would be willing to permit if the loan were not so insured. This means that the owner or developer of a project usually needs to invest less equity money to develop an FHA-insured mortgage project than to build a project secured by a conventional mortgage.

C. THE ORGANIZATION OF THE FHA

The student should have some familiarity with the way the FHA is organized in order to know where to obtain necessary information or answers to questions or to submit drafts of documents which must be approved by the FHA. The structure of the FHA is of course, subject to change, however, a brief description of its present structure may be helpful.

The main office of the FHA is in the HUD Office Building in Washington, D. C. This office is the source of general policy decisions, new and amended regulations and changes in over-all procedures. Questions of an unusual nature relating to a particular project may ultimately have to be referred to Washington for a decision.

A legal assistant is most likely to have contact with the HUD Area Office which has jurisdiction over the project on which an insured mortgage will be placed. Between the HUD Washington Office and the forty Area Offices there are ten Regional Offices blanketing the country, each of which has one or more Area Offices reporting to it. For example, the Philadelphia Regional Office is responsible for all HUD programs in Delaware, the District of Columbia, Maryland, Pennsylvania, Virginia and West Virginia (including five Area Offices—Philadelphia, Pittsburgh, Baltimore, Richmond and Washington, D. C.—and Insuring Offices in Wilmington, Delaware and Charleston, West Virginia). The Philadelphia Area Office, in turn, has jurisdiction over all HUD programs in the State of Delaware and the thirty-eight Pennsylvania counties nearest Philadelphia, with the Pittsburgh Area Office being responsible for the balance of the Pennsylvania counties.

D. TYPES OF PROJECTS ON WHICH THE FHA WILL INSURE THE MORTGAGE

The FHA is authorized to insure mortgages for a vast array of residential projects. Each program is commonly referred to by the Section or Title of the National Honsing Act which authorizes the particular program. The FHA has responsibility for insuring mortgages on such diverse projects as housing designed specifically for the elderly, cooperative and condominium housing, nursing homes, rehabilitation of run-down homes, luxury apartments, experimental housing and housing for veterans. It is neither possible nor necessary to discuss all these programs in the confines of these materials. Rather, we will consider the Section 236 Program which is for mortgages on new construction rental apartment projects.

E. TYPES OF MORTGAGES WHICH THE FHA WILL INSURE

The FHA has the power to insure several different types of mortgages. If the FHA is insuring only the permanent loan, it is said to be insuring the loan on an "Insurance Upon Completion" basis. If both the construction loan advances and the permanent mortgage loan are being insured, the insurance is said to be issued on an "Insurance of Advances" basis. Obviously, only the latter method provides insurance protection for the construction lender as well as for the permanent lender. An Insurance of Advances mortgage loan may be the only way to finance the construction or rehabilitation of projects which are located in high risk areas or which are being undertaken by a developer who lacks substantial experience and a good credit rating.

F. FHA MORTGAGE SUBSIDIES AND RENT SUPPLEMENT PROGRAMS

FHA administers certain programs by which it provides subsidized mortgages. The Section 236 Program was designed primarily for the purpose of encouraging the construction or rehabilitation by private developers of rental housing for low and moderate-income families, with a priority going to those families who have been displaced by urban renewal or other governmental actions. The "encouragement" provided by the FHA is in the form of a direct governmental subsidy of the interest payments made on the loan by the mortgagor, as well as the usual Federal insurance of the mortgage loans. In addition, in some instances described below, the FHA may make a regular cash payment to the owner to supplement a tenants' rent payments.

1. Interest Subsidy

The mechanics of the interest subsidy operate in the following manner: the mortgagor makes monthly payments to the mortgagee in the amount of the required amortization of the principal of the loan together with interest at the rate of 1% per annum on the unpaid principal balance. The FHA pays directly to the mortgagee the difference between this 1% interest rate and the interest rate set forth on the face of the note.

The project owner must pass the benefit of the interest reduction to its low and moderate-income tenants in the form of lower rents. A "basic rental" charge is determined for each apartment. The "basic rental" equals the amount of money needed each month to amortize the principal of the mortgage, pay interest on the mortgage at the rate of one percent per annum, cover the estimated operating expenses of the apartment and give the developer the percentage return on investment permitted by the FHA pursuant to the particular program. Any rental collected by the owner in excess of the "basic rents" must be returned to HUD for deposit in a revolving fund, which is used for making other interest-reduction payments.

The FHA will also determine "fair market rental" for each apartment. That is the amount which would be charged for the apartment if the project were financed conventionally. The landlord will be permitted to rent an apartment either at the basic rental for that apartment or at 25% of the income of the tenant family, whichever is greater. However, in no event may the rent exceed the fair market rental for that apartment. A family's income must be re-certified every two years and the rent charged to it adjusted accordingly.

2. Rent Supplements

Mechanically, rent supplements in Section 236 projects work as follows: as previously discussed, a tenant of an apartment in a Section 236 project would normally pay the greater of 25% of income or the basic rent for that apartment computed upon the basis of a one-percent interest rate mortgage loan. In the case of tenants whose family income is low enough to make them eligible for public housing, the basic rent for their apartment would in fact be about 35% to 40% of the family's income. The rent supplement payment fills the gap between 25% of the tenant's income and the basic rent so that the landlord would receive the full basic rent even though the tenant paid only 25% of the family's income.

Part Five

INDUSTRIAL DEVELOPMENT AUTHORITY LOANS

In order to attract industry, many communities throughout the country have created industrial development authorities, which grant low interest mortgages on both old and new industrial and commercial facilities. Interest received from units of state and local government is exempt from the federal income tax. Taxpayers who buy obligations of such a governmental unit need not pay income tax on the interest income produced. This tax exemption allows state and local governments to raise money at a lower interest rate than would otherwise be necessary to attract investors because a dollar of tax-free interest is worth more to an investor than a dollar of other interest income upon which the taxpayer must pay income tax.

Promoters of local industry have utilized these facts by creating a government authority which would borrow money from a bank, use the money to purchase or build an industrial or commercial facility, and then lease the facility to a tenant who would pay enough rent to pay off the mortgage. When the mortgage was paid in full, the authority would sell the facility to the user for a nominal price. The authority in such a case is a mere conduit, the true economic substance of the transaction being a mortgage loan from the bank to the industrial user of the building. However, since the interest was actually being paid by a governmental unit, the interest income is tax exempt. Banks are willing to lend money at a lower than normal interest rate, the benefit of which is passed on to the industrial user in the form of lower rent. Instead of a lease with rent, the transaction between the authority and the user might be an installment sale contract. In either case the user is fully responsible for the property and all of the expenses of operating, repairing and maintaining it.

While it is beyond the scope of this course to detail the steps of such a mortgage, we will describe briefly the substance of such a loan.

I. MORTGAGE LOAN FROM THE BANK TO THE INDUSTRIAL DEVELOPMENT AUTHORITY

An industrial development authority loan starts when the authority obtains a mortgage loan from a financial institution on a piece of property which the authority will acquire for an industrial user. In actuality, the user will normally approach the authority after having spotted a property which suits its purposes. The authority will not advance any of its own money. The costs of acquisition, plus construction, if applicable, will be paid from the mortgage loan. The balance, if any, will be supplied by the industrial user. The mortgage will look much like any other mortgage, with the authority as the mortgagor.

II. LEASE WITH THE INDUSTRIAL USER

In order to be assured of the funds necessary to meet the mortgage payments, the authority will lease the premises to the industrial user or will grant possession under an installment sales contract. The rent will normally equal the mortgage payments, fire insurance premiums and real estate taxes. In some instances the latter two items would not be included in the rent but would be the direct responsibility of the tenant. The lease would be what is called a "net" or a "net-net lease" meaning that authority would have no responsibilities as a landlord. All repairs and other expenses would be the obligation of the industrial user as tenant.

III. AGREEMENT OF PURCHASE

It is the intention of the parties that the industrial user will own the property when the mortgage has been paid off. The lease itself could contain the sales agreement in the form of an option to buy the property for nominal consideration, or the whole arrangement might be cast as an installment contract.

While the mechanics of industrial development authority transactions may differ from one locale to another, they all will resemble the format outlined above.

Part Six

FORM AND SUBSTANCE OF THE NOTE AND MORTGAGE

I. DRAFTING NOTES

The mortgagor's debt will be evidenced by an instrument called a note [1] and secured by a conveyance or lien on real estate called a mortgage. The note will set forth the obligation itself, the interest rate, and the terms and date of repayment.

In preparing a note, the draftsman must consider a number of items:

A. PARTIES

The draftsman has the usual concerns respecting parties and property execution. Normally the signer of the note, who is usually referred to as the "maker" or the "obligor", will be the same person

---

1. In some areas a "bond" is used in place of a note.

who owns the real estate upon which the mortgage is being given. However, this is not always the case, and it is this possibility that can create unusual concerns for the draftsman. These situations can arise in a number of different factual settings, most of which are variations upon two basic possibilities. The first of these basic situations is one in which the person borrowing the money has some interest in the real property, but there is some other person who also has an interest and who must join in the mortgage in order to grant a mortgage lien upon the entire property. The second basic situation is one in which the person borrowing the money has no interest whatsoever in the real property to be mortgaged, and the borrower requests the owner of the real property to grant a mortgage as security for the payment of the debt. The owner may accede to this request either because the owner is a related party to the borrower or because the owner is itself obligated in some way to the borrower.

Let us consider the example of Holly Singer, who wishes to borrow $25,000 from Greene National Bank. Holly and her husband Fred are the owners of 2021 Spruce Street, Centre City. Holly has other assets of her own, and is willing to be personally liable for repayment of the loan. Fred also has other assets of his own. Although he is willing to mortgage 2021 Spruce Street, and to lose it if the loan is not repaid, he is unwilling to risk any of his individual assets. Under these circumstances, Holly alone, and not Fred, would sign the note. Both Holly and Fred would sign the mortgage, but the standard language of the mortgage would probably be reworked to make it clear that the obligation which the mortgage secured was not an obligation of both mortgagors, but was only the obligation of Holly. Additionally, Greene National Bank will be concerned that there is sufficient legal consideration for the agreement of Fred to join in the mortgage and it will therefore very likely include in the mortgage a recitation that Fred is joining in the granting of the mortgage in order to induce Greene to make the loan to Holly.

Notes signed by persons under 18 years old (21 years in some jurisdictions) are voidable[2] in many cases. If the person who has signed the note is less than 18 at the time he signs it, he can disavow the note and refuse to pay it. There are certain exceptions to this general rule. The draftsman should ascertain whether the signatory is under 18 and if so, should determine whether, under applicable state law the minor signatory will be bound by the instrument. Similarly, a note signed by a person who is mentally incompetent may be voidable.

---

2. Lawyers distinguish between agreements which are voidable, and those which are void. A voidable agreement may be negated by the active denial of a person entitled to void it. A void agreement is void from its inception, and there is no requirement for anyone to perform an active denial in order for it to be void and unenforceable.

If the signatory is a trustee, the draftsman will want to examine the document under which the trust has been created to ascertain whether the trustee has the authority to sign notes and subject the trust property to the lien of the mortgage. The same applies to guardians, executors and administrators.

With reference to partnerships, the general rule is that any partner may sign for the partnership if the mortgage is necessary for carrying on the business of the partnership in the usual way. However, the rules relating to partners' authority are not always entirely clear, and there are certain legal limitations on partners' authority. In any event, it is generally considered good practice to obtain the signatures of all general partners and to obtain proof, by affidavit or otherwise, that the people who have signed are all of the general partners.

The question of authority to sign also arises in connection with corporations. A corporation is a legal entity and, as such, may sign notes and mortgages. However, the action of the corporation must be authorized by its board of directors, and the documents must be signed by natural persons authorized to do so by the board. Normally these persons will be the corporation's officers. In some states if all or a substantial portion of the property of the corporation is to be mortgaged, a note and mortgage require the approval of the shareholders in addition to the approval of the directors. This should be checked in each instance.

To satisfy itself as to the authority of the people signing the note or mortgage, the lender will want the borrower to provide resolutions of the board of directors (and the shareholders, if necessary) in substantially the following form:

> RESOLVED, that this corporation borrow the sum of $10,000.00 from the First National Bank to be repaid with interest at 10% per annum in 180 equal successive monthly installments of $107.47 each; and on such other terms and conditions as the President may deem proper;

> FURTHER RESOLVED, that to secure payment of the aforesaid loan this corporation create a first mortgage on its real estate known as 214 Main Street, Hartford, Ohio.

> FURTHER RESOLVED, that the President or Vice President be and they hereby are authorized, empowered and directed to execute, acknowledge and deliver a mortgage note and mortgage in the foregoing amount, and to execute, acknowledge and deliver such other documents and take such other steps as may be necessary or desirable to effectuate the foregoing resolutions.

B. PAYMENT

As discussed previously, residential mortgages are normally self-liquidating, level payment loans. That is, the borrower makes identical payments during each month while the loan is being repaid. The payments are applied first to accrued interest at the rate set forth in the note and the remainder of the payment is used to reduce the principal. Since the principal is constantly being reduced, the amount of interest, which is payable only on the outstanding balance of the principal, is also reduced. Each succeeding month, therefore, a smaller amount is applied to interest and a larger amount to principal. The exact allocation of each payment can be determined from amortization schedules, which most lawyers can obtain for a particular loan.

Many notes are prepared on printed forms, and the major drafting involved in the preparation of those notes is the drafting of the payment provision. The payment provision should indicate the interest being charged, the number and frequency of payments, the allocation of payments between interest and principal and the date upon which the first payment is due.

An example of a level payment provision for a 20-year loan of $25,500 with interest at the rate of 7% per annum follows:

"The principal, together with interest thereon at the rate of 7% per annum, shall be payable in 240 consecutive equal monthly installments of One Hundred Ninety Seven and 71/100 Dollars ($197.71) each, commencing on the first day of June 1977, and thereafter on the same date of each month until the principal and interest are paid in full. The final payment of the entire indebtedness evidenced hereby, together with all accrued interest thereon, shall be due and payable on May 1, 1997."

Non-residential mortgage notes often call for other than level payments. For example, a note might provide for principal to be paid in equal quarterly installments over a five-year period with interest payable at the same time on the then remaining balance. The principal payments will always be equal but the interest payments will decline as the principal balance declines. An example of such a provision in regard to a $1,000,000 loan follows:

"Beginning on January 1, 1978, principal shall be due and payable in 40 successive quarter annual installments of Twenty-five Thousand Dollars ($25,000.) each, together with interest at the rate of 8% per annum, the final installment to be in the full amount of principal and interest then remaining due and unpaid, shall be due December 1, 1987."

A variation of the above provision is one in which the periodic payments would not be sufficient to liquidate the loan. For example, a $2,000,000 loan may call for quarterly principal payments of $50,000 during a five year term of the loan. The final payment will have to include an extra $1,000,000. Such a note is said to contain a "balloon" referring to the extra large payment at the end.

PROBLEM

Prepare a repayment clause for a $1,200.00 loan bearing interest at 8% per annum. Payments are semi-annual beginning January 1, 1979 with the first two payments being interest only. Beginning with the third payment, payments shall include principal of $100.00 plus interest. Loan matures on July 1, 1986.

C.   PREPAYMENT PRIVILEGE

Another item which is frequently included in the note but not in the mortgage is the borrower's right to prepay. Particularly in periods when interest rates are high, lenders may provide either that the borrower may not make any prepayments of principal, or that the borrower may not prepay the entire loan. The borrower wants to reserve the privilege to prepay the loan at any time so that if interest rates should decline, the borrower would have the right to replace the existing loan with one at a lower interest rate. Prepayment is frequently a matter of intense negotiation between borrower and lender. Generally the lender is willing to permit prepayment but only after a number of years have elapsed and even then only upon the payment of a fee, sometimes called a "prepayment premium" or "prepayment penalty".

The prepayment penalty is generally set forth as a percentage of the amount prepaid and, in many cases, the prepayment penalty declines as the loan grows older (and the lender has received most of the interest he originally anticipated receiving). For example, it is not unusual for a note in commercial transactions to provide that no prepayment is permitted for a period of ten years; and thereafter prepayment may be made but only if the loan is paid in full and the prepayment is accompanied by a prepayment penalty which in the eleventh year is equal to 5% of the then outstanding balance. The amount of the prepayment penalty may decline each year thereafter until it is reduced to 1%, or even to nothing at all. In many jurisdictions, the failure to include a prepayment clause reserving to the borrower the right to make prepayments has the effect of barring any prepayment without the lender's consent. As a result, the prepayment provision should be included even if no penalty or premium will be charged.

PROBLEM

Prepare a prepayment clause for the situation described in the preceding paragraph.

D.   ACCELERATION

A note will generally provide for acceleration to maturity in the event of default. This means that if the borrower fails to pay even one installment when it is due the lender may immediately declare the entire balance due at one time. Without the right to accelerate, the lender would be able to sue only for the amount then due, and would have to sue each month for the most recent default in payment. The following provision is a form of acceleration provision:

> "It is hereby expressly agreed by Maker that, should any default be made in the payment of any installment of principal and/or interest as aforesaid on the date on which it shall fall due, or in the performance of any of the terms, agreements, or covenants contained in this Note, or in said Mortgage,[3] then the entire unpaid balance of said principal sum with interest accrued thereon and all other sums due by Maker hereunder or under the provisions of said Mortgage, shall at the option of Payee and without notice to Maker become due and payable immediately."

E. SPECIAL CLAUSES IN CONSTRUCTION LOAN NOTES— ADVANCE MONEY OBLIGATIONS

When a construction loan is settled, the borrower may receive at settlement only funds required to pay certain settlement costs and sometimes the cost of acquiring the land. The borrower receives the remainder of the loan as the work progresses, generally by presenting vouchers or requisitions each month to the lender for work done during the prior month. The construction loan agreement, if one is used, will describe the procedures and contingencies necessary for disbursements of the loan. The note signed at settlement will normally be in the full amount of the loan, so that the borrower and the lender do not have to prepare and sign new notes every time the borrower wants an advance. In order for the note to reflect accurately the understanding of the parties, there will normally be a reference to the fact that sums are being advanced from time to time by the lender towards the stated principal sum of the note. A note which is accompanied by a construction loan agreement might contain the following sort of clause:

> "This Note and the accompanying Mortgage are made pursuant to a written Construction Loan Agreement, signed or about to be signed between Maker and Payee, with reference to construction of certain improvements on the mortgaged premises and the advance, from time to time, of sums evidenced by this Note in payment for labor and materials incorporated into the work, and associated costs, upon terms and conditions therein set forth. Advances under the aforesaid Construction Loan Agreement shall constitute advances of the principal of this Note . . . Any breach of the aforesaid Construction Loan Agreement shall, at the option of Payee, constitute a default under this Note and the accompanying Mortgage, as a result of which Payee shall have all of the rights

---

3. The provision that a default in the mortgage is a default in the note is called a cross-default provision. There may also be cross-default provisions with a loan agreement, assignment of lease, security agreement or other collateral for the loan.

and remedies it would have in the event of default in the payment
of any principal or interest due hereunder."

If a note is to be both a construction loan note and a permanent
loan note, then certain other provisions will have to be revised from
the normal form. The note will provide for two different maturity
dates, one if the permanent lender does purchase the note and another, earlier maturity date if the permanent lender does not purchase the note. Similarly, the note will provide for payment of interest only during the construction loan period and for amortized
payments of interest (probably at a different rate) and principal if
and when the permanent lender purchases the note.

There are various drafting techniques that might be used to prepare the provisions needed to reflect the dual purpose of the note.
The most obvious technique, and one which is often difficult to perform well, is straight narrative. A second technique is to draft as if
it were a permanent loan note and then to add a proviso as follows:

> Notwithstanding any contrary terms of payment contained herein,
> no payments of principal but interest only at a rate which is 2%
> in excess of the prime rate of interest charged by Payee from time
> to time, shall be paid by Maker on amounts actually advanced by
> Payee to or for the account of Maker, payable on the first day of
> each month, until such time as this Note has been assigned to the
> Permanent Lender. The outstanding principal balance of this Note
> together with unpaid accrued interest shall be due and payable to
> Payee on _____, 19__, unless this Note has been earlier as-
> signed to the Permanent Lender.

A third technique would be to deal with each concept in the alternative as follows:

> This Note shall be repaid as follows:
> a. Until such time as Payee has assigned this Note to the Perma-
>   nent Lender, then   .   .   .
> b. From and after the date that this Note is assigned to the Per-
>   manent Lender, then   .   .   .
> This Note may be prepaid as follows:
> a. Until such time as Payee has assigned this Note to the Perma-
>   nent Lender, then   .   .   .
> b. From and after the date that this Note is assigned to the Per-
>   manent Lender, then   .   .   .

A fourth technique would be to define certain terms such as Construction Loan Period, Permanent Settlement Date and Permanent
Loan Period, and then to group together all of the terms that are particular to the different provision of the Note:

Construction Loan Period

During the Construction Loan Period the following terms and conditions shall apply: .   .   .

Permanent Settlement Date

At the Permanent Settlement the following shall occur: . . .

Permanent Loan Period

During the Permanent Loan Period the following terms and conditions shall apply: . . .

The choice of techniques, and combinations thereof, should be based upon both stylistic preferences and the particular complexities of the note in question. A careful draftsman can employ any of the techniques and still accurately memorialize the intended transaction. A less experienced draftsman might find it helpful to adopt some variation of the fourth technique, at least to the extent of defining terms. Errors and inaccuracies can often occur from a failure to define terms. For example, the permanent loan commitment might provide for no right of prepayment for the first ten years. If the prepayment clause is drafted to read "Maker shall have no right of prepayment for the first ten years of this Note", then it will be inaccurate. The commitment letter undoubtedly intended that the ten year period commence from the time the *permanent* lender makes its loan, whereas the drafted language causes the ten year period to run from the date that the *construction* lender commences to make its loan. If terms have been defined, then the draftsman could easily write that "Maker shall have no right of prepayment for ten years from the Permanent Settlement Date".

An example of a note is appended at the end of this Part Six. That example is the form of note approved by FHLMC and FNMA for use nationwide.

II. DRAFTING MORTGAGES

A mortgage is the grant of an interest in real property to secure performance of the borrower's obligations under the note. In addition, the mortgage normally includes the agreement of borrower and lender with respect to various other items such as payment of taxes, application of fire insurance proceeds, application of proceeds of any eminent domain award and repairs to the property. An example of a mortgage is appended at the end of this Part Six. That example is the form of mortgage approved by FHLMC or FNMA for use nationwide.

A. PARTIES

The first part of the mortgage sets forth the date of the mortgage, the names of the parties and the background of the transaction which led to the creation of a mortgage.

MORTGAGE, made this twenty-first day of June in the year one thousand nine hundred seventy one between [*insert name of Mortgagor*] hereinafter called Mortgagor (whether one or more than one), of the one part, and NATIONAL BANK, a national banking association organized and existing under the laws of the United States of America, having its principal place of business in the City of Dallas, Texas hereinafter called Mortgagee, of the other part:

WHEREAS, Mortgagor has executed and delivered to Mortgagee a certain promissory note of even date herewith (hereinafter called the "Note"), in favor of Mortgagee in the principal sum of One Thousand Dollars ($1,000.00) with interest thereon at the rate therein specified, and payable in the manner and at the times therein set forth and under the terms and conditions therein contained, all of which are incorporated herein by reference; [4]

AND WHEREAS, Mortgagee may hereafter make further loans to Mortgagor and it is intended that the same, with interest, shall be secured hereby." [5]

The draftsman must take care to use the precise name of the mortgagor and the mortgagor's capacity to execute the mortgage, as such appear in the last deed of record, if mortgagor is the same person as the grantee thereunder. The draftsman must also be certain that the mortgagor is in fact the party who holds title to the real estate.

B. CONVEYANCE—DESCRIPTION

Just as with a deed, a precise description of the property is set forth in the mortgage. Generally there is no disagreement between the parties concerning the description.[6] The draftsman should be sure that the description has been checked against a survey, wherever possible, to be sure that the description accurately represents the property borrower and lender intended to be mortgaged. A survey will also illustrate the location of any buildings on the mortgaged premises so that a review will show whether they are within the boundary lines and therefore subject to the mortgage.

C. PROPERTY INCLUDED

If there is a particular easement or appurtenance which is important to the property, it should be mentioned specifically and described by metes and bounds. In addition, if the lender intends to obtain a lien on certain personal property, the mortgage should de-

---

4. The practice in some areas, by force of custom or law is to recite the exact repayment terms of the note in the mortgage. Where this is not necessary, it is probably undesirable, as it can lead to question of loss of priority of right upon a modification of terms of repayment.

5. In many jurisdictions this clause is necessary in order to obtain mortgage security for other funds later advanced to the borrower. This clause does not grant priority to such further loans, but does grant security for them.

6. The most common problems arise when there has been assemblance of a large tract from several smaller tracts and an overall perimeter description is to be used.

scribe that property specifically and contain, either here or at some other place in the mortgage, a statement that the mortgage is intended to create a security interest in personal property under the Uniform Commercial Code. Generally a borrower will not object to this clause, unless the borrower intends to obtain separate financing for some or all of the personal property, or unless the borrower does not have unencumbered title to the personal property in question.

> "Together with all and singular the present and future buildings, additions, and improvements as well as any and all fixtures, appliances, and equipment of any nature whatsoever now or hereafter installed in or upon said premises or used in connection with the premises or the operation of the plant, business or dwelling situate thereon, streets, alleys, passages, ways, waters, water courses, rights, liberties, privileges, hereditaments, and appurtenances whatsoever thereunto belonging, or in any wise appertaining, and the reversions and remainders, rents, issues, and profits thereof, now or hereafter accruing."

D. HABENDUM

A mortgage will contain a habendum clause similar to the habendum clause in a deed. Although it is absolute in form, the conveyance will become ineffective as a matter of law when the mortgage debt has been paid.

> "TO HAVE AND TO HOLD said property, hereby granted, or mentioned and intended so to be, with the appurtenances (such property and appurtenances being hereinafter referred to together as the 'Mortgaged Property'), unto Mortgagee, to its own use forever, in fee."

Even though the mortgage, as a matter of law, will be ineffective when the debt has been paid, the borrower would like to include an additional clause to that effect, called a defeasement clause, substantially as follows:

> "If Mortgagor pays to Mortgagee said principal sum and all other sums payable by Mortgagor to Mortgagee as are hereby secured, in accordance with the provisions of said Note and in the manner and at the times therein set forth, without deduction, fraud, or delay, then and from thenceforth this Mortgage, and the estate hereby granted, shall cease and become void, anything herein contained to the contrary notwithstanding."

E. TAXES

In general, the lien of a mortgage takes priority over any lien which arises subsequent to the time the mortgage has been recorded. However, there are certain liens, such as real estate taxes, and some other taxes owed state and local governments by corporate borrowers, which will take precedence over the lien of the mortgage. This means that upon a foreclosure sale, the fund produced at the sale will be paid to satisfy these prior liens for taxes and then to the mortgagee. To protect itself against this situation, the mortgagee wants to be sure that all of such taxes are paid when due, and are not permitted to accumulate. The mortgagee may only require that the mortgagor present evidence of payment of such taxes before they are due (as in provision (1) below) or it may require the mortgagor to deposit in escrow each month ½2th of the estimated yearly taxes (as in provision (2) below).

Until the entire indebtedness secured by this Mortgage, including all sums due Mortgagee under the terms of this Mortgage and of the Note, with interest, is fully paid, Mortgagor covenants and agrees:

(1) *No Escrow.*

To pay when due and payable and before interest and penalties are due thereon all taxes, water and sewer rents, assessments and all other charges or claims which may be assessed or levied upon the Mortgaged Property at any time, by any lawful authority, and which by any present or future law may have priority over said indebtedness either in lien or in distribution out of the proceeds of any judicial sale, and to produce to Mortgagee on or before the last day upon which they may be paid without penalty or interest, receipts of the current year for the payment of all such taxes, water and sewer rents, assessments, charges and claims.

(2) *Escrow.*

To pay to Mortgagee, if requested, on each installment due date an additional sum equal to one-twelfth of the annual taxes, assessments and water and sewer charges, if any, on the Mortgaged Property. If the fund so held by Mortgagee shall be insufficient to pay any of the aforesaid items when due, Mortgagor upon demand shall deposit with Mortgagee such additional funds as may be necessary to remove such deficiency. All the sums deposited with Mortgagee may be comingled with Mortgagee's general funds and shall be non-interest bearing. In the event title to the Mortgaged Property passes to another party either voluntarily or by operation of law, all the right, title and interest of Mortgagor in the aforesaid fund shall pass to the new owner of the Mortgaged Property, or at the option of Mortgagee be used to reduce the mortgage debt.

Generally the mortgagor will not object to clause (1) above, although he may object to clause (2) because it forces the mortgagor to tie up money during the year in a non-interest bearing account.

In either case the mortgagor wants to be in a position to contest real estate taxes if he thinks they are excessive, without being in default under the mortgage. Accordingly, the mortgagor will want to include a clause substantially as follows:

> "However, if the Mortgagor in good faith and by appropriate legal action shall contest the validity of any such item, or the amount thereof, and, if required by the Mortgagee, shall have furnished reasonable assurance satisfactory to Mortgagee indemnifying it against any loss by reason of such contest, then Mortgagor shall not be required to pay the item or to produce the required receipts so long as the contest operates to prevent collection, is maintained and prosecuted with diligence, and shall not have been terminated or discontinued adversely to Mortgagor."

F. INSURANCE

The mortgage will contain a provision requiring the mortgagee to keep the premises adequately insured against loss by fire or other casualty. Unlike the sample clause below, the provision may require monthly payment to mortgagee of ½th of the insurance premiums due for a year. In the latter case, the mortgagee will use the fund to pay the annual premium.

> "Mortgagor shall maintain insurance on the Mortgaged Property of such kinds, in such amounts, and in such companies as are satisfactory to Mortgagee; and if said insurance or any part thereof shall expire, or be withdrawn, or become void by breach of any condition thereof by Mortgagor, or become void or unsafe by reason of the failure, or impairment of the capital of any company in which said insurance may then be, or if for any other reason whatsoever said insurance shall become unsatisfactory to Mortgagee, to effect new insurance on said Mortgaged Property satisfactory to Mortgagee; and to pay as they shall grow due all premiums for such insurance; and to lodge with Mortgagee, as further security for said indebtedness, all policies therefor, with loss payable clauses attached in favor of and acceptable to Mortgagee. In event of loss Mortgagor will give immediate notice by mail to Mortgagee, and Mortgagee may make proof of loss if not made promptly by Mortgagor. Mortgagor hereby directs any insurance company concerned to pay directly to Mortgagee any moneys not in excess of the unpaid balance of said indebtedness which may become payable under such insurance, including return of unearned premiums, such moneys, or any part thereof, to be applied at the option of Mortgagee to said unpaid balance or to the repair of the property damaged; and Mortgagor appoints Mortgagee as attorney in fact to endorse any draft therefor."

The provisions of the mortgage relating to insurance are frequently the most difficult in the mortgage. The mortgagor will not object to the requirement that he carry insurance nor will he object to the requirement that the insurance policy bear a standard form of "mort-

No test but read

gage clause" which makes losses payable to the mortgagor and mortgagee jointly. The mortgagor can understand the mortgagee's concern that in the event of fire its security may disappear. However, the mortgagor will want the mortgagee to agree to make the insurance proceeds available to reconstruct the building. Otherwise, the mortgagee may elect to apply the insurance proceeds from a substantial fire to payment of the debt, and the mortgagor may find himself with a partially gutted building and no funds with which to reconstruct. Therefore, the mortgagor will want to add a clause substantially as follows:

> "All insurance proceeds shall be made available to Mortgagor for repair and restoration of the Mortgaged Property. Such proceeds shall be paid to Mortgagee to be held in trust and disbursed to Mortgagor from time to time as the work proceeds, provided such advances shall not be made more often than twice in each calendar month and shall not exceed 90% of the value of labor and materials for which an advance is requested, with the balance due upon delivery of a certificate of substantial completion from a licensed engineer or architect."

The above clause provides some safeguards for the mortgagee by permitting it to hold the funds and disburse them from time to time as work progresses, much in the manner of a construction lender. In the case of a substantial fire the mortgagee must be sure that the building as reconstructed will be satisfactory for the balance of the loan.

G. MAINTENANCE

To protect his security, the mortgagee will want a clause requiring the mortgagor to keep the property in repair.

> "Mortgagor shall maintain the Mortgaged Property in good repair, order and condition; Mortgagor shall not remove from the Mortgaged Property fixtures, appliances and equipment of any nature covered by the lien of this Mortgage without having obtained the prior written consent of Mortgagee; and Mortgagor will not make, install, or permit to be made or installed, any alterations, additions, improvements, fixtures, appliances, or equipment of any nature to or in the Mortgaged Property without obtaining the prior written consent of Mortgagee which consent Mortgagee hereby reserves the right to refuse to grant."

The mortgagor will not object to agreeing to maintain the property in good repair. However, he may object strenuously to the portion of the above clause which prevents him from removing fixtures, appliances and equipment or making any alterations. Such a clause may restrict the mortgagor's freedom of action much more than is really necessary to afford protection to the mortgagee. The mortgagor would much prefer a clause substantially as follows:

> "Mortgagor shall maintain the Mortgaged Property in good condition and repair, reasonable wear and tear alone excepted."

H. CONDEMNATION

Governmental agencies have the power, under certain circumstances, to obtain property by condemnation. The holder of a mortgage on land which is condemned will lose its security. Therefore, the mortgagee will want to make certain that the award be first applied to pay off the mortgage. A sample provision follows:

> "Mortgagor shall notify Mortgagee promptly upon receiving any notice of commencement of any proceedings for the condemnation of Mortgaged Property, and permit Mortgagee to participate in such proceedings and to receive all proceeds payable to Mortgagor as an award or in settlement up to the amount of the unpaid principal, accrued interest and any other sums due hereunder."

As in the case of loss by fire, the mortgagor will want to have the mortgagee agree to make the proceeds available for reconstruction in the event only a part of the mortgaged premises is condemned, for example, to make way for a road. Accordingly, the mortgagor will want to add the following:

> "If only a part of the Mortgaged Property is condemned, Mortgagor shall promptly restore the remaining portion of the Mortgaged Property so that it will constitute a complete architectural unit and upon completion of such work, the condemnation award shall be released to Mortgagor to pay the reasonable cost thereof. If the Mortgaged Property cannot be restored to a complete architectural unit, or if the condemnation is so extensive that the Mortgaged Property would not, after restoration, be suitable for the use to which it was put prior to condemnation, the condemnation shall be considered a total taking."

I. FINANCIAL STATEMENTS

Some mortgages on income producing properties will provide for the mortgagor to submit financial statements to the mortgagee periodically.

> "Mortgagor shall furnish Mortgagee within sixty (60) days of the close of each fiscal year audited statements prepared by independent certified public accountants satisfactory to Mortgagee, in such detail as Mortgagee may reasonably require."

The mortgagor may want the word "audited" and the words "independent" deleted from the above clause since preparation of audited financial statements involve greater expense to a mortgagor than do unaudited statements. In addition, engaging an "independent" accountant may also involve additional expense if the mortgagor is a company which has accountants on its own staff.

J. MORTGAGEE'S PERFORMANCE FOR MORTGAGOR

In the event mortgagor fails to make any payment relating to the property which could jeopardize mortgagee's first lien or jeopardize the security itself, mortgagee will want the power to make such payment on behalf of the mortgagor and charge mortgagor for the same.

> "In the event Mortgagor should fail to pay said taxes, water and sewer rents, assessments, charges, claims, costs, expenses or fees or to maintain said insurance, or to make all necessary repairs to the Mortgaged Property, all as hereinbefore provided, Mortgagee may at Mortgagee's sole option and without notice to Mortgagor, advance sums on behalf of Mortgagor in payment of said taxes, water and sewer rents, assessments, charges, claims, costs, expenses, fees, insurance and repairs, which repairs Mortgagor hereby authorizes Mortgagee to make, without prejudice to the right of enforcement of the obligation of the Note, or the other remedies of Mortgagee as herein set forth, by reason of the failure of Mortgagor to make payment of the same; and all such sums so advanced by Mortgagee shall be added to and become a part of the indebtedness secured hereby, and repayment thereof, with interest thereon at the rate set forth in said Note, from the dates of their respective expenditures, may be enforced by Mortgagee against Mortgagor at any time."

From the standpoint of the mortgagor, the main objection to this clause is the phrase "at Mortgagee's sole option and without notice to Mortgagor." The mortgagor will not object to the above clause provided he has notice and an opportunity to make the payment. In some cases the mortgagor may have a good reason for not wanting to make the payment. For example, the mortgagor may wish to contest a tax or assessment. The mortgagor would want to insert, in lieu of the words "at Mortgagee's sole option and without notice to Mortgagor", the words "unless Mortgagor has made such payment within thirty (30) days after written notice from mortgagee to do so" and the mortgagor will also want to add at the end of the clause, a statement substantially as follows:

> "Mortgagor's obligations to make the payments provided in this paragraph within thirty (30) days after notice as aforesaid are subject to Mortgagor's right to contest taxes, assessments, and other impositions as hereinabove provided."

K. DEFAULT—REMEDIES

In the event of default by the mortgagor or any of his obligations under the note or mortgage, the mortgagee desires a full range of legal remedies to protect itself from loss. The remedies desired are

(a) foreclosure, (b) the right to take over possession of the mortgaged premises, and (c) the right to sue mortgagor for the balance of principal and interest due on the note as well as any expenses incurred by mortgagee as a result of the default.

"When said principal sum or any unpaid balance thereof shall become due and payable, or in case default shall be made in the payment of any installment of principal and/or interest on the date on which it shall fall due in accordance with the provisions of said Note, or in the performance of any of the terms, agreements or covenants contained in said Note or in this Mortgage, then Mortgagee may forthwith and without further delay:

(a) institute an action of mortgage foreclosure against the Mortgaged Property, or take such other action at law or in equity for the enforcement hereof and realization on the within mortgage security as the law may allow, and may proceed thereon to final judgment and execution thereon for the entire unpaid balance of said principal sum, with interest at the rate stipulated in said Note together with all other sums due by Mortgagor in accordance with the provisions hereof and of said Note, including all sums which may have been loaned by Mortgagee to Mortgagor after the date of this Mortgage, and all sums which may have been advanced by Mortgagee for taxes, water or sewer rents, charges or claims, insurance, or repairs to the Mortgaged Property, all costs of suit, together with interest at six percent (6%) per annum on any judgment obtained by Mortgagee from and after the date of any Sheriff's Sale until actual payment is made by the Sheriff of the full amount due Mortgagee, and reasonable attorneys' fees. Without any law, usage or custom to the contrary notwithstanding; and/or

(b) enter into possession of the Mortgaged Property, with or without legal action, and by force if necessary; collect all rentals therefrom and, after deducting all costs of collection and administration expense, apply the net rentals to the payment of taxes, water and sewer rents, charges and claims, insurance premiums and all other carrying charges, and to the maintenance, repair or restoration of the Mortgaged Property, or on account and in reduction of the principal and/or interest hereby secured, in such order and amounts as Mortgagee, in Mortgagee's sole discretion, may elect; and for said purpose Mortgagor hereby assigns to Mortgagee all rentals due and to become due under any lease or leases of the Mortgaged Property whether now existing or hereafter created, as well as all rights and remedies provided in such lease or leases for the collection of said rents.

The remedies of Mortgagee as provided herein, or in said Note, shall be cumulative and concurrent, and may be pursued singly, successively, or together against Mortgagor and/or the Mortgaged Property at the sole discretion of Mortgagee, and the failure to exercise any such right or remedy shall in no event be construed as a waiver or release of the same.

Mortgagor hereby waives and releases all errors, defects, and imperfections in any proceedings instituted by Mortgagee under this Mortgage, as well as all benefit that might accrue to Mortgagor by virtue of any present or future laws exempting the Mortgaged Property, or any part of the proceeds arising from any sale thereof, from attachment, levy or sale under execution, or providing for any stay of execution, exemption from civil process, or extension of time for payment."

"The words Mortgagor and Mortgagee whenever occurring herein shall be deemed and construed to include the respective heirs, personal representatives, successors and assigns of Mortgagor and Mortgagee; and if there shall be more than one Mortgagor, the obligation of each shall be joint and several. This Mortgage shall be governed by and construed according to the laws of the State of Pennsylvania."

Generally neither party will object to the inclusion of this clause. Ordinarily a mortgage will be construed according to the laws of the state in which the mortgaged property is located.[7]

L.   WARRANTY OF TITLE

Sometimes the mortgagee will desire the mortgagor to warrant the title of the mortgaged premises.

"Mortgagor warrants and will warrant specially the property hereby conveyed."

The Mortgagor will generally prefer to omit this clause entirely, especially in areas in which the mortgagee obtains title insurance at the mortgagor's expense. The effect of this clause is to make the mortgagor a title insurer. If the mortgagee has a title insurance policy from a title insurance company, it is unnecessary to impose this additional burden on the mortgagor.

M.   PAYMENT OF SUMS SECURED

Although it is unnecessary, mortgagees generally like to insert a clause which repeats the provision of the Note requiring the various payments to be made to the mortgagee. The mortgagor generally has no substantial objection to such a provision, unless the mortgagor is not the same person as the maker of the note. If this is so, then this clause must be deleted.

"Mortgagor shall pay to Mortgagee the principal of and interest upon the Note according to the terms of the Note secured hereby, reasonable charges fixed by Mortgagee to satisfy and discharge this Mortgage of record, and all other sums hereby secured; and

---

7. Some large lenders, especially those based in New York, require that New York law shall apply to all transactions, because their attorneys believe that the documents are satisfactory if interpreted by New York law.

shall keep and perform every other covenant and agreement of such Note and this Mortgage."

N. SECURITY AGREEMENT

As mentioned previously, the mortgagee will often want a lien against the mortgagor's personal property located at the premises, as additional security for the loan. Furthermore, a security agreement may be used to obtain a lien on property which is not clearly real property and not clearly personal property. The security agreement may be a separate document or it may be included within the mortgage.

> "This Mortgage creates a security interest in the personal property included in Premises and constitutes a security agreement under the Uniform Commercial Code. Mortgagor shall execute, file and refile such financing statements or other security agreements as Mortgagee shall require from time to time with respect to property included in Premises."

Such a provision may raise problems where a security interest has already been given in regard to certain items of personal property. For example, a mortgagor which financed with a bank the purchase of office equipment used on the mortgaged property will probably have granted the bank a security interest in the equipment. Even if some personal property is not subject to a security interest, the mortgagor may wish to use that as collateral to secure an additional loan. If either of the above problems is present, the mortgagor may refuse to grant the mortgagee a security interest in the personal property or may wish to limit the interest to specified items of personal property. This result could be accomplished by the following clause:

> "This Mortgage creates a security interest and constitutes a security agreement under the Uniform Commercial Code in those items of personal property located at the Premises as set forth in Exhibit A hereto. Mortgagor shall execute, file and refile such financing statements or other security agreements as Mortgagee shall require from time to time with respect to such property located at the Premises."

O. TRANSFER OF TITLE

Often the mortgagee will require a clause which provides that a transfer of title to the mortgaged premises is a default of the note and mortgage. The effect of such a provision is that the mortgagor cannot sell the property subject to the mortgage. Selling the property subject to an existing mortgage would be desirable if the prospective buyer is unable to obtain a mortgage as favorable as that presently on the property.

> "A transfer by sale, gift, devise, operation of law or otherwise of the fee title interest in all or any portion of the mortgaged prem-

ises shall have the same consequences as an event of default re-specting the indebtedness secured hereby, and upon such transfer, Mortgagee, without prior notice or the elapse of any period of grace or the right to cure, shall have the right to declare all sums secured hereby immediately due and payable, and, upon failure by Mortgagor to make such payment within thirty days of written de-mand therefore, Mortgagee shall have the right to exercise all reme-dies provided in the Note, this Mortgage, or otherwise at law."

This is a harsh provision which the mortgagor may resist. A "due on sale" clause gives a mortgagee the right to call the loan and thus pre-vent a sale on terms which might otherwise be desirable to the mort-gagor, particularly if interest rates have risen substantially since the mortgage was obtained. The mortgagor may argue that sale does not really endanger the loan since the sale does not diminish the per-sonal liability (if any) of the original mortgagor. However, where the property is commercial, the mortgagee may insist that its security is affected by the identity of the owner and by the owner's ability to operate the property on a profitable basis.

P.   CONSTRUCTION MORTGAGE

Where the mortgage is being used in connection with a construc-tion loan, the mortgagee will often want to include a provision which makes a breach of the construction loan agreement a breach of the mortgage.

"This Mortgage and the accompanying Note are made pursuant to a written Construction Loan Agreement, signed or about to be signed between Mortgagor and Mortgagee, with reference to con-struction of certain improvements on the mortgaged premises. Any breach of the aforesaid Construction Loan Agreement shall, at the option of Mortgagee, constitute a default under the Note and this Mortgage, as a result of which Mortgagee shall have all of the rights and remedies it would have in the event of default in the payment of any principal or interest due hereunder."

Q.   LIMITATION OF LIABILITY

There may be situations in which the lender is willing to rely entirely upon the real estate for repayment of the debt, and waive its rights to look also to the other assets of the borrower. In such a situation, the borrower will have only limited liability rather than unlimited personal liability as discussed previously. This is common-ly done in connection with income-producing property where the mort-gagee is satisfied that the income will be more than adequate to cover the debt service, taxes, insurance, and other carrying charges. The mortgagor is willing to accept the risk that he may lose the property if he fails to pay the mortgage debt, but he would certainly prefer not to expose any other assets he may have in the event the value of the mortgaged property turns out to be less than anticipated.

"Enforcement of the debt evidenced by the aforesaid note, and the obligation of the Mortgagor under this mortgage, shall be limited to the real estate described herein. The lien of any judgment against Mortgagor in any proceeding instituted on, under or in connection with this mortgage or the aforesaid note shall not extend to any property now or hereafter owned by Mortgagor other than the mortgaged premises, and the judgment index and docket will be so noted."

R.   SECOND MORTGAGE CLAUSE

A second mortgagee holds a mortgage subject to the existing first mortgage. In the event of foreclosure on the first mortgage, the funds generated at the sale will not be divided pro rata between the first and second mortgagee, but will be paid entirely to the first mortgagee up to the full amount owed to it. Only the excess, if any, will be paid to the second mortgagee and such foreclosure sale shall foreclose the second mortgagee's security interest in the property. In many cases, the second mortgagee will bid the amount of the first mortgage at the Sheriff's sale unless there is another bidder who is willing to pay the total amount of both mortgages. By acquiring the property the second mortgagee is in the position of being able to recover the debt if it can resell the property at some future date for a price equal to the purchase price plus the second mortgage.

The second mortgagee is, therefore, very concerned that the mortgagor avoid default under the first mortgage, which could give the first mortgagee reason to accelerate the mortgage debt and precipitate a foreclosure. To protect itself, the second mortgagee may require proof of payments on the first mortgage (so it will immediately be aware of any default), and in the event of such a default, it will want the right to accelerate the second mortgage loan to maturity so that the full amount of its mortgage loan will be payable at the Sheriff's sale in the event that there are bidders. The second mortgagee increases its security with every payment that is made on the first mortgage because with every payment the debt that has priority over the second mortgage is decreased. Accordingly, the second mortgagee does not want the borrower to be in a position to defer amortization (principal payments) on the first mortgage. To deal with these problems, the second mortgagee will generally insist upon a clause similar to the following in the second mortgage:

"This Mortgage is under and subject to the lien of the existing first mortgage in the original principal amount of $_____ which has since been reduced by payments on account to $_____ held by the Savings Bank (the "prior lien"). With respect to the prior lien, Mortgagor agrees as follows:

1. Mortgagor will pay the principal, interest and all other sums when due and payable under the prior lien no later than their due date, and will comply with all of the other terms, covenants and conditions thereof; and

2. Mortgagor will, upon written notice, forward to Mortgagee on or before said due date, copies of checks, or receipts or other evidence of payment satisfactory to the Mortgagee, that the aforesaid sums have been seasonably made; and

3. Mortgagor will not enter into any agreement or arrangement, without the prior written consent of Mortgagee, pursuant to which Mortgagor is granted any forebearance or indulgence (as to time or amount) in the payment of any principal, interest or other sums due in accordance with the terms and provisions of the prior lien. Any default by Mortgagor under the prior lien, by failure to make payment or otherwise to comply with the terms thereof, or any failure by Mortgagor to produce receipts, or Mortgagor's entering into an agreement contrary to the provisions of this paragraph shall constitute a default under this Mortgage, and Mortgagee shall have the right, at its election, to declare immediately due and payable the entire indebtedness secured hereby with interest and other appropriate charges. Mortgagee, at its election, and without notice to Mortgagor, may make, but shall not be obligated to make, any payments the Mortgagor has failed to make under the prior lien but such payment by Mortgagee shall not release Mortgagor from Mortgagor's obligations or constitute a waiver of Mortgagor's default hereunder."

The clause set forth above does not really protect the second mortgagee from the possibility of default under the first mortgage; it simply gives it a way of discovering such a default promptly. A much better solution for the second mortgagee is to obtain a letter from the first mortgagee pursuant to which first mortgagee agrees to give second mortgagee notice of default and a ten-day period within which to cure any default. Second mortgagees customarily ask for such a letter, but first mortgagees are not always willing to give it.

S. EXECUTION

The final section of a mortgage has one or more lines for the mortgagor's signature. This section appears in the usual forms which you have previously seen.

T. ACKNOWLEDGMENTS

In order to be valid as against other creditors of the mortgagor, the mortgage must be recorded in the proper place for the jurisdiction in which the real estate is situated. Once recorded, the mortgage becomes a public record which any other prospective creditor is bound to search for and find. To be recorded, the mortgage must be acknowledged before a proper official. The form for acknowledgments varies from state to state and the draftsman should be sure to use the proper form (individual, partnership, or corporate) for the state in which the real estate is situated. If the mortgage is signed and acknowledged in one state, but is to be recorded in another, it must bear the acknowledgment form of the state in which it is to be recorded. Acknowledgment forms can be found in Martindale-Hubbel Lawyers Directory Volume V. Generally a telephone call to the recording office in the jurisdiction in which the real estate is located can verify that the form is appropriate.

EXAMPLE:

41-13 6/76

MORTGAGE

THIS MORTGAGE is made this.........................day of.........................
19...., between the Mortgagor,...,
...................................(herein "Borrower"), and the Mortgagee,................
...., a corporation organized and existing
under the laws of. .The Commonwealth of Pennsylvania........., whose address is. .12 South 12th Street,....
Philadelphia, Pa. 19107..
....(herein "Lender").

WHEREAS, Borrower is indebted to Lender in the principal sum of...............................
....Dollars, which indebtedness is evidenced by Borrower's note
dated.........................(herein "Note"), providing for monthly installments of principal and interest,
with the balance of the indebtedness, if not sooner paid, due and payable on...........................
..................;

To SECURE to Lender (a) the repayment of the indebtedness evidenced by the Note, with interest thereon, the payment of all other sums, with interest thereon, advanced in accordance herewith to protect the security of this Mortgage, and the performance of the covenants and agreements of Borrower herein contained, and (b) the repayment of any future advances, with interest thereon, made to Borrower by Lender pursuant to paragraph 21 hereof (herein "Future Advances"), Borrower does hereby mortgage, grant and convey to Lender the following described property located in the County of......................................, State of Pennsylvania:

which has the address of................................., ...,
                       [Street]   [City]
..........................(herein "Property Address");
      [State and Zip Code]

TOGETHER with all the improvements now or hereafter erected on the property, and all easements, rights, appurtenances, rents, royalties, mineral, oil and gas rights and profits, water, water rights, and water stock, and all fixtures now or hereafter attached to the property, all of which, including replacements and additions thereto, shall be deemed to be and remain a part of the property covered by this Mortgage; and all of the foregoing, together with said property (or the leasehold estate if this Mortgage is on a leasehold) are herein referred to as the "Property".

Borrower covenants that Borrower is lawfully seised of the estate hereby conveyed and has the right to mortgage, grant and convey the Property, that the Property is unencumbered, and that Borrower will warrant and defend generally the title to the Property against all claims and demands, subject to any declarations, easements or restrictions listed in a schedule of exceptions to coverage in any title insurance policy insuring Lender's interest in the Property.

UNIFORM COVENANTS. Borrower and Lender covenant and agree as follows:

1. Payment of Principal and Interest. Borrower shall promptly pay when due the principal of and interest on the indebtedness evidenced by the Note, prepayment and late charges as provided in the Note, and the principal of and interest on any Future Advances secured by this Mortgage.

2. Funds for Taxes and Insurance. Subject to applicable law or to a written waiver by Lender, Borrower shall pay to Lender on the day monthly installments of principal and interest are payable under the Note, until the Note is paid in full, a sum (herein "Funds") equal to one-twelfth of the yearly taxes and assessments which may attain priority over this Mortgage, and ground rents on the Property, if any, plus one-twelfth of yearly premium installments for hazard insurance, plus one-twelfth of yearly premium installments for mortgage insurance, if any, all as reasonably estimated initially and from time to time by Lender on the basis of assessments and bills and reasonable estimates thereof.

The Funds shall be held in an institution the deposits or accounts of which are insured or guaranteed by a Federal or state agency (including Lender if Lender is such an institution). Lender shall apply the Funds to pay said taxes, assessments, insurance premiums and ground rents. Lender may not charge for so holding and applying the Funds, analyzing said account, or verifying and compiling said assessments and bills, unless Lender pays Borrower interest on the Funds and applicable law permits Lender to make such a charge. Borrower and Lender may agree in writing at the time of execution of this Mortgage that interest on the Funds shall be paid to Borrower, and unless such agreement is made or applicable law requires such interest to be paid, Lender shall not be required to pay Borrower any interest or earnings on the Funds. Lender shall give to Borrower, without charge, an annual accounting of the Funds showing credits and debits to the Funds and the purpose for which each debit to the Funds was made. The Funds are pledged as additional security for the sums secured by this Mortgage.

If the amount of the Funds held by Lender, together with the future monthly installments of Funds payable prior to the due dates of taxes, assessments, insurance premiums and ground rents, shall exceed the amount required to pay said taxes, assessments, insurance premiums and ground rents as they fall due, such excess shall be, at Borrower's option, either promptly repaid to Borrower or credited to Borrower on monthly installments of Funds. If the amount of the Funds held by Lender shall not be sufficient to pay taxes, assessments, insurance premiums and ground rents as they fall due, Borrower shall pay to Lender any amount necessary to make up the deficiency within 30 days from the date notice is mailed by Lender to Borrower requesting payment thereof.

Upon payment in full of all sums secured by this Mortgage, Lender shall promptly refund to Borrower any Funds held by Lender. If under paragraph 18 hereof the Property is sold or the Property is otherwise acquired by Lender, Lender shall apply, no later than immediately prior to the sale of the Property or its acquisition by Lender, any Funds held by Lender at the time of application as a credit against the sums secured by this Mortgage.

3. Application of Payments. Unless applicable law provides otherwise, all payments received by Lender under the Note and paragraphs 1 and 2 hereof shall be applied by Lender first in payment of amounts payable to Lender by Borrower under paragraph 2 hereof, then to interest payable on the Note, then to the principal of the Note, and then to interest and principal on any Future Advances.

4. Charges; Liens. Borrower shall pay all taxes, assessments and other charges, fines and impositions attributable to the Property which may attain a priority over this Mortgage, and leasehold payments or ground rents, if any, in the manner provided under paragraph 2 hereof or, if not paid in such manner, by Borrower making payment, when due, directly to the payee thereof. Borrower shall promptly furnish to Lender all notices of amounts due under this paragraph, and in the event Borrower shall make payment directly, Borrower shall promptly furnish to Lender receipts evidencing such payments. Borrower shall promptly discharge any lien which has priority over this Mortgage; provided, that Borrower shall not be required to discharge any such lien so long as Borrower shall agree in writing to the payment of the obligation secured by such lien in a manner acceptable to Lender, or shall in good faith contest such lien by, or defend enforcement of such lien in, legal proceedings which operate to prevent the enforcement of the lien or forfeiture of the Property or any part thereof.

5. Hazard Insurance. Borrower shall keep the improvements now existing or hereafter erected on the Property insured against loss by fire, hazards included within the term "extended coverage", and such other hazards as Lender may require and in such amounts and for such periods as Lender may require; provided, that Lender shall not require that the amount of such coverage exceed that amount of coverage required to pay the sums secured by this Mortgage.

The insurance carrier providing the insurance shall be chosen by Borrower subject to approval by Lender; provided, that such approval shall not be unreasonably withheld. All premiums on insurance policies shall be paid in the manner provided under paragraph 2 hereof or, if not paid in such manner, by Borrower making payment, when due, directly to the insurance carrier.

All insurance policies and renewals thereof shall be in form acceptable to Lender and shall include a standard mortgage clause in favor of and in form acceptable to Lender. Lender shall have the right to hold the policies and renewals thereof, and Borrower shall promptly furnish to Lender all renewal notices and all receipts of paid premiums. In the event of loss, Borrower shall give prompt notice to the insurance carrier and Lender. Lender may make proof of loss if not made promptly by Borrower.

Unless Lender and Borrower otherwise agree in writing, insurance proceeds shall be applied to restoration or repair of the Property damaged, provided such restoration or repair is economically feasible and the security of this Mortgage is not thereby impaired. If such restoration or repair is not economically feasible or if the security of this Mortgage would be impaired, the insurance proceeds shall be applied to the sums secured by this Mortgage, with the excess, if any, paid to Borrower. If the Property is abandoned by Borrower, or if Borrower fails to respond to Lender within 30 days from the date notice is mailed by Lender to Borrower that the insurance carrier offers to settle a claim for insurance benefits, Lender is authorized to collect and apply the insurance proceeds at Lender's option either to restoration or repair of the Property or to the sums secured by this Mortgage.

Unless Lender and Borrower otherwise agree in writing, any such application of proceeds to principal shall not extend or postpone the due date of the monthly installments referred to in paragraphs 1 and 2 hereof or change the amount of such installments. If under paragraph 18 hereof the Property is acquired by Lender, all right, title and interest of Borrower in and to any insurance policies and in and to the proceeds thereof resulting from damage to the Property prior to the sale or acquisition shall pass to Lender to the extent of the sums secured by this Mortgage immediately prior to such sale or acquisition.

6. Preservation and Maintenance of Property; Leaseholds; Condominiums; Planned Unit Developments. Borrower shall keep the Property in good repair and shall not commit waste or permit impairment or deterioration of the Property and shall comply with the provisions of any lease if this Mortgage is on a leasehold. If this Mortgage is on a unit in a condominium or a planned unit development, Borrower shall perform all of Borrower's obligations under the declaration or covenants creating or governing the condominium or planned unit development, the by-laws and regulations of the condominium or planned unit development, and constituent documents. If a condominium or planned unit development rider is executed by Borrower and recorded together with this Mortgage, the covenants and agreements of such rider shall be incorporated into and shall amend and supplement the covenants and agreements of this Mortgage as if the rider were a part hereof.

7. Protection of Lender's Security. If Borrower fails to perform the covenants and agreements contained in this Mortgage, or if any action or proceeding is commenced which materially affects Lender's interest in the Property, including, but not limited to, eminent domain, insolvency, code enforcement, or arrangements or proceedings involving a bankrupt or decedent, then Lender at Lender's option, upon notice to Borrower, may make such appearances, disburse such sums and take such action as is necessary to protect Lender's interest, including, but not limited to, disbursement of reasonable attorney's fees and entry upon the Property to make repairs. If Lender required mortgage insurance as a condition of making the loan secured by this Mortgage, Borrower shall pay the premiums required to maintain such insurance in effect until such time as the requirement for such insurance terminates in accordance with Borrower's and

[B7776]

Lender's written agreement or applicable law. Borrower shall pay the amount of all mortgage insurance premiums in the manner provided under paragraph 2 hereof.

Any amounts disbursed by Lender pursuant to this paragraph 7, with interest thereon, shall become additional indebtedness of Borrower secured by this Mortgage. Unless Borrower and Lender agree to other terms of payment, such amounts shall be payable upon notice from Lender to Borrower requesting payment thereof, and shall bear interest from the date of disbursement at the rate payable from time to time on outstanding principal under the Note unless payment of interest at such rate would be contrary to applicable law, in which event such amounts shall bear interest at the highest rate permissible under applicable law. Nothing contained in this paragraph 7 shall require Lender to incur any expense or take any action hereunder.

8. Inspection. Lender may make or cause to be made reasonable entries upon and inspections of the Property, provided that Lender shall give Borrower notice prior to any such inspection specifying reasonable cause therefor related to Lender's interest in the Property.

9. Condemnation. The proceeds of any award or claim for damages, direct or consequential, in connection with any condemnation or other taking of the Property, or part thereof, or for conveyance in lieu of condemnation, are hereby assigned and shall be paid to Lender.

In the event of a total taking of the Property, the proceeds shall be applied to the sums secured by this Mortgage, with the excess, if any, paid to Borrower. In the event of a partial taking of the Property, unless Borrower and Lender otherwise agree in writing, there shall be applied to the sums secured by this Mortgage such proportion of the proceeds as is equal to that proportion which the amount of the sums secured by this Mortgage immediately prior to the date of taking bears to the fair market value of the Property immediately prior to the date of taking, with the balance of the proceeds paid to Borrower.

If the Property is abandoned by Borrower, or if, after notice by Lender to Borrower that the condemnor offers to make an award or settle a claim for damages, Borrower fails to respond to Lender within 30 days after the date such notice is mailed, Lender is authorized to collect and apply the proceeds, at Lender's option, either to restoration or repair of the Property or to the sums secured by this Mortgage.

Unless Lender and Borrower otherwise agree in writing, any such application of proceeds to principal shall not extend or postpone the due date of the monthly installments referred to in paragraphs 1 and 2 hereof or change the amount of such installments.

10. Borrower Not Released. Extension of the time for payment or modification of amortization of the sums secured by this Mortgage granted by Lender to any successor in interest of Borrower shall not operate to release, in any manner, the liability of the original Borrower and Borrower's successors in interest. Lender shall not be required to commence proceedings against such successor or refuse to extend time for payment or otherwise modify amortization of the sums secured by this Mortgage by reason of any demand made by the original Borrower and Borrower's successors in interest.

11. Forbearance by Lender Not a Waiver. Any forbearance by Lender in exercising any right or remedy hereunder, or otherwise afforded by applicable law, shall not be a waiver of or preclude the exercise of any such right or remedy. The procurement of insurance or the payment of taxes or other liens or charges by Lender shall not be a waiver of Lender's right to accelerate the maturity of the indebtedness secured by this Mortgage.

12. Remedies Cumulative. All remedies provided in this Mortgage are distinct and cumulative to any other right or remedy under this Mortgage or afforded by law or equity, and may be exercised concurrently, independently or successively.

13. Successors and Assigns Bound; Joint and Several Liability; Captions. The covenants and agreements herein contained shall bind, and the rights hereunder shall inure to, the respective successors and assigns of Lender and Borrower, subject to the provisions of paragraph 17 hereof. All covenants and agreements of Borrower shall be joint and several. The captions and headings of the paragraphs of this Mortgage are for convenience only and are not to be used to interpret or define the provisions hereof.

14. Notice. Except for any notice required under applicable law to be given in another manner, (a) any notice to Borrower provided for in this Mortgage shall be given by mailing such notice by certified mail addressed to Borrower at the Property Address or at such other address as Borrower may designate by notice to Lender as provided herein, and (b) any notice to Lender shall be given by certified mail, return receipt requested, to Lender's address stated herein or to such other address as Lender may designate by notice to Borrower as provided herein. Any notice provided for in this Mortgage shall be deemed to have been given to Borrower or Lender when given in the manner designated herein.

15. Uniform Mortgage; Governing Law; Severability. This form of mortgage combines uniform covenants for national use and non-uniform covenants with limited variations by jurisdiction to constitute a uniform security instrument covering real property. This Mortgage shall be governed by the law of the jurisdiction in which the Property is located. In the event that any provision or clause of this Mortgage or the Note conflicts with applicable law, such conflict shall not affect other provisions of this Mortgage or the Note which can be given effect without the conflicting provision, and to this end the provisions of the Mortgage and the Note are declared to be severable.

16. Borrower's Copy. Borrower shall be furnished a conformed copy of the Note and of this Mortgage at the time of execution or after recordation hereof.

17. Transfer of the Property; Assumption. If all or any part of the Property or an interest therein is sold or transferred by Borrower without Lender's prior written consent, excluding (a) the creation of a lien or encumbrance subordinate to this Mortgage, (b) the creation of a purchase money security interest for household appliances, (c) a transfer by devise, descent or by operation of law upon the death of a joint tenant or (d) the grant of any leasehold interest of three years or less not containing an option to purchase, Lender may, at Lender's option, declare all the sums secured by this Mortgage to be immediately due and payable. Lender shall have waived such option to accelerate if, prior to the sale or transfer, Lender and the person to whom the Property is to be sold or transferred reach agreement in writing that the credit of such person is satisfactory to Lender and that the interest payable on the sums secured by this Mortgage shall be at such rate as Lender shall request. If Lender has waived the option to accelerate provided in this paragraph 17, and if Borrower's successor in interest has executed a written assumption agreement accepted in writing by Lender, Lender shall release Borrower from all obligations under this Mortgage and the Note.

If Lender exercises such option to accelerate, Lender shall mail Borrower notice of acceleration in accordance with paragraph 14 hereof. Such notice shall provide a period of not less than 30 days from the date the notice is mailed within which Borrower may pay the sums declared due. If Borrower fails to pay such sums prior to the expiration of such period, Lender may, without further notice or demand on Borrower, invoke any remedies permitted by paragraph 18 hereof.

NON-UNIFORM COVENANTS. Borrower and Lender further covenant and agree as follows:

18. Acceleration; Remedies. Upon Borrower's breach of any covenant or agreement of Borrower in this Mortgage, including the covenants to pay when due any sums secured by this Mortgage, Lender prior to acceleration shall mail notice to Borrower as provided by applicable law specifying: (1) the breach; (2) the action required to cure such breach; (3) a date, not less than 30 days from the date the notice is mailed to Borrower, by which such breach must be cured; and (4) that failure to cure such breach on or before the date specified in the notice may result in acceleration of the sums secured by this Mortgage, foreclosure by judicial proceeding and sale of the Property. The notice shall further inform Borrower of the right to reinstate after acceleration and the right to assert in the foreclosure proceeding the non-existence of a default or any other defense of Borrower to acceleration and foreclosure. If the breach is not cured on or before the date specified in the notice, Lender at Lender's option may declare all of the sums secured by this Mortgage to be immediately due and payable without further demand and may foreclose this Mortgage by judicial proceeding. Lender shall be entitled to collect in such proceeding all expenses of foreclosure, including, but not limited to, reasonable attorney's fees, and costs of documentary evidence, abstracts and title reports.

19. Borrower's Right to Reinstate. Notwithstanding Lender's acceleration of the sums secured by this Mortgage, Borrower shall have the right to have any proceedings begun by Lender to enforce this Mortgage discontinued at any time

[B7777]

prior to at least one hour prior to the commencement of bidding at a sheriff's sale or other sale pursuant to this **Mortgage** if: (a) Borrower pays Lender all sums which would be then due under this Mortgage, the Note and notes securing Future Advances, if any, had no acceleration occurred; (b) Borrower cures all breaches of any other covenants or agreements of Borrower contained in this Mortgage; (c) Borrower pays all reasonable expenses incurred by Lender in enforcing the covenants and agreements of Borrower contained in this Mortgage and in enforcing Lender's remedies as provided in paragraph 18 hereof, including, but not limited to, reasonable attorney's fees; and (d) Borrower takes such action as Lender may reasonably require to assure that the lien of this Mortgage, Lender's interest in the Property and Borrower's obligation to pay the sums secured by this Mortgage shall continue unimpaired. Upon such payment and cure by Borrower, this Mortgage and the obligations secured hereby shall remain in full force and effect as if no acceleration had occurred.

    20. Assignment of Rents; Appointment of Receiver; Lender in Possession. As additional security hereunder, Borrower hereby assigns to Lender the rents of the Property, provided that Borrower shall, prior to acceleration under paragraph 18 hereof or abandonment of the Property, have the right to collect and retain such rents as they become due and payable.

    Upon acceleration under paragraph 18 hereof or abandonment of the Property, Lender, in person, by agent or by judicially appointed receiver, shall be entitled to enter upon, take possession of and manage the Property and to collect the rents of the Property including those past due. All rents collected by Lender or the receiver shall be applied first to payment of the costs of management of the Property and collection of rents, including, but not limited to, receiver's fees, premiums on receiver's bonds and reasonable attorney's fees, and then to the sums secured by this Mortgage. Lender and the receiver shall be liable to account only for those rents actually received.

    21. Future Advances. Upon request of Borrower, Lender, at Lender's option prior to release of this Mortgage, may make Future Advances to Borrower. Such Future Advances, with interest thereon, shall be secured by this Mortgage when evidenced by promissory notes stating that said notes are secured hereby. At no time shall the principal amount of the indebtedness secured by this Mortgage, not including sums advanced in accordance herewith to protect the security of this Mortgage, exceed the original amount of the Note.

    22. Release. Upon payment of all sums secured by this Mortgage, Lender shall discharge this Mortgage, without charge to Borrower. Borrower shall pay all costs of recordation, if any.

    23. Purchase Money Mortgage. If all or part of the sums secured by this Mortgage are lent to Borrower to acquire title to the Property, this Mortgage is hereby declared to be a purchase money mortgage.

    IN WITNESS WHEREOF, Borrower has executed this Mortgage.

Witnesses:

....
                                                                        —Borrower

....
                                                                         —Borrower

COMMONWEALTH OF PENNSYLVANIA, ...County ss:

    On this, the...........day of..........................., 19...., before me, ...
......................the undersigned officer, personally appeared...................................
....known to me (or satisfactorily proven) to be the person....whose name...........subscribed to the within instrument and acknowledged that ....executed the same for the purposes herein contained.

    IN WITNESS WHEREOF, I hereunto set my hand and official seal.

My Commission expires:

                             ....

                             ....
                                        Title of Officer

EXAMPLE:

41-16   6/76

NOTE

US $........................

.............................., Pennsylvania
City

..........................., 19....

FOR VALUE RECEIVED, the undersigned ("Borrower") promise(s) to pay........................ ...., a Pennsylvania Corporation ...., or order, the principal sum of ....Dollars, with interest on the unpaid principal balance from the date of this Note, until paid, at the rate of........................ ....percent per annum. Principal and interest shall be payable at 12 South 12th Street, ... Philadelphia, Pa. 19107 ...., or such other place as the Note holder may designate, in consecutive monthly installments of.. ....Dollars (US $...........................), on the.................... ....day of each month beginning..........................., 19..... Such monthly installments shall continue until the entire indebtedness evidenced by this Note is fully paid, except that any remaining indebtedness, if not sooner paid, shall be due and payable on....................................

If any monthly installment under this Note is not paid when due and remains unpaid after a date specified by a notice to Borrower, the entire principal amount outstanding and accrued interest thereon shall at once become due and payable at the option of the Note holder. The date specified shall not be less than thirty days from the date such notice is mailed. The Note holder may exercise this option to accelerate during any default by Borrower regardless of any prior forbearance. If suit is brought to collect this Note, the Note holder shall be entitled to collect all reasonable costs and expenses of suit, including, but not limited to, reasonable attorney's fees.

Borrower shall pay to the Note holder a late charge of. **TWO** ....percent of any monthly installment not received by the Note holder within. **FIFTEEN**.................days after the installment is due.

Borrower may prepay the principal amount outstanding in whole or in part. The Note holder may require that any partial prepayments (i) be made on the date monthly installments are due and (ii) be in the amount of that part of one or more monthly installments which would be applicable to principal. Any partial prepayment shall be applied against the principal amount outstanding and shall not postpone the due date of any subsequent monthly installments or change the amount of such installments, unless the Note holder shall otherwise agree in writing.

Presentment, notice of dishonor, and protest are hereby waived by all makers, sureties, guarantors and endorsers hereof. This Note shall be the joint and several obligation of all makers, sureties, guarantors and endorsers, and shall be binding upon them and their successors and assigns.

Any notice to Borrower provided for in this Note shall be given by mailing such notice by certified mail addressed to Borrower at the Property Address stated below, or to such other address as Borrower may designate by notice to the Note holder. Any notice to the Note holder shall be given by mailing such notice by certified mail, return receipt requested, to the Note holder at the address stated in the first paragraph of this Note, or at such other address as may have been designated by notice to Borrower.

The indebtedness evidenced by this Note is secured by a Mortgage, dated............................ ...., and reference is made to the Mortgage for rights as to acceleration of the indebtedness evidenced by this Note.

....

....

....
Property Address

(Execute Original Only)

Part Seven

ASSIGNMENT, SATISFACTION AND RELEASE OF MORTGAGES

I. ASSIGNMENT OF MORTGAGES

A mortgage note or bond is an instrument which can be sold exchanged, donated or otherwise traded, much like the bonds and stocks which are commonly traded on the stock exchanges. As a matter of law, a sale of the note entitles the purchaser to ownership of the mortgage. However, it is customary to transfer both the note and the mortgage, either in separate documents for each or in one document.

The mechanics for transferring a mortgage note are fairly simple. The seller may just endorse the note substantially as follows:

"Pay to the order of [*name of buyer*] without recourse"

The words "without recourse" mean that the seller makes no guaranty as to the credit of the borrower. If the note is not paid, the seller will have no responsibility. If, on the other hand, the buyer is bargaining for the credit of the seller as well as the credit of the borrower, the note may be endorsed "with recourse". If a note assigned with recourse is not paid, the seller is obligated to repurchase the note from the buyer.

A note is sometimes assigned rather than merely endorsed. The buyer of the note will want to be sure (a) that the seller owns the note free and clear of any liens or charges or obligations in favor of third parties; (b) that it has not previously sold or assigned or agreed to sell or assign it to anyone else; and (c) that it has the right to sell the note to the buyer on the terms and conditions agreed upon. The buyer will try to protect itself by obtaining warranties to this effect (if the seller is willing to give them) and by making a search of the public records to ascertain whether the mortgage has been previously assigned. The note or bond is not, of course, a public record and there is no effective way of ascertaining whether it has been assigned except that it would be unusual for the seller to have assigned the note or bond and still retain possession of the original instrument. Moreover, it would be most unusual to assign the note or bond and not assign the mortgage.

The assignment of the mortgage instrument may be combined in the same document as the assignment of the note or may be in a separate document. Although the form of assignment will vary from state to state, a mortgage assignment will generally be in substantially the following form:

"For value received, the undersigned [*name*] hereinafter called "Assignor" hereby assigns, transfers and sets over unto [*name of assignee*] hereinafter called "Assignee" all of the Assignor's right, title and interest in, to and under a certain mortgage between [*name of mortgagor*] as Mortgagor and [*name of mortgagee*] as Mortgagee, dated _____, recorded in the Office of the Recorder of Deeds in _____ County on ___ [*date*] in Mortgage Book _____ Page ___, with reference to premises described as follows: [*description of premises*].

Together with the bond or note described in said mortgage and the money due and to become due thereon including interest. To have and to hold unto Assignee and its successors, legal representatives and assigns forever.

THIS assignment is made without recourse to and without covenant or warranty express or implied by Assignor in any event, or for any purpose whatsoever (if the Assignee has bargained for any warranties or the credit of the Assignor, this paragraph will be deleted and in lieu thereof any warranties the parties have agreed upon will be inserted here).

IN WITNESS WHEREOF, Assignor has executed this instrument the _____ day of _____.

[*Signature by Assignor*]"

The purchaser of a note may pay the seller the amount owed on the note, or may pay somewhat more (a "premium") or less (a "discount") than the amount owed. Whether or not a premium will be paid or a discount made will depend both upon the interest rate of the note as compared with the then prevailing interest rate and upon the credit of the borrower. In any event, the purchaser wants to be certain of the amount owed on the note at the time it buys the note. In order to be assured, the purchaser may require a warranty from the seller and a statement from the borrower acknowledging (i) the amount due, and (ii) that the borrower has no defenses against payments, and that there are no amounts owed him which he is entitled to deduct or "set off". Such a statement from the borrower is commonly called a "Declaration of No Set-Off" or an "Estoppel Letter".

"The undersigned, owner of the premises known as [*description of premises*] and covered by the mortgage in the amount of $_____ given by _____ as Mortgagor to _____ as Mortgagee dated _____, 19__ and recorded in the Office of the Recorder of Deeds on [*date*] in Mortgage Book _____, Page _____, hereby acknowledges that the principal amount due on said mortgage as of [*date*] is $_____; that interest thereon accrues at the rate of _____% per annum, the last such interest payment having been made on _____; that neither the mortgage nor the obligation which it secures have been modified, altered or amended in any way; and that there are no defenses, counterclaims or set offs to the aforesaid mortgage or the bond or note secured thereby.

IN WITNESS WHEREOF, the undersigned has executed this Declaration this _____ day of _____, 19___.

[*Signature*]"

II.   SATISFACTION OF MORTGAGES

As already noted, a mortgage is recorded and becomes a public document. When the mortgage debt has finally been paid, the mortgagee will return to the borrower the mortgage note or bond marked "canceled" or "paid", and will mark the mortgage "satisfied of record". The procedure for causing the mortgage to be marked satisfied on the public records varies from location to location, but in general the original mortgage is required to be presented to the recorder's office together with a statement, either endorsed on the mortgage or on a separate document signed and acknowledged by the mortgagee, confirming that the debt has been paid and instructing the recorder to mark the mortgage satisfied on the public records.

III.   RELEASE OF MORTGAGES

There may be some situations in which borrower and lender may wish to release part of the property covered by the mortgage from the lien of the mortgage, without affecting the lien on the balance of the property, or to release all of the property from the lien of the mortgage without reciting that the underlying obligation has been satisfied. Such a need could arise when a builder or developer purchases land subject to a purchase money mortgage or creates a mortgage on vacant ground on which he wishes to build in stages. As he builds, he may have to create construction mortgages or he may have to obtain releases on completed buildings so that he can convey them to the ultimate purchaser. If a mortgagor contemplates obtaining partial releases prior to payment of the mortgage debt in full, the mortgage should contain the agreement of the mortgagor and mortgagee with reference to these releases.

The mortgagor wants to be sure that he can obtain certain areas as and when he needs them and he also wants to be sure that the mortgagee will join in (or release) easement areas required for streets, roads, electric lines, recreational facilities, and the like. The mortgagee, on the other hand, wants to be sure (a) that it obtains payment for each release commensurate with the value of the security lost by release of the portion being released; (b) that the areas to be released are of a certain minimum size; (c) that they are contiguous so that if the mortgagee is required to foreclose after some (but not all) of the property has been released, the mortgagee is not left with "islands" or landlocked areas at the rear of the tract which are much less valuable than road frontage; and (d) that the release will not otherwise affect the validity or priority of the mortgage. One example of a clause which deals with these requirements follows:

> "Mortgagee agrees to release from the lien of the mortgage such portions of the mortgaged premises as mortgagor may require; provided (a) the portions to be released shall be at least one acre and shall be contiguous to the remainder of the premises not then subject to the mortgage and shall be between lines perpendicular to Jones Road; and (b) mortgagor pays mortgagee $_____ per acre for each acre and a pro rata portion of said sum for any fractional acre to be released; and (c) when the last release is delivered the payment shall be sufficient, when added to all prior payments made by mortgagor to mortgagee, to comprise the total mortgage debt. All costs incident to preparation of the releases such as surveying, preparation of documents, and recording charges shall be borne by mortgagor.
>
> The mortgagee will execute, acknowledge and deliver, without charge, any and all consents and subordinations that mortgagor may require in connection with the installation of streets, and public facilities such as water, storm drainage, gas and electricity."

After the mortgagor has ascertained which part of the property he wants released, he should deliver a survey plan, together with a metes and bounds description, to the mortgagee with a mortgage release document. The release document will vary from place to place, but will be in recordable form and will recite that the section described by the metes and bounds description is released from the lien of the referenced mortgage.

IV.   SALES UNDER AND SUBJECT TO MORTGAGES

Many situations arise in which a mortgagor wishes to sell his property without paying off the mortgage loan. In such a case, he will receive at settlement the difference between the total sales price and the amount outstanding on the mortgage.[1] Thereafter, the purchaser will make the mortgage loan payments. In Chapter Two, we discussed the relative concerns of the parties, and the different ways in which the situation is handled.

A.   PURCHASER ASSUMES DEBT

The purchaser may specifically agree to assume and pay the mortgage debt personally. If the purchaser is to be personally liable for the debt, he will either sign a note or bond in favor of the mortgagee, commonly known as a "collateral bond", or the "under and subject" section of the deed from seller to purchaser will contain a

---

1. The difference between the market value of a property and the principal balance of the outstanding mortgage loan is sometimes referred to as the owner's equity.

clause stating that the purchaser "assumes and agrees to pay" the mortgage debt. If the purchaser is not to be personally liable on the mortgage, language to that effect should be inserted in the deed and the phrase "assumes and agrees to pay" should be deleted. In either case, the legal effect is to permit the mortgagee to sue the purchaser directly for repayment of the mortgage debt. The mortgagee is an intended beneficiary of such collateral bond or such "assumes and agrees to pay" provisions and this creates the privity of contract between the purchaser and the mortgagee necessary for the mortgagee to sue the purchaser.

B. PURCHASER INDEMNIFIES SELLER

The purchaser may not agree to pay the mortgage debt personally, but he may expressly or by implication agree to indemnify the mortgagor against any loss suffered by the mortgagor by virtue of the purchaser's failure to pay the debt when it is due. The purchaser does not make himself personally liable to the mortgagee, and cannot be sued personally by the mortgagee,[2] but he is liable to the seller in the event the seller suffers an actual loss. This might occur, if the mortgagee elected to sue the seller on the note instead of foreclosing, or if the property had depreciated in value to such a point that the mortgagee did not satisfy the debt out of the property and subsequently sued the mortgagor personally. The obligation to indemnify is implied as a matter of law from an "under and subject" clause which refers to the mortgage and does not contain the agreement to "assume and agree to pay". If this is not so in the particular state in which the real estate is located, the draftsman may want to insert a clause specifically stating that the purchaser does not assume and agree to pay the mortgage, but does agree to indemnify the seller against any actual loss or damage seller may suffer by reason of purchaser's failure to make any payments thereunder.

C. NO LIABILITY ASSUMED BY PURCHASER

This is the best solution for the purchaser and the least desirable for the seller. The relative bargaining position of the parties will determine the extent of financial exposure in any given case. If the purchaser is to assume no personal liability and also wants to negate the implication of indemnification, the following language would be added to the under and subject clause which describes the mortgage:

"provided grantee does not expressly or impliedly assume or agree to pay the aforesaid mortgage debt, nor does grantee expressly or impliedly agree to indemnify grantor or any other party in connection therewith."

2. The purchaser cannot be sued personally due to a lack of privity of contract between the mortgagee and the purchaser.

V. SUBORDINATION OF MORTGAGES

Although mortgages generally take priority of right from the time they are recorded, it is possible to modify relative priorities by the agreement of the parties. For example, a developer may purchase a vacant tract of ground and give the seller a note and purchase money mortgage for part of the purchase price. Before the note and mortgage are due, the developer may want to improve the property with buildings and to do so he may need a construction mortgage loan. The construction lender will insist that its construction mortgage be a first mortgage on the property, with a priority over the existing purchase money mortgage. This requires the agreement of the purchase money mortgagee either to release the property or agree to subordinate the lien of the purchase money mortgage to the lien of the construction mortgage. In anticipation of this possibility, there may be a clause, such as the following provision, in the purchase money mortgage:

> "This mortgage is hereby made subordinate in lien, operation and effect to the lien of any institutional mortgages now or hereafter placed upon the mortgaged premises (and any subsequent mortgages substituted therefor) provided such mortgage or mortgages are for the purpose of providing Mortgagor with funds for construction of improvements on or about the mortgaged premises. This subordination shall be effective without the need for any further act or writing by Mortgagor, Mortgagee, or any other party, but Mortgagee agrees, by its acceptance of this instrument, to execute, acknowledge and deliver any further instruments that any other Mortgagee may require to evidence and confirm this subordination. All costs incident to the preparation of the aforesaid easements and subordinations, such as surveying, preparation of documents, and recording charges, shall be borne by Mortgagor." [3]

Subordination can also be accomplished by a separate agreement among the mortgagor and both mortgagees. This agreement should be in recordable form and should be recorded in the county in which the mortgages are recorded.

It should be stressed that a subordination does not effect the rights of other lien holders. Suppose that Regina Stolz holds a $1,000,000 first mortgage upon Greenacre, which is owned by Greenacre Associates. Continental Grading Co., Inc. may have obtained a $150,000 judgement against Greenacre Associates, which judgement

---

3. The quoted provision may not be acceptable to a purchase money mortgagor. There is no maximum amount to which the purchase money mortgagor agrees to be subordinate. There is no description of the sorts of improvements for which a construction mortgage may be obtained, and such improvements may be "about" the premises. Any improvements "about" the premises rather than "on" the premises should be limited to stated off-site improvements.

has been properly recorded in the county in which Greenacre is located, but which judgement is clearly inferior in time and right to the $1,000,000 Stolz mortgage. Subsequently, Greenacre Associates has obtained a $4,700,000 mortgage loan from Colonial Bank, to which Stolz has agreed to subordinate. Stolz by her subordination to Colonial should not be able to grant Colonial superior rights over Continental for the full amount of the $4,700,000 Colonial loan. The most that Stolz should be able to grant is the right of Continental to get the first $1,000,000, plus the agreement of Stolz not to get paid anything until Colonial gets its entire $4,700,000.

Thus, one possible effect of the subordination is that the proceeds of a Sheriff's sale would be distributed in the following order and priority:

1. $1,000,000 to Colonial

2. $150,000 to Continental

3. $3,700,000 to Colonial

4. $1,000,000 to Stolz

Thus, the effect if the above priority were determined by the courts,[4] would be that Colonial does not have a first lien for its entire mortgage amount, even though it has received a subordination from the undisputed first lien mortgagee. For her part, Stolz assumed she was subordinating only $4,700,000. Instead, Stolz finds that she has ended up being inferior to the $150,000 Continental lien as well, to which she had been superior and to which she had never knowingly subordinated her first mortgage lien.

Part Eight

MORTGAGE FORECLOSURE

I. INTRODUCTION

The laws and rules which govern mortgage foreclosures are local in nature, and even neighboring states often have drastically different laws regarding foreclosures. Therefore, this section is only intended to familiarize the student with concerns inherent in the concept of a mortgage foreclosure. This section is not intended as a step-by-step guide to mortgage foreclosure.

II. ACTION ON NOTE OR ON MORTGAGE

Mortgage notes are evidence of a mortgagor's debt and of his obligation to pay interest. A mortgagee has two separate means for

4. State courts have been anything but consistent and logical in their application of subordination agreements in instances where there are intervening lienors.

collecting the mortgage debt; the personal security which is the note, and the real estate security which is the mortgage. Traditionally, a bond or a note was usually accompanied by, or included, a warrant of attorney to confess judgment against the debtor, which offered a mortgagee a relatively quick and inexpensive means to collect the debt. The confession of judgment, which is now seldom used, gives the lender the right, upon a default and sometimes before a default, to appear in court on behalf of the debtor and to plead that the debtor defaulted under the obligation.

Once judgment is secured, either by a confession of judgment or by a separate lawsuit to recover the debt on the note, the mortgagee could execute upon the judgment by ordering the sheriff to seize the property (real or personal) of the debtor and sell it at sheriff's sale, generally without notice to the debtor.

Debtors were not always aware of the legal implications of signing a judgment note and even if they were, few people understood and could afford the procedures required to protect their property once a confession of judgment was wrongfully entered. Recognizing these realities, the courts have invalidated use of confessions of judgments in certain situations. Because of the possibility that these decisions might apply to a given fact situation, most lawyers, at least with respect to individual debtors, do not use the confession of judgment contained in a bond or note accompanying a mortgage as a means of collecting a debt. The mortgagee can still bring an action on the bond or note in an independent lawsuit, obtain a judgment in an adversary proceeding and execute and sell the property pursuant to that judgment. In some cases it will be better to bring a lawsuit on the note, especially when the mortgage accompanying the particular note is secured by real property less valuable than the amount of the debt or when there is substantial value in the debtor's personal property.[1] By obtaining a personal judgment in the suit brought on the note, the mortgagee will secure a lien on all the debtor's property in the county, not just the property encumbered by the mortgage which accompanied the mortgage note. Often, however, the better procedure for the mortgagee is to file a lawsuit on the mortgage.

III. THE DEFAULT

If the mortgagor is fulfilling his obligations under the bond or mortgage, the mortgagee has no right to compel the sale of the mortgaged property in order to satisfy the balance of the mortgage debt. The mortgagee's right to foreclose on the mortgage arises when the mortgagor fails to fulfill one or more of the obligations contained in the note or mortgage. For example, if the mortgage provides for re-

---

1. This assumes, of course, that the debtor's obligation is not limited to the land.

payment of the debt in monthly installments and the mortgagor fails to pay an installment in a particular month, the mortgagee may bring an action in mortgage foreclosure if the mortgage instrument so provides, which it generally does. The mortgagor's failure to make payments when due is the most common default leading to foreclosure. It is customary in installment mortgages to insert a provision in the note and the mortgage which accelerates the due date of principal, interest, taxes and insurance, upon a default in a monthly payment or in the event of other defaults in the mortgagor's obligations. The mortgagee may then institute an action to collect the debt, either by an action on the note or by mortgage foreclosure.

IV. THE COMPLAINT

A mortgage foreclosure proceeding is a kind of lawsuit and as such follows the general procedures for starting a legal action. The suit is generally instituted by filing a "complaint" with the state court in the county in which the land is located. The complaint constitutes the initial pleading of fact which the mortgagee intends to prove to the court, cites the relief requested by the mortgagee and serves to bring the defendant within the power of the court. The original complaint is filed with the court and a copy is served by the Sheriff (or comparable official) upon the defendant. The normal method of serving a defendant is to leave a copy of the complaint at his residence, or, if his address is unknown but he can be located, to hand him a copy of the complaint.

A. PLAINTIFF

The plaintiff in a mortgage foreclosure is the mortgagee or mortgagees, or his or its heirs, executors, administrators, successors or assigns.

B. DEFENDANT

Generally, the plaintiff in an action of mortgage foreclosure must name as defendants in the complaint, (1) the mortgagor and (2) the real owner of the property (if he is different from the mortgagor) or, if he is unknown, the grantee in the last recorded deed.

If the mortgagor is no longer the real owner of the property, and if the mortgagee is willing (assuming he has a choice) to absolve him of any personal responsibility and liability under the mortgage, then the mortgagor may not have to be made a party to the complaint. The rules in most states require that the plaintiff set forth in his complaint the fact that he releases the mortgagor of liability on the debt secured by the mortgage.

Persons who are in possession of the property are not required to be joined as defendants to the action in mortgage foreclosure although they may have to be served with a copy of the complaint.

The law in many states is not clear as to the consequences of failing to serve a tenant with a copy of the complaint. It is possible, for example, that a tenant who has a lease which is subject to the mortgage and, therefore, subject to divestment as a result of a sheriff's sale on a foreclosure, may not be divested if he is not served with a copy of the complaint. In any event, prudent practice requires service of a copy of the complaint on all tenants. In New York, the rules require that all parties whose interests in the land are claimed to be subordinate and subject to the mortgage must be made parties to the action. Accordingly, if a first mortgage is being foreclosed, all subordinate mortgages and all junior judgment creditors must be served and named as defendants. In California, all persons having an interest of any sort in the property must be made parties.

Federal tax liens receive special treatment in a foreclosure sale. If the mortgage was recorded prior to the federal tax lien it will be superior to the federal lien. However, the mortgagee must name the federal government as a party defendant in the foreclosure proceeding. If the mortgagee fails to name the federal government as a defendant, the federal tax lien will not be discharged by the foreclosure sale and the successful bidder at the sale will take the property subject to the federal lien.

C. DEFENSES AND COUNTERCLAIMS

Just as with any other lawsuit, there are many defenses or counterclaims that might be imposed by the defendant in a mortgage foreclosure action. We shall briefly review several possible defenses.

1. Performance and/or Waiver

The most obvious defense is that there was no default at all. More often, the defense will be either that the default has been cured within an acceptable time or that the mortgagee has by past forbearance waived its right to require strict adherence to all of the technical provisions of the mortgage. Most mortgages will contain a provision stating that forebearance, even repeated forebearance, by a mortgagee shall not constitute a waiver by the mortgagee of its right to require strict performance. Such a provision may not be completely effective and mortgagors are likely to attempt to impose a waiver defense notwithstanding the clause.

2. Invalidity of Mortgage

A mortgagor may claim that the mortgage itself was invalid for any number of technical reasons, such as failure of consideration (especially if the mortgagor was not the same party as the borrower), lack of authority of the signatories of the mortgage (where the mortgagor is a corporation or other entity) and failure to obtain the necessary signatories in their proper capacities. The mortgagee attempts to secure itself against this type of defense by requiring the mortgagor to obtain mortgagee title insurance from solvent title companies and by requiring mortgagor's counsel to supply opinion letters as to the validity of the mortgage.

3. Technical Defenses Regarding Foreclosures

The plaintiff in a mortgage foreclosure action must comply with certain requirements and rules of court. Failure to comply with those requirements and rules, such as notice provisions, may give rise to technical defenses. These may only delay the ultimate effect of the foreclosure action, but such delay may be significant.

4. Counterclaims and Offsets

In different jurisdictions, claims that the mortgagor may have against the mortgagee may be introduced into the foreclosure action. Almost certainly a mortgagor can interject a claim arising out of the mortgage relationship. This becomes very significant with a combined construction loan and permanent loan. It is not at all unusual or difficult for a mortgagor to be able to work up some claim against the construction lender based upon an alleged breach of the construction loan agreement. Since the loan agreement is referred to in the mortgage, the permanent lender, as assignee from the construction lender, would be susceptible to such counterclaims. This points up the importance to the permanent lender of the Declaration of No Set-Off signed by the mortgagor at the time of the permanent loan closing, which has the effect of estopping the mortgagor from interposing a counterclaim arising prior to the date of the permanent loan closing.

V. EXECUTION SALE

The first concept to be aware of is that the purchaser at the execution sale will take title to the mortgaged property free and clear of the mortgage. Even if there are insufficient funds to pay the mortgage in full, the mortgagee has no further rights in the property. The other important concept is that the mortgagee can bid at the execution sale without having to put up cash, except to the extent of the expenses of sale, any sums having a priority of payment to the mortgagee and except as to any amount above the total judgment that the mortgagee has obtained.

VI. CONCLUSION

The foreclosure action is the ultimate measurement of the effectiveness of a mortgage. If a mortgage is ineffective at the point of foreclosure, then it has failed to serve its basic purpose. However, foreclosure is just the strongest example of the tests that a mortgage should properly pass.   Unlike an agreement of sale or a lease, a mortgage is a peculiarly negative document.   Its only purpose is to take effect if something goes wrong, whether fire, condemnation, bankruptcy or whatever.   No draftsman can anticipate all the adverse events that might occur.   The decision for the draftsman for the lender is to determine how much is enough, a determination that may differ from transaction to transaction.

Chapter Nine

LEASING

Part One

BASIC ELEMENTS OF A LEASE

I. INTRODUCTION

The relationship of landlord and tenant is created by an agreement (either oral or written) called a lease.[1] A lease is a contract whereby one party (the Landlord or Lessor) grants to another party (the Tenant or Lessee) the right to possess real or personal property for a period of time which may or may not be fixed and usually, but not always, in return for the payment of rent. This chapter will focus on the leasing of real property. There is a great deal of common law and statutory law which governs the landlord and tenant relationship. However, almost all of the provisions of the laws governing the landlord-tenant relationship are subject to change by the parties in their written or oral agreement. Thus, the draftsman of a lease must be aware of the relevant landlord-tenant law in order to judge the effect of a lease which does not treat with specific aspects of the landlord-tenant relationship.

This chapter is devoted to a discussion of the components of lease agreements. Those elements which are common to virtually all leases will be considered first. Later parts of the chapter will deal with matters which are unique to special types of leases such as leases of undeveloped ground (a "ground lease") and leases for shopping centers and office buildings.

Before proceeding further, the reader should be aware of the importance of printed form leases to lawyers and landlords. Lawyers in most communities will have available to them standard leases covering the rental of office space, homes, apartments and retail and commercial space. Often, these standard printed forms provide the basis for the lease executed between the landlord and tenant, with minor changes or deletions being made on the printed form and additional clauses being added on separate pages attached to the printed form of the lease (often called a "rider" to the lease).

---

1. Note that the word "lease" is used both as a noun and a verb. You may recall from Chapter One that the tenant's interest created by a lease is referred to as a leasehold interest.

II. ESSENTIAL ELEMENTS OF A LEASE

There are several requisite elements which are included in virtually every lease. They are set forth below in the usual order in which they usually appear in the simplest form of written lease.

A. DATE

The date on which the agreement is executed should be included.

B. PARTIES

The lease must adequately identify the parties and should contain the correct names and addresses of the landlord and tenant. After each party's name, his or her capacity (i. e., landlord or tenant) should be stated.

1. Landlord

The landlord's name should conform exactly with the name of the party or parties holding record title (or, in the case of a sublease, with a party having the right of possession) to the property. If the landlord is not an individual, the type of entity, should be mentioned. Additional considerations which vary with the type of landlord in a particular situation are set forth below:

(a) Individual as Landlord

An individual landlord's spouse who does not have any ownership interest in the property need not join in signing the lease unless the lease gives the tenant an option to purchase the property.

(b) Partnership as Landlord

Where possible, it is good practice for all partners of a partnership to be named as well as the name of the partnership itself. For example, "A, B, and C, co-partners trading as ABC Company".

(c) Corporation as Landlord

Following the name of a corporation, include its state of incorporation. For example, "XYZ Corporation, an Illinois corporation". The authority of the officers of the corporation to lease a particular property should be ascertained. To determine whether the officers of a corporation have the authority to lease a particular property, the tenant should ask the landlord to produce a certified copy of resolutions of the landlord's board of directors, authorizing execution of the lease by the officers who propose to sign it.

(d) Fiduciaries

The name of the fiduciary and a description of his or its role should be included. For example, "John Smith, executor under the will of Betsy Jones, Deceased". The authority of a fiduciary to lease the property should be ascertained by the tenant. To determine the authority of the executor or administrator of an estate, the tenant should request the landlord to give the tenant a copy of the letters testamentary (in the case of an executor) or letters of administration (in the case of an administrator) evidencing appointment as a personal representative and certified as accurate by an appropriate official of the court which granted the letters.

In the case of a trustee-landlord, the tenant may ascertain the trustee's power to lease the property by reviewing a copy of the instrument creating the trust.

(e) Agents

If the lease is to be executed by an agent of either party, the lease should clearly indicate that the party signing the lease is acting as an agent. (E. g., "George Jackson, agent".) The authority of the agent to lease the property should be investigated by the tenant. It is best to have the lease approved in writing by the principal for whom the agent is acting.

2. Tenant

The landlord should check the status and authority of the prospective tenant to enter into an enforceable lease. The rules stated above for describing the landlord also apply to the tenant.

C. STATEMENT OF DEMISE

The lease should use the historical words for granting a leasehold estate, such as "landlord does hereby let and demise" or "landlord does hereby lease". These words have been construed by the courts in many cases and have a fixed meaning.

D. DESCRIPTION OF PREMISES

The leased ("demised") premises should be clearly identified. If the premises are an apartment or small office the street address of the building and the number of the individual apartment or office is usually considered sufficient. If part of a building comprising less than an entire floor is demised, a plan showing the space demised should be attached to the lease as an exhibit. If dimensions are set forth, they should be clearly designated as approximate dimensions or the landlord may be deemed to have warranted that the exact dimensions set forth are accurate. If an entire building is leased, a full legal description of the property is desirable.

Where the leased premises are not yet built, a reference is usually made to the location of the premises on a site plan. In addition, the plans and specifications for the erection of the building are generally included as an exhibit to the lease.

If the tenant is to have use of personal property located on the leased premises, that fact should be stated and the lease should contain an exhibit setting forth the items of personal property included in the lease.

If a tenant is leasing space in a multi-tenanted building which contains common or public areas, the lease should contain a specific grant of the right to use those areas in common with other tenants. If certain areas outside of the space actually being leased are to be for the tenants exclusive use (e. g., assigned parking or storage) then such rights of exclusive use should be set forth.

E. TERM OF LEASE

In leases for a fixed term, the term of the lease together with the commencement and expiration dates [2] must be set forth. An example of such a provision follows:

> "This lease shall be for a term of five (5) years beginning the 1st day of January, 1977 and ending the 31st day of December, 1981."

It is important to understand that the date of the lease, the date of the commencement of the term and the date of the commencement of the obligation to pay rent may be different. A lease may be signed well in advance of the intended commencement of the term. The obligation to pay rent may not commence until a substantial period of time has expired after commencement of the term, for example the tenant may have use of the property without rent for a period of time so that the tenant has the opportunity to alter and furnish the premises for the tenant's own purposes.

Not all leases are for a fixed term. Some leases are simply silent as to term. Such a lease is considered to be a "tenancy at will" and to be terminable by either party with reasonable notice (30 days in most jurisdictions). There are also leases which will terminate upon a given event, often the death of the tenant (such a tenant is said to have a "life estate" or a "tenancy for life") or of some other party (a life estate *pur autre vie*).

F. RENTAL

If the lease is one which provides for rent, then the rental is usually expressed in a fixed dollar sum. Often the total rental for the entire term is also stated, followed by a provision as to the time

---

2. The date set for the end of a lease is called the expiration or termination date. If for some reason the term actually ends prior to the expiration date (e. g., because the tenant defaults) then the lease term is said to terminate. In current legal jargon "expiration" is the natural end of a lease term, whereas "termination" refers to any end of the term, but especially a premature end.

and amount of each installment. For example, in a one-year lease, the following rental provision might appear:

> "Tenant shall pay, without demand and without set-off or deduction, a minimum annual rental of Twelve Hundred ($1,200.00) Dollars payable in equal monthly installment of One Hundred ($100.00) Dollars each, and a pro-rata portion thereof for any part of a month, on the first day of each month in advance, beginning the 1st day of January, 1977, and on the first day of each month thereafter."

The phrase "in advance" is essential because the common law provides that, without that phrase, the entire rent will be paid at the end of the term. The words "minimum rental" are used because other sums due the landlord may be classified as rent (see below). The rent clause includes the words "without demand" because in the absence of those words the landlord may not be able to take advantage of all of the remedies available to the landlord unless a prior demand for payment of the rent has first been made. The rental clause should also include the words "without set-off or deduction" or the tenant may withhold rent if he feels the landlord owes him money (whether for sufficient or insufficient reason), thereby prejudicing the landlord's or the mortgagee's financial position.

The place of payment of the rent should be stated, since otherwise rent is payable on the premises. The usual clauses direct payment to be made at the landlord's office, with his address given, or at such other place as the landlord may from time to time designate.

Often, a lease requires the tenant to pay certain expenses, such as real estate taxes and water and sewer rents. If the tenant is required to make additional payments, the lease should specifically provide that all such additional payments are collectible as rent, in the hope that all remedies applicable to the collection of rent and priorities in bankruptcy and insolvency proceedings are available with respect to the additional payments.

G. EXECUTION

If a written lease is required by the Statute of Frauds (which requirement is discussed below), then all parties must sign the lease. Corporate signatures should be in the corporate name by a principal officer such as the president or vice president, attested by a secretary or assistant secretary, and the corporate seal affixed. If a lease is to be recorded, the proper acknowledgments must be completed.

In addition to the basic elements set forth above, there are many provisions which are common to most leases. Those provisions are the subject of Section IV below.

III. THE NEED FOR A WRITTEN LEASE

In section I(B) of Chapter Two we discussed the Statute of Frauds, a variation of which has been adopted by nearly every jurisdiction. The Statute of Frauds for a particular state will usually require that leases for longer than a specified term must be in writing, or must otherwise qualify as having satisfied the Statute of Frauds, in order to be enforceable against either the landlord or the tenant.

You must realize that the landlord-tenant relationship is one that may continue over an extended period of time. During that period of time, the parties may modify the relationship by increasing or reducing the term of the lease or the rent or by amending the terms of the lease in any number of ways. The question of which amendments and modifications to a lease must be in writing and be signed by the parties is a difficult and controversial one, and many jurisdictions have not settled even some of the more obvious of the issues, such as whether an extension or reduction of the term of the lease must be evidenced by a written and signed agreement.

Consider also whether a lease which otherwise need not be in writing should be incorporated into a written agreement if it contains an option to purchase the demised premises.

PROBLEM

Determine what leases in your jurisdiction must be in writing in order to be enforceable.

IV. ADDITIONAL PROVISIONS COMMON TO ALL TYPES OF LEASES

The basic requirements of a lease establish the relationship of landlord and tenant, insure the tenant possession for a specified term and, as a matter of law, afford the landlord certain minimum benefits, including the right to collect the rent and the right to exercise the remedies provided by law for the collection of rent and for the recovery of possession of the demised premises at the termination of the lease. In addition, every lease should include specific provisions dealing with the issues discussed below. Otherwise, the common law and statutory provisions of landlord and tenant law dictate terms which are often contrary to the actual intent of the parties.

A. USE CLAUSE

If no provision as to the use of the premises is set forth, the tenant is entitled to use the premises without restriction, except that he may not commit "waste", i. e., destroy the premises or let the property fall into an unreasonable state of disrepair. If the landlord does not wish the tenant to be free to use the property for any purpose, he must provide in the lease for restrictions on the use of the property to limit tenant's use to the actual intended purpose. For example, in a dwelling or apartment house, the tenant might be limited to use of the premises as "a private dwelling and no other", or to use of the premises as a "single family dwelling, and no other".

The tenant will desire the broadest possible use clause, and the landlord, especially in a multi-tenanted building or a shopping center, will generally want to limit the use strictly.

In commercial properties, a restriction limiting the use of the demised premises to a particular business may be desired by the landlord to limit competition with other property in the vicinity owned or acquired by the landlord. In shopping centers, particular care must be taken to limit the type of business and to avoid infringement of exclusive use clauses in the leases of other tenants.

There are many other reasons for a landlord to restrict use. Heavy or inflammable material, machines causing vibration, noxious odors and the like endanger the building and annoy other tenants. Some uses impair the image of the building and either increase insurance costs or make it impossible to procure insurance.

In drafting a use provision, it is important that the actual intent or agreement of the parties with respect to the use be ascertained. The draftsman should be as specific as possible in describing the use. Although desirable, it is usually not possible to list all the items which may be sold at the premises. However, it may be possible, for example, to limit the use to "sales at retail" and further limit such sales to "retail sales of shoes" or even more explicitly, "retail sales of men's shoes". An example of a simple use provision is set forth below:

> "The premises may be used only as a restaurant for the sale of fast-food items and the incidental sale of non-alcoholic beverages for consumption on or off the premises. The premises shall not be used for any other purpose."

A tenant should know in advance whether there are any legal impediments to the use of the premises for the intended purpose. The existence of governmental restrictions can be checked by obtaining a permit from the municipality in which the premises are located, stating that the intended use is permissible. There may also exist private restrictions contained in an agreement or in a clause of a deed restricting the use of the premises. Restrictions imposed in private agreements or deeds will not affect third parties (including tenants) unless they are recorded. Therefore, the information needed by a prospective tenant, concerning private restrictions, can be obtained by searching the title to the property to be leased.

If the tenant is concerned about the legality of the use, and has not had an opportunity to check with the appropriate governmental authorities, a provision conditioning the validity of the lease upon obtaining the appropriate use permit might be inserted.

PROBLEM

Draft a clause making a lease contingent upon the tenant obtaining a use registration permit from the local municipal authorities on or before June 10, 1977 for use of the premises as a retail shoe store.

B. REPAIRS

1. Generally

At common law, in the absence of any provision in the agreement, the landlord has no obligation to repair or rebuild damaged premises except for common areas of a multi-tenanted building. Therefore, if the parties intend that the landlord will perform certain repairs, the obligations of the landlord should be set forth.

In the absence of an agreement to the contrary, the common law imposes an obligation on the tenant to make ordinary repairs. The obligation of the tenant does not extend to major repairs and does not include repairs resulting from acts of third parties or destruction by fire, wind or other act of God. Written leases often require the tenant to keep the leased premises clean and in good repair and at the termination of the lease to return the premises in the same condition as when it was leased, reasonable wear and tear and damage by accidental fire excepted.

There are various alternative approaches in leasing to the obligation of each party to repair. The tenant of an entire building, for example, is often responsible for all repairs, interior and exterior, structural or otherwise. Sometimes a landlord will agree to make repairs to the roof and exterior walls while requiring the tenant to make all interior repairs. Another alternative is for the landlord to agree to make all structural repairs while requiring the tenant to make all non-structural repairs. There is no precise definition of these terms, but in most states there are numerous cases in which the courts have decided whether a particular repair is structural or non-structural.

A lease should state specifically who is responsible for repairs to the electrical, plumbing, heating and air conditioning or ventilating systems. It is also good drafting policy to indicate the party who is responsible for replacement of plate glass windows as they are subject to a high rate of breakage and are expensive to repair.

2. Areas Outside Building

A tenant who leases an entire building or the first floor tenant in a multi-tenanted building is often responsible for maintenance of the grounds and walks adjoining the building.   A general provision to that effect follows:

> "Tenant shall be responsible for the condition of the pavement, curb, cellar doors, awnings and other erections in the pavement during the term of this lease; shall keep the pavement free from snow and ice; and hereby agrees to release and relieve Landlord and save Landlord harmless from any liability for any accidents, due or alleged to be due to their defective condition, or to any accumulations of snow and ice."

3.   Compliance with Requirements of Public Authorities

In addition to repair requirements occasioned by deterioration of the structure, repairs or alterations may be required by local authorities in order for the structure to comply with various safety codes. Therefore, the lease may include a provision, in addition to the general repair provision, obligating the tenant to make repairs or changes to the premises which are required by the authorities.   For example, a provision requiring the tenant to comply with local ordinances might render the tenant responsible for installing or repairing a fire alarm system.   The tenant should be certain that his or her responsibility is limited to requirements imposed by the authorities which relate to the particular use and occupancy of the tenant.

C.   ALTERATIONS AND IMPROVEMENTS

A tenant may wish to make alterations to the premises.   For example, in a retail store a tenant may wish to move the partition between the sales and storage areas.   However, absent a provision in the lease or permission of the landlord, a tenant may not alter the premises.   A landlord ordinarily will want to prohibit alterations unless he approves them in advance.   An example of a provision to that effect follows:

> "Tenant covenants and agrees that he will not, without the consent in writing of Landlord first had and obtained, make any alterations, improvements or additions to the demised premises.   All alterations, improvements, additions or fixtures, whether installed before or after the execution of this lease, shall remain upon the premises at the expiration or sooner determination of this lease and become the property of Landlord, unless Landlord shall, prior to the determination of this lease, have given written notice to Tenant to remove the same, in which event Tenant will remove such alterations, improvements and additions, and restore the premises to the same good order and condition in which they now are. Should Tenant fail so to do, Landlord may do so, collecting, at Landlord's option, the cost and expense thereof from Tenant as additional rent."

The above provision gives the landlord the option to keep the alterations or improvements at the termination of the lease or to require the tenant to remove them.

A professional or commercial tenant should always add a provision to the effect that the tenant will be permitted to remove trade fixtures and equipment, provided tenant repairs any and all damage caused to the demised premises by reason of the removal. Trade fixtures and equipment may include display cases, furniture, shelves, office equipment and many kinds of machinery and equipment. Whether or not other alterations and improvements which do not fall into the category of trade fixtures may be removed by the tenant is a matter which may be negotiated by the parties.

Often the parties agree that before the tenant occupies the premises the landlord or tenant is to make certain alterations or renovations to the premises in order to make the premises suitable for the tenant. The work should be described and, if possible, plans and specifications for the work should be attached to the lease and initialed by the parties.

If the landlord is performing the work, he should be obligated to complete the work by a specified time, with reasonable allowance for delays beyond the landlord's control. The tenant will want a clause permitting the tenant to cancel the lease should the landlord fail to complete alterations within the specified period. If such a clause is not inserted and the work runs beyond the specified time, state law may limit the tenant's remedies to a suit for damages. In certain cases the lease will provide that the term of the lease or the obligation to pay rent shall not commence until landlord's work is completed.

Improvements made by the tenant may be the basis of mechanics liens filed against the real estate. To protect itself, the landlord should include a provision requiring the tenant to pay for all work promptly, so that no liens are filed, and obligating the tenant to remove promptly any lien that may be filed. It is common to have language in the lease to the effect that the landlord will not be liable for work done by contractors for the tenant and that no liens shall affect the landlord's interest in the premises. It is unlikely, however, that such a provision will effectively prevent the filing or enforcement of mechanics liens. In jurisdictions where the right to file a mechanics lien may be waived by individual contractors and materialmen, or by the general contractor on behalf of all subcontractors and materialmen, then the lease might require the tenant to have the necessary waivers filed in a timely manner in the appropriate location.

D. FIRE

A lease should deal with three issues that arise in the event of a fire which causes damage to the demised property and equipment of the tenant: (1) whether the tenant will be entitled to stop paying rent if there is damage to the demised premises; (2) which party, if either, will be obligated to repair the damage to the demised premises; and (3) whether the landlord is legally responsible for any damage to the tenant's property or the tenant is legally responsible for any damage to the demised property, if the fire is the fault of the landlord or tenant or their respective employees.

1. Obligation to Pay Rent and Make Repairs

Every lease should state which party is to make repairs and restore the premises in the event of a fire. Typically, that is the obligation of the landlord. In addition, the lease should establish whether the tenant must pay rent during the period of repairs or restoration. Generally, if the premises are totally destroyed, rent abates and the tenant is not required to pay any rent. If the premises are partially destroyed and the tenant can still utilize a portion of the premises, the lease sometimes provides for an adjustment (or partial abatement) to the rent. A typical provision is set forth below:

> "In the event that the demised premises are totally destroyed or so damaged by fire or other casualty that the same cannot be repaired or restored within a reasonable time, this lease shall absolutely cease and determine, and the rent shall abate for the balance of the term.

> If the damage caused as above be only partial and such that the premises can be restored to their then condition within a reasonable time, the Landlord may, at his option, restore the same with reasonable promptness, reserving the right to enter upon the demised premises for that purpose. The Landlord also reserves the right to enter upon the demised premises whenever necessary to repair damage caused by fire or other casualty to the building of which the demised premises are a part, even though the effect of such entry be to render the demised premises or a part thereof untenantable. In either event the rent shall be apportioned and suspended during the time the Landlord is in possession, taking into account the proportion of the demised premises rendered untenantable and the duration of the Landlord's possession."

The tenant often tries to negotiate for a provision which terminates the lease if fire or casualty damage is extensive and cannot be repaired or restored within a reasonable period of time. In the sample provision above the use of the phrase "reasonable time" lacks precision, and a tenant may wish to specify a period of time within which the premises must be restored.

2. Liability for Damage Caused by Fire

Typically, the landlord [3] carries fire insurance on the building and the tenant carries fire insurance on the equipment and property

---

[3] Certain types of leases require the tenant to carry insurance. In that case the same discussion applies, but it is the landlord who needs protection in the event his or her negligent act causes a fire.

located within the building. Such insurance is intended to cover any loss irrespective of who may have caused the fire.

Under general principles of tort law, one whose negligent action causes a fire may be held liable for damages resulting from the fire. This tort liability is unconnected with the issues of the obligation to make repairs or pay rent. However, tort liability may be waived by the parties to a lease, and this is often the case. In doing so, one must consider the impact of such a waiver or release upon the insurance coverage.

The insurance company, if it is required to pay a claim of its insured for damages caused by fire, acquires the legal right (referred to as the right of "subrogation") to take over any tort claims of its insured against any person whose acts caused the damage. Therefore, the landlord's insurance company, after paying a claim for fire damage, can succeed to the landlord's right to obtain recovery from the person causing the fire, such as the tenant or his employee or agent.

If the landlord or tenant agrees not to hold the other party to a lease responsible for its negligent act in causing a fire, this will nullify the insurance company's right of subrogation. Unless the insurance company has agreed to such a provision, it may jeopardize the landlord's or tenant's insurance coverage. A solution to this problem is to request from the appropriate insurance company a "waiver of subrogation" by which the insurance company agrees to forfeit its right of subrogation without prejudice to the insured. Some insurance companies will only issue such waivers if an additional insurance premium is charged, and the lease should deal with this possibility.

The following sample clause deals with obtaining waivers of subrogation and waiving any right of recovery, as between landlord and tenant, to the extent that insurance coverage exists. The parties will not waive any claim beyond that covered by insurance as that would result in the loss being borne by the party who was innocent of any responsibility in causing the damage.

"Landlord and Tenant hereby release each other from any and all liability or responsibility to the other or anyone claiming through or under them by way of subrogation or otherwise for any loss or damage to property covered by any insurance then in force, even if such loss or damage shall have been caused by the fault or negligence of the other party, or anyone for whom such party may be responsible, provided, however, that this release shall be applicable and in force and effect only with respect to any loss or damage occurring during such time as the policy or policies of insurance covering said loss shall contain a clause or endorsement to the effect that this release shall not adversely affect or impair said insurance or prejudice the right of the insured to re-

cover thereunder. Any liability, fire and extended coverage insurance policies covering the Premises shall contain such a clause
if available without extra charge. If there be a charge the party
bearing the expense of the particular policy shall notify the other
party and, in such event, shall have the clause added to that
policy if the other party agrees to pay such extra charge."

E. OTHER CASUALTY

Fire is the usual but not the only cause of damage or destruction.
Some casualties, such as flood, are either non-insurable or are seldom
insured against. If the tenant is obligated to repair, and no exceptions are spelled out in the lease, the tenant will be required to repair
or rebuild after a flood. The tenant is protected if damage by "casualty" is excepted from the obligation to repair. If the parties intend the lease to terminate in the event of destruction, the fire clause
should provide for termination in the event of destruction "by fire or
other casualty".

F. CONDEMNATION

A taking of the entire premises by eminent domain obviously terminates a lease. A taking of only a part of the premises will not terminate a lease in the absence of a specific agreement by the parties.
In either case, eminent domain law in most jurisdictions provides
that the tenant will have a right to participate in the eminent domain
award. The landlord will not want the tenant to participate since the
value of the tenant's lease may take a substantial part of the award
otherwise payable to the landlord. The standard lease provision
states that the tenant is not to be compensated for the value of the
tenant's leasehold interest. A sample provision is set forth below:

"In the event that the premises demised or any part thereof is
taken or condemned for a public or quasi-public use, this lease
shall, as to the part so taken, terminate as of the date title shall
vest in the condemnor, and rent shall abate in proportion to the
square feet of leased space taken or condemned or shall cease if
the entire premises be so taken. In either event the Tenant
waives all claims against the Landlord and the condemning authority by reason of the complete or partial taking of the demised
premises, and it is agreed that the Tenant shall not be entitled
to any notice whatsoever of the partial or complete termination
of this lease by reason of the aforesaid. Notwithstanding the
foregoing, Tenant may obtain an award from the condemning
authority as reimbursement of Tenant's moving expenses."

The consequences which flow from partial condemnation should
be set forth in the lease. If the part taken is such that the remainder
will be insufficient for the tenant's business, the tenant will want the
right to cancel the lease. Of course, it would be advantageous to set
forth in the lease guidelines for determining when the premises are

no longer satisfactory for tenant's use.   If the parties agree to use space as a criteria, a formula could be expressed based on the amount of space taken by the condemning authority which will render the premises unsuitable for tenant.   For example, the lease could provide that it will terminate if "more than 2,000 square feet of the premises is taken".   Another provision might terminate the lease if "more than 20% of the floor area of the store on the demised premises, or more than 15% of the parking area is taken."

If the lease is not terminated after a partial condemnation, normally the rent is reduced, since the tenant will be occupying less space.   Again it is difficult to provide a formula which will precisely account for the reduced value of the premises to tenant.   An adjustment based solely on the percentage of space taken does not take into account the different value of different areas of the premises.   For example, the showroom or sales space in a store is more valuable than the storage space.   One solution is to adjust the rent by applying to it the ratio which the value of the premises after the taking bears to the value before the taking.   If such a provision is used, a method for fixing the value of the premises will have to be set forth.

Often the lease will provide that, in the event of a partial condemnation, the premises will be restored to a condition as near as possible to that which existed before the condemnation unless such restoration is physically impossible or economically impractical.   For example, if part of the parking area is taken, there might be room on the remainder of the premises to create new parking areas.   Responsibility for the expense of restoration should rest with the party who receives the condemnation award, which is normally the landlord.   A sample provision requiring the landlord to reconstruct follows:

> "If, after a partial taking of the premises as a result of the exercise of the power of eminent domain, this lease is not terminated, landlord shall do such work as may be reasonably necessary to restore what may remain of the premises to tenantable condition for tenant's use; provided, however, that landlord shall not be required to expend more than the net award landlord reasonably expects to receive as a result of the taking."

In this example, failure of the landlord to restore the property would effect a termination of the lease.

G.   ASSIGNMENT AND SUBLETTING

Unless the lease provides otherwise, either party may assign his or her interest in the lease to another.   An assignment is a transfer of the entire term or entire remaining term of the lease upon the same provisions as the original lease.   The tenant may also sublet the premises unless the lease provides to the contrary.   A sublease is a transfer of a part of the term or the entire term but with at least one new or different provision.

For a variety of reasons, in most leasehold situations, the landlord will prohibit any assignment or subletting without prior written consent.

The tenant should request that the landlord's consent shall not be unreasonably withheld. If the tenant is a corporation, the lease may provide that subletting or assignment is permitted to a parent, subsidiary or affiliated corporation or to a surviving corporation in a merger. A consent to an assignment or subletting should not relieve the original tenant from liability under the lease, and the assignee or sublessee should assume liability in writing directly to the landlord.

The standard restrictions against assignment and subletting are viewed by the courts as restraints upon the right of an individual to transfer his property freely. Accordingly, such restrictions are interpreted narrowly by courts. For example, if the lease contains a covenant barring only assignment, the court will allow subletting.

The ordinary restriction against a transfer by the tenant of his leasehold interest may be circumvented, in the case of a corporate tenant, by a transfer of the corporate stock. The transfer of stock will not cause a change in the identity of the entity holding the leasehold estate, and is therefore not an assignment of the leasehold itself. Recognizing this means of circumventing restrictions against subletting and assignment, the landlord might include a provision stating that a sale or transfer of the majority of a corporation's stock is deemed an assignment of the lease.

PROBLEM

Prepare a lease provision prohibiting a corporate tenant from assigning or subletting without the landlord's consent, taking into account the considerations set forth in the preceding paragraphs.

H.   ENTRY AND INSPECTION

The landlord often reserves a right to enter the premises from time to time during the term of a lease so that he may inspect and make the repairs and changes he has agreed, or is otherwise required, to make. The landlord also often reserves the right to effect repairs and changes which are the responsibility of the tenant, but which the tenant has failed to make. In the latter case the landlord should be entitled to charge the tenant the cost of any such work. The landlord is also concerned to reserve the right to exhibit the premises to prospective purchasers and tenants.

I.   DEFAULT PROVISIONS

1. Default by Tenant

The lease must spell out precisely what acts or omissions of the tenant will constitute a default under the lease. The most obvious event of default is failure to pay rent when due. Generally the lease will also provide that the tenant is in default if he fails to meet any obligation under the lease. The default provisions are generally combined with provisions setting forth the remedies which a landlord can pursue if the tenant is in default.

(a) Landlord's Remedies

Remedies are tied to local laws and procedures which vary from state to state. However, the basic remedies sought by landlords will be similar in all jurisdictions.

(i) Acceleration of Rent

The landlord will want the right to accelerate the rent for the balance of the term thereby making it all due at once. A strong commercial tenant can sometimes obtain deletion of the right to accelerate the rent. For such tenants the default is not usually one of payments of rent, but is more often a decision to cease to operate at that particular location, while still maintaining operations elsewhere. Such a tenant may insist that it be permitted by the terms of the lease to vacate the premises.

(ii) Landlord's Right to Reenter and Relet

The landlord will want the right to reenter and relet the demised premises for the balance of the term of the lease. In order to make clear that this does not relieve the tenant of responsibility for any loss or deficiency in rent suffered by the landlord, the landlord will relet the premises as agent for the tenant. The tenant will remain liable for the difference between the lease rental and that collected by reletting. Furthermore, any expenses (including alterations) which the landlord incurs in reletting the premises will be deducted from the rent being collected from the new tenant.

(iii) Termination of the Lease

Alternatively, the landlord will want the right to terminate the lease and cut off any further right of the tenant to possession of the premises.

(b) Landlord's Enforcement of Remedies

In addition to setting forth the events of default and the remedies available to the landlord, the lease should specify how the landlord may enforce his or her remedies. The following means of enforcement are common to most leases, although some, such as confessions of judgment, are available only in certain states.

(i) Distraint

The landlord will generally seek the right to distrain on the personal property of the tenant located on or within the demised premises. In effect, this means that the landlord may file a document and obtain a lien on the personal property of the tenant, which lien will give the landlord an interest in such personal property which is prior to any rights of lessee's unsecured creditors. The amount of the lien will be the unpaid amount due the landlord under the lease.

(ii) Judgment for Rent and for other Money Damages

The landlord, whether or not granted power by the lease, has the power to sue the tenant in a court of law and obtain a judgment for all sums due under the lease, including amounts which become due as a result of the acceleration of rent. The landlord can then enforce that judgment by executing against the property of the tenant and causing it to be sold to satisfy the judgment.

(iii) Confession of Judgment

In Pennsylvania, and a few other states, leases often contain a "confession of judgment" clause which permits the landlord to appear as attorney for the tenant in court, on the basis of the authority granted by the lease, and obtain a judgment against the tenant. The enforceability of confessions of judgment is questionable in light of recent court decisions. However, in states where confessions of judgment have traditionally been used, they are still included in most leases.

(iv) Action of Ejectment

If the landlord wishes to pursue his right to remove a tenant in default from the premises he must bring a court action known as an action of ejectment. Leases in those states in which confessions of judgment for money are used often contain a provision allowing the landlord to confess judgment in ejectment. The problems of enforcement of this provision are the same as in the case of confessions of judgment for money damages.

Set forth below is a comprehensive lease provision dealing with a tenant's default and the landlord's remedies:

"In the event Tenant (a) Does not pay in full when due any and all installments of rent or any other charge or payment whether or not herein included as rent; or (b) Violates or fails to perform or otherwise breaks any covenant or condition herein contained or any other obligation imposed upon lessee; or (c) Abandons the demised premises or removes or attempts to remove Tenant's goods or property therefrom other than in the ordinary course of business without having first paid to Landlord in full all rent and other charges that may become due as well as all which will become due thereafter; or (d) Becomes insolvent in any sense or makes an assignment for the benefit of creditors or offers a composition or settlement to creditors or calls a meeting of creditors for any such purpose, or if a petition in bankruptcy or for reorganization or for an arrangement with creditors under any federal or state act is filed by or against Tenant, or if a bill in equity or other proceeding is filed in any court for the appointment of a receiver, trustee, liquidator, custodian, conservator or similar official for any of Tenant's assets, or if any of the real or personal property of Tenant's shall be levied upon by any sheriff, marshal, or constable,

Then, and in any such event, at the sole option of Landlord, (1) The whole balance of rent and charges, whether or not payable as rent, for the entire balance of the term herein reserved and any renewal or extension thereof, or any part of such rent and charges, and also all or any costs and sheriff's, marshal's or constable's commissions, whether chargeable to Landlord or Tenant, including watchman's wages, shall be taken to be due and payable and in arrears as if by the terms of this lease said balance of rent and such other charges and expenses were on that date payable in advance; or (2) The term created by this lease shall terminate and become absolutely void, without notice and without any right on the part of Tenant to save the forfeiture by payment of any sums due or by other performance of any condition, term or covenant broken, and upon such termination, or also if there be no termination, Landlord may, without notice or demand, enter the demised premises breaking open locked doors, if necessary, to effect entrance, without liability for damages for such entry or for the manner thereof, for the purpose of distraint or execution or to take possession of the premises to minimize the loss by reason of Tenant's default, and to take possession of and sell under distraint the goods or chattels found upon the premises. Whether or not any rent due or unpaid, should Tenant at any time remove, or attempt or indicate an intention to remove, the goods or chattels from the premises other than in the ordinary course of business, Tenant authorizes Landlord to follow the same for a period of ninety days after such removal or attempted or intended removal and to take possession of and cause to be sold sufficient of such goods and chattels to meet the rent and charges in arrears, as well as payable for the balance of the full term then remaining or any part thereof.

Tenant expressly agrees that any judgment, order or decree entered in favor of Landlord by any court or magistrate shall be final, and that Tenant will not take or file an appeal, certiorari, writ of error, exception or objection to the same, or file a motion or rule to strike off or open the same or to stay any execution under the same, and Tenant releases to Landlord, all errors in the said proceedings, and all liability therefor. Tenant expressly waives the benefits of all laws, now or hereafter in force, exempting any goods within the demised premises or elsewhere from distraint, levy or sale.

After reentry or retaking or recovering the premises, whether by way of termination of this lease or not, Landlord may lease said premises or any part or parts thereof to such person or persons upon such terms as may in Landlord's discretion seem best and for a term within or beyond the term of this lease, and Tenant shall be liable for any loss of rent for the balance of the term plus the costs and expenses of reletting and of making repairs and alterations to the premises."

In addition to the extensive provisions above, the lease will provide that any remedies set forth in the lease are in addition to those the landlord is granted by law.

"All remedies available to Landlord hereunder and at law and in equity shall be cumulative and concurrent. No determination of this lease nor taking or recovering possession of the premises shall deprive Landlord of any remedies or actions against lessee for rent, for charges or for damages for the breach of any covenant or condition herein contained, nor shall the bringing of any such action for rent, charges or breach of covenant or condition, nor the resort to any other remedy or right for the recovery of rent, charges or damages for such breach, be construed as a waiver or release of the right to insist upon the forfeiture and to obtain possession."

While the lease provides for cumulative remedies, no court of law will permit a landlord to recover more than actual damages. Therefore, while the landlord has the right to accelerate all the rent due under a lease, to terminate the lease and to relet the property to another tenant, the landlord cannot expect to receive more than his or her actual damages, which will include past due rent and the difference between the rent which would have been received from the defaulting tenant and the rent which actually is received, during the remaining term of the lease, from any new tenant. A lease provides for cumulative remedies in order to permit the landlord to have the greatest flexibility in proceeding against a defaulting tenant.

(c) Tenant's Right to Cure Default

The tenant's greatest concern is that the tenant may inadvertently be in default of a lease. For example, the tenant or an employee of the tenant may simply forget to send the check for payment of rent. An even greater problem exists with regard to the tenant's obligation to maintain the premises in good condition. A defect may exist in the premises without the tenant's knowledge. In either of the above cases the tenant can be protected from being in default by providing that the tenant will not be in default unless when notified of the default by the landlord the tenant failed to remedy it (cure it) within a specified period of time. Generally a short period of time [4] will be allowed to cure defaults due to failure to pay rent or other money due and a longer period of time will be allowed to cure other

---

4. Lawyers refer to the time during which a party may cure a default as a "grace period".

defaults such as repairing a part of the premises. The following is a provision for a grace period during which tenant can cure a default:

> "Tenant shall not be in default hereunder unless and until Landlord gives written notice thereof to Tenant and Tenant fails to cure said default within (a) ten days if said default consists of the non-payment of rent or any other sums required to be paid by Tenant hereunder, or (b) thirty days if said default relates to something other than the payment of money; provided, however, in the event a default other than the failure to pay money reasonably takes in excess of thirty days to cure, Tenant shall not be in default if Tenant commences to cure said default within said thirty day period and proceeds diligently thereafter to complete the same."

2. Default by Landlord

Most leases contain little in the way of protection for the tenant where the landlord is in default of his or her obligations under the lease. The tenant generally has no recourse except to sue the landlord for any damages incurred. However, where the tenant has substantial bargaining power, the tenant may obtain remedies for certain types of defaults by the landlord. For example, if the landlord is unable to deliver possession of the premises to the tenant by a specified date, the tenant may reserve a right of cancellation or a right to collect a penalty from the landlord for each day during which the landlord is unable to deliver possession. If the landlord fails to make certain repairs, the tenant may have the right to withhold rent or to make the repairs and deduct (off-set) the cost of the repairs from rental due. Rights of deduction and set-off are strongly resisted by landlords, and by lending institutions making mortgage loans to the landlord.

J. RENEWALS

Whenever possible, a tenant will want to have the right to renew a lease beyond its fixed term. This is especially true when a tenant has spent substantial sums of money in preparing premises for use or has built up a great deal of good will with respect to a particular business location. In order to capitalize fully on good-will and improvements, a tenant will request the right, at the tenant's option, to extend the lease beyond the original terms for one or more renewal periods. Renewals may be upon the same basic terms as contained in the lease for the original term, or may provide for an increase in rent during each successive renewal term, as well as other modifications. A sample renewal clause is as follows:

> "Provided that the Tenant at the time of exercise of the option herein contained is not in default of any of the terms, covenants and conditions or agreements provided for in this lease, Tenant shall have the right, option and privilege of renewing and extend-

ing the term of this lease for two additional periods of five years each. The said option periods may be exercised by Tenant upon six months written notice to Landlord prior to the expiration of the original term hereof, or any renewal or extension terms hereof. All of the terms, covenants and conditions of this lease pertaining to the original term hereof shall equally pertain in all respects to all renewals and extensions of this lease."

Where a tenant is not granted an option to renew the term of the lease, the lease often provides that at the end of the initial term the lease will continue in effect on a month to month or a year to year basis until terminated by either party giving notice of termination on or before a fixed period before expiration of the then current term.

"It is hereby mutually agreed that either party hereto may terminate this lease at the end of the term by giving to the other party written notice thereof, at least sixty days prior thereto, but in default of such notice this lease shall continue upon the same terms and conditions in force immediately prior to the expiration of the term hereof for a further period of one year and so on from year to year unless or until terminated by either party, giving the other sixty days written notice of termination previous to the expiration of the then current term."

K. NOTICES

Every lease should provide for the manner and place for giving notice to the other party wherever required in the lease. The notice provision should state that either party may from time to time designate a different address for service of notice, and may generally be in the same format as the notice provisions in an agreement of sale, as discussed in Chapter Two.

L. RECORDING OF LEASES; ACKNOWLEDGMENTS

As discussed in Chapter Three, recording statutes operate to impose notice of the interests which exist in real property. If a person fails to record his or her interest in real property, that interest may be lost to a third party who has no actual notice of such interest.

In many states, the recording statutes do not penalize a person who is in possession of real property and fails to record that interest because the very fact of possession imposes notice upon third parties. In such states, it is unnecessary for a tenant who is in possession to record the lease. However, some states require the recording of leases which have a term of at least a certain number of years.

PROBLEM

Does your jurisdiction require the recording of leases? If so, of what term? What is the result of failure to record?

Even in those jurisdictions in which a tenant in possession is not in jeopardy by reason of failure to record the lease, various circumstances may require recording or making recording desirable:

(1) If the lease is executed but the tenant is not yet in possession of the premises, recording is necessary to protect the tenant's rights during the period prior to possession;

(2) If the lease contains an option to purchase or a right of first refusal, recording the lease will notify third parties of the tenant's rights;

(3) If the lease is to be superior to a mortgage, the lease may have to be recorded even if the tenant is in possession when the mortgage is recorded; and

(4) If a lease for a portion of a multi-occupancy building or shopping center provides that the landlord will not lease other parts of the building or shopping center for competing uses, the tenant can put other tenants and third parties on legal notice of that provision by recording all or a part of the lease.

It should be observed that landlords frequently prefer to avoid recording. If the lease should be prematurely terminated by agreement or by court action following a default, the landlord may have certain practical difficulties in clearing record title to the property subject to the lease.

As discussed in Chapter Three, many states permit recording of a short form or memorandum of lease instead of the complete lease. The memorandum usually must state the names of the parties, a description of the premises and the term of the lease. Unless recordation is being effected simply to notify third parties of tenant's right to possession, the memorandum should contain those provisions of the lease which the parties want to make matters of record, such as an option on the part of tenant to purchase the premises. The advantage of recording a memorandum or short form of lease, rather than the whole lease, is that it permits the parties to keep private those parts of the lease which they do not want to be matters of public record, such as the amount of rent.

Any document which is to be recorded must be acknowledged. If the parties intend to record a memorandum of lease, only the memorandum need be acknowledged.

M. INABILITY TO GIVE POSSESSION

A landlord may be unable to deliver possession of the premises at the commencement of the term. Therefore, a lease usually provides for release of the landlord from liability by reason of the holding over of an existing tenant, or delay in completing a new structure or alterations or repairs. The tenant may wish to add a provision giv-

ing him the right to cancel the lease if the tenant is not given possession on or before a specified date.

N. ADDITIONAL RENT

It is common in a lease for the tenant to be obligated to make
certain payments to the landlord in addition to periodic rent. Such
payments are designed to shift to the tenant certain costs related to
the ownership and operation of the premises being rented and thereby relieve the landlord of the risk of financial loss resulting from increases in such costs during the term of the lease.

In the lease agreement, payments other than periodic rent are referred to, and treated, as "rent". If the tenant defaults in his obligation to make such additional payments, the landlord wants to have
the same rights and remedies as exist upon a default in the payment
of periodic rent. A typical additional rent provision respecting increases in real estate taxes is set forth below:

> "Tenant further agrees to pay as rent in addition to the minimum
> rental herein reserved, Tenant's pro rata share of all taxes as-
> sessed or imposed upon the building of which the demised prem-
> ises are a part during the term of this lease, in excess of and
> over and above those assessed or imposed at the time of making
> this lease. The amount due hereunder on account of such taxes
> shall be apportioned for that part of the first and last calendar
> years covered by the term hereof. The same shall be paid by
> Tenant to Landlord on or before the first day of July of each
> and every year. Tenant's pro rata share shall be 22.3% of any
> such increase."

The specific items of additional rent will vary from lease to lease
depending upon the business arrangement between the landlord and
tenant.

In most municipalities which supply water and sewers, there is a
standard minimum charge for those services. In addition, with regard to water there is a charge for water actually consumed in excess
of a minimum quantity. Meters are installed to measure consump-
tion and, in multi-tenanted buildings, separate meters may be installed for each rental unit. The "additional rent" clause, in addition to
imposing the obligation on the tenant to pay all or a part of such water charges, should state which party has the responsibility of installing and maintaining these meters. In some leases the tenant will be
required to pay the entire bill for taxes and water and sewer rents,
and in other leases he will only have to pay the excess over the minimum.

Often the landlord is concerned that the activities of the tenant
on the premises may cause an increase in the landlord's fire and/or
liability insurance rates. As a result, the "additional rent" clause
may provide that the tenant shall pay for any increase in the land-

lord's insurance premiums if the increase is caused by any act or neglect of the tenant or by the nature of the tenant's use of the premises. The tenant should take care to ascertain in advance whether its intended use of the premises will cause an increase in lessor's fire insurance and, if so, to what extent.

A tenant leasing a large space with an obligation to pay a pro-rata share of real estate tax increases may want to include a provision allowing the tenant to dispute any tax increases.

O. SERVICES AND UTILITIES

If the tenant is to receive any services or utilities from the landlord, the facts must be expressly set forth in the lease. In many apartment leases, the landlord supplies water, gas and electricity. In an office building lease, the description of the services to be supplied by the landlord is especially important. Unlike the case of an apartment building, the services of an office building may be supplied only during certain hours and on certain days. For example, the lease may provide that elevator service, heat and air-conditioning will be provided only on weekdays between the hours of 9:00 A.M. and 6:00 P.M. The lease may or may not obligate the landlord to provide cleaning service for the offices. The tenant must determine whether the services to be provided are satisfactory for the tenant's purpose. If, for example, the tenant has a night office shift, the lease must allow tenant access to the building, and perhaps heat and air-conditioning, during the hours of work of that shift.

If the landlord has covenanted to supply services such as air-conditioning, heat and elevators, the landlord will normally request a "breakdown" clause which eliminates any liability which the landlord might incur due to the interruption of any service caused by the need for inspection or repair or any cause beyond landlord's control. A tenant, on the other hand, may insist upon abatement of rent if the discontinued service is not restored within a specified period of time.

P. LIABILITY AND INDEMNIFICATION PROVISIONS

The terms of a lease may allocate, as between the landlord and tenant, the responsibility for losses and damages caused to the landlord, to the tenant or to third persons which occur on or about the demised premises. Some allocations of such responsibility are discussed below.

1. Injury to Tenant or Damage to his Property

If the lease is silent and the tenant is injured or the tenant's property is damaged as a result of negligent conduct by the landlord or the landlord's servants or agents, the landlord will be responsible to the tenant for any such injury or damage. Landlords often insist, however, that the tenant release the landlord and landlord's servants or agents from any liability which may arise as a result of the negligence or misconduct of such persons. In a lease, the tenant's agreement releasing the landlord is referred to as an "exculpatory" clause, an example of which follows:

> "Landlord shall not be held responsible for, and is hereby expressly relieved from, any and all liability by reason of any injury, loss, or damage to Tenant or Tenant's property in or about the demised premises or the building due to any cause whatever, and whether the loss, injury or damage is due to any oversight, neglect or negligence of Landlord, occurring before or after the execution of this lease."

While exculpatory clauses are enforceable in most states, courts construe such clauses strictly against the landlord. This means that if there is any doubt as to whether the tenant has released the landlord from liability in a particular situation, the doubt will be resolved in favor of the tenant.

2.   Injury to Third Persons or Damage to their Property

A person may be injured, or property damaged, on or about leased premises due to the negligence of a tenant. Even if the tenant is clearly responsible, the injured party might choose to sue the landlord as well as the negligent tenant. Clearly, the landlord would want to have in the lease a provision, referred to as an "indemnification clause", which imposes on the negligent tenant the responsibility of protecting the landlord from any liability, including any costs incident to defending a lawsuit, which arises because of the tenant's misconduct. An example of such a provision, which may also be referred to as a "hold harmless" clause, follows:

> "Tenant will indemnify Landlord and save it harmless from and against any and all claims, actions, damages, liability and expense in connection with loss of life, personal injury and/or damage to property occurring in or about, or arising out of, the demised premises and adjacent sidewalks and loading platforms or areas occasioned wholly or in part by any act or omission of Tenant, his agents, contractors, customers or employees."

Going a step further, the landlord may insist on indemnification by the tenant from any liability arising from injuries to third persons or damages to the property of third persons arising from an act occurring or conditions existing on the demised premises, irrespective of who is responsible for such injury or damage. An example of such a broad clause follows:

> "Tenant agrees to be responsible for and to relieve and hereby relieves the Landlord from all liability by reason of any injury or damage to any person or property in the demised premises or any part or portion of the building of which the demised

premises is a part, caused by any fire, breakage or leakage in any part or portion of the demised premises, or from water, rain or snow that may leak into, issue or flow from any part of the said premises, or of the building of which the demised premises is a part, whether such breakage, leakage, injury or damage be caused by or result from the negligence of Landlord or his servants or agents or any person or persons whatsoever."

Such a provision is unpalatable to a tenant. One way to minimize the burden of such a clause is for the tenant to obtain insurance protection against the extra risk which he is undertaking. A second approach is to make the indemnification inoperative if the injury or damage is attributable to the negligence of the landlord, his or her servants or agents.

Q. SUBORDINATION

The landlord's mortgagee may require the tenant to agree that the lease shall be subordinate to its mortgage, or the landlord may require that the lease shall be subordinate to any future mortgages or replacements thereof which the landlord may place upon the leased premises. In addition, if the landlord does not own the premises the lease should be subordinate to any other lease or arrangement under which the landlord is in control of the premises. In either of the above cases, the lease should contain a waiver of any damages by reason of termination of the tenant's lease caused by the termination or forfeiture of the landlord's right of possession. The clause should also include an agreement by the tenant to execute any documents required by a mortgagee to confirm the lease provisions.

Without a subordination clause the landlord may be unable to effect satisfactory refinancing because many lenders insist that their mortgage have a first priority.[5] Where the lease is subordinate to a mortgage a strong tenant may request a "non-disturbance" provision stating that so long as tenant fulfills his or her obligations under the lease the mortgagee or purchaser at a foreclosure sale will recognize the lease. The tenant will, in return, be expected to execute an Attornment Agreement providing that in the event of foreclosure, the lease will not be discharged and the tenant will recognize the mortgagee or the purchaser at the foreclosure sale as its new landlord.

A provision dealing with subordination, attornment and non-disturbance is set forth below:

"Tenant hereby subordinates this Lease to any mortgage created by Landlord on the Premises and will execute any and all documents which Landlord may desire to confirm such subordination

---

5. Cf. Chapter Eight. Some lenders want the leases to be superior to the mortgages.

provided that the mortgagee under any such mortgage shall furnish Tenant with a written agreement in recordable form and binding upon the mortgagee's successors and assigns, satisfactory to Tenant providing that so long as Tenant, its assigns, successors or subtenants are not in default under this Lease, Tenant's possession of the Premises and its rights under this Lease shall not be interfered with by the Mortgagee (whether or not the mortgage is in default and notwithstanding any foreclosure action), any insurance proceeds and any condemnation award shall be applied as provided in the Lease, and the lien of the mortgage shall not cover any equipment used in Tenant's business on the Premises.

Tenant, at the request of any mortgagee, or anyone acquiring title to the Landlord's estate or the Premises by foreclosure, deed in lieu of foreclosure, or otherwise, shall attorn to the then owner and recognize such owner as landlord for the balance of the term of this lease subject to all the terms and provisions hereof. Such mortgagee or purchaser at said foreclosure sale shall not be (a) liable for any act or omission of the Landlord, (b) subject to any offsets or defenses which Tenant may have against the Landlord, (c) bound by any rent or additional rent which the Tenant may have paid to the Landlord for more than the current month, and (d) bound by any amendment or modification of the lease made without its consent."

R. SECURITY DEPOSITS

In most leases landlord requires tenant to grant some form of security deposit or advance rental payment at the time the lease is signed. A security deposit is not treated the same as advance rent. The security deposit is a fund which may be used by the landlord to discharge any unfulfilled obligation of tenant such as unpaid rent or unrepaired damage to the premises. It is generally provided that resort to the security deposit is optional for the landlord, thus preserving all other remedies.

In the event that all of tenant's obligations under the lease are discharged, the landlord is obligated to return the security deposit to tenant at the end of the term of the lease. Additionally, many jurisdictions have enacted legislation governing security deposits for residential leases.

PROBLEM

Draft a simple lease provision providing for a two months' security deposit.

S. OPTION TO PURCHASE

A tenant of an entire building often attempts to obtain an option to purchase the premises during the term or at the end of the lease. The same considerations which arise in negotiating and drafting an agreement of sale must be covered when including an option to purchase in a lease. The option provisions in the lease in and of themselves must be a complete agreement of sale, or must refer to and incorporate an agreement of sale which is attached to the lease as an exhibit.

1. Purchase Price

The purchase price should be stated in a fixed or determinable sum (such as by appraisal or by a per acre price) and the method of payment should be set forth. For example:

> "The option price shall be $100,000 Dollars payable as follows:
>
> (i) $10,000 shall be payable to lessor in cash or certified check and shall accompany the document exercising the option;
>
> (ii) the balance, being $90,000, shall be paid in full in cash or by certified check at the settlement for the purchase of the premises."

2. Manner of Exercising Option and Time of Exercise

Specify clearly the time within which the option must be exercised and specify the manner of exercise, for example, by written notice accompanied by a predetermined deposit.

PROBLEM

Draft a provision requiring written notice by December 31, 1980 for exercise of the option, exercise to be by submission of signed agreements of sale together with a 10% deposit.

3. Time of Settlement

A specific provision regarding the time and place for settlement of the purchase of the premises should be included.

4. Condition of Title

The usual clauses in an agreement of sale dealing with the condition of title should be included.

5. Other Provisions

The lease should state whether the option is to be terminated in the event of a condemnation, destruction of the building or death of either party. Provision should also be made for the application of fire insurance proceeds to the purchase price if the option is exercised after fire damage and before restoration. The landlord usually will want to condition the option upon the tenant having made no default under the terms of the lease. The tenant, in turn, may request that if a default is waived or cured, it will not forfeit the option.

A lease with an option to purchase should be recorded in order to notify potential purchasers of tenant's interest. If the option were not recorded, most recording statutes would provide that a purchaser from the landlord, who had no notice of the option, would not have to recognize tenant's option.

T. RIGHTS OF FIRST REFUSAL

A landlord may be unwilling to grant an option to purchase the premises since the value of the property may exceed the option price at the time the option may be exercised. If a tenant cannot obtain an option, he may seek a "right of first purchase" or "right of first refusal". This device does not commit the landlord to sell at any time or at any price. It merely provides that if the landlord receives a bona fide offer to purchase the property and the landlord does decide to sell pursuant to that offer, the landlord will give the tenant an opportunity to buy at the same price and upon the same terms which the landlord is willing to accept from the third party who has made the offer.

The lease provision should require the landlord to communicate the exact terms of the offer the landlord is willing to accept and should provide that the tenant must accept the offer within a specified period of time or the landlord may sell to another party. A sample provision follows:

"In the event Landlord shall receive a bona fide offer for the purchase of the property or any part thereof, whether or not in conjunction with any other property, which Landlord desires to accept, Landlord shall give written notice thereof (hereinafter called 'Offering Notice') to the Tenant. Said Offering Notice shall contain:

(a) The name and address of the proposed purchaser;

(b) An exact copy of the terms and conditions of said offer; and

(c) An offer to sell the property involved to the Tenant in preference to the proposed purchaser, and upon the same terms and conditions of the aforesaid offer made by the proposed purchaser.

Tenant shall be entitled to purchase said property offered by giving written notice thereof to Landlord within fifteen (15) days after receipt of the Offering Notice. If Tenant fails to agree to purchase said property within the time aforesaid, the Lessor shall have the right to complete the sale to the proposed purchaser who shall then hold said property subject to the provisions of this Lease Agreement and right of first refusal with like force and effect as if said purchaser had been a signator and original party hereto.

In the event of any change in the identity of the proposed purchaser or of the terms and conditions of the Offering Notice, notice thereof and opportunity to purchase shall nevertheless be given by the Landlord to the Tenant in accordance with the terms hereof."

The landlord must be careful to reserve the right to effect certain transfers of the property without triggering the tenant's right of first refusal. The situations for which landlord's right to transfer should be reserved will vary depending on the fact situation. If landlord is a corporation, it may want to retain the right to transfer the property to any parent, subsidiary, affiliate or successor by merger without having to first offer the premises to tenant. If the landlord is an individual, he may want to reserve the right to transfer the premises to certain relatives, or trusts for them, without having to first offer it to tenant.

If the landlord who has granted a right of first refusal owns land in addition to the demised premises (and especially if such other land is on adjoining parcel), the right of first refusal should deal with the possibility that landlord will receive an offer to purchase a package comprising the demised premises and the adjacent land, eliminating the right of first refusal in such a case.

U. RULES AND REGULATIONS

It is customary for the landlord in a lease for a multi-tenant building to prescribe certain rules and regulations which to each tenant must adhere to and which may be changed from time to time so long as the changes apply equally to all tenants. The initial rules and regulations must be drafted to cover the particular building or buildings with which you are concerned, as no single set can apply in all situations. A set of rules and regulations is likely to be concerned with subjects of general interest to all tenants, such as hours of access to the building, days on which the building is closed, excessive noise and nuisances.

In order to bind a tenant to comply with the rules and regulations, the lease must contain a provision giving the landlord the right to prescribe rules and regulations and requiring the tenant to comply with the same. A provision granting landlord the right to prescribe rules and regulations follows:

"The Rules and Regulations in regard to the building wherein the said demised premises are located, printed upon the fourth page of this lease, and marked Schedule 'A', and such alterations, additions and modifications thereof as may from time to time be made by the Landlord shall be considered a part of this lease with the same effect as though written herein; and the Tenant covenants and agrees that said Rules and Regulations and all alterations, additions and modifications thereof shall be faithfully observed by the Tenant, the employees of Tenant, and all persons invited by Tenant into said building."

V. AFFIRMATIVE COVENANTS

Most leases contain a provision which, in general terms, obligates the tenant to perform a variety of acts. Examples of affirmative covenants on the part of a tenant might be to pay the rent promptly, to keep the premises clean, to take all necessary precautions against fire, and keep the premises open for business.

W. NEGATIVE COVENANTS

The provision relating to negative covenants differs from affirmative covenants only in that the items listed are things which the tenant is not to do without the prior written consent of the landlord.

Most landlords include a provision to the effect that the tenant will not remove the tenant's goods or property from the demised premises otherwise than in the usual course of business, without having first paid and satisfied the landlord for all rent which may become due during the entire term of the lease. The landlord may also add that the tenant shall not vacate or desert the premises during the term of the lease. These provisions are added to protect the landlord against tenants moving in the middle of the night without paying their rent. The landlord in many states has a right of "distraint" which gives the landlord a special lien against the tenants' personal property on the premises, and the landlord will lose the advantage of the power to distrain if the tenants remove their goods. Furthermore, the landlord may want the premises occupied because in many urban areas it is difficult or even impossible to obtain fire insurance on vacant buildings.

X. MISCELLANEOUS OR "BOILERPLATE" PROVISIONS

Most leases contain the following or similar standard provisions:

1. Waiver of Custom

The landlord will wish to make clear that although he may choose not to exercise rights against tenant at any given time, any such waiver shall not prevent the landlord from exercising rights when the same or a different fact situation occurs in the future. For example, the landlord may allow the tenant to pay the rent ten days late one month. The landlord is not thereby giving the tenant permission to pay the rent ten days late in the future.

> "It is hereby covenanted and agreed, any law, usage or custom to the contrary notwithstanding, Landlord shall have the right at all times to enforce the covenants and provisions of this lease in strict accordance with the terms hereof, notwithstanding any conduct or custom on the part of the Landlord in refraining from so doing at any time or times, and further, that the failure of Landlord at any time or times to enforce his right under said covenants and provisions strictly in accordance with the same shall not be construed as having created a custom in any way or manner contrary to the specific terms, provisions and covenants of this lease or as having in any way or manner modified the same."

2. Integration Clause

The parties will desire to make clear that the written lease contains all of the provisions which govern their relationship. This provision would be substantially similar to integration clauses discussed in previous chapters.

3.　Heirs and Assigns

Generally the parties will expressly provide that the lease will be binding upon their respective heirs (in the case of an individual party), successors (in the case of a corporate party) and assigns. Furthermore, if there are several landlords or tenants acting jointly, the lease will provide that they are jointly and severally responsible. That means that each is required to perform his or her share of the obligations and, in addition, each is required to perform the obligations of his or her fellow tenants or fellow landlords, as the case may be.

PROBLEM

Prepare an "Heirs and Assigns" clause for a lease between a corporation as landlord and an individual as tenant.

4.　Captions

The draftsman of a lease may include captions or titles preceding various provisions for ease of reference. The lease should state that the captions are for reference purposes and are not to affect the interpretation of any provision.

Part Two

SPECIAL TYPES OF LEASES

The preceding discussions in Chapter Nine have been applicable to almost all leases. In this chapter, the focus will be on lease clauses which are unique to the following types of leases: commercial and shopping center leases, office building leases and net or ground leases. Each type of lease will be discussed in detail below.

I.　COMMERCIAL AND SHOPPING CENTER LEASES

Leases covering space which will be used for clothing stores, food stores, restaurants and other business activities in which goods or services are sold directly to customers at the location of the business are commonly referred to as "commercial or shopping center" leases. Significant variations exist among commercial and shopping center leases. The lease for space in a shopping center is typically more complicated than the lease of the corner drug store because of the need to deal with the existence of adjacent stores also owned by the landlord and shared common areas and facilities. Moreover, shopping center leases often reflect the interests of institutional lenders who have financed the construction of the shopping center and who depend on the leases as security for the repayment of loans. We will now consider various individual provisions of commercial and shopping center leases.

A. TRADE FIXTURES

As previously discussed, a standard lease provides that fixtures, alterations and additions remain on the premises at the termination of the lease and become the property of the landlord unless the landlord gives notice to the tenant that the landlord wants the items removed. That provision may be unacceptable to a commercial tenant who has made a substantial investment in display cases and other fixtures which can be easily removed and transferred to a new store. In addition, the commercial tenant may want the option to remove alterations or additions made to the leased space. A sample of a clause incorporating a tenant's wishes concerning trade fixtures and improvements and alterations follows:

> "Any trade fixtures, equipment and other property installed in or attached to the demised premises by and at the expense of the tenant shall remain the property of the tenant, and the tenant shall have the right at any time and from time to time, to remove any of the same so installed or attached in the demised premises, including, but not limited to counters, shelving, showcases, chairs and movable machinery. If tenant shall not remove said property at the termination of this lease, then the same shall be deemed to be abandoned by the tenant but the failure to remove said property shall not be deemed to be a holding over by tenant or a ground for claiming a renewal or extension of this lease. Tenant shall repair all damage to the demised premises caused by the removal by tenant of such property, except for necessary holes and other openings and unavoidable damage to plaster and painted surfaces resulting therefrom."

B. PERCENTAGE RENT

Percentage rent generally means that the tenant pays a basic annual rent plus an amount of rent calculated by reference to the volume of business transacted by the tenant at the premises. Often the percentage rent applies only when the volume of business exceeds a specific amount set forth in the lease. Percentage rent is common in leases for retail stores in prime commercial locations and for stores in most shopping centers. The advantage to the landlord is to insure rental income commensurate with the economic value of the location (which is measured in part by the volume of business conducted at the location). The advantage to the tenant is the possibility of a low base rent which will be increased only if the tenants' volume of business at the premises is good. In addition, in an inflationary period, the landlord will be more willing to grant a lease for a long term where the rent will increase as the dollar volume of the tenant's business increases. A percentage rent gives to the landlord reasonable assurance that the rent will increase to keep pace with inflation.

There are several possible percentage rent provisions:

1.　Straight Percentage Rent

It is possible to write a lease in which there is no basic rent. Instead rent is merely a percentage of the tenant's volume of business at the premises. Obviously, such a lease is risky from the landlord's standpoint because the landlord cannot, with any degree of certainty, predict the volume of business and therefore the amount of rent which will be received. Generally, in order to finance a shopping center, the landlord must show the prospective lender that the leases for the project will provide for a sufficient amount of fixed rent to cover debt service, real estate taxes and basic operating expenses. Thus it is rare that a straight percentage rent will be agreed to. In addition to being risky for a landlord, such a lease is unlikely to be acceptable to a mortgage lender.

2.　Minimum or Basic Rent Plus a Percentage

The most commonly used percentage rental provision calls for the tenant to pay a basic fixed minimum rent plus a percentage of the volume of business at the premises. Generally, the percentage rent is based on the amount of sales in excess of a minimum amount. For example, a lease might provide that the tenant pays basic rent equal to $20,000 per year plus 2% of the tenant's sales (which term must be carefully defined) at the premises in excess of $1,000,000. Since $20,000 is 2% of $1,000,000, this example suggests that the tenant is simply paying a rent equal to 2% of sales and is bearing the risk that sales will at least equal $1,000,000.[1] In most cases, the amount of "basic rent" will reflect a judgment of the volume of business which could be expected if the tenant's business is moderately successful.

PROBLEMS

(1) In the example above, if the tenant has sales in a year of $1,500,000, what would be the total rent which the tenant would pay?

(2) In the example given in the footnote, how much total rent would the tenant pay in a year in which sales equal $1,200,000?

A lease may provide that there are circumstances, such as fire damage, which cause a suspension of the payment of basic rent. If this is the case, then the lease must provide for the consequence of such abatement upon the amount of percentage rent which is payable. For example, if there is an abatement in basic rent, there may be a

---

1. It is very common for the percentage rent calculation to be based upon a minimum amount which when multiplied by the percentage factor will equal the minimum rent. However, this need not be the case. For example, the rent could be a minimum of $10,000 per year plus 5% of sales in excess of $800,000.

corresponding reduction in the minimum volume of sales above which the percentage rent is computed.

3.   Definition of "Sales"

Percentage rent is generally based on the tenant's "gross sales" or "gross receipts" at the premises. These terms must be defined in each lease, since there are no commonly accepted definitions for these terms. From the landlord's perspective, the definition should include all sales of merchandise, or charges for services, made in, upon or from the leased premises, whether by cash or credit, and, if on credit, irrespective of whether the sales price is actually collected or not. Furthermore, the definition should include orders received at the demised premises regardless of the place from which delivery is made. Sales by concessionaires [2] should be included as sales by the tenant, or rental received by the tenant from concessionaires, multiplied by a factor to approximate the amount of sales of concessionaires, should be included as sales by the tenant. The tenant will seek to have excluded from the definition of sales all sales to employees, all sales on credit where payment is never received, income derived from services (such as repair work), the sale of trade fixtures, and transfers of merchandise to other stores of the tenant. Certain items such as returns, exchanges, sales taxes or their equivalent are typically excluded from the definition.

4.   Record of Gross Sales

The lease should require the tenant to keep records of all sales and such records must be in a permanent form and in accordance with accepted accounting procedures. The tenant should be required to make periodic reports of gross sales (monthly or quarterly); to furnish an annual report certified by a certified public accountant or the proprietor, partner or chief officer; to retain copies of sales slips or cash register tapes for inspection by the landlord; and to permit the landlord or a representative of the landlord to examine all books and records of the tenant relating to purchases and sales, as well as copies of tax returns.

5.   Time for Payment of Percentage Rent

If a tenant's volume of business creates the obligation to pay percentage rent, the landlord will typically want to receive all or a portion of such percentage rent on a regular monthly or quarterly basis, and not wait until the end of each year before any percentage rent is paid. Since the exact amount of percentage rent payable under a lease cannot be ascertained until after the end of each year, the tenant would make periodic payments based upon advance estimates

---

2.   Many commercial tenants devote part of their space to a concession which pays the tenant for the right to operate on tenant's premises. For example, the shoe department of a clothing store may be operated as a concession rather than being directly operated by tenant.

of the percentage rent, with an annual adjustment when the actual amount is determined. Many tenants, especially those whose sales are particularly seasonal, will successfully resist the requirement for interim estimated payments.

PROBLEM

Why would particularly seasonal tenants object most strongly to interim estimated payments?

6. No Partnership

Often the landlord will require a provision stating that payments based on a percentage of sales are rent only and that the landlord has not become a partner in the tenant's business and is not responsible for the tenant's debts.

A sample percentage rent provision incorporating many of the considerations discussed above follows:

"In addition to the minimum rent, Tenant shall pay to Landlord a percentage rental for each lease year (as herein defined) during the term hereof equal to the amount by which six (6%) percent of the gross sales (as herein defined) made by Tenant on or from the Premises exceeds the minimum rent actually paid. A lease year is hereby defined as the yearly period beginning with the first day of the calendar month succeeding the commencement of the term of this lease and thereafter the lease years hereunder shall begin on the same day of each succeeding year during the term.

The term 'gross sales' as used herein is hereby defined to mean the selling price of all merchandise whatsoever sold and charges for all services rendered by Tenant, or any licensee or concessionaire of Tenant, on or from the Premises, whether such sales or services be for cash or credit, less refunds or allowances made for returned or defective merchandise or improperly performed services. The term 'gross sales' shall not include the amount of any sales or gross receipts tax or other imposts upon sales levied directly on sales by City, County, State or Federal authorities, and collected from customers, provided, that specific record is made at the time of each sale of the amount of such sales or gross receipts tax and the amount thereof is charged separately to the customer.

Within thirty (30) days after the end of each lease year, commencing with the first lease year, Tenant shall deliver to Landlord a complete statement signed and certified by Tenant or by a duly authorized officer or representative of Tenant acting on Tenant's behalf, showing accurately and in reasonable detail, on a monthly basis, the full amount of Lessee's gross sales in the Premises during the immediately preceding lease year and the percentage rent computed for that lease year. At the same time, Tenant shall pay to Landlord the full percentage rent payable for that lease year, if any. Each lease year during the term of this Lease shall be deemed a different and distinct accounting year, and there shall be no adjustment from one lease year to another. Tenant agrees to keep at its principal offices, a complete record of all gross sales in accordance with its regular system of accounting now in effect or hereafter adopted and in accordance with good accounting practice. Landlord shall at reasonable times during business hours of Tenant, but not more often than four times during each lease year, have the right of access to the sales records pertaining to the business upon the Premises, and to have the said sales records examined for the purpose of verifying the gross sales or Tenant's statements concerning them, or audited by a Certified Public Accountant chosen by Landlord at Landlord's expense; but no examination of the sales records of any other stores or premises shall be permitted.

If it is determined that the actual gross sales for any period covered by the statement required pursuant to this Paragraph shall exceed by five (5%) percent or more the amount of gross sales shown in that statement, Tenant shall pay all the reasonable expenses incurred by Landlord in determining the actual gross sales for that period.

Tenant further agrees that in the event Lessee shall at any time during the term hereof enter into a sublease with a sublessee for all or a portion of the premises hereby demised, as hereinafter provided, or a license or concession agreement with a licensee or concessionaire, such sublease or agreement will contain provisions that such sublessee, licensee or concessionaire shall submit to Landlord annual statements of gross receipts of the sublessee, licensee or concessionaire, shall maintain records and books of account at the Premises, and shall give to Landlord the right to make examinations of such books and records, all in the same manner as is herein provided with respect to Tenant.

Nothing contained in this Lease shall be deemed or construed to create a partnership or joint venture between Tenant and Landlord or confer upon Landlord any interest in the business of Tenant, or cause Landlord to be responsible in any way for the debts or obligations of Tenant."

7. Other Considerations Applicable to Percentage Rent

In addition to that part of the lease which describes percentage rent, the following sections of the lease relate directly to percentage rent:

(a) Active Operation

Since the percentage rent depends upon the volume of the business done, the landlord will want to include as an express covenant that the tenant will actively and continuously operate his business throughout the lease term. The provision may simply state that or may be expanded to include (a) the obligation to staff the store with adequate personnel and merchandise to produce the maximum possible amount of gross sales in and from the demised premises; (b) the obligation to keep the store open every day excepting Sundays (if local law or custom so dictates) and legal holidays usually observed in the area; (c) the obligation to open the store daily for the minimum hours customary for the area and the type of business; and (d) a statement that temporary closing due to strikes or similar circumstances beyond the tenant's reasonable control shall not constitute a breach of tenant's obligation to be open for business. The above provisions are usually found in the affirmative covenants section of the lease.

PROBLEM

Consider whether a covenant to operate provides any significant guaranty that a tenant will in fact remain open for business. Is a court likely to try to grant specific enforcement? If the usefulness of the provision is really just to establish a right to damages beyond the minimum rent, is there a better way to try to do so?

(b) Diversion of Sales

Since the landlord is depending upon tenant's sales at the premises to produce percentage rent, the landlord should protect himself against diversion of sales by tenant to a nearby branch store. This may be done by a covenant in the lease that the tenant will not directly or indirectly [3] operate a business from any other location within a specified radius or distance from the demised premises during the term of the lease. If tenant has an existing store which violates the non-competition provision and that store is to remain open, the non-competition provision must be phrased so as to except the existing store from its coverage.

C. COMMON AREAS

1. Use, Location and Control

A shopping center has extensive facilities, called "common areas", which are for the use of the customers of all the tenants, including parking lots, walkways, and enclosed areas. The lease normally grants the tenant and tenant's customers the non-exclusive right to use the common areas along with other tenants and their customers.

A prospective tenant of a shopping center is vitally interested in the number of people walking past the store or business. This volume of traffic is determined in part by the relationship of the tenant's space to the shopping center's common areas. In a completed

---

3. Indirect control could result from the use of related parties or entities under joint or common control.

and operating center, the tenant can ascertain by physical inspection the relationship of the tenant's space to the common areas and can be reasonably certain that the relationship will not change in the future. If the shopping center is not complete, the architectural plan of the center, showing the common areas and the tenant's space, may be incorporated into the lease so as to assure the tenant of the location of common areas. The landlord will want to maintain control of the common areas and to reserve the right to change the location of common areas. The differing interests of landlord and tenant become the subject of negotiation.

2. Common Area Maintenance Expenses

In most shopping center leases the landlord is obligated to maintain the common areas. However, the tenant is generally required to pay part of the cost of operating and maintaining the common areas and facilities. The specific common area for which a tenant is making contribution payments should be clearly defined in the lease. The amount of the tenant's payment is usually based on the ratio of the square footage of the demised premises to the square footage of the gross rentable area in the shopping center. Sometimes a landlord will insist that the tenant's contribution be based on the ratio of the square footage of the demised premises to the square footage of all of the occupied space in the shopping center. The latter formula is more favorable to the landlord since he does not absorb the contribution relating to any unoccupied store space. When the tenant is required to contribute to maintenance and operation of common area,[4] it is advisable to specify the items of expense for which tenant is responsible, such as cleaning, fire protection, snow removal, lighting, rubbish removal, landscape maintenance and supplies, liability and other insurance premiums, fire insurance premiums, wages for those employed in maintenance, and workmen's compensation. Sometimes depreciation on maintenance equipment and personal property taxes are included.

Some shopping center leases specify a flat sum for each tenant to pay toward common area maintenance costs based on the area leased by tenant, without regard to the actual costs of maintenance. Such a provision is normally coupled with an escalation clause, which computes increases in the CAM charge by reference to increases in a cost of living index. A provision of this sort eases the accounting burden of the landlord and is often an acceptable alternative.

3. Heating, Ventilation and Air Conditioning

If the lease is for space in an enclosed mall, the obligation on the part of the landlord to supply heating, ventilation and air condition-

---

4. Such expenses are referred to in the trade as common area maintenance (CAM) expenses.

ing (commonly referred to as "HVAC") for the mall, should be clearly set forth in the section of the lease dealing with common areas. The tenant usually shares the cost for such services either by including such costs under a common area and facility provision such as that above or by including a separate provision.

4. Merchants' Association

In order to promote the business of the shopping center, most landlords require the formation of a merchants' association. Generally, the leases require all tenants to join and contribute toward the advertising and public relations expenses of the association. Sometimes, however, large food and department store tenants who do their own advertising are not required to join the merchants' association. Merchants' associations are usually formed as associations or as non-profit corporations. It is customary for the landlord to contribute between 20 and 30 percent of the budget adopted by the association. The leases of the individual tenants will set forth contributions applicable to each tenant. Many tenants will covenant that they will join a merchants' association only if a specified percentage (by number or by square footage) of tenants in the shopping center, other than department store tenants, are similarly required to join.

D. COMMENCEMENT OF THE TERM AND RENT

1. Where the Shopping Center is in Existence

Where the shopping center is in existence, the commencement of the term of the lease and the payment of rent will be specified in the lease.

2. When the Shopping Center is Not Completed

Even though the shopping center is not yet completed, some leases are written to provide that the term of the lease shall start immediately upon signing. In such cases, the tenant is subject to the obligations of the lease immediately upon execution, with certain exceptions:

(a) Payment of Rent

The commencement date for the payment of rent might be keyed to the earlier of (1) the date of opening for business by the tenant or (2) a specific number of days after notice from the landlord that the store is ready for occupancy by the tenant, which in many cases means only that the landlord's work is completed and not that the premises are ready to be opened for business.[5]

---

5. Occasionally a landlord will agree that it will completely fixture the store for the tenant and will deliver the store in reasonable condition. Such a transaction is called a "turn-key" deal.

(b) Fixturing Period

The provision outlined in (a) above allows the tenant a rent-free period of time to "fixture" the store by installing display cases and making improvements and alterations and to stock the store prior to the opening for business. Often a lease will provide that tenant's work may be carried on while some of the landlord's finishing work is being completed, if the tenant's work does not interfere with the landlord's work. From the time that the tenant starts fixturing and stocking the premises, the tenant should be obligated by all of the lease terms other than the payment of rent.

(c) Indemnification

In the event that the lease term commences immediately upon execution of the lease, the tenant should not be obligated under any tort indemnification provision in favor of the landlord until such time as the tenant actually enters the premises.

(d) Store Openings

The prospective tenants in a shopping center are vitally interested in the time at which their stores will open and each desires to time his own opening to coincide with a joint opening of several tenants. The lease may require each tenant to defer opening, at the landlord's request, to make possible a joint opening.

Another approach, which is desirable from the standpoint of an individual tenant, is to condition the tenants' obligation to open (and pay rent) upon the prior opening of a specified percentage of tenants or square footage of store space of the shopping center. The small tenant can expect only to condition his or her opening upon the prior or coincident opening of one or more major tenants, who are recognized as the most important draw of any shopping center. A major tenant, on the other hand, may condition its opening upon (1) a certain percentage of the gross rentable area of the center also being open for business; (2) the shopping center being substantially completed; (3) the parking being minimally adequate, even if not 100% completed; and (4) certificates of occupancy being issued for the building and the particular premises. A fair compromise might be that a tenant would be required to open before all such conditions are met, but would pay only a percentage of gross sales and no fixed minimum rent until all conditions were met by the landlord.

Some tenants will request a deferment of the requirement of opening for business during certain periods of the year. For example, a department store which does a large volume of its annual business in the Christmas season may request a provision in the lease that if occupancy is not available by October 1, they will not accept occupancy prior to February 1 of the following year. It is not unusual for landlords to acquiesce to such requests when they are based on a sound business reason.

E. NON–DISTURBANCE AGREEMENTS

Usually, a shopping center will be encumbered by at least one mortgage. The law in most jurisdictions provides that if a lease is subordinate or subordinated to a mortgage and there is a foreclosure upon the lien of the mortgage, then either the lease is automatically terminated or the mortgagee and/or the tenant will lose a very valuable location in which the tenant has a substantial investment. To protect against such a situation, a strong tenant will insist, as a condition to subordinating the lease to a mortgage, on being provided a "Non-disturbance Agreement" from the holders of any mortgages respecting the premises. The non-disturbance clause is usually conditioned on the lease being in good standing. The following is a strong non-disturbance provision for a tenant:

"Tenant shall, at any time upon request of Landlord, execute for recording an agreement whereby Tenant will subordinate the estate hereby demised to any new institutional first mortgage placed by Landlord upon the Demised Premises or any property of which the Demised Premises are a part, provided and upon condition that said agreement shall contain specific provisions against the disturbance of the possession of Tenant and the following additional provisions:

(a) So long as Tenant continues to pay the rent as in said Lease reserved and otherwise complies with the terms and provisions of the said Lease, the right of possession of Tenant of the Demised Premises, and the terms and provisions of said Lease shall not be affected by Mortgagee in the exercise of any of its rights under said mortgage or the bond or debt secured thereby, or otherwise by law provided;

(b) In the event that Mortgagee comes into possession of or ownership of the title of the Demised Premises by foreclosure of the said mortgage, or by proceedings on the said bond or otherwise, said Lease and all rights of Tenant thereunder shall continue in effect and shall not be terminated by any of said proceedings;

(c) In the event that the Demised Premises are sold or otherwise disposed of pursuant to any right or any power contained in the said mortgage or the bond, or as a result of proceedings thereon, the purchaser of the Demised Premises at such sale, or any person acquiring title through or by virtue of said sale, shall take title subject to said Lease, and all rights of Tenant thereunder;

(d) If the Demised Premises are damaged by fire or other casualty, for which under any of the insurance policies therefor the loss is payable to the Mortgagee, Mortgagee agrees that such insurance funds when payable to it, will be made available for the purpose of repair or rebuilding of the Demised Premises, as provided in said Lease;

(e) This Agreement shall be binding upon and inure to the benefit of Mortgagee, Landlord and Tenant, and their respective heirs, executors, administrators, successors and assigns.

In the event that the Shopping Center, or any portion thereof, or the Demised Premises shall be subject to any existing mortgage as of the date of execution of this Lease, Landlord shall obtain and deliver to Tenant the agreement of each holder of such mortgage or mortgages simultaneously with the execution hereof in the form hereinabove provided, and until delivery of such agreement or agreements, Tenant shall not be obligated to perform any of its agreements or covenants hereunder.

The word 'mortgage' as used herein includes mortgages, deeds of trust or other similar instruments, and modifications, extensions, renewals and replacements thereof, and any and all advances thereunder. 'Institutional Mortgagee' shall mean either a savings or commercial bank, trust or insurance company, governmental agency or bureau, pension or retirement fund, labor union, teachers' association or an educational or philanthropic institution regularly engaged in lending money secured by mortgages."

A non-disturbance agreement in favor of a tenant will normally be conditioned upon tenant executing an attornment agreement.

F. INSURANCE

1. Fire and Extended Coverage Insurance

The buildings comprising the shopping center must be insured against fire and extended coverage risks such as wind. It is customary that the landlord carry the fire and extended coverage insurance on all or the major portion of the shopping center. However, a major tenant, such as a department store, sometimes pays for and carries the fire insurance on his own building, especially in those circumstances where the department store tenant has the concomitant obligation of fully repairing or restoring the building in the event of fire damage.

Where the landlord carries the insurance, the tenant usually covenants to pay any increases in the landlord's fire insurance premiums if they are caused by the nature of the use or occupancy of the tenant or any act of negligence or violation of the insurance policy provisions by the tenant. The lease customarily prohibits the tenant from bringing combustibles onto the premises and requires the tenant to follow insurance company or underwriting bureau recommendations for lowering premium rates, such as installing fire extinguishers.

2. Liability Insurance

In addition to insuring against damage to the premises due to fire and other casualty, it is customary to insure against damage to persons or property caused by the negligence of landlord, tenant or the servants, agents or employees of either. An insurance policy granting this coverage is referred to as a general liability and property damage policy. In the normal shopping center or office building leasing situation, the tenant is obligated to carry his own general liability and property damage insurance. If the tenant has indemnified the landlord then the policy must insure against acts of landlord as well as tenant. The dollar limits of coverage of the insurance policies must be set for each particular leasing situation. Required limits have been increasing due to the magnitude of verdicts in personal injury cases. The standard provision usually requires that the tenant be the insured and the landlord (and often the managing agent and the mortgagee) be named as an additional insured. Generally the tenant is required to deliver a certificate from the insurer to the landlord. The certificate sets forth the general terms of the coverage as well as the dates of commencement and termination of the insurance. The landlord should require that no termination or amendment of the insurance coverage can occur unless the landlord has received 10 days prior written notice thereof from the insurer. Therefore, if the tenant has failed to pay for a renewal of the policy, the landlord will be notified and will have ten days in which to make the payment in order to continue the coverage, or to get the tenant to do so.

G. WORK TO BE DONE BY LANDLORD

The lease must describe in detail the obligations of the landlord regarding construction of the building and the store premises. It may be that the landlord is to produce a "turn key" job, which means finishing the building sufficiently that the tenant needs only to move in stock before opening for business. The landlord may be obligated only to build the shell of the store and the common facilities. In the latter situation the lease will likely specify that it is tenant's obligation to finish the interior work in accordance with plans and specifications approved by the landlord. In such a case a landlord would sometimes agree to pay the tenant a certain amount of money (called the "tenant allowance") as reimbursement for finishing the premises. If a tenant allowance is payable, the lease should state when and upon what conditions it is to be paid. The lease should identify the party responsible for insuring the premises while work is in progress and should require that suitable workmen's compensation and protection against mechanics' liens are procured.

H. EXCLUSIVES [6]

A tenant who opens a particular type of store in a shopping center may want assurance that he will not have competition from other similar stores in the shopping center. In order to gain that assurance, a tenant who is to open a bakery will request that his lease con-

---

6. Exclusives and their counterpart, radius restrictions (see Section V(A) (2)(j) of this Chapter) are becoming much less common due to the application of antitrust laws establishing that such provisions are, at least in certain circumstances, illegal restraints upon trade.

tain a provision granting him the "exclusive" right to operate a bakery in the shopping center. The landlord tries to avoid granting exclusive use provisions to specific tenants, since they reduce flexibility in leasing space. Furthermore, with the tendency of larger stores to sell diversified lines of goods and services, tremendous overlappings occur. For example, a department store might have a baked goods department. Therefore, lease provisions such as "landlord covenants not to permit any other tenant to sell . . ." should be avoided. Such a clause should instead be drawn in terms of an agreement by the landlord not to "lease any space in the shopping center to a tenant whose primary or main business is . . ." The use of such language will permit some overlapping of the sale of similar merchandise. The exclusive might not cover the department stores, whose leases sometimes permit any lawful use, or any tenants who have already been granted or to whom the landlord anticipates granting a similar use. Also, a landlord will want to draft the exclusive very narrowly. For example, the exclusive may be in terms of "high fashion women's shoes" rather than just "shoes".

Holders of mortgages upon shopping centers dislike exclusives. Mortgagees are especially concerned about the possibility of a tenant being able to terminate a lease due to violation of the exclusive use provision. Therefore, in granting an exclusive, the landlord should limit the tenant's remedies for breach of such an obligation, as the following example illustrates:

> "In the event the landlord violates the provisions of this section, tenant's remedies shall be limited to injunctive relief and/or the recovery of money damages, but in no event shall tenant be entitled to any other remedy, including but not limited to cancellation, recision of the term of this lease, the withholding of rent or set off against rent, all of which latter remedies tenant hereby expressly waives."

I. TAX ESCALATION

Shopping center leases typically have a lease term of 5, 10 or 15 years. In setting the rent, a shopping center landlord must strike a balance between making sure that the rent is currently competitive with alternate locations and making sure that he is not stuck with rental income which is insufficient to pay increased expenses, including real estate taxes, during the term of the lease. To aid in striking this balance, shopping center leases almost always contain a "tax escalation" provision which requires a tenant to pay a pro rata share of increased taxes on the shopping center over the real estate taxes imposed in a base year, which is usually the initial year of the lease term.[7] Even if the landlord were willing to forego such a provision,

---

7. An escalation provision which requires a tenant to pay a share of some expense over some base (whether the base is the cost in a year or a set

the mortgagee would probably insist on a tax escalation clause to insure that the landlord's expenses in future years did not exceed rental income. Similarly, most leases require the tenants to share assessments for public improvements that benefit the shopping center as a whole, such as sewer lines, widened streets and sidewalk installation.

1. Tenant's Share of Escalation

The usual escalation provisions require the tenant to pay a proportionate share (as defined in the lease and usually based upon the amount of space leased) of the increase in real estate taxes on the shopping center over the taxes in a designated base year. As discussed in another context in Section V(A)(3) of this Chapter, one of the problems inherent in a provision requiring the tenant to bear a "proportionate share" is the question of whether the landlord or the tenant bears the burden of the vacant space. If the landlord is to bear that burden, the tenant's share would be computed by a formula based on tenant's space divided by the space in the center which can be rented (the rentable space). If, on the other hand, the tenants are to bear the burden of the escalation attributable to vacant space, the formula would be based on the tenant's space divided by the space in the center actually rented to other tenants.

2. Base Year

Escalation of taxes, or of any other expense, must have reference to a base year. In an established, fully-assessed shopping center any year could be used. In a new center, however, taxes will increase for the first few years due to the increased value of the center as new stores are completed. The tenant will not want to pay for any increases that are due solely to new construction. The parties therefore often agree that the base year shall be the year during which the shopping center was first assessed as a fully completed shopping center.

A sample provision for a new shopping center is as follows:

"Commencing with the calendar year next following the calendar year in which the total real estate tax assessment (whether based upon a fiscal or calendar year) upon Landlord's property in the Shopping Center shall reflect the completion of the building of which the demised premises are a part, Tenant shall pay to Landlord each year on demand, as additional rent, 'Tenant's share of excess real estate taxes', if any, as hereinafter described. Tenant's share of excess real estate taxes for any such calendar year shall be an amount equal to the product obtained by multiplying the number of square feet of gross floor area leased by Tenant by

figure not tied to a year) is known in the shopping center industry as a "stop", and such a provision relating to real estate taxes is called a tax stop. If a tenant agrees that it will pay for such increases, but not beyond a certain maximum, then the maximum is referred to as a "cap".

the excess, if any, of the 'current tax per square foot' in such year over the 'basic tax per square foot'. The 'basic tax per square foot' shall be computed by dividing the amount of the total real estate taxes levied on the Shopping Center in the first year for which the assessment thereof reflects the completion of the building of which the demised premises are a part, by the total number of square feet of rentable floor area in the Shopping Center reflected in such assessment. The 'current tax per square foot' for any year shall be computed by dividing the amount of the total real estate taxes levied in the Shopping Center for such year by the total number of square feet of rentable floor area in the Shopping Center reflected in the real estate tax assessment thereof for such year."

3.   Deduction of Tax Escalation from Percentage Rental

Tenants often take the position that they should be able to deduct real estate tax and other escalation payments from any percentage rental due. A landlord would not want such an offset right to be cumulative; that is, he would want to make sure that the tenant would only offset against percentage rent due during any year the escalations paid during that year. Many business compromises are possible in this area.

PROBLEM

Prepare a lease clause which provides that the tenant may offset against 50% of percentage rent, non-cumulatively, the amount by which the aggregate escalations for real estate taxes and CAM charges which tenant pays in any year exceeds $1.00 per square foot of rentable space in the Demised Premises.

4.   Tenant's Right to Contest Increased Taxes

Where a tenant leases a substantial amount of space and its share of tax increases amounts to a significant sum of money, the tenant may request the right to contest tax increases with the governmental authorities. A sample provision follows:

"If Landlord shall fail or refuse, on demand of Tenants of the Shopping Center whose stores aggregate at least 75% of the leasable store area of the Shopping Center, to take any necessary steps to contest the validity or amount of the assessed valuation or of the real estate tax for any tax escalation year, then such tenants at their own cost and expense, may undertake, by appropriate proceedings, in their own name, to review the validity or amount of the assessed valuation or of the real estate tax for any tax escalation year. Any documents required to enable tenant to prosecute any such proceeding shall be executed and delivered by landlord within a reasonable time after demand therefore."

5. Tax Escalation Due to Additional Construction

Escalation due to increased construction is not an unforeseen expense of the landlord. In addition, if the new space produces new rent, the tenants of that space will bear the expense of those taxes. Therefore, the tenant should try to protect against tax escalation due to additional construction. An appropriate provision follows:

> "In the event of any increase in rentable space, or any increase in land area comprising the shopping center site, or any additional improvements made to the shopping center over and above those upon the shopping center site at the time of the base tax year, the real estate taxes resulting therefrom shall not be considered for Landlord's tax increase, nor shall the gross square foot area of such increased area or space improvements be included within the computation of the gross square foot area in all of the buildings of the shopping center."

6. Caps

A strong tenant may be able to set a maximum upon the potential liability under an escalation clause and such a maximum is known as a "cap". The cap may be an absolute maximum, usually expressed as a dollar figure, or may be the maximum amount by which the charge may be increased in any year, with no absolute maximum.

7. Tenants Pay All Taxes and Operating Costs

The discussion in this Section has been concerning tax escalation provisions. In such situations the landlord has set the initial fixed minimum rent at a figure which the landlord believes will be sufficient to enable him to pay landlord debt service and all initial operational costs of the shopping center, including real estate taxes. Thus the minimum rent has a real estate tax factor in it, as well as factors for common area maintenance and HVAC, which are other operating costs for which escalation provisions are common. However, the factors are just a guess on the part of the landlord, and if the guess is on the low side of actual expenses, he will never recover the difference. Thus if the real estate tax factor in the minimum rent is $1.00 per square foot and the actual real estate taxes assessed during the base year works out to $1.50 per square foot, the tax stop provision will only require the tenant to pay increases from $1.50. In a year in which the actual taxes are $2.00 per square foot, the landlord will only be receiving $1.50 per square foot from the tenant ($1.00 as built in to minimum rent and $.50 from the tax stop), and the remaining $.50 per square foot will come out of and reduce the profit factor built into the minimum rent.

Some landlords have found that the guesses of what taxes and other operating costs will be in the base year are too difficult to make and that the consequences of a wrong guess are too serious. Therefore, some landlords have taken the usual operating cost factors out of the minimum rent and have provided in their leases that the tenant shall share in the entire costs of real estate taxes and other operating costs without regard to any base year. The relevant provisions are not escalation provisions or stops, but are a pro rata share in such expenses "from the first dollar".

PROBLEM

Using the tax stop provision as a guide, prepare a clause requiring the tenant to pay its pro rata share of all real estate taxes imposed upon the shopping center.

J. PARKING

The amount and the ease of parking is a major item of concern for the tenant at a shopping center. Major tenants will often require the landlord to covenant that there will be a given number of parking spaces available in the shopping center and that the landlord will stripe, clean, light and maintain and in some instances police the parking areas. The expenses of doing so will usually be borne by the tenants ultimately to the extent that they pay a share of common area maintenance and operating expenses.

A major tenant will generally require a landlord to provide a minimum number (often 5) of parking spaces for each 1,000 square feet of gross rentable area in the shopping center. The landlord generally tries to avoid guaranties as to the number of car spaces that will be provided for each 1,000 square feet of rentable space and, in lieu thereof, the landlord will try to guarantee a gross number of spaces regardless of the gross rentable area in the shopping center. The landlord may want to expand the store area at the expense of parking area if the center turns out to be highly successful. If there are non-shopping center retail spaces, different minimum parking requirements will apply to such spaces.

The landlord will normally restrict the tenant and employee parking to certain areas of the parking lot, although it is very difficult to enforce such a provision.

K. ESTOPPEL CERTIFICATES

At various times it may be necessary for the landlord to be able to prove that all of the leases are effective and that he is not in breach of any lease. For example, a prospective buyer of the shopping center or a prospective mortgage lender will want to know whether there are unfulfilled obligations of the landlord for which the buyer will be responsible. The best evidence of the facts would be a document signed by each tenant certifying that the lease is in good standing; that tenant has accepted possession of the premises; that there are no defaults on the part of either party; that the tenant has no claims against the landlord; and also confirming the basic data of the leases, such as the rent, term and expiration date. Such a certificate is referred to as an "Estoppel Certificate". The landlord will want a provision in the lease obligating the tenant to tender such a certificate (to the extent the facts are true) upon request.

L.   CLAUSES OF CONCERN TO MORTGAGEE

During negotiations with the tenant, the landlord must consider the mortgagee's requirements. Indeed, usually all leases are subject to the approval of the mortgagee. In the event of default under the mortgage, the mortgagee must be able to sell the shopping center at a foreclosure sale or take over the operation as owner of the center. The following are some of the clauses that are of particular interest to the mortgagee:

(1) Self-help clauses which give the tenant the right to cure landlord's defaults and recoup the cost out of rent will be acceptable to the mortgagee only if the deduction comes out of percentage rent and not out of minimum rent.

(2) Any clause giving the tenant the right to cancel a lease or surrender the premises or abate the payment of rent, except in the event of destruction or eminent domain, might be unacceptable to a mortgagee.

(3) Clauses which give tenants exclusive rights which generally limit competition and which, if breached, might in some circumstances give rise to cancellation of the lease by the tenant might be unacceptable to a mortgagee.

(4) Clauses restricting competition on land owned by the landlord outside of the shopping center are often unacceptable to mortgagees, unless such provisions exclude application to a mortgagee.

(5) Clauses requiring or giving the tenant the right to make improvements for which tenant is to be reimbursed by the landlord, or which require the landlord to do the work, such as future expansion of the store, may trouble a mortgagee. Since the mortgagee may have to step into the landlord's position vis-a-vis a tenant, the mortgagee is alert to any circumstances which would permit the tenant, upon failure by the landlord to act, to do work at landlord's expense and to recoup the cost of such work by offsetting the cost against the rent or by acquiring a lien on the land. Furthermore, these provisions will alarm a mortgagee because any default by the landlord may give rise to a right by the tenant to cancel the lease.

(6) An option to purchase the store premises or the center may be unacceptable to the mortgagee. In some states an option is considered an encumbrance which prevents a regulated lender, such as an insurance company, from making a first mortgage loan. Because a shopping center usually contains many tenants, it is unusual for a shopping center developer to grant an option to any one tenant, but

the department store tenant in a one-major center might demand and receive such an option.

(7) Clauses committing the landlord to make repairs after fire, regardless of the adequacy of insurance proceeds, are generally unacceptable to a mortgagee.

(8) Provisions which allow a tenant to share in any condemnation award, without first applying the award to pay off the mortgage in full, are unacceptable to a mortgagee.

(9) Regardless of the law of any particular state, some mortgagees, as a matter of policy, prefer their mortgage to be subordinate to the major leases so as not to run the chance of the lease being terminated automatically by reason of a mortgage foreclosure. In most cases, an attornment provision will cure the problem of a lease which is subordinate.

Part Three

OFFICE BUILDING LEASES

Much of the preceding discussion in Chapter 9 of general lease provisions and shopping center and commercial lease provisions has application to office building leases. The following discussion considers those provisions which tend to be unique to office building leases.

I. IN GENERAL

A. SERVICES

As mentioned previously, an office building landlord usually furnishes heat, water, electricity, air conditioning, elevator service and janitor service. However, some or all of these services are usually provided only during certain hours and on certain days of the week. The tenant should require enumeration of the services to be furnished and the periods during which they are furnished in order to make certain that the space will serve tenant's purposes. The landlord should be careful to include a release of liability for interruption of services due to causes beyond the landlord's control. An example of a provision imposing requirements on the landlord is set forth below:

"So long as Tenant is not in default under any of the provisions of this lease, Landlord shall

(a) provide elevator facilities on business days from 8 a. m. to 6 p. m. and on Saturdays from 8 a. m. to 1 p. m. and have an elevator subject to call at all other times;

(b) furnish heat to the demised premises, when necessary, on business days from 8 a. m. to 6 p. m. and on Saturdays from 8 a. m. to 1 p. m.;

(c) furnish air-conditioning to the demised premises, when necessary, on business days from 8 a. m. to 6 p. m. and on Saturdays from 8 a. m. to 1 p. m.;

(d) clean or cause the demised premises to be kept clean, provided the same are kept in order by Tenant;

(e) furnish a reasonable amount of electricity, as Landlord may determine, for normal office use in the demised premises during business hours;

(f) furnish a directory with names of tenants of the building on the first floor or lobby of the building."

B. CONSUMER PRICE INDEX ESCALATION

For a number of years the steady inflation has caused a continual increase in the cost of operating rental property. Rental rates which are reasonable one year are too low the next because of increases in real estate taxes, wages of building personnel and the cost of gas and electricity. One method for the landlord to protect against inflation, is to include the standard additional rent provisions covering among other expense items, real estate taxes, water and sewer rents and insurance. However, such provisions merely reimburse the landlord for excess costs and do not give the landlord the benefit of increased rental values or any compensation for the lower purchasing power of his or her profit. A common method for assuring the landlord of increases in rent during the term of the lease and, therefore, making the landlord more receptive to accepting a longer term lease, is to provide for rental adjustments on a regular basis in accordance with increases in the cost of living. These rental adjustments might be in addition to increased real estate and operating expenses escalation provisions. Such provisions can be found in all types of commercial leases and, recently, can even be found in some apartment leases.

"A. As used herein:

(1) 'Index' shall mean the 'Revised 1953 Consumer Price Index (New Series) for Urban Wage Earners and Clerical Workers (1957–59 = 100) for all Items for Philadelphia, Pennsylvania, issued by the Bureau of Labor Statistics of the United States Department of Labor';

(2) 'Lease Date' shall mean the date of this lease;

(3) 'Anniversary Date' shall mean the date which is one year after the Lease Date and each successive such date thereafter;

(4) 'Percentage Increase' shall mean the percentage of increase in the Index on each Anniversary Date equal to a fraction the numerator of which shall be the Index on the Anniversary Date and the denominator of which shall be the Index on the Lease Date.

B. The minimum annual rent shall be adjusted on each Anniversary Date such that the rent from that Anniversary Date to the next succeeding Anniversary Date shall be the greater of:

(i) the minimum annual rent reserved pursuant to § 501 hereof; and

(ii) the product of the minimum annual rent reserved pursuant to § 501 hereof multiplied by the Percentage Increase.

C. In the event the Index shall hereafter be converted to a different standard reference base or otherwise revised, the determination of the Percentage Increase shall be made with the use of such conversion factor, formula or table for converting the Index as may be published by the Bureau of Labor Statistics."

C. ACTUAL COST ESCALATION

We have already mentioned cost escalation as a device whereby the landlord can be protected from increases in the cost of operating rental property. In lieu of, or in addition to, an adjustment in minimum rent based on an increase in a price index, office leases may contain cost escalation provisions whereby the tenant pays its share of the actual increases in operating costs. Such a provision may be similar to the real estate tax and common area maintenance escalation provisions used in shopping center leases, except that the description of what constitutes operating expenses will differ considerably due to the different categories of cost encountered in the different commercial settings.

A common variation of the actual increased operating cost provision is an escalation provision keyed to increases in one or more specific areas, such as a porter's wage and the cost of fuel. This method is less accurate, but greatly reduces the paperwork needed to document the requested increases.

D. LANDLORD'S WORK

The owner of a new office building will generally agree to perform certain work on the space to be leased to each tenant. Typically, the landlord agrees to provide certain standard lighting fixtures in the ceiling, to partition the space into offices, to paint the walls of the space and to provide other minor services for the new tenant. Many tenants find the landlord's work to be inadequate for their particular needs and will want to make changes in the work performed by the landlord and additional improvements to the space. It is customary for a work letter to be signed by the landlord and the tenant specifying exactly what work each is obligated to perform in order to put the space into the condition desired by the tenant. The letter should state the specifications of the landlord's standard work and indicate substitutions which may be made. If the tenant requests the landlord to perform work beyond that which the landlord normally provides, the extra cost to the tenant and the method of payment should be described. If, on the other hand, the tenant wants to employ his own contractors to do work which the landlord would otherwise do, the amount of credit allowed the tenant by the landlord should be specified.

II. NET AND GROUND LEASES

Businesses often find that capital can most profitably be invested in machinery and inventory rather than in real estate needed for plants, offices or stores. A long term lease gives the industrial or chain store tenant most of the advantages of ownership without the permanent investment of a large amount of capital. Moreover, tax considerations make leasing attractive to the tenant since the entire amount of rental payments is deductible in computing federal income taxes whereas, for an owner of a building, that portion of the mortgage payment which is applied to reduce the principal of the mortgage is not so deductible. In addition, the tenant will be able to insure its use of the property through a long-term lease with renewal options.

For a landlord, a long-term lease to a single tenant of a plant or store can be more like a passive investment than the traditional active landlord's position. To insure that the landlord-investor will realize a fixed return on the investment, the "net lease" is utilized. The tenant under a net lease bears all operating costs, utilities, taxes, insurance, and other expenses and risks which are normally incident to ownership of the property. The tenant also pays the landlord-investor an amount of rent sufficient to pay the debt service on any mortgaged loans secured by the property and to provide a satisfactory return on the investment in the property. The term of the lease is normally computed so as to coincide with or exceed the length of any mortgages on the property.

A. INTENT CLAUSE

Although there are many variations, a completely net lease contemplates the landlord receiving the rent free and clear of any expenses relating to the property except debt service on any pre-existing mortgage loans and with no obligations to incur any expenses respecting the property whatsoever. This intent is expressed in a general provision which is supplemented by specific provisions dealing with specific costs and expenses:

> "It is the purpose and intent of Landlord and Tenant that the rent shall be absolutely net to the Landlord, so that this Lease shall yield, net to the Landlord, the minimum net rent specified herein in each year during the term of this Lease and that all costs, operating expenses, impositions, premiums, fees, interest, charges, expenses, reimbursements and obligations of every kind and nature whatsoever relating to the demised premises, excepting only certain taxes of Landlord, which may arise or become due during or out of the term of this Lease, shall be paid or discharged by the Tenant as additional rent, and that the Landlord shall be indemnified and saved harmless by Tenant from and

against such costs, operating expenses, impositions, premiums, fees, interests, charges, expenses, reimbursements and obligations."

B. IMPOSITIONS

In a completely net lease situation, the tenant pays all taxes and assessments on the real estate:

"As additional rent, Tenant shall pay throughout the term hereof, at least ten (10) days before any fine, penalty, interest or cost may be added thereto for the non-payment thereof (or sooner if elsewhere herein required):

(a) all levies, assessments, water and sewer rents and charges, liens, license and permit fees, charges for public utilities (including, without limitation, charges for electricity, gas, light, heat, steam, power and telephone service) and all other charges, imposts or burdens of whatsoever kind and nature, whether or not particularized by name, and whether general or special, ordinary or extraordinary, foreseen or unforeseen, which at any time prior to or during the term of this Lease may have been or may be created, levied, assessed, confirmed, adjudged, imposed or charged upon or with respect to the Premises or any improvements made thereto;

(b) all real estate taxes levied or imposed against the Premises in excess of those levied for the calendar year in which the term hereof commences.

Provided, however, if any imposition shall be created, levied, assessed, adjudged, imposed, charged or become a lien with respect to a period of time which commences before or ends after the commencement and expiration dates of the term of this Lease respectively (other than by reason of breach of the terms hereof by Tenant), then Tenant shall only be required to pay that proportion of such imposition which is equal to the proportion of said period which falls within the term of this Lease. Nothing herein contained shall require Tenant to pay any income or excess profits taxes assessed against Landlord, or any corporation capital stock and franchise taxes imposed by Landlord. Tenant shall furnish Landlord, no later than ten (10) days prior to the last day upon which they may be paid without any fine, penalty or interest, evidence satisfactory to Landlord of the payment of all impositions."

C. INSURANCE

Under a net lease, the tenant usually pays for and maintains the fire insurance, boiler insurance and public liability and property damage insurance. A provision to that effect is set forth below:

"(a) During the term of this Lease or any extension thereof, Tenant, at its expense and for the respective interests of Landlord and Tenant, shall keep the buildings and improvements on the Premises insured against loss or damage by fire and the hazards included in the standard extended coverage endorsement, in an amount equal to one hundred (100%) percent of the replacement value. Said policy shall provide for at least ten (10) days notice to Landlord before cancellation and shall be issued by a responsible insurance company authorized to do business in the state in which the Premises are located and approved by Landlord, which approval shall not be withheld unreasonably. If there is a mortgage on the Premises, such policy shall have attached standard non-contributory mortgagee clauses making losses payable to the mortgagee. Tenant shall pay all premiums or assessments on such insurance to the insurer and from time to time shall furnish Landlord (and the mortgagee of the Premises, if any) with a memorandum of such insurance.

(b) Tenant shall also at its expense provide and keep in force general liability insurance in which Landlord shall be named as an additional assured, said policy to contain minimum limits of liability in respect to bodily injury (including death) of Five Hundred Thousand Dollars ($500,000.00) for each person, One Million Dollars ($1,000,000.00) for each occurrence and property damage of One Hundred Thousand Dollars ($100,000.00). Such policy shall cover the entire Premises including the sidewalks and streets abutting thereon, and shall provide for at least ten (10) days notice to Landlord before cancellation. Tenant shall, from time to time, furnish to Landlord at its request a memorandum of such insurance.

(c) Upon Tenant's failure to supply and/or maintain any of the policies of insurance referred to in subparagraphs (a) and (b) above, Landlord shall have the right to purchase such insurance or any part thereof, and the cost of such insurance shall become due and payable as additional rental hereunder, to be collectible by Landlord in the same manner as herein provided for the collection of rent."

D. REPAIRS

In a net lease, the tenant usually makes and bears the expense of all repairs and improvements, ordinary and extraordinary, including rebuilding in the event of destruction. A sample provision to that effect follows:

"Tenant covenants throughout the term of this lease, at Tenant's sole cost and expense, to take good care of the Premises, and, subject to the provisions of this lease elsewhere set forth, to keep the same in good order and condition, and promptly at Tenant's own cost and expense to make all necessary nonstructural repairs to the interior of the Premises, ordinary as well as extraordinary, foreseen as well as unforeseen. When used in this Article, the term 'repairs' shall include replacements and renewals, and all such repairs made by Tenant shall be at least equal in quality and usefulness to the original improvements and equipment."

Sometimes the landlord is responsible for repairs to the exterior and/or structural portions of the premises. That obligation would be undertaken as a result of negotiation between the parties and would constitute a deviation from a completely net lease.

E. GROUND LEASES AND LEASEHOLD MORTGAGES

It is often common for a tenant to decide to lease vacant property for a long-term (often as long as one hundred years), in order to construct on the property an office building, hotel, shopping center or industrial plant. For the tenant-developer of the property, the use of a lease permits the avoidance of an outlay of funds necessary to purchase the property. In such a case, the rental paid for the property will reflect the value of the undeveloped property and not the value of the property and improvements that are ultimately to be constructed on it. At the end of the lease term (or any renewals), the property will revert back to the owner of the property, who will also at that time receive title to the improvements.

The developer will usually seek financing for the construction of the improvement on the leased property. As security for its loan, the lender will want a "leasehold mortgage", which is a security interest in the tenant's rights under the lease and which gives to the mortgagee the right to take over the tenant's position under the lease. The tenant's interest in the lease (often referred to as a "leasehold interest") is valuable because the tenant has the right to use the property for a long time, during which the rental payments under the lease relate only to the value of the unimproved land, while the earning power of the tenant is directly related to the value of the improvements constructed on the land. For example, Mr. Smith, a developer, may have entered into a lease for the unimproved property requiring rental payments of $10,000 per year. Mr. Smith then constructed an industrial plant which he leased to a major corporation under a "net lease" at a rental of $100,000 per year. Mr. Smith, as the owner of the leasehold interest, receives $90,000 per annum (the difference between the rent received from the tenant of the plant and the rent payable to the owner of the land). The net amount received by Mr. Smith is intended to reflect a rate of return for the investment made by Mr. Smith in constructing the leasehold improvements. Mr. Smith is in a position to give his leasehold as security, for any loan incurred to construct the leasehold improvements, and that leasehold interest has a value measured by the annual excess of the rent received from the corporation above the rent payable to the owner of the unimproved property.

If there is to be a leasehold mortgage, the lease with the owner of the unimproved property should contain certain provisions which one would expect the mortgagee to require. Since the mortgagee's security is the leasehold interest, the mortgagee will want to protect itself against a premature termination of the lease caused by the default of the tenant by being able to cure any such defaults. In addition, the mortgagee will want a voice as to whether a renewal option will be exercised. The mortgagee will also want to establish its rights to the proceeds of any condemnation award or fire insurance policy applicable to the leasehold improvements. In effect, the leasehold mortgagee wants to have rights in the leasehold improvement which are in many ways prior to the rights of the landlord. The leasehold mortgagee is concerned about two types of possible tenant defaults under the lease:

1. Defaults Which May Be Cured by Payment of Money

A default caused by failure to pay rent, real estate taxes, water and sewer rents, insurance obligations and the like can be cured by the mortgagee paying the requisite amount. The leasehold mortgagee will want the lease to require that it receive notice of such defaults and an opportunity to cure them before the lease may be terminated.

2. Defaults Consisting of a Failure to Repair

If a default is due to the failure of the tenant to make repairs or perform work necessary to make the premises comply with the law, the leasehold mortgagee can not cure the default unless it can obtain entry to the premises. The only sure way for the mortgagee to gain entry is by obtaining possession of the premises. Therefore, the leasehold mortgagee can be protected against this type of default if it is given enough time to acquire the leasehold interest of the tenant by foreclosure or other similar procedure. However, if the default relates to non-compliance with the law the landlord may be exposed to fines or other penalties due to the delay. An improper assignment of the lease by tenant, insolvency and other breaches of the lease can not be prevented or cured by the mortgagee. Again the only real protection for the mortgagee is time to acquire the tenant's rights by foreclosure or otherwise.

The leasehold mortgagee can obtain effective protection if the lease provides that in the event of breach by the tenant, the landlord will enter into a new lease, identical to the old one, with the mortgagee as tenant. The mortgagee would be obligated to cure any defaults of the tenant as a condition to obtaining the new lease.

The danger to the mortgagee arising from an unexercised renewal option can be avoided by giving the leasehold mortgagee the right to exercise any renewal right which the tenant fails to exercise. If the mortgagee exercises such a renewal right, it would become the tenant.

Before granting a mortgage, a prospective leasehold mortgagee can be expected to require an estoppel certificate stating that the lease is in good standing and that all obligations of tenant to date have been met.

F. ALTERATIONS

A long term net lease often permits the tenant not only to make alterations but to demolish completely an existing building and build a new one. The landlord usually requires prior approval of plans and specifications and adequate assurance against mechanics' liens which might be a lien upon the landlord's interest in the property.

G. CASUALTY

In a net lease, the tenant usually carries the fire insurance and agrees to restore the premises with no abatement of rent during the period of restoration. The landlord will generally specify the amount of insurance to be carried. The replacement value of the building should be appraised from time to time and the insurance coverage adjusted if inadequate.

H. CONDEMNATION

For many purposes, the tenant of a long term ground lease can be considered as the real owner of the property, subject to an agreement to turn the property over to another party someday. Condemnation poses an especially difficult problem, because state law regarding entitlement to proceeds of condemnation might have more to do with strict legal questions of title than with economic reality. Therefore, it is not unusual for the landlord and tenant to include elaborate condemnation provisions which attempt to divide condemnation proceeds along the lines of economic reality. Such clauses often resort to formulae and appraisals in an attempt to describe what the value of the respective parties will be at any time during the lease term that condemnation might occur.

I. SALE AND LEASEBACK TRANSACTIONS

Ground or net leases have often been used in sale and leaseback transactions. A ground lease is often more of a financing transaction than a typical lease transaction. The financing aspect is even clearer in the sale and leaseback situation.

Traditionally, the owner of a property who wants to develop or substantially renovate the property, or who has a developed property but needs cash, will obtain a loan and will grant a mortgage encumbering the property. The loan is often relatively long-term (25–35 years) and self-amortizing, in whole or in part. However, a variety of factors, including lending limits and criteria, accounting practices and tax considerations, sometimes dictate that some other financing technique is more attractive than a mortgage in a particular situation. The "other financing technique" is often a sale and leaseback. A sale and leaseback involves a sale by the user of the property to the financial institution for a cash purchase price (the economic analog of the principal amount of the loan) and a simultaneous net lease from the financial institution to the user for a long term (the analog of the term of a mortgage) and at a specified minimum rent (the economic analog of the debt service on a mortgage). The concerns of the institutional investor in a sale and leaseback transaction are directly analogous to the concerns of a permanent lender secured by a mortgage, and the documents will be similar in many respects. In preparing documents for a sale and leaseback transaction, a legal assistant shall therefore consider the mortgagee's typical concerns, as discussed in Chapter Eight.

J. CLOSE CORPORATION/PARTNERSHIP NET LEASE

One task which you may have as a legal assistant is to prepare net leases from an individual or partnership that owns the property to a corporation closely held by that individual or partnership. The occasion for such a lease would arise due to tax and business planning considerations. It might be advantageous to persons who want to own property out of which they plan to operate a business for them to acquire the real estate in a partnership,[1] but to incorporate for the actual operation of the business. In these situations the parties usually intend to let the corporation bear all economic risks and to shield themselves and the property from the economic risks of the operation of the business. Thus, a net lease is usually appropriate. However, the net lease may not be a completely net lease in the sense that we have described a completely net lease. For example, the parties may not want to require the corporation as tenant to reconstruct the property after a fire or other casualty if the damage is such that the corporation will be forced to cease operations for a substantial period of time. An analysis should be done in preparing a net lease in this situation to determine the appropriateness of the typical net lease provisions. The conceptual difficulty in doing so is that at the start the ultimate parties in interest are identical. This identity of interest may not continue to exist, due to deaths,[2] bankruptcy of either the partnership or the corporation, or changes in personnel due to public sale of corporate stock, stock options to key employees or the like. The draftsman must try to consider all of the possibilities and arrive at some reasonable determination.

PROBLEM

Using a common printed form of commercial lease available in your area, prepare a net lease between Hardy and Wilkins, Co-Partners as the owner of 14 King Street and H and W, Inc. as the tenant, for a term of 10 years at $12,000 per year. Presumably, this assignment will require you to delete certain provi-

---

1. Problem: What are the reasons for electing to acquire the real property in partnership rather than corporate form?

2. The partnership agreement and the stockholder's agreement may vary as to the consequences of the death of a partner/shareholder.

sions of the lease, to modify others (either by interlineation or by rider) and to add other provisions entirely, presumably by a rider.

III. SURETY OR GUARANTY AGREEMENT

Where the tenant's credit is not established or not adequate and especially if the tenant is a newly-formed corporation, it is not unusual for the landlord to obtain a guaranty of the lease from a person or entity having substantial assets. In order to serve its intended purpose, the guaranty must make clear that the guarantor's obligations will not be affected by (a) the release or discharge of the tenant in any type of bankruptcy proceeding; (b) the impairment, limitation or modification of the liability of the tenant or its estate in bankruptcy, or any remedy for the enforcement of the tenant's liability under the lease, resulting from the operation of any present or future provision of the National Bankruptcy Act or other such statutes; (c) the rejection or disaffirments of the lease in any such proceedings; (d) the assignment or transfer of the lease by the tenant; (e) any disability or other defense of the tenant; or (f) the cessation from any cause whatsoever of the liability of the tenant. The guarantor often requires that he receive adequate notice and have an opportunity to cure any default.

IV. ASSIGNMENT OR SUBLETTING

Generally, a tenant may assign or sublet all or part of the premises which he is leasing. However, virtually all printed leases, such as apartment leases, office leases and leases for small stores, prohibit assignment and subletting without the consent of the landlord. Unless the landlord is in a strong bargaining position, often the only concessions a tenant can obtain are an agreement by the landlord not to withhold consent unreasonably and an agreement to permit assignment to an identified category of persons or entities (e. g., wholly owned subsidiaries).

According to proper legal terminology, a transfer of part of the tenant's interest in all or part of the premises is a sublease, whereas, a transfer of all of tenant's interest in all or part of the premises is an assignment. It is often important to determine whether a sublease or an assignment has occurred. One reason is that a landlord may not directly sue a subtenant for breach of a subtenant's lease (since the landlord is not a party to that lease). However, the landlord may sue an assignee to enforce the lease which has been assigned. In either case the original tenant remains liable to the landlord for fulfillment of the original tenant's obligations under the lease if the assignee or subtenant fails to meet those obligations. Generally it is difficult for a tenant who has assigned his or her rights to regain possession of the premises if the assignee defaults. Therefore, the tenant may end up performing under the lease while not having possession of the premises. On the other hand, it is possible for a sublessor to regain possession if the sublessee defaults under the sublease.

A subtenant incurs several risks over and above those incurred by an ordinary tenant. First of all, the prime lease must permit subletting, or the prime landlord must have consented, in order for the sublease to be valid. Since the sublease derives its entire interest from the prime lease, the subtenant can retain possession only so long as the tenant under the prime lease (the subtenant's landlord) retains his right of possession under the prime lease. If the prime lease ends either by normal termination, due to breach, or otherwise, the subtenant will lose his right to possession of the premises. In order to be assured of continued possession, the sublessee needs an agreement with the prime landlord stating that the sublease will not be terminated by reason of a default by the prime tenant (the sublessor) without first giving the subtenant notice of the default and an opportunity to cure the same.

When the landlord's consent to an assignment is requested, most landlords of shopping centers or office buildings require a three-party agreement to be entered into between the landlord, tenant and the assignee. This agreement includes language to effect the actual assignment. It also includes a consent to the assignment by the landlord. Such agreements will reiterate that the original tenant's liability continues in full force and effect after the assignment. Finally, the assignee assumes the obligations under the lease and submits to the special remedies provided in the jurisdiction in the event of a default under the lease.

A sublease usually looks exactly the same as the prime lease with the exception of the term and the rent. The use of the sublease has become very common recently in office buildings. A tenant may lease a certain amount of space which is adequate for its present needs. However, the tenant may want the ability to expand to additional space as the tenant grows through the years. Landlords are very reluctant to agree to hold space available for the tenant in the future. Therefore, the tenant may lease the expansion space right from the beginning of the lease. The extra space is then either subleased by the tenant to third party or leased back to the landlord for a relatively short term.

V. CONCLUSION

As we have seen, leases have their uses in many different situations, and the particular nature of a transaction shapes the kind of lease to be used. If the variety of lease transactions seems overwhelming, it may be helpful for the student to remember that many of the basic concepts of leasing go back to early English history. Land was leased, as is, to persons who would cultivate it, live on it and in many ways treat it as their own, subject to payment of rent. The landlord had no obligations whatsoever, and was often very much an absentee landlord. The complications have come in due to the leasing of space (not land) in multi-tenanted structures, in which the consideration for the rental includes services, maintenance, availability of parking and even the proximity of desirable fellow tenants. As landlord and tenant become ever more entangled in a joint project, such as a shopping center, more agreements must be included in the lease to deal with the points of tangency between the parties. The art of drafting leases is to seek out the points of tangency, and to put into legal language the business decisions with respect to the issues raised.

Chapter Ten

Deeds of Conveyance

I. INTRODUCTION

Title to real property is normally transferred by the signing and delivery of a legal instrument called a deed of conveyance. The body of laws, rules, procedures and customs relating to the transfer of title to real property is known as conveyancing.

The rules regarding the transfer of real property differ greatly from those dealing with transfers of personal property. Most items of personal property, such as clothes, books, and furniture are able to be delivered in a physical sense. Title to such personalty can and does pass from one person to another by mere physical delivery, although formal documents evidencing title are sometimes prepared and used to make a written record of the transaction. On the other hand, real property cannot be moved [1] and, therefore, cannot be physically delivered. During the earliest days of the common law, title to real estate was transferred without any written documentation. Instead, the seller of medieval times simulated the physical delivery of title to the real estate by meeting the purchaser on the land to be conveyed and delivering a symbol of the land, such as a clod of earth or a twig. It was necessary to have witnesses present at the ceremony so that, if challenged, the purchaser could prove the terms of the oral conveyance. Such a method of conveyancing was satisfactory when transfers of title were infrequent and actual possession was the best evidence of ownership. However, the constant subdividing of land into small parcels, more complicated family arrangements for the descent of land, and the rise of more modern forms of commercial enterprise required more permanent records of land transactions.

Two basic forms of written records of the transfer of title to real property developed—the indenture and the deed poll.

A. THE INDENTURE

An indenture was originally a deed between two or more parties written out twice on the same long piece of paper. The duplicate copies were separated by cutting or tearing along a jagged or indented line. Each party signed both halves and received one of the counterpart copies. The reason the grantee signed the deed was to prove that he had accepted the property and the deed, including grantor's covenants contained in the deed. The grantee could not enforce the

---

1. Indeed upon being removed, it ceases to be real property. Thus, felled timber or mined ore becomes personal property.

361

covenants unless he had signed the deed. If the authenticity of the deed was ever questioned, the issue could be resolved by fitting together the two indented counterparts and comparing them. Although we no longer prepare deeds by cutting one piece of paper into two parts, the most common modern form of deed is still called an "indenture". However, in the modern form the indenture deed does not require the signature of the grantee.[2]

B. THE DEED POLL

The other early form of deed, the deed poll, was distinguished from the indenture by the fact that it was not executed in counterpart. It was signed only by the grantor, and its top was "polled" (i. e., shaved or cut straight), not indented. If there were no covenants contained in the deed which the grantee was required to accept, only the grantor had to sign, and a deed poll could be used. The deed poll survives today in the typical form of Sheriff's deed, which will be discussed later in this chapter.

II. THE ELEMENTS OF A DEED

A. STANDARD LANGUAGE AND FORMS

The common law form of deed of conveyance was developed to perform a relatively simple task. It served to memorialize the intent of the grantor to transfer to the grantee title to a certain interest in a particular parcel of real estate. Although modern deeds are sometimes quite long and complicated, they contain only a few essential elements which can be simply expressed.

A deed should recite that the grantor intends, by delivery of the deed, to transfer to the named grantee title to a specific interest in a described piece of real estate. By custom, particularly when the grantee is to pay a price for the real estate, the grantor warrants to the grantee that (a) he, the grantor, owns the real estate, (b) he has the right to transfer it, (c) that no one has any claim against the real estate or any other interest therein and (d) that he will defend the title being transferred if any adverse claimant attacks it.

As the modern form of deed of conveyance developed during the last few hundred years, the words lawyers used to describe the grantor's intentions to convey and warrant have been construed by countless courts and, in the tradition of the common law, have been given very precise meanings. Because of the certainty gained by use of these words, the forms of deed commonly used today have a rather quaint flavor and style of language. Each state has developed standard forms which are almost universally used by the lawyers of that jurisdiction. In fact, the forms are so well defined and widely ac-

---

2. The party conveying the property is called the grantor and the party to whom the property is being conveyed is called the grantee.

cepted that they are printed by local legal stationers with blank spaces for the names of the parties, the price and the description of the real estate. At this point you should review the sample deed set forth at page 393, which has been prepared on a form customarily used in Pennsylvania.

B.   PARTS OF DEED

There are three main parts of the typical common law indenture: the premises, the habendum, and the conclusion. The *premises* includes the date; the names of the parties; a recital of the consideration; the grant; the legal description; exceptions and reservations, if any; the recital; the encumbrance clauses, if any; and the appurtenance clause. The *habendum* includes the "to have and to hold" clause; a reference to or repetition of the exceptions, reservations, and encumbrances, if any; and the covenants and warranty. The *conclusion* consists of the execution clause, a receipt for the consideration (in some cases) and the acknowledgment (for recording purposes). We will now consider each of the sections of the deed in detail.

C.   PREMISES

1.   Date

Title to real estate passes upon the delivery of a deed, rather than on the date of its execution. Nevertheless, good conveyancing dictates that the date of execution be inserted in the heading of the deed. Unless other evidence is brought forth, it will be presumed that the deed was delivered to the grantee on the date of execution as indicated in the heading. In order for the deed to be recorded, it cannot be dated after the date on which the grantor gave his or her acknowledgment before a notary public. (The acknowledgment will be discussed below.) In drafting a deed for use at a settlement which will take place in the future, it is best to leave blank the day and the month. This can be filled in by hand at settlement when the deed is executed.

2.   Names of the Parties

Following the date the names of the grantor(s) and grantee(s) appear as follows:

"BETWEEN MARY R. BURNS, singlewoman, of 100 Blackacre Lane, Philadelphia, Pennsylvania (hereinafter called the Grantor), of the one part, and ROBERT B. DAVIS of 642 Greenacre Road, Philadelphia, Pennsylvania (hereinafter called the Grantee), of the other part."

Names should be stated with the greatest possible accuracy and completeness. If an individual party has a middle initial or uses a title such as "Jr.", it should be included as part of his name. Nicknames should be avoided. It is a wise practice to indicate the marital status of the grantor (e. g., Mary R. Burns, singlewoman; or Mary S. Bell, widow; or Joseph P. Dobbs, singleman; or Frank R. Green, widower). If the parties are husband and wife, their relationship should be indicated. Such information helps those who search the chain of title to determine whether it is necessary for a spouse to join in the deed. If a corporation is a party to a deed, its official name should be used and its state of incorporation mentioned, to avoid confusion with other entities having similar names (e. g., BCP Associates, Inc., a Pennsylvania corporation).

Before preparing a deed it is helpful to obtain a copy of the deed by which the grantor acquired title to be sure that he or she is using the same name in conveying title. Of course, in many cases, the named grantee in the last recorded deed will not be the title holder, or the title holder's name will have changed since the last recorded deed. For example, when real estate has passed at the death of the record title holder to an heir the property records may contain no evidence of such transfer. Other examples are when the grantor was an unmarried woman when she acquired title, but has since married and changed her name, and when a corporation merges into another corporation or changes its name after taking title. In such cases, a brief explanation is necessary to keep the recording officials from mis-indexing the deed. Consider, for example: "Jane B. Doe, widow (formerly Jane A. Burns)"; or "RCA Corporation (formerly known as Radio Corporation of America)"; or "ITT Corporation (successor by merger to The Sheraton Company)".

Similar care should be taken to designate the grantee in precisely the name in which title is intended to be taken. For example, when the grantee is to be a partnership it is necessary to determine whether title is to be held in the name of the partnership without mention of the names of the individual partners, or whether title is to be held in the individual names of the partners.[3]

3. Consideration

As you recall from previous Chapters, consideration is a legal term for the payment or inducement which one gives in exchange for a promise or services, goods or real estate. At common law there had to be consideration given for a deed. The consideration clause of the model deed set forth on page 393, is as follows:

"WITNESSETH that the said Grantor for and in consideration of the sum of Twenty Thousand Dollars ($20,000.00) lawful money of the United States of America, unto her well and truly paid by

---

3. See Chapter Seven respecting partnerships.

the said Grantee, at or before the sealing and delivery hereof, the receipt whereof is hereby acknowledged."

Traditionally, the amount of the consideration or price is not important so long as the deed recited that the grantor had received some consideration. When the actual consideration for the transfer of title is something other than money (e. g., an unrelated contractual undertaking) or when the price is substantial, but the parties wish to avoid disclosing the real price, it has become the custom to insert "one dollar" as the consideration. A recital of one dollar is also used when the grantor intends to make a gift of the real estate to the grantee.

For most purposes the recital of the consideration is merely a formality and not conclusive. It may be contradicted and the real consideration established by other evidence. In many states, however, taxes are imposed upon the transfer of real estate or the recording of the deed. Such taxes are based upon the actual consideration paid for the real estate or, in the case of a gift, upon the market value of the real estate. In such cases, actual consideration or the market value is usually established by an affidavit which accompanies or is attached to the deed.

4. Granting Clause

The granting clause follows the recitation of the consideration. In the deed set forth as on page 393 the granting clause is as follows:

"has granted, bargained, and sold, released and confirmed, and by these presents does grant, bargain and sell, release and confirm unto the said Grantee, his heirs and assigns,"

The purpose of the granting clause is to state the grantor's intention to convey title to the grantee. The words above have been construed many times by the courts of Pennsylvania and their meaning is now well defined by the case law. In fact, the legislature has defined the meaning of some of the words by statute. It should be pointed out that, although these are the customarily used words of grant in Pennsylvania, in other jurisdictions other words of grant have the same effect. Similarly, in other jurisdictions variations on this formula have become sacred over the years as a result of their continual use and interpretation by the courts.

PROBLEM

In your jurisdiction what are the customarily used words of grant? How do they differ from the Pennsylvania format?

(a) Implied Warranty

In many states the courts have construed the words used in the granting clause to imply certain covenants, promises and warranties by the grantor in favor of the grantee. In other states the legislature has affirmatively defined by statute the customarily used words of the granting clause to include certain covenants and warranties. For instance, in Pennsylvania, the words "grant, bargain, sell" have been defined to be an express covenant to the grantee that the grantor holds a title which cannot be defeated by another, that the land is unencumbered (i. e., not subject to claims of mortgagee or other creditors) and that the grantee shall not be disturbed or evicted from the premises by the grantor or her heirs.

Certain kinds of deeds for limited purposes require the words of the standard granting clause to be changed. For example, when the grantor wishes to negate any implications of covenants or warranties, the grantor delivers a "quit-claim" deed. Such a deed is in reality a "release" in favor of the grantee or whatever interest the grantor may have in a parcel of real estate. A quit-claim contains no representation as to quality of title and no express warranty clause in the habendum (to be discussed below). Such a deed would not include the words "grant, bargain, sell" in the granting clause, or the warranties sought to be avoided would arise by implication. Accordingly, the quit-claim deed uses the following form of granting clause:

> "has remised, released and quit-claimed, and by these presents does remise, release and quit-claim unto the said party of the second part, and to his heirs and assigns forever"

(b) Words of Inheritance

The words "his heirs and assigns" which appear at the end of the granting clause had great significance in the early days of the common law. If such words were not used, the grantee did not obtain a fee simple estate, but only a life estate (that is, the right to ownership of the real estate was limited to the duration of grantee's life) which he could not pass on to his heirs after his death. For that reason, the words "his heirs and assigns" are called words of "inheritance". In most states today either court decisions or statutes have made words of inheritance superfluous and, therefore, unnecessary. Nevertheless, attorneys are reluctant to tamper with time-revered language and words of inheritance continue to be used in nearly all forms of deeds.

(c) Nature of the Estate Granted

In Chapter Six we discussed the various forms in which title to real estate may be held. Conveyancing puts into action the decision respecting the choice of a titleholder. At the end of the granting clause the conveyancer inserts words which indicate the nature of the estate granted to the grantee or grantees. If no estate is expressly stated, the law of most jurisdictions will imply a particular estate depending on the nature of the grantees. If the grantees are husband

and wife and the nature of their estate is intended to be a tenancy by the entirety, the words "as tenants by entirety" should be added at the end of the granting clause. Some states have held as a matter of law that the designation of the grantees as husband and wife creates the legal implication that they hold a tenants by the entirety unless some other tenancy is specified, such as tenants in common. Other jurisdictions hold directly to the contrary, and tenancy by the entirety will not be implied but must be specified. If individual grantees intend to hold title as joint tenants, the phrase "as joint tenants with right of survivorship and not as tenants in common" should be used. If there is more than one grantee, and they are not husband and wife, it will be assumed that they hold title as tenants in common in *equal* shares. If that is not the case, it is extremely important to indicate the fractional share which each tenant receives. For example:

> "in the undivided portions or shares of one-third to A, his heirs and assigns, one-ninth to B, his heirs and assigns, two-ninths to C, her heirs and assigns, and one-sixth each to D and E and their respective heirs and assigns."

It is particularly important to describe the nature of the estate conveyed to tenants in common when two of them are husband and wife. In such a case in many jurisdictions there is a strong legal presumption that the husband and wife are intended to take one share as tenants by entirety as between themselves. Therefore, if B and C are husband and wife, a conveyance to A, B, and C may be construed to be a conveyance of a one-half interest to A and the other one-half interest to B and C (who will hold their one-half interest as tenants by entirety) rather than a conveyance of one-third interests to A, B, and C each. If a father wishes to convey a one-third interest in the family home to his wife, "A", and the remaining two-thirds interest to his son and daughter-in-law, "B" and "C", the granting clause should indicate that the grantees hold their unequal shares as follows:

> "in the undivided portions or shares of one-third to A, her heirs and assigns, and two-thirds to B and C, his wife, their heirs and assigns, as tenants by entirety as between B and C, his wife, and as tenants in common as between them as such tenants by entirety, and A."

Where real estate is to be conveyed to A and B, who are to be business partners and not merely tenants in common or joint tenants, it is important to indicate that they will hold "as tenants in co-partnership for the uses and purposes of the co-partnership".

In the rare case where a conveyance is limited to a life estate, the granting clause should indicate that the grantee holds "for the term of his natural life only".

5. Description

In a practical sense, the legal description of the real estate being conveyed is the most crucial part of the deed and requires the greatest accuracy in drafting. As we have seen, legal descriptions are usually prepared by surveyors, title insurance companies or other experts. They are often based upon professional surveys, official city plans or prior conveyances. Since this subject has been dealt with in Chapter Five only a few points need be mentioned here.

The legal description must be sufficiently clear and precise to enable a surveyor (but not necessarily a lay person) to locate and identify the property to the extent that the surveyor is able to place boundary markers at each corner of the parcel of land and at any other point along the entire perimeter. This does not mean that a full metes and bounds description is necessary. In many cases although the real estate has not been surveyed, the boundary lines are ascertainable by reference to visible and reasonably permanent markers or other boundaries such as roads, streams or party walls.[4]

Occasionally, the legal description is based upon an official plan of survey or a plan of survey prepared by a registered surveyor or civil engineer. Some attorneys and title insurance companies refer to such a survey in the introduction to the legal description even when the survey has not been recorded among the official local land records. The practice is based on the theory that a future purchaser or interested party will be able to obtain a copy of the plan either from his grantor or from the surveyor who drew the plan. Where it is permitted by the rules and practices of the local recording office, it is becoming common to attach to the deed a copy of the plan referred to in the legal description.

In some jurisdictions, recording offices maintain a "map file" in which original copies of survey plans may be filed or recorded. When residential communities are created in accordance with an officially approved plan of subdivision, the plan is normally filed or recorded and the deeds to the purchasers of subdivision lots contain a reference to that plan. In other jurisdictions (for example New York City) it is the practice not to refer to any plan of survey, on the contrary theory that the deed should stand on its own and not depend on, or even suggest that, reference to another document or plan is necessary to locate accurately the land referred to in the legal description.

---

4. Party walls are walls which are located on the common boundary of two parcels of land. Such walls are generally shared by buildings on the adjoining properties. Party walls are especially common in the older cities of the east and in modern town house developments. There is a considerable amount of common law regarding the rights, duties and obligations of the owners of party walls.

Whenever possible, the legal description to be used in the deed should be checked against any plan of survey to which it refers, as errors in transferring information from a survey are common.

6. Recital

The recital is a clause which follows the legal description and serves to explain how the grantor acquired his title to the real estate. The deed on page 393 contains the following recital:

> "BEING the same premises which Charles Clark and Dorothy Clark, his wife, by Indenture dated July 8, 1945 and recorded in the Office for Recording of Deeds in and for the County of Philadelphia (now the Department of Records of the City of Philadelphia) in Deed Book J.M.H. No. 2286, page 354 &c., granted and conveyed unto the said Mary R. Burns, singlewoman, in fee."

The recital is not a legally necessary part of the deed. However, it is a valuable aid to conveyancers and those who search the land records to examine the chain of title. It also may provide evidence of the grantor's intention in certain respects. For example, the recital may indicate that the premises being conveyed are "the same premises" which the grantor acquired by a specific prior deed or that they are only "a part of" certain premises which the grantor acquired by a certain deed.

In cases where the granting clause of the deed leaves the extent of the grant uncertain or vague, the recital may be deemed to reveal the grantor's true intent. A court may construe the recital to restrict general words to a narrower meaning if the intent to do so is clear. In most states, however, it cannot enlarge a clearly defined grant. If the operative words of the granting clause and the recital conflict, the operative words of the granting clause will prevail, so long as they are certain and definite.

Recitals can be concisely drafted whenever the grantor obtained title by one deed and there have been no subsequent changes in the grantor's name or the nature of his title. However, there are many situations which require more complicated recitals, such as the following:

(a) Deed to the Grantor Signed by an Attorney-in-Fact

Often, a grantor will not be available to execute a deed. In such situations the grantor may appoint another his attorney-in-fact with power to execute deeds on his behalf. When the deed to the present grantor was signed by an attorney-in-fact for the previous grantor a recital such as the following must be inserted in the new deed:

> "BEING a part of the same premises which James P. Monroe, III by his attorney-in-fact, William C. Hamilton (by virtue of a power of attorney given by the said James P. Monroe, III, dated

April 8, 1971, and recorded in the Office for Recording of Deeds in and for the County of Montgomery, Pennsylvania, in Miscellaneous Book No. 4331 at page 24) by Indenture dated April 20, 1971, and recorded in said Office in Deed Book No. 778 at page 578, &c., granted and conveyed unto George Q. Andrews, in fee."

(b) Grantor Received Sheriff's Deed

When the deed to the grantor was given by the Sheriff or other judicial officer after a foreclosure sale, a recital such as the following should be employed in a new deed given by the grantor:

"BEING the same premises which William M. Lennox, Sheriff of the County of Philadelphia, by deed-poll dated February 10, 1971 and recorded in the Department of Records of the City of Philadelphia for the consideration therein mentioned, by virtue of a certain Writ of Execution therein recited, granted and conveyed unto Donald L. Stone and Susan B. Stone, his wife, in fee, as tenants by entirety."

(c) Name of Corporate Grantor Changed

When the corporate grantor has changed its name or has merged into another company since acquiring title, language such as the following should be inserted in the deed.

"BEING the same premises which Clyde Hanson by Indenture dated September 4, 1969 and recorded in the Office for the Recording of Deeds in and for the County of Montgomery, Pennsylvania, in Deed Book No. 345 at page 765, &c., granted and conveyed unto Atlas Harness and Buggy Whip Manufacturing Company, a Pennsylvania corporation, in fee."

"AND on October 10, 1970, a Certificate of Merger evidencing the merger of Atlas Harness and Buggy Whip Manufacturing Company, a Pennsylvania corporation, with and into Aberfoyle Petroleum Refining Co., Inc., a Pennsylvania corporation, was issued to the said corporation by the Secretary of the Commonwealth of Pennsylvania, changing its name and corporate title from Atlas Harness and Buggy Whip Manufacturing Company to Atlas Corporation."

("AND on October 10, 1970, a Certificate of Merger evidencing the merger of Atlas Harness and Buggy Whip Manufacturing Company, a Pennsylvania corporation, with and into Aberfoyle Petroleum Refining Co., Inc., a Pennsylvania corporation, was issued by the Secretary of the Commonwealth of Pennsylvania to the surviving corporation, the name and corporate title of which is Atlas Corporation.")

(d) Real Estate Being Conveyed Was Assembled in Multiple Transfers

When the real estate being conveyed has been assembled by several conveyances to the grantor several recitals are required to show the prior conveyance of each piece, each beginning:

> "BEING, AS TO A PART THEREOF, the same premises which . . . ."

When several grantors own separate interests which they are conveying together, but which they acquired at different times, several recitals are again necessary to give the history of each piece. Each such recital would begin as follows:

> "BEING THE SAME PREMISES which A . . . granted and conveyed unto B, in fee, as to a one-third interest therein."

(e) Entireties Property Where One Spouse Has Died

When the real estate was acquired by husband and wife as tenants by entirety, but one spouse has since died, the following clause is added to the normal form of recital:

> AND the said Frank D. Bennett died on November 21, 1968, and title to the property passed to the said Emma J. Bennett by operation of law."

PROBLEM

Prepare a deed recital for the following fact situation on January 21, 1958, BCR Associates, Inc., an Iowa corporation conveyed certain property to Frank Z. Conn and Mary R. Conn, his wife, as tenants by the entirety. The deed was recorded in Blackhawk County in Deed Book 113, page 272. On November 15, 1969 Frank Z. Conn died, leaving Mary as his widow. On October 19, 1972, Mary R. Conn married Joseph W. Moore, and she is now known as Mary Conn Moore. Mary, joined by her husband, is now conveying the property to the grantee.

7. Encumbrance Clauses

A deed may convey property which upon agreement of the buyer, is subject to various encumbrances such as pre-existing mortgages, restrictions created by prior deeds, or other liens, easements, exceptions, and reservations. Such encumbrances are each set forth in one or more clauses referred to as the "encumbrance clause" or, more commonly, the "under and subject" clause. The latter phrase is derived from the introductory words commonly used in such a clause, an example of which follows:

> "UNDER AND SUBJECT, nevertheless, to certain conditions and restrictions as appear of record in Deed Book W.S.M. No. 231, page 253, &c."

The grantee will acquire title subject to all encumbrances that actually exist, whether or not the deed mentions them or lists them in the encumbrance clauses. However, by mentioning and listing encumbrances the grantor gives the grantee notice of their existence and thereby limits the scope of her covenants and warranties of title to encumbrances not mentioned. Accordingly, the grantor should attempt to list all the encumbrances upon his title of which he has knowledge. Good conveyancing practice calls for inclusion of the full text of each encumbrance to be included in the text of the deed. However, such text may be many pages in length. It is usual, therefore, merely to refer to each encumbrance by setting forth the recording data which will enable the grantee, his attorney, or the title searcher, to locate in the local land records the document creating the encumbrance. Such a reference to the encumbrance is sufficient to limit the grantor's warranty of title with respect to a particular encumbrance.

If the grantor is not certain of the particular encumbrances which remain in a chain of title, he may attempt to limit the scope of his covenants and warranties by using a general encumbrance clause such as the following:

> "UNDER AND SUBJECT to all agreements, covenants, liens, reservations, exceptions, restrictions and other encumbrances of record."

The grantor may also limit his warranties by use of a "special warranty deed" or deed with covenants only "against the acts of grantor", both of which shall be examined in Section D(2)(d) below.

In some cases, the grantee may object to reference being made in the deed to obsolete restrictions and encumbrances which may have expired by passage of time or may be extinguished by other circumstances. Such an objection is especially pertinent when restrictions or encumbrances are referred to by a catch-all provision referring to all encumbrances of record. Many lawyers feel that mention of such obsolete restrictions might be viewed as evidence that the parties wish to revive them or continue to treat them as binding and enforceable. A compromise solution is achieved by changing the wording of the catch-all encumbrance clause to the following:

> "UNDER AND SUBJECT to all agreements, covenants, liens, reservations, exceptions, restrictions and other encumbrances of record, to the extent still valid, subsisting, and enforceable."

A similar change in language can be used at the end of a provision listing specific encumbrances and restrictions.

Reference to existing encumbrances should appear both in the "under and subject" clause in the premises portion of the deed and again, by reference, in the habendum. It is also good practice to refer to encumbrances a third time, in the warranty clause. Reference to encumbrances in the habendum and warranty clauses will be discussed below.

8. Use of the Encumbrance Clause for Creation of New Restrictions

In addition to conveying subject to former encumbrances, the grantor may wish to create new restrictions by her own conveyance.

(a) Purposes

Restrictions are most often created by residential developers who, for the benefit of all homeowners, impose limitations on use upon each lot in their subdivision. Limitations might relate to the kind and quality of buildings and improvements which may be constructed and on buildable lot area. Such restrictions serve as private zoning and building codes and attempt to prevent the establishment of any nuisances in the subdivision community. Customarily these restrictions appear in the developer's deed for each lot and are enforceable by and against each lot owner in the subdivision.

Restrictive covenants are also used when a business, such as a retail furniture store, moves from its original location to a nearby location and wishes to prohibit its grantee and future owners of the original location from opening a competitive retail furniture enterprise. Gasoline companies use such restrictive covenants to limit the number of service stations in prime areas.

Another common use of deed restrictions is to assure the seller of a portion of a large tract of land that the land conveyed will be used for purposes compatible with the use of the remainder of the grantor's land. For example, a farmer may be willing to have the purchaser of his or her south sixty acres develop that land for residential purposes, but not for commercial or industrial uses. The farmer is protected by inserting a restrictive covenant in the deed to the purchaser.

(b) Covenants Running with the Land

Restrictions may be of two types, those for the personal benefit and protection of the grantor only and those for the protection of others (such as neighbors in a subdivision) including the grantor's successors in title. A restriction of the first type is enforceable only by the grantor who creates it, whereas a restriction of the second type is intended to be of continual benefit to the original grantor as well as her heirs and successors in title. Such a restriction is known as a "covenant running with the land."

In order to determine whether a particular covenant is the type that runs with the land, a prospective purchaser, and the courts, if necessary, must determine the intent of the parties who created the restriction. Books are filled with legal theory and precedent on this subject. However, good drafting will forestall many disputes. By adding a clause such as the following to the deed restrictions, any question about the grantor's intention will be eliminated:

> "And the Grantee, for himself, his heirs and assigns, by acceptance of this indenture, agrees with the Grantor, her heirs and assigns, that the restrictions and conditions set forth above shall be covenants running with the land, and that in any deed of conveyance of the above-described premises or any part thereof to any person or persons, such restrictions and conditions shall be set forth therein or shall be incorporated by reference to this indenture and the record hereof."

(c) Limitations on Restrictions

Even though the grantor may want her restriction to be a covenant running with the land, she may not wish it to be a perpetual restriction. In such cases, she must indicate a time limitation, such as ten, twenty or fifty years. This is becoming an advisable practice, since courts are more frequently holding restrictions to be unenforceable in light of changing circumstances. For example, if the adjoining neighborhoods become commercial or industrial, land located in or near the heart of a city which was originally restricted for dwelling purposes only, may become undesirable for such use. If there is no time limit on the restriction for dwelling purposes imposed on such land, courts are likely to hold that the restrictions have become obsolete and are unenforceable. Restrictions limited to twenty or thirty years have a much greater chance of being upheld as reasonable until they expire by their own terms.

In most jurisdictions today deed restrictions which impose limitations upon the use of real estate based upon race or national origin have been held unconstitutional and unenforceable. When such restrictions appear in a chain of title, they may safely be ignored.

(d) Drafting

Where there is any doubt as to the meaning of a restriction, a court will construe the language in a manner most unfavorable to the grantor.[5] Therefore, restrictions must be very carefully drafted, lest either the restriction be construed in an unintended manner, or be completely unenforceable because of its ambiguity. For example, it is important in drafting a restriction to make clear whether you are trying to limit the kind of building which may be erected or the use to which a building may be put, or both. For example, a restriction intending to prohibit construction of any dwelling other than a dwelling house for commercial or quasi-commercial purposes such as a real estate broker's office or a doctor's office.

---

5. The theory on which such a rule is based is that where the language of a restriction is unclear, it is better to leave the land unencumbered.

9. Encumbrance Clause for Mortgage Liens

If the grantor has borrowed money and created a mortgage debt during her ownership of the real estate to be conveyed, her title is burdened with another type of encumbrance, a mortgage lien. Often the grantee will be willing to receive the property subject to the mortgage lien. In such a case the grantee would take a credit against the purchase price in an amount equal to the unpaid balance of the mortgage debt.[6] If the grantee is willing to take title subject to the mortgage, the grantor will certainly want to limit the granting clause and her warranties by adding to the deed an "under and subject" clause such as the following:

> "ALSO UNDER AND SUBJECT to the lien of a certain mortgage debt created by David G. Metropolis in favor of East Kalamazoo Savings and Loan Association by Mortgage dated January 6, 1971 and recorded in the Office of the Recorder of Deeds in and for Montgomery County, Pennsylvania in Mortgage Book No. 3168 at page 405, in the original principal amount of $35,000.00 but since reduced by payments on account to $33,600.00, with interest thereon as the same may become due and payable."

Such an encumbrance clause should be inserted in the premises section of the deed and referred to again in the "to have and to hold" clause and in the warranty clause of the habendum.

(a) Personal Liability of Grantee to Mortgagee

As previously discussed in Chapter Eight, under the terms of some mortgage loans, the debtor's liability is personal, whereas liability under certain other mortgage loans is limited to the land. In the latter case, the holder of the mortgage can satisfy his debt only from the value of the mortgaged real estate.

It is important to determine whether, under the law of the local jurisdiction, the words chosen to refer to the existence of the mortgage lien create any personal liability upon the grantee for payment of the mortgage debt. The grantee may be willing to take title subject to the likelihood that if he does not pay the sums due on the mortgage debt, the mortgagee will foreclose and cause the real estate to be sold at foreclosure sale. However, he may not be willing to risk personal liability for the payment of any balance due on the mortgage if the foreclosure sale does not produce sufficient funds to pay it in full. In Pennsylvania, for example, the use of the words "under and subject" have been statutorily defined to eliminate the implication that the grantee has assumed personal liability for the mortgage debt. In some cases, however, the grantor may insist that the grantee become personally liable to the mortgagee, and the grantee may agree. In such cases it is necessary to add the phrase "which the grantee

---

6. Please refer to Chapter Eight for a discussion of financing the purchase of real property by taking under and subject to an existing mortgage.

hereby assumes and agrees to pay", to the above form of encumbrance clause referring to an existing mortgage debt.

(b) Indemnification of Grantor

In the event the grantee assumes the mortgage of the grantor, the grantor will be concerned about protecting himself in the event the grantee fails to perform his obligations under the mortgage. Such a problem, of course, need only concern a grantor who will remain personally liable for the mortgage debt. The protection normally desired by a grantor is indemnification from the grantee.[7]

In choosing the wording for a mortgage encumbrance clause, one must consider whether the law of the state implies any right of indemnification by the grantee in favor of his grantor in the event the mortgagee sues the grantor on her original mortgage note (following a default by the grantee). Since the grantor allowed the grantee a credit against what would otherwise have been the purchase price, on the understanding that the grantee will pay the installments on the mortgage debt, the grantor ordinarily expects to have such a right of indemnification; and in many states, including Pennsylvania, the law implies one. If the parties agree that the grantee will not indemnify the grantor, it is necessary to negate the implication of such a right of indemnification in those jurisdictions where it would otherwise be implied. The following sentence, when added to the encumbrance clause (omitting, of course, the words "assume and agree to pay") accomplishes that aim:

> "But it is expressly agreed that the grantee herein shall not be held liable to indemnify or reimburse the grantor for any loss which the grantor may sustain by being required to pay the mortgagee or its successors in interest, or the grantor's predecessors in title or any of them, in satisfaction of such mortgage debt or any part thereof for which such mortgage was given as security, and that any and all such liability which may arise by operation of law is hereby expressly released."

Such an agreement could be the subject of a separate agreement, but it is preferable to include it in the deed immediately after the mortgage encumbrance clause which would otherwise give rise to the implied right of indemnity.

(c) Effect Upon Statement of Consideration

Whenever an encumbrance clause refers to a judgment, mortgage lien or other obligation payable in money, it is best not only to refer to the relevant recording data, but also to indicate the original principal amount of the debt and the outstanding principal balance thereof as of the date of conveyance. This latter sum is the amount

---

7. Indemnification is a previously defined Glossary item.

of the "credit" which the grantor allows the grantee in reduction of what would be the purchase price if the real estate were to be sold free and clear of the lien of the debt. Some lawyers prefer to state the amount of this credit in the consideration clause of the deed to avoid confusion. In such cases the consideration clause may be phrased as follows:

> "for and in consideration of the sum of One Million, Two Hundred Thousand Dollars ($1,200,000.00) lawful money of the United States of America, Two Hundred Thousand Dollars ($200,000.00) of which has been paid in cash and the balance of which, One Million Dollars ($1,000,000.00), is the outstanding principal balance of a certain mortgage lien hereinafter referred to."

In some localities, it is the custom to state in the consideration clause only the amount of cash and other consideration (such as a purchase money mortgage note) paid to the grantor.

10. Encumbrance Clause for Easements

Another form of encumbrance on title is the easement. If the grantor's title was subject to an easement when he acquired it, the encumbrance clause referring to it is drafted in a manner similar to that for restrictions:

> "ALSO UNDER AND SUBJECT to the easement of a certain 25 foot-wide driveway, as set forth in an Easement Agreement between Potter M. Brenner and Mary R. Burns dated January 8, 1971, and recorded in the Office of the Recorder of Deeds of Norfolk County, Massachusetts, in Deed Book Volume XV at page 91."

Of course, if the actual text creating the easement is not unduly long and complicated, it is preferable to repeat it in full in the deed. As is the case of other encumbrances, the "to have and to hold" and warranty clauses should also refer to the encumbrance of the easement.

11. Exceptions and Reservations

Often the grantor wishes to create a new easement for his own purposes across the lands being conveyed. Creation of such an easement may be accomplished by "excepting" or "reserving" such easement from and out of the interest in the real estate being conveyed. An "exception" is created by withholding from the operation of the deed some existing right which would otherwise normally pass to the grantee. A "reservation" creates a new right which had no previous existence. An exception does not require words of inheritance to be used in order to survive for the benefit of the grantor's heirs and assigns because title to that which is excepted was part of what the grantor and his heirs and assigns owned prior to the present conveyance. It continues to be held by the grantor and his heirs. A reservation, however, does require words of inheritance since it is a newly created right and not part of an existing estate of inheritance. Obviously, it is difficult in practice to distinguish between exceptions and reservations. Conveyancers may avoid the problem by referring to the grantor's right as both an exception and reservation and by using words of inheritance. Such a clause may be drafted as follows:

"EXCEPTING AND RESERVING unto the grantor, her heirs and assigns, the full, free liberty and right at all times hereafter forever, in common with the grantee, his heirs and assigns, to have and use as a passageway and driveway that certain strip of land twenty-five feet (25') in width, extending in a northerly direction for a distance of one hundred fifteen feet (115') from the northerly right-of-way line of State Highway 100 (50 feet wide), across the premises herein conveyed to the grantee, to the southerly boundary of other premises of the grantor on the north; the centerline of such twenty-five feet wide passageway and driveway being parallel to and at a distance of twelve and one-half feet (12½') from the easterly sideline of the premises herein conveyed to the grantee."

(a) Drafting Easements

When drafting such easements, it is important

(i) to specify the limited purposes for which the easement is granted, for example:

"as a driveway and parking lot for pedestrian and vehicular traffic."

(ii) to state whether or not the easement is to be perpetual or limited in duration, for example:

"for a period of twenty-five (25) years from the date of this indenture" or "at all times hereafter forever."

(iii) to indicate whether the easement is an exclusive right of the grantor or whether the grantor must use it in common with the grantee (or with the grantee and also his heirs and assigns) for example:

"unto the grantor, and his heirs and assigns, including future owners, mortgagees, and tenants and their respective customers, invitees and permitees, in common with the use thereof by the grantee, his heirs and assigns."

(iv) to describe the land to be burdened by the easement (using a full metes and bounds description or other form of legal description where necessary);

(v) to describe, when appropriate, the lands to be benefitted by the creation of the easement (e. g., if the grantor has retained a large tract of land, but the grantee is willing to have the easement benefit only a small portion of that retained land); and

(vi) to list any conditions imposed by the grantee upon the exception and reservation, for example:

> "subject to the duty and obligation of maintaining such passageway and driveway in good order and repair, including maintaining a smooth, hard surface thereon with curbs and adequate drainage."

(b) Deed of Grant

Easements may be created by a document which does not convey any other interest in the burdened real estate, such as when one neighbor grants an easement for driveway purposes to another neighbor years after the parties acquired their respective lots. Such a document is identical in form to an indenture but is called a "Deed of Grant" or "Deed of Easement"; instead of conveying the fee title to the described real estate, only an easement therein is granted.

(c) Declaration of Easements and Reciprocal Easement Agreement

Occasionally, the owner of a tract of ground anticipates its subdivision for resale or for mortgage purposes and wishes to impose certain reciprocal rights and easements on each part of his land for the benefit of every other part. For example, the owner of a garden apartment complex may want to assure future owners of sections of the complex the right to use recreational facilities, roads and a common entrance gate. This may be done by a unilateral "Declaration of Easements". Such a Declaration of Easements might be used in a rental garden apartment project either because different sections will be syndicated to different limited partnership, thus creating different ownerships immediately, or because different sections will be separately financed, creating the possibility of different ownerships in the future due to foreclosure upon one or more sections.

The establishment of a condominium creates certain reciprocal easements as well as common ownership of the common area within the condominium. If a complex is to contain several separate condominium sections, then the entire complex may first be subjected to a Declaration of Easements, for the same reason as described above.

Declaration of Covenants and Easements are sometimes used to create mandatory homeowners associations. Such a Declaration might be used in a development of single family residences to create certain reciprocal easements. However, a Declaration of Covenants and Easements for a homeowners association goes beyond a simple Declaration of Easements, for it would contain the affirmative covenant of each homeowner to join an association. The association would own certain common use area, including perhaps roads and recreational facilities, and would have the power to assess the homeowners for a share of the costs of maintaining the common use area. In addition, a Declaration of Covenants and Easements would ordinarily also include a variety of restrictions, such as a restriction against non-residential use. The association is a form of self-government, with the right to regulate certain aspects of life within the complex, such as policies covering fences, pets and plantings. In many ways, the Declaration of Covenants and Easements is analogous to the creation of a condominium, but without benefit (and restrictions) of an enabling statute.

If two or more neighbors wish to join in dedicating a portion of their respective real estate for common use by all of them, they may do so by joining in a "Reciprocal Easement Agreement". Reciprocal Easement Agreements are very common in connection with the development of shopping centers. Each major department store may obtain title to the land upon which its store is constructed, but dedicates a large portion of it for use as a part of the common system of driveways and parking lots.

(d) Creation of Easements by Other Means

Easements may arise by operation of law rather than by express language in an indenture or deed of grant. For example, a "way of necessity" is an easement which arises by implication when a portion of a larger parcel of land is conveyed without any express grant of an easement, but the land conveyed is so situated that access to it from a public highway can be had only by passing over the retained land of the grantor. Such an easement is known as an "easement by implication". Easements by implication also arise when an owner of land subjects part of it to an open, visible, permanent and continuous easement in favor of another party and then conveys either part. The purchaser's title is subject to the easement or is benefitted by it, as the case may be, even though it is not referred to in the deed.

Easements "by prescription" arise in a manner similar to the acquisition of title by adverse possession [8] where continuous open, visible, hostile and adverse use of a right continues for 21 years or more. Even though no written document may ever have existed, the law presumes that at some time in the remote past such a right or easement was granted. Whenever an easement is known to exist, even though it was not created by express language in a deed and is not of record, the prudent grantor will insert a reference to it in an encumbrance clause when she conveys title.

12. Appurtenances

As a matter of law in most jurisdictions, all easements, rights and incidents which belong to the property conveyed and are necessary to its full enjoyment will pass with the conveyance of that property as "appurtenances" without specific mention of them in the deed. But those which are merely "convenient" and not "necessary" will not pass unless they are apparent at the time of conveyance and

8. See Glossary.

are not expressly excepted or reserved. Therefore, it is important to determine, for example, whether, under the law of the jurisdiction, a conveyance of the surface of the land will include, without specific mention, title to the gas, oil and minerals beneath the land. Note that the model Pennsylvania deed, page 394, includes the following clause, beginning with the words "together with", following the encumbrance clauses in the deed:

> "TOGETHER with the free and common use, right, liberty and privilege of the aforesaid alley as and for a passageway and watercourse at all times hereafter forever."

If the tract of land conveyed acquired the benefit of an easement by a prior deed or by a deed of grant made after the grantor acquired the original tract, care should be taken to refer to the recording data of such instrument, and if possible, the full text of the easement should be set forth.

Because of the complicated rules and common law precedents which determine which of the grantor's rights will pass to the grantee and which will not, the legislatures of some states have statutorily defined the rights and interests which are deemed to pass. Although Pennsylvania has such a statutory definition, nearly all printed forms of deed continue to contain a general appurtenance clause with language nearly identical to the statutory definition (requiring only the insertion of a reference to any buildings or other improvements which may be situated on the land). The model deed for Pennsylvania contains the following clause:

> "TOGETHER with all and singular the buildings, improvements, ways, streets, alleys, driveways, passages, waters, water-courses, rights, liberties, privileges, hereditaments and appurtenances, whatsoever unto the hereby granted premises belonging, or in any wise appertaining, and the reversions and remainders, rents, issues, and profits thereof; and all the estate, right, title, interest, property, claim and demand whatsoever of them, the said Grantor, as well at law as in equity, of, in and to the same."

The general appurtenance clause is unnecessary since it follows the language of the Pennsylvania statute, but it is advisable to use it since lawyers expect it to appear in the deed. The general appurtenance clause usually follows all of the encumbrance clauses and precedes the habendum portion of the deed.

D. HABENDUM

1. "To Have and To Hold" Clause

The second section of the deed, the habendum, begins with the "to have and to hold" clause which, in our model form of Pennsylvania deed reads as follows:

> "To have and to hold the said lot or piece of ground above described with the buildings and improvements thereon erected, heredita-

ments and premises hereby granted, or mentioned, and intended so to be, with the appurtenances, unto the said Grantee, his heirs and assigns, to and for the only proper use and behoof of the said Grantee, his heirs and assigns forever."

Strictly speaking, the purpose of the foregoing clause is to designate the quantity of the estate which is to pass to the grantee. The "to have and to hold" clause may be used to explain, limit, qualify, or vary the estate granted by the granting clause. For example, it may provide that the grantee is to have and to hold the real estate only "as long as it is used as a church or other place of worship" or "as long as it is used for residential purposes". The effect of such limiting language is to create an estate in the grantee which may terminate upon the violation of the condition imposed. If the estate is terminated, title to the real estate will revert back to the grantor who imposed the condition or his heirs and assigns. In the early days of the common law, it was a common practice to impose limitations to keep title to the family domain in the hands of the direct male descendants of the grantor. Today, however, the "to have and to hold" clause is generally used to merely suggest to the grantee the purpose for which the grantor *hopes* the grantee will use the real estate. For example, the provision may say, "as and for a school for the training of doctors, nurses, and other medical personnel". In such cases, the words of grant are not legally limited by the words of the habendum and title does not revert to the grantor or his heirs when the real estates ceases to be used for the desired purpose. In some instances, however, the habendum clause is used to create conditions, subsequent to which, if broken, will either provide for a reversion back to the grantor or to a grant over unto a third party.

The "to have and to hold" clause serves no useful purpose that could not be fulfilled by the premises portion of the deed. Therefore, it could be eliminated, thereby preventing disputes about inconsistencies between the granting clause and habendum. Nevertheless, in Pennsylvania, as well as elsewhere, it continues to be perpetuated by lawyers who revere its ancient common law history. Most printed forms continue to contain the "to have and to hold" clause.

It is necessary to limit the effect of the "to have and to hold" clause when the grant itself is limited, such as when there are encumbrance clauses referring to restrictions, mortgage liens or exceptions and reservations. In such cases, it is customary not to repeat the entire text of the encumbrance clauses, but only to refer to them by adding at the end of the "to have and to hold" clause the words "under and subject as aforesaid". If the estate granted is not an unqualified fee, such as when the grantees hold as tenants by the entirety, the "to have and to hold" clause should make reference to that limitation by adding the phrase "as tenants by entirety" at the end of the clause.

2. Warranty Clause

(a) Covenants in General

A "covenant" has been defined as any writing under seal whereby a party guarantees the truth of certain facts or binds himself to perform or give something to another. Covenants can be of many kinds and used for many purposes. General covenants can be expressed in or implied from the grant.

(b) Covenants for Title

Although general covenants do not appear in most deeds, covenants for title have been and continue to be of great importance. Naturally, the grantee wishes to obtain as much assurance as possible that he is getting that title to the real estate for which he has bargained. For hundreds of years, grantees have required grantors to include in deeds of conveyance specific covenants whereby the grantor personally guarantees the existence of certain facts and agrees to protect the grantee if the title conveyed to him is attacked by others.

Historically, covenants for title dealt with six subjects: seisin, the right to convey, freedom from encumbrances, warranty, quiet enjoyment and further assurances. The grantor covenants that he is lawfully "seised of" ("owns") the premises he purports to convey, and that he has a "right to convey" the described premises. He also guarantees that the premises conveyed are "free and clear of all encumbrances". The meaning of such a covenant in any particular jurisdiction depends upon the meaning there of the term "encumbrance". "Encumbrances" usually include unpaid tax liens, assessments, mortgage liens, building restrictions, encroachments, and easements. The grantor's covenant for warranty is an agreement to compensate the grantee for any loss which he may sustain by virtue of the failure of the title which the deed purports to convey. This form of covenant is the most important today. A similar covenant is that of quiet enjoyment, whereby the grantor guarantees that his grantee will not be disturbed by the holder of a paramount title. The covenant for "further assurances" binds the grantor to do those things which may be required to perfect the grantee's title.

(c) General Warranty

In many states the meaning of the ancient covenants has been defined by statute. They are implied from the words of grant and do not have to be set forth in full. However, in most jurisdictions at least the warranty of title is still set forth. The so-called "general" warranty is the grantor's assurance that neither he nor any predecessor of his title, nor anyone else, will disturb the grantee's use and enjoyment of the real estate by reason of any paramount title or encumbrance. This form of warranty is closest to the original medieval form of covenant and is still widely used. In Pennsylvania deeds it is worded as follows:

> "AND the said Grantor, for herself, her heirs, executors and administrators does covenant, promise and agree, to and with the said Grantee, his heirs and assigns, by these presents, that she, the said Grantor and her heirs, all and singular the hereditaments and premises hereby granted or mentioned and intended so to be, with the appurtenances, unto the said Grantee, his heirs and assigns, against her, the said Grantor and her heirs, and against all and every person and persons whomsoever lawfully claiming or to claim the same or any part thereof, shall and will, warrant and forever defend."

(d) Special Warranty

In areas where real estate is reconveyed every few years, such as in residential sections of our large cities, grantors have developed a reluctance to give such a broad warranty when their predecessors in title were not family members. In order to feel comfortable about giving such a warranty, the grantor would have to have a search made of his title. Indeed, in many jurisdictions it is still the obligation of the grantor to present to the grantee, before the closing, an attorney's certificate evidencing the state of title. Sometimes grantors simply refuse to make such broad warranties and agree to give only "special" warranties. A special warranty, also known as a "covenant against the grantor's acts", is limited to an assurance that the grantor himself did not create any encumbrances during his period of ownership to which the conveyance will be subject. Use of such a limited warranty is the custom in most large cities today. The availability of owner's title insurance, issued by large and financially responsible corporations, has minimized the grantee's risk of relying on so limited a warranty.

In our model form of Pennsylvania deed a special warranty is established by the following language:

> "AND the said Grantors, for themselves, their heirs, executors and administrators do covenant, promise and agree, to and with the said Grantee, his heirs and assigns, by these presents, that they, the said Grantors and their heirs, all and singular the hereditaments and premises hereby granted or mentioned and intended so to be, with the appurtenances, unto the said Grantee, his heirs and assigns, against them, the said Grantors and their heirs, and against all and every person whomsoever lawfully claiming or to claim the same or any part thereof, by, from or under him, her, them, or any of them, shall and will, warrant and forever defend."

The critical words which distinguish the special warranty from the general warranty appear in the limitation of the grantor's obligation to defend title to only those actions which may be brought by the grantor and her heirs or any other person lawfully claiming *"by, from or under her, him, them or any of them"*. If those "magic" words are omitted from the warranty clause, the deed becomes a general warranty deed and, except for any listed encumbrances, the grantor must defend the grantee's title against all mankind. Before preparing a deed for any transaction, it is imperative to determine whether the agreement of sale requires the delivery of a general warranty deed.

(e) Fiduciary's Warranty

The warranty normally required of a trustee, executor or administrator of the grantor's estate is limited in much the same manner as a special warranty. A fiduciary covenants only that *he* did nothing to encumber title during the time of his ownership. In Pennsylvania, a fiduciary's deed contains the following covenant:

"AND the said Grantors, for themselves and their respective executors, administrators and successors, do covenant, promise and agree, to and with the said Grantee, his heirs and assigns, by these presents, that they, the said Grantors, have not done, committed, or knowingly or willingly suffered to be done or committed, any act, matter or thing whatsoever whereby the premises hereby granted, or any part thereof, is, are, shall or may be impeached, charged or incumbered, in title, charge, estate, or otherwise howsoever."

(f) Quit-Claim Deed without Warranty

The grantor, for many reasons, may not wish to give the grantee the benefit of any warranty. Title to a particular piece of real estate may be quite complicated and confused and the grantor may not be sure what interest he really owns or how free of encumbrances his title may be. However, for a given price he is willing to sell and convey whatever estate and title he has. In such cases the grantor delivers a deed without warranty, also called a "quit claim" deed, which is very similar in form to a release. Quit-claim deeds are often used when purported heirs or adjoining property owners wish to convey and release any rights which they may have in property, the title to which is disputed.

(g) Reference to Encumbrance Clauses

As indicated elsewhere, if any encumbrance, exception, or reservation is referred to in the granting clause and the "to have and to hold" clause, it is wise to refer to it again in order to expressly limit the scope of the warranty. In Pennsylvania deeds, it is sufficient to insert the words "subject as aforesaid" or "excepting and reserving as aforesaid" prior to the words "warrant and forever defend" or at some other appropriate place at the end of the warranty clause.

E.   CONCLUSION

1.   Execution Clause

The first clause appearing in that part of the deed called the conclusion is the clause beginning "In witness whereof".   It is known as the "testimonium" or "execution" clause.   The exact language used is not critical.

(a) Individual

Where individuals are the grantors the following form is appropriate:

> "IN WITNESS WHEREOF, the parties of the first part (or 'the Grantors') have hereunto set their hands and seals, the day and year first above written."

(b) Corporation

The customary form of testimonium for corporate grantors is as follows:

> "IN WITNESS WHEREOF, the party of the first part (or 'Grantor') has caused this Indenture to be signed by its President, duly authorized thereunto, and has caused its corporate seal to be hereunto affixed and attested by its Secretary.   Dated the day and year first above written."

2.   Signatures

(a) Individual

The signature lines for individual grantors usually call for witnesses:

SEALED AND DELIVERED
in the presence of us:
WITNESS:

_____   _____ [Seal]
                                                    John Q. McDonald

_____   _____ [Seal]
                                                    Alexa S. McDonald

(b) Corporate

The typical form of corporate signature calls for the signature of the President or Vice President to be witnessed or "attested" by the

Secretary or Assistant Secretary, who also impresses the seal of the corporation:

AJAX CORPORATION

By _____

John Q. McDonald
Vice President

Attest: _____

Alexa S. McDonald
Assistant Secretary

[Corporate Seal]

The officers signing and attesting the signing of the deed on behalf of the corporation or other entity must be authorized to do so by the board of directors or other managing body. The signing officer may be a president, vice-president, trustee, partner, chief executive officer, dean or other authorized representative. Since local laws vary, it is wise to check with the local recording office to determine whether a deed signed by such an officer or attested by an officer other than a secretary (such as a cashier, treasurer or clerk) will be accepted for record.

(c) Attorney-in-Fact

If an individual signs by his attorney-in-fact, it should be indicated thus:

SEALED AND DELIVERED
in the presence of us:
WITNESS:

_____   _____ *[Seal]*

Alexa S. McDonald, by her attorney-in-fact, John Q. McDonald, duly authorized by Power of Attorney dated November 13, 1970

3. Receipt

In some jurisdictions a clause may be inserted after the execution clause to serve as a receipt for the consideration paid to the grantor. Such a provision need not be included where the consideration is only nominal.

"Received on the day of the date of the above Indenture, from the above-named grantee, the full consideration above mentioned."

WITNESS:

_____   _____ *[Seal]*

John Q. McDonald

_____   _____ *[Seal]*

Alexa S. McDonald

4. Certification of Grantee's Address

With the growing complexity of our local taxing systems, it has become common for local authorities to require all deeds to contain a certification of the address of the grantee so that notices and tax bills may be forwarded to him. The signing party need not be the grantee. In Pennsylvania the following form is used on the back of the deed or following the signatures:

"The address of the above-named grantee is 642 Greenacre Road, Philadelphia, Pennsylvania.

/s/ _____
On behalf of the Grantee"

5. Acknowledgment

The final clause of the deed is the acknowledgment. The grantor must appear before an officer qualified by law to take acknowledgments and "acknowledge" that he signed the deed or other instrument. The officer, who is usually a notary public, must sign the acknowledgment clause in the required manner. Although the execution and the delivery of the deed and its acceptance by the grantee is sufficient to vest title in the grantee, the acknowledgment is a critical part of the deed. Without it, the deed will not be accepted by the local recording officer and the grantee will not obtain the benefits of the recording system. At one time every state had its own required form of acknowledgment. The Uniform Acknowledgment Act has eliminated some of the technical difficulties in this regard and those states subscribing to the Uniform Acknowledgment Act will accept deeds acknowledged in other jurisdictions in the form provided by that Act, even when it varies from the preferred form. If, however, the jurisdiction in which the deed will be recorded has not adopted the Uniform Acknowledgment Act, the acknowledgment form used must be the one acceptable to the recording state. In the model form of Pennsylvania deed, the acknowledgment (in the form adopted by the Uniform Acknowledgment Act) appears as follows:

Commonwealth of Pennsylvania }
County of Philadelphia } ss.

On this, the 26th day of May, 1971, before me, a Notary Public in and for the Commonwealth of Pennsylvania, the undersigned Officer, personally appeared MARY R. BURNS, singlewoman, known to me (satisfactorily proven) to be the person whose name is subscribed to the within instrument, and acknowledged that she executed the same for the purposes therein contained.

IN WITNESS WHEREOF, I hereunto set my hand and official seal.

_____

Notary Public

My commission expires: _____

[*Notarial Seal*]

The important elements to be set forth in the acknowledgment are:

(a) The *venue*, or place where the acknowledgment is taken, in our example, in the Commonwealth of Pennsylvania and County of Philadelphia;

(b) The *date* on which the acknowledgment is made and taken. An acknowledgment may be made at any time after execution of the deed. An acknowledgment cannot be made before execution of the deed since it is impossible to acknowledge an act which has not yet been performed. Although the acknowledgment need not be made on the same day that the deed is signed, it is best to have the deed signed in the presence of the notary public, usually a settlement clerk, who may immediately complete the taking of the acknowledgment.

(c) The *name* of the person taking the acknowledgment and

(d) his *official position* (e. g. "Notary Public").

(e) The location of the *office* of the officer (that is, the state and county, city, township or borough which he serves);

(f) the *date of expiration* of his commission. Of course, the officer must sign the acknowledgment and impress his official seal next to his signature.

Depending upon the jurisdiction, there may be limitations upon those who are qualified to take acknowledgments. For example, a Pennsylvania notary public may not act as such for any bank of which he is a director or an officer. Therefore, when a bank officer's signature is to be acknowledged, the notary public should certify below the acknowledgment as follows:

"I certify that I am not an officer or director of the above-named bank, banking institution or trust company."

In some jurisdictions, the corporate acknowledgment takes the form of a deposition and requires the attesting officer of the corporate grantor to sign the acknowledgment in addition to the notary public. The following is a form widely employed in New Jersey:

STATE OF NEW JERSEY ⎤
                     ⎬ ss.
COUNTY OF CAMDEN ⎦

BE IT REMEMBERED, that on this 26th day of May in the year of our Lord one thousand nine hundred and seventy-one before me, a Notary Public, personally appeared ALAN L. BURNS who being by me duly sworn, on his oath saith, that he is the Secretary of COUNTRY VILLAGE, INC., the grantor within named, and that WAYNE EMERSON is the President; that deponent knows the common or corporate seal of said grantor and that the seal annexed to the within Deed of Conveyance is such common or corporate seal; that the said Deed of Conveyance was signed by the said President and the seal of said grantor affixed thereto in the presence of deponent; that said Deed of Conveyance was signed, sealed and delivered as and for the voluntary act and deed of said grantor for the uses and purposes therein expressed, pursuant to a resolution of the Board of Directors of said grantor; and at the execution thereof this deponent subscribed his name thereto as witness.

Sworn and Subscribed the
day and year aforesaid
                 —————————————
                 Alan L. Burns, Secretary
——————————————————
     Notary Public

My Commission expires: —————————

[*Notarial Seal*]

III. STATUTORY FORM OF DEED

Many jurisdictions have attempted to shorten, simplify and standardize the language and forms of deeds by adopting a statutory form. One of the purposes of such legislation is to eliminate the verbosity that the old common law deed forms perpetuate. However, as is the case in many fields, lawyers and conveyancers have felt more comfortable with the tried and true common law forms and have been reluctant to use the statutory form.

IV. DELIVERY OF DEEDS

The final requirement for the effectiveness of a deed is that it be delivered to the grantee and accepted by him. No special ceremony is necessary to deliver the deed so long as it is the intention of the grantor that the deed be passed from his control into the hands of the grantee or the grantee's agents. Even though the grantor may have signed a deed, it is not sufficient delivery if it is stolen and delivered to the grantee.

A. DELIVERY IN ESCROW

Delivery may be made to a third person, such as an escrow holder. When a lawyer, real estate broker or title insurance company holds the document in escrow, the condition precedent to the delivery of the deed to the grantee is that the grantor or grantee comply with specific conditions established by mutual agreement. Such conditions should be very clearly spelled out in the escrow agreement so that there will be no dispute as to whether the escrow holder should return the deed to the grantor or deliver it to the grantee. In such cases, delivery to the escrow holder is complete delivery so far as the grantor is concerned.

B. ACCEPTANCE OF DELIVERY BY GRANTEE

A grantor cannot unilaterally convey title to real estate to an unwilling grantee. (This could occur where the property is worth less than its annual taxes.) Acceptance by the grantee is a necessity. Such acceptance may, however, be implied from the acceptance by the grantee of the benefits of the deed.

V. SPECIAL DEEDS AND DEED CLAUSES

A. SHERIFF'S DEED

When real estate is sold at a public auction sale, pursuant to the law and procedural rules of the jurisdiction, in execution upon a judgment for money damages or a judgment in mortgage foreclosure, or upon a lien for unpaid taxes, the Sheriff or other authorized judicial officer delivers a deed conveying title to the successful bidder at the sale. The former owners of the real estate sold at the sale are not required to sign the deed. The Sheriff's deed resembles the common law form of deed-poll. It recites the consideration paid to the Sheriff by the successful bidder, but it does not contain the customary granting clause. However, it does use the words "grant and convey", and, in Pennsylvania, those words are statutorily defined to mean that the purchaser obtains the entire estate which the former owner held. The Sheriff makes no warranties. The deed contains an explanation of the basis for the judicial sale; it refers to the court, term, and number of the case which led to the judgment upon which execution was held at the public auction sale.

B. DEED OF CONFIRMATION OR CORRECTION

The purpose of a deed of confirmation is to correct an error in a prior deed of conveyance and thereby confirm the grantee's title. The deed of confirmation may take the form of an ordinary indenture with a special recital to indicate that the purpose of the deed is to confirm title already held by the grantee and to convey to him any outstanding interest or claim against his title which may exist by reason of a defect in the original conveyance, such as a typographical error in the legal description or improper recording; in some cases it is wise to explain the error in the recital. Such deeds are also used when an owner desires to record a perimeter legal description of a number of lots which he has acquired by numerous separate deeds containing overlapping or otherwise inconsistent legal descriptions. In such cases the owner "conveys" to himself and the recital explains how each part of the entire described premises was acquired and that the purpose of the deed is to describe the same properties in accordance with a new perimeter description. This form of deed is usually exempt from recording or transfer taxes because its purpose is not to convey any additional real estate.

C. CONDOMINIUM DEED

Condominium is a form of ownership of real estate by co-tenants. Each tenant owns a specified part of the real estate, either on, above, or below the surface of the land, and a proportionate undivided fractional interest in common with the other tenants in other parts of the real estate. In most states where condominiums have been developed, there are special statutes which prescribe how a condominium may be established and how the fee title to a part or unit of the condominium may be conveyed. Condominium deeds are not necessarily any different from ordinary indentures, except that the legal description does not usually refer to metes and bounds which can be traced upon the ground, but incorporates by reference the description of the condominium unit as set forth in the Declaration of Condominium which must be recorded prior to any sale of a condominium unit. Also, in some jurisdictions, by statute or by practice, the grantee of a condominium unit deed signs the deed agreeing to be liable for condominium maintenance assessments.

D. COAL AND OTHER MINERAL SEVERANCE CLAUSES

Some jurisdictions, by statute, require deeds conveying the surface of land where there is or has been a severance of the underlying coal or other minerals or a severance of the right to surface support, to include a prescribed form of notice or warning that such document (a) may not, or does not, include or insure title to underlying minerals and right of support under the surface, (b) that the owner of the minerals may or does have the right to remove such and (c) that damage to the surface and any buildings thereon may result therefrom. Such a clause is appropriately inserted before the general appurtenance clause.

The following are examples Fee Simple, Sheriff's and Quit-Claim Deeds.

EXAMPLE: Fee Simple Deed (Pennsylvania)

Printed for and Sold by John C. Clark Co., 1326 Walnut St., Phila.

This Indenture Made the   26th   day of

May   in the year of our Lord one thousand nine hundred and   seventy-seven   (19 77)

Between ALAN L. BURNS and MARY R. BURNS, his wife, of 100 Blackacre Lane, Philadelphia, Pennsylvania

(hereinafter called the Grantor), of the one part, and

ROBERT B. DAVIS of 642 Greenacre Road, Philadelphia, Pennsylvania

(hereinafter called the Grantee), of the other part,

Witnesseth That the said Grantor s

for and in consideration of the sum of

Twenty Thousand Dollars ($20,000.00)   lawful money of the United States of America, unto   them   well and truly paid by the said Grantee , at or before the sealing and delivery hereof, the receipt whereof is hereby acknowledged, have granted, bargained and sold, released and confirmed, and by these presents do   grant , bargain and sell, release and confirm unto the said Grantee , his heirs   and assigns,

ALL THAT CERTAIN lot or piece of ground with the buildings and improvements thereon erected, bounded and described in accordance with an official survey and plan thereof by Adam Smith, Surveyor and Regulator for the First District, dated April 10, 1971, as follows:

SITUATE on the North side of Blackacre Lane at the distance of three hundred sixty-eight feet (368') westward from the West side of Bond Street in the Tenth Ward of the City of Philadelphia;

CONTAINING in front or breadth on the said Blackacre Lane fifty feet (50') and extending of that width in length or depth northward between parallel lines at right angles with the said Blackacre Lane eighty-one feet, six inches (81' 6") to the middle of a certain three feet (3') wide alley leading eastward and westward from Bond Street to Abbey Road.

BEING known as No. 100 Blackacre Lane.

BEING the same premises which Charles Clark and Dorothy Clark, his wife, by Indenture dated July 8, 1945 and recorded in the Office for Recording of Deeds in and for the County of Philadelphia (now the Department of Records of the City of Philadelphia) in Deed Book J.M.H. No. 2286, page 354 &c., granted and conveyed unto the said Alan L. Burns and Mary R. Burns, his wife, in fee, as tenants by entirety.

[B7778]

UNDER AND SUBJECT, nevertheless, to certain conditions and restrictions as appear of record in Deed Book W.S.M. No. 231, page 253 &c.

TOGETHER with the free and common use, right, liberty and privilege of the aforesaid alley as and for a passageway and water-course at all times hereafter forever.

AND

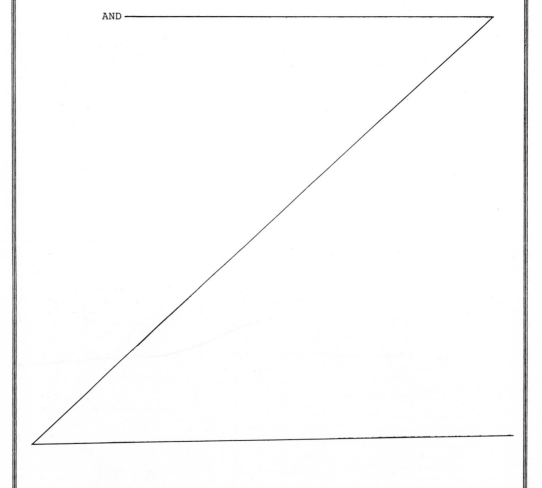

Together with all and singular the buildings, improvements, ways, streets, alleys, driveways, passages, waters, water-courses, rights liberties, privileges, hereditaments and appurtenances, whatsoever unto the hereby granted premises belonging, or in any wise appertaining, and the reversions and remainders, rents, issues, and profits thereof; and all the estate, right, title, interest property, claim and demand whatsoever of them

the said Grantor s, as well at law as in equity, of, in, and to the same.

To have and to hold the said lot or piece of ground above described with the buildings and improvements thereon erected, hereditaments and premises hereby granted, or mentioned, and intended so to be, with the appurtenances, unto the said Grantee , his heirs and assigns, to and for the only proper use and behoof of the said Grantee , his heirs and assigns forever.

UNDER AND SUBJECT, nevertheless, to certain conditions and restrictions of record, as aforesaid.

Covenants

And the said Grantors, for themselves, their heirs , executors and administrators do covenant, promise and agree, to and with the said Grantee , his heirs and assigns, by these presents, that they , the said Grantors and their heirs, all and singular the hereditaments and premises hereby granted or mentioned and intended so to be, with the appurtenances, unto the said Grantee , his heirs and assigns, against them, the said Grantors and their heirs, and against all and every person and persons whomsoever lawfully claiming or to claim the same or any part thereof, by, from or under him, her, them or any of them, shall and will SUBJECT as aforesaid, WARRANT and forever DEFEND.

In Witness Whereof, the parties of the first part have hereunto set their hands and seals . Dated the day and year first above written.

Sealed and Delivered
IN THE PRESENCE OF US:

_____(SEAL)
Alan L. Burns

_____(SEAL)
Mary R. Burns
[B7780]

Commonwealth of Pennsylvania
County of Philadelphia   } **ss:**

On this, the 26th **day of** May , 1977, **before me,** a Notary Public in and for the Commonwealth of Pennsylvania,   **the undersigned Officer,**

personally appeared ALAN L. BURNS and MARY R. BURNS, his wife,

known to me (satisfactorily proven) to be the person   whose name   is (are) subscribed to the within instrument, and acknowledged that   he   executed the same for the purposes therein contained.

In Witness Whereof , I hereunto set my hand and official seal.

_____
Notary Public

My Commission expires:_____
(Notarial Seal)

Deed.

ALAN L. BURNS et ux.

TO

ROBERT B. DAVIS

Premises:

No. 100 Blackacre Lane
10th Ward
Philadelphia, Pa.

753-S   John C. Clark Co., Phila.   1977

The address of the above-named Grantee

is 642 Greenacre Road,

Philadelphia, Pa.
On behalf of the Grantee

[87779]

EXAMPLE: "Quit-claim Deed (Pennsylvania)"

Quit-claim Deed   No. 664/S   Printed for and Sold by John C. Clark Co., 1326 Walnut St., Phila.

This Indenture, Made the

12th   *day of*   April   *in the year of our*

Lord one thousand nine hundred   seventy-seven (1977)

Between VILLAGE GREENE, INC., a Pennsylvania corporation, having an office at 13th Floor, 401 Walnut Street, Philadelphia, Pennsylvania, party of the first part, and

P E S ASSOCIATES, a partnership, having an office at 1001 Wilmington Pike, Dover, Delaware, party of the second part,

Witnesseth, *That the said part*   *of the first part, for and in consideration of the* *sum of* Two Thousand Five Hundred Dollars ($2,500.00)

lawful money of the United States of America, to   it   *well and truly paid by the said* *part*   *of the second part, at and before the* *sealing and delivery of these presents, the* *receipt whereof is hereby acknowledged,* has   **remised,** *released and quit-claimed, and by these presents,* does   **remise,** *release and quit-claim unto the said part* y   *of the second part, and to* its successors

and assigns forever, **ALL** THAT CERTAIN tract of land SITUATE in the Township of Upper Gwynedd, County of Montgomery, Commonwealth of Pennsylvania, bounded and described according to a Plan of Survey made for Village Greene, Inc. by Urwiler and Walter, Inc., dated April 1, 1977, as follows, to wit:

    (Legal description and recital, although the recital is
      sometimes omitted.)

    CONTAINING, five and five hundred seventy-four one-thousandths
(5.574) acres of land, more or less.

[B7783]

𝕿𝖔𝖌𝖊𝖙𝖍𝖊𝖗 *with all and singular, the tenements, hereditaments and appurtenances thereunto belonging, or in any wise appertaining, and the reversions, remainders, rents, issues and profits thereof:* 𝕬𝖓𝖉 *also, all the estate, right, title, interest,*

*   property, claim and demand whatsoever, as well in law as in equity, of the said part   of the first part, of, in, or to the above-described premises, and every part and parcel thereof, with the appurtenances.*

𝕿𝖔 𝖍𝖆𝖛𝖊 𝖆𝖓𝖉 𝖙𝖔 𝖍𝖔𝖑𝖉 *all and singular the above-mentioned and described premises, together with the appurtenances, unto the said part   of the second part,* its successors

and assigns forever.

𝕴𝖓 𝖂𝖎𝖙𝖓𝖊𝖘𝖘 𝖂𝖍𝖊𝖗𝖊𝖔𝖋, the party of the first part, by its proper officers thereunto duly authorized, has caused its name and corporate seal to be hereunto affixed. Dated the day and year first above written.

𝕾𝖊𝖆𝖑𝖊𝖉 𝖆𝖓𝖉 𝕯𝖊𝖑𝖎𝖛𝖊𝖗𝖊𝖉 }
IN THE PRESENCE OF US: }

                                   VILLAGE GREENE, INC.

                                   By_____
                                      Albert F. Village, President

                                   Attest_____
                                         Albert F. Greene, Secretary

Commonwealth of Pennsylvania } SS.
County of

On this, the   day of   , 19   , before me, the undersigned Officer,

*   , personally appeared*

*   known to me (satisfactorily proven) to be the person   whose name   is (are) subscribed to the within instrument, and acknowledged that   he executed the same for the purposes therein contained.*

𝕴𝖓 𝖂𝖎𝖙𝖓𝖊𝖘𝖘 𝖂𝖍𝖊𝖗𝖊𝖔𝖋, *I hereunto set my hand and official seal.*   [B7784]

Commonwealth of Pennsylvania
County of Philadelphia   }   ss.

On this, the   12th   *day of* April   19 77 , *before me*, a Notary Public, in and for the Commonwealth of Pennsylvania, *the undersigned Officer, personally appeared*   ALBERT F. VILLAGE
who acknowledged himself to be the   President   *of* VILLAGE GREENE, INC.
      , *a corporation, and that*   *he as such* President
      , *being authorized to do so executed the foregoing instrument for the purposes therein contained by signing the name of the corporation by himself (herself) as*   President.

In Witness Whereof, I hereunto set my hand and official seal.

_____
Notary Public

My Commission expires
(Notarial Seal)

DEED.

VILLAGE GREENE, INC.

TO

P E S ASSOCIATES

Premises:

Upper Gwynedd Township
Montgomery County
Pennsylvania

1976   John C. Clark Company, Philadelphia.   664/S

The address of the above-named Grantee is 1001 Wilmington Pike
Dover, Delaware
On behalf of the Grantee

[B7782]

EXAMPLE: Sheriff's Deed (Pennsylvania)

Printed for and Sold by John C. Clark Co., 1326 Walnut St., Phila.

Know all Men by these Presents

THAT I, WILLIAM M. LENNOX, ***Sheriff of the County of*** Philadelphia, ***in the Commonwealth of Pennsylvania, for and in consideration of the sum of*** six hundred ($600.00)

dollars, to me in hand paid, Do hereby grant and convey to HARDCASH SAVINGS BANK, a Pennsylvania corporation, its successors and assigns,

ALL THAT CERTAIN lot or piece of ground with the two-story brick building thereon erected, SITUATE on the East side of 50th Street at the distance of four hundred thirty-nine feet (439') northward from the North side of Main Street in the Thirty-fourth Ward of the City of Philadelphia;

CONTAINING in front or breadth on said 50th Street fifteen feet (15') and extending of that width in length or depth eastward between parallel lines at right angles to said 50th Street ninety feet (90') to a certain three feet (3') wide alley extending northward and southward between Main Street and Rosetree Lane.

BEING known as No. 159 North 50th Street.

TOGETHER with the free and common use, right, liberty and privilege of the aforesaid alley as and for a passageway and water-course at all times hereafter forever;

[B7785]

the same having been sold by me to the said grantee   , *on the*   3rd   *day of*

May   *Anno Domini one thousand nine hundred and*   seventy-seven   *after due*

advertisement, according to law, under and by virtue of a writ of Execution

~~issued   Decree entered~~☆ *on the*   25th   *day of* April   *Anno Domini*

one thousand nine hundred and   seventy-seven *out of the*   Court of Common Pleas of

Philadelphia County, Trial Division *as of* April   *Term, one thousand nine*

hundred and   seventy-seven *Number*   734   *at the suit of* Hardcash

Savings Bank v. Alan L. Burns and Mary R. Burns, his wife, Real

Owners.

       In witness whereof, I have hereunto affixed my signature, this   27th

day of   May   *Anno Domini one thousand nine hundred and*   seventy-seven.

SEALED AND DELIVERED   WILLIAM M. LENNOX, SHERIFF
IN THE PRESENCE OF

          By   _____

            James Browne, Chief Deputy **Sheriff**

☆ Eliminate which not applicable.   [B7787]

Commonwealth of Pennsylvania

County of Philadelphia   } *ss.*

On this, the   27th   *day of*   May,   **19**77   , *before me*

the undersigned Officer, personally appeared   JAMES BROWNE, Chief Deputy *Sheriff of the County of*   Philadelphia   , *known to me (or satisfactory proven) to be the person described in the foregoing instrument, and acknowledged that he executed the same in the capacity therein stated and for the purposes therein contained.*

In Witness Whereof, *I hereunto set my hand and official seal.*

Prothonotary

Writ No. 232/73.

Deed=Poll.

WILLIAM M. LENNOX,   **Sheriff.**

TO.

HARDCASH SAVINGS BANK, its successors and assigns

Hardcash Savings Bank   C.P.   Apr. T. 1977.   **No.** 734

vs.

Alan L. Burns Mary R. Burns

Premises:

159 North 50th Street

2-69   John C. Clark Company, Philadelphia.

The address *of the within-named* **Grantee is** 620 E. Spring Road Philadelphia, Pa.

On behalf of the Grantee

[B7786]

Chapter Eleven

SETTLEMENTS AND CLOSINGS

I. GENERAL INFORMATION

The settlement or closing is the time at which the real estate transaction is consummated. The format of a closing varies markedly, as a matter of tradition, from one part of the country to another. In some areas it is common for all of the parties or their representatives to conduct the settlement as a face to face meeting. In other jurisdictions, most settlements for the purchase of residential real estate take place without the presence of the parties. Instead all of the necessary documents and consideration are forwarded to one person, normally an employee of a title company or bank, who acts as an escrow agent. When everything has been received, the escrow agent consummates the closing without the parties being present.

This chapter will focus on settlements or closings at which the parties are present, but the preparation for an escrow closing would be virtually identical. Several different kinds of settlements will be considered, but the major emphasis will be on purchases of residential property which involve a mortgage supplied by an institutional lender.

This chapter considers settlements as if they were being conducted by a title insurance company. This will not always be the case, and the settlement may be conducted by an attorney or an agent. The principles remain the same, whoever actually conducts the settlement.

II. PREPARATION FOR SETTLEMENT—PURCHASE— SALE OF PROPERTY

The closing itself is often anti-climactic. If the parties are well organized and prepared for the closing, the event becomes a mere formality. It will make a favorable impression on a client if the lawyer representing the client has anticipated everything needed for the settlement and has all of the documents in order.

In order for an attorney or a paralegal to prepare for a closing concerning the sale or purchase of property, he must review the relevant documents, which usually include the agreement of sale, the title report or abstract, and, if a mortgage is being used by the purchaser, the mortgage commitment and any disclosure forms required by federal or state law. This review will help provide a list of things that must be done prior to the settlement as well as the documents and consideration which must be produced at the closing.

A. PREPARATION BY SELLER

There are a number of documents which must be produced by the seller at or before the settlement.

1. Deed

The seller's basic obligation at a settlement is to tender a deed to the buyer. The party responsible for the preparation of the deed will vary from one jurisdiction to another. In Pennsylvania, tradition dictates that a deed be prepared by the purchaser and delivered to the seller for review prior to settlement. In many states, such as New Jersey, preparation of the deed is the responsibility of the seller. The deed should be reviewed by both the seller and the purchaser in order to make certain that the legal description conforms to the property being sold.

If one or more of the grantors will not be present at the closing, it is necessary to obtain the absent party's signature in advance, along with an acknowledgment of that signature. If all parties who will execute the deed will be present at the closing, they can execute the deed at that time.

2. Objections and Exceptions in the Title Report

(a) Mortgage Pay-off Statement and Satisfaction

If the property is subject to a mortgage which is to be removed at the time of settlement, it will be necessary to obtain from the mortgagee a statement of the exact amount of principal, interest and other charges, if any, which will be due on the date of settlement in order to satisfy the mortgage.[1] Normally, the mortgagee will send a letter stating the aggregate amount owed on that date, and indicating the daily interest which should be added to that figure in the event that settlement occurs a few days late. The party in charge of the settlement will forward a check to the mortgagee who will return a satisfaction of mortgage in recordable form. In some instances the mortgagee will send an executed satisfaction to the settlement with the understanding that it will be recorded only after the sum necessary to satisfy the mortgage has been sent to the mortgagee.

(b) Real Estate Taxes

The agreement of sale will usually require that the property be conveyed free and clear of all liens for taxes. It will typically be necessary for the seller to produce at the settlement tax receipts for the prior two or three years.[2] If taxes for the current year have not

---

1. If a mortgagee has been escrowing for the payment of real estate taxes, the payoff letter will show that funds currently held in escrow are being applied in reduction of principal.

2. The exact number of years of tax receipts required will depend on the statute of limitations relating to tax sales for unpaid taxes.

been paid, the seller should produce the bill for those taxes if it has been received. Prior to settlement the receipts and the bill referred to above should be obtained. If the receipts cannot be found, one can write to the taxing authority and request a letter acknowledging payment of the taxes. If taxes have been escrowed under the existing mortgage, the receipts may be held by the lender. Often the party conducting the settlement will rely on the written statement of the mortgagee [3] that taxes have been paid without requiring production of receipts.

(c) Water and Sewer Rents

If water and sewer services are supplied by a municipality, and if the municipality has the power to impose a lien for unpaid charges, it will be necessary for the seller to produce receipts evidencing payments of these bills for several years prior to settlement. Again, any outstanding bill should be produced at the settlement.

In many areas, a minimum charge for water is made periodically. Less frequently the meter on the property is read and the owner is billed for any excess water usage. If possible, the seller should arrange to have the meter read near the date of settlement so that the seller can pay for any excess charges incurred to the date of closing. Otherwise, it will be necessary to make provisions for those charges at settlement as discussed below.

(d) Judgments

In the event that there are outstanding judgments against the premises, the seller must either arrange with the judgment creditor to have the judgment satisfied of record prior to settlement or the seller must deposit at settlement an amount of money sufficient to pay any such judgment so that it may be satisfied by the party in charge of the settlement.

Often the title searcher picks up judgments against people whose names are similar to seller. If, in fact the judgments are not against seller, they will normally be removed from the title report if seller signs an affidavit to the title insurer stating that he is not the judgment debtor.

(e) Miscellaneous Title Objections

There may be any number of miscellaneous objections which will arise in a title report. Miscellaneous title objections are often removed by the title company in reliance upon a sworn affidavit of the seller verifying the existence of facts which satisfy the objection.

---

3. Title companies are often willing to rely upon such statements from local, institutional mortgage lenders, but would be unlikely to do so if the mortgagee were a private individual or non-institutional lender not familiar to them.

For example, there may be a standard objection on a title report relating to the competency of the seller to sign the deed. That objection might be removed by an affidavit to the effect that the sellers are of legal age and have not been declared to be legally incompetent. Other objections will require more than an affidavit for removal. If, for example, the seller is presently unmarried, but had been previously married and divorced, the seller might have to produce a copy of the divorce decree.

3. Documents Needed for Special Situations

The following documents will be necessary for settlements where the seller is not an individual or where certain facts are present, such as the existence of leases.

(a) Corporation as Seller

If the seller is a corporation, the title company will require the seller to produce a certified copy of resolutions of the board of directors authorizing the sale of the property.[4] In addition to corporate resolutions, it may be necessary to produce the corporate charter at the closing in order to prove the existence of the corporation. In the event that the corporation is a foreign corporation,[5] it may be necessary to obtain a certificate of authority from the state in which the property is located. That certificate should indicate that the seller is registered to do business and is in good standing in the state in which the property is located. Sometimes, where the seller is a corporation, the state may have a lien against the property for payment of state corporate taxes. Depending upon the procedures in the particular state, either such taxes may be paid at the settlement or a certificate which allows the property to be transferred clear of state taxes may be obtained in advance. If the seller is a corporation, often the deed will have to be signed by two officers. The corporate seal normally will be affixed to the deed.

(b) Leased Property

The agreement of sale must be reviewed in order to determine what is to be done concerning occupancy leases for the property, if any.

(i) Termination of Leases

Where the leases are to be terminated prior to settlement, it is necessary to send the appropriate termination notices and take appro-

---

4. The title company will often also require certified resolutions from a purchaser corporation, especially if the purchaser is obtaining a purchase money mortgage loan.

5. A foreign corporation is simply one which is not chartered under the laws of the state in question. If a settlement involves land in Alabama, then as far as that settlement is concerned, a Georgia corporation is a foreign corporation.

priate steps to free the premises for occupancy by the purchaser. Sometimes, because of the length of time by which notice must be given to an existing tenant, the property will not be vacated by tenants until after settlement. In such a case, it is necessary to tender at the settlement proof that the seller has sent the proper termination notices.

(ii) Assignment of Leases

If the existing leases are to be assigned to the purchaser, it is necessary for someone to prepare an assignment of those leases, to be presented at the closing. In addition, someone should prepare notices to each tenant, to be signed by the landlord, indicating that future rental payments are to be made to the purchaser. These notices will be delivered by the seller at the settlement. The question of which party actually prepares the assignment and the notices will vary from one jurisdiction to another and from one transaction to another.

(c) Purchase Money Mortgage

In the event that the property is to be conveyed subject to a purchase money mortgage to be given by the purchaser to the seller, it will be necessary for someone to prepare the note and the mortgage to be signed by the purchaser at the closing. Again, these may be prepared by the seller or by the purchaser. In either event, the party preparing the documents should submit them to the other party well in advance of the settlement for review and possible revision. The seller-lender may also have to make certain disclosures to the purchaser, as discussed in section III of this chapter.

(d) New Construction

Where the premises to be conveyed are newly constructed, several documents relating to the construction may have to be tendered at the settlement.

(i) Release of Liens and Proof of Payment From Contractors and Subcontractors

In order to satisfy provisions in the Agreement of Sale concerning conveyance of the property free and clear of liens, it may be necessary to produce a release of liens signed by all contractors, subcontractors and materialmen who were involved in work at the premises. In the event that the signature of any such party has not been obtained on a release, the seller may submit receipts or other proofs of payment, including affidavits.

(ii) Subdivision Approval

If the property to be conveyed is part of a subdivision the seller may have the responsibility of submitting proof that the subdivision plan has been approved by the appropriate local authorities.[6]

(iii) Use and Occupancy Certificate

Often, in the case of new construction, it is the obligation of the seller to produce at the closing a certificate from the appropriate local authorities indicating that the building has been inspected and that construction has been performed in compliance with the local building codes. Without such a certificate, often called a certificate of occupancy, it may be impossible for the purchaser to occupy and use the building.

(e) Conveyance Where Record Owner is Deceased

A variety of problems may arise where one of the record owners of the premises has died.

(i) Joint Tenant Survives

In the event that the property is owned by a husband and wife as tenants by the entirety, or is owned by joint tenants with the right of survivorship, and one of the spouses or joint tenants dies, the property automatically passes to the other spouse or joint tenant. If this has happened, it will be necessary to produce at settlement proof of the death of the deceased spouse or joint tenant. Proof of death may be in the form of any actual death certificate or it may be sufficient for the remaining spouse or joint tenant to give an affidavit concerning the death of the deceased spouse or joint tenant.

(ii) Property Now Owned by One Not Named In the Last Recorded Deed

If the grantee named in the last deed is not the present owner, it will be necessary for the present owner to establish right of ownership at the time he sells the property. If the named grantee was an individual who has died, then in order to establish that right, the seller would normally have to produce a certified copy of the recorded will of the decedent. If there is no will, then he must submit proof of distribution of the property to the present owner. In addition, proof of the death of the grantee named in the last deed would be necessary. If the prior grantee were a corporation that had dissolved with the property passing by law to the shareholders, then the shareholders would have to show proof of such dissolution and of their status as shareholders.

---

6. In some circumstances, the purchaser may have the responsibility for obtaining subdivision approval, especially in instances where the purchaser is acquiring land for development.

If the property is being sold by the executor or administrator of the estate of the grantee named in the last deed, the personal representative would have to submit at the closing proof of appointment as the personal representative of the decedent. That proof would typically take the form of a certified copy of the Letters Testamentary or Letters of Administration granted to the personal representative.

(iii) Inheritance and/or Estate Tax Waivers

In the above cases relating to a deceased prior owner, it will be necessary to obtain from the taxing authorities (state and federal) either documents indicating that the estate tax due by the estate of the grantee in the last deed has been paid or documents waiving the right of the taxing authority to seek payment from the property to be conveyed.[7]

(f) Residential Property

An agreement of sale for residential property often provides for certain miscellaneous documents to be tendered to the purchaser at the closing.

(i) Termite Certificate

The residential agreement of sale may provide for the seller to tender at the closing a certificate of a termite control company stating that the premises are free and clear of termites and damage from termites.

(ii) Miscellaneous Certificates

Sometimes the agreement of sale requires the seller to have various systems within the premises, such as the heating, plumbing and electrical systems, inspected prior to settlement, and to provide at settlement certifications respecting the satisfactory functioning of those systems. If the property is being sold to a purchaser receiving either an FHA or VA mortgage, the rules of those agencies will require many of these certifications.

(g) Commercial—Industrial Properties

There are certain documents in addition to those mentioned above which often must be obtained in connection with the settlement of commercial or industrial properties.

---

7. A title company may be willing to accept a letter from a party which it trusts, such as a local bank or law firm, stating either that the estate is not subject to inheritance or estate taxes or that the party writing the letter will make sure that the taxes are paid. The bank or law firm might be willing to give such a letter because it is executor of the estate, or counsel to the estate.

(i) Zoning Classification Certifications

Often the agreement of sale will provide that the seller must tender to the buyer at settlement a certification setting forth the zoning classification of the property and declaring that its present use is consistent with the zoning ordinance.

(ii) Licenses

If the purchaser is purchasing the property in order to continue an existing business, it may be necessary for the seller to transfer to the purchaser at closing various licenses or permits relating to operation of the premises.

(iii) Bill of Sale

Where the property to be conveyed is a commercial or industrial site, there may be valuable personal property transferred in connection with the purchase and sale. In such a case, it is often the custom to have a bill of sale executed by the seller transferring the personal property tendered at settlement.

(iv) Inventory of Supplies at the Premises

If any supplies to be used in the operation of the property remain at the time of settlement, they must be valued just prior to settlement so that the seller can charge the purchaser for those items. An example of supplies would be heating fuel remaining in the tanks. The inventory process can be much more complicated if the sale of the real estate is in conjunction with the sale of a business, such as a grocery store.

B. PREPARATION BY THE PURCHASER

The discussion which follows is intended to outline the purchaser's preparation for settlement. The purchaser must prepare certain documents and review others to insure that he is receiving what he has been promised. In addition, the purchaser must obtain the money to be tendered to the seller at settlement.

1. Title Report

The first step in preparing for the settlement is normally to order a title search or a title report on the property. Once the title report has been received by the purchaser, he should send a copy to the seller in order to inform the seller of the objections that the seller must remove in order to convey good title. The purchaser should also send a copy of the title report to the proposed mortgagee, if any. The title report will also be useful as the source of the legal description to be inserted in the deed.

2. Deed

The purchaser may be responsible for the preparation of the deed. If requested to do so, the preparer should send the deed to the other party for review in advance of settlement.

3. Survey

If the purchaser desires or is required to have a survey, it will be necessary to contact a surveyor or engineer and arrange for the preparation of the survey. The attorney for the purchaser should make certain the survey includes all of the property described in the agreement of sales.

4. Inspection of Property

Where the agreement of sale grants the purchaser a right of inspection prior to settlement, the purchaser should arrange for such an inspection.

5. Mortgage

When the settlement has finally been scheduled, the purchaser must notify the mortgagee of the exact time and place of settlement several days in advance.[8] The mortgagee will either prepare the necessary mortgage documents or forward blank forms to the purchaser for preparation by his attorney. The mortgage commitment should be carefully checked for any other requirements imposed by the lender, which may include advance receipt of insurance policies, termite certificates or the like. In any event, the purchaser should receive the documents in advance of settlement to review them.

The attorney for the purchaser will also have to determine from the mortgagee the amount, if any, of prepaid interest, tax escrow and fees which the purchaser will be required to pay at settlement. Calculation of prepaid interest and the various methods of disclosing the costs relating to closing and to the loan are discussed later in this chapter.

6. Fire Insurance

It is desirable to arrange in advance of settlement to obtain a fire insurance policy covering the premises to be purchased. A mortgagee will insist upon insurance being in effect as of the time of settlement and will insist upon receiving a copy of the policy at settlement. The policy must contain a clause acknowledging the interest of the mortgagee in the proceeds of the fire insurance. It is important for the purchaser's attorney to make certain that the purchaser has secured the necessary policy well in advance of settlement and

---

8. Often the mortgage commitment requires that such notice be received within a specified number of days.

brings a copy with him to the settlement. The amount of the fire insurance policy must at least equal the principal sum of the mortgage.

7.   Public Utilities

The purchaser should notify the various public utilities whose services he will require of the date on which he will want the premises served. For example, it will be necessary to arrange in advance for electricity, gas, telephone and water service to begin on a specific date.

8.   Advance Calculation of Funds Needed to Complete Settlement

The purchaser's major obligation at a closing is to tender the consideration for the premises. As you realize by now, the amount of money which the purchaser will need to complete the settlement will differ from the remainder of purchase price left to pay. The purchaser's attorney will have to calculate the amount of money which the purchaser will need to complete the settlement. In doing so, the attorney, or paralegal, will have to apportion taxes and other apportionable expenses, and contact the various parties as to what charges they will impose at settlement, such as charges by the mortgagee and the title insurance company. Expenses such as transfer taxes, notary fees and recording costs will also have to be calculated. Some of these items might change because the date of settlement might change. The calculation of the apportionments and expenses will be discussed in detail later in this chapter.

When a determination of exactly how much the purchaser will need to complete settlement has been made, the purchaser's attorney should send a letter setting forth this amount.[9] The letter should specify the type of check (e. g., certified) which the purchaser must bring to the settlement. The letter should also indicate the exact day, time and place of settlement.

9.   Notice of Settlement

If the agreement of sale calls for either party to give notice of settlement to the other, such notice must be prepared and sent as specified in the agreement.

10.   Special Situations

The discussion which follows relates to tasks which have to be performed only where the purchaser is a corporation or where the property is subject to a lease.

---

9.   Often, a purchaser's attorney will add a certain sum to the calculation of the settlement costs in order to have a cushion in case there was some error in the calculations or in case there is some unexpected expense at settlement. Any excess will be reimbursed to the purchaser at settlement.

(a) Purchaser as Corporation

Where the purchaser is a corporation, the following documents may be needed for the settlement:

(i) Corporate Resolutions

The seller may require that the purchaser present at the settlement a certified copy of resolutions of the board of directors authorizing the purchase of the premises. If there is to be a mortgage, then the lender or the title company will almost certainly require such resolutions, which must include authorization for creation of the mortgage.

(ii) Corporate Charter

It may be necessary to produce the corporate charter at the closing as evidence of the corporation's existence.

(iii) Certificate of Authority

In the event that the corporation purchasing the premises is a foreign corporation, it will often be necessary to present at the settlement a certificate of authority to do business, as well as a "good standing" certificate evidencing the continued qualification of the corporation to do business in the state in which the property is located. Such certificates are available from the state's corporation bureau.

(b) Property Subject to Lease

If the property is subject to one or more leases, an assignment of lease and notice to tenants will be needed. Again, depending upon the custom of the jurisdiction in which you work, the assignment of lease and notices to tenants may be prepared by the purchaser or by the seller.

III. SETTLEMENT FOR THE PURCHASE AND SALE OF PROPERTY

The next section of these materials will focus on the problems of the actual settlement. Most of the documents needed for the settlement have been referred to above. In the event that the preparation for settlement has been carefully carried out, the settlement itself will be quite simple. If the transaction is very complex, it may be wise to arrange for a rehearsal of the closing. The purpose of a rehearsal is to make certain that all documents which are necessary for the settlement are complete and that there are no matters which must still be negotiated. In addition, all of the computations concerning the purchase price may be made in advance.

A. PLACE OF CLOSING

The place at which a closing is held will vary according to the practice in your part of the country. It is common to hold settlements for the purchase of real estate in the offices of title insurance companies, real estate brokers and attorneys.

B. SETTLEMENT CLERK

In order to expedite the settlement, it is normal for one person to act as a clerk in charge of the settlement. That person is the recipient of all signed documents and money. It is the clerk's task to make certain that each party receives the appropriate documents, that all checks are drawn and forwarded to the appropriate recipients and that any documents requiring recordation are in fact recorded and then returned to the appropriate parties. Where the purchaser's title is being insured by a title insurance company, it is common for the title insurance company to provide a settlement clerk. It is also common for a real estate agent, attorney or employee of a bank to perform the same duties.

C. MECHANICS OF THE SETTLEMENT

The discussion which follows is intended to familiarize the student with the various activities which take place at settlement.

1. Record of Parties Present

In order to obtain a complete record concerning the closing, the attorneys for each party should prepare a list of all of the persons present.

2. Execution and Exchange of Documents

At the settlement all of the documents which we have discussed in the previous sections of this Chapter must be signed, acknowledged and tendered to the settlement clerk or to the party who is to receive the document. In many instances the settlement clerk will be a notary public and make take any necessary acknowledgements.[10]

3. Conforming Copies of the Documents

In addition to the original documents which are tendered at the settlement, each party should make certain to retain several extra copies in order to maintain a complete record of the transaction.

---

10. If the settlement clerk is not a notary public, then the parties will have to make some advance arrangement for a notary public to be present, unless one of the other parties to be present is permitted in to take acknowledgements in that jurisdiction. As you may recall, in many states an attorney of that state is permitted to take acknowledgements.

These may be conformed copies. A conformed copy is an unexecuted copy of an original document. The unexecuted copy is marked to indicate that the original has been executed. Typically this is done by printing the name of the person or persons who have signed the document on the signature line. In addition, the symbol "/s/" is printed prior to the name. An example of a conformed signature is set forth below:

/s/ John Seller

_____

John Seller

4. Computation of the Amount to be Paid by Purchaser

As mentioned above, there are various adjustments, apportionments and calculations which must be made in order to determine how much money the purchaser needs to bring in order to complete settlement.

(a) Purchase Price

The purchaser must pay the purchase price to the seller at settlement. In calculating how much of the purchase price the purchaser needs to bring to settlement, you should credit towards the gross amount of the purchase price the sum of the following:

(i) any deposit which the purchaser has already paid;

(ii) the amount of any purchase money note which the seller has agreed to accept; and

(iii) the amount of any third-party mortgage financing.

(b) Apportionments

The following are income and expense items relating to the property which are typically apportioned between the parties. Apportionment means that an expense (or an income item) is allocated so that each party bears a burden (or obtains a benefit) proportionate to his share of the time for which the expense accrued.

(i) Real Estate Taxes

If the real estate taxes for the year of settlement have been paid by the seller, or are to be paid by him at the closing, it will be necessary for the purchaser to pay the seller for the purchaser's proportionate share of taxes for the remainder of the tax year after the date of closing. On the other hand, if the tax bill will be paid by the purchaser, the seller must give the purchaser a credit for the seller's pro rata share of the bill.

Example: Suppose that the real estate taxes are $3600, are assessed for the calendar year and paid in advance. If settlement is held on September 15, then the purchaser should reimburse the seller for 3 months and 15 days worth of taxes. Each month's share is $300 and each day's share is $10. Thus the purchaser must pay the seller an additional $1050 for the apportionment of taxes ($3 \times$ $300 plus $15 \times$ $10).

(ii) Water and Sewer Rents

If minimum charges for water and/or sewer rents have been prepaid by the seller for periods extending beyond the date of closing, those minimum charges should be adjusted by requiring the purchaser to pay his pro rata share. If, on the other hand, the purchaser will receive a bill after closing, which would cover a period prior to closing, it will be necessary for the seller to make an adjustment in favor of the purchaser.

Example: Suppose that minimum water rents are $45 for a 3-month period, assessed every 3 months from January 15th of every year and paid in arrears. If settlement is on September 15, the seller must give the purchaser credit for the 2 month period from July 15 to September 15, which would equal $30 ($\frac{\$45}{3} \times 2$).

If the water meter has not been read immediately prior to closing, an adjustment will also have to be made for any excess water which may have been consumed by the seller since the last meter reading. That amount can be estimated based on previous bills which have been paid by the seller. Alternatively, the seller may be required to place a portion of the proceeds of sale in escrow to be applied to the excess water bill after the meter has been read.

(iii) Rental Payments

If the premises being sold are subject to one or more leases, an adjustment will have to be made for rental payments. If the purchaser will or may receive rental payments from tenants covering periods prior to the date of settlement, the agreement of sale may provide that those payments will be apportioned and that the seller will receive his pro rata share of the payments only after they are actually paid by the tenant or it may provide that the rent will be apportioned at settlement as if they were already received.

Normally rents are prepaid. Therefore, the only adjustments which will be made at settlement will pertain to those rental payments which have already been paid to the seller and which cover periods after the date of settlement. The seller must credit the purchaser at the closing with the purchaser's pro rata share of such income. For example, if a tenant has paid $200 rent to the seller on the first day of the month, and settlement occurs on the 15th day of that month, the purchaser would be entitled to a $100 credit as his share of the rent for the remaining one-half of the month.

(iv) Security Deposits

If tenants have made security deposits, it will be the obligation of the purchaser as the new owner of the building, to return the deposits at the end of the lease terms. Therefore, the seller must either credit the purchaser with the total amount of such deposits, or assign the deposits to the purchaser.

(v) Insurance

Often, the seller will assign the existing fire insurance policy to the purchaser. In that event, the purchaser will have to pay the seller a pro rata share of any premium already paid by the seller.

(vi) Miscellaneous Apportionments

A variety of miscellaneous apportionments covering such matters as fuel and other supplies on the premises, salaries of employees at the premises, and related matters, may be made at the settlement depending upon the circumstances of the purchase and the provisions of the agreement of sale.

(c) Expenses of Settlement

The purchaser will also incur a variety of expenses relating to the purchase of the premises and the obtaining of mortgage financing for the purchase. These expenses are normally paid at or prior to the settlement.

(i) Title Insurance Charges

If the purchaser's title is to be insured by a title insurance company, the premium is normally paid by the purchaser at the settlement. Each title insurance company publishes a schedule of its premiums. Normally the premiums increase as the amount of title insurance increases.

(ii) Recording Fees

The purchaser will incur recording fees in connection with the recordation of the deed and the mortgage.

(iii) Brokerage Charges

In most transactions involving the purchase of real estate, brokerage commissions will be born by the seller. However, the parties sometimes agree that some or all of the commission is to be borne by the purchaser. In that event, the purchaser will pay a share of the commission at the closing.

The broker may also perform certain extra services for the purchaser for which he will be compensated at the closing. These may include preparation of the deed, if that is the purchaser's responsibility.

(iv) Attorney's Fees

Depending upon the practice of a particular attorney and the custom of the community, the fee due the attorney for representation of the purchaser may be paid at the settlement or a bill may be rendered at a later date.

(v) Extras

In the event that the premises being purchased are being constructed by the builder/seller, the purchaser may have agreed to purchase certain extras from the builder. The cost of those items will be added to the purchase price and paid in advance or at settlement, as provided in the agreement of sale.

(vi) Personal Property

In the event that the purchaser has agreed to purchase items of personal property from the seller, the cost of such property must be added to the purchase price. In addition, if the personal property is extensive, a bill of sale may be tendered at the settlement.

(vii) Payments to Mortgagee

(aa) Placement Fees and Service Charges

It may be necessary to make a variety of payments to the mortgagee at the settlement. The mortgagee may impose a commitment fee and may also make charges for credit reports, appraisals, preparation of documents and other related matters. The charges which must be tendered at settlement will be set forth in the mortgagee's commitment letter. In addition to the above charges, the mortgagee may require the purchaser to pay the fee of the attorney representing the mortgagee.

(bb) Prepaid Interest

Typically the first mortgage payment of principal and interest will not be due for several weeks after the closing. One must contact the mortgagee in advance of settlement in order to determine when the first payment of principal will be due. In many instances, the mortgagee will require the buyer to prepay at settlement the interest charges from the date of settlement to the date of the first principal payment, or to the date which is one month (or other regular interest period) prior to the date of the first principal payment. As you remember from Chapter Eight, the question of the date to which prepaid interest will be paid depends upon whether interest is to be paid in arrears or in advance. If it is to be paid in advance, then interest must be prepaid to the date of first payment of principal and interest. For example, if the buyer is borrowing $50,000 from the mortgagee at 8% interest (in advance) and if 36 days will elapse between the date of closing and the first mortgage payment, the prepaid interest is calculated as follows: 8% interest per annum on $50,000 equals

$4,000. The interest for 36 days equals $4,000 $\times$ $^{36}/_{365}$ or approximately $394.00.[11]

(viii) Mechanics' Lien Insurance

In the event that the premises to be purchased are new, or have undergone extensive repairs in the recent past, the mortgagee may require insurance against the possibility of a mechanics' lien being filed against the premises. Such insurance is normally issued as an endorsement to the basic title insurance policy. The cost of the endorsement is generally based on the amount of mortgage title insurance being purchased.

(ix) Transfer or Recording Tax

If the state or local government levies a transfer or recording tax, the amount of that tax to be borne by the buyer is paid by buyer at settlement.

Typically all payments are made directly to the order of the bank, title company or the law firm for whom the settlement clerk works. The settlement clerk then aggregates the sums paid, and then breaks down that sum into separate checks in order to make the necessary payments to tax authorities, sellers, attorneys, brokers, mortgagees, recording offices and real estate agents. The settlement clerk will also issue a check covering any overpayment made at the settlement by the purchaser.

5. Payments by the Seller

The apportionments between the purchaser and the seller affect the total sum which the seller will take from settlement. From the proceeds, the seller must pay all of the expenses of sale, which might include commissions, payoffs of mortgages and judgments, attorney's fees, transfer taxes, payment for certification and the like. The amount that the seller takes from settlement is the net proceeds.

6. Settlement Sheet

Generally, it is the obligation of the settlement clerk to prepare a "settlement sheet" which sets forth all of the payments and apportionments which must be made by both parties. If the Real Estate Settlement Procedures Act applies to this transaction, the Uniform Settlement Form must be used.

---

11. Remember, many banks treat the year as consisting of only 360 days, with each month having 30 days. In such case the calculation would be $\frac{4000 \times 36}{360} = \$400.$

7. Escrow Accounts

In the event that the seller has been unable or has failed for any reason to complete any of the pre-closing obligations, or in the event that payment of an unknown amount such as for excess water must be made after closing, the seller may be required to place a portion of the proceeds in an escrow account to be used to discharge a specific obligation. For example, if the seller has not obtained the satisfaction of a $1,000 judgment, the parties may agree that the seller should place $1,500 in escrow. As a result of the money being placed in escrow, the title insurer will be willing to insure the purchaser's title free of the judgment.

8. Marked-up Title Report

It is the duty of the settlement clerk to mark up the report of title indicating which objections will be removed and, therefore, not appear on the insurance policy to be issued to the purchaser. Those objections which remain appear as exceptions to the policy of insurance. The purchaser's attorney should retain a copy of the marked-up title report as that is the insurer's commitment to issue a policy.

IV. POST CLOSING—PURCHASE—SALE OF PROPERTY

After the settlement, several matters must still be attended to.

A. RECORDING

The deed and mortgage, if any, have been taken by the settlement clerk for recording. After the recorder has recorded and indexed the documents, he will normally forward them to the settlement clerk. The settlement clerk will send the deed to the purchaser's attorney who will usually forward the original directly to the client after making a copy for the attorney's own files.

B. TITLE POLICY

Some time after the documents have been recorded the title insurer will normally issue the actual title policy. The original title policy is usually forwarded to the client, and a copy of the title policy is retained for the attorney's file.

C. ESCROW

As mentioned above, escrow accounts may have been created at the settlement for payment of various sums. The items relating to the escrow accounts should be attended to, and any excess in the accounts should be returned to the seller promptly.

D. TENANT LETTER

If the premises are acquired subject to a lease, then the seller delivers at settlement letters to the various tenants indicating that rent should now be paid to the purchaser. The purchaser will send the letters to the various tenants after settlement.

E. BINDER

For ease of future reference, many lawyers prepare a binder containing all of the important documents relating to the transaction. A binder for the purchase of real estate might include a deed, mortgage, note, corporate resolutions of the seller, assignments of leases, notices to tenants, a survey, the Agreement of Sale, the marked-up title report, a copy of the final title policy and a closing report. The binder should contain a table of contents listing the documents it contains and identifying the transaction. The closing report will contain a list of the parties present at closing and a recitation of what took place at closing, including a discussion of any problems which arose and how they were resolved. It might also set forth a checklist of items that remain to be done.

Binders, including closing reports, are often the responsibility of a paralegal to prepare.

In Chapter Eight we discussed in detail the subject of mortgages. The following sections of this chapter will contain a brief review of the process of closing construction and permanent mortgages.

V. CONSTRUCTION LOAN CLOSING

A. PREPARATION FOR CLOSING

If the key to a closing is preparation, then the key to preparing for a construction loan closing is a close review of the commitment letter of the construction lender, the commitment letter of the permanent lender and the title report. These documents will set forth the items necessary to prepare for the closing. The following documents are those which typically must be prepared for the closing, by one party or another.

1. Note and Mortgage

The note and mortgage will normally be prepared either by the borrower on forms supplied by the permanent lender or by counsel for the lender. The terms of the note will be such as comply with the commitment letters.

2. Plans and Specifications

A complete set of plans and specifications will usually have to be submitted to the permanent lender and the construction lender for their approval in advance of closing.

3. General Construction Contract

The general construction contract will be executed in a form approved or supplied by the construction lender.

4. Corporate Resolutions

If the borrower is a corporation, a certified copy of corporate resolutions authorizing the borrower to incur the debt and create a mortgage should be prepared by the borrower for submission at the closing. It is preferable to have the form of resolution approved by the permanent lender, construction lender and title insurer before adoption by the borrower.

5. Survey

In addition to the plans and specifications, the construction and permanent lenders will normally want to review a survey of the property prior to the time of the closing.

6. Insurance

The commitment letters will undoubtedly contain requirements for fire insurance and in some cases liability insurance. Such policies must be obtained well in advance of settlement, and must set forth limits of liability consistent with the commitment letters. The commitment letters will require that the policies contain clauses recognizing the interest of the mortgagee.

7. Completion or Performance Bond

In the event that a completion or performance bond is required by the construction loan commitment, it must be obtained by the prospective general contractor in order to be tendered at settlement.

8. Construction Loan Agreement

The construction loan agreement between the borrower and the construction lender may be prepared by the borrower's attorney or by the lender's attorney. In any event that document will have to be approved by the borrower and the construction lender in advance of settlement.

9. Building Permit

The commitment letter will usually require the developer to submit at the closing, permits of the appropriate local authorities evidencing permission to build the proposed improvements. Such permits must be obtained in advance of closing.

10. Security Agreement and Financing Statements

If the commitment letter requires the borrower to execute a security agreement granting the lender a lien on personal property, then that document, along with the requisite financing statements, would typically be prepared by the borrower's attorney for approval of the lender's attorney in advance of closing.

11. Declaration of Cross Easements or Declaration of Reciprocal Easements

As discussed in Chapter Eight, certain transactions will require a reciprocal easement agreement.   Such an easement agreement would usually be prepared by the borrower's attorney, for approval of the lender's attorney, and for recording.

12. Buy-Sell Agreement

The buy-sell agreement is typically prepared by the construction or permanent lender and will be executed by both lenders and the owner at the construction loan closing.

13. Leases

If either or both of the commitment letters are conditioned upon certain leases being in existence at the time of the closing, then executed copies must be produced at or before closing.   In addition, it may be necessary to present estoppel certificates at the closing evidencing the fact that the borrower (as landlord) is not in violation of any lease as of the date of closing.

14. Assignment of Lease

Any leases that are in existence at the time of closing will be assigned to the construction lender, who will assign the assignment of leases to the permanent lender when the permanent lender purchases the note and mortgage.

15. Subordination Agreement

In the event that an existing lease would be superior to the construction mortgage and is to be subordinated, a subordination agreement must be prepared and tendered at the closing.

16. Attornment/Non-Disturbance Agreement

If there are to be leases on the premises subordinate to the mortgage, the lender and lessee may require the existence of an attornment/non-disturbance agreement at the time of the closing. The lessee will probably not be present at the mortgage loan closing and, therefore, all documents to be signed by the lessee, such as the lease, estoppel certificate, and attornment/non-disturbance agreement must be signed by the lessee in advance of closing.

17. Waiver of Mechanics' Lien

If a waiver of mechanics' lien is to be filed at the closing, the borrower must obtain the executed waiver from the general contractor prior to the closing.   In addition, the title company may require that photographs of the premises be taken prior to closing evidencing that no work has begun.

18. Letter of Permanent Lender Approving Documents

The construction lender will often require that all of the documentation for the closing be submitted to counsel for the permanent lender in advance of the closing and that counsel for the permanent lender issue a letter to the borrower and the construction lender indicating that the permanent lender has reviewed and approved the documents.

19. Title Report

If the lenders require the issuance of a title policy certifying that its lien is a valid first lien, then the borrower must order the title report and distribute copies to the permanent and construction lenders. Often the title company will indicate, after consultation with the borrower, which of the objections on the title report it expects to remove at the closing. The lenders may require that information in advance.

20. Letter Confirming Date of Closing

When all of the documents have been drafted, reviewed and approved by the parties, one of the parties (usually the borrower) will send all the parties a notice letter confirming the date, time and place of closing.

21. Rehearsal for Closing

Because of the complexity of many construction loan closings, the parties to a particular transaction may conduct a rehearsal (sometimes called a dry closing) in order to determine what remains to be done.

B. CLOSING

1. Place of Closing

As in the case of a purchase, the closing might take place at a title company, a lawyer's office or a bank. In the event that a title company will insure the title of the mortgagee, it is typical for an employee of the title company to act as the settlement clerk.

2. Parties Present

As in the case of the purchase of property, a list should be prepared setting forth information concerning the parties present at the closing.

3. Mechanics of Closing

Closing itself will be very similar to the closing for the purchase of property. The parties will exchange various executed documents. Some documents, such as the mortgage, financing statements, and possibly a memorandum of lease, assignment of lease or a reciprocal easement agreement, will be left with the settlement clerk for recording. The attorneys should be certain to prepare conformed copies of all documents for their files. In addition, the borrower will be required to make certain payments.

(a) Expenses of the Borrower

(i) Placement Fees

If there are any placement fees or similar charges to be paid by the borrower at the time of the closing, such items may be deducted from the proceeds of the loan. If there is to be no disbursement on the loan at the closing, or if any such fees may not be taken from the proceeds of the loan, the borrower must pay such expenses at the closing.

(ii) Tax Escrow

If the borrower is required to escrow $\frac{1}{12}$ of annual taxes monthly, it may be required to make payments into the escrow account at the closing.

(iii) Discharge of Liens

If there are objections to title based on taxes due, judgments against the borrower or prior mortgages, these items must be discharged at the closing by the borrower depositing sufficient funds with the settlement clerk.

(iv) Lender's Attorney's Fee

Often the commitment letter will provide that borrower must pay the fee of lender's attorney relating to the loan being closed. That payment will normally be made at the closing.

(v) Title Insurance Premium

Borrower will be required at the closing to pay the premium for the policy insuring lender's lien.

(vi) Miscellaneous Expenses

Borrower may incur additional expenses for items such as recording costs, notary fees, and mortgage taxes, which may be minor or may be a substantial expense.

(b) Settlement Sheet

As in the case of a purchase, a settlement sheet will be prepared by the settlement clerk. The settlement sheet will evidence payment of the items discussed above.

(c) Marked-Up Title Report

The settlement clerk will mark up one or more copies of the title report indicating the state of title which will be insured to the mortgagee.

C. POST CLOSING

As in the case of the purchase of property, there are several steps which must be taken after the closing.

1. Recordation of the Mortgage and Other Documents

The mortgage must be recorded and forwarded to the lender by the settlement clerk after recordation. In addition, any financing statements, leases and reciprocal easement agreements must be recorded.

2. Issuance of Title Policy

Typically the title insurance company will not issue a policy until the loan is bought by the permanent lender. Instead, the commitment will be kept open and, although the lender has a right to have a policy issued, the lender will normally not require the issuance of a policy unless a claim arises.

3. Binder

Because of the large number of documents involved, many attorneys prepare a binder similar to that for an acquisition settlement.

Some time after the construction loan closing, the construction on the premises will presumably be completed and conditions for closing the permanent loan will have been met.

VI. PERMANENT LOAN CLOSING

A. PREPARATION FOR CLOSING

Where a permanent loan is not part of a package with a construction loan, then preparation is similar to preparation for a construction loan, except that there will be no buy-sell agreement, no construction loan agreement and no construction contract. Settlement of a permanent loan pursuant to a buy-sell agreement will involve some or all of the following:

1. Assignment of Mortgage

An assignment of the mortgage from the construction lender to the permanent lender must be prepared, and executed by the construction lender.

2. Certificate of Occupancy

In many instances, the permanent commitment letter will require as a condition for closing that the local governmental authorities must have issued a certificate acknowledging that construction is sufficiently complete that the premises may be occupied for their intended purpose. Such a certificate must be obtained by the borrower for submission at the closing.

3. As-Built Survey

Often the permanent lender's commitment letter will require that the borrower submit an as-built survey at the time of closing. The purpose of this survey is to insure the lender that the buildings and on-site improvements are within the title line of the premises and that the buildings and improvements have been constructed in the locations shown by the plans and specifications, with the normal allowances for field conditions.

4. Rent Roll

If disbursement under the permanent loan commitment is contingent upon achievement of a certain minimum rent roll, it will be necessary for the borrower to submit to the lender a list of all leases in effect. In addition to the list, the lender may want to examine each of the leases.

5. Estoppel Certificates

If leases are to be assigned to the mortgagee, the permanent lender will require estoppel certificates from some or all tenants evidencing that the owner is not in default in its obligations as landlord.

6. Declaration of No Set Off

The declaration of no set off assures the permanent lender, who takes the mortgage by assignment from the construction lender, that it is not accepting the mortgage subject to defenses of the borrower against the assignor.

7. Security Agreements and Financing Statements

Either a new set will be prepared or the old set will be assigned by the construction lender to the permanent lender.

8. Corporate Resolutions

A certified copy of corporate resolutions of the borrower, authorizing the permanent loan, must be prepared by the attorney for the borrower and submitted at the permanent loan closing. These may already have been delivered as a part of the construction loan closing.

9. Advance Arrangements for Pay-Off of Construction Lender

At the closing, the permanent lender will disburse the amount of his mortgage or a percentage of that amount if a rental achievement has not been met. The sum to be disbursed by the permanent lender will be used to pay off the construction lender. If the mortgage is for a substantial sum, the borrower will desire to expedite the transfer of funds from the permanent lender to the construction lender in order to minimize interest payments. Interest will have to be paid to the permanent lender from the date of the permanent loan closing. Interest will be paid to the construction lender each day until the construction lender's account has been credited with repayment of the loan. If the parties merely tender checks at the closing and put the checks through for normal deposit, the overlap could require the borrower to pay interest to both lenders for several days. In order to prevent that, the borrower will often arrange for the permanent lender to deposit its funds at the closing either by tendering at the closing a check drawn directly on the Federal Reserve Bank of the district in which the closing takes place (and putting that check through for immediate deposit), or by wiring funds from the permanent lender's account directly into the account of the construction lender without a check being tendered at settlement. In the event that you are working on a permanent loan closing, you should inquire of the lawyer for whom you are working whether special arrangements should be made in order to minimize interest charges to the borrower. These arrangements obviously must be made in advance.

10. Title Bring Down

Some time prior to settlement the title insurance company must be notified to undertake a bring down search from the date of the construction loan closing to the date of the proposed permanent loan closing.

11. Notice to Parties

The borrower normally notifies the lenders of the date, time and place of settlement by a letter.

B. CLOSING

The closing for the permanent loan will again be very similar to the other closings we have considered.

1. Place of Closing

The closing will take place at a bank, title company or law firm.

2. Parties Present

At a permanent loan closing the borrower and representatives of the permanent lender, construction lender and title company will usually be present. Again, there will be need for a settlement clerk to record documents and handle the exchange of funds. As in the case of all closings, a list of parties present should be prepared for inclusion in the closing report.

3. Mechanics of Closing

The closing will be relatively simple as there are only a limited number of documents to be exchanged. In addition, the construction lender will be paid off.

(a) Exchange of Money

(i) Pay-Off of Construction Lender

The permanent lender will purchase the construction loan note for the amount due on the note. If the permanent loan is to be advanced in stages and if the first advance is insufficient to purchase the note, then the borrower must first repay the excess principal balance of the note to the construction lender. If the permanent loan disbursement exceeds the sum due on the note, then the borrower will first receive the excess from the construction lender as a loan. In either event, the new principal balance of the note will be the amount disbursed by the permanent lender, whether that amount is equal to or more or less than the principal balance that had been due to the construction lender prior to settlement.

(ii) Final Interest Payment to Construction Lender

The borrower must make a final interest payment to the construction lender covering the interest due from the date of the last interest payment to the date of closing (or later, if the funds paid to the construction lender at closing are not immediate funds).

(iii) Return of Borrower's Stand-By Fee

Most permanent lenders require a prospective borrower to make a substantial deposit in order to secure the obligations of the borrower under the commitment. Such a deposit may be refundable at the time that the permanent loan is closed.

(iv) Escrows

In addition to normal tax escrows, the permanent lender may require other escrows, especially for work that has not been completed and for tenant space finishing work that the borrower has contracted to perform in the various occupancy leases.

The discussions under construction loan closings relating to tax escrows, lender's attorney's fees, title insurance premiums and miscellaneous expenses also apply to the permanent loan closing.

(b) Settlement Sheet

A settlement sheet will be prepared by the settlement clerk setting forth all of the items referred to in (a) above.

(c) Marked-Up Title Report

The title policy will be marked up and assigned to the permanent lender. A copy of the marked-up report will be given to each party.

C. POST CLOSING

After the closing has taken place, the settlement clerk will record the assignment of the mortgage and any financing statements or assignments of financing statements. The assignment of mortgage and copies of the financing statements will be returned to the lender.

In the event that the full amount of the loan was not disbursed at closing, because of failure to meet a rental achievement, further disbursement may take place in the future as new leases are presented to the permanent lender. A closing may or may not be necessary for payment of those further sums, depending on whether the sums are already evidenced by the note, or whether another note will be required.

After the permanent loan closing the title company will issue a policy in favor of the permanent lender. The policy will usually be forwarded to the attorney for the permanent lender.

Following the closing a binder of documents should be prepared.

VII. DISCLOSURE AND THE REAL ESTATE SETTLEMENT PROCEDURES ACT OF 1974

A. INTRODUCTION

Continuing a long tradition in western civilization, the various American state governments have enacted a variety of laws to protect individuals with respect to the lending of money or extension of credit. The oldest tradition is of proscriptive statutes, and all the states still have some form of proscriptive statutes. The most familiar is a usury law, which in its strictest form sets a legal maximum interest rate above which no lender or borrower may legally go, no matter how well informed the borrower or how necessary it is for the borrower to borrow the money. American usury laws, as we have previously noted, are a patchwork and vary from states that now have no such limit, to states that do not apply the limit to certain borrowers (such as corporations) or to certain loans (business loans over a certain amount or any loan over a larger amount), to states that apply the strict standard described above to all loans and all lenders. Other forms of proscriptive laws carve out areas in which only certain regulated institutions are permitted to act, such as commercial banks, building and loan associations, savings banks or associations, and the like.

The second major kind of statute is the disclosure statute. The impulse behind the proscriptive statutes is that there are certain transactions that society will simply not permit. The impulse behind the disclosure statute is that the consumer needs certain information in order to be able to operate effectively in the market and that the supplier will not provide that information unless forced to do so by competition or by law. Thus, the various disclosure acts are a requirement upon lenders, particularly institutional lenders. Again, state disclosure acts vary tremendously, but there is a common thread of requiring disclosures for those thought to be least able to demand it. The laws that we would be concerned with most pertain to real estate mortgage loans, and the disclosure laws are generally applicable only to single family or small multi-family residential mortgages.

State disclosure laws still exist in many states, but have been in large measure superseded by the federal Real Estate Settlement Procedures Act of 1974, known everywhere as RESPA. RESPA was a hybrid in that it was also a proscriptive statute, prohibiting certain forms of kickbacks, and referral fees, for example. But the major thrust was to provide uniform standards for disclosure of relevant information in a timely fashion. To that extent, RESPA represents a sharpening and extension in a limited field of the requirements of the federal Consumer Credit Protection Act of 1968, known commonly as the Truth-in-Lending Act, which governs disclosure respecting the lending of money and extension of credit much more generally, and not just in the context of a residential mortgage loan. RESPA by no means supplants Truth-in-Lending, indeed they are governed by different sets of regulations and even by different departments of the government.[12] Instead, RESPA supplements Truth-in-Lending.

This Chapter is not designed to make the reader an expert on RESPA or Truth-in-Lending. If your future job is with a lender, you might be required to work closely with disclosure and regulatory laws, and in that case you will be trained in their use by your employer. We will, however, take the opportunity of a brief review of RESPA to examine a settlement sheet for a hypothetical settlement to familiarize you with the type of information disclosed, the form of settlement sheet presently required by RESPA and the relationship between disclosure and the actual settlement costs.

B. SCOPE OF RESPA

1. Transactions Covered

Briefly, RESPA covers real estate mortgage loans in connection with the purchase of residential real estate. Residential real estate includes condominiums, mobile homes and cooperatives as well as traditional residences, and includes the purchase of a duplex, triplex or quadruplex. The loan must be made by a federal lender, as defined in the Act. The definition is so broad that almost any institutional lender falls within its definitions. The effect of the qualification is to exclude from RESPA only those residential purchase settlements in which either there is no mortgage involved or the mortgage involved is a purchase money mortgage given to the seller or a regular mortgage loan from a relative or friend.

---

12. RESPA is administered by the Department of Housing and Urban Development and the regulations relating to RESPA are generically known as Regulation X. Truth-in-Lending comes under the Treasury Department and the regulations are known as Regulation Z.

2. Prohibition Against Kickbacks and Unearned Fees

In many parts of the country, lenders, brokers and title insurance companies customarily paid referral fees to persons, such as brokers and lawyers, who directed a seller or purchaser/borrower to them. RESPA characterizes such referral fees and fee splitting as kickbacks and prohibits them in connection with a transaction covered by RESPA.

3. Limitations on Escrows

We have previously discussed, and shall review, the concept of escrow payments for taxes and insurance. RESPA places limitations on the amounts that a lender can require to be escrowed. The limitations have no effect on common practices and reach only to abuses.

4. Uniform Settlement Sheet

HUD has devised a uniform settlement sheet that is intended for use throughout the country, with only minor local variations permitted. The sheet must be used for all settlements to which RESPA applies. HUD believed that settlement sheets used in some areas were not complete and failed to disclose all that transpired at settlement. You must become familiar with the sheet and be able both to explain the sheet to a client and to use the sheet as a source of information after settlement. Section VIII(D) of this chapter is devoted to a discussion of the RESPA sheet.

C. DISCLOSURES

RESPA has already undergone significant revisions since its enactment in 1974. Many of these revisions related to changes in the pre-settlement disclosure requirements of RESPA, which many found to be unworkable and unproductive, if not counterproductive. As of 1977, RESPA and Truth-in-Lending required between them the disclosure of the items discussed below to the borrower, at various times during the transaction (but at latest at settlement). The lender is the party required to make the disclosures. Some of the disclosures required are of costs that are beyond the lender's control, but are costs that one can reasonably expect will in fact be incurred. To the extent that the lender does not control such costs, it may make good faith estimates, clearly marked as such with an "(e)" following the estimated figure (a figure rather than a range must presently be given).

1. Booklet

Each lender is supposed to supply to an applicant for a RESPA-covered loan a booklet prepared by HUD explaining home loan financing, the settlement costs that might be expected and the use of escrows for taxes.

2. Finance Charges and Annual Percentage Rate

At the time that the lender issues its commitment letter, it must disclose to the borrower, on a form conforming with Regulation Z, the basics of the loan. A copy of the presently permissible form is included in the Appendix on p. 455. These basics include:

a.   The amount of the loan, which is the purchase price less any downpayment, is shown as line I.D. on the Form.

b.   Prepaid finance charges, which are charges paid to the lender at or prior to settlement, and which include any commitment fee (presently 1% of loan amount by custom in the Philadelphia area), any prepaid interest (usually from the day of settlement through the end of the month), mortgage guaranty insurance and points (even though paid by the seller). This figure can be very misleading to a borrower if the borrower thinks that these represent the total of his closing costs. Care must be taken to explain that the term "prepaid finance charges" is a term of art [13] used to define only certain specific charges that are deducted in order to compute the Annual Percentage Rate as defined by Truth-in-Lending. The total prepaid finance charges are shown as line I.E.6. on the Form.

c.   The finance charge consists of the sum of prepaid finance charges, interest paid through the anticipated term of the loan and any other finance charges which are not prepaid. The total finance charge is shown as line II.D. This amount is treated as if it were all interest and is calculated using as the base the amount financed, rather than using the principal amount, over the stated term of the loan. The result is the Annual Percentage Rate. Whenever there are prepaid finance charges, then the annual percentage rate will be greater than the simple annual interest rate set forth in the note and as understood by home mortgage lenders and borrowers. As an example, a 1% service fee on a 25 year loan has the effect of making the annual percentage rate 8.25% on an 8% interest loan. You must be able to explain this difference to clients, as the result is often confusing to them.

d.   The Form also requires disclosure of the repayment terms (e. g., 300 equal and consecutive monthly payments) late charges, prepayment penalties and the security being taken for the loan.

3. RESPA Disclosures

RESPA originally required certain disclosures to be made at least 12 days prior to settlement, which requirement had the effect of

---

13. "Term of art" is itself a term of art; that is, a phrase or word having a defined meaning within a trade, profession or business.

not permitting parties to meet deadlines because they had to wait 12 days after disclosure even if everyone wanted an earlier settlement. As of 1977, RESPA requires the following disclosures at or before settlement:

a.   The cost of all settlement services charged to the borrower, which includes (inter alia) title charges, document preparations, inspections and certifications, appraisals, services rendered by an attorney or broker, and surveys.   Good faith estimates must be made if not known.   The reference to "services rendered by an attorney" does not apply to a fee to an attorney freely chosen by a borrower of their own volition and representing only the borrower and not the lender. Note that the total of settlement service charges of taxes and similar charges has many more components than prepaid finance charges.

b.   The remainder of the purchase price, the apportionments between buyer and seller and the amounts to be escrowed with the lender.

The sum of a. and b. should equal a good approximation of the total cash that the purchaser will have to pay before settlement, or bring to settlement to the extent not paid before settlement.

D. SETTLEMENT SHEET

The form of settlement sheet to be used in a RESPA settlement is included in these materials below. We will review this form by showing how it would be filled in at a settlement based upon the following hypothetical situation:

Example: Albert Browne is purchasing a home at 49 W. Landview Drive from Rose Sadowski for $50,000. Browne is obtaining a loan from Upper Dublin Bank for $40,000, for a term of 25 years at 8% per annum simple interest. Settlement is to take place on October 10. Real estate taxes are paid on a calendar year basis and are due on March 15 of each year. Presently, taxes are $1200 per year. Water and sewer are paid on the same bill, quarterly in advance, with a reading for excess every six months. The quarterly minimum is $35, and the average 6 month excess for this house is $24. The agreement of sale requires Sadowski to pay for a termite inspection and the 6% broker's commission to Hill 'N Dale Brokers. The mortgage commitment requires real estate tax escrows, a prepaid fire insurance policy, a survey and Pennsylvania endorsements 100 and 300 to the title insurance coverage given to the mortgage. The lender charges a 1% commitment fee (of which $75 has been paid with the application) and an appraisal fee of $90.

EXAMPLE: Settlement Sheet

A.		B. TYPE OF LOAN	
U.S. DEPARTMENT OF HOUSING AND URBAN DEVELOPMENT **DISCLOSURE/SETTLEMENT STATEMENT** APPLICATION No. *COMMONWEALTH LAND Title Insurance Company*		1. ☐ FHA 2. ☐ FMHA 3. ☐ CONV, UNINS, 4. ☐ VA 5. ☐ CONV. INS.	
		6. FILE NUMBER	7. LOAN NUMBER
If the Truth-in-Lending Act applies to this transaction, a Truth-in-Lending statement is attached as page 3 of this form.		8. MORTG. INS. CASE NO.	

C.   NOTE: This form is furnished to you prior to settlement to give you information about your settlement costs, and again after settlement to show the actual costs you have paid. The present copy of the form is:

☐ ADVANCE DISCLOSURE OF COSTS. Some items are estimated, and are marked "(e)". Some amounts may change if the settlement is held on a date other than the date estimated below. The preparer of this form is not responsible for errors or changes in amounts furnished by others.

☐ STATEMENT OF ACTUAL COSTS. Amounts paid to and by the settlement agent are shown. Items marked "(p.o.c.)" were paid outside the closing; they are shown here for informational purposes and are not included in totals.

D. NAME OF BORROWER	E. SELLER	F. LENDER
Albert Browne	Rose Sadowski	Upper Dublin Bank

G. PROPERTY LOCATION	H. SETTLEMENT AGENT	I. DATES	
49 W. Landview Drive Upper Dublin, Penna.	**COMMONWEALTH LAND TITLE INSURANCE COMPANY**	LOAN COMMITMENT	ADVANCE DISCLOSURE
	PLACE OF SETTLEMENT OFFICE CLOSER _____ NO.	SETTLEMENT	DATE OF PRORATIONS IF DIFFERENT FROM SETTLEMENT

J. SUMMARY OF BORROWER'S TRANSACTION		K. SUMMARY OF SELLER'S TRANSACTION	
100. GROSS AMOUNT DUE FROM BORROWER:		**400. GROSS AMOUNT DUE TO SELLER:**	
		401. Contract sales price	*50,000*
101. Contract sales price	50,000	402. Personal property	
102. Personal property		403.	
103. Settlement charges to borrower *(from line 1400, Section L)*	2,518.86	404.	
104.		Adjustments for items paid by seller in advance:	
105.		405. City/town taxes 10/10 to 12/31	266.66
Adjustments for items paid by seller in advance:		406. County taxes to	
		407. Assessments to	
106. City/town taxes 10/10 to 12/31	266.66	408. *WATER/SEWER RENT* 10/ to 12/31	31.20
107. County taxes to		409. *SCHOOL TAXES* to	
108. Assessments to		410. to	
109. *WATER/SEWER RENT* 10/ to 12/31	31.20	411. to	
110. *SCHOOL TAXES* to		**420. GROSS AMOUNT DUE TO SELLER:**	50,297.77
111. to			
112. to		NOTE: *The following 500 and 600 series sections are not required to be completed when this form is used for advance disclosure of settlement costs prior to settlement.*	
120. GROSS AMOUNT DUE FROM BORROWER:	52,816.72		
200. AMOUNTS PAID BY OR IN BEHALF OF BORROWER:		**500. REDUCTIONS IN AMOUNT DUE TO SELLER:**	
		501. Payoff of first mortgage loan	15,352.47
201. Deposit or earnest money	5,000	502. Payoff of second mortgage loan	
202. Principal amount of new loan(s)	40,000	503. Settlement charges to seller *(from line 1400, Section L)*	3,562
203. Existing loan(s) taken subject to			
204.		504. Existing loan(s) taken subject to	
205.		505. *TAXES to*	
Credits to borrower for items unpaid by seller:		506. *WATER/SEWER RENT to*	
		507.	
206. City/town taxes to		508.	
207. County taxes to		509. *ESCROW FOR:*	
208. Assessments to			
209. *WATER/SEWER RENT* 7/1 to 10/10	13.55	Credits to borrower for items unpaid by seller:	
210. *SCHOOL TAXES* to			
211. to		510. City/town taxes to	
212. to		511. County taxes to	
		512. Assessments to	
220. TOTAL AMOUNTS PAID BY OR IN BEHALF OF BORROWER:	45,013.55	513. *WATER/SEWER RENT* 7/1 to 10/10	13.55
300. CASH AT SETTLEMENT REQUIRED FROM OR PAYABLE TO BORROWER:		514. *SCHOOL TAXES* to	
		515. to	
301. Gross amount due from borrower *(from line 120)*	52,816.72	**520. TOTAL REDUCTIONS IN AMOUNT DUE TO SELLER:**	18,927.80
		600. CASH TO SELLER FROM SETTLEMENT:	
302. Less amounts paid by or in behalf of borrower *(from line 220)*	45,013.53	601. Gross amount due to seller *(from line 420)*	50,297.77
		602. Less total reductions in amount due to seller *(from line 520)*	18,927.80
303. CASH (☐ REQUIRED FROM) OR (☐ PAYABLE TO) BORROWER:	7,803.39	603. CASH TO SELLER FROM SETTLEMENT	31,369.71

810-35-1981   (B7773)

COMMONWEALTH LAND TITLE INSURANCE COMPANY   APPL. No.   *Page 2*

L.	SETTLEMENT CHARGES	PAID FROM BORROWER'S FUNDS	PAID FROM SELLER'S FUNDS
700.	SALES/BROKER'S COMMISSION based on price $ 50,000 @ 6 %		
701.	Total commission paid by seller		3,000
	Division of commission as follows:		
702.	$ 3,000 to Hill N' Dale Realty		
703.	$ to		
704.			
800.	ITEMS PAYABLE IN CONNECTION WITH LOAN.		
801.	Loan Origination fee 1 % ($400 less $75 prepaid)	325	
802.	Loan Discount %		
803.	Appraisal Fee to Upper Dublin Bank	90	
804.	Credit Report to		
805.	Lender's inspection fee		
806.	Mortgage Insurance application fee to		
807.	Assumption/refinancing fee		
808.			
809.			
810.			
811.			
900.	ITEMS REQUIRED BY LENDER TO BE PAID IN ADVANCE.		
901.	Interest from 10/10 to 10/31 @ $ 8.88 / day	195.36	
902.	Mortgage insurance premium for mo. to		
903.	Hazard insurance premium for yrs. to	140	
904.	yrs. to		
905.			
1000.	RESERVES DEPOSITED WITH LENDER FOR:		
1001.	Hazard insurance mo. @ $ / mo.		
1002.	Mortgage insurance mo. @ $ / mo.		
1003.	City property taxes 8 mo. @ $ 100 / mo.	800	
1004.	County property taxes mo. @ $ / mo.		
1005.	Annual assessments mo. @ $ / mo.		
1006.	*SCHOOL TAXES* mo. @ $ / mo.		
1007.	mo. @ $ / mo.		
1008.	mo. @ $ / mo.		
1100.	TITLE CHARGES:		
1101.	Settlement or closing fee to		
1102.	Abstract or title search to		
1103.	Title examination to		
1104.	Title insurance binder to		
1105.	Document preparation to		20
1106.	Notary fees to	5	5
1107.	Attorney's Fees to		
	(includes above items No.:)		
1108.	Title insurance to COMMONWEALTH LAND TITLE INSURANCE COMPANY	340	
	(includes above items Nos.: 1101 - 1104)		
1109.	Lender's coverage $ 40,000		
1110.	Owner's coverage $ 50,000		
1111.	*DISBURSEMENT CHARGE to COMMONWEALTH LAND TITLE INS. COMPANY*	13.50	
1112.	*ADD'L CHARGES TO CLTIC* Endorsement 100, 300,		
1113.			
1200.	GOVERNMENT RECORDING AND TRANSFER CHARGES		
1201.	Recording fees: Deed $ 5 ; Mortgage $ 5 Releases $ 7	10	7
1202.	City/county tax/stamps: Deed $; Mortgage $	250	250
1203.	State tax/stamps: Deed $; Mortgage $	250	250
1204.			
1300.	ADDITIONAL SETTLEMENT CHARGES		
1301.	Survey to XYZ ENGINEERS	100	
1302.	Pest inspection to ZYX EXTERMINATORS		30
1303.			
1304.			
1305.			
1400.	TOTAL SETTLEMENT CHARGES (entered on lines 103 and 503, Sections J and K)	2,518.86	3,562

NOTE: *Under certain circumstances the borrower and seller may be permitted to waive the 12-day period which must normally occur between advance disclosure and settlement. In the event such a waiver is made, copies of the statements of waiver, executed as provided in the regulations of the Department of Housing and Urban Development, shall be attached to and made a part of this form when the form is used as a settlement statement.*

810-36-1982   [B7774]

Using this information, let us fill in the settlement sheet. Blocks A through I are self-explanatory, and we will do Blocks J, K and L.

1. Block J.   Summary of Borrower's Transaction

(a) Section 100

Section 100 relates to the gross amount due from the purchaser (who is characterized on the form as being the borrower) before credit apportionments, credit for deposit monies and amount of the mortgage. It indicates the gross amount that the borrower will have to produce from all sources.

Line 101 is the purchase price, in this instance $50,000.

Line 102 is the price of any personal property being sold by the seller to the purchaser and not included in the purchase price. In our example, there is none.

Line 103 relates to the total settlement charges to be paid by the borrower, as calculated in Block L. As we shall see from our review of Block L, this equals $2518.86.

Lines 104 and 105 are for any other direct charges that do not apply elsewhere.

Lines 106 through 112 are for items paid in advance by the seller for which the seller is entitled to some reimbursement. Lines 106 and 107 can be used for different real estate taxes. Here there is only one real estate tax and we will show the amount on Line 106 alone. The taxes are $1200 per calendar year and have been paid for the year of settlement. The seller is entitled to be reimbursed from October 10 through December 31. Roughly, we can call this 2 months and 20 days using a 30 day month, as is often done for ease of calculation. The total due the seller is $266.66, which is obtained by dividing $1200 by 12 to get the monthly rate and then by 30 to get the daily rate, and by multiplying the monthly rate of $100 by 2 (for November and December) and the daily rate of $3.33 by 20. The space on line 106 should indicate the period of apportionment as 10/10 to 12/31.

Line 109 can be used for the apportionment of prepaid sewer and water. Sadowski has paid the entire quarterly minimum charge of $35 for October, November and December. Using artificial quarters of 90 days, this equals a per diem rate of $.39, which should be multiplied by 80 days, for a total adjustment on line 109 of $31.20. Again the period of adjustment should be indicated.

Lines 110 through 112 will remain vacant here. They could be used to apportion prepaid insurance, unpaid rent from a tenant or similar items, where appropriate.

Line 120 is the sum of all the items filled in in Section 100. In this case, the sum of $52,816.72 should be entered on line 120.

(b) Section 200

Section 200 indicates all amounts for which Browne will receive credit towards the amount due, or which will be paid by others on Browne's behalf.

Line 201 equals the deposit money, in this case 10% which is $5,000.

Line 202 equals the amount of the mortgage loan, which is $40,000. Note that this is the actual amount of the loan, not the "amount financed" as defined by Truth-in-Lending.

Line 203 would be vacant here, as there is no mortgage being assumed by Browne.

Lines 206 through 212 are the converse of lines 106 through 112. They are items which Browne must pay, but for which Sadowski is at least in part responsible. In our case there are no unpaid taxes, so lines 206, 207 and 208 will be vacant.

Line 209 will contain an apportionment of estimated excess water and sewer. In our example, the normal 6 month excess is $24 and the period is from July 1 through December 31. Browne is entitled to reimbursement from July 1 through October 10, which is 3 months and 10 days. The monthly rate is $4 and the daily rate is $.13, giving a total credit of $13.33, which should be entered on Line 209.

Line 220 is the total of the items shown in Section 200, which in this case is $45,013.33.

(c) Section 300

Section 300 reconciles the information contained in Sections 100 and 200 by subtracting Line 220 from Line 120. This result, shown in Line 303, is the total cash that Browne must pay at settlement.

2. Block K Summary of Seller's Transaction

(a) Section 400

Section 400 is roughly analogous to Section 100. The section calculates the total amounts due to Sadowski, before deductions for her various expenses.

Line 401 is the purchase price, again $50,000. Again line 402 is blank.

Line 405 will be $266.66, the same as line 106. Line 408 will be $31.20, the same as line 109.

Line 420 is the sum of items in Section 400, in this case $50,297.-77.

(b) Section 500

Section 500 includes the reductions in the gross amount which the seller is due to receive.

Line 501 is the amount needed to pay off any first mortgage with which the seller had encumbered the property. In our case let us suppose that the payoff (equal to unpaid principal, accrued interest and any prepayment penalty) is $15,352.47. We will assume that there are no other mortgages or judgments, and that line 502 will be blank.

Line 503 relates to the total settlement charges to be paid by the seller, as calculated in Block L. As we shall see from our review of Block L, this equals $3562.

Lines 504 through 509 are blank here, as there are no loans being assumed by Browne.

Lines 510 through 515 are analogous to lines 206 through 212. Again, the only entry is $13.33 for estimated sewer and water excess, which would go in line 513.

Line 520 is the sum of items in Section 500, in this case $18,927.80.

(c) Section 600

Section 600 reconciles Sections 400 and 500, by substracting line 520 from line 420. This result, shown in line 603, is the total net proceeds of settlement to be paid to the seller.

3. Block L Settlement Charges

(a) Section 700

Section 700 includes all brokers commissions to be paid by either party. Line 701 is for commissions paid by the seller, and the sum of $3000 ($50,000 × 6%) should be entered under the column marked "Paid From Seller's Funds" (which will hereafter just be referred to as under "Seller", and "Paid From Borrower's Funds" will just be referred to as under "Borrower").

Line 702 will indicate that the entire $3000 is being paid to Hill 'N Dale Realty. If the commission were being split, then some lesser amount would be paid to Hill 'N Dale and the remainder would go in line 703 as being paid to the cooperating broker.

Line 704 is blank because the borrower is not paying any broker's commission.

(b) Section 800

Section 800 includes items payable in connection with the loan, whether paid to the lender or some other party.

Line 801 would read $400 (less $75 prepaid), for a total of $325 under Borrower.

There are no points being paid, so line 802 is blank.

Line 803 is an appraisal fee to Upper Dublin Bank of $90, under Borrower.

In our case, we have no further entries in Section 800.

(c) Section 900

Line 901 would indicate interest for 22 days from 10/10 to 10/31 at $8.88 per day for a total of $195.36 under Borrower.

Line 903 will be filled in if Browne is paying for his hazard insurance policy at settlement. Let us assume that he is and that the premium is $140, which would be entered under Borrower.

(d) Section 1000

Section 1000 is for escrowed items. Here we are only escrowing for real estate taxes and there is only one real estate tax, so the only entry will be line 1003. We have said that Upper Dublin Bank needs to have a full year's taxes in escrow after receipt of the payment due on March 1. Since each monthly payment will be accompanied by an escrow payment of 1/12th of the taxes, Upper Dublin Bank will only have received 4/12ths by March 1, being the payments for December (the first payment date), January, February and March. In order to have 12/12ths available on March 15, Upper Dublin Bank will require reserves paid at settlement by Browne of 8/12ths of the year's taxes. As we have seen, the monthly rate is $100, which means that line **1003** will show $800 under Borrower.

(e) Section 1100

The first entry we would have in Section 1100 would be in line 1105, where we would enter $20 under Seller for preparation of the deed.

Line 1106 would have entries of $5 each under Seller and under Borrower, for notary fees.

We will assume that line 1107 will be blank, either because none of the parties are represented or because the only attorneys are independent (i. e. they were not selected by Upper Dublin Bank) and do not elect to be paid at the settlement.

Line 1108 would be $340 under Borrower, for the basic title company charge. Line 1109 would indicate that the lender's coverage was $40,000. Line 1110 would indicate that the borrower's coverage was $50,000. Line 1111 would refer to Pa. Endorsements 100 and 300, for which $13.50 would be entered under Borrower.

(f) Section 1200

Line 1201 would show recording fees of $5 each for deed and mortgage (and $10 under Borrower) and $7 for the mortgage release (under Seller).

Lines 1202 and 1203 would indicate $500 each under Borrower and Seller, the two $500 charges being the 1% transfer tax to the municipality and the 1% transfer tax to the state.

(g) Section 1300

Line 1301 would show a $100 charge paid to XYZ Engineers for the survey, listed under Borrower.

Line 1302 would show a $30 charge paid to ZYX Exterminators for the termite certificate, listed under Seller.

(h) Section 1400

Section 1400 simply represents the sum of items under each of the columns. The line 1400 total under Borrower is inserted into line 103 in Block J. The line 1400 total under Seller is inserted into line 503 in Block K.

VIII. SUMMARY

A. CLOSING AGENDA

The preparation for any closing is greatly facilitated by the use of some form of check list. One helpful form of checklist is an agenda which can be revised as the closing nears and can be used as an actual agenda for conducting the closing itself. The elements of a good closing agenda are as follows:

1. Personae

The agenda should contain a list of the full and correct names of all the persons and entities involved, their respective roles in the transaction and their addresses and telephone numbers. Listing all of these in one place simplifies matters for secretaries and typists and serves as a reminder of the necessary parties to receive drafts of documents, copies of notices and the like.

2. Documents

The agenda should contain a listing of all of the documents which are involved in the closing, including the basic documents, such as the commitment letter, and including all items which must be produced or tendered at settlement. The list can initially be produced by a review of the basic documents, the title report and binders of past similar transactions to see what documentation is specifically required to be produced or which may be expected to be a part of the transaction. There should be a separate folder in the file for every one of the documents listed in the agenda, and drafts should be maintained in these folders.

3. Status and Responsibility

As each document is listed, there should be an indication of which party is responsible for drafting or otherwise producing the document and which parties have rights of approval. There should be a status report indicating at different times at what stage the document then is (e. g. first draft out for review by permanent lender; comments received from construction lender on March 3).

4. Disposition

The expected disposition of each document should also be listed, including the parties who will be receiving executed or conformed copies and the number of copies they are to receive. Indicating whether or not the document is to be recorded will also provide a checklist of which documents need to be acknowledged by a notary.

The agenda is not intended to be a fixed document. In addition to status changes, there will likely be revisions in the list of documents, and may even be revisions in the parties to the transaction. As settlement approaches, the agenda should change less, except in terms of status, but it is very common for additional documents to be prepared and executed at settlement itself to deal with a specific, unanticipated problem or situation. New documents at settlement should be included on the agenda so that they are not overlooked.

Normally, in a large transaction each party begins with its own agenda. However, the parties often exchange their agendas in order that they may agree upon a common agenda. This is particularly important with regard to disposition of documents and the list of documents itself. There are certain items which some lenders and title insurance companies will require and which others will not, and whether or not they will be required is not always obvious from the face of the commitment letter or title report. For this and other reasons, the copies of agendas that are first exchanged will often be edited versions of the actual agenda then under consideration by a party, especially by a borrower.

The agenda acts as a checklist at settlement of all the documents that need to be produced, exchanged, executed, acknowledged and delivered for recording. At the end of the settlement, the parties can review their own agendas, or the common agenda if one agenda is being used in common by all parties, to determine whether they have received all the documents to which they are entitled.

The agenda serves two other functions. If the attorney working on the matter should become indisposed or unavailable for any reason, then the agenda will provide crucial information to the attorney who takes over the matter. The agenda serves as the basis for the creation of a binder after completion of the transaction.

B. CLOSING REPORT AND BINDER

Human memory being what it is, fallible and selective, the attorney or paralegal should immediately after settlement write a settlement report. The closing report should summarize the transaction, which can be understood in detail from the underlying documents, and should provide a more detailed account of any problems or other situations that arose at settlement, and any concessions, compromises, promises or representations that were made at settlement. The closing report really serves three functions. The first is to provide a narrative account of the transaction for persons not directly involved with the mechanics of the transaction but having some interest in it, such as accountants, corporate officers and other attorneys in the office. The second purpose is to memorialize the events of settlement, especially the concessions and the like mentioned above, for assistance in settling later disputes. The third is to serve as an introduction into the documents themselves in the event that someone five or ten years hence has to review the file for any reason, such as a dispute. Even the closing attorney may forget the basics of the transaction in the meantime, and an attorney or paralegal who was a stranger to the transaction would certainly appreciate an introduction before plunging into a binder of documents.

The document binder should contain copies of all documents relevant to the transaction, which may be as few as fifteen documents or may exceed one hundred. The documents should be arranged in some sensible order, probably culminating in a settlement sheet and a closing report. As recorded copies are returned from the recorder, they should be inserted in place of the photocopies of those documents.

Many binders are just made in the office, using fasteners. Some binders are literally bound, as hard-cover books. The method used will depend on cost and custom. In any event, a determination will have to be made as to how many copies to produce and who will retain which original documents.

Occasionally, as an aid to interpreting what a document really means, a court will want to review prior drafts of the document. For this reason, prior drafts are often maintained, at least for a number of years, for major transactions. To reduce the bulk of the main file, the prior drafts may be placed in some ancillary file.

The binder and the correspondence folder, with an occasional assist from the prior drafts file, should serve as complete records of a transaction. An attorney picking up the file years later should be able to trace the entire transaction from these sources alone.

*

GLOSSARY

Abatement—The suspension or cessation, in whole or in part, of a continuing charge, such as rent.

Adverse Possession—One may gain title to or a right to use over real property by adverse possession. Adverse possesion is open, continuous (for a specified period of time), adverse (in such a manner as is contrary to ownership being in another) use and without right (the owner has not consented).

Agency—The legal relationship between a person (the agent) who is acting on behalf of another person (the principal). Most of the law respecting the agency relationship deals with the duties and responsibilities of an agent to his principal, and the responsibilities of the principal to third parties for the acts of his agent.

Amortization—The payment or repayment of a principal amount over a period of time in installments. A self-amortizing mortgage is one in which the entire principal amount will be repaid by the regularly scheduled payments, with the result that no large portion of the loan is due upon the maturity of the loan. A standing loan is one in which the principal is not repaid or reduced during the term of the loan, but is due in full at maturity.

Apportionment—The allocation of a charge or cost such as real estate taxes between two parties, often in the same ratio as the respective times that the parties are in possession or ownership of property during the fiscal period for which the charge is made or assessed.

Assignment—The transfer by a party of all of its rights to some kind of property, usually intangible property such as rights in a lease, mortgage, agreement of sale or a partnership. Tangible property is more often transferred by possession and by instruments conveying title such as a deed or a bill of sale.

Assumption—The agreement of a party to be responsible and liable for performance of the obligations of another party. A person to whom intangible property is assigned, such as the rights of a tenant under a lease, often agrees to assume the obligations of the assigning party under the contract being assigned.

Attornment—The agreement of a person to recognize a third party as a permissible successor party to a contract; most often, the agreement of a tenant to pay rent to a new landlord, especially a mortgagee who has foreclosed.

Beneficial Owner—One who does not have title to property but has rights in the property which are the normal incident of owning

445

the property. The persons for whom a trustee holds title to property are the beneficial owners of the property, and the trustee has a fiduciary responsibility to them.

Capital Contribution—The money or other property which a partner invests in a partnership. Normally, personal services are not considered property that may be contributed to a partnership as capital.

Completion Bond—A form of surety or guaranty agreement which contains the promise of a third party, usually a bonding company, to complete or pay for the cost of completion of a construction contract if the construction contractor defaults.

Condition Precedent—In a contract or other document, a specified event which must occur before all or part of the contract or document takes effect. This is to be distinguished from a condition subsequent, which is an event the occurrence of which will have the effect of rescinding or supervening some or all of the document or agreement which otherwise is in effect.

Condominium—A form of ownership of real property which includes exclusive ownership and use of some portion, such as an apartment in a high-rise building, and joint and common use of the non-exclusive areas. The condominium concept was not rooted in English common law and most condominiums in the United States are formed in accordance with specific state enabling statutes.

Consideration—That which is given in return for the agreement or act of another person. The consideration for most contracts is the mutuality of the promises set forth in the contract.

Convey—Transfer; usually the transfer of legal title to property by deed or bill of sale.

Corporation—An organization established in accordance with a state or federal enabling law and having the legal status of a person. A corporation's identity is considered to be separate and distinct from its shareholders, officers and directors.

Covenant—A promise, in a deed or contract, either to do something (an affirmative covenant) or to refrain from doing something (a negative covenant or a restrictive covenant). Normally the covenant specifically affects the property which is the subject of the deed or contract.

Creditor—One to whom a debtor is obligated to pay money.

Debt Service—The periodic payments that must be made in payment of a debt, including interest and principal.

Debtor—One who has an obligation to pay money.

Declaration—A document by the owner of property which is recorded in order to establish a legal order upon the property, such as a condominium (by a declaration of condominium or master deed), a system of cross-easements (by a declaration of easements) or a homeowners association (by declaration of covenants, restrictions and easements).

Default—A failure to perform a contractual obligation in a timely manner.

Defeasible Deed—A deed containing a condition subsequent the happening of which will cause title to the property to revert to the grantor or to go to some third party.

Demised Premises—That property, or portion of a property which is leased to a tenant.

Depreciation—A tax accounting concept which may be applied to investment properties. The assumption is that physical structure and equipment, such as a building or an airplane (but not land) diminishes in value over time due to physical deterioration or obsolescence. Therefore, income to the taxpayer from the investment property (or from other sources) should not be taxed to the extent that the property itself has diminished (depreciated) during a tax year. The reduction in taxable income is called depreciation. Claiming depreciation on an investment property results in an equivalent reduction in the taxpayer's tax basis in the property. If property is eventually sold above the tax basis, then the taxpayer will recognize income from the sale, so that the claiming of depreciation may result in taxable income being realized at the time of sale.

Devise—To leave real property by a specific provision in a will. Real property is "devised", while personal property is "bequeathed".

Dissolution—The winding up and conclusion of a corporation (but not necessarily a partnership) as a business.

Distraint—The inchoate right and interest which a landlord has in the property of a tenant located on the demised premises. Upon a tenant's default, a landlord may in some jurisdictions distrain upon the tenant's property, generally by changing the locks and giving notice, and the landlord will then have a lien upon the goods. The priority of the lien will depend on local law.

Easement—A right of use over the property of another. Traditionally the permitted kinds of uses were limited, the most important being rights of way and rights concerning flowing waters. The easement was normally for the benefit of adjoining lands, no matter who the owner was (an easement appurtenant), rather than for the benefit of a specific individual (easement in gross). The land having the right of use as an appurtenance is known as the dominant tenement and the land which is subject to the easement is known as the servient tenement.

Eminent Domain—The paramount right of the government to take the property located within the state. In the United States, the power of eminent domain is found in both the federal and state governments. However, the constitution limits the power to taking for a public purpose and prohibits the exercise of the power of eminent domain without just compensation to the owners of the property which is taken. The process of exercising the power of eminent domain is referred to as "condemnation".

Encumbrance—Any continuing restriction or obligation upon real property, which may include a lease, mortgage, easement, ground rent, license and the like.

Equity—The difference between market value of property and the aggregate of the current outstanding balances of all mortgages upon and other liens against the property is often referred to as the owner's equity. The term came from the development in English courts of equity of the right of an owner of property to redeem his property even after a foreclosure, which right came to be known as the equity of redemption. The existence of the right was predicated on the property being of far greater value than the debt owed to the party that foreclosed.

Escrow—The holding in safekeeping by a third party (the escrowee) of certain property, documents or money which is the subject of a dispute, or which the parties simply wish to be held pending the occurrence of specified events. Deposit money for an agreement of sale is often held in escrow by an attorney or agent pending settlement.

Estoppel Certificate—A signed statement by a party, such as a tenant or a mortgagee, certifying for the benefit of another party that a certain statement of facts is correct as of the date of the statement, such as that a lease exists, that there are no defaults and that rent is paid to a certain date. Delivery of the statement by the tenant prevents (estops) the tenant from later claiming a different state of facts.

Exclusive—A right granted to a tenant in a shopping center to be the only tenant in that center (with perhaps some specified exception) permitted to sell certain items.

Execution—(a) Execution of an agreement or document by a party is the valid signing and sealing of the agreement with all of the formalities required by law and by all of the persons necessary to bind that party. (b) Execution upon a judgment is the legal process of enforcing the judgment, usually by seizing and selling property of the debtor.

Fee Title and Fee Simple Absolute—Fee title is any kind of present ownership of real property. The fee estate is distinct from other interest, such as a leasehold estate (a tenant's interest) or an easement. Fee simple absolute is the most common kind of fee interest in the United States, and represents full ownership without any restrictions or limitations in the quality of title itself.

Fiduciary—A person who holds, controls or manages money or property for the benefit of others in a situation such that the beneficiary has the right to expect a high degree of trust and confidence. The status of being a fiduciary gives rise to certain legal incidents and obligations, including the prohibition against investing the money or property in investments which are speculative or otherwise imprudent.

Financing Statements—A form of public notice of the existence of a security interest in personal property.

Fixtures—Items of personal property which are affixed to land or to a building in such a way that they become part of the real estate itself.

Habendum—The "to have and to hold" section of a deed. When quality of title is to be limited to something less than fee simple absolute, the limitation is likely to be set forth in the habendum.

Hereditament—Something which can be inherited. Some interests in real estate are potential interests rather than present interests. Some of these potential interests are hereditaments and some are not.

Indemnification—The promise of one party to vouchsafe another party from financial harm with respect to a particular property or transaction.

Interest—(a) A right in something; one having some right in particular real property is said to have an interest in the property, which may be a leasehold interest, fee interest, security interest or other right (b) payments made for the loan of money, in addition to repayment of the loan, are called interest, interest being normally expressed as an annual percentage of the principal amount of the loan.

Intestate—Dying without leaving a valid will. The intestacy laws of the various states control how property is to be distributed when a person dies intestate.

Joinder—The consent to an agreement or document by a party who has an interest in the subject matter of the agreement or docu-

ment, but who is not himself an active party to the agreement or
document.

Judgment Note—A form of note (a promise to pay money) which contains a warrant of attorney authorizing the holder of the note to
enter (confess) judgment against the debtor without first having
any legal proceeding in which the debtor can take part.

Lease—The grant by the owner of real property of the right to use
the property for a period of time, usually for the payment of rent.
The tenant under a lease has a leasehold interest in the property,
which is a form of non-fee interest in the land.

Liquidated Damages—An agreed sum of money which will serve as
the full payment of damages to be paid to a party to a contract
upon the default of the other party.

Mechanics Lien—Various states have a statute giving to persons who
work on constructing or improving real property a right to impose a lien upon the real property, and in some cases to obtain
special priorities, if they are not paid for their work.

Lis Pendens—A notice entered on the public records indicating that
there is a suit pending, the outcome of which could affect title to
specified real property.

Metes and Bounds—A way of describing land by listing the compass
directions and distances of the boundaries.

Mortgage—A document granting an interest in real property as security for the payment of a note or performance of some other
obligation.

Non-Disturbance Agreement—Usually part of an attornment agreement, it is an agreement by a mortgagee that it will not cancel a
non-defaulting tenant's lease if it forecloses on the property.

Note—A document evidencing the obligation to pay money.

Option—The contractual right to purchase property, but with no obligation to purchase. Options to purchase are sometimes included
in leases for real property.

Partnership—A form of business organization consisting of two or
more persons. The traditional form of partnership is a general
partnership, in which all of the partners take part in the business
and have personal liability for partnership obligations. A limited
partnership is a statutory hybrid between a general partnership
and a corporation, and includes passive investors who do not have
personal liability for partnership obligations.

Personal Liability—A kind of responsibility for the payment or performance of an obligation which exposes the personal assets of the
responsible person to payment of the obligation.

Personalty or Personal Property—Any form of property whether tangible (a necklace) or intangible (a loan evidenced by a note), which is not real property. The distinction is not always an easy one to make, for example, the interest of a partner in a partnership is considered to be personalty even if the only asset of the partnership is real property.

Points—Usually, one percent. Often, in loan transactions the borrower is charged a loan fee which is expressed as a percentage of the principal loan amount or as points. The term is also used in setting interest rates. If the prime rate of interest is 7% per annum, then an interest rate of two points over prime would be 9% per annum.

Precedent—Courts attempt to decide cases on the basis of principles established in prior cases. Prior cases which are close in facts or legal principles to the case under consideration are called precedents.

Prime Rate of Interest—Usually defined as the lowest rate of interest from time to time charged by a specific lender to its best customers for short term unsecured loans. Prime is often used as the measuring rod for interest rates on other loans.

Priority—The order in which claims may be satisfied out of the sale of real property.

Privity of Contract—Persons who are either parties to a contract or are intended beneficiaries of the contract are said to have privity of contract. Only parties having privity of contract may sue for enforcement of the contract.

Profit—(a) Most commonly, the gross proceeds of a business transaction less the costs of the transaction. (b) at English common law, a profit à prendre was a kind of property right being the right to remove certain items (such as wood or specified minerals) from the land.

Purchaser—Buyer, vendee; one who has contracted to purchase property.

Purchase Money Mortgage—(a) Generally, any mortgage given to secure a loan made for the purpose of acquiring the land on which the mortgage is given, (b) more particularly, a mortgage given to the seller of land to secure payment of a portion of the purchase price.

Remedies—The rights given to a party by law or by contract which that party may exercise upon a default by the other contracting party, or upon the commission of a wrong (a tort) by another party.

Recission—A remedy at law, the right of recission is the right to cancel (rescind) a contract upon the occurrence of certain kinds of default by the other contracting party. Not every default in a contract will give rise to a right of recission.

Restriction—A limitation, often imposed in a deed or lease respecting the use to which the property may be put.

Security Agreement—An agreement granting a creditor a security interest in personal property, which security interest is normally perfected either by the creditor taking possession of the collateral or by filing financing statements in the proper public records.

Security Interest—A form of interest in property which provides that the property may be sold in order to satisfy the obligation for which the security interest is given. A mortgage is used to grant a security interest in real property.

Seller—Vendor; one who has contracted to sell property.

Settlement—Closing; the culmination of a particular transaction involving real property, such as the purchase and sale of the property, the execution of a lease or the making of a mortgage loan.

Straw Party—Nominee; one who acts as an agent for another for the purpose of taking title to real property and executing whatever documents and instruments the principal may direct respecting the property.

Subordination Agreement—An agreement by which the subordinating party agrees that its interest in real property should have a lower priority than the interest to which it is being subordinated.

Subrogation—The lawful substitution of a third party in place of a party having a claim against another party. Insurance companies, guarantors and bonding companies generally have the right to step into the shoes of the party whom they compensate and sue any party whom the compensated party could have sued.

Tender—To offer; at a settlement under an agreement of sale the seller tenders the executed deed to the purchaser, who tenders the remainder of the purchase price to the seller. Although the requirement for tender may be waived in the agreement of sale, in instances of default by either party, the non-defaulting party will often go to the place of settlement at the appointed time, even though the other party is not there, and make tender.

Termination—(a) Of a lease or contract, an ending, usually before the end of the anticipated term of the lease or contract, which termination may be by mutual agreement or may be by exercise of one party of one of his remedies due to the default of the other party. (b) Of a partnership, a winding up and cessation of the business as opposed to only a technical ending (as upon the death of a partner) which is a dissolution. A dissolved partnership may terminate or may be continued by a partnership of the remaining partners, including perhaps the estate or heirs of the deceased partner.

Torrens System—A system of registering titles to lands that presumes an adjudication of title each time a deed or claim is filed.

Usury—Collectively, the laws of a jurisdiction regulating the charging of interest rates. A usurious loan is one whose interest rates are determined to be in excess of those permitted by the usury laws.

Warranty—A promise that certain facts are truly as they are represented to be and that they will remain so, subject to any specified limitations. In certain circumstances the courts will presume a warranty, known as an implied warranty.

*

APPENDIX

FEDERAL TRUTH-IN-LENDING STATEMENT

(As Part of Disclosure/Settlement Statement)

I. A. Cash price (contract sales price) $_____

       1. Less any cash downpayment $_____

           Total Downpayment $_____

   B. Equals unpaid balance of cash price $_____

   C. Plus any other amounts financed:

       1. _____ $_____

       2.   Total other amounts financed $_____

   D. Equals unpaid balance $_____

   E. Less any prepaid finance charges:

       1. Origination fee or points paid by borrower $_____

       2. Mortgage guaranty insurance $_____

       3. _____ $_____

       4.   Total prepaid finance charge $_____

   F. Equals amount financed $_____

II. The FINANCE CHARGE consists of

   A. Interest (simple annual rate of _____%) $_____

   B. Total prepaid finance charge (I. E. 4.) $_____

   C. PMI for life of loan $_____

   D.   Total FINANCE CHARGE $========

III. A. The ANNUAL PERCENTAGE RATE on the amount financed is _____%

   B. If the contract includes a provision for a variation in the interest rate, describe _____

IV. Payments for principal and finance charge, excluding mortgage insurance premium, on this transaction will consist of _____ monthly installments of $_____ (consisting of principal and interest) beginning on the first day of _____ and due on the first day of each month thereafter through _____. In addition, added as part of this monthly payment will be a monthly mortgage guaranty insurance payment the first of which will be required on _____ in the amount of $_____. Such payments will be made over a total of _____ months and the last monthly payment for mortgage insurance will be due on _____ and will be $_____. Thereafter, remaining monthly payments will be in the amount of $_____. The total of payments is $_____.

In addition to the above, your monthly payment may be increased if your mortgage commitment requires escrow payments for Hazard Insurance, Life Insurance, Accident and Health Insurance or Taxes.

V.   The finance charge begins to accrue on _____*.

VI.   In the event of late payments, charges may be assessed as follows: 4% of the total payment after 15 days.

VII.   Conditions and penalties for prepaying this obligation are:

VIII.   Insurance taken in connection with this obligation: Fire insurance and extended coverage in the amount of the mortgage required. Also Title Insurance is required.

IX.   The security for this obligation is mortgage on premises:

---

* Indicates a date, rate or amount that is estimated and may be subject to change. (FOR USE WITH CONVENTIONAL MORTGAGES REQUIRING PMI.)

INDEX

References are to Pages